About the author

The journalist, author and broadcaster Spencer Leigh was born in Liverpool, England, and is an acknowledged authority on the Beatles. He has been broadcasting his weekly show, *On the Beat*, on BBC Radio Merseyside for 30 years and has interviewed thousands of musicians. He has written over twenty-five books, hundreds of album sleeve notes and he writes obituaries of musicians for *The Independent* and the *Oxford Dictionary of National Biography*. He is an Honoured Friend at Sir Paul McCartney's Liverpool Institute of Performing Arts (LIPA) and he has a Gold Badge of Merit from the British Academy of Composers and Songwriters. Spencer continues to live on Merseyside.

His acclaimed book, *Best of the Beatles: The Sacking of Pete Best*, is published by McNidder and Grace and is available in paperback and ebook.

Thanks

When it comes to acknowledging help, I must first credit the late Len Scarratt from the Wirral who has no idea that he has helped me in any way. He was a well-organised Sinatra collector whose possessions were removed in a house clearance. They were given to the Literally bookshop in New Brighton and its owner, Cathy Roberts, passed them to me. Another long-time collector, Babs Freckleton, passed over some VHS tapes which otherwise would have gone to a charity shop. Thanks to Billy Butler, Andrew Doble, Peter Doble, Peter Grant, Denny Seyton and in particular to David Roberts of *poppublishing* who did much to drum up interest in this project.

A special thank you to my wife, Anne, who has had to put up with my obsession with Frank Sinatra: she read the Kitty Kelley biography when it was published in 1986, decided that he was despicable and has had no further interest in him: I hope this is a more balanced view than Kelley's although Frank Sinatra certainly had his dark side.

I acknowledge the use of the British Library, the library attaching to the BFI Southbank and the BBC Written Archives in Caversham. These are all brilliant places with helpful staff. My thanks to Marion Leonard and the Institute of Popular Music at the University of Liverpool: they possess a wonderful vinyl archive with several shelves of Sinatra albums but, strangely, hardly anything by Dino.

I am very glad that Andy Peden Smith of McNidder & Grace was as intrigued by this subject as I was and I hope I haven't let him down. I am grateful to the readers for this book – David Charters, Fred Dellar and Patrick Humphries – their comments were invaluable. David was asked by his son why he was spending so long on the book. 'Is it longer than *War and Peace?*' he asked. 'No, it's not quite that long,' said David, 'but the themes are similar.' Thanks also to publicist Linda MacFadyen and the book's designer Bryan Kirkpatrick.

Contents

Illustrations

Between pages 166 and 167

Frank meets Queen Elizabeth II at the British premiere of *Me and the Colonel*, 1958.

Long before Beatlemania, note this crowd for Frank outside the London Palladium in 1950.

Frank at Sunshine Home for the Blind, Northwood, London in 1962 was asked, 'What colour is the wind?'

Frank and daughter Nancy attend a film premiere in Hollywood, 1955.

'You married the wrong guy, honey'. Frank and Princess Grace in London, 1970.

Frank as Danny Ocean gives Patrice Wymore the key to his room in *Ocean's 11*, 1960.

A rare shot of Frank conducting, 1962.

Frank at the Royal Festival Hall, 1978.

Sweatshirt with Ol' Blue Eyes is Back – and he was, 1973.

Handbill from 1953.

In 1953 Frank visited Ma Egerton's, which is behind the Liverpool Empire. In 2015, the visit is still used to promote their pizzas.

Frank honoured by the US postal service, 2008.

Frank Sinatra song sheets.

Page 350

UK journalist Stan Britt asked Dave Dexter to help him with a Sinatra biography. Dave doesn't pull his punches, 1988.

The general format of Frank Sinatra: An Extraordinary Life *is to split the chapters into two parts: the first describes the background to something significant in Frank Sinatra's life, and the second continues Frank's story on a day-to-day basis. If you just want Frank's life story, the second sections on their own form a continuous story. In Chapter 1 the first section describes life in Italy and America before Frank was born and how so many Italians found themselves in the United States.*

Foreword

by Sir Tim Rice

In March 1965, I forked out the largest sum I had ever invested in a vinyl gramophone recording when I purchased a triple LP – a compilation of Frank Sinatra's greatest Capitol tracks entitled 'Sinatra – The Great Years'. This mono package set me back £5 at a time when that was the exact sum I was earning every week as an articled clerk in a solicitors' office in London. In the 50 years since I handed over my hard-earned cash to Christopher Foss Records of Paddington Street, W.1., I have never regretted my extravagant purchase. The album (the 13th – and I suppose the 14th and 15th – I had ever bought) still holds an esteemed place in my collection and is still a regular on my turntable.

But half a century later, I realise that the financial aspect of my transaction was not the most important one. This was the first time I had bought a record that was not a rock era disc; indeed nearly half the tracks on it were recorded before Elvis Presley broke through with 'Heartbreak Hotel' in 1956. From that year onward, although Sinatra and many of his refined colleagues, such as Dean Martin, Nat 'King' Cole and Tony Bennett, continued to hit the charts, there was a definite "them and us" divide within the music-buying public; adults liked Sinatra and co. and were square (or sophisticated), kids were with-it (or moronic) and went for Elvis, Cliff and in due course the Beatles and the Rolling Stones. No-one was supposed to cross the generational barrier. But of course many did, in both directions, and what is more, found themselves perfectly happy on both sides of the fence. Spencer Leigh was clearly one of these open-minded music lovers. Frank Sinatra was not.

I have known and admired Spencer's work as a music historian for many years. When he describes music and musicians of a bygone age, we become aware of so much more than the songs and performers – the era itself returns to life and we are reminded that all art, notably popular art, is inspired by, and inseparable from, its time and place, and if we don't understand that background, the story is far from complete.

Spencer is primarily known, through his radio shows and his two dozen or so books, as a chronicler of the British pop and rock scene from 1955 to 1980 or thereabouts, but he has ventured Stateside on more than one occasion (Paul Simon, Buddy Holly) and revealed his great knowledge of popular music before he was born in such publications as *Brother, Can You Spare a Rhyme*. In his mammoth and wonderful tome on Frank Sinatra, he has superbly given us Americana through the long life and career of his subject which began way before his did. Sinatra's agents, lovers, dodgy associates, show biz friends and enemies, passions, hatreds, bravery and recklessness, finesse and crudity, worldly wisdom and naiveté, are all part of the complex whole and Leigh captures them all.

The sleeve note of 'Sinatra – The Great Years' asked "were better records by a singer ever made?" This is a pretty bold question, but on the other hand, someone must have made the greatest vocal recordings of all time and there are plenty who would support Sinatra's claim to that honour. I would certainly place two or three of these great 1953–1960 Capitol sides in an all-time Top 40 male vocal performance chart, 'One For My Baby', 'The Tender Trap' and 'All The Way' being my favourites this week. Whether there has been a better telling of the Frank Sinatra story than Spencer Leigh's version only someone who has read all the myriad other attempts can say – I can say for sure that after reading *Frank Sinatra: An Extraordinary Life* you may want to read more about him, but you won't need to.

INTRODUCTION

Set 'em up, Joe

Many think that Frank Sinatra's career is summed up in the title of his 1939 recording, 'All Or Nothing At All', but it's not. Frank's career is summed up in that first word, 'All': he wanted everything and 'nothing at all' had no appeal for him. He was a winner, the ultimate winner, and all losers were schmucks. Being a Democrat or a Republican didn't matter much to him: Frank would switch allegiance according to whom was in the White House.

Sinatra's story is incredible. He was a man with a remarkable constitution, drinking heavily and involved in numerous projects at any one time. He slept badly and yet he had the stamina to maintain the Cresta Run of his life. It's a cliché but he said it: he did it his way – and his way was the only way that mattered.

His life was full of making friends and falling out, a love of family life but continual love affairs, enormous grudges and spontaneous fights, a fascination with gangsters, dicey financial decisions, the most sublime recording sessions, thousands of personal appearances, radio and TV shows and numerous starring roles in the movies.

Frank Sinatra loved hard, worked hard and played even harder. It is an extraordinary fact that Sinatra set aside $1,000,000 each year for his gambling losses. That's right. Frank Sinatra was at ease with losing $1,000,000 a year on the tables in Las Vegas. Despite his reputation for the party life, he always wanted to keep working. He would choose a mediocre film or lacklustre songs rather than do nothing at all.

It is extraordinary that his most valuable asset, his singing voice, did not deteriorate with all his smoking and drinking and insomnia. It did change in timbre over the years but for most of the time, Frank could sing the Great American Songbook better than anybody on earth.

I want to tell this remarkable story as though for the first time. If you are a newcomer to Sinatra and know little of his background, I can guarantee you will be exhausted just by reading about it. Imagine living it or even worse living with him. It was like being perpetually in a storm. Maybe Sinatra's greatest achievement is not what he did but the fact that he did it – his energy, determination and ability is remarkable.

Frank Sinatra has been under my skin for years as I've always been fascinated by him. I have spoken to scores of musicians, songwriters, fellow performers, fans and even the Mob about him, and their stories and reflections appear throughout the book along with the results of my research. I have made a point of listening to all his official recordings, and tracked down as many of his media appearances as I could find. I have watched all his films – some of which made me cringe, but never mind. Although I knew many of the films and records already, I wanted to see everything afresh and where possible, in chronological order, as I felt the story would benefit from this. If you want, you can undertake this journey with me, all you need is the internet. You can hear any of Frank's records on YouTube or Spotify without cost and even many of his films can be viewed in full for free.

Please remember as you read the story that Frank could not see into the future: he didn't know what would happen on the next page – and very often it took him by surprise.

Given Frank Sinatra's famed loathing of the press, I found many more interviews than I expected. Some, like his famed *Playboy* interview, were ghosted, although he would have signed it off. His infamous, inflammatory barbs about the rock'n'roll explosion of the 1950s were also ghosted but it is clear from his private conversations that they reflected his thoughts. Although he later worked rather uncomfortably with Elvis, he never apologised for calling him 'a cretinous goon'. Indeed, he probably never changed his opinion.

Given the fact that Sinatra gave relatively few in-depth interviews, his stage performances provide a valuable alternative source for what he was thinking. Frank Sinatra didn't know that his concert in Blackpool in 1953 was being recorded and so he can never have expected his comments to travel outside Lancashire. They are deliciously indiscreet and tell us a lot about him and his relationships. Hearing one show after another, particularly in Las Vegas, is by no means tiresome as you are never sure what he is going to say next. Indeed, in his later years, he would even programme a seven-minute rap into his set, mainly to regain his breath but also to comment on whatever was on his mind. In this regard, he and Elvis were similar. On the other hand, Dean Martin, who cultivated his image of a lovable lush, gave very little away on stage; he rarely finished a song, let alone an anecdote.

What makes an entertainer want to be so frank with his public? Is it just egotism or is it that, as he got older, he realised that there were experiences about living that he wanted to share with his audience? Whatever, once you know the Sinatra story and the personalities involved, a seemingly throwaway remark can resound with meaning.

There is one huge plus in telling Frank Sinatra's story. As far as I can tell, once he was a celebrity, he never did anything alone, so, over the years, there have been several friends, lovers, employees and acquaintances who have told it how it was. Even though some of their memories may have been exaggerated, a consistent picture emerges, and having read so many books and articles, I think I can determine what is true and what isn't.

I hope I have written this biography objectively, though my opinions will intrude from time to time. Hardly surprising, given the subject matter. So sit back and relax, and enjoy this rollercoaster of a life story from a safe distance. If life is strange, then few have been stranger than Frank Sinatra's.

CHAPTER 1

New York, New York

'I am not Italian. I was born in Brooklyn.'
Al Capone

I. Italian-Americans

Frank Sinatra is a classic rags to riches story, a classic rage to riches story too. He was born in poverty to immigrant parents in Hoboken, New York in 1915 and he died in 1998 worth at least $200,000,000 – and probably a whole lot more too. In between he became the most famous singer in the world with successes like 'I'll Never Smile Again', 'Young At Heart', 'I've Got You Under My Skin', 'All The Way', 'Strangers In The Night', 'My Way' and 'New York, New York'. He won an Oscar for his role in *From Here To Eternity* and starred in *High Society, Ocean's 11* with his so-called Rat Pack, and one of the definitive war films, *Von Ryan's Express*.

Frank Sinatra's passport said he was American but he certainly felt that he was a man with dual nationality and often his Italian roots were of prime importance. Mostly, and certainly musically, this was beneficial, but he was often associated with the Mafia and these connections came close to destroying his career as well as making him behave erratically. Frank Sinatra was fond of saying, 'I'm a victim because my name ends with a vowel.' This is overstating the case, as there are plenty of successful Italian singers with no known connection to organised crime.

One thing is certain: his Italian background and his torrid relationship with his mother gave him a warped view of the world. Time and again in this book, you will see Sinatra making a decision, with the choice of going down one path or the other, and he invariably chooses what any reasonable person would say was the wrong one. But we are talking about Sinatra and in a funny kind of way, it was always the right path for him. The whole of his life was a crapshoot.

You can also be sure that when everything was going right for Sinatra, he would find a way to mess it up. Whatever he was doing, he wanted to move on to the next project, so anecdotes about his impatience, bad temper and intolerance are legion. He would learn his lines for a film script and want to make it single takes, an approach which set him at loggerheads with Marlon Brando when they were making *Guys And Dolls*.

This book describes how Frank Sinatra operated, thought and lived and much of that was filtered through his Italian background. Before we get onto his life, it worth having a potted history of Italy and finding out how so many Italians came to be in America.

There is nothing unusual about dual identity in America. Millions of Americans in his era came from first or second generation immigrant stock and while many of them regard themselves as American first and foremost, some regard their heritage as equally significant. The further somebody is from their immigrant ancestors, the more American they feel.

On the other hand, the film director, Frank Capra, although born in Palermo, Sicily, in 1897, would always refer to himself as American.

After the fall of the Roman Empire in the fifth century AD, Italy became politically fragmented until unification in 1861. In that sense, the country is younger than America. Not that there has been much consistency since that unification. Although Italy is a major European country with a population of over 60 million, it often acts like a banana republic.

For centuries, Italy has been a tourist destination and the Grand Tour would not have been so grand without Venice or Rome or even Florence or Verona. Thomas Cook would have been proud of the slogan, 'See Naples and die', which dates from the 18th century. The Rat Pack equivalent, taking into account the many voluptuous and tempestuous Italian actresses, was 'See Nipples and die.'

Italy is famed for its historical buildings, many of them not commercialised. However, not much money has been spent on preservation and many sites are in ruins and even appreciated for it such as Pompeii and the Coliseum. But their neglect is not solely down to time, as artisans have been chipping away bits for their own use. After Leonardo da Vinci had painted his mammoth fresco *The Last Supper*, the Pope, making home improvements, wanted a door just by Christ's feet. In more recent times, the nightclub by the Spanish Steps which was featured in *La Dolce Vita* (1960) has become a McDonald's.

The most debauched and evil period in Italy's history was in the late 15th century when it had a Borgia pope. The TV series with Jeremy Irons as the scheming Pope Alexander VI drew many parallels with the Mafia, one of its subheadings being 'The original crime family'. Pope Alexander VI was able to quell foreign invaders and indeed, all who opposed him. The Borgias were Spanish, which weakens the argument that the Italians are genetically programmed for such destructive behaviour.

In 1796 Napoleon invaded Italy, intending to capture it for France. His stock fell when he met his Waterloo in 1815, leaving Italy as a loose collection of states, run by the Pope, the Habsburgs and the Bourbons. Political turmoil and revolts led finally to unification in 1861, when Victor Emmanuel was crowned king. Giuseppe Garibaldi was considered the darling of fashionable society in England but opinions about him are mixed. Was he a champion of the oppressed or did plant the seeds which led to Europe's dictators? In some circles, he is only remembered by a biscuit.

In the 19th century there was a huge nautical trade bringing cotton from America to Europe and the ship owners wondered what they could transport on the outward journey and the answer was people, hundreds of thousands of them. The ships hadn't been built for passengers and the journey could take several weeks with the possibility of disease as the travellers were crammed in tight. Because times were hard, millions of people were prepared to endure hardships and risk their lives in order to reach America.

America called itself 'the land of the free' and the Statue of Liberty in New York harbour, which was a gift from the people of France in 1886, welcomed immigrants with open arms, but the prospects were not good. There was plenty of room, but there were no financial handouts or housing benefits for the arrivals.

The first settlers went to mining towns but the later ones opted for an urban existence in the developing huge conurbations of New York and Chicago. Close to New York, Hoboken was taken from the name of a city in Belgium, so it is reasonable to assume that the Flemish had some say in its name. It was founded by John Stevens in 1784 and he established a ferry service across the Hudson River between Hoboken and New York. At first, Hoboken became home for many German and Irish immigrants. The large waterfront included a recreational area and New Yorkers would go there for Sunday picnics. When Charles Dickens came to

America in 1842, he commented on how busy Hoboken was. In 1855 Hoboken became a city in its own right.

Meanwhile, Italy was a country in crisis: it was in debt and badly managed with poor roads and widespread poverty, especially in the south. Over the years a gulf had developed between the urban north and the rural south. On the map, Sicily, the largest island in the Mediterranean, looks like a football being kicked by the mainland and that is how it felt for the inhabitants.

Sicily had been the cause of one of the bloodiest conflicts in ancient history. It had originally belonged to the Greeks but they lost it to Carthage in Tunisia. Carthage with its teeming city, booming port and extensive trading empire could be seen a template for New York.

With the help of mercenaries, the Romans gained control of Sicily in the First Punic War (264–241 BC). The Carthaginians then moved into Spain and Hannibal destroyed several Roman armies. Hannibal hoped to regain Sicily but in 146 BC, Rome destroyed Carthage, fearing that the armies might rise again.

Sicily has a population of around five million, and yet an extraordinary number of players in this biography are of Sicilian extraction: Frank Sinatra and his family, Louis Prima, Frankie Laine, Vincent Minnelli, Liza Minnelli, Frank Capra, Joe DiMaggio, Sonny Bono, Cyndi Lauper, the author of *The Godfather*, Mario Puzo and a real life godfather, Sam Giancana. To them, we can add the bodybuilder Charles Atlas, Al Pacino, Martin Scorsese, Sylvester Stallone, Frank Zappa, Jon Bon Jovi and Lady Gaga. Sicily rules, OK?

But back in the 19th century, Italy's problems were magnified in Sicily. The landowners controlled the jobs and many working men felt that they were forgotten or disregarded. A self-help group, the Fasci, was formed to resist their oppression. *Fasci* means a bundle or sheaf. The implication was that you might be able to break a single stick, but you couldn't break a bundle. This has a direct link to rise of Italian fascism in the 1920s. Strikes, violence and arson were commonplace in Sicily. The Fasci Siciliani was dissolved in 1894 and over 1,000 members were forcibly deported. As a result, the poor were even more demoralised and many were desperate to emigrate.

Italy's strongest asset, its good agricultural land, was being wasted through overuse. Amongst Italy's drawbacks were its volcanoes. Mount Vesuvius hasn't erupted since 1944 but it can't be much fun living in its shadow.

The country's politicians were often inefficient and corrupt and there were food shortages and mass unemployment. This has meant that Italians have great allegiance to their family and friends, seeking support from and helping those around them. Because of the poverty, many Italians wanted to leave the country and set up new lives for themselves and their families abroad.

Emigration from Italy started on a small scale around 1850 and in the next 40 years around half a million Italians went to America. Then, between 1890 and 1914, 4 million Italians went to America. As the ships sailed into New York harbour, the immigrants would see the Statue of Liberty and cheer, but when they landed at Ellis Island or Castle Garden they were confused and bewildered. They were given medical tests and, if satisfactory, were allowed into the country. They brought their belongings with them but their possessions were often stolen within hours of arriving in America. The now derogatory term of 'wop' comes from the immigration process where it stands for 'without papers'. They were living on their wits and it was survival of the fittest.

Many of the Italians joined the Germans and the Irish in Hoboken. As elsewhere, the hatred between the different communities was occasioned by fear, the thought that these people were not like us with their different cultures, languages and religion. One positive result of this bigotry was that the Italians from the north and south, although rivals in their homeland, felt they had to bond in this new land. Paul Anka says, 'The Irish were Frank's natural enemies when he was in Hoboken so he was always a bit suspicious of them.' We will see how this plays out in Sinatra's relationship with the Kennedys.

A portrayal of the racism of the time can be seen in D W Griffith's film, *The Birth of a Nation* (1915). Although acclaimed as an early cinematic masterpiece, it was effectively a long commercial for the Ku Klux Klan, whose members at the time hated all immigrants.

Hoboken became a major transatlantic port and in 1917 became the embarkation point for American forces going to Europe. This was when America dropped its neutrality by joining the Allies. The Government originally thought that it wasn't their fight but then many Americans lost their lives with the sinking of the Lusitania in 1915.

There was a slogan, 'Heaven, Hell or Hoboken by Christmas'. By seizing the docks for military use, less revenue came into the city, and for one very good reason: the authorities had closed all bars within half a mile of the port. The German parts of the city were placed under martial law and many Germans were incarcerated at Ellis Island.

It was a difficult time for German-Americans, but the First World War gave some hope to Italian-Americans. The USA did not enter the war until 1917 and the American casualties have been placed at 50,000, far fewer than the loss in Vietnam. Nevertheless, many Italian-Americans had fought for the USA, some being wounded or killed, and they had earned the right to be called Americans. Hoboken was no longer dominated by the Germans as they had lost their standing. Two Jewish-German immigrants, Jerome Kern and Oscar Hammerstein II, set their 1929 Broadway musical, *Sweet Adeline*, in a beer garden in Hoboken in 1890, although it did not have a score to match their earlier success, *Show Boat*.

Of the four million Italians, mostly from southern Italy, who settled in America, most did not want to farm as they thought the land might again be overused. Those who did want to farm settled around New Orleans, but the majority wanted to live in the cities. Most of them were illiterate so were forced into manual work – any manual work would do. Frank Sinatra said of his forefathers, 'They took any kind of job and you know why? So their kids wouldn't have to do those jobs. So I wouldn't have to do it.'

Or as Tony Soprano told his therapist: 'When America opened the floodgates and let us Italians in, what do you think they were doing it for? Because they were trying to save us from poverty? No, they did it because they needed us – they needed us to build their cities and dig their subways and make them richer.' His shrink responds, 'That might be true, but what do poor Italian immigrants have to do with you?'

In Italy, the *padrone* system operated: the boss would find employment for the workers. The *padrone* system could work but at the extremes, it became the Mafia, and it came to America. The word *mafia* is a Sicilian word for 'daring', itself taken from an Arabic word for 'bragging'. Although associated with organised crime, the Mafia was respected as well as feared in the community. They could bribe police, judges and politicians. They could curry favour and solve disputes. The aim was to make as much money as possible, no matter what it took.

The American Mafia did not become a social problem until Prohibition in the 1920s and with the advent of such gangsters as Al Capone, turf wars and gangland killings became commonplace. Generally speaking, the Mafia refers to Italian gangsters, while the Mob widens the term to include Jewish and Irish gangsters. There is a code of honour with the Mafia – they look after their own, hence the Italian word *omertà*.

The families often had legitimate businesses as a front: one owned its own funeral parlour where special coffins with false bottoms were manufactured so that two people could be buried at once. It's hard to make a conviction stick if you can't find the body. Once the families moved to Las Vegas, it was easy to lose bodies in the desert.

In 1891 in the Catholic part of New Orleans, several Italian immigrants were accused of murdering a corrupt policeman, David Hennessy. Nineteen were charged with the crime but several were not tried and the rest were acquitted. For the first time, the press talked of the Mafia, a society which conferred hidden powers to a relative handful of hoodlums, bound by blood oaths. It was suggested that the Mafia had bought off the jurors. There was a public outcry and 11 of the accused were killed, mostly lynched or shot. The press didn't criticise their behaviour and Sinatra was to comment, many years later, 'We've been there too, man. It wasn't just black people hanging from the end of those ropes.' Indeed, the Italians were not seen as Caucasians and were often despised A tv movie about this lynching, *Vendetta*, starring Christopher Walken, directed by Nicholas Meyer, was made in 1999.

Italians also came in large numbers to America after the Great War and huge family communities were established. Although cholera was largely eradicated through better sanitation, one of the Italian areas became a focal point for polio and they were blamed, unfairly, for the disease. The Italians didn't mingle much with other groups as they formed friendships within their communities. They had pride in who they were. Gianni Russo, the adopted son of the Mafia leader, Frank Costello, told me, 'I have nine sons and every Italian thinks he can sing and can make love. I thought I could do those too but I tell my kids not to do them at the same time. (Laughs)'

Dozens of American cities had their Little Italys; apart from Hoboken, there was a Little Italy around Mulberry Street in nearby Manhattan. These areas were based around their old culture and the residents could speak Italian all day if they wished. They lived in cramped conditions with several to a room. The police were hostile and the newspapers derided them. They clung to their faith, the vast majority being Roman Catholics, and they concluded that it was still better than what they left behind.

There was the clichéd image of the Jews as clever and wealthy, the blacks as athletic and sexually potent, and the Italians as criminals and psychopaths. Curiously, the Jewish singer, Al Jolson found international fame by wearing blackface, while the Jewish comic actor, Chico Marx, made his reputation by imitating Italian-Americans. He used his comic accent for mispronunciations and malapropisms. In *Animal Crackers* (1930) Groucho Marx asked his brother, 'Hey, how did you get to be an Italian?' Good question.

The Italians were associated with gangsters and anarchists, the gangster image persisting to this day. Even if not criminal, the immigrants were regarded as hot-headed and temperamental. In the late-1920s, an Italian-American, Tony Lazzeri, became a very successful baseball player; it was unusual to find an Italian excelling in this most American of sports. Lazzeri also had a secret – he was epileptic but fortunately he never had a seizure on the field.

In 1922 Mussolini turned Italy into a fascist state, and he made his peace with the Pope in 1929 with the creation of Vatican City. When Mussolini entered the war on the German side against Britain and France in May 1940, Churchill gave the order to 'collar the lot' with reference to the Italian immigrants in the UK. These poor men and women – tailors, hairdressers, shop owners – were imprisoned on the Isle of Man or sent to Canada, without any thoughts for human rights. When Mussolini announced that Italy was at war against America in December 1941, the US government had a much more difficult problem, as there were millions of citizens of Italian origin already established there.

President Roosevelt had antipathy towards Italian-Americans and he asked the head of the FBI, J Edgar Hoover to draw a list of anyone who was a threat to national security. Consequently, Sinatra's mother could not understand why her son supported Roosevelt.

Many Italian-Americans joined the armed forces and some ended up fighting their blood relatives. There were severe losses of Italian lives when the ships, Arandora Star and Laconia, were torpedoed. Italy was invaded by the Allies in 1943, and many Italian-Americans must have nursed mixed feelings. Mussolini was imprisoned and Italy did an about-turn and declared war on Germany. In 1945 Mussolini and his mistress were shot dead by communist partisans and their bodies were hung from meat hooks at a local petrol station in Milan, where they were defiled by the public.

In 1946 Italy became a republic and for a few years, all was well as Italy was a founder member of NATO and the European Union. However, its internal politics returned to pandemonium and often the residents neglected to pay their taxes with no official action being taken. In the 1990s there were allegations of corruption in public office and it was as though the country had learnt nothing from its history. The upshot has been short-lived governments and constant turmoil, and Silvio Berlusconi with his bunga bunga parties became the laughing-stock of Europe.

Today there are nearly 300 million people living in the USA. Over 50 million people have German ancestry, which is the largest group, followed by 40 million African-Americans, largely descended from the slaves. Those of Italian origin number 18 million and the race has certainly punched above its weight in terms of the arts, fashion and cuisine: by now pizza is as American as apple pie.

A director of the Grammys, Bob Santelli, says, 'I am an Italian-American, born a mile and a half from Frank and it is very hard to shake off this Mafia image. The image may have become worse as *The Sopranos* shows the Italian immigrants in the worst light possible. My grandfather was born in Italy, but my father was born here and he said that we had to call ourselves Americans and not Italian-Americans. I couldn't take Italian at school as he told me to choose another language. We were Catholic though and my grandmother had three pictures in her house, Pope John XXIII, John F Kennedy, the first Catholic president, and Frank Sinatra. The blessed Trinity.'

Although there has now been a black President and Oprah Winfrey has become one of the richest Americans, there is still considerable racial tension in many cities, which was exposed by the O J Simpson trial in the 1990s, and continues to be exposed on a regular basis given the police shooting unarmed black people in recent times. This undercurrent of one community not wanting to be associated with another is played out in all manner of ways in the Frank Sinatra story.

When a concert was staged to celebrate Frank Sinatra's 80th birthday in 1995, Bob Dylan, of Russian-Jewish stock, chose to perform his little-known 'Restless Farewell'. Dylan had written the song when he was only 23 but the whole song encapsulates Sinatra's life: the chaotic spending, too much booze, treating women badly, ignoring bad press and being true to your code. The defiant 'I'll make my stand and remain as I am' could have come from 'My Way' and 'I'll bid farewell and not give a damn' would have been Sinatra's preferred way of saying goodbye. It's a brilliant song and the most significant verse relates to racial tension; Dylan makes the pertinent observation, 'Every foe that ever I faced, The cause was there before we came' – in Sinatra's case, being of Italian origin in America. Sinatra never sang this song and he might not have picked up on Dylan's diction, but it's the best song ever written about Sinatra, even though Dylan presumably wrote it about himself.

II. Day In–Day Out, 1915–1934

From an archivist's standpoint, the record-keeping at Ellis Island was not all that it should have been, and assumed or incorrect names were often recorded. We do however know that over 200 people called Sinatra (or something similar) arrived at Ellis Island between 1892 and 1910, but it's not possible to pinpoint the entry date for all of Frank Sinatra's grandparents into America.

The Latin *senex* means 'old man' and *senatus* stood for the 'senate', so the wise elders of a land came to known as senators. The name 'Sinatra' evolved as a corruption of this. It was the perfect surname, distinctive but not too much so, and ironically, having 'sin' as the first syllable. In view of Frank Sinatra's eminence, it is surprising that very few children have been christened Sinatra. Sinatra Presley sounds as good a stage name as Elvis Costello.

Francesco and Rosa Sinatra lived in Lercara Friddi in the province of Palermo, Sicily, and their son, Frank's father, Antonino Martino (known as Marty) was born on 4 May 1892. As it happens, a Mafia boss, Lucky Luciano, who figures in this story, was born in Lercara Friddi in 1897.

Francesco picked grapes for a living and thought he could do better in America. He sailed to Hoboken and worked first as a boilermaker. Then he moved to the American Pencil Company, making a reasonable $11 a week. In 1903 he was joined by Rosa and her two sisters. In time, Rosa was able to open a little grocery store.

In the 19th century, the port of Genoa was prosperous, and Sinatra's maternal grandfather worked there as a lithographer. Sinatra's maternal grandparents, the Garaventes, sailed to America and settled in Hoboken. Their daughter was called Natalina because she was born on Christmas Day 1895. They gave her the nickname, Dolly; she had blue eyes and stayed petite, being five foot and weighing seven stone.

Marty worked for a shoemaker but he felt that he might have more success boxing, a sport then more associated with the Irish than the Italians. Because he had blue eyes, he felt he could pass himself off as an Irishman and so he fought as Marty O'Brien. Marty met Dolly in 1912 and they were soon an item. As boxing was a male sport, Dolly would dress as a boy and attend his fights.

There was still some prejudice about northern Italians dating southerners, but Dolly was determined to marry Marty. Her parents said no; Marty was from Sicily, he was illiterate, he had tattoos, but the fact that he was a boxer was not a drawback as Dolly's two brothers, Dominic and Lawrence, were also fighters.

They married without parental approval at Jersey City Hall on Valentine's Day 1913. Marty listed his occupation as an athlete. Both families were outraged: in their view, a marriage ceremony had to be conducted by a priest. The families soon accepted their commitment and a priest married them the following year. Marty and Dolly lived at 415 Monroe Street, one of eight families in the tenement.

Frank Sinatra was born at home on 12 December 1915. As Dolly was small, it is surprising that he weighed nearly a stone at his birth. The doctor used forceps for a breech delivery, not too efficiently as he damaged the baby's neck, cheek and ear as well as puncturing his eardrum. He wasn't breathing and he might just have been another stillborn baby but Rosa had other ideas. She held him under the cold water tap until he breathed. Dolly told Marty, 'That's my Christmas present to you. We can't afford anything else.'

In 1955 Frank told Peggy Connolly, a singer he was dating, that 'they were just thinking about my mother. They ripped me out and tossed me aside.' Because of the permanent marks on his left jaw, he was called Scarface by his school friends and the doctor was the first person he ever wanted to beat up (but he never did). Although he was nowhere near as precious as some Hollywood stars, he preferred to be photographed from his right side.

Because of the complications of the birth, Dolly was unable to have further children. So Frank was an Italian rarity: an only child. The birth certificate says Francis Sinestro (sic), no doubt a clerical error, with no mention of Albert. Having the wrong name officially recorded bugged Sinatra and in 1945, a sworn affidavit from Dolly declared that the intended name was Francis A Sinatra, though Albert was still not given in full. On the birth certificate, Marty gave his occupation as chauffeur, but he was still fighting.

Dolly was still recuperating and not well enough to attend her son's christening at St Francis Roman Catholic Church in Hoboken on 2 April 1916. With a view to stepping up in the world, his godfather was Frank Garrick, a family friend who worked for the *Jersey Observer* and was a nephew of the Hoboken police captain. The priest asked Garrick his name, thinking him the father, and continued by christening the baby, Frank. So he was christened Frank Sinatra, and again no Albert. Recordkeeping was slapdash: the 1920 census shows the family as Tony, Della and Frank Sonatri.

The young child had plenty of relations living nearby. Both sets of grandparents were alive and there were five uncles, three aunts and twelve cousins. A second cousin, Ray Sinatra, who had been born in Sicily in 1904, was to become, independently of Frank, an arranger and conductor. He was Mario Lanza's musical director but he had few dealings with Frank, and only worked with him occasionally.

Dolly had been hoping for a girl and often dressed Frank in pink baby clothes. As he grew up, Dolly gave him the smartest clothes she could afford, which Frank later likened to Little Lord Fauntleroy. She associated dirt with poverty and she instilled in Frank the need to be fastidiously clean.

Although Dolly had a day job in a sweet factory, she found time to help the local community, often reading letters from home for illiterate Italians. She spoke English well and knew the various Italian dialects so she provided invaluable help with legal matters such as citizenship papers.

The politicians in Hoboken were impressed by Dolly's personality and saw how she could be used to attract voters. She became politically motivated, campaigning for the Democrats, and even chained herself to the city hall railings in 1919 in support of women's suffrage.

The US Temperance Movement had been advocating prohibition and the legislation for banning alcohol was passed in 1919 across much of America. The intention was that the population would sober up. It was the craziest legislation imaginable but perhaps the drinkers were too busy drinking to combat the prohibitionists.

Producing alcoholic drinks was one of the biggest businesses in America; now this was all declared illegal. Prohibition came into effect on 16 January 1920. The saloons held farewell parties, giving the last rites to John Barleycorn. Only it wasn't over. The law only encouraged an underground world of mobsters and bootleggers, and illegal drinking clubs, known as speakeasies, opened up. It wasn't difficult to bribe corrupt officials who would ignore what was happening. As Frank Sinatra commented, 'The Mob was invented by those self-righteous bastards who gave us prohibition. It was never going to work.' Not true, but it certainly made the Mob more powerful.

Alcohol was also used for paint thinning, antifreeze and had many other uses. The Government warned that such products must not be consumed, but many citizens were drawn to poisonous cocktails.

There were thousands of illicit stills and the mobsters added gambling and prostitution to the mix. F Scott Fitzgerald's 1925 novel, *The Great Gatsby*, romanticises bootleggers, although the source of Gatsby's own wealth is unknown. Many of the key figures such as Al Capone were evil and highly dangerous. Al Capone was known as Scarface, though not, of course, to his scarred face. It is highly probable that Joe Kennedy, the patriarch of the Kennedy family, made some of his wealth by illegally importing spirits into Boston with the help of the Mafia, but Joe was too clever and too manipulative to be caught. Kennedy invested some of his capital in the 1926 silent film, *Rose of the Tenements*, which was about New York gangsters.

In 1921 Dolly's brother Lawrence, who fought as Babe Sieger, was arrested for driving the getaway car in an armed robbery which left a railway worker dead. He could have been executed so he was fortunate to receive 10 years hard labour.

Also in 1921 Marty decided that he'd had enough. He had fought 30 professional fights, sometimes losing and after both breaking his wrist and being knocked out, he wanted to retire from the ring. He had a short spell as a boilermaker but the working conditions exacerbated his asthma. For a time, he worked for some bootleggers by collecting whiskey from Canada. However, having suffered a head injury while protecting his cargo he looked for something more stable.

As a result, Dolly borrowed some money from her family and they bought a bar on the corner of Jefferson and Fourth called Marty O'Brien's, although it was officially listed as a restaurant. A noted bootlegger Waxey Gordon (real name Irving Wexler) was a regular customer who replenished their stock of illegal booze.

Marty was not a perfect landlord but he could keep order. He was grouchy and didn't enter into small talk with the customers, but he liked practical jokes. Once at a friend's house, he slipped him a laxative after spreading glue on the toilet seat. Another time he took a sick horse to a rival saloon and shot it dead in the doorway. Not only does this have echoes of *The Godfather* but this paragraph could have been written about his son. But, as we shall see, it was Dolly's personality that really matched Frank's.

Dolly was always scheming and could be abusive and vengeful. She once pushed Frank downstairs, knocking him unconscious, and she often beat him with a small truncheon. She dunked his head in the ocean, an incident which led to him becoming an expert swimmer. 'My mother had the most wonderful laugh. She was wonderful,' he would say, but he both sought her out and avoided her in equal measure. It's possible that some of Frank's attitudes towards women came from his upbringing. Possibly he learned to trust no one because of his mother's outlook.

Like mother like son when it came to foul language. Dolly was surprisingly uninhibited for a woman in the 1920s and her favourite expression was 'son of a bitch bastard'.

Sometimes Dolly would sing in the bar; one of her favourite songs, 'When Irish Eyes Are Smiling', was in keeping with the Irish pseudonym. There is a photograph of Dolly holding a guitar in 1925 so presumably she knew some basic chords.

While Marty and Dolly were managing the bar, the young Frankie might be left with a neighbour. One was the Jewish Mrs Golden, from whom he assimilated some Yiddish phrases which occasionally drifted into his stage act.

In the early 1920s it was possible to buy radios fairly cheaply. Although a family might not be able to afford theatre tickets, they could hear Enrico Caruso or the Paul Whiteman Orchestra in their living rooms. You could argue that Caruso was the key performer in establishing gramophone records; Bing Crosby then introduced intimate singing through a microphone; Sinatra encouraged the sale of LPs; Elvis 45rpm singles; the Beatles rock albums; Queen stadium rock; Dire Straits compact discs; and Radiohead downloads. It's simplistic, but there you have it: the history of popular music in one sentence.

The young Sinatra was entranced by what he heard and from 1924 onwards, he would sit on the piano in the bar and sing in his unbroken voice for customers. He favoured 'Honest and Truly', a ballad written by Fred Rose, the co-founder of the music publishing giant, Acuff-Rose. He was also singing in the choir at St Francis.

Marty's cousin Vincent Manzola had been wounded in the First World War and he came to live with them in 1926. He was shell shocked and slow-witted, but he held down a job on the docks, where he was called Citrullo, the Italian term for blockhead. He was another of Dolly's problems but he did bring extra income into the house.

Another unwelcome nickname was attached to Marty's wife: Hatpin Dolly. She was a trained midwife and was known for walking around with her little black bag. Living in a Roman Catholic community, abortions were not officially allowed in any circumstances, but Dolly set herself up as the local abortionist. She saw herself as saving local embarrassment, but she was arrested in both 1937 and 1939, the second time just after Frank's first wedding.

In 1927 Dolly used her influence to secure Marty a job with the Hoboken fire brigade, which was very much an Irish domain. Marty was able to bypass the written test. This meant that there were three incomes in the household and they moved from 415 Monroe Street to a flat ten blocks away: 705 Park Avenue. It had three bedrooms, cost $65 a month and was a step up the social ladder – they were now living in a German/Irish neighbourhood.

Frank was scrawny but healthy, his only operation being an appendectomy when he was twelve. He was mocked by his classmates in the David E Rue Junior High School for his short temper. He didn't enjoy being taught, and did poorly, but he shielded this from Dolly by purloining a blank report card and completing it himself. His most mischievous stunt was to release some pigeons during the school play, *Cleopatra*, which led to his expulsion in 1928. He signed on briefly at the Stevens Institute, the oldest college of mechanical engineering in the US, and located in Hoboken. His friends called him Slacksy O'Brien because he had so many trousers.

Frank had his own room and he would listen to his Atwater Kent radio. Radio was recognised as the most important form of communication; two key networks had started broadcasting: the future giants NBC (1926) and CBS (1927). Frank would dream of singing over the radio.

One of his favourite songs was Irving Berlin's 'Oh! How I Hate to Get Up in the Morning', a theme that resonated with his own life. The song was introduced by Eddie Cantor and popularised through a hit recording by Arthur Fields. Bing Crosby's crooning appealed to him and he loved jazz bands, especially Louis Armstrong's. The jazz musicians would sometimes take liberties with the original melodies, something which horrified Jerome Kern, who wanted his songs performed as they had been written. Frank approved of this free and easy approach to a song and, as we shall see, sometimes the songwriters did not approve of Frank did with their songs.

As everyone who attends pub quizzes knows, the first 'talkie' was *The Jazz Singer*, starring Al Jolson, but it was anything but a jazz film. The story concerned a young singer from an immigrant family who defies his parents as they only want him to sing in the synagogue. Jolson, who sang schmaltz with exaggerated mannerisms, has few followers today, but his repertoire was amazing: 'Alexander's Ragtime Band', 'Swanee', 'California Here I Come', 'Sonny Boy' and 'Mammy', the last two being idealised pictures of family life which Frank would hardly recognise. Jolson started wearing blackface because his dresser had told him, 'You'd be much funnier, boss, if you blacked your face like mine. People always laugh at the black man.' At the time, nobody thought Al Jolson's approach was offensive.

Although *The Jazz Singer* was immensely successful and at the forefront of new technology, it was also dated as Al Jolson had not modified his approach following the introduction of stage microphones in 1924. He still sang as though he was bellowing to the back of the stalls. Now Bing Crosby had developed his crooning style with immaculate diction and a laidback, friendly approach. In other words, the voice on records was sounding more like a normal voice. Frank pinned his picture on his bedroom wall and once Dolly threw a shoe at Frank and hit the picture. Frank would impersonate the way he sang. 'Every time Bing sang on the radio,' said Frank, 'it became a duet and I was the other singer.'

There is a wonderful story, probably apocryphal but worth telling. Around 1930 Bing Crosby was in Hoboken and was arrested for being drunk. Sinatra couldn't believe his luck: Bing was in the local jailhouse! He went over there and found the cells were in the basement with windows at street level. Sinatra located where Bing was being held and Bing responded with a 'Go away, kid.' If that's not true, it certainly should be.

His uncle Dominic had given him a ukulele but he didn't take the instrument seriously. Frank never mastered a musical instrument nor read music, although he could play a few notes on the piano and a few chords on the guitar. Whenever he could, he would see Jascha Heifetz play violin. He had no wish to play the violin but he was intrigued by the way that Heifetz could hold notes and sustain them. Almost without thinking, his own vocal style developed from that. He would improve his diction by watching films starring Clark Gable and, from 1932, the British actor Cary Grant, the George Clooney of his day. A reporter once told Grant, 'Everybody wants to be Cary Grant' and he replied, 'So do I'.

Unlike Jolson, Rudy Vallée, the star most associated with megaphones, adapted well to the new techniques. He became the host of one of the first variety shows, *The Fleischmann Hour* on NBC. He had a major success with 'The Stein Song', the rights of which were bought by NBC, an early example of a media organisation moving into associated fields.

In 1930 Marty was fed up with Frank hanging around the house. Rather like Aunt Mimi with John Lennon, he told him, 'Go out and get a job, but no singing.' Admittedly, this was a tough order during the Depression when there were over four million unemployed in the US. Although a job didn't materialise, he did go to New Jersey and sing in a bar. The song he chose was 'Am I Blue' which Ethel Waters sang in the film, *On with the Show*. He was paid with cigarettes and a sandwich.

In 1931 Frank enrolled at the A J Demarest High School and his parents had hopes that he would settle down and train to be an engineer. No such luck; Frank lasted 47 days. Sinatra's lack of a formal education was his own fault, but he became self-conscious about it and this insecurity manifested itself from time to time.

The family moved to a three storey house with four bedrooms and central heating at 841 Garden Street, effecting a mortgage for $13,000. Dolly bought Frank a used Chrysler convertible for $35. He kept himself fit by pitching in an amateur baseball team, his favourite sport; his team wore orange and black, his favourite colours.

Frank loved gangster films, his favourites being *Little Caesar* (1931) with Edward G Robinson and *Scarface* (1932) with Paul Muni. Both actors were playing a character based on Al Capone, but neither actor was of Italian origin. Sinatra saw the gangsters as romantic figures like Robin Hood, and he was to develop this thought into a Rat Pack film. Oddly, the craze for gangster films was short-lived as the 1933 film code banned 'bigotry or hatred among people of different races, religions or national origins'. This reduced the number of Italian gangsters on screen, but certainly one young Italian-American did not see them that way. Bing Crosby, who was invariably diplomatic, did once let slip that 'I think Frank has always had a secret desire to be a hoodlum.'

Meanwhile, the real life gangsters were having a hard time. Al Capone was inside for, of all things, tax evasion, and Legs Diamond was shot to death in his hotel room.

Also in 1931 Bing Crosby had a huge success with his radio show for CBS and had one of the biggest hits of his career with 'Just One More Chance'. The following year he appeared on the same bill with Bob Hope at the Capitol Theatre on Broadway. They worked a few light-hearted routines together, which cemented their partnership.

Meanwhile Frank was still being coerced into finding regular employment. In 1932 he had a terrifying job at the Teijent and Lang shipyard in Hoboken. He had to catch hot rivets while swinging on a harness 40 feet in the air. He dropped one which singed his shoulder and it scared him so much that he left. He had lasted three days and he was still only 16.

After that he was unloading books for a publisher in Manhattan and then back on the docks for a nightshift in the dead of winter. His job for United Fruit Lines was to remove parts of the condenser units, clean them and restore them. He hated the dirt and he hated the drudgery.

Then Dolly had a brainwave. She went to the *Jersey Observer* to ask Frank's godfather, Frank Garrick, now the circulation manager, to give him a job. For a short while, he bundled newspapers onto delivery trucks, but Frank wanted to be a sports writer. When one of the sports journalists was killed in an accident, Dolly demanded that Frank take his job. Very foolishly, she instructed Frank to sit at his desk. Bad move. The editor asked what he was doing and he said, quite wrongly, that Mr Garrick had given the post. The editor sacked him. Frank was furious – he was always angrier when he knew he was wrong – and he blamed Garrick for not supporting him. Dolly was equally furious and never spoke to Garrick again.

In 1933 Bing Crosby sang the lighthearted and gently self-mocking 'Learn to Croon' in the film, *College Humour*, and Frank was soon performing the song with a megaphone (as microphones were expensive) in little bars and clubs. The patrons would throw cents into the funnel. This was way out-of-date and he persuaded Dolly to spend $65 on a portable public address system in return for him performing at some local meetings for the Democrats. He was a Bing Crosby tribute act as he sang 'Please', 'Just One More Chance' and 'I Found a Million Dollar Baby', but he also included an impression of Jimmy Cagney in the gangster film, *Public Enemy*.

Everyone knew that Prohibition wasn't working and the laws were repealed in 1933. Many of the bootleggers who ran the speakeasies remained in the night clubs after drinking became legal, and many of them retained their links with the gangsters.

In 1934 Frank went to Long Branch on the New Jersey shore, where Dolly's sister Josie had rented a holiday home. There, he met the 17-year-old Nanicia (Nancy) Barbato. She was on the front porch giving herself a manicure and Frank sang to her with his ukulele. Nancy became his first steady girlfriend. She lived in Jersey City and her father Mike was even stricter than Marty. As he said, 'No work, no girlfriend.' In 1935 he worked with Nancy's brother, Bart, as a plasterer's assistant, but his heart was not in it. It was the last time Frank Sinatra would accept a day job.

Towards the end of 1934 Frank took his girlfriend Nancy Barbato to see Bing Crosby at the Journal Square Theatre in Jersey City. He was just 19 and he was seeing his idol on stage for the first time. He later commented, 'I thought, if he can do it as easily as that, I'm going to take a whack at it myself.' Straight after this engagement, Bing played the Capitol Theatre on Broadway with the comedian Milton Berle and Eddy Duchin's band. It was a tour de force as Bing clowned with Berle on stage, but bizarrely, they were Bing's last performances as a touring concert attraction until 1975. He had found other things to do.

CHAPTER 2

You must be one of the newer fellas

'A voice like Sinatra's comes along once in a lifetime. Why did it have to be mine?'
Bing Crosby

I. Anything Bing Can Do...

A continuous thread through this book is Frank Sinatra's relationship to Bing Crosby as a young admirer, as a fellow entertainer, as a friend and as a rival. Their paths crossed frequently, not always in favourable circumstances.

Bing was born Harry Lillis Crosby in Tacoma, Washington on 3 May 1903 which made him twelve years older than Frank. Bing's father worked for the city treasury, but soon after his son was born, he was offered a new job as a bookkeeper at the new Inland Brewery in Spokane, Washington. The young boy picked up his nickname from a strip cartoon character, Bingo, in a local newspaper. He was bright and did well at high school, planning to be a lawyer.

Once at university, Bing both sang and played drums with a Dixieland jazz band led by Al Rinker and he considered singing for a living. Rinker's sister, the jazz singer Mildred Bailey was working with Paul Whiteman and his Orchestra and she arranged an audition. Bing, Al and Harry Barris became the Rhythm Boys and were an added attraction on Whiteman's appearances. Their songs included 'Ol' Man River', 'Mississippi Mud' and 'I'm Coming Virginia'. Harry Barris wrote 'Wrap Your Troubles in Dreams', which became a standard after Bing recorded it in 1931.

Paul Whiteman was featured in an early talkie, *King of Jazz* (1930) and he could claim that title, not because he was a jazz musician (he wasn't) but because the real claimants such as Louis Armstrong were black. Bing's warm, friendly appearance in the film made him a star overnight, and with his brother Everett as his manager, he branched out as a solo performer. Everett liked to call himself 'the wrong Crosby'.

Electrically amplified microphones had been introduced for both public performances and recording studios. Although Al Jolson found it difficult to get away from his declamatory delivery, the new technique was ideal for Bing Crosby. He adopted a laidback, intimate style that drew audiences to him. His conversational singing became known as crooning. He had an easily identifiable voice and the public loved the lowdown 'ba, ba, ba, boom'. Sinatra started by imitating Bing, despite having a higher voice.

In 1931 Bing had several hit records including 'Just One More Chance' and 'Out Of Nowhere' ('You came to me from out of nowhere' – how apt!). He made three films and hosted a daily radio series for CBS. By the end of the year, he was a major star.

Despite this impressive work load, Bing was not the only singer in town and NBC hired Russ Columbo to start a series which would follow Bing's. Columbo was the twelfth child of Italian-American parents in New Jersey. The press were told it was 'a battle of the baritones', a contest that paved the way for Crosby vs Sinatra, Beatles vs Stones and Blur vs Oasis. As you might expect, Russ Columbo was roundly beaten in the ratings by Bing Crosby but he did have substantial successes with 'Sweet and Lovely' and his own song, 'Prisoner of Love', later a huge hit for Perry Como. In September 1934, when Columbo was showing a friend his antique guns, one of them accidently went off and Columbo took a bullet to the head and died. Russ Columbo's signature tune was 'You Call It Madness'.

In 1932 Bing starred in *The Big Broadcast* (actually a film), which had a feeble storyline attached to several cameo performances. Besides Bing, there were songs from Cab Calloway, the Mills Brothers and the Boswell Sisters. The film established George Burns and Gracie Allen as comedy stars.

In the same year Bing recorded a tremendous 'St Louis Blues' with Duke Ellington and his Orchestra, complete with exhilarating scat singing. In 1930 the country singer Jimmie Rodgers had recorded 'Blue Yodel No. 9' with Louis Armstrong, but it was still rare for a white singer to perform with black musicians and even more so to do it with credibility. Hear this record and you will realise why the bandleader Artie Shaw called Bing 'the first hip white man in America', a comment that otherwise seems anomalous today.

Bing's brother, Bob, led one of the most popular jazz bands in America, Bob Crosby's Bob Cats but they rarely worked together. Like Bing, Bob Crosby was modest about his abilities and would say, 'I'm the only guy in the band business who made it without talent.' He was probably right although he was a reasonable vocalist. Bob Crosby's big records included 'South Rampart Street Parade' and 'Big Noise from Winnetka', recently revived by Clint Eastwood and his son, Kyle.

Also in 1932 Bing scored with an acutely telling song about the Depression, 'Brother, Can You Spare a Dime'. This song was as surprising to the listening public as 'Blowin' in the Wind' was to pop pickers in 1963. It was a frank song about mass unemployment and the beggar in the song simply wants a dime to keep him going until the next day. The lyricist, Yip Harburg later remarked, 'It was a terrible period. You couldn't walk along the street without crying, without seeing people standing in breadlines.'

As Bing's *modus operandi* was to be reassuring rather than disturbing, it is much to his credit that he recorded this controversial song and a shame that he shunned such material in subsequent years. I wouldn't have expected Bing to record Woody Guthrie's 'Deportee' or 'Vigilante Man' but there were plenty of songs which could have worked. On the other hand, he was a Republican whilst most of this material came from left-wing writers.

'St Louis Blues' and 'Brother, Can You Spare a Dime' are impressive exceptions. On the whole, Bing preferred to cruise along, giving the impression that anyone could sing as well as he could. Of course they couldn't, but the fact that everyone could sing along with Bing contributed to his success. Indeed, to add to his man-in-the-street appeal, Bing sometimes whistled. Bing often put himself down, describing himself as a crooner, but he knew that he didn't possess Sinatra's interpretive skills. Rather like Dean Martin, Bing wanted to work quickly and then go to the golf course.

Both Bing and Frank were custodians of what is now called The Great American Songbook, but Bing spread his net wider. He often recorded hymns, country and western songs, excessively sentimental songs, patriotic flag-wavers and what would now be called world music. Can you imagine Frank singing 'Hey Jude'? Can you imagine Bing singing 'Hey Jude', but he did. For every album like the superb jazz collection, *Bing Sings While Bregman Swings* (1956) with Buddy Bregman, there were several *Join Bing and Sing Along*s. His phrasing and his artistry on the album with Bregman are comparable to anything that Sinatra recorded in the 1950s, but unlike Sinatra, Crosby did not like recording at night.

He liked a morning session which would be over by noon and then it was over to that golf course.

An example of the contrast between the two stars came in 1962 when they both decided to record albums with London musicians. Sinatra recorded an album of slow, intense ballads, *Great Songs from Great Britain*, while Bing made *On the Sentimental Side*, a project which predates the *Sing Along A Max* LPs of Max Bygraves. The *Sing Along* albums reveal that Bing was not at all concerned with his legacy; how could such albums merit inclusion in a history of music?

Bing's casual approach worked especially well on duets. Both Bing and Frank worked with the singers of the day and Bing's generally comes off best because the duets brought out his affability and geniality. Just listen to how relaxed he sounds on *Bing and Rosie – The Crosby-Clooney Radio Sessions*, a double CD released in 2010. When they let rip on the uptempo jazz of 'Chicago Style', he starts with an 'Everybody duck' and concludes with 'Anybody hurt?' As they harmonise on 'Easter Parade', Bing adds, 'Damn good, hey?'

Typical of his good humour is the gentle ribbing when he and Sinatra appeared together on radio:

Frank: *"Hey, Bing, do me a favour."*
Bing: *"What?"*
Frank: *"Retire."*

Bing loved Dixieland jazz. Writing in his autobiography, *Call Me Lucky*, which was published in 1953, he says, 'When all is said and done, my favourite music is Dixieland music. I can get up in the morning after a restless night, feeling blue and depressed, put on a few LPs featuring Eddie Condon's band or Red Nichols or Louis Armstrong – or any practitioner of the cult, for that matter – and after half an hour of this music, I'm picked up and ready to go again.' It's disconcerting to hear of Bing being 'blue and depressed' but for 'blue and depressed' read 'hung over'.

Bing was a staunch Catholic, but when his record company wanted him to record carols for Christmas, he wasn't sure that this was the right thing to do: should someone profit from singing the hymn book? He relented when the company agreed to donate all profits to a mission in China. So in 1935 Bing Crosby had a best seller with a very respectful arrangement of the carol, 'Silent Night', the first ever million selling charity single.

From then on Bing became associated with songs for the holidays. When Irving Berlin gave him 'White Christmas' for the film, *Holiday Inn*, in 1942, Bing simply said, 'You don't have to worry about this one, Irving'. It became the biggest selling record of all time. I accept that One Direction or No Direction may have claimed this title by now, but I'm talking about the days when record sales mattered and the fact is, 10 million people got on their feet, went into record stores and physically bought 'White Christmas'. What's more, for next Christmas and all the Christmases to come, there will no escaping Bing's wish that all your Christmases be white.

In 1937 Bing starred in *Waikiki Wedding*, which prompted a run of Hawaiian hits, notably 'Sweet Leilani'. He loved performing with steel guitars and ukuleles and, oddly enough, his only album with the arranger Nelson Riddle was *Return to Paradise Islands* for Frank Sinatra's Reprise label in 1964. It could be argued that Bing was being contemporary as Elvis Presley had scored with the film, *Blue Hawaii*.

Unlike today, where there is normally only one version of a hit song, a potential success might be sung by a dozen different performers. All the big labels wanted their own version of a winner. Hence, Bing and Frank often vied for the charts with the same song and sometimes there was little to choose between them. Bing recorded definitive versions of 'Pennies from

Heaven', 'Blue Skies' and 'Moonlight Becomes You'.

However, for all his good phrasing and diction, Bing does little more than sing the song in a conversational manner. There is little of the sexuality that Sinatra put into his performances, a different kind of bedside manner if you like as Bing was more suited to lullabies. As Bing told Michael Parkinson, 'Frank creates a mood. I don't think that I create a mood when I sing.'

Although they might have discussed hair loss when they were together, Bing was photogenic and looked good on the screen. Most directors realised that he was best when someone was close to him and he was speaking naturally. His speech was always very musical and at times, it sounded like singing. Often he was playing a priest or clowning around in some good-natured comedy. It certainly worked as he was the top star at the US Box Office between 1944 and 1949, a considerable achievement when you consider whom he had to beat. He made it seem effortless and he titled his autobiography, *Call Me Lucky*.

Bing won an Oscar for playing the Irish priest, Father O'Malley in *Going My Way* (1944) directed by Leo McCarey. The priest was optimistic, musical, down to earth and full of good humour and he became a priest to help others. The role played to Bing's strengths and the songs included the Oscar-winning 'Swinging on a Star' with a boys' choir and the lullaby, 'Too-Ra-Loo-Ra-Loo-Ra' where he sends an old priest to sleep. Bing was so convincing that he would receive fan letters addressed to Father Crosby. Pope Pius XII said that it was good to have the priesthood humanised. Indeed, the film changed the way that Catholics were perceived in the USA. When Bing played Father Conroy in *Say One for Me* (1959), he is seen performing Catholic rites and services.

Bing was given his Oscar for Best Actor by Gary Cooper and Bob Hope and when it looked like he was too overcome to respond, Hope gave him a prod and told him to say something. Bing said, 'It just goes to show what a great and democratic world we live in, when a broken-down crooner like myself can win this Academy crockery. If Leo McCarey can lead me through a picture like this one, he can find me a horse to win the Kentucky Derby."

In December 1932 both Bing Crosby and Bob Hope were booked to appear at the Capitol Theatre on Broadway and Bing invited Bob to join him for some knockabout banter. They found that witty repartee came easily to them. In particular, they would both try and impress each other with impressions which always sparked off their humour. They were soon best friends and would continue their dialogue on golf courses, with Bob often sniping about Bing's wealth and his meanness (whilst ignoring his own). Although this was following similar jokes about Jack Benny, it had a basis in truth. Bing was a very shrewd investor and when he died, he was worth millions.

Although Bing always had retirement at the back of his mind, he was easily persuaded to make *The Road to Singapore* with Bob and Dorothy Lamour. As Bing said, 'I was intrigued with the idea of working with Bob and Dottie because it seemed to me it would be a winning combination: a foreign land, natives, music, Dottie in a sarong, Bob being a clown, me singing the ballads.' Spot on. It was 1940, the world was at war, and this was perfect light relief and led to series of other *Road* films, nearly all of them about cannibals who had to be won over with humour.

Although featuring exotic locations, the *Road* films are very American and full of wisecracks, usually from Bob although Bing could deliver one-liners better than Sinatra. Often they would deviate from the script and ad-lib. Hope said to one of the writers, 'If you recognise one of your lines, shout 'Bingo!'" Their repartee is still amusing but Hope on his own is no longer funny.

In the *Road* films, Bing and Bob played good-natured guys who were down on their luck: single guys but loving girls and usually betraying each other. The concept was that the cinemagoers would laugh at Bob Hope, the inept seducer, and identify with Bing Crosby. Bing was usually cool, while Bob was sparkling with energy but full of false confidence. Although his image was as the good guy, Bing often got the upper hand by trickery. In the final reel, Bing won the girl, usually by singing romantically. The films were not without risks. In *The Road to Utopia* (1946), Bing and Bob have a routine with a bear; the day after the filming, the bear tore off one of its trainer's arms.

Bing refused to appear as a priest in one of their comedies as mocking religion, however light-heartedly, was a definite no-no for him. He took his public image seriously, although he did play golf with one of the Hollywood bad boys, Humphrey Bogart.

Crosby's legend was built around being the nicest guy in town, though we now know that wasn't true. He was a family man but he did not treat his children well, although none of this was revealed until after his death in 1977. In particular, too much booze would make him unpleasant.

In his later years, Bing was often grouchy, and Engelbert Humperdinck's manager, Tony Cartwright recalls, 'Bing Crosby was a grumpy old man who hated pop singers and anything new. He didn't care for either Tom Jones or Engelbert. He was doing *Hollywood Palace* and it was his first TV series in years. Humperdinck was looking forward to seeing him as he loved meeting the old greats. I knocked on Bing's dressing-room door and I said, 'It's Tony Cartwright, Engelbert Humperdinck's manager.' 'What do you want?' 'Can I come in?' 'No, you can't.' Our whole experience was like that."

Frank was no lover of David Bowie and when it was mooted that Bowie was going to play him in a film, he stated that he was not going to be played by 'that faggot'. Bowie didn't have the voice but at times he did have the look with his trilby hat and cashmere overcoat. On the other hand, Bing Crosby recorded a schmaltzy duet with him. Seymour Stein, the owner of Sire Records, says, 'I do regard Bing Crosby as more important than Frank as he totally changed popular music – and he also did that nice little duet of 'Little Drummer Boy' with David Bowie just before he passed away. But when it comes to the actual quality of the voice, I would pick Nat 'King' Cole's over both of them. I just loved his voice.'

In March 1977 Bing fell into an orchestra pit after completing a show in Pasadena. He was put in hospital and he told the press, 'I gotta change the act and find a new finish.' His back injuries took it out of him and the plans for a final *Road* film were dropped. In September he was well enough to record a Christmas special in London and his family recommended David Bowie as a guest star. Bowie wrote a countermelody for 'Little Drummer Boy' called 'Peace on Earth' and Bing called him 'a clean-cut kid'. After the special he went to play golf with his friends in Spain and he collapsed and died after a round on 14 October. His final words were 'That was a great game of golf, fellas.'

Bing's musical legacy has dimmed with the years and his records can only be heard in an historical context today while many of Sinatra's still seem contemporary. There are many reasons for this: his arrangements were coated in sugar; his lack of gravitas let him down; and Sinatra understood the LP age much better. But most of all, it's because his image was in the Perry Como/Val Doonican bag, while Sinatra had a bad boy reputation that today's rebels can only dream about. It gave his work an authenticity that Crosby lacked. Bing's blue of the night may have faded into Sinatra's day, but for all that, Frank Sinatra could never eclipse Bing Crosby's record sales.

II. Day In–Day Out, 1935–1939

Having seen Bing Crosby perform in December 1934, the 19-year-old Frank Sinatra was determined to become a professional entertainer. He played at small clubs in Hoboken and landed a 15 minute spot, unpaid, on WAAT in Jersey City, where he sang with his friend Matty Golizio on guitar. Although this was only a community station, it began his love for performing on radio.

A singing group of three Italian boys from Hoboken, the Three Flashes, played at the Rustic Cabin, a roadhouse in Alpine, New Jersey. The venue was notorious as a private haunt for married men with their girlfriends as there were little private cabins in the showroom itself.

Edward Bowes made movie shorts and he used the Three Flashes. Sinatra heard about this and he made his film début as a waiter in *The Nightclub* and as part of a blackface chorus in *The Big Minstrel Act*, both shot in the Bronx for Biograph and distributed by RKO. So the first time the American public would have glimpsed Sinatra was in top hat, bowtie and spats with a black face and wide, white lips. This was not a one-off as Frank put burnt cork on his face for a show at a New Jersey fire station in 1936; back then, nobody thought this insensitive.

However, Bowes' main interest was his NBC radio show, *Major Bowes and his Original Amateur Hour*, which discovered new talent. Bowes wanted the Three Flashes to perform and Frank asked Dolly, a formidable ally, to persuade them to become a quartet. This involved a change of name to the Hoboken Four. The show was broadcast live from the Capitol Theatre on Broadway. If the audience objected to a performer, they could jeer and a large gong would sound, telling him to stop. Otherwise, the acts would be assessed by a clapometer and the winner duly announced.

The Hoboken Four broadcast on 8 September 1935, when Bowes introduced them as 'singing and dancing fools'. Bowes spoke to them and they said they had worked on amateur shows. 'What about him?' said Bowes, indicating Sinatra. 'Oh, he's never worked a day in his life,' one of them retorted. They performed 'Shine', a song which had been written in 1910 for a travelling black show, *His Honour The Barber*. It had been recorded by both Bing and Louis Armstrong in 1931 and Frank emulated Bing's scat singing.

The Hoboken Four won easily, but Frank felt uneasy. He had acne, was very skinny and put lifts in his shoes to raise him above five foot seven. But he was already very attractive to young women and he made the best of it.

Major Bowes put the Hoboken Four on his touring show. It was nothing very glamorous as they stayed in fleabag hotels and tensions ran high. One evening in Spokane, of all places, Sinatra joked about another member, Fred Tamburro on stage. After the show, Tamburro was annoyed and Frank said, 'Just my sense of humour, Tamby.' 'Here's mine,' said Tamburro and knocked him out. Frank left the tour and went home for Christmas.

Frank returned to WAAT with Matty Golizio and billed himself locally as 'Major Bowes Radio Winner'. He enjoyed going to the New York Paramount which would feature a live act with a new film and once you had a ticket, you could stay all day watching the combination of live show and film as it came round again and again. He found the perfect combination in Artie Shaw's band with Bing Crosby's film, *Pennies from Heaven*. At Bing's insistence, the movie featured Louis Armstrong and it is an early example of a black performer receiving a leading role alongside white actors in a commercial release.

In 1936 Frank met two people connected to music publishing, one a song plugger and one a songwriter, both of whom would play significant roles in his career. Hank Sanicola from the Bronx was a former boxer and now a song plugger and pianist. Like Frank, he was of Sicilian extraction. Sanicola told Frank that he was singing too high in his throat and he should take singing lessons to improve his technique and use his diaphragm. Frank took lessons from John Quinlan, a former member of the Metropolitan Opera, who had been dismissed for drunkenness. Quinlan told him, 'You can't sing what you can't understand,' and from this developed an appreciation of good songs.

The second contact was Chester Babcock, a tall, good-looking pianist who was to write under the name of Jimmy Van Heusen, taking his first name from the actor James Stewart and the surname (a non-American one!) from a shirt manufacturer. He was related to the father of American songwriting, Stephen Foster, and had been born in Syracuse, New York in 1913. Van Heusen met Sinatra at Toots Shor's bar in New York and they were to have much in common: notably booze, broads and ballads. Van Heusen is often portrayed as a coarse, sex-mad heavy drinker. This is true but he was also, like Sinatra, a man of great sensitivity which came out in his music. One of his first successes was 'Darn That Dream', sung by Mildred Bailey in 1940.

Sinatra's second cousin, Ray Sinatra, was working as an arranger for NBC and secured him a little work, singing for 70 cents a song and once working with Dinah Shore. He performed 'Exactly Like You' with his ukulele on *Town Hall Tonight*, another amateur show, this time hosted by Fred Allen. In 2001, a lacquered aluminum eight inch record was discovered, which almost certainly is Sinatra's first recording. Backed by Walter Costello's accordion, he sang a British song, 'Roses of Picardy'.

Although Sinatra hoped for a residency at the Rustic Cabin, the bandleader Harold Arden, while admiring his talent, took a dislike to his personality and wouldn't hire him. Once again Frank turned to Dolly. She contacted her friend, the local mayor, who in turn spoke to the formidable James Caesar Petrillo, president of the American Federation of Musicans – but more of him later. He was a tough cookie but for the moment they were on the same side and Frank became a singing waiter at the Rustic Cabin.

Frank often took his regular girl friend, Nancy Barbato to the Rustic Cabin, but he couldn't ignore whatever fate threw his way and he had affairs with Marian Brush and Toni Penta. The inevitable happened in November 1938 when Nancy and Toni met on the same night. They fought over him and, these times being very different from today, he was put in jail for the night. Frank told the police it was a case of mistaken identity. There is the infamous photograph of Frankie with a police number under his picture and looking like a convict, which at the time he was. He must have been tempted to use that photograph on an LP sleeve.

Toni told a different story. She had had a relationship with him under a promise of marriage and now she discovered that he was going to marry Nancy. This was reported in the *Jersey Observer* as *Songbird Held in Morals Charge*, not, you note, *Former Sports Reporter Held in Morals Charge*.

Dolly used her contacts to get her son released and there was a catfight between Toni and Dolly with Toni being arrested for disorderly contact. When it transpired that Toni was already married, the case was dismissed but not before Toni tried again and had him charged with adultery. The legislation was somewhat unrealistic back then and this charge was soon dismissed. However, Dolly, who liked Nancy, thought that her boy should be married as soon as possible in order to prevent future incidents: Frank was too vulnerable when he was single.

For all her misgivings, Nancy adored Frank and she completely approved of his singing career, even giving him $15 for publicity photographs. On the day before the wedding, Frank went into a recording studio in Manhattan to make another demonstration record. The saxophonist Frank Mane wanted to cut a couple of tracks with some musicians to see if he could further his career as a dance band leader and he asked Sinatra to sing on one of them. The song he chose, 'Our Love', worked perfectly as a wedding present. It was a romantic ballad adapted from a theme in Tchaikovsky's *Romeo and Juliet*. It had been a success for Tommy Dorsey and his Orchestra with their vocalist Jack Leonard and an arrangement from Axel Stordahl. It also did well for Tommy's brother, Jimmy with his Orchestra and singer Bob Eberly.

On 4 February 1939 Frank Sinatra married Nancy Barbato at Our Lady of Sorrows Church in Jersey City. Nancy was working as a secretary and so they were able to move into 487 Garfield Street at $42 a month. Frank loved her cooking and loved her but they disagreed over Dolly as Nancy did not want him running to Dolly at every available opportunity. Later in the month, relations were strained when Dolly was arrested for botching an abortion as the girl had nearly died. She was put on probation for five years.

Frankie's voice was improving all the time. On his nights off he would watch other singers; he admired Mabel Mercer's enunciation and Ethel Waters' feeling for the blues.

Mabel Mercer was born in 1900. Her father was a black American musician and her mother a white UK vaudeville singer, and she had been raised in Burton-on-Trent, Staffordshire. She was educated at a convent school in Manchester, hence her fine elocution and manners. She had done well in the south of France and moved to New York in 1938 for an engagement at Le Ruban Bleu in Manhattan. She stayed in America following the outbreak of war and married Kelsey Pharr of the Delta Rhythm Boys, probably just to keep her in the US. In 1942 she made her name at the Three Deuces cabaret club. This was when the big band era went in decline and vocalists like Sinatra and Peggy Lee were interested in cabaret, realising the importance of a more personal approach to the lyrics. Sinatra saw Mercer as the ultimate cabaret singer. Her accompanist from 1946 to 1949 was Bart Howard who wrote 'Fly Me to the Moon.'

Ethel Waters, born in Pennsylvania in 1896, was the first person to sing 'St Louis Blues' and she became famous for singing 'Stormy Weather' in Cotton Club revues. Although well known as a blues singer, she crossed to the popular field and became a successful Broadway and Hollywood actress. Billie Holiday acknowledged her influence but said, "She sings as though her shoes are too tight."

Much as Frank loved Ethel and Mabel, nobody could compare with Billie Holiday. She had been born in Philadelphia just a few months before Frank and she put such anguished feelings into her performances that the listeners felt she was singing from experience. The rock musician J J Cale described her appeal: 'Many musicians are laidback, I didn't invent it. Billie Holiday is probably the biggest exponent of laidback there is. She always sang behind the beat and I loved that. Pausing gives you a different kind of sound from when you're playing right on the beat.'

Frank couldn't have said it better.

CHAPTER 3

Start spreadin' the news

'There was no such thing as a man crossing his legs on the bandstand. You had to sit there straight in your chair, legs together, with both feet flat on the floor.'

Tex Beneke, saxophonist and vocalist with Glenn Miller

I. Big Band Swing

After the First World War ended, there was a feeling of euphoria in America and liveliness and frivolity marked the decade which came to be known as the Roaring 20s. Beautiful girls with bobbed hair and short skirts flapped around and swung their large necklaces to the Charleston and the Black Bottom. Everything seemed so positive: in 1927 Charles Lindbergh flew from New York to Paris and the possibilities of air travel became a reality. In 1928 Alexander Fleming discovered penicillin and so many diseases could be eradicated or cured.

The artistic scope of entertainment was vastly increased in the mid-1920s by the advent of talkies and the use of microphones for both recorded sound and live entertainment. There were exciting films which advanced technology, and the chariot race in *Ben Hur* (1925) would take some beating today – indeed, today's health and safety regulations would make this impossible. The first 'talkie', *The Jazz Singer* (1927) made Al Jolson an international star and there were classic comedies from Charlie Chaplin, Buster Keaton and Laurel and Hardy. What fun, what jolly japes; everything looked rosy and share prices were going up and up.

And then it crashed. Wall Street crashed in fact.

In 1929 the share prices tumbled so fast and to such a degree that some investors and stock brokers were climbing onto the parapets of tall buildings and diving to the ground. Everything looked bleak and a badly devised strategy for recovery only made it worse. The Wall Street Crash was followed by the great Depression of the 1930s, which was a huge and prolonged downturn with mass unemployment. To make it even worse, the farms in Texas and other southern states were devastated in the Great Dust Bowl. Nobody was doing well and millions were on the breadline.

In 1932 Franklin D Roosevelt became the Democratic President with the promise of a New Deal, although this was far easier to say than deliver. Most importantly, he introduced social security benefits to help the ordinary citizens. He realised that the crash had been caused by the free market spiralling out of control and he wanted future governments to intervene through the provision of safety nets.

You might assume that this would have dramatically affected entertainment. In the early 1970s, we had the rise of the singer/songwriter, one man with his guitar; it's conceivable they arrived 40 years too late. Such an inexpensive form of entertainment did not find much favour in the early 1930s. There was the singing brakeman, Jimmie Rodgers (a man with two jobs during the Depression!) and a young Woody Guthrie, but such entertainment was of limited appeal. What the public *en masse* wanted was the full sound of the big bands.

The 1930s is known as the big band or the swing era. As Duke Ellington recorded in 1932, 'It Don't Mean a Thing If It Ain't Got that Swing', the first time swing was mentioned in a song title.

The first successful big band was Paul Whiteman's – it had been popular since 1920. These big bands played dance music and they were helped by several developments. Sorry, tuba players, but the string bass was more flexible and more suited to quick tempos. Similarly, the strident banjo was replaced by the much more versatile guitar, which, thanks to the new microphones, could be heard in a dance band environment.

There could be up to 20 musicians in a big band but the average was a dozen. There would be a powerful brass section of trumpets, trombones and saxophones with a rhythm group of piano, guitar, bass and drums. Strings were a rarity. The bands invariably had a male vocalist and sometimes a female and a vocal group as well.

Although they might make great music, the bands were static. They looked smart, wearing uniforms with creased trousers and playing behind monogrammed stands. The singers and the soloists stood up for their contributions and then sat down again. Even comedy numbers and novelties were presented in this fashion unless there was a particularly comical front man such as Cab Calloway.

The arrangements would usually start with the band playing the song through and a musician, usually the bandleader, taking a solo. After 50 seconds, the singer would add a verse and a chorus, and then it would be back to the instruments. The singers were not regarded as the most important members and pride of place went to the arrangers, who might be the bandleaders themselves.

The most critically acclaimed big band belong to Duke Ellington, best known for his beautiful 'Mood Indigo', but he was essentially a serious composer who happened to work in jazz. Count Basie's band too was special as they were based around the blues and one of their biggest successes was 'One O'Clock Jump'.

The black band leader Fletcher Henderson had to contend with his trumpet soloist, Louis Armstrong, a musician of total brilliance. Listen to his recordings with the band and compare him to the rest of the musicians. Louis stole the show every time. From 1925 Louis Armstrong had his own bands, sometimes a Hot Five, sometimes a Hot Seven, sometimes an orchestra and he was unique: a magnificent trumpet player and a very recognisable vocalist with his gravel voice. Both Bing Crosby and Frank Sinatra admired his phrasing. Times have changed and Armstrong with his rolling eyes and perpetual mugging is viewed as an Uncle Tom, a throwback to minstrel shows, but that wasn't his intention. He was simply a brilliant entertainer and he wanted everyone to notice him.

Paul Whiteman (and never has a band leader been so aptly named) liked jazz but he didn't want to play anything abrasive or daring. He wanted a jazz feeling but it had to be a safer version of the music with little improvisation. As he was very successful, the other band leaders at first took their cue from him.

The white bandleaders certainly admired Ellington, Basie, Henderson and Armstrong, but they also wanted something that was very commercial and would appeal to dancers. They would eschew complex rhythms and harmonies, and the soloists performed with the melody in mind rather than going off into some improvisation or variation on the theme. The result was often soothing and unexciting.

The black bandleader Jimmie Lunceford insisted on absolute precision in the physical movements of his musicians. The trumpeters would pick up their mutes at precisely the same moment and the trombonist would point their slides at the ceiling at the same angle. As one of his records went, ''Taint What You Do (It's the Way that You Do It)'. This concept was continued by Glenn Miller in the late 1930s.

This was music for dancing. The bands performed in huge ballrooms and the mirrored balls would throw the light around the room making the jitterbug and the Lindy Hop seem even more exciting.

One of the earliest bands was led by the clarinetist Benny Goodman, who had played on both Bessie Smith's final record and Billie Holiday's first. His orchestra were featured on the weekly three-hour radio show, *Let's Dance*, in 1934/5 and he had hit records with 'Bugle Call Rag', 'I Want to be Happy' and naturally, 'Let's Dance'. The band had a powerful sound in keeping with Goodman's unstable personality, although to be fair, he was in constant pain from a bad back. Despite the arguments, he kept some remarkable musicians in his band including Teddy Wilson, Gene Krupa and Lionel Hampton.

If one particular day could be said to highlight the big band explosion, it would be 21 August 1935 when Benny Goodman and his Orchestra played the Palomar Ballroom in Los Angeles. They were a little disillusioned, thinking that their music needed more zest and life. Benny's friend, Fletcher Henderson, was off the road and Benny was studying some of his arrangements. The Palomar was a live radio date and he took the spontaneous decision to play them. The dancers loved them and so did the listeners. This moment was akin to an Ed Sullivan moment with the Beatles.

Back then the music was released on 10-inch 78s, which meant a maximum playing time of three minutes on each side. Some classical music was released on 12-inch 78s where the playing time could stretch to four and a half minutes. In 1937 Benny Goodman and his Orchestra recorded an eight minute version of a new tune by Louis Prima, 'Sing, Sing, Sing', spread over the two sides of a 12 inch disc. It was innovative and commercially successful.

Goodman was so successful that on 16 January 1936, his orchestra was the first to play the prestigious Carnegie Hall in New York, supported by Count Basie and his Orchestra. When the programme was being arranged, Goodman was asked how long an intermission he would like. He replied, 'I don't know. How long does Toscanini have?'

In 1937 the Savoy Ballroom in Harlem decided to hold a Battle of the Bands, judged by audience reaction and covered by the newspapers. The local heroes Chick Webb and his Orchestra with Ella Fitzgerald would battle it out with Fletcher Henderson (28 February), Duke Ellington (7 March) and Benny Goodman (11 May). Webb won the first two and was determined to win the third. He told his band, 'Anyone who misses notes tonight doesn't need to apologize. Just don't return to work.' No pressure then. Over 4,000 attended the dance that night with just as many outside. Webb's band was declared the winner.

In 1938 Artie Shaw and his Orchestra released one of the most famous of all big band records, their version of Cole Porter's 'Begin the Beguine'. There were many more successful big bands led by the Dorsey brothers, Glen Gray and Guy Lomardo. Then Stan Kenton came along with some adventurous, some would say discordant sounds.

There was a specific Glenn Miller sound – romantic and sentimental through the interweaving of clarinets, saxophones and trombones. The vocals were largely wordless harmony singing and the effect was devastating. From 1939 to 1941, Glenn Miller released a string of hits including 'In the Mood', 'Chattanooga Choo Choo' and 'A String of Pearls'. Although the vocals were integrated into the overall sound, Frank Sinatra did, nevertheless, ask Glenn Miller about a job in 1938, but Miller hired Ray Eberle instead.

Another band singer Bob Eberly was the brother of Ray Eberle but they had little time for each other and couldn't even agree on how to spell their surname. When Miller sacked his arrogant Eberle, Ray hoped to repeat Sinatra's solo success but he only made a few B-pictures for Universal.

Following the Pearl Harbour attack of 1941, Glenn Miller wanted to join the army, although he was too old at 37 and had poor eyesight. They made him a captain and he led the Army Air Corps Band. His plane disappeared in fog across the English Channel in 1944 when he was flying for a concert appearance in Paris, and his death remains a mystery to this day.

Glenn Miller had a terrific army band because so many good musicians had been conscripted. The bands back home suffered: the band buses were often requisitioned by the military and they were losing personnel to the forces. Two recording strikes, of which more later, didn't help.

The servicemen and their sweethearts wanted songs to be reminded of each other, so a preference developed for vocal records as opposed to big band records with vocal refrains and also for romantic ballads like 'Miss You' instead of dance numbers.

In 1942 Benny Goodman had Peggy Lee as his female singer and she scored with 'Why Don't You Do Right' and also with Goodman's guitarist, Dave Barbour, whom she married. She became one of the biggest singers during the war and retained her popularity in peacetime.

By the end of the war, the big band era was on the wane and Benny Goodman, Woody Herman, Harry James and Tommy Dorsey were all to disband their orchestras. If they reformed them later, it would be a case of booking musicians for particular recording dates or tours rather than offering full-time employment. The last big instrumental hit by a big band was Les Brown's revival of Irving Berlin's 'I've Got My Love to Keep Me Warm' in February 1949.

II. Day In–Day Out, 1939 – Harry James

Harry James was born into a circus family in Albany, Georgia on 15 March 1916 and so was three months younger than Frank Sinatra, although he was to be his boss. His mother was a trapeze artist and trick rider for the Mighty Haag Circus, and when he was six he was nearly trampled by a horse. As a small boy Harry played the drums and then switched to trumpet, playing in his father's band at the circus. His father recognised his ability and made him practise every day. However, his basic education was poor and he became self-conscious about his lack of learning – rather like Sinatra in that respect. It made him somewhat cold and distant and people would say that he loved his trumpet more than his women.

In 1931 the family settled in Beaumont, Texas and Harry James started playing with local jazz bands. In 1934 he was playing with Art Hicks and his Orchestra and he was attracted to their new vocalist, Louise Tobin, then only 15. They married in May 1935 around the time he achieved some national recognition in Ben Pollack's band.

At the start of 1937 Harry James joined Benny Goodman creating the formidable trumpet line of Harry James, Ziggy Elman and Chris Griffin. He was nicknamed The Hawk because of his ability to sight read and his fellow musicians joked that if a fly landed on the score, he could play it. He could hit really high notes on the trumpet. His reputation grew and he left in December 1938 to form his own 17 piece band, the Music Makers, which would be based in Philadelphia.

In June 1939, Harry James and his Music Makers secured a two week engagement at the New York Paramount, an impressive booking for a new band. His wife wasn't singing at the time but helping with the administration and his girl singer was Marie Antoinette Yvonne Jamais whom he had renamed Connie Haines. Connie was another winner from Major Bowes' talent shows.

One Sunday evening just before midnight, Louise Tobin heard Sinatra singing on WNEW's Dance Parade, which was broadcast live from the Rustic Cabin. Acting on her recommendation, Harry James went to the Rustic Cabin the following night, his night off. As it happens, Sinatra normally had his night off on Monday but this particular week he had swapped with the girl singer who had a date. As soon as he opened with 'Begin the Beguine', Harry James knew his wife was right: he had to have him in his band.

Sinatra came to see the Melody Makers on Tuesday and Harry James offered him a two year contract at $75 a week, which was three times his current earnings.

James considered the name Sinatra too Italian. Frank had previously thought of becoming Frankie Trent but he had stuck with Sinatra. His cousin Ray said to him, 'Are you kidding? Sinatra's the most beautiful name in the world. It's so musical.' Harry James wanted him to be Frankie Satin. Sinatra hated that name and said in the 1970s, "If I'd done that, I'd be working the cruise ships today."

Sinatra made his début with the Melody Makers at the Hippodrome, Baltimore on 30 June 1939 when he sang 'My Love for You' and the Glenn Miller hit, 'Wishing (Will Make It So)' from the film, *Love Affair*. When they had a residency at the Roseland Ballroom, New York in July, the critic George T Simon wrote in *The Metronome*, 'Featured throughout are the very pleasing vocals of Frank Sinatra, whose easy phrasing is especially commendable.'

There were unexpected bookings. Frank found himself singing at the ice rink at the New Yorker Hotel and in August 1939 the Melody Makers were featured for two weeks at the World's Fair in Queens, New York. They played during the day and continued at the Roseland in the evening.

Although New York had been very good, the band did less well on a month's residency at the Sherman Hotel in Chicago where they were featured alongside the Boogie Woogie Trio, namely Meade 'Lux' Lewis, Albert Ammons and Pete Johnson, who had starred in the Carnegie Hall concert *From Spirituals To Swing,* the previous year. This Chicago engagement should have been a huge success but the attendance was only moderate. The hotel manager disliked Sinatra telling James, 'Take that little scarecrow out of the show.' James replied, 'He's my singer. He stays in.'

Harry James and the Melody Makers also failed to draw crowds in Denver.

But worse was to come.

The band was due to play the Palomar in Los Angeles in early October but the ballroom burned down just before they arrived. Harry James secured a replacement residency at Victor Hugo's restaurant on Sunset Boulevard but only at a reduced rate, which meant dropping the female singer. The band was not sweet enough for the diners and there were cancellations. The restaurant refused to pay them and the band became demoralised. Nancy sent Frank a pair of gloves with a dollar bill inside each finger

While the band had been at the Sherman Hotel, they had taken part in a show for union funds with Tommy Dorsey and his Orchestra. Dorsey had noticed Frank Sinatra and been impressed.

In November 1939 Tommy Dorsey's singer, Jack Leonard, left the band and the replacement vocalist, Alan DeWitt, took one look at the hot-headed Dorsey and ran. Tommy's manager asked Sinatra to visit him in Chicago. Tommy Dorsey offered him $125 a week. As Harry James hadn't been paying Sinatra his wages, he had reneged on his contract and Sinatra was perfectly in order to walk but Sinatra politely asked him if he could leave. James said, 'If we don't do any better in the next few months, try to get me in there too.' Red Norvo also heard that Frank might be moving and offered him a job but he was too late.

Frank Sinatra made his final appearances with Harry James at Shea's Theatre in Buffalo, New York. The bill also featured the clown Red Skelton (catchphrase, "I doodit") and Burt Lancaster, then with his trampoline act.

Although Frank Sinatra was only with Harry James for six months, he never forgot the experience and was always grateful to James. 'I was young and full of zip, zap and zing and I was also full of myself,' said Sinatra in 1965.

Several recordings, either for radio or commercial release, have survived and show his voice and confidence developing but not with much zip, zap and zing. The most significant is 'All Or Nothing at All', an excellent performance which features his vocal throughout and can be seen as a precursor to 'All The Way' – 'Half a love never appealed to me'. It was recorded on 31 August 1939, the day before Hitler marched on Poland. It was issued as a single and sold 8,000 copies initially, not enough to make it a hit, but promising nevertheless. Still, he had a long way to go before he could match Bing Crosby who had 27 different songs on the charts in 1939.

Another performance, 'From the Bottom of my Heart' was captured at the Roseland Ballroom and found its way across the Atlantic as Sinatra received his first radio play on the BBC on 19 July 1939. Frank's first recorded duet, 'White Sails (Will Find a Blue Lagoon)' is from the Roseland with Connie Haines, who then moved on and was replaced by Marie Carroll.

Although many wonderful songs were written in the 1930s, some reveal flowery language and bad writing then and now. What could any singer do with lines line 'Love is a whimsy, as flimsy as lace' ('Melancholy Mood') or "My love is like the great elation that Shelley knew when he found inspiration' ('My Love for You')? 'Moon Love' is typical of its time, being based on a classical theme, this one by Tchaikovsky.

The standards include 'Stardust', 'If I Didn't Care' and 'My Buddy', a song of male companionship first recorded by Al Jolson in 1922. Harry James copied the style of Tommy Dorsey's 'Marie' with 'It's Funny to Everyone but Me' as the band chanted humorously behind Sinatra as he sang. There was a vocal version of James' signature tune, 'Ciribiribin (They're So in Love)', an Italian song with an English lyric dating from 1898.

It's good to report that things turned out okay for Harry James as he was a decent man. By 1941 he was $40,000 in debt but he turned things around with hit records including 'You Made Me Love You' and 'By a Sleepy Lagoon', an English tune by Eric Coates, which became the theme music for *Desert Island Discs*. James' speciality was a frenzied 'Flight of the Bumble Bee'. During the recording strike of 1943, his 'Two O'Clock Jump', a version of Count Basie's 'One O'Clock Jump', filled with trumpet triplets, was reissued and became a dance floor favourite.

Meanwhile, Harry's wife, Louise Tobin had joined Benny Goodman and found success with 'There'll Be Some Changes Made', an ominous title from 1941. Despite two children, Harry (born 1941) and Tim (born 1942), their marriage didn't last and Harry James married Betty Grable, the girl with the $1m legs, in 1943. He kept on drinking, womanising and gambling.

CHAPTER 4

Getting sentimental

*'Frank Sinatra was a skinny kid with big ears, and yet
what he did to women was something awful.'*

Tommy Dorsey

I. Brotherly Love

St Paul wrote 'Let brotherly love continue', an indication that he didn't have a brother or that he really was a saint. The spats, fall-outs and arguments between brothers in popular music have been at times spectacular and merit a book in their own right.

In the 1950s there were the country disharmonies of the Louvin Brothers and the off-and-on feuding of the Everly Brothers, who ended up with separate managers. The grudges that Ray and Dave Davies held against each other fuelled the music of the Kinks and there were fraternal problems within the Bee Gees and the Beach Boys. David Knopfler left Dire Straits because Mark only wanted to do his own songs. What 1990s fallout was more explosive than the rows between Noel and Liam Gallagher of Oasis? There have been brothers who have existed side by side, notably Charlie and Craig Reid, the twins in the Proclaimers, but I would argue that they are the exceptions rather than the rule.

The award for the most argumentative of all musical brothers would have to go to the Dorsey brothers. Jimmy and Tommy only had to see each other to fall out. Although they appreciated each other's musical ability, they argued constantly and may well have continued their disputes beyond the grave. Whatever, they were two awkward so-and-so's.

Both Jimmy and Tommy Dorsey were born into a mining community in Shenandoah, Pennsylvania: Jimmy a leap year baby in 1904 and Tommy on 19 November 1905. The family was of Irish extraction and their father was a miner who played in an amateur jazz band; he had Jimmy paying cornet when he was only seven.

By his teens, Jimmy was concentrating on clarinet and alto saxophone, while Tommy switched from trumpet to trombone. They worked together in Dorseys' Novelty Six and Dorseys' Wild Canaries, one of the first jazz bands to broadcast on this new-fangled invention, the radio. During the Depression, they were both working as studio musicians; Jimmy, for example, is featured on 'Singin' the Blues' by Bix Beiderbecke.

They both played with other bands and from 1928 onwards, they recorded occasionally as the Dorsey Brothers Orchestra. In 1934 they formed a permanent band, playing first at Plunkett's Saloon in New York, with musicians including Charlie Spivak and Glenn Miller and vocalists Bob Crosby and Kay Weber. Tensions were high as the brothers would frequently argue, sometimes violently.

In 1935 the orchestra was playing at the Glen Island Casino on Long Island. Jimmy was conducting and when they came to their hit record, 'I'll Never Say "Never Again" Again', of all things, Jimmy stopped the musicians and said to Tommy, 'Isn't that a little too fast?' Tommy left the bandstand and indeed the orchestra, leaving Jimmy to continue the engagement on his own. Their friend Bing Crosby attempted to mediate but it was hopeless. Jimmy ran the orchestra on his own and had minor successes with 'Long John Silver' and 'Parade of the Milk Bottle Caps'.

Tommy, on the other hand, took over the dance band led by Joe Haymes. He was highly ambitious and determined to outstrip his brother, employing great arrangers like Axel Stordahl and Sy Oliver. Jack Leonard, who had recommended Stordahl and Yank Lawson, and who played trumpet for Dorsey at the time, commented, 'Axel Stordahl was the third trumpet but he didn't like it. He wanted to be an arranger. He couldn't play worth a damn anyway but he was a great arranger.'

It took courage for Dorsey to employ Oliver, the only black musician in the band. Sometimes he wrote arrangements in New York while the band was touring down south. Sammy Cahn recalled, 'The Jimmie Lunceford band was for me the single best band in all of music, and I say this with the knowledge that there was also Chick Webb, Count Basie and Duke Ellington. The single best band for both watching and listening was Jimmie Lunceford's. He had Sy Oliver's arrangements, and Tommy Dorsey was bright enough to take this incredibly talented man away from Jimmie Lunceford. The Sy Oliver arrangements had a vast, vast effect on the Tommy Dorsey Orchestra.'

Their signature tune was 'I'm Getting Sentimental over You', which featured Dorsey's own legato trombone playing. He employed some remarkable musicians including Bunny Berigan, Buddy Rich, Yank Lawson and Gene Krupa but musicians could be hired and fired at a moment's notice and Dorsey worked his way through 250 musicians in the first 10 years.

One of Tommy Dorsey's earliest successes was in 1937 with a revival of Irving Berlin's 'Marie' featuring Jack Leonard with witty repartee from the orchestra chanting other popular song titles behind him. Edythe Wright made her mark with 'The Dipsy Doodle', a No.2 in 1938. Usually the band would play the first chorus featuring Dorsey's trombone, then would come the vocal refrain and the band would finish with a flourish.

In November 1939 Jack Leonard, fed up with Dorsey's volatile nature, walked out. His replacement was a teenage vocalist, Alan DeWitt and Dorsey also signed the vocal group, the Pied Pipers with Jo Stafford. However, Alan DeWitt quickly fell out with Dorsey and was replaced by Frank Sinatra. DeWitt became an actor and had minor roles in several films and TV series including *A Star Is Born* (1954).

Tommy Dorsey was only 34 when Sinatra joined the band but he was so pernickety and temperamental that he was known as the Old Man. He wanted to establish the top band in the USA and so he needed discipline. However, great talent can bring great problems and he had difficulty in bringing his drummer Buddy Rich into line. One night Joe Bushkin had a fight with Rich, and Dorsey was mad with them, not for fighting, but because they had dirtied their stage jackets. It was a blue jacket night and the whole band had to change into red.

Without looking in the mirror, Dorsey liked to refer to 'the three SOBs', namely, Buddy Rich, Frank Sinatra and Adolf Hitler. Dorsey and Sinatra were both quick tempered, egotistical and uncompromising. Dorsey would frequently threaten Sinatra with the sack and even suggested his replacement, Bob Allan from Hal Kemp's band. As it happens, Allan did join Dorsey in 1944. To teach him a lesson, Dorsey once replaced Sinatra with Milburn Stone (later an actor in *Gunsmoke*) but Sinatra quickly apologised (a rare word in this book) and returned.

Tommy Dorsey had to walk a tricky tightrope. He had to please the dancing public, radio producers, music publishers and RCA records. He planned his ballroom dates carefully and he was one of the first musicians to appreciate the importance of an acceptable running order. He knew how to change moods and how to build an act so that his show was never just a collection of songs for dancing.

Buddy Rich commented, 'Dorsey's wasn't a hot band and it never professed to be. It was a dance band with good musicians. When he hired Sy Oliver, he started getting some jazz arrangements and then that band would kick as well as any for that time.'

Meanwhile, Jimmy Dorsey and his Orchestra were making good, having huge successes with 'The Breeze and I' (1940) and 'Maria Elena' (1941), both featuring his vocalist Bob Eberly. Generally speaking, Bob Eberly would perform the first part of the recording in ballad mode, which would be followed by an up-tempo instrumental section, at which point female singer, Helen O'Connell, would then bring the proceedings to an end . Such hits as 'Amapola', 'Yours', 'Green Eyes' and 'Tangerine', all arranged by Tutti Camarata, followed this template. Jimmy Dorsey loved Latin-American tunes and the band hit additional paydirt with 'Besame Mucho' (1944), featuring Bob Eberly and Kitty Kallen.

In an unexpected move, clearly motivated by money, Jimmy and Tommy did recreate their differences for the film, *The Fabulous Dorseys*, in 1947. Around this time, both bands were having difficulty in continuing because the public had moved away from the big band sound.

In 1953 Jimmy Dorsey realised that he would have to disband his orchestra and he and a couple of his musicians joined Tommy Dorsey in a new venture which was tellingly called the Tommy Dorsey Orchestra featuring Jimmy Dorsey. In 1954 they were fortunate enough to secure a weekly TV series *Stage Show* for CBS and between January and March 1956, they featured Elvis Presley six times. They were the first to feature Bobby Darin on national TV.

After a heavy meal followed by some sleeping pills, Tommy Dorsey choked to death in his sleep on 26 November 1956. Jimmy took over the band for a short while and, out of the blue, the Jimmy Dorsey Orchestra had a No.2 US hit with 'So Rare', a song he had originally performed in 1937 but was associated with Guy Lombardo. However, Jimmy was being treated for cancer and died on 12 June 1957. Five days later, Lee Castle took the musicians into the studio and cut another hit single, 'June Night', a tune associated with Fred Waring's Pennsylvanians. Jimmy Dorsey had his name on a hit record on which he was not featured and was recorded after his death.

Then Warren Covington fronted a new version of the Tommy Dorsey Orchestra and they had an international best seller with 'Tea for Two Cha Cha' in 1958. This success has led to many bands being reformed after their leaders' deaths, including Ted Heath, Bert Kaempfert, Harry James and Glenn Miller.

II. Day In–Day Out, 1940–1942 – Tommy Dorsey

In January 1940 Frank Sinatra took a train from New York to Rockford, Illinois to meet up with Tommy Dorsey and his Orchestra as their new male vocalist. He arrived during the day and his first task was to join the band for softball. He rehearsed with the band and he had to perform two songs that they had performed with Jack Leonard, their big hit, 'Marie' and the current No.1 for Glenn Miller, 'My Prayer'.

Sinatra's two years with the Tommy Dorsey Orchestra is exceptionally well-documented as scores of records and radio performances have been preserved. The first recordings followed a formula. The band played for 70 or 80 seconds, with Dorsey taking the first solo, and then Sinatra took a chorus, usually without the Pied Pipers. He sang very competently but he was not specifically sounding like Frank Sinatra. He was doing his job very tunefully with excellent diction but the idea of putting his personality and indeed some sexuality into his singing didn't start until May 1940 when he recorded 'I'll Never Smile Again'.

The first recording session for RCA in Chicago on 1 February 1940 was to record a new song arranged by Axel Stordahl, 'The Sky Fell Down', also being recorded by Benny Goodman, Woody Herman and Glenn Miller. It was a pleasantly romantic song, but nothing special, so it's hard to see why it was given so much attention. The band covered Bing Crosby's 'Too Romantic' from *The Road to Singapore*. The Pied Pipers made their first recording with Dorsey, '(What Can I Say) After I Say I'm Sorry', and Frank sat that one out.

On 26 February the band recorded in New York. Frank sang 'Shake Down the Stars', his first song with music from Jimmy Van Heusen, 'Moments in the Moonlight' (with a vocal lasting for 75 seconds, something of a record for Dorsey at the time!) and a tremendous 'I'll Be Seeing You'. When it was written in 1938, it was about responding to being dumped. It developed a new poignancy during the war and was the title song for a film about post-traumatic stress disorder (how topical is that) with Ginger Rogers and Joseph Cotten in 1944. Then it was recorded by Bing Crosby but the reissue by Dorsey and Sinatra did well.

In March 1940 Tommy Dorsey and his Orchestra and the comic Red Skelton had a short season at the New York Paramount, playing six live sets a day and taking their breaks while *The Road to Singapore* was being screened. Young girls were starting to fall for the frail male and Dorsey could sense something was happening. Jack Leonard, on leave from the army, went to see the band at the Paramount and felt humiliated when he saw how good Sinatra was and the reaction he was getting.

And not just young girls; Sammy Cahn too: 'I would go to the Paramount Theatre and see the pit rise with Tommy Dorsey starting 'Getting Sentimental'. They would go into 'Marie', which again was down to the genius of Sy Oliver. After that would come Connie Haines, and then there were the Pied Pipers. Dorsey would feature Ziggy Elman on trumpet, Buddy Rich on drums and himself on trombone. When all these showstoppers had finished, out stepped a young fella, thinner than my pinkie, and that was Frank Sinatra. He sang 'South of the Border' and he topped everything that had gone before. He was incredibly talented.'

The young Tony Bennett would sit through the entire day. 'In the early 1940s I would get out of classes to see the Tommy Dorsey orchestra at the Paramount. I'd stay for seven shows a day and watch Sinatra over and over again. Just imagine: in those days, you had Dorsey's band with Jo Stafford, the Pied Pipers, Buddy Rich and Ziggy Elman as well as a dance team, a great juggler or a comic. Plus Frank Sinatra! All that for 75 cents.'

They recorded 'Polka Dots and Moonbeams' which, despite the dreadfully twee title, was the first song from a new team, Johnny Burke and Jimmy Van Heusen. It had a cute lyric and was an early indication that there was something special about Frank Sinatra. It was his first hit single and it outsold another version from Glenn Miller. A much better Burke and Van Heusen composition is 'Imagination', with a superb lyric that is deftly handled by Sinatra: 'Imagination is funny, It makes a cloudy day sunny.' Sinatra returned to the song, rather more playfully, in 1961.

Judging by the polls in music magazine, Bunny Berigan was the country's top white trumpeter and second only in ability and popularity to Louis Armstrong. However, he was a hard drinker and ill-disciplined, and attempts to form his own band were misguided. With some reluctance, Dorsey allowed him back into the fold in March 1940. Berigan was broke and Dorsey wanted to give him another chance. Dorsey, however, couldn't tolerate his behaviour and sacked him in August. In that short period Berigan recorded several fine solos including one in an excellent dance band novelty, 'I Haven't the Time to Be a Millionaire' in which Frank said he was too interested in observing nature to be making money. Oh yeah?

Berigan died from cirrhosis in June 1942 and Tommy Dorsey paid for his funeral.

Eight of the musicians, renamed the Dorsey Sentimentalists, recorded 'East of the Sun (And West of the Moon)' with an arrangement by Sy Oliver. Dorsey probably revived the song so that he could repeat the 'Marie' trick of shouting phrases. One of Dorsey's trumpeters, Zeke Zarchy, remarked, 'Tommy instantly saw how Frank would enhance the band. We had this arrangement for 'East of the Sun' and Frank sang that tune with a jazz feel, like he was playing a horn. We'd never heard anybody take a ballad and sing it like that, but that was Frank.'

Then they cut the big one, 'I'll Never Smile Again'. Unusually for the time, it had words and music by a female, Ruth Lowe. Ruth Lowe had been part of Ina Ray Hutton's all-girl orchestra and she had married the music publisher Harry Cohen. When Cohen died shortly after their wedding in 1938, she poured her feelings into a song. She asked Percy Faith to arrange a demonstration disc and she gave it to Tommy Dorsey's guitarist, Carmen Mastren. Jack Leonard was keen to record it with the orchestra, but Dorsey thought the song more suited to Glenn Miller. When Miller's version was not a success, Dorsey cut it with Sinatra. At Sinatra's suggestion, Joe Bushkin played celesta to add a bell-like sound. The song was cut twice, the second time giving more prominence to Sinatra. Sinatra received $25 from each session and was not entitled to royalties.

From the beginning of June, Tommy Dorsey and his Orchestra played at the reopening of the rooftop venue at the Hotel Astor roof garden in New York – Deluxe dinners: $2.25. Dorsey was now playing to Sinatra's popularity, letting him sing 'Smoke Gets in Your Eyes' acappella (which Dorsey found amusing) and featuring him on a sizzling 'Begin the Beguine', although Dorsey never recorded it with Sinatra. Sinatra knew he was making an impact and when he asked George Simon to feature him on the cover of his music magazine, *The Metronome*, he added, 'Bing won't be around forever.' They were featured in a Tuesday evening radio series for NBC sponsored by Pepsodent toothpaste, which ran nationally throughout the summer. This was broadcasted live from the Rockeller Centre, later the home of *The Ed Sullivan Show* and the *Late Show with Letterman*.

On 8 June 1940 Frank and Nancy had their first child, Nancy Sandra, who was born in Jersey City. At the christening, Tommy Dorsey was the godfather.

Frank was immensely happy about being a father but he was not a model husband. Far from it. He had an affair with a blonde actress, Alora Gooding, who happened to be married, and he was also dating 16-year-old Rita Maritt and a Long Island debutante, Mary Lou Watts. There was an affair with a showgirl, Dorothy Bunocelli, who gave birth to a daughter, Julie, on 10 February 1943. She has a striking resemblance to Frank and although she has never been officially acknowledged as Frank's daughter, she received $100,000 from Sinatra's estate.

Dorsey and Sinatra revived 'Whispering' with a similar arrangement to 'I'll Never Smile Again', and Sinatra recorded his first Sammy Cahn song, 'I Could Make You Care'. Sammy Cahn recalled, 'My relationship with Frank began with Axel Stordahl. Having written 'Rhythm Is Our Business', I was established as a band writer, so Axel took me round to meet Tommy Dorsey and likewise, I met Frank Sinatra. I have met each and every one of the band leaders – Glenn Miller, Glen Gray, Charlie Spivak, Harry James – but Tommy Dorsey was to me the most impeccably trained orchestra leader.'

In 1924 the bandleader Isham Jones had been given a new piano by his wife. He was so delighted that he sat playing it all night and by the morning he had written three melodies, which were given lyrics by Gus Kahn. They were 'Spain', 'It Had to Be You' and 'The One I Love (Belongs to Someone Else)', the last no doubt being a title which appealed to Sinatra.

The song had been performed by Al Jolson and Sophie Tucker, and Tommy Dorsey and his Orchestra cut it in June 1940. The arrangement was very effective, although Sinatra didn't appear for two minutes. At one point he hummed beguilingly behind the Pied Pipers.

Prior to July 1940 there had only been sheet music charts; *Billboard* published its first record chart on 22 July. It was the heart of the swing era, yet there was a ballad at the top.

Position	Title	Performer
1	I'll Never Smile Again	Tommy Dorsey
2	The Breeze And I	Jimmy Dorsey
3	Imagination	Glenn Miller
4	Playmates	Kay Kyser
5	Fools Rush In	Glenn Miller
6	Where Was I	Charlie Barnet
7	Pennsylvania 6-5000	Glenn Miller
8	Imagination	Tommy Dorsey
9	Sierra Sue	Bing Crosby
10	Make Believe Island	Mitchell Ayres

The Dorsey Brothers and Glenn Miller account for six of the hit singles. 'I'll Never Smile Again' was Tommy Dorsey's biggest hit, although really it was Frank Sinatra's success.

The No.6 song 'Where Was I' was written by the 20-stone Al Dubin, who scribbled his lyrics on the backs of menus. It was the title song from a Merle Oberon film about a dying woman falling for a criminal about to be executed. The New York bandleader, Charlie Barnet, had a wild life style, marrying six times, and broke racial taboos by hiring black musicians for his band.

The final position in the chart is taken by Mitchell Ayres, the world's first one-hit wonder, with 'Make Believe Island'. It was written by Wilhelm Grosz, a concert pianist who worked with the classical composer, Richard Strauss and had fled from the Nazis. Although he didn't have further hit records, he became Perry Como's arranger. He retired in 1963, but his retirement was short-lived when he was killed crossing a New York street.

Interestingly, none of the ten hits had war themes, but then America was not yet at war. There were no British artists on the US chart and an equivalent UK chart (which only came into being in 1952) would probably have strongly featured Vera Lynn and such songs as 'A Nightingale Sang in Berkeley Square', 'Whispering Grass', 'There'll Always Be an England' and 'We'll Meet Again'. Once the US entered the war in 1942, 'The White Cliffs of Dover' and 'Remember Pearl Harbour' were big sellers.

Sinatra and Crosby found themselves head to head with 'Trade Winds', an exotic song about finding romance where the trade winds 'play' Bing Crosby accompanied by the Dick McIntyre Harmony Hawaiians had a more authentic sound and took the song to No.1.

After having enormous success with *Babes in Arms*, Judy Garland and Mickey Rooney were teamed in another 'let's put on a show' movie, *Strike Up The Band*, in 1940. In his autobiography, wittily entitled *Life Is Too Short*, Mickey said that 'Our Love Affair', which he sang with Judy, was 'one of the most beautiful love songs ever written.' The song was nominated for an Oscar and was successful for both Tommy Dorsey and Glenn Miller. Note the reference to *Gone with the Wind* in the lyric: 'From Adam to Eve to Scarlett and Rhett.'

Another substantial hit for Dorsey was 'We Three (My Echo, My Shadow and Me)', a new song written by three songwriters and probably inspired by 'Me Myself and I' from 1937, also by three writers. It was intended as a B-side but became a big hit record, being even bigger for the Ink Spots, their first No.1 and featuring their usual sonorous recitative in the middle.

Look at any picture of the drummer Buddy Rich and he's scowling. This man was trouble but he was also one of the best drummers in the country and was earning $750 a week with Dorsey, against Sinatra's $400. He was listed separately on posters for the band and he hated it when Sinatra was given higher billing. From time to time, he would speed up the tempo or play extra loudly, just to annoy Sinatra. Once when they were arguing, Sinatra threw a water jug at him. Buddy Rich often roomed with him: 'I thought then that he was the greatest singer I'd ever heard and but he used to sit up in bed, late at night, and clip his fingernails slowly. Like click, click, click, click, you know, in the middle of the night. It used to drive me up the wall.' Rich referred to him as 'Lady Macbeth' as he was always showering and washing.

In August 1940 Frank Sinatra met two Hollywood stars, Lana Turner and Ava Gardner. They were good friends and they were both high-spirited and independent with a love for bullfighting and, it must be said, bullfighters. Lana Turner was dating Buddy Rich but Sinatra wanted her. One night Rich was beaten up by two thugs, whom, it transpired, came from Hoboken. Let's not jump to conclusions, but Frank did sometimes refer to himself as 'the hoodlum from Hoboken'.

Because of delays, Tommy Dorsey and his Orchestra played the Los Angeles Paramount for two weeks and then opened the Hollywood Palladium on Halloween night. Many Hollywood stars attended the opening and the ballroom and dining rooms could take 8,000 customers, making it the largest venue of its kind in the world. It can be seen in the film, *The Blues Brothers*. It was a busy period as the band had to be up at 5am to film *Las Vegas Nights* for Paramount, directed by Ralph Murphy and featuring Phil Regan, Bert Wheeler and Constance Moore. Even busier for Frank as he had an affair with the blonde who looked lovingly at him during 'I'll Never Smile Again'.

Las Vegas Nights was an apt title for Sinatra's first film and one of the first acknowledgements of the variety scene in Las Vegas. It featured Anne Miller as an armed forces disc jockey and although Sinatra sings with the orchestra, his performance is unbilled and he earned just $15 a day extra. The film was released in April 1941 and the hit song was Frank Loesser's 'Dolores', an infectious song with irritating rhymes. In a taste of things to come, Sinatra gave the song a star performance leaving Bing Crosby's cover version far behind. There is also a comic version from Bert Wheeler in *Las Vegas Nights*.

As for Frank's feature film début, George Simon wrote in *The Metronome*, 'He sings prettily in an unphotogenic manner.' Another critic, John T McManus added, 'His voice is pleasant... a kind of moaning baritone with a few trick inflections.'

Tommy Dorsey and his Orchestra were featured in *Fame and Fortune*, a new weekly radio series for the autumn. It was sponsored by a laxative, Nature's Remedy from Missouri, which is hard to understand. You wouldn't make a programme for a young audience today and seek sponsorship from Stannah Stairlifts. A regular feature was to be *Memory Melody* which was to rival Glenn Miller's *Something Old, Something New*.

Most significantly, Dorsey wanted to encourage amateur songwriting, with Dorsey taking the publishing on anything half-decent. Amateur songwriters could pick up entry forms from their local drugstores. The winning songs which included 'One Red Rose', 'When Daylight Dawns' and 'When Sleepy Stars Begin to Fall' were performed by Sinatra, which sounds like a prize in itself, but the songs were not hit parade material. The best was Virginia Sloane's 'You're Part of My Heart' and Dorsey must have considered this had potential as he gave it a very well-planned arrangement.

The radio programmes included some delightful performances with Sinatra and the band often camping up 'Marie', making it funnier than the record. With Jack Leonard it was as though the singers were making faces behind him, but here it was all part of the fun. They used the call-and-response technique on several other songs, both on record and on radio. You can hear this in 'Who', 'Yearning', 'Sweet Sue', 'How Am I to Know', 'Deep Night', 'Blue Skies' and the hit single, 'Do I Worry'. My favourite moment occurs in 'Blue Moon' as when Frank sings, 'And there suddenly appeared before me', the band yells 'Boo!'

The band returned to New York for the Christmas season at the Paramount from 18 December. Frank invited them to meet his parents and Marty cooked them all spaghetti.

The Christmas hit was 'Stardust', although it was Artie Shaw's instrumental version that topped the charts. Sinatra was immensely fond of this Hoagy Carmichael song, first hearing it from Bing Crosby in 1931. The record label said, says 'Stardust-Fox-Trot' and both Frank Sinatra and Jo Stafford had solo parts on the recording. Frank was named the outstanding male vocalist of the year by *Down Beat* magazine, the first person for seven years to beat Bing Crosby.

At the start of 1941 the Selective Service Act required all males between 21 and 31 to register for the draft. Frank Sinatra completed his form, requesting deferment as a married father. This protected him until autumn 1943 when such deferment ended.

Sinatra did not get on well with Dorsey's female vocalist, Connie Haines. She was 20 years old and pretty with a delightful voice, but she came from Savannah, Georgia and he thought her stage presence was too cornball. He didn't like her demonstrating the Lindy Hop and teasing the soldiers. She also travelled with her mother, which meant 'Hands off!'

Frank and Connie had a huge success with 'Oh, Look at Me Now', written by Dorsey's pianist Joe Bushkin. The single was only kept from the top by Jimmy Dorsey's 'Amapola'. On this playful recording, Sinatra is starting to develop his Rat Pack persona with 'Man, I've really come on' and 'Jack, I'm ready.' He and Connie covered the score of the new Hope and Crosby film, *The Road to Zanzibar*, taking two songs apiece. Sinatra's 'It's Always You' was a hit single on reissue in 1943.

The songwriters of the day were affiliated to the union ASCAP (American Society of Composers, Authors and Publishers) and the officials (who were often songwriters) had become increasingly bitter as records were being played without payment on radio. Irving Berlin, who was always counting his pennies, was particularly annoyed. The songwriters were ordered to strike but this had repercussions as a rival group, BMI (Broadcast Music Incorporated) was established. When the matter was settled in October 1941, the ASCAP writers had to accept lower fees than they wanted and had to acknowledge their competitor, BMI. Rather cleverly, Dorsey was able to milk his amateur songwriters on his *Fame and Fortune* programme as, by definition, they were not affiliated to anyone. There was a similar protest over the USA's 200,000 jukeboxes. A licensee might install one in a bar and this could take work away from live musicians.

In May 1941 Billie Holiday recorded the blisteringly honest song, 'God Bless the Child'. It was her song title and the writer, Arthur Herzog, was not affiliated to ASCAP so this extraordinary song, which was still commercial, had more air play than in normal times.

In concert, Tommy Dorsey and his Orchestra played a five minute arrangement of the spiritual-like 'Without a Song', arranged by Sy Oliver and it was issued on a 12-inch single. It starts with a trombone solo and then a fine vocal from Sinatra, arguably the best of his career but marred now by a reference to 'darkies'. Note that Sinatra does not take a breath when going from 'in my soul' to 'I'll never know': he could do it effortlessly. This was something he had learnt from Dorsey.

How had Sinatra learnt to sing so well, indeed, better than anyone else around? A fellow singer, Billy Eckstine, said, 'Frank Sinatra is a great technician and so is Jo Stafford. They learnt that from Tommy Dorsey. He took an interest in his singers and they weren't just there to fill up the instrumentals.' Eckstine had a deeper voice than Frank's but for a time he was dubbed the 'Sepia Sinatra'.

From his teenage years, Frank had been interested in learning how to hold his notes. He had watched Jascha Heifetz to see if he could match the sustained feeling he got from his violin. He found that Tommy Dorsey was doing something similar on the trombone, and Dorsey recommended underwater swimming, which he did. That enabled him to increase the capacity of his lungs.

Sinatra loved Crosby but he didn't want to emulate his easygoing style. In *Life* magazine in 1965, he likened his approach to classical singing. 'When I started singing in the mid-1930s, everybody was trying to copy the Crosby style – the casual kind of raspy sound in the throat. It occurred to me that the world didn't need another Crosby. What I finally hit on was the *bel canto* Italian school of singing, without making a point of it. That meant I had to stay in better shape because I had to sing out more. It was more difficult than Crosby's style, much more difficult.'

Tommy Dorsey's encouragement certainly helped Frank Sinatra musically but on the debit side, he taught him how to hold a grudge. Nobody was to hold a grudge better than Frank Sinatra.

When Jo Stafford recommended two young songwriters, Matt Dennis and Tom Adair, to Tommy Dorsey, he appreciated that they were a cut above the amateurs who had been submitting songs to *Fame and Fortune*. He gave them a cubicle in the Brill Building and told them to write. The first hit song by the team – and there were to be many more – was 'Everything Happens to Me' which Dorsey recorded with Sinatra in February 1941. It would suit the British comedian Jack Dee as this is a song about a man who constantly complains, thinking he is jinxed. The lyric is packed with wry humour: 'Your answer was goodbye, there was even postage due' and 'I guess I'll go through life just catching colds and missing trains.' It was an excellent song that Sinatra revisited on several occasions.

Their second hit, 'Let's Get Away from It All', had such witty and perky lyrics from Tom Adair that Dorsey was reluctant to delete some of the verses and he spread them over both sides of a single. This is an ensemble piece featuring Sinatra, Haines, the Pied Pipers and a trumpet solo from Ziggy Elman. In these days of twerking, it seems mild but it was risqué at the time. There are some fabulous lines: 'Let's catch a tuna way out in Laguna' and being a travelogue, it is relatively easy to come up with new, but not necessarily better, lyrics. Rather like 'Let's Do It', the song can be rewritten to order. The recording refers to 'all the 48' but there are 50 states now. Sinatra goes 'Ouch!' when he hears 'cha cha' rhymed with 'watch ya' and when Connie sings, 'I'll get a real southern drawl', Sinatra goes 'Another one?' The duo also recorded a bright patriotic song about the benefits of democracy, 'Free for All': 'Just remember son, life is so much fun, when it's free for all.'

In 1926 Irving Berlin added a ballad for Belle Baker to the score of the Richard Rodgers and Lorenz Hart musical *Betsy*. When Baker forgot the words on the opening night, Irving Berlin rose from his seat in the front row and sang it for her. Despite this setback, 'Blue Skies' was an instant success and was performed by Al Jolson in *The Jazz Singer* in 1927. Benny Goodman recorded a swing version in 1935, which took liberties with the melody.

'That was the most incredible playing I've ever heard,' said Berlin, 'Never do it again.' Berlin was fighting a lost cause as this tune was perfect for jazz and swing arrangements. Dorsey recorded a fine version with Sinatra in the style of 'Marie', also written by Berlin. The public loved it but Berlin told Dorsey's producer, 'You tell that Irish bastard not to mess around with my songs.'

In August 1941 Tommy Dorsey and his Orchestra were back at the Paramount in New York. Young girls were grabbing the stage as it was lowered at the end of each show and at one performance, two girls grabbed opposite ends of Frankie's bow-tie and wouldn't let go. They had to be pulled away by Connie Haines and Tommy Dorsey.

Sinatra's popularity was such that he even co-authored *Tips on Popular Singing* with John Quinlan, which was published by one of Dorsey's companies. Although Frank never lost his New Jersey accent, he always enunciated clearly when he sang.

Sinatra liked the idea of having his own publishing company and talked about it with his friend, Hank Sanicola. When they heard a new song by Sol Parker, Frank said, 'Let's make it more commercial.' Frank revised the lyric and took it to Matt Dennis for approval so who knows exactly what Sinatra did for his songwriting credit? 'This Love of Mine' was recorded by Dorsey with a pleasing vocal from Frank. It went to No.3 on the charts in October 1941 which prompted some cover versions. Frank himself cut a darker, sadder version of the song in 1955.

In December, Sinatra, dressed in a sailor's hat and an open-neck shirt that was not tucked in, cut a song with the line, 'The world may rock and rumble', but he wasn't being prophetic. This was a love song 'Two in Love' written by Meredith Willson with the feel of 'I'll Be Seeing You'. It was another Top 10 single.

Of more interest is 'How About You' from *Babes on Broadway,* where it was sung by Judy Garland and Mickey Rooney. Frank's voice is deeper than usual and his phrasing more deliberate and he sings, "And Franklin Roosevelt's looks give me a thrill." Would anyone say that about a British politician? When Frank recut the track in 1956, he substituted it with Jimmy Durante's looks. He's kidding, isn't he?

The Dorsey band returned for a season at the Hollywood Palladium and made the film *Ship Ahoy* for MGM during the daytime. As *Holiday Inn* was being made in a neighbouring studio, Frank and Bing got to know each other. When Bing came to the set, he said, 'Real nice, Frank, you're going to go far.'

Alas *Ship Ahoy* was no *Holiday Inn,* nor did it lend its name to a new chain of hotels. Still it was a decent musical comedy and a good vehicle for both the Dorsey band and the tap dancer Eleanor Powell.

The Dorsey band including Sinatra are all in white sailor suits with spats, and indeed, Frank played a serviceman in 11 films. The highlight of the film is a great dance number where Powell plays drums with Buddy Rich, who, for once, seems to be enjoying himself. He has a tomtom solo in 'Not So Quiet Please'. Eleanor Powell dances while Frank sings 'Moonlight Bay'; this song and dance is crucial is to the plot as Powell is tapping out a message in morse code. In the novelty 'Snootie Little Cutie', written by Bobby Troup, Frank and Connie trade affectionate names – 'pert little skirt', 'kissy little missie' and 'vain little Jane'. It is in the same vein as Irving Berlin's 'Snookey Ookums'.

Ship Ahoy was originally titled *I'll Take Manila* and the comic song, 'I'll Take Tallulah', was retained. Following Dorsey's 'Delores', the song is a succession of exotic names, and Dorsey himself has a couple of lines. It's a dreadful song even for its time. It has none of the sharpness of Paul Simon's '50 Ways to Leave Your Lover', which has a similar lyrical vein.

The film's title had been changed for good reason. It would have been insensitive to call it *I'll Take Manila* after the Japanese occupation of the Philippines. The world was falling apart and America, which had been officially neutral, was now at war after the attack on Pearl Harbour in December 1941. In these times of trouble, Frank created a gift for one hundred of his special friends: a medallion with a St Christopher on one and the Star of David on the other.

Frank Sinatra was feeling restricted. He wanted to move away from dance band recordings and cut romantic ballads with strings. He knew someone who might help him: Emanuel 'Manie' Sacks was born in 1902 and after working in his father's tailoring shop in Philadelphia, he went into the entertainment business. He arranged comedy series for Jack Benny and George Burns on CBS and then moved to Columbia's record division. Frank knew him through Harry James and asked him to take him on as a solo artist. Manie said yes, if he were free of Tommy Dorsey. Sinatra didn't want to cut free of Dorsey so he had a word with the Old Man who said that RCA were prepared to run a trial session with strings. The normal RCA records cost 75 cents but the results would be on their budget label, Bluebird, and sold for 35 cents, an incentive to fans with little money.

The Bluebird recordings took place in Hollywood on 19 January 1942 and in retrospect, this session heralded the end of the big band era. Tommy Dorsey and his Orchestra were not present but Dorsey allowed Axel Stordahl to write the arrangements for the session musicians. Strings were featured and these were intimate and restrained performances with no drums. Frank wasn't going to have Buddy Rich messing up his big day.

Harry Meyerson, the A&R manager at RCA, who produced the 1942 sessions said, 'Frank was not like a band vocalist at all. He knew exactly what he wanted. Most singers tend to begin with the humble bit. At first they're licking your hand. Then, the moment they catch the big one, you can't get them on the phone. Popularity didn't change Sinatra. On that first date he stood his ground and displayed no humility, phony or real.'

Frank was allowed to choose the four songs; they were by writers who meant a lot to him. Matt Dennis and Tom Adair wrote the only new song, the immensely sad ballad, 'The Night We Called It A Day'. Tommy Dorsey had been thinking of recording this with his band but let Frank have it.

'The Lamplighter's Serenade' is among the forgotten songs in Hoagy Carmichael's catalogue. To Sinatra's embarrassment, Bing Crosby heard his record and did it himself. The song was well suited to Bing's warm tones and it became a hit. The song is rarely performed today because lamplighting has disappeared, but the melody retains its beauty. Note how Sinatra hummed at the end: he could have gone into 'dooby, dooby, do'.

'The Song Is You' was a Jerome Kern and Oscar Hammerstein song from the 1932 Broadway show, *Music in the Air*. Sinatra turned in a beautiful performance and the way it built to his falsetto is like a classic performance from the 1950s. Doesn't the song sum up Sinatra himself: 'The music is sweet, the words are true, the song is you'?

In the early 1930s Fred Astaire did a screen test for RKO and the assessment was 'Can't sing. Can't act. Balding. Can dance a little.' He made *Dancing Lady* (1933) for MGM and a smash for RKO with *Flying Down To Rio*.

In 1932 Cole Porter had written a Broadway musical, *The Gay Divorce*, for Fred Astaire. There were many dance numbers in the production and Porter, a resourceful composer, needed a song that would both help Astaire regain his breath and not tax his pleasant, but limited, vocal range. He had heard a call to worship in Morocco and he had taken down its notes. He worked them into a song, 'Night and Day', which was the only song retained in the 1934 film version, retitled *The Gay Divorcée* by RKO. Irving Berlin wrote to Cole Porter: 'Dear Cole, I am mad about 'Night And Day' and I think it is your high spot. I could not resist the temptation of writing to you about it.'

Frank sang this song without the opening verse and it became his first solo hit, being even bigger when it was reissued in 1943. *Down Beat* commented, 'Sinatra hits the bull's eye squarely with his relaxed, effortless ways and smart phrasing.'

On 8 February 1942 Lana Turner was 21 years old. The so-called 'Sweater Girl' was already a star and had enough money for her own presents but Sinatra always wanted to buy gifts for the women in his life, sometimes with disastrous consequences. Frank gave her some silver wine-tasting cups. They were to have an on and off love affair for many years, which suited them both.

Artie Shaw, whose marriage to Lana Turner in 1940 had not lasted a year, was five years older than Sinatra but was going into the services. He disbanded his orchestra which included a string section. Tommy Dorsey, who had been impressed by Sinatra with strings, took over the string section as he thought it would add to the sound of the Sentimentalists, but it was a risky venture as it would put up the band's expenses at a time when revenue was falling.

Dorsey's first recording with strings was 'Street of Dreams', which was known through Bing Crosby's version from 1932. Untypically, Crosby's version starts with a dark verse about an opium-induced dream and Sinatra and Dorsey omitted this. They also covered 'Be Careful It's My Heart', which Bing Crosby sang in *Holiday Inn*. The film was a huge hit and combined with the *Road* films, Crosby was becoming Hollywood royalty.

Another risky venture in the summer of '42 was the determination of the songwriters Johnny Mercer and Buddy DeSylva to start their own record label with the retailer Glenn Wallichs. Requirements for the war had led to a shellac shortage. The trio set up their label in Hollywood and called it Capitol. They were determined that it wasn't going to be a small independent but a giant. Decca was having the pick of singers and musicians on the east coast, so the best prospects were on the west. They scored immediately with 'Cow-Cow Boogie' from Freddie Slack and his Orchestra with Ella Mae Morse. Capitol cleverly appealed to both the black and white pop markets with Nat 'King' Cole and Nellie Lutcher and combined pop and country with Tennessee 'Ernie' Ford.

One of Capitol's early signings was the arranger Paul Weston, who had been working with Tommy Dorsey. He was a master at arranging a good tune for a full orchestra. He kept his link with Tommy Dorsey as he was to marry one of the Pied Pipers, Jo Stafford.

In June 1942 Tommy Dorsey and his Orchestra recorded 'Dig Down Deep', a very cheery flagwaver that encouraged citizens to buy war bonds. They performed this many times on radio as 'the band that you love the best is asking you to invest'. The money will be spent on 'bombers for our fighting yanks'. The song says, 'Let us finish what we started', even though the US had come late into the war.

In all, Frank Sinatra cut 83 titles with Tommy Dorsey and his Orchestra and the final sessions were on 1/2 July 1942, although neither Dorsey nor Sinatra knew it at the time. The very smooth 'There Are Such Things' features Frank with the Pied Pipers and promises hope for the future. It touched a nerve as the record spent six weeks at No.1.

In the same mood is 'Light a Candle in the Chapel', a spiritual song, again reflective of war. The purpose of such a song is obvious but the BBC objected to it when it was released in the UK. They banned it for bogus religiosity in 1942, which was reaffirmed on appeal five years later. There was no arguing with the Head of Religious Broadcasting: 'I feel very strongly that the ban on the broadcast of this song should be maintained for two reasons. One: the song is so nauseatingly sentimental that it debases the Christian religion, and two: in any view the treatment of this kind of subject by a dance band is entirely unsuitable.'

Having said that, Frank Sinatra was loathed by at least some of the Dance Music Policy Committee and they banned what they could, commenting in March 1945, 'It is Frank Sinatra's interpretation of songs that matter and not that the songs themselves are passed or banned.'

When Tommy Dorsey's father died, Frank Sinatra hosted the radio programme and also conducted the orchestra. Although Sinatra could not read music and relied on Joe Bushkin's help with the new arrangements, he was nevertheless prepared to conduct, something to which he returned from time to time.

Frank Sinatra was becoming much more than a band vocalist and he was so popular that he was now closing the band's shows. He was fed up with working with Dorsey and he wanted to be freed from his contract. As he told a friend, 'The Old Man has goosed me with his trombone for the last time. I'm leaving the band.' Tommy Dorsey agreed to Frank Sinatra leaving the band, providing he could have a good slice of future earnings. Frank wanted to go and didn't really consider what he might be signing.

As with Harry James' band, Frank's replacement was Dick Haymes. Haymes was nine months younger than Sinatra and had been born in Buenos Aires, Argentina. Helped by his mother, who was a professional voice teacher, he became an excellent singer, especially on ballads. He had been with Harry James from 1939 to 1941 and even though James was having hits, he wasn't sure if he was going to be paid. Once James paid Haymes his salary, he wanted to borrow it back. Haymes was teased by band members because he was a hypochondriac and always feared the worst, and he was never fully comfortable on stage as he refused to wear spectacles. There could be high jinks in the band and James was furious when band members had a water pistol fight using ink. After Harry James, Dick Haymes joined Benny Goodman's band.

On the farewell broadcast with Tommy Dorsey on 3 September 1942, Frank Sinatra introduced Dick Haymes. This was followed by Sinatra's last show with Dorsey at the Circle Theatre, Indianapolis. He ended with a brilliant version of 'The Song is You' as if to say to Haymes, 'Beat that!'

CHAPTER 5

The house I live in

'Irving Berlin has no place in American music. He is American music.'

Jerome Kern

I. The Great American Songbook

Starting in 2002, Rod Stewart has released a series of best-selling albums under the generic title, *The Great American Songbook*. As the first album included two songs which were British, Stewart's definition, and possibly the public's, of the term was imprecise, but then you will find Billy Bragg's CDs amongst the Americana collection in record stores and what we call R&B today has little to do with the R&B of the 1950s.

The Great American Songbook is meant to cover popular songs which were written from around 1920 to the birth of rock'n'roll in 1955. They could be crafted in the Brill Building for specific performers or they could be for stage musicals or films. As a rule of thumb, the theatre songs were more sophisticated and had a wider vocabulary than the ones for mainstream Hollywood musicals. In both instances, they were often different from the standard popular song as they were based around plot and characterisation.

Many of the songs were written by legendary composers like Irving Berlin, but of his 2,000 compositions only the ones which have endured would be included in this Songbook. When someone remarked to Berlin, 'I don't know anyone who has written as many hits as you have', he retorted, 'I know there's no one who has written so many failures.'

As no committee has ever decided what should go into the Great American Songbook, its definition and therefore its contents are somewhat nebulous. The first performer to acknowledge this body of work was Lee Wiley who, starting with the Gershwins in 1939, released a series of 78rpm albums devoted to individual composers or songwriting teams. The most monumental attempt to quantify the work has been Ella Fitzgerald's *Songbook* albums, which began with Cole Porter in 1956. Sinatra could have taken the same approach but by and large he preferred thematic albums, selecting songs from a wide variety of sources. This meant that he could include lesser-known writers, that is, songs that are overlooked by the Wiley/Fitzgerald approach. Indeed, Frank Sinatra can be viewed as the champion of the neglected song.

Almost by definition, a great American song is one that has been recorded by Frank or Ella. It is disappointing that Rod Stewart's research hasn't stretched far beyond their albums. With thousands of songs that are never heard nowadays, he could have found a few great but little-known songs to surprise us.

Whatever definition you choose, the origins of the Great American Songbook are rooted in Tin Pan Alley.

The origins of Tin Pan Alley lie in New York, a musical city if there ever was one. During the later part of the 19th century, the music publishing companies started clustering on West

28th Street between Broadway and Sixth Avenue. The booking agencies for the theatres and music halls were nearby. The new, enterprising publishers would encourage vaudeville artists to perform their songs: they might tour all year and then return to Tin Pan Alley for new material, some of which would be written for them. This was the start of performers wanting songs to suit their stage personas.

The publishers would distribute sheet music to American stores, where they would usually be sold for piano use at home. Family sing-songs are rare today, but then it was a major source of entertainment. For many years, the public preferred buying sheet music to records, perhaps believing that DIY was better than something professional. Even in the 1950s, many homes still had piano stools stuffed with music. It wasn't only cheerful, friendly songs that would be sung around the piano. In the Victorian era, both tear-stained ballads and hymns were very popular. In the UK in the 1930s, the *News of the World* regularly printed a page of sheet music. This can be seen as the forerunner to the freebie CD or DVD given away with newspapers and magazines.

The presentation of sheet music changed very little with the years. Usually, it was a simple four page manuscript, the front page contained the title, the composers and an illustration, and the remaining three gave you the music. The artist pictured on the cover might not be the one most associated with the song: for example, the British sheet music for Buddy Holly's 'That'll Be the Day' showed Larry Page, who had recorded a cover version. A love for old sheet music came across in Dennis Potter's imaginative TV serial, *Pennies from Heaven* (1978). The play took place in the mid-1930s and Bob Hoskins as a sheet music salesman, dreamt of the idyllic happiness that he found in songs like 'Painting the Clouds with Sunshine', 'There's a Goldmine in the Sky' or 'I Only Have Eyes for You'.

The publisher realised the value of marketing when in 1892 Chas Harris both wrote and published a very popular song, 'After the Ball'. He did everything he could to encourage performers to sing his songs, especially that one. Through his efforts, everything became less genteel and by the turn of the century, there was a bustling trade. The publishers hired pianists who would write with lyricists at their upright pianos or would play potential successes to visiting performers. There was no sound-proofing or air conditioning, so the windows would be open and a stroller might hear a cacophony, which resembled tin pans being clashed together. The phrase, 'Tin Pan Alley', was first used by the songwriter, Monroe Rosenfeld, in an article in 1899, although he may not have coined it.

From then on, Tin Pan Alley reigned supreme. Sheet music sales boomed, and around ten songs a year sold over a million copies in the first decade of the 20th century. The songwriters counted for nothing if they couldn't write to order – if 'coon songs' (and that is what they were called) were wanted, then the writers would grind them out. If it was ragtime, they would switch to ragtime, and so on.

Irving Berlin wanted to convey the colour and excitement of the ragtime era, although 'Alexander's Ragtime Band' was more of a march and lacked the syncopation of ragtime music. He played the tune for Jesse Lasky, Samuel Goldwyn's brother-in-law, who was developing a cabaret show, *Folies Bergère*, in New York. He played it three times and then asked, 'Do you think it's good?' 'I wouldn't go as far as that,' said Lasky, 'but I may use it.' It was tried for one performance and then dropped, with Berlin regarding it as a failure. Berlin worked on another show, *Ziegfeld Follies*, and when that was successful, he wrote ragtime lyrics to his troublesome composition. It was included in a new revue in 1910, *The Happy Whirl*, but when that folded, it looked as though the song was destined for obscurity. However, when other performers picked up on the song, the publishers' 75 pluggers were instructed to promote it and within a year, a million copies of the sheet music had been sold.

Irving Berlin appreciated his own ability and the value of copyrights and so, in 1914, he established his own company, Irving Berlin Limited.

With no trouble at all, the songwriters showed their patriotism by writing songs for the First World War (not, of course, called the 'First World War' at the time as nobody had any idea that there would be another. Indeed, the Americans referred to it at first as the European War.) The Tin Hat Alley included 'Over There' and 'Oh! How I Hate to Get Up in the Morning'.

Music publishing became a legitimate trade, and it became even more lucrative after legislation. The publishers received two cents a copy on sheet music following the Copyright Law of 1909. The American Society of Composers, Authors and Publishers (ASCAP) was formed in 1917. As a test case, they sued a restaurant for playing their members' music without permission or payment. They won, and some years later, scored similar victories against cinemas, radio stations and record companies. Cylinders were gradually replaced by flat discs from 1897, but it wasn't until the 1920s they merited enough sales to attract Tin Pan Alley.

Most of the early songwriters were hacks and they did not need to be good musicians as special pianos enabled them to switch keys by pressing levers. Irving Berlin, the first major songwriter to come out of Tin Pan Alley, used such a device as he could only play in F sharp. By the 1920s, the Alley was attracting more literate and sophisticated writers like George Gershwin, Jerome Kern and Cole Porter, and the standard of the work dramatically improved. Irving Berlin's work could match anyone's but he must have felt intimidated when George Gershwin, a concert pianist, was around. Jerome Kern said to him, 'Irving, you must learn how to write music. You've got to be able to sit down and write your notes.' Irving Berlin respected Jerome Kern so he started very laboriously to study music. After a month, he said, 'Why, that son of a bitch! While I was learning musical notation, I could have written twelve songs.'

In 1942 Irving Berlin became the only person in the whole history of the Academy Awards to give himself an Oscar when he won the Best Song with 'White Christmas'. That was just as well, as he would have inconsolable if he'd had to hand it to the writers of 'How About You' or 'I've Heard That Song Before'.

With the popularity of Broadway musicals, Tin Pan Alley moved to a street off Times Square and then came the 'talkies' from Hollywood. *The Jazz Singer* with Al Jolson was an awe-inspiring start but the Depression reduced cinema audiences. In 1933, *42nd Street* with a score by Harry Warren and Al Dubin, became a major success, and one Hollywood musical followed another. It was the California Gold Rush for songwriters: some songwriters moved east and others mailed their efforts from New York.

Tin Pan Alley during the 1920s and 1930s can be summed up as rhythm and Jews. The majority of the songwriters, and indeed the publishers, were male Jewish immigrants, whose parents may have come from Russia or Poland. Some of this can be attributed to peer pressure and to the fact that the offices were close to the Jewish communities in New York, but that doesn't explain why they were able to write so well. Quite possibly, many of the families had had to learn English as a second language, and the wordsmiths became intrigued with the use of words and their meanings. There is a book, *When Boxing Was a Jewish Sport*, so it is not only songwriting.

Music historian Paul Gambaccini observes, 'With both popular music and comic books, it was the Jews and the Italian-Americans who tended to be the great creators and artists. *Superman*, *Batman* and *Captain America* were created by Jews and you can have a lot of fun with sociological theories bearing in mind that they were invented between 1938 and

1940. Most of the music business was centred in New York, and that is where the Jewish immigrants were based and where those wonderful writers came to the fore.'

Several writers found inspiration in the Jewish hymnal. Sammy Cahn recalls, 'Cole Porter said to me one time, "I envy you where you were born. Had I been born Jewish, I would have been a true genius." If you listen carefully to Cole Porter's melodies, they are often Hebraic in the minor tones. (Sings) "I love Paris in the springtime, I love Paris in the fall", "What is this thing called love?" They are both beautifully and melodically constructed on the minor chords, so if you want to write a really lovely melody with great passion, you could try the deep minor chords, the Hebraic tones.'

Some wrote alone, but most songs were written by two-man teams with a distinct demarcation between words and music. Some had exclusive partnerships, but most writers were willing to try new partners.

In 1927 and at the last minute, the lyricist Oscar Hammerstein felt *Show Boat* needed a song about the Mississippi itself but Jerome Kern was preoccupied with other work. Hammerstein told him not to worry: if he slowed down the banjo music in Act One, he would have a suitable tune. Sometime later, an admirer told Mrs. Kern how much he admired *Ol' Man River*. Mrs. Hammerstein corrected him: 'Mr. Kern wrote "Dum-dum-dum-dum",' she said, 'My husband wrote "Ol' man river".'

Don't believe her, as Alec Wilder wrote of that composition, 'The song is a singers' delight, having a wide range, drama and no difficult melodic hurdles to jump. Since it does have a very wide range, an octave and a sixth, it requires a true singer to perform it.' And who better than Frank Sinatra whose version was voted the best vocal performance of all-time by listeners to AFN (American Forces Network)? If, however, you feel how have heard this song once too often, please try the extraordinary performance from Screamin' Jay Hawkins: I don't want to describe it as that would spoil the surprise.

There is often a thin line between what makes a hit and what doesn't. Jerome Kern wrote around 40 Broadway shows and his biggest flop was *Very Warm For May* (1939), which, like *Show Boat*, was written with Oscar Hammerstein II. The show did badly – only 20 people bought tickets for the second night! – but it had one of Kern's best scores. Kern thought 'All the Things You Are' was too complicated to be a hit but then he heard somebody whistling it and changed his mind, an early example of the old grey whistle test. Also, the rather precocious nine year old Stephen Sondheim saw the show and recognised its qualities.

Though Dorothy Fields provided the lyrics for over 400 songs, many of which appeared in Broadway shows and movies, there were few female composers and it was not until the 1960s that one became nationally known, namely, Carole King. I have never found a satisfactory explanation of why songwriting was so male dominated. Plenty of women wrote novels at home, so why didn't they write songs?

The British version of this writers' block developed in the 1920s with the publishers, Francis Day and Hunter, Feldman's and Lawrence Wright, among others. The companies were based around Denmark Street, a short, narrow thoroughfare off Charing Cross Road. At first, the publishers had licensed songs from America and indeed, Americans wrote many of the familiar British music hall songs. Then the British composers, Ivor Novello and Noël Coward, showed themselves to be as adept as their US counterparts. Up until the Beatles led the revolution for artists writing their own songs, performers and their managers would trudge up and down Denmark Street, picking up manuscripts whenever they entered a pokey office and hoping that they had found the elusive hit.

The record producer Wally Ridley was born in 1913: 'I started work at Feldman's when I was 15, and Feldman's, Francis Day and Hunter, and Chappell's were the main publishers.

We used to publish ten songs a week every week of the year, and the film songs of Harry Warren and Al Dubin and Johnny Burke came through us. I used to play them first in the written key, and then I would transpose them, up a semitone, down a semitone, and so on, so that I could play them in any key. If anybody came in to hear new songs, I could play them in their key, which is enormously important as a singer can't get to grips with a song if he has to sing it in a key which is unsuitable. It has to be in the right key for him, and in the end, I could transpose anything on sight.'

Once the singer had agreed to perform the song, an orchestration had to be supplied. The film composer, Ron Goodwin, recalled his early years: 'I was working for a music publisher in London and the hit song when I went there was 'Whispering Grass'. The publisher would persuade all sorts of people to broadcast it, and then orchestrations would have to be made for whichever orchestra they were with. I was the lowly copyist who copied the parts for the musicians from that score. You do it one instrument at a time. First of all you copy the first flute part, and then you copy the second one, and so forth. It's really just copying in a neat hand for the orchestra to be able to play what the orchestrator has written on the score. One of the orchestrators was a wonderful chap called Harry J Stafford. Harry was prone to taking extended lunches, you know propped up against a bar somewhere, and he would come back a little the worse for wear. One day the manager said, "Where's that bloody orchestration I wanted?" Harry drew himself up with the full dignity of alcohol, picked up the piano copy of 'Whispering Grass', put in on the floor, stood on it and said, "I'm on it now."'

The music publisher Freddy Bienstock described the American scene during the 1940s: 'I had a cousin in New York who had a job as a song-plugger at Chappell Music and he would visit all these glorious bandleaders like Benny Goodman and Tommy Dorsey and persuade them to play Chappell's songs on their radio broadcasts. This seemed the most heavenly thing one could possibly do, but when I asked him about a job, he said that I was too young. I had to wait until I was 16. In 1943, he told me that he had a job for me at Chappell's, starting in the stock room. It was only $16 a week, but nevertheless, I came to New York and started to work in their stockroom. I got great satisfaction in 1984 when I bought Chappell's.' Lucky man!

With much laughter, Freddy recalled his first day at Chappell's. 'This man was being sacked and he said to the great Max Dreyfus who was sacking him, "Mr Dreyfus, my fate is in your hands." He said, "How can you say a thing like that? Don't you know your fate and my fate are in the hands of God?" I thought, "My god, he's firing him and he's passing the buck to God."'

Fortunately, Max Dreyfus didn't sack Freddy Bienstock. 'I was there for ten years. I had two years in the stock room and worked my way up to become a song-plugger. My job was to visit the various bands which had airtime from the Waldorf Hotel, the Commodore and the like and ask them to play the songs that I was assigned to promote. Chappell was promoting the songs of Jerome Kern and Cole Porter so it was a lovely, easy, glamorous existence. I didn't have to be at the office before 11 o'clock in the morning and I would visit radio stations for daytime programming, and at night I would go from one nightclub to another. I would get paid for it and I had an expense account, so it was marvellous.'

The songs were often plugged by the composers themselves. The US singer, Jerry Wayne, who is the father of Jeff Wayne of *The War Of The Worlds* fame, recalled, 'I remember a composer calling me up and saying, "I have a new song that I would love you to hear" and as we didn't have cassettes, I had to go in and hear it. I said, "Yeah, lovely song" and so I was the first to record 'Room Full of Roses'. I used to go from publisher to publisher and even Frank Loesser and Jule Styne worked as rehearsal pianists. You could go in and rehearse a programme you were doing. They would do it for free but they would expect you to perform one of their songs.'

The main haven for songwriters was the large office block, the Brill Building, at 1619 Broadway in Manhattan, and although I wish that 'Brill' was short for 'Brilliant', it's not true. The site belonged to the Brill brothers who had a men's clothing store and they leased it to a developer. He completed most of the 11 storey *art deco* building but then ran out of money and besides, who, in the Depression, wanted new office space?' The answer was 'Songwriters'.

The Brill brothers foreclosed, completed the building and named it after themselves. Rather than go for Wall Street companies, they marketed it to one music publisher and then another and soon everybody wanted to be in the Brill Building. They had all been working in tiny offices around Broadway and now they were a community with agents and promoters also seizing the opportunity to secure tenancies at knockdown prices. Hundreds of composers including Cole Porter and Irving Berlin operated from the Brill Building. Sinatra's company, Barton Songs, was to have an office there in the 1950s.

Contemporary lyrics in one decade may seem outdated the next. So many pre-war love songs were about getting married and their sentiments would fall on deaf ears today. 'Turtle dove' was a very handy rhyme for 'love' but it has no credibility now. Similarly, 'gay', another neat word for rhyming, has a different connation today and is hardly ever used to mean 'happy'. Similarly, many pre-1960s songs referred to praying, which would sound bogus today. If there is a 1920s song which started, 'When I'm happy and gay, She says, 'Let us pray'", no one would sing it. And what song today would have a line similar to 'You told me love was too plebeian' from 'Cry Me A River'?

Because Irving Berlin wrote in so many styles, there is no such thing as a Berlin song. But we can describe a Cole Porter song: witty, urbane, sophisticated and perhaps, in both senses of the word, gay. George Melly believed that his songs had a built-in and sometimes hidden melancholy. 'There is a lot of feeling and tension in Cole Porter's work that is under the surface. 'Night And Day' is full of feeling, but frustrated feeling as he was gay and although he wrote love songs apparently to women, they were really to men, just as Noël Coward did.'

Cole Porter enjoyed putting contemporary references in his songs which date them but give them a certain charm. To this end, it is fortunate that he often wrote more verses than were necessary so the singer can select what would work today.

Nor are melodies safe in the ageing process. Michael Feinstein says, 'If you play what is written on the page, it may sound stilted. 'Someone to Watch over Me' was written in 1926 and the original recording by Gertrude Lawrence is sung with a bit of a lilt and a bit of rhythm. It sounds odd now because we have evolved. Such songs are generally sung slower now than when they were written.'

The structure of the popular song was set by Tin Pan Alley, usually consisting of some or all of verse 1, chorus, verse 2, chorus, bridge, verse 3, chorus. Many pre-war songs had introductory verses, which were particularly evident in film and theatrical productions where the preambles set up the songs. On film, Bing Crosby explained that it was a sunny December in Los Angeles before he sang 'White Christmas'. A few introductions survived in the rock'n'roll era, notably 'Poetry In Motion', 'Runaround Sue' and 'Take Good Care Of My Baby'. Many singers preferred to cut to the chase and so many introductions were omitted, but Sinatra was keen on their inclusion, once in 1961 recording the introduction to 'Stardust' on its own, that is, 'And now the purple dusk of twilight time' and omitting 'Sometimes I wonder'. Hoagy Carmichael sent Frank a short note, 'I wrote a whole song!'

Prior to the 1960s a good song would be covered by numerous performers; there are several excellent versions of say 'Unchained Melody' or 'The Way You Look Tonight' to choose from. Sinatra's strength lay in his interpretation. He would study a lyric like a poem and he would say, 'I'm trying to understand the point of view of the person behind the words. I want to understand his emotions.' He often chose Broadway songs which had been introduced by females, possibly because women were generally given more melancholy material.

Sinatra recorded a lot of late night, barroom songs because he was a late night, barroom person himself. Indeed, some listeners are not attracted to Sinatra because the songs are too sleazy. In 1993 Carly Simon wouldn't join Frank for a duet of 'One for My Baby' because the song advocated drinking and driving: certainly no one would write about having one more for the road today.

It is tempting to look for the autobiographical touches in Sinatra's performances. Although there are examples of this, most of the time he is simply able, like an actor, to immerse himself in the character required by the song. He did have a wild, rollercoaster life and so he experienced many intense emotions, which came out in his performances even if he was not feeling that way at the time. He often sang of undying love when practising nothing of the sort.

Freddy Bienstock described how the songs came to be written. 'The Brill Building was the home of all the main music publishers and a songwriter might start on the penthouse floor where we had our office and if we didn't take his songs, he would go to the 11th floor and so on until they found a home. There's a legend around Walter Donaldson who was always betting on racehorses and always needed money. He was a great writer and he would sell, say, 'My Blue Heaven' to three different publishers and then they would have to sort out their interests. Of course the publishers should have been furious with him but they weren't as they wanted his next song.' Fats Waller was also known to sell songs many times over in order to pay for his lifestyle.

The Brill Building songwriters could write whatever you wanted – love ballads, show tunes, sambas, fox-trots and novelties – but they had difficulties in the mid-1950s in coming to terms with rock'n'roll. Most of the older songwriters detested the music, and this typical remark about Elvis Presley came from Billy Rose, who wrote 'Happy Days And Lonely Nights': 'Not only are most of his songs junk, but in many cases they are obscene junk, pretty much on a level with dirty comic magazines. It is this current climate that makes Elvis Presley and his animal posturings possible.'

Paul Evans was one of those rock'n'roll songwriters: 'The established writers were disgusted with us and with what we were writing, and the tragedy is that some of us bought into that. They kept telling us that we were writing garbage, that we would be very lucky if we ever had another hit and that no-one would ever hear of our songs again. They thought rock'n'roll writers couldn't write standards but they were wrong. I'm doing very well with my old rock'n'roll songs."

Part of their antipathy was because rock'n'roll was changing the market, reducing the demand for sheet music and increasing it for records. However, the writing of the new songs in the rock'n'roll era was precisely the same. The songwriter shut himself in a tiny cubicle and hoped for inspiration. Doc Pomus was a blues songwriter, who turned to rock'n'roll: 'When I decided to become a full-time songwriter, I thought the best way to survive was to write an extraordinary amount of songs. I realised that if I wrote by myself there was no way I could write an extraordinary amount of songs, so the best thing would be to find a co-writer. My cousin knew Mort Shuman, who knew a lot about young people's songs. I locked him up in a room with me, and right from the beginning, every time I wrote I would give him a little piece of the song. This went on for the longest while and as he contributed more and more, I gave him larger percentages of the songs. Then one day I said to him, "Mort Shuman, you are my full partner."'

Some people wrote so many songs that they thought they had better use pseudonyms. The manager and British songwriter, Bunny Lewis wrote songs with Norrie Paramor: 'Norrie was the head of A&R at Columbia and a lot of people wouldn't record his songs on other labels if they knew he'd written them. To get round this, he had 34 pseudonyms. Eventually, the Performing Right Society issued an edict to the effect that no one could have more than five pseudonyms.'

Strictly speaking, the Brill Building was not the home of rock'n'roll. That was over the road at 1650 Broadway. In 1958 the songwriter and publisher, Don Kirshner, created his own songwriting teams: Carole King and Gerry Goffin, Barry Mann and Cynthia Weil, and Neil Sedaka and Howard Greenfield among them, and most were Jewish writers from the same area of Brooklyn. They were talented songsmiths, who, naturally, were at one with the young audience, and so their songs hit the right emotional spots. By 1962, Aldon employed 18 writers and the oldest was only 26. It was a positive, competitive atmosphere and so successful that Kirshner set up a second office on the west coast, thus supplying songs for surfing bands. The 1996 film *Grace of My Heart* was loosely based on Carole King's life and is a reasonably accurate portrayal of the teen factory.

Although Otis Blackwell wrote 'Don't Be Cruel', 'All Shook Up' and 'Paralyzed' by himself, the label says 'Blackwell-Presley'. Elvis, it appeared to me, was doing nothing new: Al Jolson used to claim credits on songs he didn't write and so did George Formby. Freddy Bienstock commented, 'It's not quite the same thing. In the early days, Elvis would show dissatisfaction with some lines and he would make alterations, so it wasn't just what is known as a 'cut-in'. After 1956, his name did not appear as a writer, but if Elvis liked the song, the writers would be offered a guarantee of a million records and they would surrender a third of their royalties to Elvis.'

The hit songwriter Cynthia Weil recalls, "One of the advantages of writing in cubicles was that you had everybody around you, and it was a turn-on to hear what everybody else was doing. It was so inspirational and competitive that it got you all jazzed up to work harder and write faster and do more. There were friendly rivalries between the writers but as we matured, the rivalries disappeared and the friendships continued."

'There were two restaurants in the Brill Building where the writers hung out,' Paul Evans adds, 'The older ones would be in Dempsey's and the younger ones in The Turf. I was in The Turf when the dreadful news about the Big Bopper, Buddy Holly and Ritchie Valens came through. The place just emptied as they were all racing to pianos to write songs about the plane crash.'

So the younger writers were, in some ways, like the older ones. They could write to order and they could be astonishingly prolific. Paul Evans continues: 'Barry Mann is one of the greatest pop writers of all-time, usually writing with his wife Cynthia Weil. When we were kids in New York, he was racing down the street out of breath and I said, "Stop, Barry, congratulations!" and he said, "Paul, what are you congratulating me for?" I said, "You have three songs in the Top 10, congratulations!" and he said, "Paul, they're all on the way down!", and he was off to write another song.'

In 1963 Don Kirshner sold Aldon to Screen-Gems Columbia for $2m, although he was still running day to day operations. In 1964 Kirshner thought he had done well with the sale as the upsurge of the Beatles and Bob Dylan encouraged performers to record their own material and there was not such a demand for Screen-Gems material. It was not hip to have your songs written by some third party. Some writers found a lifeline with the Monkees and then the Archies, both groups being manufactured (in very different ways) by Kirshner. We can now see that $2m was a knockdown price but who could have predicted the true value of these copyrights due to reissues, revivals, tribute bands and commercials?

The Brill Building is still functioning – Paul Simon has an office there – but there are now major publishers in other American cities. Indeed, there are now more songwriters in Nashville than New York, and not all of them are writing country. 'Most of the songwriters in the US have retreated to Nashville, it is like the keep,' says Jimmy Webb, 'They are making their last stand down there as songwriting as an art form is in decline. Certainly the role of the songwriter and the importance of the songwriter is not what it once was in America.'

Intriguingly, the Nashville publishers usually insist that songs are co-written – not one lyricist and one music man, but two songwriters. The publishers therefore have their risks reduced by having their wagon pulled by two horses instead of one.

Shortly before his death in 2009, Freddy Bienstock thought standards had deteriorated: 'Everything was done on a much more personal basis at that time – now it's all about money and guarantees and so forth. I also think that the quality of the songs was higher. A song was presented to a publisher and it was discussed and then given to an artist, who had some input into it, and so by the time Tony Bennett, Frank Sinatra or Perry Como recorded the song, the song had been fashioned into something that was just right. The standards fell with the advent of albums as so many more songs were needed and it was difficult to cherry pick in the same way. Very often the performer or his advisers thought they could write them themselves. That is why we have so few new standards nowadays.'

One great Tin Pan Alley story is that songs had to pass the old grey whistle test. If the doorman could remember it after one hearing, it stood a chance of being a hit. The 1960s writer (now retired) Mitch Murray says, 'If you look at my songs, they only have four or five chords maximum as that's all I know. That may sound amateurish but it forced me to write very melodic songs. I couldn't rely on clever chords to make them sound beautiful, and today's writers can really fool you with their chords. At the end of it, they won't stand up as songs you can whistle. Nowadays, they are record writers. In my day, the songs were often hits despite the records but you can't say that now. They have to be good records."

II. Day In–Day Out, 1943–1945

If Frank Sinatra wanted to build on his success with Tommy Dorsey, he had to establish himself on four fronts: as a recording artist, as a radio performer, as a live attraction and as a film star. He and his family had moved to 220 Lawrence Avenue, New Jersey, where a Mafia boss, Willie Morettia, was a close neighbour. Morettia was born in 1894 and had already done time for robbery. Nancy's cousin, John, had worked for Morettia, who himself was related to another crime boss, Frank Costello, who made his fortunes from slot machines in New York.

What should have been the simplest task for Frank Sinatra, namely, establishing himself as a recording artist, was to prove elusive for almost a year. Within a few weeks, Manie Sacks had given him a contract with Columbia Records, which was owned by CBS, so Frank had what he wanted, but because of the musicians' strike, he wasn't able to record, although Columbia did eventually find a way around this. The obvious solution which was to make records in Canada was not pursued by any of the labels, possibly because the Canadian musicians might have claimed solidarity with their American counterparts and escalated the problems.

Maybe that hiatus was a good thing for Sinatra as the market might have been flooded with his product. Victor were still issuing tracks he had recorded with Tommy Dorsey and his Orchestra and there were Top 10 singles with 'Take Me', where he sang the chorus as a tenor, 'Daybreak', based on a classical theme, and the mellow 'It Started All Over Again'.

The most effective way to become a national celebrity was to work regularly on the radio and for the next 10 years, Frank Sinatra took everything that came along, often hosting two shows in a week with several guest appearances. There were many local stations which were big in their own areas, but Sinatra favoured working for the giants, CBS and NBC, largely because they had decent budgets as well as audiences. He had to follow the rules: if he offended a sponsor, he was out of a job.

His success on radio was immediate. From October 1942 to February 1943 he presented a twice-weekly show, *Songs by Sinatra* for CBS. It was broadcast from 6 to 6.15pm and featured Frank with a small group led by the pianist, Skitch Henderson. Skitch was fond of using quirky phrases like 'skitchadudawawa', which Sinatra was to copy. *Songs by Sinatra* featured familiar material but there were quirky selections like 'Rose Ann of Charing Cross'. Sinatra made one-off appearances on the radio specials, *Your Broadway and Mine* and *America Salutes the President's Birthday*. In January 1943, he recorded 16 songs for the *Treasury Song Parade* with an accordion-led combo.

A guest appearance in a musical film, Columbia's *Reveille with Beverly,* came straightaway as there were no restrictions on musicians working on film soundtracks. There was no plot to speak of as Ann Miller played an armed forces DJ introducing Duke Ellington (performing in a train carriage), Count Basie, Bob Crosby, Ella Mae Morse and the Mills Brothers. The most electrifying sequence is Ann's tap dance, *V For Victory*, which, like several Fred Astaire's routines, has you wondering how they did it – and even if you knew, you would still be amazed. Sinatra appeared in white tie and tails, singing 'Night And Day' and surrounded by pretty girls playing violins and pianos. He visited each piano in turn as the girls looked lovingly at him. Sinatra received $1,000 for his three minute slot and when the film was released in February 1943, his name was on the marquee as though he were the star. The press told of a Sinatra fan who saw it 120 times.

In November 1942 Bob Weitman, the manager of the New York Paramount, saw Sinatra in Newark. He had previously booked Sinatra with Dorsey at the Paramount and now he was very impressed with his solo performance. He had Benny Goodman's band scheduled for a month from 30 December and he wanted Frank as an added attraction. The band would play alongside Bing Crosby and Bob Hope's film, *Star Spangled Rhythm*. There would be early shows because of the school holidays and because many people were working shifts because of the war.

Benny Goodman's regular vocalist was Peggy Lee. She had joined him in 1941 but the record executive, John Hammond, hadn't been impressed and had urged Goodman to sack her. Goodman refused and she was to have a huge success in January 1943 with 'Why Don't You Do Right', which they performed in *Stage Door Canteen*. Like *Reveille With Beverly* and *Star Spangled Rhythm,* this was a let's-put-on-a-show film. As the only woman in the ensemble, Goodman became very protective towards Lee and when one of the band members, Dave Barbour, dated her in March 1943, he sacked him. Dave and Peggy were to marry and both of them became friendly with Sinatra. The band had a tough schedule because after playing all day in between the showings of the film at the Paramount, they had late night sets at the New Yorker Hotel.

Frank Sinatra was staying in the Times Square area at the Astor. He would arrive at the Paramount at 9.30am and take hot tea with honey to loosen his voice. After the final show, he might go to CBS to record a *Songs by Sinatra*.

Benny Goodman knew that Frank was popular but he was stunned by the reaction when he announced, 'And now Frank Sinatra'. The band struck up the wedding song, 'For Me and My Gal' and from then on it was wall-to-wall screaming. The theatre did such good business that Sinatra continued for another month, singing with the bands of Sonny Dunham, Johnny Long and, would you believe, Dolly Dawn and her Dawn Patrol.

This booking is regarded as the start of Sinatramania, which might be true, but Sinatra had booked a press agent, George Evans, who had handled Glenn Miller, Duke Ellington Louis Prima and Lena Horne. He was a skilled manipulator, akin to a spin doctor today. The hysteria was there, no doubt about that, but he knew how to intensify it and make out that Sinatra was like nobody else.

His first job was to rewrite history: Sinatra was now born in 1917, had an excellent school record and had worked as a sports reporter. He was keen on boosting Frankie's fees in a press release so that he was earning $25,000 a week at the Paramount, not that there would be much left after paying George Evans. Sinatra was actually receiving $2,500. Evans must have been delighted when the crime novelist Damon Runyon of all people succumbed to the hype and wrote, 'Frank Sinatra's about as normal as any 23-year-old who's just made a million bucks.'

Evans told Sinatra that he should wear his wedding ring on stage and that he should fiddle with it as he sang 'Embraceable You', an unusual strategy for a matinee idol. He hired uninhibited girls to start the screaming and he told Frank that he must say 'we' and not 'you' when talking to his fans from the stage. Evans encouraged fans to respond to songs so that when he started 'She's Funny That Way' with 'I'm not much to look at...', they would shout back, 'Oh yes, you are!' Shades of John Otway! The fans would yell 'Hubba hubba Frankie, hey!' which is surprisingly close to the Ramones' 'Gabba gabba gabba, hey!'

George Evans helped organised Sinatrics to establish fan clubs, a New Jersey one being called the Sighing Society of Sinatra Swooners. An editorial said, 'I wish Frankie were twins, one for me and one for Nancy.' George created a family image, passing out information (or misinformation) about the two Nancys and as a result, they were welcomed by fans and received presents in their own right. Fans often slept with a Frank Sinatra pillow, but they didn't know that Frank was sometimes so busy that his mother would sign his autographs. Dolly, to add to her eccentricities, now had a pet monkey.

And why was Frankie busy? He knew the Bronx boxing champ, Tami Mauriello, and he had his trainer come to the Paramount for breathing exercises to build up his lungs. He maintained his friendship with the trainer and gave him a corner man role in a fight scene in *The Joker Is Wild* (1957).

In comparison to Elvis Presley and what was to follow, Frank Sinatra was a fairly tame performer: he just stood there and sang. However, the fans loved his lean and hungry look and wanted either to mother him or jump into his bed. George Evans told him to caress the microphone and said he must wear a different suit and floppy bow tie for each performance in the day. He should have a curl over his forehead that girls would want to put back in place; it looked like Bill Haley's kiss-curl.

The bow ties, some of which were made by Nancy, became his trademark. Indeed as late as *The Man with the Golden Arm* (1955), Frankie Machine wears a 'Sinatra', the name for his bow tie. The 'Sinatra style' was acknowledged in the novelty song, 'Tabby the Cat', recorded by Anita O'Day with Stan Kenton and his Orchestra.

George Evans asked radio stations to hold Frank Sinatra days and, most cleverly of all, he called him 'The Voice', actually 'The Voice that Thrills the World' but it was soon abbreviated. I don't know what George Evans charged but whatever it was, it was worth it.

Sinatra was so popular that the windows in his dressing-room at the Paramount had to be covered as the sight of him from the street caused traffic jams. Journalists referred to 'this mass self-debasement of women' and 'the desperate chemistry of adolescence'. There was no such word as 'teenager' back then. The girls came to be known as 'bobbysoxers', a reference to their white cotton socks with saddle shoes.

Some analysts said that this was due to 'wartime degeneracy' as Sinatra became the replacement for the eligible men in the services. At the time, Frank said, rather immodestly, 'The war has nothing to do with it. It just so happens that I am the greatest singing sensation of the past ten years.' He did revise this opinion some years later by saying, 'I think it had a lot to do with the time period. It was important for people to have someone to root for during the war years. I always felt that I was, in their minds, one of the kids from the neighbourhood who made good.'

Latin lovers were also nothing new: do we not still use the term Romeo for a loving dude and Casanova for a randy one? Rudolph Valentino was an Italian who had come to Hollywood in 1926 and became an iconic romantic figure without saying a word. He died before the talkies came in and there were hysterical crowds at his funeral.

Bing Crosby was of Irish extraction but his biggest rivals for a time were the singer and actor, Rudy Vallee, an Italian-American who was billed as 'The Vagabond Lover', and Russ Columbo, another Italian-American who died when he was only 26. However, Bing Crosby never pretended to have any sex appeal and was now pleasing the pipe-and-slippers brigade. Bing was calm, confident and unpretentious and he figured that people liked him because he sounded like the average man in the shower.

On the other hand, George Evans had turned Frank Sinatra into a pop idol. The cover feature of *Billboard* on 27 March 1943 said that 'Frank Sinatra is the biggest threat in years to Bing Crosby's reign as king of the vocalists' and remarked that he was 'young, good looking and heavily romantic'. George Evans could have written the piece himself and probably did.

Based in New York, John Walters wrote a feature for the *Daily Mirror* in October 1943. He described how girls rushed the stage when Frankie sang the lines, 'Come to papa, come to papa, do' in 'Embraceable You'. He said, 'The Voice is rather a weak baritone, magnified by the microphone into which he warbles' and he concluded, 'Whenever I hear Sinatra on the wireless, I switch it off and open the window to let in some fresh air.'

CBS had a weekly chart show, *Your Hit Parade*, from 9 to 9.30pm on Saturday nights. It had been broadcast since 1935 and was sponsored by Lucky Strike cigarettes with their slogan, 'So round, so firm, so fully packed, so free and easy on the draw' As if to balance this, Frank was voicing radio ads for the American Cancer Society, although the link between the two was not yet known.

Your Hit Parade featured the most popular songs of the week based on sheet music sales, record sales, radioplay and jukebox plays, although its accuracy was never questioned and the producers never said how they balanced the four components. The chart placings could have been back-of-the-envelope stuff for all we know. The songs were performed live with resident male and female singers and the group, the Hit Paraders. Lennie Hayton, Lena Horne's husband, had been its first conductor and Ray Sinatra had worked on the show in 1936. Frank Sinatra took over from Barry Wood on 13 February 1943 and, in his first stint, was to go through until the end of 1944. His co-star was Joan Edwards and the orchestra was conducted by Mark Warnow.

Sinatra could see the huge advantage of being featured, but he knew the drawbacks. He might be told to perform songs that he had antipathy towards; he might prefer more sensual arrangements as CBS wanted everything quick-moving and cheerful. He preferred to ad lib rather than stick to a script. Still, on the whole it worked well. Taking an episode not quite at random, on 27 March 1943, the date of the *Billboard* cover feature, Frank sang 'Moonlight Becomes You', 'There Are Such Things' (his own hit), 'You'd Be So Nice to Come Home to' and 'That Old Black Magic'. Nothing wrong with that.

Frank sang 'God Bless America' for *I'm an American Day*, which featured the Mayor of New York, Fiorello La Guardia. Gangsters notwithstanding, the best-known Italian-Americans of the moment were La Guardia, Frank Sinatra and Joe DiMaggio, who batted safely in 56 consecutive baseball games in 1941.

In April 1943 Sinatra had wanted to play the prestigious nightclub, the Copa, but was turned down. To show them what they were missing, he accepted a three week booking at another sophisticated venue, the nearby Riobamba club on East 57th Street in Manhattan. It was a small club which only paid him $750 a week but it enabled him to develop a more intimate style where he could work with a pianist, Skitch Henderson, and walk around the tables singing and talking. The club was in serious trouble as its owner, Louis 'Lepke' Buchalter, was awaiting execution as a hit man for the Mafia. He had formed the hit squad known as Murder Inc. The Riobamba was being run in his absence by his wife and Sinatra was keeping it open. He must have liked it as he stayed for another seven weeks. Buchalter was executed in March 1944, the only Mob boss to be executed.

Because there was always the possibility of being executed, most Mafia bosses spent their day standing up, saying that they didn't want their clothes creased. But in truth it is far easier to stab someone when he is sitting down, and what's more, the victim cannot draw a gun as fast if he is seated.

On somewhat larger stages, Sinatra took part in a war bond rally in Central Park and in a charity event for war relief in Madison Square Garden. He returned to the Paramount, where he was going to work with Gene Krupa and his Orchestra, but Krupa had been jailed for possessing marijuana. *Down Beat* commented on Sinatra, 'His spell is not as artless as it looks. He knows his feminine audience and fires romance – moonlight moods – at them with deadly aim.'

In May, Frank became a resident in another CBS show, *Broadway Bandbox*, on Friday nights with Axel Stordahl arranging and conducting. Here he worked alongside Benny Goodman, Harry James, Orson Welles and the Golden Gate Quartet.

The musicians' strike rumbled on and the record companies wanted to break the deadlock. Columbia had had Sinatra on their books for several months without doing anything with him.

Some smaller labels, away from New York, ignored the ban and the musicians continued to work for them. Capitol and Decca settled with the unions but Columbia and Victor held out convinced that Congress would call the strike unconstitutional, especially in times of war. In the meantime, they had a temporary solution. The singers could not record with musicians but why not make acappella recordings with a choral backing? Both Bing Crosby and Dick Haymes made acappella recordings before Sinatra, and it is interesting to speculate why the singers didn't support the strikers and refuse outright. In Sinatra's case, nothing got in his way if he wanted to do something, though I doubt that his mother would have approved.

On 7 June 1943 Sinatra recorded the first sides with the radio choir, the Bobby Tucker Singers. The songs were arranged by the serious-minded Alec Wilder, whom Sinatra called the Professor. He had arranged a chamber music accompaniment for Mildred Bailey, which Frank loved, and so he had been asked to help out.

The first song was a new one, 'Close to You', published by the vaudeville performer, Ben Barton, who wanted to be a music publisher. The result was a beautiful combination of voices and a superb recording. Later, Sinatra did rework it with an orchestral accompaniment from Axel Stordahl, but the original is fine.

'You'll Never Know' was performed by Alice Faye in the 1943 film, *Hello, Frisco, Hello*. She crooned the ballad into a telephone and its melody recurred throughout the film. It won the Oscar for Best Song, but because of the strike, she did not record it and both Sinatra and Dick Haymes sang it acappella.

The other songs were 'Sunday, Monday Or Always' from the Bing Crosby film, *Dixie*, 'If You Please' and two songs from the new stage musical, *Oklahoma!* The choreographer Agnes de Mille had not wanted 'People Will Say We're in Love' in the show, telling Richard Rodgers that 'It's not up to your standard.' Sanity prevailed but it is odd to hear Sinatra sing, 'Give me my rose and my glove' as it clearly should be a girl's song or a duet. The light and shade of the voices is brought out magnificently in 'Oh, What a Beautiful Mornin''.

'All Or Nothing at All' was going down well in concert and Sinatra wanted to make a new orchestral version but he was stymied by the strike. Instead Columbia reissued the original recording Frank had made with Harry James and his Orchestra. It went to No.1. Other Dorsey tracks did well including 'In the Blue of Evening' and 'It's Always You'. In the same way, an old recording of 'I'll Get By' that Dick Haymes recorded with Harry James was No.2.

Still, 'Close To You' went to No.4 but 'You'll Never Know' became a US No.1 for Dick Haymes and the Song Spinners with Frank at No.2. Both Bing (with Trudy Erwin) and Frank put the same two *Oklahoma!* songs on a single, both acappella, with Sinatra getting to No.6 and Bing climbing to No.2.

In July 1943 his *Broadway Bandbox* show was replaced by a second series of *Songs by Sinatra*, again with Axel Stordahl. The closing theme was 'Put Your Dreams Away', another composition by Ruth Lowe. It was the perfect way to say goodnight to an audience and proved popular, prompting Frank to record a full version in 1945. Among the songs he performed on the new series were 'My Ideal', which had been written for Maurice Chevalier in 1930 and had been revived by Margaret Whiting, and 'Speak Low', a brilliant song from the Broadway show, *One Touch Of Venus*, written by the German composer Kurt Weill, who had escaped to America, and the poet Ogden Nash.

Sinatra undertook some major concerts including ones with the Cleveland and New York Philharmonic Orchestras, the latter at Lewisohn Stadium in New York. He played a bizarre gig with Benny Goodman and his Orchestra in Central Park. It was sponsored by the American Legion and the audience was requested to bring along old records, which were sold for recycling.

The American trade magazine, *Variety*, had a headline in August 1943 saying, *Frankie Goes to Hollywood*. He was leaving New York for Hollywood, and he was going by train, but he didn't arrive at Los Angeles Central Station. He and his entourage got off in Pasadena, that is on the eastern side of Los Angeles, supposedly to avoid the crowds. Somehow he was met by his fans who had got wind of it. How did they know? Well, look at the photographs and you will see that the steps are the property of RKO. Some of the fans were RKO starlets and the policemen were, as likely as not, actors too. According to press reports, there were 5,000 fans at Pasadena Station and it took the police two hours to clear the site. Rubbish: there were only a couple of hundred, but it worked. Well done, George Evans, but an eagle-eyed journalist could have wrecked the story.

Shortly after arriving Frank appeared at the Hollywood Bowl where the orchestra played an hour of the classics and then accompanied Sinatra. Ten thousand fans attended the concert which was a huge success.

Two days later Frank was appearing on radio from the Hollywood Canteen, which was a club for servicemen. He endeared himself to them by joking, 'Well, nobody in this crowd's gonna faint.' Later the Hollywood Canteen was a setting for yet another let's-make-a-show film.

All this was handy publicity but the main purpose of his visit was to make a new film, *Higher and Higher*, for RKO. The property had been a Broadway musical starring Jack Haley, who was retained for the film. He had played the Tin Man in *The Wizard of Oz* and judging by his acting here, that role was about right for him.

The Broadway show had been written by Richard Rodgers and Lorenz Hart, a lyricist who had a maxim, 'Prepare to make thy metre', above his bed. He was a dazzling wordsmith but now alcoholic and incapable of working to order. Indeed, Hart died in November 1943. Harold Adamson and Jimmy McHugh were recruited to write new songs and in the event they wrote four to which was added Rodgers and Hart's 'Disgustingly Rich'. Sinatra was annoyed that the Broadway songs were dropped and he would often perform one of the originals, the stunning ballad, 'It Never Entered My Mind'.

Still, the new songs were good and Frank knew it. 'I Couldn't Sleep a Wink Last Night', performed with Dooley Wilson at the piano, was nominated for an Oscar. McHugh suffered from insomnia, hence the song title, and it's just as well he couldn't get to sleep as he rang Adamson at 3am after his radio had gone dead. He told him, "Here's the title for the big number, 'The Music Stopped'." Also, it would seem, an apt title for the musicians' strike; the two songs could only be recorded for Columbia with the Bobby Tucker Singers. For all that, Sinatra's version of 'I Couldn't Sleep a Wink Last Night' is amongst his greatest performances and was a Top 10 single.

Higher and Higher was a silly film with a silly plot about an implausible scam and anyway, Frank's role was at a tangent to the storyline. He did persuade the heroine not to enter a loveless marriage, but this type of role was more suited to Bing and, indeed, Bing did precisely that in *The Big Broadcast* (1932). The producers had planned a cameo in which Bing and Frank would pass each other on bicycles and stick out their tongues – but it didn't happen.

Sinatra's first speaking line in a film was 'Good morning. My name is Frank Sinatra' at which Marcy McGuire fainted and he caught her before she hit the floor. *Higher and Higher* featured a teenage Mel Tormé acting like an ersatz Mickey Rooney – but we all have to start somewhere. Dooley Wilson was excellent as the chauffeur/pianist while that great Dane, Victor Borge stole the film as Sir Victor Fitzroy-Victor KB OBE. One character says that he 'sounds like a radio station'. The cast are surprised when Sir Victor is exposed as a fake, but as he is so clearly not British, it would have been obvious to the entire audience from the start. However, when he is revealed to be 'Joe Brown from Newcastle', you wonder what the scriptwriters were taking.

Sinatra trousered $25,000 for his trouble but he hated retakes and whenever possible, films would be made his way. He'd learn his lines, do one take and move on; romantic scenes being the exception, of course. Reviewing *Higher and Higher* for the UK publication, *The Listener*, Dilys Powell wrote, 'Frank Sinatra is the new craze in America: a crooner who gets 3,000 fan letters a week. There are 1,000 Sinatra fan clubs in America, and women faint when they hear his voice. I thought he seemed quite a nice young man.'

For much of October 1943 Frank was in New York at the Wedgwood Room at the Waldorf-Astoria. It was a prestigious supper club, but the room could only hold 300 patrons.

The guest list often included show business luminaries and Sinatra began his practice of giving name checks from the stage. Having them in the audience helped to make him look good. One evening he was so excited at the prospect of performing that he slipped coming out of the shower and twisted his ankle.

A heckler fed up with his wife's sighing shouted, 'You stink!' and Sinatra challenged him to a fight. The heckler backed down and returning to the microphone, Frank said, 'Ladies and gentlemen, I like to sing. I'm paid to sing. Those who don't like my voice are not compelled to come and are under no obligation to stay.' The audience applauded. Having been fed the story by George Evans, *Down Beat* ran the headline, *Don't Say Sinatra Stinks Unless You Can Punch!*

Sinatra was now on air with the continuing *Your Hit Parade* and a new series of *Songs by Sinatra*, which was broadcast for 15 minutes every Sunday night from October to December. He opened each show with a snatch of 'This Love of Mine' which went back to Dorsey days, and in the first show, he sang 'Paper Doll', a witty No.1 from the Mills Brothers which promoted pin-up mags. He was a guest on *The Burns and Allen Show* with George Burns adding asides while he sang. Burns had once cancelled a radio appearance by Frank Sinatra for $250 as Burns could have a vocal trio, the Smoothies for the same money. Frank often thanked him for not doing for his career what he had done for the Smoothies.

Because Frank was a family man, he had been exempt from serving in the US forces, but this loophole was removed in the autumn of 1943. On 22 October 1943, he was considered fit, that is classified 1-A, with his height, incidentally being 5 foot 7 inches and his weight 8 stone 7 pounds. Sinatra was a driven man and he didn't relish putting his career on hold or for that matter, being a German or Japanese target. His career was too much on the rise but he knew audiences were fickle and he could lose this momentum through being conscripted.

George Evans knew what to do. Sinatra managed to have himself reclassified 4-F. Capt Weintrob said he had mastoiditis and he was also 'neurotic, afraid to be in crowds or go in an elevator.' I'll buy the eardrum, but fear of crowds, duh! And some people say Sinatra wasn't a good actor! Some servicemen were asking their girlfriends, 'Why do you like him? This guy didn't fight for us', and according to the social commentator, William Manchester, Frank Sinatra became the most hated man of World War Two – but he must have been exaggerating for effect. However, this reassessment didn't harm Sinatra's career nearly as badly as Dick Haymes' tactics. He signed an affidavit of non-belligerency as he had been born in Argentina. It was a clever move, but the public didn't buy it at all. After all, their sons and their boyfriends were out there fighting.

Maybe somebody thought that keeping Frankie at home and keeping the girls happy was a better contribution to the war effort than fighting on some distant front. I don't know; many entertainers had gone into the forces including Clark Gable, James Stewart and Glenn Miller. The songwriter Jimmy Van Heusen had a secret life as a test pilot at Lockheed for three days a week. Bing Crosby was exempt because, at age 40, he was too old to serve, but he did the next best thing by undertaking personal appearances for the troops.

Because of the recording strike, there were few new records for the forces, and so the concept arose of making records especially for them – called Victory Discs or V-Discs, the name prompted by Churchill's trademark V-sign – with the performers waiving all royalties and fees. George Simon of *Metronome* was asked to sign up the artists and negotiate with the record companies. The 12-inch 78s, which were pressed by Victor, had up to six minutes playing time on each side and they were shipped every month directly to the troops, often on the front line. Victor made them virtually unbreakable and by the time they finished producing V-Discs in 1949, there had been 900 different releases with 3,000 songs. Over

8m singles had been pressed.

The authorities found that the armed forces, like the girls, wanted romance. They preferred Bing, Frank or Peggy singing dreamily to the big band blasting away or Gene Krupa's drum solos. The unions allowed the performers to record with musicians for V-Discs, but many of the tracks were taken from radio shows or film soundtracks. Sometimes they issued the final rehearsal before a live show which often worked better on record. Because of the recording strike, it is ironic that Frank Sinatra's first new recordings with an orchestra were going to servicemen and not bobbysoxers.

Frank Sinatra was to release 55 titles on V-Discs between 1943 and 1947 and the first ones are of particular interest as there were no compatible commercial releases and they illustrate his early work with Axel Stordahl. The first track, cut in October 1943, was 'I Only Have Eyes for You'. It opens with Frank saying 'Hiya, men' before going into a four minute version of the song: when Frank did record it commercially in 1945, he had to take it faster and cut the opening verse so as to fit a 10 inch disc.

His friend Joe Bushkin had written the flagwaver, '(There's Gonna Be a) Hot Time in The Town Of Berlin', which was too lighthearted for the subject in hand but nevertheless served its purpose. Sinatra did not think it suited an acappella treatment so Buskin gave the song to Bing Crosby who recorded it with the Andrews Sisters for US Decca, which had settled with the unions. Frank recorded his Dixieland version as a V-Disc and Bing's 'They're gonna start a row and show 'em how' was replaced by the dubious 'I'm gonna grab a frau and show her how'. Frank performed the song in a short propaganda film, *The Road to Victory*, as well as joining Harry James and his Orchestra for 'Saturday Night (Is the Loneliest Night of the Week)' in a US Treasury film to encourage the sale of war bonds. The movie also featured Bing Crosby, Betty Grable (now married to Harry James) and Harpo Marx.

At a party at Johnny Burke's house, the comic actor Phil Silvers cracked a joke that made Bessie, Burke's wife, laugh. He called her 'Bessie with the laughing face'. Jimmy Van Heusen said that was a song title and Burke said, 'It's my day off, you two write it.' Phil Silvers wrote the lyric in 20 minutes and Van Heusen wrote the melody. They changed the title to 'Nancy' and sang it to Frank's daughter as a fourth birthday present. Frank performed it for Vimms Vitamins and then cut it as a V-Disc.

Taking George Evans' advice, Frank had made arrangements to relocate to Hollywood. Frank became a California resident in January 1944 and remained that way for the rest of his life. He stayed in a Castle Argyle apartment until his new home in Valley Spring Lane, Toluca Lake, Palm Springs was ready. It had belonged to Mary Astor and he lived close to Bing Crosby, Bob Hope and W C Fields.

Frank and Nancy's second child, Franklin Wayne Emanuel Sinatra, was born on 10 January 1944, but in Jersey City as Nancy had not yet moved. Two days later he dedicated a song for 'the little fella' on the radio but it would be two months before he went back east. The 'Emanuel' was for Manie Sacks, and when the priest refused to let the child have a Jewish godfather, Sinatra stormed out of the church.

Nancy was pleased to move the family to Hollywood as the area smelt of orange groves rather than smog. Indeed, her parents and her siblings were to follow her there. She hoped that Frank would be making more movies as this would keep him at home, but these were false hopes as he would be working with beautiful Hollywood stars. Still, Frank did love having meals with the family around him. He sailed in a paddle boat on the lake with his friends and took the young Nancy rowing on a wooden raft.

In January 1944 *Songs by Sinatra* was replaced by the 30-minute Wednesday night programme, *The Frank Sinatra Show*, broadcast from Hollywood and sponsored by Vimms

Vitamins. Sinatra was sleeping badly and losing weight and so he needed some Vimms Vitamins himself. As the Bobby Tucker Singers were renamed the Vimms Vocalists, he was lucky to escape Frank Vimmatra. This time Frank was involved in crooning, commercials and comedy. Sometimes he had not read the script beforehand which gave his links some spontaneity. Nearly all the Sinatra and Stordahl arrangements were tested on this show and then recorded. Studying them carefully was an up-and-coming trombonist in the studio orchestra, Nelson Riddle.

Among the songs Frank didn't record commercially were the poignant 'Last Time I Saw Paris' and the wondrous 'Long Ago and Far Away', both written by Jerome Kern, and the Cuban ballad, 'Poinciana'. His guests included Ginger Rogers and his duets with Eileen Barton included 'Come Out Wherever You Are', written by Sammy Cahn and Jule Styne, and 'You're Getting To Be a Habit with Me'. He worked with Tommy Dorsey again on *Your All-Time Hit Parade*.

The singer Jerry Wayne recalls, 'The *Hit Parade* show was really in two parts: there was a Friday night show called *The All-Time Hit Parade*, which was old classics and standards and there was the Saturday night show, *Your Hit Parade*, which was the current hits of the week. I did the Friday night show and Sinatra the Saturday. I worked with him on lots of things and he was a wonderful singer; how could anybody deny that? He was a big favourite of mine. He had wonderful phrasing and a lovely voice and a real feel for the songs.'

Frank was a guest on Bing's radio shows and vice versa. He and Bing mocked their reputations in a seven-song parody, while they were joined by Bob Hope for a comic 'You're the Top'. Frank was so taken with the arrangement for 'These Foolish Things' on Bing's *Kraft Music Hall* that he went out of his way to thank the orchestra.

On a *Command Performance* recorded for servicemen, Frank played Bing's singing instructor and performed 'Learn to Croon'. Weirdly, Sinatra's first foray into Oscarland was when a Duffy Duck cartoon, *Swooner Crooner*, written by Frank Tashlin, was nominated for an award.

Still continuing with *Your Hit Parade*, Frank sang 'I'll Get By', 'Sweet Lorraine' and a high-pitched 'The Very Thought of You', a British song from Ray Noble. His final song on *Your Hit Parade* at the end of 1944, though he would be back, was 'Don't Fence Me In'. He acted in radio theatre versions of *The Gay Divorcée* with Gloria DeHaven and *Wake Up and Live* with Marilyn Maxwell, who became another of his conquests.

Gloria DeHaven gave Frank his first screen kiss in his next film, *Step Lively*, directed by Tim Whelan. Frank didn't mind the kiss but he did refuse to act in a scene where Gloria wore a large hat. She was taller than him and he would have been swamped.

In 1937 *Room Service* was a Broadway farce and Zeppo Marx had persuaded RKO to turn it into a celluloid comedy for the Marx Brothers. It flopped and now RKO wanted to remake it as a musical, *Step Lively*. Frank Sinatra played an author who gave $1,500 to a crooked producer (George Murphy) who lived in a plush hotel in Manhattan. Murphy had no intention of staging his play but when he heard Sinatra sing, he added him to his current production to save it.

The songs by Cahn and Styne are good – 'Some Other Time' (a duet with Gloria), 'Come Out Wherever You Are', 'Where Does Love Begin', 'As Long as There's Music' – and could have been successful, but Sinatra was stuck with the recording ban.

Frank had not called his son Franklin after himself but in honour of President Roosevelt. In September he met Roosevelt in the White House and, even though the country was at war, he was able to donate $7,500 to the Democrats. When Frank gave a speech at a political rally at Madison Square Garden, Alistair Cooke reported that it was 'the simplest, the most nervous, the most honest and the best political campaigning speech I certainly have ever heard.' The fans wore buttons, 'Frankie's For FDR'.

Although it is commonplace today, a politician in the 1940s might be considered lightweight for associating with celebrities, but George Evans knew this was a sound idea. Frank himself was to parody his visit in a rewrite of an early hit:

'They asked me down to Washington
To have a cup of tea,
The Republicans started squawking
They're as mad as they can be,
And all I did was say hello to a
Man named Franklin D
Everything happens to me.'

Still, the possible controversy surrounding this was dwarfed by what happened a fortnight later, namely, the Columbus Day Riot on a schools holiday, 12 October 1944. It was the most intense demonstration of teenage hysteria to date and it took place, naturally enough, at the Paramount Theatre in Times Square, New York.

The Mayor of New York had instituted a 9pm curfew for juveniles but this was ignored as fans camped outside the Paramount from 4.30pm on the previous day and had no intention of budging.

When Frank arrived at 6am for rehearsal with the Raymond Paige Orchestra (how he must have hated that), over a thousand girls were waiting outside. The doors opened at 8.30am and Frank was to perform in between showings of a Paramount film, *Our Hearts Were Young and Gay,* a cute comedy starring Gail Russell and Diana Lynn. The audience was 80% female, mostly between 12 and 16 with many of them copying Sinatra by wearing bow ties. In between the film showings, Sinatra only performed four songs – 'There Are Such Things', 'Embraceable You', 'Everything Happens to Me' and 'She's Funny That Way' – and fans had to wait two hours for each appearance.

When the first show was over, only 250 of the 3,500 capacity audience left. The rest were there for the day. The theatre's policy of allowing patrons to stay all day was questioned as riots took place outside and the ticket booth was destroyed. Perhaps they should shown some really terrible movie which might have driven out the fans.

The other days were more controlled as children were supposedly back at school but truancy figures were up. An 18-year-old boy, Alex Dorogokupetz, threw eggs at Sinatra, one of which hit him, and Alex was then struck with a pair of binoculars. It turned out that he had been paid $10 to throw eggs by a reporter, but it did prompt a genuine reaction as some sailors went to the Paramount and hurled tomatoes at Frank's poster.

Newsweek was befuddled by this hysteria: 'As a visible male object of adulation, Sinatra is baffling. He is undersized and looks underfed – but the slightest suggestion of a smile brings squeals of agonised rapture from his adolescent fans.'

The Mayor of New York did not comment on this excitement as he felt it might add support to Roosevelt's campaign. Frank had a special show on election night for CBS and Roosevelt was re-elected by a landslide, the only US President to win four times.

When Sinatra returned to cabaret, he sang new lyrics to 'Don't Blame Me':

'I don't blame the guy who threw an egg at me
If my gal swooned, I'd do the same as he.
It's tough to sing
I wish they'd do the same to Bing.'

All this delighted Tommy Dorsey. He had let Sinatra go but only on the most stringent terms. Sinatra, who rarely thought ahead, had signed papers for Dorsey to receive one-third of his future earnings and this was for all-time. He had been stitched up good and proper. Oddly enough, both sides made this public knowledge. Sinatra even sang 'I'll Be Seeing You' as 'I'll Be Suing You' and Dorsey would joke on air about getting his commission. The columnist Walter Winchell said that there was a new word, 'To be Sinatra'd was the past tense of a verb meaning to cut up into several financial pieces.'

Suddenly it was no more: Dorsey accepted a one-off financial settlement and the contract was void. The rumour was that the Mafia had extricated Frank from the contract by putting the frighteners on Dorsey. It's a possibility, but why would they have given him a cash payment? It is more likely that clever Hollywood lawyers realised the terms were unfair and threatened Dorsey with legal action.

Frank Sinatra was placed alongside Gene Kelly and Kathryn Grayson in a lavish MGM film musical, *Anchors Aweigh*, a two hour spectacular directed by George Sidney. When Sidney told the producer he wanted Frank he was told he was 'too skinny'. They should have been more concerned that the Technicolor processing would show up lined features. As a result, both Sinatra (28) and Kelly (32) looked too old for their youthful roles.

Frank was given the role and Louis B Mayer (the second M in MGM) asked him whom he wanted to write the songs. Did he want Richard Rodgers, Irving Berlin or Jerome Kern? Frank said, 'None of them. I want Sammy Cahn.' Frank was being Frank, typically awkward, as he would have been happy with any of those composers. Mayer said, 'I don't mind hiring him, but who is he?' Frank said, 'Since you're not going to be singing the songs, don't let it concern you. I know who he is and I want him to write for me.'

Such hubris caused brouhaha and Cahn was asked to reason with Frank. Cahn said, 'Look, Frank, yesterday nobody knew me and today they all hate me. Why not wait? There will be other pictures.' Frank said, 'If you're not there Monday, I won't be there Monday.'

Sammy Cahn concluded, 'That is what separates Frank from the rest of us. I did the songs for *Anchors Aweigh* and the one I love the most is 'I Fall in Love too Easily', which he sang at the Hollywood Bowl at the piano. I also love the song he does with Gene Kelly at the start of the film, 'I Begged Her', and then there's 'What Makes the Sun Set'.'

As the songs by Sammy Cahn and Jule Styne are excellent, Frank's belligerence was not a problem, and his bravado was masking the real problem – he wasn't sure if he could dance well enough, particularly alongside Gene Kelly. Fortunately, Kelly was a thoroughly decent individual and a born teacher. He had no intention of embarrassing Frank but told him that it would be hard work. Frank called him 'the Irish taskmaster'. It would have undermined the film if Frank Sinatra couldn't match Gene Kelly Gene scaled himself down to what Frank could do. As a result, Frank never looked amateurish.

There is one extended sequence that they have to dance together. The two sailors sing 'We Hate to Leave' while they are jumping over beds in a dormitory. Frank was prepared to spend time rehearsing but when he took a rest because he was exhausted, Mayer told him to get back to work. Gene Kelly told Mayer to lay off: this really was hard work. The end result is remarkably good but the scene that everyone remembers is when Gene Kelly dances with the cartoon Jerry from *Tom and Jerry*, one of several instances where they leave the plot behind. There is a grand finale in which all six leads are dancing and they rush to the camera for a mock 3-D effect. Bear in mind that this extraordinary story was supposed to take place in one day.

Gene Kelly, who was nominated for an Oscar, did his own choreography but he acted overbearingly for much of the film. Still, his partner, Frank Sinatra (as Clarence Doolittle) was stuck in an equally irritating, girl shy, 'gee whiz' role: he dialed the speaking clock while the other sailors phoned their dates. Considering he was a real life sex symbol, it seems ridiculous to depict him so sexlessly. On the other hand, the wonderful 'I Fall In Love too Easily', which Frank sang on an empty stage, was a superb sequence but the song was far too confident for a weak character. Who cared? Cinemagoers swooned when he sang it.

José Iturbi, the Hollywood conductor and pianist, played himself in an amusing cameo where Frank mistook him for the piano tuner. Kathryn Grayson was excellent as Aunt Suzy, but she let a young boy fend for himself while she undertook a singing engagement, and none of the characters remarked on this woeful childcare. There was a mawkish moment when Frank sang Brahms' 'Cradle Song' to the young boy, played by Dean Stockwell.

Spencer Tracy met Frank Sinatra on the MGM lot and as Frank was in a sailor suit, he asked him where he was stationed. Frank kidded him along and said, 'Right here', and they became friends.

In the film, Frank falls for Pamela Britton and he calls her 'Brooklyn' because of her thick accent. It's amusing too as the real life Sinatra never lost his own dese, dem, dose accent.

A reporter picked up some chance remarks by Sinatra: 'Pictures stink. Most of the people in them do, too. I don't want any more movie acting. Hollywood won't believe I'm through, but they'll find out I mean it.' Sinatra threatened libel when this was published but did he say it or not? It was his first big blow-up with the press.

Anchors Aweigh was released in August 1945 and was a commercial hit, probably as much for Gene Kelly as Frank Sinatra. Pauline Kael called it 'stupidly wholesome', but it was just the ticket for the end of the war. It was nominated for several Oscars but lost out to *The Lost Weekend* for both Best Film and Best Actor. George Stoll won an Oscar for his scoring. Recently his family put his Oscar up for auction and Kevin Spacey bought it and returned it to the Academy. Frank had Gene Kelly as a guest for a *Songs by Sinatra* special to promote the film and in 1947, Frank, Gene and Kathryn took part in a one hour radio adaptation of the film.

The musicians' action against the record companies was settled on a piecemeal basis, Both Decca and Capitol settled in 1943 but Columbia and Victor held out until 11 November 1944. It was agreed that the musicians would receive royalties from records played on radio and on jukeboxes. Soon Columbia and Victor were making up for lost time.

On 14 November Sinatra recorded 'If You Are but a Dream', a popular music adaptation of Anton Rubinstein's 'Romance in E Flat', and 'Saturday Night (Is the Loneliest Night of the Week)', a Sammy Cahn and Jule Styne song. You could argue that it is a song for a girl whose man is in the forces but the public preferred Frank's version to the King Sisters, Nancy Norman or Phyllis Lynne, and Soul Brother No.l James Brown declared it had been one of his favourite records.

Fortunately, Frank was now able to able to record the songs from *Anchors Aweigh*: 'I Begged Her', 'The Charm of You', 'What Makes the Sun Set' (with a more exotic arrangement than in the film) and 'I Fall in Love too Easily'. What is a more apt line for Sinatra than the reflective 'I fall in love too easily, I fall in love too fast', but oddly the best selling version came from the former Casa Loma Orchestra vocalist Eugene Baird with Mel Tormé and his Mel-Tones providing backup. The song was nominated for an Oscar but it lost out to 'It Might as Well Be Spring'.

The *Sunday Times* critic, Derek Jewell, recalled, 'The first Sinatra record I bought was a 78 of 'The Charm of You'. It was surefire aid to breaking the ice in the affairs of late adolescence. The words were pretty mushy but they seemed to do the trick every time. In Sinatra's mouth they really did have the ring of the finest poetry.'

When Frank recorded 'The Cradle Song', a lullaby written by Johannes Brahms, it was rather soporific so it served its purpose. The BBC still considered Frank Sinatra its bête noire and this single was banned. A committee member noted, 'Although I am myself the devil's advocate, I am considering transferring my allegiance to the side of the angels after listening this morning to Frank Sinatra singing Brahms' 'Cradle Song'. As an emetic, I know of nothing to equal it.'

Because George Gershwin died in 1937, he never heard Frank Sinatra sing any of his songs. Sinatra gave a new life to many of them, especially 'Embraceable You', which at first excited the bobbysoxers but became a song he returned to again and again. It had been sung by Ginger Rogers and Allen Kearns in the 1930 Broadway show *Girl Crazy* and it had been a favourite of Gershwin's father. He would ask George to play it and when he reached the line, 'Come to papa do', he would beam with pride. This fine version from 1944 includes Billy May on trumpet, thus bringing the musician into Sinatra's firmament.

Another stage favourite committed to wax was 'She's Funny That Way', written by Richard Whiting (Margaret's father) and popular for Gene Austin in 1929. Frank chose to record this intimately with a small group. It's about a couple who have little but faith in each other. Frank's wife, Nancy, loved this song and Frank would often dedicate it to her and yet he was singing, 'She loves to work and slave for me ever day.'

The most ambitious recording was a four minute 'Ol' Man River' for a 12 inch single. The song had been made famous by Paul Robeson, and Frank Sinatra was to call it 'the most important song in my repertoire'. He felt that it commented significantly about racial tension and he retained the references to the 'white boss'. The lyricist Oscar Hammerstein called it 'a song of resignation with a protest implied.' When the composer Jerome Kern died in 1945, Sinatra sang it in a tribute concert at the Hollywood Bowl.

A few months later the producer Louis B Mayer heard Sinatra sing 'Ol' Man River' at a benefit for a Jewish charity. He was so impressed that he asked Sinatra to perform the song in his film biography of Jerome Kern, *Till the Clouds Roll By*. I don't know how Robert Walker came to impress Mayer as his portrayal of Kern is from the Timberland school of acting. You have to wait over two hours for Sinatra and if you are still awake, he performs 'Ol' Man River' in white suit and tails on a white dais, but at least not in blackface. Louis B Mayer loved his performance but it seems a high watermark in kitsch today.

The other side of this single was another song connected to racial issues, the bluesy Cotton Club song, 'Stormy Weather' from the repertoire of a key influence, Ethel Waters. She recorded it in 1933 and later said, 'I sang 'Stormy Weather' from the depths of my private hell in which I was being crushed and suffocated.' It was featured with great success by Lena Horne in the 1943 film called, would you believe, *Stormy Weather*. Sinatra took it a little too upbeat (after all, everything he has is gone) but it's a beautiful performance with a trumpet solo from Billy Butterfield.

The first single from the next session was 'White Christmas'. The song had been the biggest-selling single of all-time for Bing Crosby so why on earth did Sinatra want to cut it? It may simply be that Columbia wanted to have a version on their books. In any event, it entered the *Billboard* chart on 21 December and reached No 7 and, get this, it stayed in the Top 10 for nine weeks! Just who was buying 'White Christmas' in the middle of February?

Frank Sinatra was involved in a short film for RKO called *The House I Live In*, directed by Mervyn LeRoy, who had directed *Little Caesar*. At the start of the film, we see Frank recording 'If You Are but a Dream' and when he takes a break outside, he sees a young Jewish boy being bullied. He tells the bullies, 'God created everybody. He didn't create one people better than another.' He then sings 'The House I Live In', an Earl Robinson and Lewis Allen composition, which is sometimes known by its opening line, 'What is America to me?' The script was clunky but this song was a masterpiece of dramatic timing. In 1993 Frank recorded a melodramatic version that was way over the top but blame his duet partner, Neil Diamond, for that. How sad that Sinatra's last studio session should lead to his worst recording.

In 1939 Lewis Allen had written Billie Holiday's 'Strange Fruit' about lynchings in the south and oddly enough, Sinatra didn't record the original version of 'The House I Live In'. It had been performed by the Golden Gate Quartet in *Follow the Boys* a few months earlier.

The film was shot in a day and everybody worked for free. In March 1946 the producer Frank Ross, Mervyn LeRoy and Frank Sinatra collected a special Oscar for promoting tolerance. Frank sang 'The House I Live In' at the ceremony. Tony Bennett saw the film as a young serviceman and said it had a profound effect on him, but a few years later the film was cited as an example of Sinatra's communist leanings. The FBI's first suspicions came in March 1945 when Frank spoke at the World Youth Rally at Carnegie Hall, an event regarded by the FBI as communist-infiltrated.

In the run-up to Christmas, Nancy had noticed a package from Tiffany's in the glove compartment of Frank's car. It was an expensive bracelet and she expected it as her gift. Instead she was given some earrings.

Frank and Nancy held a New Year's Eve party and Frank invited the actress, Marilyn Maxwell, who was living apart from her husband, the actor John Conte. She had recently worked with Frank, and Frank was taking a chance as he was having an affair with her. Quite unknowingly, she came to the party with the bracelet on her wrist so Nancy realised what was going on. She asked her to leave and said to Frank, 'How dare you shame me in my own house?' Nancy would later say, 'What made it bearable for me was that I was always his No.1 fan.'

Frank Sinatra finished 1944 with his final appearance, for the moment, on *Your Hit Parade*. CBS had dropped him because he wanted to record in Hollywood rather than New York. His replacement was an operatic baritone, Lawrence Tibbett, a talented but unlikely choice for the pop songs of the week. He was friendly with Frank and they sang together on *Songs by Sinatra* in November 1945 when they combined their talents for the Stephen Foster compositions, 'Camptown Races' and 'Beautiful Dreamer'. Frank commented, '"I'm a big doo-dah man.' Frank was still to guest on *Your Hit Parade* from time to time and he gave a swinging, uptempo treatment to 'Oh, What a Beautiful Mornin''.

The sponsors Max Factor were happy to give him another show, also with CBS, and so *The Frank Sinatra Show* started on 3 January 1945 and continued until 16 May 1945. The first guest was Rudy Vallée but the programme was broadly *Frank Sinatra in Person* with a different sponsor. The regulars were Eileen Barton and announcer Bill Goodwin; the arranger was Axel Stordahl; and vocal accompaniment came from the Ken Lane Singers. Once again the opening song was 'This Love of Mine' and the closer 'Put Your Dreams Away'. One guest was Sy Oliver, still in uniform, and they did a surprisingly hip 'Yes Indeed!' together with such exchanges as 'Groovy like a movie' and 'Let me hear you holler!'

Frank continued to make guest appearances including *The Charlie McCarthy Show*, a show hosted by a ventriloquist's dummy (on radio!) and a *Command Performance* spoofing Dick Tracy with Bing and Bob and another with Bob Hope, Judy Garland, and the Andrews Sisters. The Andrews Sisters played three girls, May, June and July, and Bob Hope wanted July because 'She's hot'. Bob called Frank, 'a pipe cleaner in suspenders'. Frank sang 'I Wonder Who's Kissing Her Now' with Bing Crosby and Judy Garland and 'My Romance' with Judy Garland. There was a new novelty number, 'Dick Haymes, Dick Todd and Como' with lyrics by Sammy Cahn. Dick Todd was the Canadian Crosby and Perry Como was the new crooner on the block, so laidback that Bing seemed wildly animated.

The oddest *Command Performance* was when Bing and Frank squabbled over who will be Judy Garland's leading man with Bob Hope as the judge. It was only a comedy show but the insults must have hit home. In the end, Garland chose Sinatra but he declined and sang 'Bingy Boy' to the tune of 'Sonny Boy'.

In February 1945 Frank was back in front of the draft board. It was determined that he had a job 'necessary to the national health, safety and interest' as well as being physically unfit to serve. There was a proviso that he could be given essential war work in a factory. As the hearing was open, the newspapers carried such headlines as *Is Crooning Essential?*

The first album chart was printed in *Billboard* on 24 March 1945, but the albums were not as we know them now, as each comprised a collection of four 78rpm singles bound together. Still, it was the start of something big. At No.1 was *A Collection of Favourites* from Nat 'King' Cole.

For the moment, Frank was making singles. 'Dream' was an immediate hit. Johnny Mercer, who wrote both words and music, called it 'a kind of 'Whispering' sideways'. The bandleader Paul Weston had heard his melody and said it could be a theme tune for *The Chesterfield Supper Club*. As the radio show was sponsored by a tobacco company, Mercer wrote a lyric which referred to smoke rings.

Paul Weston himself co-wrote 'I Should Care' with Sammy Cahn and Axel Stordahl. It is a lovely, whimsical song and a testimony to muddled thinking, rather like 10cc's 'I'm Not In Love'. Another orchestra leader, Gordon Jenkins, wrote 'Homesick, That's All', an ideal song for a GI's longing for home.

Another new song was the inspirational ballad, 'You'll Never Walk Alone' by Richard Rodgers and Oscar Hammerstein for *Carousel*. Frank Sinatra was the first to record it. Oddly enough, it became a favourite with rock'n'roll performers – Conway Twitty, Roy Hamilton, Gene Vincent – and then, in 1963, Gerry and the Pacemakers completed their hat-trick of No.1s with the song. It was taken up by the Kop choir at Liverpool Football Club and in 1985 Gerry Marsden led a chart-topping all-star recording for the Bradford City fire appeal. In 1996 it was No.1 yet again for the TV actors Robson and Jerome.

Frank recorded 'Where or When' as a ballad although he was later to swing it, the glorious 'All the Things You Are' and 'Mighty Lak' a Rose' a song about a parent's love for his child, published in 1901.

In May 1945 Frank had a session with the Charioteers, a four man black group which had been formed 10 years earlier and had been featured by Bing Crosby on radio shows. Their Top 10 single with Frank was 'Don't Forget Tonight Tomorrow' with a nutty falsetto standing out and they recorded two gospel songs together: 'Jesus Is a Rock (In a Weary Land)' and 'I've a Home in That Rock'. Another session saw Frank going south of the border with Xavier Cugat and his Orchestra, although the performances were better than the songs, 'Stars in Your Eyes' and 'My Shawl'.

Frank would often eat at restaurants on Sunset Strip and fraternising with other Hollywood celebrities. Humphrey Bogart's wife, Lauren Bacall, said to him, 'They tell me that you have a voice that makes girls faint. Make me faint.'

Frank had met the actress Ava Gardner when she was 20 and married to Mickey Rooney. Now they were divorced and she was in a relationship with the tycoon Howard Hughes. Famously, Robert Mitchum asked Hughes if he could sleep with her, and Hughes said, 'You might as well. Everyone will think you're a fag if you don't.' Now Frank met her again, but for the moment it was hands off as she was about to marry the bandleader, Artie Shaw. She was a bewitching and beautiful temptress, known for the flecks of gold in her green eyes. She laughed a lot but, like Sinatra, she had little humour about herself.

Lana Turner had had an affair with Mickey Rooney, married Artie Shaw and had an affair with Frank, so she and Ava had some lovers in common, although Lana had been there first. Lana had sampled Howard Hughes and the gangster Johnny Stompanato before Ava and it is said that the two girls, along with Ann Sheridan the 'Oomph' girl, liked to compare the genital size of their men, but the finest lovers were not necessarily the ones they wanted to stay. Jackie Gleason once compared the naked Sinatra to a tuning fork so undoubtedly he did well in these discussions.

In 2007 when Mickey Rooney was playing pantomime in Sunderland (cripes!), a Sinatra record was played during in the interval. A fellow actor, Les Dennis said that the mere sound of Frank's voice made him irritable as Ava would have been his if it weren't for Sinatra. This wasn't quite true but he had seen her first.

The war in Europe had ended with a victory for the Allies and the sheer atrocities that Hitler had authorised in concentration camps was revealed. The film, *The House I Live In,* seemed highly appropriate and George Evans encouraged Frank to talk to schools about intolerance. Admittedly, he could go off message: when he spoke to white students at a school in Gary, Indiana who refused to integrate with black ones, he added, 'I can lick any son of a bitch in this joint.' On another occasion and overcome with emotion, he said that he was going to adopt 12 war orphans, but unlike with Madonna, this never happened.

In other words, Frank was being marketed as something more than a popular singer, but George Evans was concerned that Frank was accused of dodging the draft and he talked to Phil Silvers about touring with Frank for troops in Europe and North Africa in June 1945. Phil had also missed the draft but it was evident from his thick glasses that his eyesight was poor. The tour seemed a good antidote to the bad publicity and it would be the first time Frank had left the US.

Phil Silvers would mock Frank on stage and make the usual thin jokes, 'He weighed 12 pounds when he was born and he has been losing weight ever since.' Or again: Phil, 'I got a girl in Maine.' 'Bangor?' 'I just met her.' Frank said that the servicemen threatened to squirt him with tomato juice if he didn't sing 'Paper Doll'; he did.

In a hospital, Frank talked to an amputee who had driven a cab in New York. He said that Frank got in and 'those goddamn bobbysoxers had kicked in my fenders'. It was the first time that Frank had really laughed in months.

Frank learnt that his music was well known in England because the public as well as the servicemen listened to AFN. He found out that when German soldiers masqueraded as British soldiers, they spoke good English but they were often caught because they didn't know who Frank Sinatra was.

The powers-that-be were able to arrange for Frank and Phil, who was Jewish, to have an audience with Pope Pius XII. The Pope asked Sinatra what sort of singing he did, was he an opera singer? Phil Silvers brought out some rosary beads and asked the Pope to bless them for Bing Crosby. The Pope then dropped them into Phil's tin, so that the next person to touch them would be Bing. On the way out, Frank said to him, 'You creepy bum! I take you in to see the Pope and you're plugging Crosby!'

When Frank asked for requests, he found that the soldiers wanted 'Nancy' which they had heard on V-Disc. The song made them think of their wives and families back home. Frank knew that he must record Phil Silvers' song commercially when he got home. They played 17 shows for 100,000 troops and they were received magnificently. Frank even sang in a castle that Goering had once requisitioned. He had left a grand piano behind so they were able to use it for the concert. They flew home with 50 nurses who were returning from Burma and Frank sang to them in the plane.

Frank returned with some enemy weapons as souvenirs but they were confiscated at the airport. When he got home, he spent three days ringing the families of servicemen. Phil took the rosary beads to Bing Crosby. He opened the box and said, 'The last hand to touch these was the Pope's.' Bing responded, 'Always kidding, huh?'

Rather foolishly, Frank complained about the organisation of the trip in the forces' newspaper, *Stars and Stripes*, though he should have stayed quiet. Marlene Dietrich told him he was naïve: he couldn't expect five star treatment as Europe had been ravaged by war. In September Bing, Frank and Dinah Shore performed songs from *Porgy and Bess* in a *For the Wounded* concert at the Hollywood Bowl.

In his autobiography, Phil Silvers compared Bing and Frank. He said that Frank would often flare up and get angry in order to get his way, but 'Bing in his relaxed, pipe-puffing way always did what he wanted'. The biggest film of 1944 was Bing's *Going My Way*; he was doing things his way long before Frank.

By avoiding the draft, Frank Sinatra had been a lucky man as, despite some awkward moments, his career had not been tarnished. The bad publicity could have been disastrous for his career, but not as disastrous as if he had died in active service.

Encouraged by Manie Sacks, Frank was keen to make one of these new-fangled albums. It was to be a collection of eight tender and sophisticated romantic songs called *The Voice of Frank Sinatra* and would be recorded with an intimate group rather than a full orchestra. 'I Don't Know Why (I Just Do)', made famous by Russ Columbo in 1931, opened with George Van Epps' guitar and moved onto calm, gentle strings. Frank sounded equally sublime on the Gershwin ballad, 'Someone to Watch Over Me' and the intoxicating 'You Go to My Head' from Billie Holiday's repertoire, but the best performance comes on the British song, 'These Foolish Things'. He pays tribute to Bing with 'The song that Crosby sings, These foolish things remind me of you.' When the actor Dirk Bogarde recorded the song, he replaced that line with 'The sound Sinatra sings'.

For some unknown reason, Frank didn't get round to completing this project for another four months when he added Bing's own composition, 'I Don't Stand a Ghost of a Chance with You', Cole Porter's 'Why Shouldn't I' and another Russ Columbo hit, 'Paradise'. Best of all was a stunning 'Try a Little Tenderness' which included an opening verse and contained more than a little tenderness. The four 78rpm pack, *The Voice of Frank Sinatra*, was released in 1946 and topped the album chart for seven weeks.

During those four months, Frank recorded several songs for single release including 'The House I Live In', 'Day by Day' and 'You Are too Beautiful', a Rodgers and Hart song recommended by Sammy Cahn. At long last, Frank recorded 'Nancy'. By now there were two lyrics for 'Nancy': one for a little girl and one for romance with Nancy being compared to a film star. Anticipating the baby boom, Frank chose the former and indeed, it worked so well that Ernest Borgnine called his own daughter, Nancy. The record opened with violins, violas and cellos. As Sinatra came in, so did the harp and it was a magical performance. Did Stephen Sondheim get the idea for angels singing in 'Maria' from the middle sequence of this record?

'Nancy' was a Top 10 single and somewhat out of character. Buddy Rich said, "Nancy' was the first bit of music that my daughter ever heard when she was brought home from the hospital when she was about 10 days old so that record has always had a sentimental value to me.'

The lyric did vary in performance and 'Sorry for you, she has no sister' could become the witty 'Just give me some time and she'll have a sister'. In 1981 Sinatra sang the song with a completely fresh lyric for the First Lady, Nancy Reagan.

The choice of material for 27 August 1945 was all over the place as Frank recorded the patriotic ballad, 'America the Beautiful', the carol 'Silent Night', a daft song about 'that Cupid fella', 'The Moon Was Yellow' and the supremely sublime, 'I Only Have Eyes for You' with a choir and a lavish arrangement. The song had been written by Harry Warren and Al Dubin for a Busby Berkeley extravaganza in the 1934 film, *Dames*, in which all the dancers resembled Ruby Keeler. Dick Powell performed the song in *Dames* and 25 years later, it was transformed into a doo-wop classic by the Flamingos. Taking his cue from the Flamingos, Art Garfunkel's version topped the UK charts in 1975.

In September 1945 another cigarette manufacturer, Old Gold, presented the weekly *Songs by Sinatra*, again with Axel Stordahl arranging and conducting, but with the Pied Pipers providing vocal accompaniment. One programme reunited them with Tommy Dorsey for the tenth anniversary of his band.

This CBS show, which ran through until June 1946, captured Sinatra at his peak and he devoted whole programmes to Jerome Kern, Johnny Mercer and Irving Berlin. The opening theme was now 'Night and Day' but Frank was still closing with 'Put Your Dreams Away'. The guests on the first programme were Bing Crosby's children! During the series, Frank sang 'The Night is Young and You're So Beautiful' (with Dinah Shore). 'Empty Saddles' (with the Andrews Sisters) and 'Exactly Like You', the only time he sang with Nat 'King' Cole and it's a loss that they didn't do more together. Guesting on other programmes he sang 'I Like To Recognise the Tune' with Rudy Vallée and 'Blue Skies ' with Louis Armstrong.

The radio shows could be a hindrance but salvation was coming. In the 1930s Bing Crosby found it an imposition to be broadcasting live shows for different time zones across America. He had discovered that the Germans had developed technology during the war which would allow programmes to be recorded in perfect quality on tape. Subsequently, he invested $50,000 in Ampex, a tape company. On 1 October 1947 Bing Crosby's radio programme became the first network show to be broadcast on tape in different time zones and soon everybody would follow, paying Crosby a suitable royalty. Magnetic tape would be used right up to the digital age and Bing's $50,000 investment was to make him a multi-multi-millionaire and one of the richest men in America.

Frank was also getting back to performing and after three weeks at the Capitol Theatre in Los Angeles, he generously hosted a Thanksgiving Day meal for everybody in the show. Then it was back to the Wedgwood Room with Dick Stabile's band, and Cole Porter came to hear him sing 'Night And Day'. As Sinatra's singing dates were confined to the big cities, usually New York or Los Angeles, you can appreciate the importance of radio, films and records for getting him to other parts of the country.

In November 1945 Sinatra had his first orchestral date without Axel Stordahl since the start of his solo career. Alec Wilder had told Frank that 'Old School Teacher' was his type of song, a whimsical piece about a country school teacher written by Willard Robison who was noted for American lieder. Frank wasn't too sure but he went along with it as an experiment. They also recorded Wilder's own song 'Just an Old Stone House' about the joys of rural living.

Alec Wilder played Frank two of his classical compositions that he had recorded for the BBC in London. Frank thought that they merited an album but Columbia said that there was only enough shellac to press records by major artists. The arranger Mitch Miller suggested that Frank's name could appear as conductor, and Manie Sacks agreed. Frank said, 'I don't know the first thing about conducting, but I know this music and I love it, and I think we can get it down.' The late night sessions took place after Frank had been singing all day at the Paramount. The result was *Frank Sinatra Conducts the Music of Alec Wilder* with Frank insisting that his name should not be in larger type than Wilder's. Mitch Miller is featured on 'Air for English Horn'.

Wilder had a therapeutic habit in that he would write letters to his associates but not post them. *Letters I Never Mailed* was published after his death and following these sessions, he wrote, 'In the wildest of those dreams, I couldn't have made up anything as marvellous as what you did for me.' No reason why he shouldn't posted that letter of course, but there are other examples which we will come to.

Sinatra was back with Stordahl for 'Full Moon and Empty Arms', based on a theme by Rachmaninoff and an American version of the aria, 'O Marenariello', now called 'I Have But One Heart' and later a big hit for Vic Damone. In May 2014 Bob Dylan, of all people, kicked off the centenary celebrations with a slow, deliberate version of 'Full Moon And Empty Arms' with prominent steel guitar and, taking into account the limitations of his voice, it was performed rather well.

Frank and Nancy hosted a new year's eve party at Toluca Lake and a private show was staged for the guests. Earlier in the year Phil Silvers had married Miss America, Jo Carroll, and Sammy Cahn and Jule Styne wrote a special song for her, 'I'm the Wife of the Life of the Party'. Part of the lyric went:

'He's a riot at every party
In calm or rainy weather,
He's the life of every party
Except the one we have together.'

This was exceptionally close to the truth. By 1950, Jo had had enough. She left their home but Phil Silvers continued to live there with his mother-in-law.

CHAPTER 6

Kissing bandits

'Sinatra's idea of paradise is a place where there are
plenty of women and no newspapermen.'
Humphrey Bogart

I. Viva Lost Vegas

Las Vegas is hell on earth. If someone were to tempt you by saying, 'I'd like you to come to one of the hottest places in the world where the temperature could be 130 degrees Fahrenheit and while you are there, I will relieve you of your money', the odds are that you wouldn't go. But you do. Millions do.

The biggest gamble in Las Vegas has to be the city itself. Some gangsters and businessmen believed that the place would work, and it did. Spectacularly, this woebegone city thrives on entertainment for adults and indeed made its reputation with activities which were illegal elsewhere. The Mafia's control of the city and its casinos is infamous; yet initially Las Vegas was created by the church.

Las Vegas Valley in the Mojave Desert was named by some Mexican scouts around 1830. Although it was desert, some artesian wells supported meadows (*vegas* in Spanish), hence the name. The Mormons, who were based in Salt Lake City, Utah and San Bernadino, California, built a midway fortress which was both a resting place for travellers and a home for the missionaries who were attempting to convert the local residents, the Palute Indians. The conversion was doomed to failure from the start: how could you persuade them that they might burn in hell when they already were? Ultimately, the Mormons settled in Salt Lake City and stopped using the fort.

The railway brought new life to the area in 1905 when the settlement was officially called Las Vegas and then incorporated as a city in 1911. Not that many people would want to live there. It was exceedingly hot and Death Valley was named Death Valley for good reason.

In 1928 President Coolidge approved the building of a dam in Black Canyon, some 30 miles south-west of Vegas. It was to provide electricity for the region. Construction work started the following year and continued throughout the stock market crash. Over 20,000 men, nearly all white, worked in blisteringly hot temperatures. The Hoover Dam was completed in 1936, an engineering masterpiece, although it cost 100 lives.

The workers lived in a new town, Boulder City, and Las Vegas provided their entertainment. Barrooms and brothels sprang up and, in a critical piece of legislation, gambling in Nevada was made legal. From a fiscal viewpoint, the move was highly successful and the casinos have been so lucrative that the state can thrive through taxing their profits. Prostitution is officially illegal within the city but takes place discreetly and many Vegas hookers have over 1,000 clients a year. There have been official brothels outside the city such as the notorious Chicken Ranch.

It wasn't until 1941 that the first resort hotel opened for business, El Rancho Vegas, with 100 rooms, a swimming pool and a casino full of showgirls. It was partly funded by the Marx Brothers, and we shall see how Zeppo Marx's love for showgirls plays into our story. A rival attraction, the Frontier, followed, continuing the penchant for western names. These hotels were on the Strip and this dusty stretch of highway was about to become valuable real estate. A Roy Rogers film, *Helldorado* was shot in Vegas in 1946.

In 1941 Frank Sinatra had been in Vegas with Tommy Dorsey and his Orchestra for the film, *Las Vegas Nights*. He was quick to spot its potential. The Hoover Dam brought water, neon lights and, most importantly, air conditioning. Gambling was legal; there was little law enforcement and it was effectively a gangster's paradise. Being only 270 miles from Los Angeles was a bonus as it was a short plane journey to a major conurbation and hence, to some very wealthy patrons with money to burn. Many rich Americans were going to casinos in Havana but this was much more convenient.

Frank Sinatra told his friend, the gangster Benjamin 'Bugsy' Siegel, that fortunes could be made and that he himself could be a main attraction in the showroom.

Bugsy was a dangerous criminal who was proud of his good looks. He used face creams and was known as Baby Blue Eyes as well as Bugsy – not that anyone would be daft enough to call him Bugsy or Baby Blue Eyes to his face. He disregarded danger and probably committed every crime in the gangsters' handbook, if there is such a thing. Additionally, his baby blue eyes had vision. He knew that the Mafia did well by pooling its efforts on the east coast but the families on the west had little coordination. He called the leaders together and brought solidarity to their businesses, admittedly taking a share of the profits for his trouble. Anyone who objected met with a sticky end.

Sinatra was in very hazardous territory where a wrong move could cost you your life, but as a result, Bugsy Siegel established a two-thirds interest in a new, large hotel complex which he called the Flamingo, his girlfriend's nickname. Bugsy wanted real life pretty flamingos to greet the guests but they quickly died in the heat – the flamingos, that is, not the guests, though some of them probably did too.

The neon nightmare, the Flamingo opened on Boxing Day 1946 with Frank Sinatra and the bandleader Xavier Cugat as the main attractions. The casino closed three months later as too many people had won. When they reopened, they had found a way to fix the odds in their favour, but Siegel's cards were already marked and he was shot dead in June 1947 on orders from another gang boss, Charlie Fischetti. The 1991 film, *Bugsy,* starred Warren Beatty as Siegel. It was a good film but it failed to acknowledge that El Rancho Vegas and the Frontier were there first.

One of the rules that Bugsy established was that no violence should take place on the Strip. There was no point in scaring the clients who might not return. No, far better to take the offending person and beat him up in the desert. You could even bury him there as no one would ever find him. Take for example, the gambler, Louis Strauss, known as Russian Louie. He had won handsomely on the tables but Meyer Lansky, who had taken control of the Flamingo within half an hour of Bugsy's death, told Louie, 'That's the last time a Jew will cheat a Sicilian in this town.' Russian Louie was taken for a ride in the desert and was never seen again. Who knows how many bodies are buried in the desert? It was far too convenient.

And who killed Jimmy Roselli, another casino owner? In 1976 his body was found washed up in a steel drum off the Florida coast. His legs had been cut off and there were rags stuffed in his mouth.

The Flamingo set the template – gaudy neon signs, exotic architecture, large swimming pools, lavish landscapes, and the best in food and drink and entertainment. The prices seemed surprisingly reasonable but the idea was to keep everybody happy. Everything was the trimmings for the main attraction, gambling – and the aim was to keep the gamblers playing as long as possible because even successful players would lose eventually. There were no clocks or windows in the casinos as the gamblers were to lose track of time. From then on, most of the casinos would be funded by Mafia money. It really didn't matter that the owners were gangsters: they were going to get your money anyway.

This raises an interesting point about casino management, which Marc Almond noted in the 1980s. 'I was surprised when I first went to Vegas as the hotel rooms were quite dingy, you know, the television didn't work properly and things like that. I soon realised it was deliberate. The casinos don't want you in the bedrooms. They want you out on the floor, spending money on the tables and in the slot machines. If they gave you a gorgeous hotel room, you might want to say there and use room service.'

The Desert Inn, which opened in 1950, was built for Moe Dalitz, who ran a crime syndicate in Cleveland before moving to Vegas. He was a vicious thug who spoke softly and told jokes. His enterprise was partly funded through Jimmy Hoffa's management (or rather, mismanagement) of the pension funds of the International Brotherhood of Teamsters, not that the union members knew much about it. Its Painted Desert Room only seated 450 customers but it became a prestigious place to play. They also funded Caesars Palace and the Dunes.

Normally, pension funds were invested in safe securities rather than risky investments. The Teamsters, a massive union for truckdrivers and warehousemen, had millions of dollars to invest and its management thought that building casinos in the desert in conjunction with gangsters was the way forward (these were not the subprime mortgages of the day). Las Vegas blossomed, but Hoffa was creaming off the top and Bobby Kennedy was determined to 'Get Hoffa'. He was eventually arrested for improper use of the Teamsters' money by lending large sums to criminals. By then, the casinos had been built and Las Vegas was flourishing. As far as the mobsters were concerned, they had built heaven on earth. Hoffa was imprisoned from 1967 to 1971 and President Nixon decreed that he could no longer undertake any union work, but he was still involved in shady deals. He disappeared in 1975 and was probably murdered, the ending chosen for the 1991 biopic, *Hoffa*, starring Jack Nicholson.

More huge casinos opened in the 1950s – the Sahara (1952), the Sands (1952), the Riviera (1955, the first high riser with Dino's bar, to boot) and the Tropicana (1957). The accessories were nothing if not original – the Dunes had a 30 foot sultan to welcome you. The Sands, with its logo 'A place in the sun', had an innovative floating crap game so you could lose your money as you swam. Frank Loesser was so amused that he wrote a song about it for *Guys and Dolls*. All these casinos upped the ante for slot machines and you would have to pass the cashiers' cage and walk through the aptly-named one-armed bandits to reach your room. There were no TVs or minibars in the rooms as the owners wanted guests to go to the casinos for entertainment. As a result, meals were astonishingly cheap and the steaks were so large at the Sands that they would come over the side of the plates. The Sahara had a special adult playground called House of Lords where the Rat Pack would often mingle with the showgirls.

Ah, the showgirls. The *Playboy* clubs had a rule that the bunnies were not to date the clientèle – on the surface at any rate, as Hugh Hefner pretended that the clubs were respectable. It was different in Vegas. The showgirls were ordered to sit in the lounge after performances and mix with the customers. They might encourage the high rollers to bet heavily and be given a few chips for their support. Zsa Zsa Gabor, obviously at the high end of the market, was once with the Wall Street financier, Lou Wolfson, who lost $400,000 in a night. If you had money to burn, you could pick up a showgirl very easily – in Sinatra's case, it was just 'Hello, what's your name?'

The girls might also be called for other services; Vegas was also a home to full-time prostitutes and to massage parlours which were not rubbing the same muscles as their brochures implied. In 1962 a law was passed in Vegas which made it illegal for women to massage men unless approved by a doctor, and it would be intriguing to learn how this legislation was administered. Then there were the prostitutes themselves – the going rate in 1964 was $100 but you could get a quickie in a slow period for $50.

One of the first performers at the Desert Inn, Phil Silvers, told the audiences of a gambler who had won a fortune in Vegas. Would this lucky individual stand up and take a bow? His plant, sometimes Sammy Cahn, stood up covered in bandages. It was a good joke but not far from the truth. Look at how a gambler with a winning streak is beaten up in *Casino*: it couldn't happen because the games were fixed so he must be cheating.

At first, no laws had been introduced to stop the owners from skimming the take and there were no limits on the size of the bets, other than what the owners would allow. The casinos became the perfect place for money laundering.

Buddy Greco comments, 'Clubs are run by gangsters all over the world. I would say that maybe 60% of the clubs and theatres I've worked, at one time or another, were associated with gangsters because they had the money to put behind them. I have never associated with them. I just say hello to them as I would say to anybody else.' This is the Sinatra defence, and indeed Frank wouldn't have lasted long if he had ignored 'the boys' (as he called them) in Vegas.

You could argue that the US government encouraged Mob involvement. Much of the profit was ploughed back into the city, so it was money well spent. Moe Dalitz from the Desert Inn built a hospital in Las Vegas as well as ensuring that it had some patients.

In 1940 there had only been 8,000 people living in Las Vegas but by 1950, it was 65,000 and rising fast. It had become the biggest city in Nevada. Indeed the entire population of the state had only been 100,000. *Time* magazine ran a cover story about corruption and the place was dubbed 'Sin City', later the title of a poignant song by Gram Parsons, who also wrote 'Ooh Las Vegas' with the refrain that Las Vegas 'ain't no place for a poor boy like me'.

It was an open secret that Las Vegas encouraged gambling addiction and it wasn't until 1986 that a centre to help addicts was established. Step 1 of the 12-point plan was to leave the city.

This 'live and let live' policy gave the whole area a feeling of freedom. The first and perhaps biggest star to emerge from Vegas was the glittering pianist, Liberace, the product of an Italian father and Polish mother. He was gay (surely you could tell?) and he could live his life without persecution by the police or vigilante groups in Vegas. He appealed to wealthy, middle-aged and elderly Jewish ladies who would attend his shows while their husbands gambled.

The British agent Tony Cartwright says: 'If you saw Bobby Darin, you would guess that he was having trouble with his hair as the wigs weren't good, but if you saw Liberace, you would say "What a beautiful head of hair!" I used to think, "I wish I had hair like that" and then I found out it was a wig. Liberace has been the biggest star of all time in Las Vegas. He grossed twice as much as Elvis Presley. He was very Jewish and the people who came to see him were the wealthiest of the wealthy Jews. Their jewellery was amazing. They would buy expensive gifts and gamble and it was great for Vegas.'

The blue-rinsed ladies could fawn over the preening pianist while their husbands took in the topless shows or the massage parlours. Striptease was fashionable on the strip with beautiful girls often brought over from France. The Lido de Paris show at the Stardust ran for 30 years; you didn't need to go to Paris to see the Folies Bergère.

There were strict unwritten rules about booking performers for Vegas as a young British agent, Malcolm Feld, learnt to his cost in the early 60s. Performers could only work in their designated casino. 'I went out there and I did deals for all the acts I was representing including Bobby Darin and I thought, "How wonderful and how easy all this is and what nice people they are." Two days later Milton Stein who owned Talent Artists Corporation called and told me to pack up everything and return to New York. I thought I was being transferred to New York because I had done such great business. When I got there, he said, "You're booked on the flight back to England – tonight – and you'd better be on it." I said, "Why?" and he said, "It's safer." The Mafia controlled Las Vegas and they didn't like the way I had been booking artists into different casinos. I was lucky. They had probably figured, "He's English, he's just a kid, what does he know?" If I'd been any older, I probably would have been supporting a highway.'

To give you an idea of what Las Vegas had to offer in one week in September 1960, the entertainment was Sammy Davis (Sands), Louis Prima and Keely Smith (Riviera), Tony Martin (Desert Inn), Billy Eckstine (New Frontier), Teresa Brewer (Sahara) and Andy Williams with Sarah Vaughan (Flamingo). There wasn't much high culture in Vegas as one badly-chosen booking revealed. Leonard Bernstein, conducting the New York Philharmonic, declared it a culture desert in 1960. He thought the audiences were boorish and said that he wouldn't be back.

More to the audiences' liking was a Hollywood actor, Ronald Reagan, who appeared at the Frontier in 1954. He told jokes, sang with a vocal quartet, danced with showgirls and read sentimental poems. It might be seen as an embarrassing spectacle by a future US President but it was typical of its day and a number of stars, including Peter Lawford, followed his example. You could get by with little genuine talent so long as you were a celebrity and the audience could get to know you.

Anthony Newley knew the secret: 'The difficult lesson that you have to learn is that Las Vegas is not theatre, it is not variety and it is not even cabaret as we know it. It is something much more subtle. It is about being who you are. Sammy Davis explained it to me before I opened in 1969. He told me that I should just sing the songs that I had written and made famous and should just be myself. It became very clear to me over the years that the closer you get to being who you are, the more successful you become. I remember Tommy Steele coming here and he didn't understand that principle. The show is not about 13 girls dancing behind you and some trick scenery. The great night club performers are the ones who come out like Sammy, Frank and Dean and create an evening out of who they are; they put in asides and they stop the orchestra if they want to. That rapport with the audience is very important because then the great night club act is happening right here in front of you. It is not choreographed, it is not rehearsed, it is happening here and if something happens, you stop and you talk to the girl serving the drinks or you talk to your musical director. It is a Zen experience and the great performers know that.'

Even Elvis did not know that initially and his first appearance at the Frontier in April 1956 was a disaster, involving the worst shows of his career. The audience didn't want to hear 'Heartbreak Hotel', 'Blue Suede Shoes' and 'Long Tall Sally' and he was paid off early. There would have been few teenagers in Vegas and the middle-aged audience had no interest in Elvis. When he returned in triumph in 1969, it was a very different Elvis and the show was all about being Elvis. His indiscreet raps on stage became legendary – the audience was seeing the man, admittedly with some loss in integrity as the performances of his early hits were a travesty. Still his first trip to Vegas did have some benefits: while there he heard Freddie Bell and the Bellboys performing 'Hound Dog' and decided to do it himself.

The experience can't have hurt Elvis too much as he made a film musical, *Viva Las Vegas!* (1964) with Ann-Margret which included scenes in the Sahara, the Tropicana and the Little Church of the West. In that same year the Beatles appeared at the Convention Centre, next to the Sahara Hotel. The lobby was overrun with adolescent Beatle fans who had persuaded their parents to come to Vegas.

The Beatles were instructed not to go into the casino because juveniles might follow them. Instead, slot machines were taken to the penthouse suite so that they could play them privately. They came down at 2.30pm for a soundcheck in the Convention Centre, which was next door to the hotel and they performed against a backdrop of the US flag. Although the official capacity was 7,500, the management let in another 1,000, some standing and some sitting behind the Beatles. There was a huge chant of 'Ringo for President' in the build-up for the Beatles. In the audience were former child star Shirley Temple, Liberace and Pat Boone with his four daughters.

The presence of the young fans was just about acceptable for the management as they had come with their parents who could lose their money in the casinos. When Elvis conquered Vegas in 1969, he created a different problem. Elvis's fans were adults but on the whole they had come to Vegas solely to see him and didn't want to gamble. The fans were lookie-loos, that is, people who only watched the gamblers, and the ticket prices had to accommodate that. Even so, Elvis at the International and the Hilton was a mammoth PR boost for the city.

The lookie-loos might witness some extraordinary sights. The Australian Kerry Packer, not a mobster but a super-wealthy tycoon, once gambled $1m on a single bet. The croupier stated that such a large bet was not permitted. Packer told him that if he didn't take the bet, he would buy the hotel. The bet was placed and he lost. Another time, Packer asked a waitress how much her mortgage was – she said $125,000 and he paid it off.

The UK manager Tony Cartwright was mesmerised by what he saw, 'The gangsters were the high rollers and they followed the artists. If you owned a restaurant and a load of gangsters came in, you would want to serve them if they were orderly. They might be ordering expensive wine and spending two grand a day. It was much better than having punters who only spent a few dollars. These Mob guys brought their money and would be throwing it around. They liked having attractive girls with them and it was all part of that culture. People are fascinated by it and that is why we have the big films like *The Godfather, Casino* and *Goodfellas* and ten years of *The Sopranos*. Everyone is fascinated by the Mafia and I was glad to see something of it first hand. Sometimes they were all pals together and sometimes they were at war with each other. Sometimes I thought that they were funny but other times I thought I might end up in the desert.'

Martin Scorsese's dazzling *Casino*, in particular, from 1995 offers a stunning analysis of the Mob in Vegas. Though based on fact, the plot may be far-fetched, but it showed in great detail how the casinos operated. We learn how skimming went on and how the public were watched with security staff in the ceiling. In addition, there were security men spying on security men and so on. When someone hits the jackpot three times in a day, Sam 'Ace' Rothstein (played by Robert DeNiro) knows it's a scam because the slot machines are not programmed to be so generous. Watch this film if you are thinking of going to Vegas and you may change your mind; there is no regard for the public at all – everyone is there to be fleeced.

The Hotel Tangiers in *Casino* is in reality, the Stardust Casino, which had been built in

1958 with millions of dollars money from the Teamsters pension fund. The bad practices in the film may be historic, but it is remarkable that Scorsese was allowed to make such a negative film about the gambling world on location.

Everything is very elegant in Casino. None of the Mob look like gangsters (well, maybe a few), but they are stylishly dressed and super polite until they get riled. They have left Las Vegas now and that elegance has gone with them. For example, in those days you had to be smartly turned out for the casino; now you can play in shorts and trainers.

The top performers were paid enormous fees to perform in Vegas but the casino owners were always hopeful of getting it back. Some owners would give the performers an extra 10% if they would take it in chips. Frank Sinatra fell for that whereas Paul Anka was very careful about hanging onto his earnings. He would accept the extra payment and then cash the chips in, preferring to spend his spare time riding horses in the desert in the early morning. By way of contrast, Fats Domino usually left Vegas a poorer man. Billy Eckstine, who played Vegas for many years, said, 'I don't mind playing gambling casinos. It's like working in an ice cream parlour. You don't eat ice cream all the time.'

The major problem for some performers was beating the Vegas throat. The climate was so dry that there was a strong chance that you might lose your voice. The precautionary action was to put Vaseline up your nose. Then there was the endless whirring of the air conditioning systems, a constant irritant for someone with sensitive hearing.

Caesars Palace opened in 1966 and quickly became a major player. They have had some great stunts such as the stunt rider Evil Knievel attempting to jump the fountain at Caesars Palace on his motorbike and breaking several bones – even he couldn't win in Vegas. Caesars has played host to Formula 1 drivers in their gigantic car park and the casino was featured in *The Electric Horseman* (1979)

In 1973 there was a sumptuous opening for the MGM Grand. 'Showgirls are so dumb,' cracked Joan Rivers, 'They can't even spell MGM.'

Not everyone with money was welcome in Vegas. At first the casinos operated a whites only policy; even if black entertainers were booked, they could not reside there. Sammy Davis performed as part of the Will Mastin Trio, and when they played El Rancho Vegas in 1947, they had to stay in shabby rooms on the Westside.

The racial intolerance came to a head in 1954. A big star, Eartha Kitt, was at least able to insist on her own bungalow at El Rancho Vegas. Pearl Bailey confronted Bugsy Siegel at the Flamingo and even though she wasn't allowed to stay there, he did arrange for a Buick to transport her between the Westside and the Flamingo. A few months later Lena Horne would only play the Flamingo if she could stay there. Siegel agreed but he gave instructions for her sheets to be burned every morning. When another star, Josephine Baker took a dip in the pool, the white residents insisted that it should be drained and cleaned. Unbelievable – but it happened.

Frank Sinatra was at the Sands at the same time as Nat 'King' Cole, who was about to eat in his dressing-room. Sinatra caused controversy by insisting that he joined him in the Garden Room. Harry Belafonte, a noted advocate for equal rights, finished his second show at the Sands and went into the casino to play blackjack and wasn't thrown out.

Note Sammy Davis's demeaning role in the Rat Pack film, *Ocean's 11* (1960). Even though it is fiction he still can't have a job inside the casinos because they hadn't been desegregated. Instead, he plays the garbage man, so, without intending to, the film reveals something about the real Vegas.

The first casino in Vegas to admit both black and white customers was the Moulin Rouge in May 1955. One of the investors, the boxer Joe Louis greeted visitors at the door. It only lasted six months but that was long enough to make the case for desegregation. The MC and singer from the Moulin Rouge, Bill Bailey, then took the cause forward.

By 1960 the times they were a-changin'. Dr James McMillan, a physician in Las Vegas, was going to organise a protest on the Strip against the casino's policy of segregation. He ignored threats and in the end, the casinos relented without the march taking place.

As if the racial problems weren't enough, Las Vegas had a potentially life-threatening disaster on its doorstep. The Sands had the slogan, 'A place in the sun', which was open to several interpretations.

In April 1952 the Government approved nuclear testing, known as Operation Big Shot, some 75 miles from Vegas. The press was allowed to view the tests through protective goggles and no one raised health and safety issues. Nowadays we realise that you would have had to be mad to live in Vegas with all that close at hand, but not then. Vegas capitalised on the event with pictures of showgirls straddling rockets, and hatched plans to separate the nuclear workers from their salaries. The Sands dubbed a showgirl 'Miss Atomic Energy' and the Frontier billed Elvis as the 'Atomic Powered Singer'. In1954 Mickey Rooney made a comedy, if you will, about radioactivity in the area, *The Atomic Kid*.

A state senator, Dina Titus, remarked, 'Up until that point, we were just a spot in the desert. We were prostitution; we were gambling. Suddenly we were helping to win the Cold War and people could grab a hold of that because it was good for democracy.'

Well, maybe, but broadly speaking, the major powers were playing nuclear poker.

In 1958 there was a moratorium on nuclear testing agreed by the USA and the USSR, but three years later, the Americans discovered that the Russians were still testing. The Americans resumed testing and then a limited test ban treaty drove the activities underground. By 1964, the test site in Nevada covered 1,350 square miles and only those involved knew what was happening.

When Howard Hughes was installed as the new saviour of Las Vegas in 1967, he wanted the testing to stop. He offered huge cash donations to the political parties associated with Presidents Johnson and Nixon, but the testing continued. This didn't appear to affect Las Vegas' commercial appeal but from time to time there were protests. Thousands of US citizens went to Nevada to protest in 1989 and the final test took place in 1992.

In 1987 a dump for nuclear waste was set up at Yucca Mountain; this has remained a contentious issue to this day. Nevertheless, the whole area still attracts plucky tourists and there is a museum and souvenir shop on site. The US government has acknowledged that nuclear tests have affected health and furthermore it could be to blame for 100,000 cases of thyroid cancer.

Nowadays there's no need to go to Las Vegas for a casino. There are casinos in every city and Atlantic City has attractions to rival Vegas. Nor is there a need to leave home as many people gamble on line. With the recession, you might have expected Las Vegas to go to the way of Detroit, but that hasn't happened.

Key films have been made in Vegas including *Indecent Proposal* (1993), *Leaving Las Vegas* (1995), *Fear and Loathing in Las Vegas* (1996), *What Happens in Vegas* (2008) and *Lost Vegas* (2013). Top rock acts have performed there and Beyoncé released *I Am…Yours: An Intimate Performance at Wynn Las Vegas*. Intimate? I doubt that. Las Vegas goes from strength to strength and in many ways it has become *the* rock'n'roll city: how Sinatra would have hated that.

Performances took place in showrooms which were rather like small theatres. They were only separated from the gambling by a curtain, and seeing the lounge acts was free. Sometimes one of the bigger acts might be demoted to the lounge and not like it. However, the hotels discovered that gamblers didn't need music and so instead bigger showrooms were built to separate the entertainment from the gambling. The lounge acts had disappeared by 1973.

In the 1960s many convention centres were built. This changed the clientèle and there was a further move to encourage family entertainment. Nowadays there are lavish shopping malls and specific entertainments for children. It is not unusual to find a casino/hotel with 25 floors. The city has changed a great deal; the big corporations now own the casinos and everything is much more legitimate. There is constant building work as casinos come and go – huge casinos are often replaced by even larger ones. Very little of the old Vegas is left.

Las Vegas now boasts a resident population of 600,000 and the tourist population is enormous. It is possible to be both married and divorced much quicker than elsewhere, and sometimes the two go hand in hand. In 2004 Britney Spears impulsively married Jason Alexander but she had little memory of getting married and the marriage was annulled two days later. There are over 100,000 marriages a year in Vegas and you can get married in the *Star Trek* chapel or be given away by an Elvis Presley or Michael Jackson impersonator. There are even 'drive thru' marriages.

The British country singer Hank Wangford recalls, 'Las Vegas is a completely potty place, totally mad. The weekend that Virgin Atlantic had their first direct flight to Las Vegas was the time that my son was getting married by 'Elvis' in the Viva Las Vegas wedding chapel. If you want your marriage to last, don't get married by 'Elvis' in Las Vegas. I was on the tour bus and the guide was saying, "Over there is Paris and over there is London and over there is Venice, and where in the world can you get London and Paris and Venice in the same place?" and a little voice piped up, "Europe".'

II. Day In–Day Out, 1946–1949

The weekly *Songs by Sinatra* radio show featured some superlative singing but its charm lay in its looseness and the fact that Frank wasn't taking it too seriously. One week, for example, he allowed the gravel-voiced Jimmy Durante to sing his closing theme, 'Put Your Dreams Away'. Durante said that he has been with Frank in Palm Springs, adding, 'You were always under my nose. It was the only shady place in the desert.' The scripted comedy with Teenage Tina played by Janet Waldo was lamentable.

The show's guest list had the usual camaraderie with stars who appeared on each other's shows like Bob Hope's. Frank's duets of 'Exactly Like You' with Nat 'King' Cole and 'You Brought a New Kind of Love to Me' with Peggy Lee revealed how well they worked together. Even though they all ended up on Capitol, where it would have been easy to arrange duet albums, it never happened.

Frank had fun singing the soft shoe shuffle 'Whispering' with the bandleader Skinnay Ennis and turned to parodying opera with Carlos Ramirez, who had been in *Anchors Aweigh*. He and Jack Carson shared goodhearted banter in 'Don't Bring Crosby', a rewrite of 'Don't Bring Lulu'. He ventured into country music by singing 'You Are My Sunshine' with its credited composer, Jimmie Davis and around this time, the city-based Sinatra recorded 'Home on the Range', the most inappropriate song he ever recorded.. When he did 'Blue Skies' with the pianist Skitch Henderson he fell behind and commented 'Never made it, did I?'

Among the songs were 'Rock-A-Bye Your Baby with a Dixie Melody' and the bizarre 'Chickery Chick', a Sammy Kaye chart-topper which ended, 'The chickery chick is me.' 'How Cute Can You Be' had the line, 'I've seen lassies with fine looking chassis'; indeed he had but it's an odd way of saying it. 'Oh, What It Seemed to Be' sounded like an audition for Fagin in Lionel Bart's *Oliver!*

Frank assumed a South American accent for the romantic 'No Can Do' sung with Lena Romay, a vocalist with Xavier Cugat, adding jokes about Dick Haymes and Perry Como and ending with 'Nancy's very jealous so we no can do'. When he performed 'All Through the Day', he added an anecdote about his shoelaces and little Nancy. All very nice and cozy but the paparazzi did catch him being affectionate with Lana Turner and with his wedding ring on display. They might have missed the main story as apparently Frank and Lana went on a double date with Howard Hughes and Ava Gardner and at some stage in the evening they changed partners. Sinatra was cited in Josephine Ingildsen's divorce petition; she was the wife of a building executive and apparently had had it away with Frank Sinatra on the day after her marriage.

These stories didn't have enough exposure to harm his record sales. Frank was all over the charts as hit followed hit – he had to share the sales with Perry Como on Jerome Kern's sublime 'All Through the Day' and he made the Top 10 with 'Oh, What It Seemed to Be' and 'Day by Day'. Frank went to No.1 with Sammy Cahn and Jule Styne's 'Five Minutes More', which Phil Brito had sung in the film, *The Sweetheart of Sigma Chi*. Again, note Frank's playful 'come on' at the end.

There was yet another wedding song in 'From This Day Forward' and a strange obsession with his wife's suitcase in 'Something Old, Something New'. Curiously there were relatively few cheating songs, though most of them were in country music. For the teenage fans who dreamed of Frankie there was the playful 'Could'ja', a big band novelty about the daft things that he liked – Tootsie Rolls and Kentucky Special Juleps amongst them. Don't dismiss this song as frivolous as it contains Frank's personal credo: 'I just want what I want when I see what I want.'

This was a truly golden period for Frank Sinatra as he recorded classic songs which he would return to again and again. He loved Cole Porter's 'Begin the Beguine', which had been written for the Broadway show *Jubilee* in 1935 and been a success for Artie Shaw and Tony Martin. Alex Stordahl wrote a gentle swinging arrangement which went into an impassioned finale and Sinatra had to stretch himself for the final notes.

The lyricist Johnny Mercer had loved the reference to voodoo in Cole Porter's 'You Do Something to Me' and wanted to explore it in a whole song. Hence, he and Harold Arlen wrote 'That Old Black Magic' for *Star Spangled Rhythm* in 1942 where it was sung by Johnny Johnston and danced by Vera Zorina, although it was written by Mercer for his girlfriend of the time, Judy Garland. Sinatra took it as a slow swinger but later he would belt it out.

When Irving Berlin's son died on Christmas Day 1928, he poured his feelings into a new song, 'How Deep Is the Ocean'. It asks a series of impossible questions, 'How many times a day do I think of you?' and Sinatra gave this great song the passion and intensity that it deserved. It had been a hit for Bing Crosby in 1932 and Peggy Lee revived it at the same time as Frank, who also sang it in the film, *Meet Danny Wilson* (1952).

In 1945 Jerome Kern was commissioned to write a Broadway musical about the western heroine, Annie Oakley, called *Annie Get Your Gun*. Irving Berlin took over the project on his death and although it was an unlikely Berlin subject, within a few days he had written 'Doin' What Comes Naturally', 'Anything You Can Do', 'They Say It's Wonderful' and the rousing and extremely witty finale, 'There's No Business like Show Business'. When Berlin wrote an opening verse for 'You Can't Get a Man with a Gun', he realised he had something that would stand alone and so another hit song was born, 'The Girl that I Marry'. Sinatra loved the score and recorded 'The Girl that I Marry' and 'They Say It's Wonderful', which became another Top 10 single. It's hard to be frequently employing superlatives about Frank's work but note the magnificent way he sings 'grand, and' as he goes into the chorus, a little touch maybe but evidence of his vocal perfection. Later in the year he sang 'There's No Business like Show Business', an amusing song that holds home truths.

Frank revived Jerome Kern and Oscar Hammerstein's 'The Song Is You' from *Music in the Air* (1932), a characteristic example of how songwriters like writing songs about writing songs, and this beautifully poetic lyric is among the best of them.

Frank had previously recorded 'You'll Never Walk Alone' and 'If I Loved You' from Rodgers and Hammerstein's musical *Carousel*. and now he returned to the most difficult song in the libretto, the eight minute 'Soliloquy' in which Billy wonders how he will measure up as a father. Manie Sacks allowed him to record the full version which was issued over both sides of a 12-inch single. He did, however, insist that Frank amended the words as Broadway songs could be a little more risqué than the general public would normally accept: 'fat-bottomed' became 'flat-footed'; 'bastard' went to 'bully'; 'virgin' to 'wench'; and "by God' to 'by gosh". Nevertheless, Frank was very pleased with his recording and he would play it to his friends and say, 'This is what I what I want to do.' So why didn't he do a Broadway musical? Too much discipline and too much work.

There were plans to star Frank Sinatra in a film of Rodgers and Hart's Broadway show, *Jumbo*. He would have been cast alongside the original Broadway star Jimmy Durante but nothing happened. The film was made with Durante and Doris Day, but it was a sprawling mess rather than a lavish extravaganza with Stephen Boyd lamentable in what would have been Sinatra's role. When Sinatra recorded his first duet in 1946, he sang the sweet but not saccharine 'My Romance' from *Jumbo* with Dinah Shore.

Frank had the No.1 album, *The Voice of Frank Sinatra* and won a special Oscar for *The House I Live In*. A three-part profile by E J Kahn for *The New Yorker* revealed that Frank knew his worth: 'He regards his voice as an instrument without equal, and although he tries scrupulously to be polite about the possessors of other renowned voices, he is apt – if the name of a competitor comes up abruptly in conversation – to remark, "I can sing that son of a bitch off the stage any day in the week!"' Sounds like Frank.

Frank had returned to concert dates after the war, usually earning $25,000 a week plus 50% of gross above $60,000. On 23 March 1946, fifty-six adolescent fans were taken into custody at 4.30am in San Francisco as they were waiting for Frank Sinatra to start performing at 10.30am at the Golden Gate Theatre. The curfew laws prohibited anyone under 18 from being on the streets from 11pm to 6am. Similarly, a rise in school truancy was noted when he performed in Detroit. He had worked out a great entrance – the screen went dark and just two green florescent drum sticks could be seen for the start of 'Night And Day'.

There was talk of UK dates but the London promoter Harold Fielding abandoned his plans after bad publicity. The press felt that he shouldn't pay a US entertainer when the dollar shortage was preventing food imports.

President Roosevelt had died in office in April 1945; on the first anniversary of his death, his widow, Eleanor gave their home to the nation. Frank was attending the ceremony and so 2,000 fans came to the event.

You might have thought that supporting Paul Robeson's anti-lynching march on Washington was hardly controversial, but Sinatra was pilloried by all but the liberal press. He was said to be attacking a very American way of life as though lynching was perfectly fine! The journalist Westbrook Pegler defended lynching as an American institution, and a short while later Sinatra punched him on the nose. Orson Welles sent Sinatra a congratulatory note; he didn't know what Pegler had done but he was sure he deserved it.

On 4 July 1946 Frank held a fireworks party for Nancy and Frank Jr. The neighbours were invited and watched Frank load fireworks onto a raft and then sail out with them to the middle of the lake. He asked his wife to start 'The Star Spangled Banner' on the record player and the plan was that guests would stand and salute as the record played and fireworks whizzed through the air. Everything started okay but Frank had some pinwheels on a flagpole and one of them fell off and dropped into a box of fireworks. Then the real fireworks started and there was a large explosion and Frank disappeared. He was a good swimmer and he soon reappeared, unscathed, and the neighbours put out the fire. Frank was annoyed that his plans had misfired and also that his watch had stopped as it was supposed to be waterproof.

As Sinatra's press agent, George Evans, had his work cut out because his client had a whole second life that he wanted to keep private. Evans felt that Sinatra's affair with Marilyn Maxwell was a step too far and could escalate into unfavourable newspaper copy. However, she was under contract to MGM and the studio had a morals clause. He told her that if her affair with Sinatra reached the newspapers, MGM could cancel her contract and she would become unemployable. Maxwell listened to reason and told Frank that they would have to break up. Soon after that, she started an affair with another married man, Bob Hope. This affair became so open that friends would refer to Maxwell as 'Mrs Bob Hope'. Frank became resentful about this; he bore Hope a grudge and even after her death in 1972, he never really forgave him.

It should be said that Sinatra had an MGM contract with the same morals clause, which Sinatra was breaking from Day One, but it was more of an issue with actresses. Sinatra's contract which he renegotiated in 1946 gave him $260,000pa and he was permitted to make one film a year for another studio. He had the publishing rights to the music in every other film.

As often happened, Frank turned to Lana Turner, but she was having an affair with Tyrone Power. Frank decided to ease off, but Lana then sent him begging letters and started calling him at home. In October, Frank announced his separation from Nancy and was back with Lana, but returned to Nancy by the end of the month. For the moment, Lana contented herself with Peter Lawford and Mel Tormé.

There was a sad postscript to these shenanigans. During 1946 Tyrone Power held a party at his house which led to an amorous version of hide and seek. David Niven joined in the fun with his wife, Primmie, but during the playfulness, Primmie fell down the basement steps. She suffered fatal injuries and died the following day.

As so often with Sinatra, his acquaintances were either 'in' or 'out', and their status could change in a second. On 5 September 1946 Marlon Brando and Paul Muni opened on Broadway in *A Flag is Born*, a play about resistance fighters and the creation of a Jewish state. At the after show party at Toots Shor's, Brando and Sinatra met for the first time. Soon Brando was at the top of Sinatra's 'out' list but the first meeting was cordial. They both agreed that Spencer Tracy was a great actor.

Frank's friend, the comedian Rags Ragland played a policeman in *Anchors Aweigh* and in October 1946 he was scheduled to appear at the Copa in a double act with Phil Silvers. He died shortly before the opening and Phil Silvers was preparing to go it alone. Frank was in New York filming *It Happened in Brooklyn* and so he turned up at the club with the words, 'Hi, Phil, what do we open with?' For once, it is unlikely that Frank had flings with any of the showgirls. For some misguided reason, the owner of the Copa had told them all to dye their hair purple.

Recording a witty song from a Copa revue, Frank had another hit single with 'The Coffee Song'. It was a delightful track but it did end dodgily with Frank saying in a mock-

Latin voice, 'Hey Pedro get the flashlight, I cannot find the sugar.' He must have enjoyed this as a few months later, he closed 'I Got a Gal I Love' with 'Hey Pedro, hold the hoss.' There was a slow and almost parlando 'Among My Souvenirs', a mournful 'I'm Sorry I Made You Cry' (See, Sinatra can apologise when he wants to) and 'None But The Lonely Heart' (based on Tchaikovsky).

Although 'September Song' was superbly recorded, he was still too young for its sentiments. Another of Kurt Weill's melodies was 'Lost in the Stars', the title song of a Broadway show, although not staged until 1949, about racial injustice in South Africa. Sinatra saw that it had a resonance for events at home and this show challenged an audience in the way that Stephen Sondheim would. The show was a foretaste for the 'Is God dead?' debate of the late-60s:

'And sometimes it seems maybe God's gone away,
Forgetting the promise that we've heard him say,
And we're lost out here in the stars.'

In total contrast, Sinatra recorded novelties like 'Hush-A-Bye Island (on rockabye bay)', 'The Dum Dot Machine' (about two children buying gum) and 'Why Shouldn't It Happen to Us' which was a blatant crib of Cole Porter's 'Let's Do It' but good fun in its own right:

'There's even been a rumour
That it has happened to a puma
Why shouldn't it happen to us?'

The first recorded wordplay on his name comes in 'I Want to Thank Your Folks' with the phrase, 'To be perfectly Frank'.

One of Sammy Cahn's best songs, the forlorn 'Guess I'll Hang My Tears Out to Dry', has the cryptic line, 'I'll know how the lady in the harbour feels.' Sammy is just playing with words on 'I Got a Gal I Love' where Frank has to choose between a girl in North Dakota and a girl in South Dakota. Way ahead of the campaigns for healthy living today, Frank cut 'It's All Up to You' with Dinah Shore. But this was two-faced: Frank mocked health food shops in Songs by Sinatra and the programme, sponsored by Old Gold cigarettes, had the slogan, 'Anytime you want a treat instead of a treatment.'

Undoubtedly, Sinatra was at his best on 'All of Me', where he brought out the vulnerable quality in the lyric. Still, it is hard to pick a definitive version however as there are also excellent interpretations from Billie Holiday, Louis Armstrong and Willie Nelson.

Sinatra saw the Page Cavanaugh Trio in a club and asked them to record with him. They recorded a country song by Eddy Arnold 'That's How Much I Love You', which was fair enough but Sinatra added a mock and unnecessary southern accent at the end. It marked the first time that the guitarist Al Viola recorded with Frank and he was to become one of his favoured guitarists. Frank did a benefit in Galveston with the trio for the victims of the Texas City petroleum explosion and in 1949, he worked with them in Atlantic City and in Canada.

Throughout the year, Frank was making various one-off appearances: appealing for funds for the March of Dimes, singing for wounded servicemen and paying tribute to Al Jolson on his 60th birthday. In December 1946 he was featured in an award winners show for Metronome jazz magazine and as a result he took part in a recording of 'Sweet Lorraine' by the so-called Metronome All Stars with Nat 'King' Cole (piano), Coleman Hawkins (tenor), Johnny Hodges (tenor) and Buddy Rich (drums). The song had been popular since Rudy Vallée's recording in 1928 and had been a hit for the Nat 'King' Cole Trio in 1944. It is a fine performance but it is rather short – those musicians could have created a ten minute masterpiece.

In December 1946 Sinatra was voted the Least Cooperative Star by the Hollywood Women's Press Club. Probably true, but his aversion was to journalists of either sex. Around that time he had an argument with Erskine Johnson of the *New York Daily News*. He said, 'Just continue to print lies about me and you will get a belt in your vicious and stupid mouth.' Johnson offered to fight him at a local boxing stadium, but it never happened. Sinatra only hit out when the odds where in his favour.

Still, goodwill to all men and Frank was again back in the Top 10 with 'White Christmas' and he saw 1947 in at the new Flamingo hotel in Las Vegas, no doubt cementing his relationship with the owner Bugsy Siegel, but his loyalty would soon be called into question.

Frank was big business. There were 2,000 Frank Sinatra fan clubs in the US alone with an average membership of 200. The membership fee was around $1 a year and for that the fan received four mimeographed newsletters. There was little hard news and Frank's philandering was ignored. Mostly the pages were filled with sentimental poems and dreams about Frank. Sinatra was ambivalent about fan clubs. The blues singer, T-Bone Walker, referred to Frank in his song, 'Bobby Sox Blues'; until Chuck Berry started recording in 1955, it was highly unusual for a black artist to comment on white culture.

Frank was cultivating an older audience and the screaming on a live broadcast like *Songs by Sinatra* was a turnoff for servicemen and older listeners. He commented, 'They don't like all the noise and I don't blame them. With everyone clapping, it sounds like a Chinese laundry.'

The autumn series of *Songs by Sinatra* had begun in September and a couple of programmes highlighted the talented, 17-year-old pianist, André Previn, whom Frank kept calling 'Andrew Previn'. In time, they would both marry Mia Farrow. The songs included 'Wait Till the Sun Shines, Nellie', 'My Melancholy Baby', 'If I Had My Way', 'You Keep Coming Back Like a Song', and a current hit for Peggy Lee, '(I Used to Love You But) It's All Over Now'. Where have I heard that title before? Frank and Jimmy Durante sang together on 'You Gotta Start Off Each Day with a Song' and 'I Ups to Him, He Ups to Me', while Frank sang a parody of 'Ole Buttermilk Sky' with Fred Allen. Frank took part in a radio drama, *Room for a Stranger*, sponsored by Reader's Digest.

Despite getting Previn's name wrong, the young pianist ghosted for him in the MGM film, *It Happened In Brooklyn*. Frank was seen singing a new Sammy Cahn and Jule Styne song, 'Time After Time' while playing the piano. We didn't see his hands as the playing was done off-screen by Previn.

Frank commented, 'In *Anchors Aweigh*, I was cast as a friendly little sailor with nothing much to say for himself. In *It Happened in Brooklyn*, I was a friendly little GI with nothing much to say for himself.' He came to loathe Louis B Mayer for making him play naïve and shy characters but at least Mayer had put him in the forces. Once, talked into it, he did have Mayer as a guest on *Songs by Sinatra*. Things were cooling between them as Mayer wanted actors who would do as they were told and wouldn't argue. He wanted actors who would turn up on schedule and not take days off at will. In fact, he wanted the complete opposite of Frank Sinatra.

It Happened in Brooklyn was not one of the lavish MGM musicals but a workable, good-natured movie with plenty of songs. The combination of the four leads – Sinatra, Durante, Kathryn Grayson and Peter Lawford – worked very well. Lawford, in his first film with Sinatra, had a winsome smile, though we saw little of it. Durante was hilarious throughout, similar to the way that Tommy Cooper was. He is just funny and at his best when talking nonsense. Picking up a hat, he says, 'That's a very fine chateau.' If the outtakes are still around, this could be a great DVD package.

The opening scene, supposedly set in England, showed GI Sinatra about to return home. Back in New York, he walked on the deserted Brooklyn Bridge and sang about why it means so much to him. It was tempting fate to cast Frank as a GI when there had been so much controversy over his classification. Frank's character wanted to be a songwriter and he and Durante, a school caretaker, successfully auditioned 'The Song's Gotta Come from the Heart', for a music publisher, Sinatra impersonated Durante during the song and Grayson did the same elsewhere. Although Sinatra wanted single takes, he frequently cracked up when he saw Durante's face.

Frank sang 'Black Eyes' in Russian and he and Grayson attempted an aria from *Don Giovanni* in Italian. Cahn and Styne's 'I Believe' was written to impress a troubled boy, a 'High Hopes' moment. 'It's The Same Old Dream' had a dual purpose, working as a ballad for Frank and as a jive number for the kids in the music store. The records were tossed around, so clearly the purchasers weren't buying product in pristine condition. Peter Lawford did a jive version of 'Whose Baby Are You' in the music store and moved like a rock and roller.

Sinatra's character (or Sinatra himself) denigrated the 'jive stuff' and said he wanted to win a girl with a ballad. The enduring song from the film was 'Time After Time' and as we shall see, there weren't too many great songs that Frank introduced in his films; Fred Astaire certainly had a better run.

It Happened in Brooklyn had generally favourable reviews but not from Lee Mortimer of the *New York Daily Mirror*. Mortimer, perhaps not so incidentally, had had a song rejected by Sinatra, and he was not a popular man, regarded as mean and unpleasant.

Frank had recorded 'Always' in 1946 but he felt that he could do it better and on 9 January 1947 that is precisely what happened. The song had an unusual genesis which was a testament to the benefits of filing. Irving Berlin had a secretary, Arthur Johnston, who transcribed his songs. One day Irving was chatting to Johnston's girlfriend and she asked if he would write a song about her sometime. Always one for showing off, he said, 'Why not now?' and wrote 'I'll Be Loving You, Mona'. Arthur dutifully jotted it down. Some months later, Irving Berlin came across the song – he couldn't recall writing it and Arthur was no longer dating Mona. With slight adjustments, the song became 'Always' and it was published in 1925. Irving Berlin was getting married, so he assigned the copyright to his bride as a wedding present. This is an unparalleled act of generosity in Berlin's life, although he was still keeping it in the family.

On the same day Frank recorded a lovely Cole Porter ballad, 'I Concentrate on You', which had been written for the wartime film, *Broadway Melody Of 1940*, but had never been a hit. The film had starred Fred Astaire but the song had been given to the little-known Douglas McPhail, who had since committed suicide.

A few weeks later Frank was back in Columbia's Hollywood studio for his most commercial single for some time, 'Mam'selle', although the song is forgotten now. The melody was the theme music for the 1946 film of W Somerset Maugham's *The Razor's Edge*, directed by Edmund Goulding. Frank's record went to No.1 but it was also a hit for Art Lund, Dick Haymes, the Pied Pipers and Ray Dorey.

Frank was always up for songs from a good new Broadway musical and he recorded 'Almost Like Being in Love' and 'There But for You Go I' from Alan Jay Lerner and Frederick Loewe's *Brigadoon*. He released a charming version of 'Tea for Two' including the introductory verse as a duet with Dinah Shore.

Frank made an early TV appearance on the *Hoffman Hayride*, a country show hosted by Spade Cooley and his Orchestra. Spade Cooley was a national star with such records as 'Shame on You' but in 1961 he beat his wife to death and received a life sentence. On another TV show, Bing and Frank sang 'Stardust' on a strange set that had them together yet apart.

On 29 January 1947 Frank took three weeks' sick leave from *Songs by Sinatra*. He recuperated (if indeed there was anything wrong with him) at a house in Miami Beach, Florida belonging to Joe and Rocco Fischetti. They were cousins to Al Capone and Frank also knew Al Capone's brother, Ralph.

While there, he was invited to Cuba and on 11 February 1947, he met Lucky Luciano in Havana. Luciano had been imprisoned but had had his sentence commuted for helping the Allies land in Sicily. Under the terms of his parole, he was meant to return to Italy but instead he went to Cuba where he continued planning underworld crime in America, especially the importation of drugs. Sinatra met him in Cuba and it has been said that he was delivering money, but there is no proof of this. What cannot be denied is that Frank gave him an inscribed cigarette case, 'To my dear pal Lucky, from your friend, Frank Sinatra'.

Lucky Luciano said of Sinatra, 'He was a good kid and we were all proud of him', not an endorsement you would actively seek. Frank was a party animal too. He had promised Nancy he would join her in Acapulco for Valentine's Day but he was delayed by an orgy that Luciano had arranged in his honour. Well, you can hardly say no, can you?

Frank later said that he had been booked to appear at the Grand National Casino and the fact that Mafia was there was a coincidence. Frank was photographed with several Mafia bosses, but not Bugsy Siegel. Bugsy was too busy establishing himself in Vegas and anyway, he was a marked man. Even if we believe Frank's explanation, how come he was booked to sing at the wedding of the daughter of another mobster, Willie Moretti?

Because of his affairs and his unpredictability, Nancy was feeling humiliated. She was pregnant and was unsure about having a third child. She was a staunch Catholic so she must have tormented even to think of abortion. She found a doctor in Los Angeles who was willing to terminate the pregnancy while he was in Cuba. When she met Frank in Acapulco, she told him what she had done. Sinatra was mortified and said, 'Don't ever do that again.' Soon she was pregnant again and this time she followed it through.

Nancy didn't know that Sinatra was having yet another affair. This time it was a long on-off relationship with Peggy Lee, which had started because Peggy had told him that she was unhappy with her husband's drinking.

As well as his affairs, Nancy was concerned about his expenditure. Ten years earlier he had nothing and now he was giving away gold cigarette lighters to anyone who did him a favour. In 1946 alone, he gave away 300 lighters at a cost of $150 each. He possessed a huge wardrobe – one fan feature said he owned 50 suits, 25 sports jackets and 100 pairs of trousers, all of them high quality. No wonder that when he sang 'I Got Plenty o'Nuttin'', the fans would shout, 'No, Frankie, you got everything.'

The columnist Lee Mortimer had another pop at Frank calling him Frank 'Lucky' Sinatra, indicating that he knew of his Mob connections. On 8 April Frank saw him dining in Ciro's on Sunset Strip, now the Comedy Store. He called Mortimer 'the garter belt Mafia' and hit him as he left and was arrested. Frank pleaded not guilty on the grounds that he had been provoked that night by Mortimer, but that story might have been spun to hide Frank's bad temper. Frank had just been granted a gun permit (don't know what for) and this was promptly suspended.

An exasperated Louis B Mayer ordered Sinatra to settle as a war with the Hearst newspapers would be bad for business. Mortimer received $9,000 and an open letter from Frank to his fans on MGM stationery was printed in the newspapers. Of course, Sinatra never really regretted hitting Lee Mortimer, and the Hearst press would now be making jibes at Sinatra. He was to be accused of being a communist by Westbrook Pegler and George Sokolsky

Springing to his defence, Ed Sullivan, then a sports writer and gossip columnist, wrote, 'Basically Sinatra is a warm-hearted decent person and I think it's about time they stopped kicking him around.' Naturally, Frank sent Ed a present – in this case, a gold watch with the inscription, 'Ed, you can have my last drop of blood, Frankie.'

Songs by Sinatra lost its impetus despite special programmes devoted to key songwriters. There were fewer guests and they tended to be old favourites like Phil Silvers and George Burns. The series had discovered 17-year-old Jane Powell and she was featured in many shows often singing duets like 'People Will Say We're in Love' and 'Make Believe' with Sinatra, an impressive way to start your career. She was to play the lead in the 1954 film musical, *Seven Brides for Seven Brothers*.

Among the songs performed by Sinatra were '(I Love You) For Sentimental Reasons', 'I'll Close My Eyes', and 'April Showers'. When he sang Charles Chaplin's 'Anniversary Song' in April 1947, he said, somewhat mysteriously, 'I'd like to dedicate this song to two people who have been very good to me – one in Detroit and one in Hollywood.' He appeared in a radio comedy, *Too Many Husbands*, with Bob Hope and Lucille Ball in which he sang 'So Happy to be Loving You'.

On NBC, Fred Allen told a joke about an executive which was faded down. An NBC executive said that station executives were not to be mocked and no other network was to be mentioned. This prompted Bob Hope to say on his next programme, 'Las Vegas is the place where you can get tanned and faded at the same time. Of course Fred Allen can get faded at any time.' A fortnight later, Frank was the guest on Bob Hope's Pepsodent Show. Bob Hope told him that he would see him the following night on his CBS show.

Not that it did Frank's ratings much good. They were falling and Old Gold dropped *Songs by Sinatra*. Instead, the public was falling in love with another Italian-American singer, Perry Como. Admittedly he was three years older than Frank but there were no scandals in his love life and no involvement with gangsters; he was a regular Joe and his records tended to be light and easy-going with little of Sinatra's intensity. The underlying reason was that Old Gold wanted to invest in TV instead and the company couldn't be bothered to bring *Songs by Sinatra* up to standard. Still, Sinatra was still a huge name and his latest collection of four 78rpms, *Songs by Sinatra* was the No.1 album.

Then Sinatra made an odd move. He returned to *Your Hit Parade* on 6 September. The programme was glad to have him as its ratings had fallen from No.5 to No.15. Once again he would be singing other people's hits but there was a bonus. His female counterpart would be Doris Day, who had been born Doris Van Kappelhoff in Cincinnati, Ohio in 1924. She became Doris Day when she sang with Bob Crosby's band in 1940. She had a No.1 record in 1945 with 'Sentimental Journey' with Les Brown's orchestra and the song became a standard. Her three month stint with Sinatra was another stepping stone. She would soon be a major film star and would work with Frank again. Although her singing voice was sultry, she had a clean-cut, wholesome image – a tomboy vitality really – and she was different from most Hollywood stars in that she had little interest in expensive jewellery. She would say, 'All I can think of is how many dog shelters those diamonds could buy.' Doris Day was, in turn, replaced in *Your Hit Parade* by another excellent singer, the British-born Beryl Davis, who was still singing when she was 80. Frank himself continued with *Your Hit Parade* for almost two years, finishing on 28 May 1949.

Frank was able to state his terms for the show. Alex Stordahl would write the arrangements and *Metronome* commented that 'Axel plays murderous, rag-timey junk that he, with his impeccable taste, must abhor.' However, Frank could sing an 'all-time favourite' each week such as 'Over the Rainbow'. The first song he sang on his return was an indifferent version of Bing Crosby's current success, 'Feudin' and Fightin'', an amusing song which needed a comedy vocal, and among the more unlikely songs were 'The Lady From 29 Palms' (Andrews Sisters), 'The Dickey-Bird Song' (sung by Jeanette MacDonald and Jane Powell in *Three Darling Daughters*), and 'I'll Dance at Your Wedding' (Peggy Lee).

Frank and Doris's duet of 'There's No Business like Show Business' was better than Sinatra's solo recording, except for one little thing. Doris Day changed 'your favourite uncle' to 'your father died', so the next line about your ma and pa parting made no sense. Frank appeared on *The Jack Benny Show* in a well-worn sketch in which they argued over fees.

In June 1947 Frank promoted his first fight which was between Jersey Joe Walcott and Joey Maxim at Gilmore Stadium, Hollywood. Walcott won but it was Frank who was knocked out as he lost $50,000 – this was the first and only time he was a boxing promoter. He was better out of it as the Mafia was arranging for fights to be thrown such as Jake LaMotta (*The Raging Bull*) losing to Billy Fox at Madison Square Garden later that year.

Hoboken was so proud of Frank that it declared 30 October 1947 Frank Sinatra Day and gave him the keys to the city. He spent a month at New York's Capitol Theatre, performing eight shows a day between showings of *Her Husband's Affairs* with Lucille Ball. Over Christmas he was back in Los Angeles, singing for children in a hospital on Christmas Day, which was just as well, as there were blizzards and 26 inches of snow in New York. Still, the New Yorkers could listen to a radio adaptation of *Anchors Aweigh*, courtesy of Lux soap, with the three main leads: Frank, Gene and Kathryn.

Frank Sinatra had been actively recording in the latter half of 1947. As usual, he was recording Christmas songs in July including 'Have Yourself a Merry Little Christmas' which Judy Garland sang in *Meet Me In St Louis*. In sentiment and execution, the song isn't far removed from 'White Christmas' – if one word can make a song, it is the use of the world 'muddle'.

During August 1947, he started one session with two excellent revivals, 'That Old Feeling' and 'If I Had You' and then moved onto a very slow and stately version of a Glenn Miller hit, 'The Nearness of You'. As if that wasn't enough, the magic happened with 'One for My Baby', and composer Harold Arlen described his melody of 43 bars as 'a tapeworm'. In *The Sky's the Limit* (1943), Fred Astaire got sozzled and ended up breaking glasses and throwing a barstool through the mirror, so that his drunken dancing was featured more than the song, 'One for My Baby'. Frank set the scene with the words, 'It's a quarter to three' and then told the story with a barroom piano, ending with a little whistling, and a fade-out which was rare at the time. Fred Astaire said it was 'one of the best pieces of material that was written especially for me' and Frank considered it 'a great Johnny Mercer lyric that has all the wit you wish you had and all the love you ever lost.' The reference to 'Set 'em up, Joe' inspired another songwriter, Richard Berry, to write 'Louie, Louie'.

A 1944 film mystery, *Laura*, starring Gene Tierney in the title role of a murdered girl and directed by Otto Preminger, had a haunting, romantic theme. The melody proved popular and Oscar Hammerstein was asked for a lyric, but the producers wouldn't agree to Hammerstein's company publishing it. Irving Caesar failed to write a satisfactory lyric so it went to Johnny Mercer. Once he had got the feel of 'footsteps in the dark', he was away. Cole Porter said it was his favourite song, outside of his own catalogue. 'Laura' was successful for Woody Herman and Stan Kenton and their orchestras as well as Dick Haymes and Frank Sinatra, who had a stunning arrangement bringing out its dreamlike state.

Both 'A Fellow Needs A Girl' and 'So Far' come from the Rodgers and Hammerstein musical, *Allegro*. The show did not last on Broadway and revivals have been unsuccessful. The theme of the musical, a caring doctor who becomes a politician, was about how people may give up what they do best and that could apply to Rodgers and Hammerstein themselves. Sinatra also recorded 'Can't You Just See Yourself' and 'You're My Girl' from *High Button Shoes*, a Broadway musical starring Phil Silvers and written by Sammy Cahn and Jule Styne.

Frank recorded a brilliant version of Johnny Mercer's 'Fools Rush In (where angels fear to tread)', although in this case the songwriter took the title from Alexander Pope's *Essay On Criticism*. Sinatra once explained his craft by drawing attention to this record, 'It's important to know the proper manner in which to breathe at given points in a song because otherwise what you're saying becomes choppy. The song says, "Fools rush in where wise men never go, But wise men never fall in love, So how are they to know?" That should be one phrase because it tells the story right there. But you'll hear somebody say, "Fools rush in" and breathe. You should do it all in one breath as that's the whole story.'

Some of Frank's sessions were low-key. He heard Alvy West and the Little Band in a club and he invited them to record 'It All Came True' with him, the closest he came to Klezmer. He had a session with a jazz trio, the songs including 'My Cousin Louella' which was a nod to the gossip columnist, Louella Parsons. Another song, 'We Just Couldn't Say Goodbye' is equally inconsequential but does have the line, 'The chair and the sofa, they broke right down and cried', which is a precursor to the silent chair in Neil Diamond's 'I Am... I Said'.

Other less noteworthy material included the quirky 'If I Only Had a Match' and 'I Went Down to Virginia', a curious ad for the state. Dave Mann, who later wrote 'In the Wee Small Hours of the Morning', said, 'Frank did record a lot of dogs and I wrote one of them, 'I Went Down to Virginia'.'

There is neat punning word play of 'Mean to Me' and 'Spring Is Here' and some classic standards, 'Autumn in New York', 'It Never Entered My Mind' and 'I've Got A Crush on You', which remained one of his favourites. 'I've Got a Crush on You' featured Bobby Hackett on trumpet, who also shines on 'Body and Soul'. It is the only song to contain the line, 'Pardon my mush' although the word 'mush' is, for obvious reasons, also in 'Lush Life'. Manie Sacks told Sinatra that they would have to record it quicker or they would have to edit it for a single.

Mitch Miller who was hired to play oboe, chipped in, 'We could fit the whole thing on a record over at Mercury.'

Sinatra exploded, 'You mean a big fucking outfit like Columbia can't do what a nickel record company like Mercury can do?'

Maybe this inspired Columbia to invent microgroove but the immediate outcome was that Manie Sacks told Mitch Miller that he wasn't welcome at Columbia anymore. As it happens, it was Manie Sacks who moved on.

It hadn't been what Manie had wanted to hear. Around the same time, Sinatra had asked him to set up a recording with session with Duke Ellington and Manie had turned it down as Ellington wasn't selling.

A highlight from December 1947 was an interracial duet with Pearl Bailey of the two-part 'A Little Learnin' Is a Dangerous Thing'. The witty song was written by Sy Oliver who devised an imaginative arrangement which gave both Pearl and Frank plenty of breathing space. At one stage, Pearl impersonated a trumpet and it was all great fun.

But the potential of one song was missed. The pianist Ken Lane, who worked on *Your Hit Parade*, had written a new ballad for Frank, 'Everybody Loves Somebody'. Frank recorded it but he was never keen on songs about universal love. Dean Martin liked the song and when Ken Lane was his pianist, they recorded it for Reprise in 1964. As it was a US No.1 and released on Frank's label, Reprise, I should think that, Frank, for once, was happy to be wrong. Ken played the harassed white haired pianist on the 60s TV series, *The Dean Martin Show*.

The reason why Frank Sinatra and many other performers had been recording frantically during the latter months of 1947 was because another union strike had been announced. It started on New Year's Day 1948 and the matters wouldn't be settled for 11 months.

The songwriter eden ahbez – no capitals please as he felt only the deity deserved them – was the first hippie. His real name was Alexander Aberle. He had a straggly beard and lived as a hermit under the Hollywood sign. His only possessions were a sleeping bag, some wooden flutes and a bicycle. He wrote the idyllic 'Nature Boy' and felt that Nat 'King' Cole could do it justice. Dressed in rags, ahbez turned up at the stage door, passed over his music and left without leaving an address. He returned a week later by which time Cole had put the song into his act. His record, cut before the strike with a brilliant use of strings arranged by Frank DeVol, soared to the top. Cole had been recording with small jazz combos and now he was doing a Sinatra. Frank Sinatra loved the song and often sang it on *Your Hit Parade*. Once again he couldn't record it with musicians but he cut a lovely acappella version with the 20-strong Jeff Alexander choir, which sold very well.

'Nature Boy' sounds full of eastern mysticism but the publishers of a Jewish music company sued for plagiarism. A cash settlement was reached as ahbez had plagiarized 'Hush, My Heart' by Herman Yablokoff as well as the second movement of Dvorak's Piano Quintet No. 2 from 1887.

The big film for the first holiday season in 1948 was, naturally enough, *Easter Parade*, an MGM musical starring Judy Garland, Fred Astaire and Peter Lawford and boasting a brilliant score from Irving Berlin. Berlin was paid a huge cash sum but when he complained in his usual way to another songwriter that it would be better to have the sum in installments, he was told, 'Good idea, Irving. Why not ask for $1 a year?' Both Frank and Perry Como had advance notice of the songs and they went head to head on 'It Only Happens When I Dance with You'. They had split sales and Frank sounded like Fred on this one.

Frank covered the song that Peter Lawford sang to Judy Garland, 'A Fella with an Umbrella', so Frank was singing the Peter Lawford Songbook. If I'd made that joke to Frank, I would have been punched. It's a delightful song – Frank is the fella with an umbrella looking for a girl who has saved her love for a rainy day, and he la-la's along delightfully in the instrumental passage.

Oh, that Frank had made a film like *Easter Parade*. He had two films released in 1948 and both, in their different ways, were disasters. *The Miracle of the Bells* was an adaptation of a best-selling book by Russell Janney. Copying Crosby as the good-natured priest in *Going My Way*, Frank played a cleric at a down-at-heel church that suddenly became nationally known. The heroine, Alida Valli, was in a coffin for the whole film but she was seen in flashback. Frank sang just one song, a Polish folk song with English lyrics, 'Ever Homeward'.

Okay, it's fiction, but how come the authorities allowed the bells from the five churches to ring continuously for three days and nights? Didn't anyone complain about it other than the mine owner? Fred MacMurray played the press agent who was spinning the story of the young actress who died, but even if he had worked on the film itself, he couldn't have saved it. Perhaps Frank was doing his own spinning by passing himself off as a better person through this fictional portrayal.

In an attempt to discipline him, Frank had been loaned by MGM to RKO to make *The Miracle of the Bells*, At first he was happy although he later called it hokum. According to the press release, Frank, a former altar boy (oh yeah?), was giving part of his $100,000 earnings to the Catholic church. In the Golden Turkey awards, Frank won one for the worst performance as a clergyman or nun. He wasn't that bad, but the film was.

Frank was so embarrassed that he didn't want to attend the première of *The Miracle of the Bells* in San Francisco. But because he was forced to go, by way of retaliation, he ran up an enormous hotel bill. He ordered 88 Manhattan cocktails and left them untouched on the waiter's trolley. But worse was to come – *The Kissing Bandit*.

Back with MGM and with a score from André Previn, *The Kissing Bandit* was bad in every respect, so it was hardly surprising that the director was replaced during the shoot. It was set in a Spanish colony with Frank in a Zorro-like role. The trailer said, 'Between hold-ups and pin-ups, he's a busy little bandit.' The poster had him playing a guitar and said it was 'The boldest story ever told in song, spectacle and Technicolor.'

Frank played Ricardo who, returning home after his father's death, found he was expected to take over his outlaw band.So he became an inn-keeper by day and a kissing bandit by night. Frank looked a geek in his embroidered costumes; everybody else was overacting like mad. Frank had his first fight on screen, this one with his love rival, Carleton Young, The four songs, one with Kathryn Grayson, were forgettable, with 'If I Steal a Kiss' being the best. The only scene that worked was Sono Osato with her ferocious dance with a bullwhip. Frank was looking scared, but that was probably in the script.

The Kissing Bandit was as bad as its title. Frank said, 'I hated reading the script, hated doing it, and most of all, hated seeing it. So did everyone else.' This means that you can't justify the film as a spoof or a parody. It had the thumbs-down from both critics and public alike and Orson Welles commented, 'It should be the new birth control method as you can't make love while you're asleep.' A saving grace is that *The Kissing Bandit* has amused children. They like seeing Frank falling off a horse and having other mishaps. Nancy Sinatra said she enjoyed it as a child and commented, 'I thought he was the handsomest man in the world.'

Moreover, it was bad timing to release such a poor effort when he was being challenged by a crop of new singers: Eddie Fisher, Frankie Laine, Johnnie Ray and Tony Martin. By January 1949, Sinatra had fallen to No.5 in the top male singers in the *Down Beat* poll. George Evans offered some sound advice: go home to Nancy, drop all the women, cut down on the booze and stay away from people with underground connections. As you might expect, all that was easier said than done.

Frank continued on *Your Hit Parade* singing such successes as 'Little White Lies' (Dick Haymes), 'Ballerina' (Vaughn Monroe), 'Haunted Heart' (Perry Como), 'Now Is the Hour'(Bing Crosby) 'It's Magic' (Sammy and Jule for Doris Day) and 'A Tree in the Meadow' (Margaret Whiting). Ella Fitzgerald joined him for a duet of her own hit record, 'My Happiness'. The problem came when he was asked to perform songs he loathed, notably 'Woody Woodpecker' from the cartoon film *Wet Blanket Policy*. It had been recorded by Mel Blanc, who incidentally was allergic to carrots despite being the voice of Bugs Bunny. When it first hit the charts, Frank left it to the vocal group, but when it made No.1, he was ordered to sing it so he did. He made his feelings known to *Metronome*: 'Outside of show tunes, you can't find a thing. The music business must give people things that move them emotionally.'

Frank made guest appearances with Jack Benny and Spike Jones and his City Slickers, and he starred in a radio adaptation of *The Miracle of the Bells*. There was a neat acknowledgment to his fame in the Orson Welles, film, *The Lady from Shanghai* where a crowd gathered round a jukebox to listen to Sinatra.

Some dangerous liaisons were giving his press agent, George Evans, food for thought. In March 1948 Sinatra met Teddy Kollek who was buying arms in America and smuggling them out of the country. Frank helped him make contacts and so became a benefactor for the Israeli cause. Frank later commented, 'It was the beginning of that young nation. I wanted to help. I was afraid that they might fall down.'

Much more damaging personally was his tempestuous relationship with the actress Ava Gardner. Sammy Cahn and Jimmy Van Heusen had an apartment in Sunset Towers, Hollywood, and Ava was a neighbour. Frank would stay up drinking with them and they would shout to Ava from their balcony. He asked her for a date and she knew that he was married. She said in her autobiography, 'He sure was attractive so what else could I do?' The date ended with some heavy petting and Ava feeling guilty, but not for long. Much to the consternation of George Evans, their dates became public property, especially when they drove around drunk, shooting out street lighting.

George Evans knew that Frank was playing with dynamite regarding Ava Gardner. She didn't care about her career and did just what she wanted – just like Frank, in fact. Anything could happen, and the inevitable did happen as Frank fell out with George Evans.

Frank even received a telegram from the gangster, Willie Moretti: 'I am very much surprised by what I have been reading in the newspapers between you and your darling wife. Remember you have a decent wife and children. You should be very happy. Regards to all.' When a Mafia boss is dispensing home truths, you are in trouble.

The mechanics of making long-playing records had now been resolved and *The Voice of Frank Sinatra* could be purchased as a single LP instead of four 78 rpm singles. His seasonal songs were collected for *Christmas Songs by Sinatra,* which reached No.7 on the *Billboard* album charts. The unbreakable (so they say) 45rpm had also been invented but the 78rpm was to continue for some years.

Back in December with the strike over, Frank could start recording again. The first song was 'Sunflower', written by Hal David's elder brother, Mack, and arranged by Alex Stordahl. It was a cheerful song about the sunflower girl from the sunflower state, that is, Kansas. Sinatra recorded it with a steel guitar and a small combo and so the result was close to country. It was quickly forgotten until, in 1964, someone spotted its similarity to Jerry Herman's 'Hello Dolly!' Jerry Herman wrote in his autobiography, 'Well, this was some hillbilly tune and of course I had never heard it in my life.' I don't believe that: it had been a major hit for several artists including Sinatra. Because the film musical might not have been made with such a cloud hanging over it, the matter was settled out of court for $200,000.

In 1948 the songwriter Frank Loesser had the concept of recasting the British farce, *Charley's Aunt,* as a Broadway musical, which he called *Where's Charley?* It was Loesser's first musical; his second, two years later, was *Guys and Dolls.* The delightful love song, 'Once in Love with Amy', captures love within the quadrangles of Oxford University. Sinatra's initial piano rehearsal with Henry Rowland as well as the full orchestration was recorded, which enables you to hear how Sinatra worked. The lyric itself was rather self-satisfied, but when you hear the orchestration, you realise that the lyric was being treated humorously.

Frank recorded two songs with the Phil Moore Four, going for a similar sound to the Nat 'King' Cole Trio but with added clarinet. 'Why Can't You Behave' is a little-known song from Cole Porter's *Kiss Me Kate* with Frank going 'Baby I'm all confused' at the end. 'Bop! Goes My Heart' has some forced hipness about it, and Frank adds, 'I ain't the square I used to be".' Giving a taste of things to come, Frank sings,

'Lips as sweet as muscatel
Make me jingle like a bell.
Ding a ling, zang zoom, a dizzy spell
Bop! goes my heart.'

Early in 1949 he recorded two more songs with the quartet. One was 'Kisses and Tears' from his forthcoming film, *Double Dynamite* and the other was a neat, don't give up song from Jimmy Van Heusen and Johnny Burke, 'If You Stub Your Toe on the Moon'. It described how an inventor could become an ace repairman.

Frank didn't write 'Comme Ci Comme Ça' but no doubt he identified with the lyric,

'It seems my friends have been complaining
That I have been acting rude.
But I have never liked explaining
Which may explain my attitude.'

Frank rounded off the year with another wedding song, but what a classic. In 1944, Edith Piaf heard Jean Villard sing his uplifting story of 'Les Trois Cloches'. She loved the song and decided to record it acappella with Les Compagnons de la Chanson, which constituted three tenors, three baritones and three basses. The way their voices chimed behind Piaf's lead vocal was delightful and the record was very successful. The song became an English language hit with two different lyrics – 'When the Angelus Was Ringing' (Frank Sinatra, Anne Shelton) and 'The Three Bells' (The Browns, Brian Poole and The Tremeloes and, with heavily accented voices, Les Compagnons themselves.) Frank's version is sung in English with no mention of Jimmy Brown.

After falling into the crater of *The Kissing Bandit*, Frank was given a decent MGM musical, *Take Me Out to the Ball Game*, a baseball story developed by Gene Kelly. Considering it was Gene's story and he had the main role, scored the winning hit and got the girl, it was anomalous that Frank got top billing. Instead, Frank won his admirer, played by Betty Garrett who picked him up – physically! Frank was called a 'skinny little runt' in the script, which is an odd way to treat your star performer.

This story, full of Irish-American bonhomie, was set in 1910 when the Wolves had a new owner, a woman. At the time (1948), female managers in sport were a rarity and so a modern day audience will pick up on the fact that K C Higgins will be a woman long before the cast does. Frank and Gene were the star players, but they were also vaudeville performers and the oddity of this was never remarked upon. Their clowning pre-match antics were inspired by real-life players, Nick Altrock and Al Schacht.

The film was going to star Judy Garland but she was unfit and unreliable. An alternative, June Allyson, turned down the role as she was pregnant. Esther Williams was brought in, an actress known for swimming sequences directed by Busby Berkeley. As Berkeley was working on this film (his final assignment), a swimming scene was added. Both Gene Kelly and the director Stanley Donen had doubts about Esther Williams but she was fine. Frank matched Gene Kelly when they were together but in one sequence notice how high Gene can jump compared to Frank.

There were no classic songs but they worked in context. The title song showed that Sinatra and Kelly could have been a vaudeville duo for real and there was the Irish blarney of 'The Hat My Dear Old Father Wore Upon St Patrick's Day', a typical Gene Kelly dance tour de force in 'Where Did You Get that Hat', and the witty 'O'Brien to Ryan to Goldberg' (with Jules Munshin). Some songs had to be dropped as the film was too long. In the final song, they referred to themselves by their real names and even threw in a reference to Astaire – post-modernism in 1948. It is a Fellini touch and something that Sinatra repeated in *Ocean's 11*.

The film cost MGM $2m and grossed $4m. It could have grossed more but baseball films meant nothing outside the US. Indeed, for the UK it was rebranded as *Everybody's Cheering*. Very few baseball movies have had success outside the US but the short list includes the musical *Damn Yankees* (1958), Robert Redford's *The Natural* (1984) and Kevin Costner's *Field of Dreams* (1989).

Frank made a second film in 1948 but it was so mediocre that it didn't escape until

1951. On paper, it must have looked fine – Jane Russell, Frank Sinatra and Groucho Marx – but the film had no idea what it wanted to be. The well-endowed Jane Russell was the *Double Dynamite* of the title and yet her famous figure was hidden in a dark dress for much of the film, so what was the point of that? There were not enough songs to make it a musical, which makes it jarring when they appear: 'Kisses and Tears' which Frank and Jane sang in bed from their different apartments, and 'It's Only Money' which Frank and Groucho performed on a treadmill. However, the director got the perspective wrong and they looked too tall compared to the citizens walking past. Still, there was true wit in Sammy Cahn's lyric and the scene in which Groucho wanted to deposit money with the bank was worthy of any Marx Brothers film.

Frank played a timid bank teller earning $42 a week who wanted to marry another clerk, Jane Russell. By chance, he helped someone who was being mugged. That someone was the racketeer, Hot Horse Henry, who gave him $1,000 which with appropriate bets becomes $60,000. Meanwhile there had been money embezzled at the bank and Frank dared not reveal his winnings as he might be accused. It transpired that Jane had a faulty adding machine and so no one was guilty.

Frank and Groucho were at loggerheads for much of the film. When Frank turned up late, Groucho turned up later and so on until they called a truce, but the film was not as bad as some critics have suggested. The producer Howard Hughes shelved the film for three years, partly because he had come to loathe Sinatra. Then he released it to create confusion with his then current film, *Meet Danny Wilson*.

Although the recording ban had been lifted, Frank was too busy making his next film *On the Town* and performing on radio shows to record much in the early months of 1949. However, the score of Rodgers and Hammerstein's new musical, *South Pacific*, appealed to him and he wanted to have a crack at 'Some Enchanted Evening', which became a big hit for Perry Como and 'Bali Ha'i', which he recorded Hawaiian-style with steel guitars. *Down Beat* was highly critical of this track but it sounded fine and Frank was to be commended for trying something different.

He recorded two songs from another new show, *Miss Liberty*, the latest from Irving Berlin. He sang 'Let's Talk an Old Fashioned Walk' with Doris Day and the way they swap lines is very engaging, even if improbable. In reality, Doris would be walking her dogs and Frank would be dipping into the nearest bar. There was some banter before they sang and just listen to the way Frank rolls his r's on the word 'romantic'. 'Just One Way to Say I Love You' sounds like a song Irving Berlin wrote in his sleep and probably did.

A most intriguing session took place on 10 April 1949 when Frank recorded with the Ken Lane Quintet and was produced by George Siravo. Andy Gibson, who had been Harry James' arranger in 1939, had taken a riff from Charlie Parker's 'Now's the Time' and had written a song around it, a dance tune 'The Hucklebuck'. Sinatra started his vocal with 'Not now, Moose, I'll tell you when' and went into a song that was ascloseasthis to 'The Twist', so you could argue that this is a contender for the first rock'n'roll record, a claim that Sinatra would hate. The song became a Top 10 success for Sinatra and at the same session he recorded the odd 'It Happens Every Spring':

'Your dad rolls up his sleeves to clean the attic,
Your sixteen year old sister goes dramatic.'

It's hard to tell whether this was a romantic song or a comic one and *Melody Maker*, reviewing it for spring of 1950, said, 'Sinatra makes the worst of it. He intones what surely must be his most indifferent vocal to date. Frankie frankly sounds as though the whole business was a bore.' A sad postscript to this session is that the big band saxophonist Herbie

Haymer was hit by a car while crossing the street on his way home and was killed. Meanwhile Frank's second cousin, Ray Sinatra, was conducting for Mario Lanza and recording his classic, 'O Sole Mio'.

On 28 May 1949 Frank said goodbye to *Your Hit Parade* for good. He sang both 'Some Enchanted Evening' and 'Bali Ha'i' as well as two huge hits, Doris Day's 'Again' and Vaughn Monroe's '(Ghost) Riders in the Sky'. Frank got into the spirit of the song and had fun with the yippee-i-ay.

Possibly an indication that his fans were ageing is that he participated in the Arthritis And Rheumatism Foundation broadcast and sang 'A Dream Came True ' and 'Anything You Can Do', both with Bob Hope, as well as 'On a Slow Boat to China'.

Frustrated by *The Miracle of the Bells* and *The Kissing Bandit*, Frank wanted a film that he could believe in. He had read Willard Motley's novel, *Knock on Any Door*, and he lobbied to play opposite Humphrey Bogart in the courtroom drama. Bogie would be the attorney while Frank would play the kid from the slums who had killed a policeman in frustration. It was felt that Frank was too old and the role went to John Derek, who was 10 years younger. Derek's impressive tally of wives included Ursula Andress, Linda Evans and Bo Derek.

Not to worry as MGM had something very attractive on hand. Leonard Bernstein's musical, *On The Town*, had been very successful and he was being touted as the successor to George Gershwin. The plan was to film it by teaming Frank and Gene Kelly for the third time. They would be joined by Betty Garrett and Jules Munshin from *Take Me Out to the Ball Game*. The film was about three sailors on 24-hour shore leave in New York and it is very enjoyable if you overlook the daft and improbable plot. In a sense, it's a remake of *Anchors Aweigh* with New York for Hollywood. Betty Garrett's career, along with that of her husband Larry Parks, who played Al Jolson in *The Jolson Story*, came to an abrupt end during the Communist witch hunt. She later performed a one woman show about her career, *Betty Garrett and Other Songs*.

The Broadway musical opened with the three sailors singing 'New York, New York, it's a helluva town' but the film dilutes this to 'New York, New York, it's a wonderful town'. Indeed, can you imagine three sailors going through a series of stressed-out events and not even swearing once? I told you it was improbable.

Although many servicemen had travelled with the forces, the vast majority of the public were not used to the sights of the world which is why so many films right up to the 1960s had a travelogue aspect. However, this magic carpet ride was unusual as few large production numbers had been shot on location before. There are scenes at the Empire State Building (where health and safety precautions seem non-existent), the Statue of Liberty, Radio City Music Hall, Fifth Avenue and Coney Island fairground (where Frank was seen in drag). It was all in glorious Technicolor. This high definition was unflattering to Sinatra himself as it reveals the lines on his face and he was made to wear backside padding to avoid looking too thin. Nevertheless, his snack of choice was a Mars bar.

There were strong dance sequences featuring Gene Kelly but the score was radically changed with Sinatra being sore that 'Lonely Town' had been dropped. Sinatra sang 'You're Awful' to a girl he loved but the wittiest moment was the line, 'As the adding machine once said, 'You can count on me'.' There were delightful in-jokes. The collapse of the dinosaur at the museum prompted a reference to Dinah Shore, and Jules Munshin says to Sinatra, 'Who you got waiting for you in New York? Ava Gardner?' Sinatra smiled wryly.

When someone in the canteen told Frank that Mayer had been injured by falling off a horse, he joked, "Naw, he fell off Ginny Simms", referring to the actress who was Mayer's girlfriend. (They were all at it.) This was repeated to Mayer, who was furious and told Sinatra that there would be no more MGM films for him. Mayer didn't have this trouble with Lassie. Frank's final job with MGM was recording a Cole Porter song, 'Farewell Amanda' for the Spencer Tracy film, *Adam's Rib*. Only a few seconds were heard in the film and the master tape has been lost.

Frank Sinatra was on good terms with the head of Columbia Pictures, Harry Cohn, though this would change. Cohn had made a comedy, *Miss Grant Takes Richmond*, with Lucille Ball and William Holden, which looked like a flop. He saw that Frank had been booked for the Capitol Theatre in New York for four weeks and the engagement would sell out irrespective of the film being screened. Sinatra thought the film was okay and persuaded the management to screen it during his engagement. Frank did good business so the film did well, but Frank got a throat infection in the third week and had to withdraw. He stayed at Manny Sacks' apartment and Cohn flew to New York to see him. Cohn told him jokes and kept his spirit up but added on the way out, 'You tell anybody about this and I'll kill you.'

In June 1949 Frank recorded a pilot for yet another radio series, *Lite-Up Time*, sponsored by Lucky Strike cigarettes. He was to be featured in the show with the New York Metropolitan opera star, Dorothy Kirsten and sometimes, his previous singing partner Jane Powell (whom he called Little Miss High Notes), Mindy Carson and Margaret Whiting. Sinatra enjoyed working with Kirsten and he would note how she maintained her voice, though he still smoked the sponsor's cigarettes. She was game for anything singing duets of 'The Hucklebuck' and the folk song 'Hey Lolly Lolly' with Frank as well as the more predictable 'Some Enchanted Evening' (which worked well for two voices) and 'If I Loved You'.

There would be five 15-minute shows a week at 7pm but they were taped in batches and produced in Hollywood with Jeff Alexander usually conducting, but sometimes Ziggy Elman and Skitch Henderson. Alexander was to work on *The Tender Trap* and *Jailhouse Rock*.

Lite-Up Time was to run from September 1949 to June 1950, and each programme consisted of two solos by Sinatra, one by Kirsten and one duet. Sometimes there would be a medley and the theme music was 'Night And Day' and 'Put Your Dreams Away'. Always there would be two minutes of commercials for Lucky Strike, so it was hardly surprising that he was crowned the Tobacco Festival King in Richmond, Virginia in November 1949 when he sang to 6,000 fans from the flat roof of a department store. (Who says the Beatles were first?) As Frank received $10,000 a week from Lucky Strike, he must have sold a lot of cigarettes. Because he was given free product, Frank was always handing out packs to his friends. Contrast with his friend, Milton Berne, who was sponsored by Texaco and could only hand out bubble gum with their name on it.

Sinatra's solos include 'Envy' (Fran Warren), 'You're Breaking My Heart' (a No.1 for Vic Damone), 'There's a Yes Yes in Your Eyes', 'Nothing Less Than Beautiful', 'Them There Eyes' and 'Meadows of Heaven'. Even though millions were listening, it's very much one take Sinatra. When he sang 'You're The Cream in My Coffee', he ad-libbed that he has just repeated a line, and on the same show, he missed a note on 'A Man Wrote a Song' and started again. He was singing well but standards were slipping.

This looseness can be contrasted with his record sessions for Columbia. Quite by chance, Sinatra's comments to the orchestra for 'It All Depends on You' were recorded and have been preserved. He was very precise about how he wanted it to sound and he says, 'Trombones – you may have to face the microphone. I'd like to hear all six of you as a unit. Guitarist – move in a shade closer, that's enough.' It was a good version too as Sinatra assumed that the audience knew the Al Jolson hit well, enabling him to play around with the lyric.

Frank Sinatra was impressed by a new Haven Gillespie song, 'That Lucky Old Sun', which he saw as another 'Ol' Man River'. Everybody wanted to record it but Vaughn Monroe had obtained a six-week exclusive which meant that his version came out first. It did well, but then Frankie Laine topped the charts and there were decent sales for Sinatra, Sarah Vaughan and Louis Armstrong. The song found unexpected popularity in Russia where it was promoted as an anti-capitalist anthem. Another Haven Gillespie song is 'The Old Master Painter' is full of colour and wit but at 1 minute 55 seconds in, doesn't Frank sing 'the old masturbator'? Had he got away with it – until now!

Frank recorded an answer version to 'Lili Marlene', 'The Wedding of Lili Marlene', which was very sentimental but that was the point. 'Sunshine Cake' was a nonsense song about a confectionary packed with vitamins L, O, V, E. Frank sang 'Sorry' with Glenn Miller's former vocal group, the Modernaires, who had previously backed Doris Day on 'Thoughtless', a far better recording. When Frankie recorded 'Don't Cry Joe' with the Pastals vocal group and Sy Oliver arrangement, he said, "This is a great song and should be a big hit." It was a Top 20 single.

Frank sang partly in Italian for '(On the Island of) Stromboli', the theme from an Ingrid Bergman film, written by Ken Lane. The dramatic film was matched by the drama off screen as the Swedish actress was having an affair with the director Roberto Rossellini and the press reported that she was pregnant. She left her doctor husband, had the baby and married Rossellini, resulting in a fierce backlash from the American press which harmed her career for many years. The bad publicity should have made Sinatra cautious about his own life.

Frank had moved with Nancy and their children to 320 North Carolwood Drive in Holmby Hills, Los Angeles, a large, sprawling property behind a high wall, but they had a bad start with the basement flooding when the water heaters burst. Frank established a library and he loved collecting books signed by their authors. But was it that idyllic? Nancy told the songwriter Jimmy McHugh, 'I'd give anything to be back on the road again with Harry James and making onion sandwiches.'

Their third child, Christina (Tina), was born on 20 June 1948 and named after Nancy's sister. It was Father's Day but Frank was not playing father that day. He was a party playing charades. He got called away for the birth and when he returned, he drew an hourglass figure in the air and held up his fingers for the weight.

The Sinatras settled in well, being friendly with Barbara Stanwyck and Robert Ryan and their families. As Bing was often arguing with his kids, they could go round to the Sinatras. Walt Disney lived across the street and had a model railway around the perimeter of his property. On Saturdays at 1pm, he would give rides to the local children which presaged the start of his magic kingdom.

Walt Disney's animated features can be regarded as mini-musicals and he used many great singers and songwriters. Surprisingly, he never employed his neighbour, Frank Sinatra, although Peggy Lee was to have enormous success by both writing and singing the material for *Lady and The Tramp*. Maybe Frank was a little bit too raunchy for that Disney image. In 2007 Jamie Callum mimicked Frank with *Where Is Your Heart At*, written by Rufus Wainwright for the animated feature, *Meet the Robinsons*.

A young Gianni Russo recalls his first meeting with Sinatra. 'Being an Italian-American from Hoboken, I related to him and saw what he had done with his life. He was like my mentor although I hadn't met him. My stepfather Frank Costello told me to go the Sands Hotel when I was 18, not even realising it was December 12 and that Frank and I shared the same birthday. I was sitting ringside in the Copa Room at the Sands. There are 400 people in the room and every major star was there to celebrate his birthday. After the third or fourth song, he looked down at me. He said, "Kid, I don't know who you are but I know whose table that is."'

Newsweek reported in September 1949 that Frank Sinatra was in 'staggering financial debt'. Possibly his new mortgage had a lot to do with that but he was earning $10,000 a week from his radio show and his records were selling steadily if not spectacularly. However, the loyal fan base was falling apart: the scandal sheets were writing about his affairs and he seemed disloyal and untrustworthy. To add to his problems, the Revenue was claiming a large amount in back taxes.

In December 1949 the MGM musical *On the Town* opened and did well though it was more Gene Kelly's film than Frank's. To boost his earnings and after a gap of two years, Frank went on a movie theatre tour.

1949 had been a bad year for Columbia Records. Frank Sinatra was not selling as well as before, Buddy Clark had been killed in plane crash, and Dinah Shore had moved to Victor. Manie Sacks would soon be poached by Victor, and Mitch Miller was recruited to turn Columbia around. Previously, record producers had accurately reproduced what the musicians were playing but Miller saw the potential for adding echo, multi-tracking and overdubbing. At Mercury Records he had made the atmospheric and bombastic 'Mule Train' with Frankie Laine and this sold a million within a month. With his cigar and goatee beard, he could have played the Devil, but Columbia loved him.

Columbia had given Frank a large advance to pay his back taxes. They had to recoup the money and more and they thought Mitch Miller was the man to do it.

Frank didn't agree.

CHAPTER 7

I'm a fool to want you

*'I feel sorry for people who don't drink. When they wake up,
that's as good as they're going to feel all day.'*

Frank Sinatra

I. Rat Packers

When it comes to the Rat Pack, everyone knows that Frank Sinatra was the Chairman of the Board, the A No.1, King of the Hill, Top of the Heap. Most people know that Dean Martin and Sammy Davis were in the Rat Pack and some more would add Peter Lawford, but after that, where do you go? You have to be a real Sinatra nut to add Joey Bishop; however, I'm not sure if there was anyone else. The term, Rat Pack, was given to a loose collection of drinking buddies and Sinatra himself never publicly acknowledged its existence and he hated the name. Certainly Shirley MacLaine, Jimmy Van Heusen, Jilly Rizzo and Mort Viner would associate with them, but did that make them Rats?

For the purposes of this book, the Rat Pack will refer to the five performers who took the stage for a short season at the Sands in Las Vegas in 1961: Frank Sinatra, Dean Martin, Sammy Davis Jr, Peter Lawford and Joey Bishop. At the time Sinatra regarded Vegas as his personal fiefdom and the very phrase, the Rat Pack, is synonymous with Vegas.

There are scores of books and hundreds of articles about Sinatra but precious few about Dean Martin: Nick Tosches' 1992 biography and a memoir from a daughter, and that's about it. There is good reason for this: Dean's image is appalling. He is seen as a night club entertainer with a drink in one hand, a cigarette in the other, making off-colour remarks about cocktail waitresses. What talent he had is assumed to have come naturally and as he is seen to lack artistic integrity, so what is there to write about? If you were asked to name a show-business personality who personified wine, women and song, most people would pick Dean Martin.

Some associates maintained that he was permanently sozzled, others that the glasses contained apple juice. It may have been apple juice, but wouldn't it be boring if it was? Don't we all buy into the image of Dean as the tipsy crooner, and didn't he encourage that dissipated image for all it was worth? His car number plate was DRUNKY and in the 1964 film, *Kiss Me Stupid*, he played an inebriated, womanising singer named Dino.

'No one really knew how drunk Dean was on stage,' says the British manager, Tony Cartwright, who worked in Vegas for many years, 'but whenever I saw him, he was always right on cue, so he knew exactly what he was doing. In reality, he was a very serious bloke, and everything had to be just right. When Sinatra was drunk, I've seen Dean take over and be the boss.'

'He was both a stage drunk and a real drunk,' said the singer Malcolm Roberts, 'When he was a stage drunk, he was controlled and he knew exactly what he was doing, a real pro.

96

He did the same show, year in, year out. I was in Vegas once and two ladies said, 'He'll knock the water over now', and sure enough, he did. He was lovely off stage and very philosophical when he wanted to be.'

Dean had his Vegas routine: he would do his drunk act, chat to his fans, do his drunk act again, go to bed, get up and play golf. Sammy Cahn said, 'That drinking is a crutch. Dean was not a heavy drinker, but he would come on stage and he would down a glass of apple juice and the audience would go, 'Look what he's doing.' It was to give the impression that he was loose and free.'

Tommy Sands agrees, 'Dean was always in control of himself but he also was a bit of a drinker. He just got funnier and funnier when he drank and everybody liked him, I can't think of one person who didn't like Dean.' The California Highway Patrol once stopped him when he had been drinking. 'We'd like you to walk in a straight line,' said the cop. 'Not without a net,' said Dean.

It is intriguing to have these contradictory views on his drinking. Dean had very adroitly created a mystery around himself – was he a lush or was it all an act? Well, you have to be reasonably sober to pull that off, and by doing this, he created a ceaseless talking point.

Dean Martin's life is the American dream come true as he came up the hard way. Dean Paul Crocetti was born on 7 June 1917, the son of a barber in Steubenville, Ohio. Ironically, it was a premature delivery as, in later life, he rarely did anything until it was absolutely necessary. Dean's background has much in common with Frank Sinatra's, which helps to explain their friendship. Both were from families of Italian immigrants, both lived in working-class-towns, both were poorly educated, both were singers who idolised Bing Crosby, both adored their mothers, and both were fascinated by gangsters. Indeed, Steubenville was known as 'Little Chicago'. In order to improve its image, a Dean Martin Day was created in Steubenville on 6 October 1950, and Dean remarked, 'I love getting the keys to the city. When I lived here, my folks wouldn't give me the key to the house.'

The barber shop did well but Dean's parents were not like most Italians of the period. They did not flare up, and they maintained a chilly indifference about what they were doing and, indeed, towards their children. Dean didn't grow up unloved but he was lonely and unhappy as a child and wanted to drop out of school as soon as he could. This reserve stayed with him for the rest of his life. Apart from golf clubs, it was never important for him to join anything; he had an air of self-sufficiency about him. This had catastrophic effects on his personal life as he always did what he wanted and hated confrontation.

Dean's family insisted that English should be the main language, although Dean could get by in Italian. Dean dropped out of school when he was 13 and the only book he'd finished was *Black Beauty*; he never read another, much preferring *Superman* comics. He became proficient at playing pool and shooting craps, which held him in much better stead in later life. At one stage he was making $150 a week as a croupier in an illegal gambling hall. From time to time he took regular employment, even working in a steel mill, but usually he was peddling bootleg whiskey or trying to be a prize-fighter. He got a broken nose in one fight; later, he felt it was holding back his success. Maybe it was, because as soon as he had had his nose reshaped, courtesy of the Mafia, he became famous. So the Mob fixed noses as well as breaking them.

Dean broke some fingers, possibly while boxing, so his hands curved inwards. He had huge hands so he could easily palm cards when he was a dealer and also perform card tricks. Tony Cartwright continues, 'Dean Martin was as handsome as Elvis Presley, but his fingers were like sausages. They were the biggest fingers I've ever seen and he put make-up on them to try and make them look smaller. Someone told me that he got those hands after a crooked card game in Cleveland. Somebody had taken a baseball bat to them. Years later I asked his manager Mort Viner if this story was true. He said, "Tony, if you believe the story is true, then it is true."'

In 1941 Dean had a relationship with a snake charmer, Zorita, and then met an Irish girl, 18-year-old Betty McDonald, whom he soon married. They had a son, Craig, in June 1942, but Dean was determined to live his life as though he were single, and if another Zorita came along, so be it.

Dean was to record a song called 'If I Could Sing Like Bing' and that was his aim in the early years. He cultivated the same easy-going delivery. He was at his best if he was relaxed, so he never tried too hard. He worked with one band, then another, eventually having bookings in New York and Chicago. He said, 'I don't remember why I changed my name. I guess there were enough Italian singers around and most of them sang opera. I wanted to do my own thing.'

Although Dean had seen Frank singing at the prestigious Riobamba in Manhattan and enjoyed his performance, he wasn't sure if he wanted to make his own living this way. When Sinatra had to cancel an engagement at the Riobamba in September 1944, Dean took his place. Dean commented, 'I got by. Nobody threw tomatoes at me.' Least of all, Frank's nemesis, the journalist Lee Mortimer, who commented favourably on his act.

Richard Havers, a Sinatra biographer, says, 'Part of Frank's great gift was getting inside the lyrics of a song and presenting it in a way that was totally unique. Dean on the other hand sings it like we would all would sing it, so you can sing along to Dean Martin. It is very hard to sing along with Frank as he put his unique timing into the songs which makes it almost impossible. Dean was really a very, very good pub singer!'

Dean cited a little-known album he loved, *Phil Brito Sings Songs of Italy* (1946) and, in that same year, he would go to a friendly record store for several days on end and ask an assistant to play, *The Voice of Frank Sinatra*. He was entranced by Frank's singing (though he didn't buy his records!) even though he knew he couldn't reach that level of interpretation himself. According to Sammy Cahn, Dean was doing Bing Crosby when he sang and Cary Grant when he acted. According to Paul Anka, another key influence was Donald Mills of the Mills Brothers.

Dean's maxim was simply, 'Show up and get paid.' When he started, Dean gave a percentage of himself to different agents and just like *The Producers*, he gave away more than 100% of himself. Dean didn't care as he wasn't going to pay them anyway. Sooner or later he was going to get a nasty shock and calling someone 'pallie' wasn't going to save him.

Then Dean Martin met Jerry Lewis.

Jerry Lewis was born Jerome Levitch into a Russian immigrant family on 16 March 1926 and he started performing in between his father's shows at the Empire, Newark, New Jersey. His father sang Al Jolson's hits and Jerry started by comically miming to records. He developed this into his own adult act, where he would act out records like 'Indian Love Call' and it was described, somewhat pretentiously, as 'satirical impressions in pantomimicry'. In 1966 Jerry Lewis revived this feeble act for, of all things, his starring role in the Royal Variety Performance. When viewers discussed the show at work the following day, everybody said how wretched he had been, one of the biggest mistakes by a comedian in the whole history of television as nobody found his pantomimicry funny.

In 1945 both Jerry and Dean were working the club as single acts and they were introduced to each other by the singer, Sonny King. Jerry, a frenetic, anxious, desperate personality loved Dean's coolness and saw how easily he attracted women. To emphasise their closeness, Jerry would refer to Dean by his second name, Paul. Neither of them had done war service, both being classed 4-F: Jerry for a heart murmur and Dean, first by being married with a son and then for a double hernia. (There seems to be a trend here: John Wayne also avoided military service and his widow said that his guilt over this led to his patriotism in the 60s.)

In March 1946, for a bit of fun, Jerry interrupted Dean's act by playing an insane waiter at the Havana-Madrid on Broadway. The audience loved it and in July 1946, the owner of the 500 Club in Atlantic City, Pasquale (Skinny) D'Amato had the idea of billing Martin and Lewis together. Skinny, a smart-looking dude, had done time for transporting prostitutes across state borders and he became a close friend of the Rat Pack.

The showroom only held 250 customers so they thought they would give it a go: if it didn't work, hardly anyone would know. The whole act was based around Jerry as the clown and Dean as the Latin crooner, but it was evident that Dean, in his own way, could be as funny as Jerry. It worked superbly and by a stroke of luck, Sophie Tucker was in the audience, who raved to the press about them. Soon, the crowds were lining up to see the duo.

Dean decided to emphasise the difference between them. Using his barbering skills (or maybe the lack of them), he gave Jerry that famous crew-cut. It provided Jerry with a simian look and kitted out with additional buckteeth, he became Dean's wacky sidekick, Seymour. By April 1948, they could command $2,500 as a double act at the Copa, sharing the bill Vivian Blaine (Miss Adelaide from the Broadway production of *Guys and Dolls*) and several scantily-clad showgirls. The club was owned by the crime boss, Frank Costello, with a front man, Jules Podell, hardly the face of respectability given his prison record and history of bootlegging. Like a real life Seymour, Jerry was intimidated by these thugs, but Dean took them in his stride.

Dean's first record was 'Which Way Did My Heart Go' for the Diamond label in 1947 and it was followed by records for Apollo and Embassy. In 1948 he signed to Capitol and the first record was with Jerry, namely 'That Certain Party'. Although Jerry had a separate contract with Capitol, they only recorded four titles together and Dean's duet of 'Open Up the Doghouse' with Nat 'King' Cole was more humorous than any of them. While he was with Capitol, Dean had several duet partners including Peggy Lee (the frolicsome 'You Was'), Line Renaud (the sensual 'Two Sleepy People'), Helen O'Connell and Margaret Whiting.

In December 1948 Dean cut 'Powder Your Face with Sunshine' with the Paul Weston Orchestra and it became his first hit single. Like many singers of the day, he cut cover versions of popular songs for his label ('Be Honest with Me', 'Who's Sorry Now', 'If'), but, from the start, he enjoyed Latin songs and the opportunity to sing part of the lyric in Italian.

Dean Martin and Jerry Lewis – note how you always say Dean's name first and how that must have rankled with Jerry – signed up with the producer Hal Wallis to make films for Paramount. The first two, based on a radio series, were *My Friend Irma* (1949) and *My Friend Irma Goes West* (1950). Their 1952 film, *Sailor Beware*, cost $750,000 and grossed $27m. Dean had hated making the film as he felt claustrophobic inside a submarine. Like Sinatra, he didn't even like riding in lifts. The one thing Dean would never do was play a policeman as he regarded them as 'low life'.

When rehearsing for the first film, Jerry realised that the role wasn't right for him and the script was changed so that he could effectively be Seymour. They got the girls though. Both were married, but Dean was dating June Allyson and Jerry Gloria De Haven, and despite the possibility of unfavourable press and trouble at home, they would go on foursomes.

Born in 1899, Hal Wallis was the publicist for *The Jazz Singer* in 1927 and had been in the film industry ever since. He was a stocky, well dressed man with little humour. It took Hal Wallis some time to appreciate Jerry Lewis's style and he once sacked him for ineptitude without realising that the silliness and the little-boy voice were part of the act. Their films were more manic than the *Road* films but Bing and Bob had created the template. When Bing and Bob were making *The Road to Bali* (1953) with Dorothy Lamour, she said to them, 'You'd better watch them as they're funnier and younger than you.' Hope retorted, 'Be careful how you talk to us. We could always replace you with an actress.' To give Hope his due, he had his funniest moment ever when he shared a bed with Trigger in the film, *Son of Paleface* (1952).

Everybody wanted Dean Martin and Jerry Lewis and they became one of the most successful show-business partnerships. In their eight years together, they made 16 feature films and appeared on numerous TV shows. There was conflict in their stage shows as Jerry Lewis wanted to dominate the act and usually did. At one stage he added his father to do Al Jolson impersonations! The bitterness between them sharpened their humour, and one night Dean put his foot down so hard on Jerry's toes that he broke two of them.

You can sense the tension between them in the outtakes at the end of the CD in the series, *The Golden Age of Comedy*. Dean and Jerry are reading from a script for *The Colgate Comedy Hour* and Dean fluffs his line. He thinks Jerry has made the mistake, and you hear recriminations going back and forth. Although they are playing to the audience, you can sense that this is for real. In another outtake, Dean and Jerry are reading commercials for their 1953 film, *The Caddy*. Their language makes them sound like today's alternative comedians.

In June 1953 they sailed to the UK on the Queen Elizabeth to appear at the London Palladium. The music journalist Fred Dellar notes, 'I saw Martin & Lewis at the Palladium and while Jerry struggled to put his humour across, Dean emerged as one of the smoothest and most assured singers to play the London theatre at that time.' The press reports were mixed and they did receive some hostile reviews. Back in America, Dean said on stage that he was never going back to England. He was acting ridiculously as he was only drawing attention to the bad reviews.

Martin and Lewis were contrasting personalities both on- and off-stage . As well as coming from different cultures, Dean Martin was the smooth-talking lover: everything came to him so easily – and if it didn't, so what? Jerry Lewis was a perfectionist and a workaholic, always tightening scripts to improve their comic impact.

The guitarist Ron Anthony says, 'I played with Dean in Vegas a couple of times and he was good. He would sing a lot of country songs but he was more of a personality and entertainer. I never thought of him as a great singer but he was a nice stylist much in the tradition of Bing Crosby. Dean was such a good looking guy that the women were crazy about him. He was taller than Frank and about two years younger than him. They liked each other an awful lot and Frank had a lot of respect for Dean's comedic abilities. His timing as a comedian was perfect. Frank loved him and he copied a lot of his comedy lines. Dean loved Frank's singing so they definitely had a mutual admiration thing. Dean was a wonderful straight man for Jerry Lewis but then he could come up with something off the top of his head. I'm not sure that Jerry liked that but Frank would fall over laughing when Dean did that to him.'

Certainly there was no love lost between Jerry Lewis and Bing Crosby. Martin and Lewis were the new kids on the block when they appeared with Hope and Crosby on a telethon in 1952. When introduced, Jerry Lewis leapt onto Bing Crosby, which spooked him so much that Hope had to joke about it to get the show back on course. Jerry should have apologised but he didn't and Crosby and Lewis didn't speak for several years. As the Jerry Lewis character, played by Kevin Bacon in *Where the Truth Lies* says, 'Having to be a nice guy is the toughest job in the world when you're not.'

In 1953 Dean Martin and Jerry Lewis made a film called *The Caddy*, which includes a famous scene of Jerry roller-skating through a china shop. Jerry had told the songwriter Harry Warren that in order to retain the balance, he must write a big hit song for Dean in the film. He and a Liverpool-born composer, Jack Brooks, wrote an Italian novelty, 'That's Amore'. Dean thought the song was an insult – he hated the cod-Italian of 'When the moon hits your eye like a big pizza pie, That's amore.' The lyric had been written by a Russian Scouser who had moved to Hollywood, and as Jack Brooks was sensitive about his own background, the last thing he would have done was insult Dino. Indeed, it's a great line and the song was ideal for him – and Jerry. Watch the scene on YouTube and you will see Jerry take over in his inimitable way. Sinatra incidentally didn't sing many faux Italian songs, but Dean made a career out of it.

'That's Amore' gave Dean his first gold record and established him as an international singing star, but you can hear the conditions in which he recorded it in the Capitol Collector's Series as he complains about the cigar smoke in the studio. The song went to No.2 both in Britain and America, and became an integral part of Dean's act. Although he sang it at the Oscar ceremony, it was beaten by a not so 'Secret Love', sung in *Calamity Jane* by Doris Day. At the time Dean and Jerry were earning far more than Frank Sinatra for night club appearances.

Dean had plenty of secret loves, but despite his playboy lifestyle, he liked a woman at home. Dean and Barbara had a son and three daughters before they were divorced in 1949. He then married Jeanne Biegger, who was the Orange Bowl Queen at the Beachcomber Club in Miami. They had two sons and a daughter. Their second house was next to a golf course in LA. Jeanne was to say, 'I married him knowing nothing about him. I divorced him 23 years later and I still knew nothing about him.' She was a tough cookie though and Frank referred to as 'the U-boat commander'.

Then came the family song.

The songwriter, Terry Gilkyson, is a great, unheralded songwriter. His daughter, the folk singer and songwriter, Eliza Gilkyson, says, 'He hated people looking for hidden meanings in his songs and he wrote them as a job. He went to the office every day and often wrote about us. 'Memories Are Made of This' is about our family: it's about him meeting my mother and having three kids. He left us a wonderful legacy.'

On the other hand, Dean Martin was going through hell in 1956. His second marriage was on the rocks (although he saved it) and so was his comedy partnership with Jerry Lewis (although they broke up). He told Gilkyson that memories were made of shit as far as he was concerned ('All I want is a bottle of Scotch and a blow-job'), but he recognised it as a hit song. Capitol didn't think it was suitable – a strange decision as he had cut some real dogs for them. Dean was adamant and when they relented, 'Memories Are Made of This' became a transatlantic No.1 in the early months of 1956. It topped the US charts for six weeks, which was good going when rock'n'roll was around.

Dean only had one UK No.1, but with a little luck, he might have had five. 'That's Amore' (1954), 'Return to Me' (1958), 'Volare' (1958) and 'Gentle on My Mind' (1969) all faltered at No.2. His other US No.1, 'Everybody Loves Somebody' (1964) only made No.11 in the UK and his novelty, 'Little Ole Wine Drinker Me' wasn't a UK hit at all. He couldn't have cared less; all he wanted was that Scotch and a blow-job.

Although 1956 marked the end of the Martin and Lewis partnership, they went out on a high. Their last three films were their best – *Artists and Models* (a frantic comedy with Shirley MacLaine and Anita Ekberg), *Pardners* (a western with Cahn and Van Heusen songs) and *Hollywood or Bust* (the bust belonging to Anita Ekberg). Given a choice, Dean would always want to make a western but *Pardners*, made for their own York Productions, was shot in terrible weather in Phoenix and it only exacerbated the tensions between them. Both Dean and Jerry do some fine gun tricks, but note the slapdash ending with the remark, 'We're not ready for the end yet.' Had they torn out the final pages of the script?

Shirley MacLaine was a Broadway dancer, whose first film role was in *The Trouble with Harry* for Alfred Hitchcock in 1955 – she played a kooky girl so start as you mean to go on. Jerry Lewis saw her on Broadway in *The Pajama Game* and then took Hal Wallis to see her. She was signed for *Artists and Models*. She maintained that Dean played a heightened version of himself on stage and was really the funny one. He would often amend songs so that 'It Happened in Monterey' became 'It Happened in Martha Raye'. She noted his odd habits such as never wearing a pair of socks more than once.

Success was getting to the duo – Jerry wanted to direct and he liked endless rehearsals while Dean didn't want to rehearse at all. He told Jerry, 'There is no love between us. To me, you're nothing but a dollar sign.'

Dean was making dollar signs of his own. In 1954 they had been booked into Ciro's in Hollywood and when Jerry caught hepatitis, Dean did the prestigious bookings as a solo act and did fine. Going solo was no problem. He subsequently said, 'The two greatest turning points in my career were, first, meeting Jerry Lewis and second, leaving Jerry Lewis.' However, Dean couldn't be bothered to bear grudges and he would have happily been civil with Jerry, but with Jerry it was all or nothing at all, and he chose nothing.

Equally, Jerry Lewis's 1982 autobiography, *In Person*, is unkind to Martin, but he does say this about Dean's ability: 'I'll use a metaphor to explain what our on-stage partnership represented. Imagine a day at the circus. There at centre ring is the flier winging his way high up on a trapeze while thousands watch his every move, not realising that if it weren't for the catcher below, the flier would be nothing. And Dean was my catcher – the greatest straight man in the history of show business. His sense of timing was so flawless, so infinite and so fragile it almost looked as if he didn't do anything at all. Which, of course, was the magic, giving form and substance to the act. It's what made Martin and Lewis work. The truth is, I wouldn't have done as well with anyone else.'

Jackie Gleason commented at the time, 'Dean's got a great sense of timing. He gives the impression that he's a nice guy which audiences love. He's coordinated which means he can dance when he sets his mind to it. Wait and see – in a couple of years, Dean will be bigger than Jerry.'

Jackie Gleason notwithstanding, the sensible money was on Jerry Lewis becoming the big solo star, but Dean found a good manager, Mort Viner, who stuck with him throughout his career. Dean was able to take advice while Jerry wanted to do everything his way.

Jerry Lewis made films such as *The Nutty Professor* (1963) and *The Patsy* (1964) which were even more eccentric than before – you had to be very childish or very clever to enjoy them and he became a cult hero amongst the French cognoscenti. Personally, I find the greater part of all of his films insufferable but there are usually a few moments of sheer genius, some beautifully orchestrated mayhem.

In August 1956 Jerry Lewis had taken over from Judy Garland in Las Vegas when she had a bad throat. He was welcome to use Garland's arrangements and he alighted on Al Jolson's success, 'Rock-A-Bye Your Baby with a Dixie Melody', which, oddly enough, had previously been recorded by Dean. It went down well and to everyone's surprise, it was released as a single and became a million-seller. In addition, Jerry Lewis did a vast amount of good with his annual telethons for charity: such telethons are commonplace now but Jerry

Lewis was there at the beginning. Indeed, Frank Sinatra first worked with Martin and Lewis in March 1952 on an early telethon.

Jerry should have known where he was with Dean. He was the sort of person who would always let you down. If Jerry's animosity towards Dean hadn't been so strong, maybe they could have worked together from time to time and been like Bob Hope and Bing Crosby. As it is, they didn't speak to each other for twenty years.

In the end, Dean Martin didn't quite make the first division. Even those who don't like Frank Sinatra would concede that he was a great singer. Dean Martin didn't have Frank Sinatra's dazzle, Tony Bennett's phrasing, Vic Damone's technique and certainly not Sammy Davis's energy, but he developed a warm, friendly act. His records sound sloppy, full of slurred notes, but that's the way he wanted it and it makes him instantly recognisable. He was Frank-lite, the world's best-loved drunk, and to quote his philosophy of life, 'Everybody should have fun', to which he could have added, even if some people get hurt along the way.

There is an Italian word, *menefraghista*, which sums him up – Dean was somebody who didn't give a fuck.

The Sammy Davis story is remarkable. He was born in Harlem on 8 December 1925. His mother was Cuban but later he would say that she was Puerto Rican to avoid being dragged into the Cuban crisis and being thought unpatriotic. His parents were vaudeville dancers – hence Sammy Davis Sr – and he was performing on stage from the age of three, being billed somewhat unfairly as he was only a baby as 'Silent Sam, the Dancing Midget'. He never had a day's formal schooling. As a youngster, he had tap-dancing lessons from the legendary Bill 'Bojangles' Robinson, who worked with Shirley Temple. In later years, Davis would sing Jerry Jeff Walker's 'Mr Bojangles' as a tribute to Bill Robinson, but Walker was really writing about someone else. Walker didn't want to tell him in case he stopped doing the song. Leslie Bricusse likens Sammy's performance to Olivier doing Hamlet: it was that good.

In 1943 Davis was conscripted for wartime service and he suffered racial prejudice in the army. He was painted with distemper to make him white. He came through by entertaining the troops and they appreciated him after that, and it's almost the story of his life.

After the war Sammy sang with his father and Will Mastin in the Will Mastin Trio. They appeared at the top night clubs, often supporting Jack Benny, Bob Hope and Frank Sinatra. When Frank was with Tommy Dorsey in 1941, he met Sammy for the first time and then in 1945, Sammy was in the audience for a *Songs by Sinatra*. In 1947 Frank and the Will Mastin Trio were on the same bill at the Capitol Theatre in New York, providing the entertainment in between *Her Husband's Affairs* with Lucille Ball.

Although Mastin's name was on the billing, everybody was applauding Sammy for his singing, dancing, drumming, comedy and impressions. He could mimic both Martin and Lewis to perfection at a time when it was unusual for black artists to imitate white performers. When Sammy went solo in 1954, he had hit records such as 'Hey There' from *The Pajama Game*. An album, *Starring Sammy Davis Jr*, topped the US charts.

In 1950 he danced so frenziedly on TV that the host, Eddie Cantor, mopped his face. This led to national outrage – a white man mopping a black man's face, what was he thinking of? Eddie Cantor and Sammy Davis were close friends: he introduced Sammy to Judaism and he gave him a religious medallion which he wore until he left it in his dressing room at the New Frontier on 18 November 1954.

Sammy had a recording session the next day and he and his valet drove to Hollywood. As they neared the studio, an elderly lady made a U-turn as she had gone the wrong way. She smashed into Sammy's car and he was driving. Sammy lost his left eye, and this is where

Sinatra showed himself to be a true friend. He had Sammy as a house guest, allowing him to convalesce and helping him rebuild his confidence. When Sammy lost his eye, his doctor showed him his face in the mirror and he responded with customary wit, 'I never was a debutante but this is ridiculous.'

In 1955 Sammy returned to performing and was given a standing ovation at Ciro's for his courage. Further hits followed with 'Something's Gotta Give', 'Love Me or Leave Me' and 'That Old Black Magic' and in 1956 and now with a glass eye, Sammy made his Broadway début in *Mr Wonderful*, which featured Will Mastin and Sammy Davis Sr. It ran for over a year and featured two hit songs, 'Mr Wonderful' (recorded by Peggy Lee) and 'Too Close for Comfort' (a hit for Sammy).

Sammy's talent was so extraordinary that he wanted to do everything and he became known as the world's greatest entertainer. The BBC producer Dennis Main Wilson made a television special with Sammy in 1964. Dennis Main Wilson told me, 'I spent five weeks watching his act at the London Palladium. I was there every night and he was always doing something different. He'd say, "You haven't seen my guns yet, have you, Dennis?" and he'd go out and put some fast draw tricks in his performance. Bernard Delfont didn't like at all. He complained that we were using the Palladium shows as a rehearsal for the BBC.'

The British dancer Lionel Blair recalls, 'Sammy loved coming to the UK. Even though he was a big star, he couldn't believe that he could go anywhere. I invited him to the Tropicana and he got his valet to check first that it was okay.'

When appearing with Sammy on a Royal Command Performance, Lionel saw Sammy's generosity. 'Even though he was Sammy Davis, he never wanted to upstage me. We were rehearsing a routine and he said, "I'll walk off and you finish the number." I said, "But, Sammy, you're the star." He said, "But you're my friend" and he let me do that.'

Sammy's shows were all snap, crackle and pop, and Tommy Sands recalls, 'Sammy was wound up tighter than a snare drum. He was a little ball of nerves and it showed in his performances because he was so brilliant, doing everything so fast and so well. He tapped, he did comedy, he sang, he played all the instruments and he did it with blinding speed and competence.'

In many ways, Sammy lived up to his publicity: he was the world's greatest entertainer but his act was too intense and in your face for some. His talents made him restless as he was forever trying new things. There is a beautiful album, *Sammy Davis Jr Sings, Laurindo Almeida Plays* (1966), which is just Sammy's voice with the distinctive Brazilian jazz guitarist and it's a pity that there are not more recordings like this.

The only Brit in the Rat Pack was Peter Sydney Ernest Lawford. He was born illegitimate in London on 7 September 1923, the son of a general in the First World War. He loathed his mother who had dressed him as a girl in his early years and once told Louis B Mayer that he was homosexual. He appeared in a film, *Poor Old Bill*, in 1931 and during a visit to California in 1938, he played a cockney in *Lord Jeff*. Lawford was exempt from military service as he had a damaged right hand with two of his fingers bent and immobile. He was self-conscious about this but he disguised it well and you would never notice it in his film appearances.

In 1942 while most young British men were in the forces or involved in war work, Peter Lawford was in Hollywood, working as an ensemble actor for MGM. He wasn't much of an actor but he could cash in on his good looks, his British accent and being debonair. In 1945 he was voted the most popular actor in Hollywood, but he didn't have enough self-esteem to campaign for better roles. Women loved him and he lived a playboy lifestyle in both his films and real life and he had an affair with Lana Turner and probably another with Ava Gardner.

Lawford's numerous credits include *Son of Lassie* (1945), *It Happened in Brooklyn* (1947) where he worked with Frank Sinatra, *Easter Parade* (1948), *Royal Wedding* (1951) and *It Should Happen to You* (1954). He described Lassie as a 'vicious bastard' and he gave Elizabeth Taylor her first screen kiss in *Julia Misbehaves* (1948). In 1952 Lawford was to have a supporting role in a film about the Pilgrim Fathers, *Plymouth Adventure* starring Spencer Tracy. Tracy was very unhappy about the casting as he thought Lawford was a poor, unprepared actor and something of a lightweight. Fortunately, the producers could drop Lawford without hurting his pride by offering him a lead role in the romantic comedy, *You for Me*.

In 1954–5, Lawford starred in the TV series, *Dear Phoebe*, in which he played a college professor who is also an agony aunt, but he is best known for the comedy mystery series, *The Thin Man* (1957/9) with Phyllis Kirk and a fox terrier, Asta. The series was made for NBC and at the time it had far higher ratings than Frank Sinatra's programmes.

Frank would regularly tease Peter Lawford by calling him Freddie Bartholomew, the English child actor who had played the title role in the 1936 film, *Little Lord Fauntleroy*, but Sinatra needed Lawford for one good reason.

His talent was by the way. The key factor was that he had married Pat Kennedy on 24 April 1954 and so was now part of the Kennedy dynasty. Frank wanted to be on the inside track and he became best pals with Peter and schmoozed with Pat. In 1958 they named their daughter, Victoria Francis, after him. By July 1961, they had four children but the marriage was unhappy. His place in the Rat Pack had little to do with talent and as if to emphasise the point, he was referred to as the brother-in-Lawford.

Joey Bishop was born Joseph Abraham Gottlieb in the Bronx on 3 February 1918, but he was raised in South Philadelphia. After graduating, he formed the Bishop Brothers Trio with some friends. Following war service, he became a stand-up comedian and he achieved national fame as a regular panel member of the game show, *What's My Line*.

In 1958 Joey Bishop had supporting roles in two significant war films, *The Deep Six* with Alan Ladd and especially *The Naked and the Dead*, the film of Norman Mailer's novel, entrusted to the nearly blind and critically ill director Raoul Walsh and starring Aldo Ray and Cliff Robertson.

As a comedian, he was one of those glum New York Jewish comedians in the Jackie Mason style and his catchphrase was 'son of a gun'. He starred in *The Joey Bishop Show* (1961–4) in which he played a talk show host. He was soon playing it for real as he often stood in for Johnny Carson on *The Tonight Show*. He was a good comic who struck lucky: he was in the right place (Las Vegas) at the right time (1959). Outside of *Ocean's 11*, his best known film is *Valley of the Dolls* (1967).

II. Day In–Day Out, 1950–1952

On New Year's Eve 1949 *Billboard* carried a feature on the possibilities for albums. Were they going to be the way forward? Frank Sinatra thought yes and said that artists would now have to think differently. He said, rather stiltedly even though his name was still on it, 'Artists and A&R men will have to pioneer in the use of script material in conjunction with music, the representation of musical sketches, commentary, narrative and mood music.' In his opinion, LPs 'will call for much more of a production package' – which could hardly have been a clearer declaration of intent.

Elsewhere his declarations of intent were getting the better of him. In January 1950, he played the Shamrock Hotel in Houston and he took Ava Gardner with him, even flaunting her to the audience during the show. Frank managed to assault a photographer from *Houston Post* but what did he expect? The next morning everybody would know about it anyway.

Frank played further concerts in Hartford, Connecticut, again with Ava by his side, so it was hardly surprising that Nancy said that they were separating. She told the press on Valentine's Day, 'Married life with Frank has become most unhappy and almost unbearable' The press wrote that Hurricane Ava destroyed anything in its path.

Unfortunately for the Sinatras, the man who might have smoothed all this over, George Evans, had died from a heart attack on 26 January 1950. The sheer strain of having Sinatra as a client might have exacerbated his condition.

In New York, Frank and Ava stayed at Hampshire House where they had separate bedrooms with an adjoining living room. Ava always did what she wanted and so she visited her former husband, Artie Shaw and his girlfriend. Frank, who disliked Shaw intensely, became jealous and had a row with Ava. She went to her bedroom and he called her and said he was going to kill himself. Ava heard a shot but he had fired the bullet into his mattress. Frank's man, Hank Sanicola, replaced the mattress with one from his own room and by the time, the police had arrived, Frank was going, 'Shot? What shot?' in a performance that merited an Oscar. Perhaps it was just as well that Ava had to leave to film *Pandora and the Flying Dutchman* with James Mason in England and Spain.

Frank had been having some trouble with his throat. He thought that doing too many shows a day would be bad for him, not to mention the five radio programmes a week and his recording sessions. In the past, he had turned down the Copa in New York because he did not want to do three shows a night. However, he agreed to a two month residency on which he would be accompanied by pianist Skitch Henderson. He needed some special material and who better to provide it than Sammy Cahn? He and Sammy had fallen out but he called Sammy and Sammy, as always, was there for him.

Rather underlining his troubles, Frank opened with 'I Am Loved' from Cole Porter's new musical, *Out Of This World*, and he had tremendous reviews. However, because of the scandal, the sophisticated New York public was not queuing to see him. The manager of the Copa, Jack Entratter, cut his season from eight weeks to six, but the season had to be cut short anyway.

On 26 April 1950, Frank lost his voice at the 2.30am show. He had dedicated 'I Have but One Heart' to Ava and was starting 'Bali Ha'i' but as he went for a high note, nothing happened. He whispered goodnight and left the stage. He was to say, but clearly not at the time, 'I was never so panic stricken in my whole life. There was absolute silence.'

No doubt all the singing was a contributory factor but there was also too much whiskey and too many cigarettes as well as considerable stress. He coughed up blood and was told that his vocal cords had haemorrhaged. Billy Eckstine was brought in as a replacement at the Copa and Jeff Clark on *Lite-Up Time*. Frank was told to rest his voice for a month. He stayed in a mansion in Florida owned by the gangster Charlie Fischetti where presumably hoarse whispers were the norm.

Lite-Up Time had been going well but Sinatra had been playing fast and loose with the scheduling. He began one 15 minute show with an extended version of 'Begin the Beguine' which took up half the programme and when he and Dorothy Kirsten sang 'A Fine Romance', Sinatra added, 'We'll buy a minute from NBC and do another chorus.'

Although Frank repeated songs on *Lite Up Time* (usually his current releases!), the programme called for him to perform several new ones, so he sang a wide variety of classics and instantly forgettable numbers plus some genuine curios: 'O Sole Mio' in Italian, and the Cockney caper, 'I've Got a Lovely Bunch of Coconuts', which had been recorded by Merv Griffin and Danny Kaye. He introduced 'It Isn't Fair' with the innuendo-laden words, 'I suppose you know why Tommy Dorsey hired me. I was the only singer who could get up in his trombone and clean it. When I was real good boy, he used to let me ride on the slide.'

Among his repertoire were 'I Beeped When I Should Have Bopped', 'Sitting by the Window', 'My Blue Heaven', 'A Man Wrote a Song', 'Why Remind Me', 'Body And Soul' and his latest singles, 'Chattanoogie Shoe Shine Boy' and 'American Beauty Rose'. The duets with Dorothy Kirsten included 'When We're Alone (Penthouse Serenade)', 'Isn't It Romantic', 'Strange Music', 'Let's Fall in Love' and Jo Stafford and Gordon MacRae's nostalgic hit, 'Dearie'.

Mitch Miller was born of Russian extraction in Rochester, New York on 4 July 1911. As a child, he was recognised as a gifted pianist but he switched to oboe and at 15, he was playing with the Syracuse Symphony Orchestra. He won a scholarship to the Eastman School of Music and graduated in 1932. Moving to New York City, Miller was in the pit orchestra for the Broadway première of *Porgy and Bess* (1935), later touring with its composer, George Gershwin. He was with the CBS Symphony Orchestra when they performed the score for Orson Welles' controversial broadcast of *The War of the Worlds* (1938). Miller became a record producer in the 1940s, first with Mercury Records and then, in 1950, with Columbia. He still played the oboe from time to time, notably on some of Charlie Parker's recordings for Mercury in 1949 including 'April in Paris' and 'Summertime'.

Although big band singing was the order of the day, he wanted to make records with small groups of musicians if that suited the songs. In 1949, he took 'Mule Train' from a little-known western *Singing Guns* and gave it to Frankie Laine. Laine's bellowing performance was accompanied by Miller himself adding the whip-cracks. 'We only had a few musicians – accordion, rhythm, string bass,' said Miller, 'so I was too embarrassed to put my name on it as a conductor.' Two years later, Miller replaced Laine with throbbing guitars for 'Jezebel'. 'I liked working with Mitch very much,' Laine once told me, 'He liked to arm wrestle before we started recording.'

The Mitch Miller sessions with Sinatra started on 10 March 1950 and to be fair, they were generally successful and Frank's bitter reminiscences were selective. Mitch thought that Frank should record more rhythm songs, and there's nothing wrong with that, providing he picked the right ones. The first was a new song, 'American Beauty Rose', which had a lyric by Hal David. Frank had brought Ava to the studio and she wore a very low-cut dress. As it was distracting the musicians, Frank told her to leave and then nailed the song in one take. The original single was labelled 'Dixieland with a beat'.

When Frank sang the western sounding 'God's Country', the songwriter, Haven Gillespie was given a special award for preserving 'the American way of life'. Frank was not too far from R&B with 'Chattanoogie Shoe Shine Boy' and he sang an old blues song from Leroy Carr, 'When the Sun Goes Down' which had the engaging couplet:

'I got my hoss and he's my pal
But what does it mean without a gal?'

Dinah Shore was going to record 'Peachtree Street' with Frank, the reference being to an address in Atlanta, Georgia, but she thought it was a terrible song and said, knowingly, 'Did you publish this, Frank?' Frank was furious as he was not only publishing the song but also had his name down as co-writer. Frank told Manie Sacks that he would record it with somebody else and asked, 'Who was the last chick you signed?' Manie said, 'Rosemary Clooney' and he sang it with her. Clooney also thought it was a terrible song but she kept stum as to be singing with Frank would prove a great start to her career.

Frank had sessions with George Sivaro and his Orchestra for a new 10 inch album, *Sing and Dance with Frank Sinatra*. George Siravo wrote arrangements to get Frank swinging for the first time and Frank must have approved as he re-recorded seven of the eight songs for

Sinatra's Swingin' Session!!! (1961). His phrasing gave a taste of what he would be doing with Capitol and Reprise. When he sings 'When You're Smiling', Frank drew out 'you' in 'you bring on the rain', and he has fun with the lyrics of 'It's Only a Paper Moon' and 'My Blue Heaven'.

Frank's voice was back to normal by the end of May and he had a full schedule of engagements. On 27 May 1950 he made his first TV appearance on a variety show for NBC, *Star Spangled Rhythm*, which was hosted by Bob Hope. He looked good and he sang 'Come Rain or Come Shine' with total confidence and swapped jokes with Hope, similar to the banter from the *Road* films with Hope and Crosby.

While Frank had been recovering, he had gone to Spain to join Ava on location. He thought that she might have been having a fling with Mario Cabré, who was playing the bullfighter in her film and, having a hard time, as the producers, by accident, had found some vicious bulls for him to fight. Still, it would be admirable training for dealing with Sinatra.

Ava's autobiography confirms that Frank was right, but whether he found out or not, they remained a romantic couple. He bought her an emerald necklace. While travelling home via Paris he was smitten by his conscience and bought Nancy a gold charm bracelet. It proved of no avail; on 28 September 1950 Nancy was granted custody of their children and given their house in Holmby Hills.

In June 1950 Frank Sinatra came to the UK for his first concert appearances. He was in good spirits as he and his pianist Ken Lane performed for passengers on the plane to London. His first UK show was at the Tooting Granada, backed by a British band, Woolf Phillips and the Skyrockets with arrangements from Axel Stordahl and George Sivaro. Both the *New Musical Express* and the *Melody Maker* called it a triumph. The reception at the Blackpool Opera House was so ecstatic that Frank told a journalist, 'They love me, don't they? I could become mayor of this town.'

He was with Ava and they both attended the premiere of Noël Coward's new musical, *Ace of Clubs*. She became irriated because Frank kept signing autographs, and when a photographer snapped them before the curtain went up, Frank leapt at him and dragged him out of the theatre, which was more exciting than anything on the stage. When they went to see Margot Fonteyn in *Sleeping Beauty*, it was Ava who attracted attention, watching the performance while chewing bubble gum.

Frank performed a 50 minute set as part of a variety package for two weeks at the London Palladium where the supporting acts included Max Wall and the sand dancers, Wilson, Keppel and Betty. Frank told the audience that he had to get special permission to sing 'Soliloquy' because *Carousel* had not yet come to London. As he was also singing 'Ol' Man River', he wasn't going for the easy options – a contrast with Dean Martin, who would never have tackled such demanding songs in public. Press photos show huge crowds outside the Palladium and under the heading "An Orpheus for your Time": the critic for the *Guardian* wrote, 'Not to be outdone by their American sisters, a mob of respectable young women surged and moaned outside the theatre throughout the evening.' Noël Coward attended the show and joked to Frank that he had behaved impeccably as he had not beaten up photographers.

The most intriguing review was from James Leasor in the *Daily Express*. Under the heading of *Miserabilism*. A miserabilist is someone who enjoys misery and Frank looks the part: 'He is thin-faced, tired-looking, and carries that world-weary look which comes of being for so long a totem for the tearful.' Instead of Sinatra 1950, this reads more like a review of Leonard Cohen 1970.

On returning to America, Frank recorded 'London by Night' and Ivor Novello's 'If

Only She'd Look My Way' from his new West End musical, *Gay's the Word*, for a special UK release. It was a charity single for the National Playing Fields Association with a spoken introduction from the Duke of Edinburgh.

Back in that recording studio, Mitch Miller was making his presence felt. You could argue that Mitch was easing Frank back into recording by giving him a simple folk song to perform with a choir (the Mitch Miller Singers, no less!) but Frank didn't see it that way. The song was Huddie Ledbetter's 'Goodnight Irene' in which the singer says that he is going to stay home with his wife and family. The hit version came from the Weavers with an arrangement by Gordon Jenkins but Frank's version was a respectable No.5. Frank could sing folk songs well – look at 'It Was a Very Good Year' – but overall they didn't provide him with any challenge and even though he had a Top 10 hit, he refused to perform it in Atlantic City in August. When a radio presenter, Ben Heller, told him, 'You oughta do a lot of songs like that, Frank', he replied, 'Don't hold your breath.' At the same session Frank recorded a cloying song from 1919, 'Dear Little Boy of Mine': the title says it all.

The studio tapes from previous years reveal that Frank Sinatra and Axel Stordahl or George Sivaro had been controlling the sessions, telling the band what to do and the producers (though that term was not used in the 1940s) were making sure that the technicalities were right. In total contrast, Mitch Miller wanted complete control in order to get Frank selling again. From that point of view it was working, but Frank didn't thank him for it and at one Columbia session he shouted, 'Mitch – out!'

Frank had punched a columnist who had implied he was a communist. He paid a fine for the incident and years later, after the newspaperman died, he pissed on his grave. Perhaps to put paid to such rumours, the FBI's files show that in September 1950 Frank, rather rat-like, contacted them to say that he could supply the names of subversives – but we do not know whom he had in mind. (Elvis, later, would do something similar.) The Deputy Director said, 'We want nothing to do with him', which was endorsed by the FBI's supremo, J Edgar Hoover. We don't know what possessed Frank Sinatra to suggest this but he was acting on impulse and surely would have changed his mind.

Louis B Mayer had been against his film stars performing on TV as he felt that the public would no longer pay to see them at the box office. Now that Frank had been sacked by MGM, he was able to appear regularly on TV and his first series, *The Frank Sinatra Show*, started on 7 October 1950, a half-hour programme sponsored by Bulova Watches and made for CBS. The guests included Perry Como, Sarah Vaughan and the actors J. Carrol Naish and Ben Blue. On the whole, the Saturday night series was not a success because Sinatra hated rehearsing. Are you seeing a pattern here?

Although the acting and comedy content were poor the music was good and Sinatra was starting to use arrangements by Neal Hefti. *Variety* said that CBS had saddled him with 'bad pacing, bad scripting, bad tempo, poor camera work and an overall jerky presentation.' Jack Gould of the *New York Times* declared, 'Frank Sinatra walked off the television high dive on Saturday night, but unfortunately fell into the shallow end of the pool.' Frank sang a new lyric to 'Everything Happens to Me' which described the pitfalls of working on TV – but why draw attention to them? A programme with Phil Silvers worked particularly well, probably because Silvers knew how to perform on TV and also how to handle Sinatra.

On the whole, the recordings with Mitch Miller were decent enough. Okay, 'One Finger Melody' deserved one finger, but as it was published by Sinatra's own Barton music, he must accept the blame.

The highlights were a sublime 'I Guess I'll Have to Dream the Rest', a singalong 'Nevertheless' and the wonderful 'April in Paris'. This masterpiece about the joys of being in love was written by Vernon Duke and Yip Harburg. Unfortunately, Vernon Duke was so argumentative that most lyricists only worked with him once. In addition, there is 'Come Back to Sorrento', which despite the English title, is the only track that Frank recorded completely in Italian. A few months later Dean Martin recorded 'Luno Mezza Mare', a little known gem sung in Italian but judging by the remark at the end, he knew he wasn't very convincing.

The songwriter Jack Wolf wanted to write lyrics for the *Andante* section of Brahms' *Third Symphony in F Major*. Joel Herron added a bridge and Wolf called the song, 'Take My Love'. They took it to Ben Barton at Barton Music, hoping that Sinatra would record it. Frank recorded it and even though he sang it on TV, it went nowhere, but it was used on film soundtracks.

The novelties fared less well. Admittedly, 'Cherry Pies Ought to be You' was one of Cole Porter's famed list songs, but it was taken from his new musical, *Out of this World*, and showed that Porter lived in a different world from most people – 'Orson Welles ought to be you' and 'Towels from The Ritz ought to be you.' Desperate stuff. Still, Frank and Rosemary Clooney did their best and it is superior to their other duet, the saccharine 'Loves Means Love'. There was the blatant product placement of Sammy Cahn and Axel Stordahl's 'Meet Me at the Copa', which rhymes 'museum' and 'see 'em' some years before Joni Mitchell's 'Big Yellow Taxi'.

Frank Sinatra was fed up with Columbia Records anyway. He had complained about fellow artist Doris Day, saying that she was recording his songs, 'That Old Feeling' and 'You Go to My Head', but both songs were standards and had been recorded by others long before Sinatra's interpretations.

In November 1950 Mitch Miller set up a recording session. He had two highly commercial new songs for him: 'My Heart Cries for You', written by Percy Faith and Carl Sigman, and 'The Roving Kind', an update of an English folk song, 'The Flagship', written around 1650. Miller knew that they were surefire hits. Sinatra arrived at the studio in the afternoon and Mitch Miller showed him what he had planned for that evening. Sinatra, who was not in the best of moods, said, 'I'm not doing any of that crap.'

Mitch Miller had booked the musicians and so he looked for an immediate replacement. He had heard a singer, Al Cernic whom he liked and he asked him to come in that evening. The session went very well and Miller told Cernic that he had to have a new name. 'I didn't want to change my name as I thought my family might think I was trying to disown them or was ashamed of it,' the singer once told me, 'but Mitch Miller couldn't pronounce it and he said, "Look, I changed my name so why shouldn't you?" I took part of his name and as I used to say "Hi, Guy" when people said hello, I became Guy Mitchell. I could see 'My Heart Cries for You' was a hit song. Mitch had a way of spotting things and that's why he was a fine A&R man. He had Tony Bennett, Rosemary Clooney, Patti Page, Frankie Laine, Johnnie Ray and myself on his books at pretty much the same time. Before every record session, he liked to wrestle for about five minutes. He had been a champion wrestler. I'm sure he could have won every time but he didn't want to hurt his singers.'

Guy Mitchell had struck lucky – he had gone from nowhere to stardom overnight as both songs became gold records for him and he then married a Miss USA. Presumably the songs would have done much the same for Sinatra and he might have got a Miss USA out of it too.

The main tension between Frank and Mitch Miller arose because Mitch Miller saw himself as the boss and Frank did not like being ordered around. Frank Sinatra notwithstanding, Miller had an exceptional talent for matching the singer with the song.

Frankie Laine always thanked Mitch Miller for finding the songs, 'That Lucky Old Sun', 'Answer Me' and 'I Believe' for him, but in 1951, Miller did threaten to tear up Rosemary Clooney's contract if she didn't record 'Come On-a My House'. She did as she was told and had her first million seller.

Although Miller could spot strong ballads like 'Rags to Riches' and 'Stranger in Paradise' for Tony Bennett, he was especially adept at finding novelty songs and encouraged his friend, Bob Merrill, to write distinctive material for his acts. Merrill wrote many of Guy Mitchell's hits as well as Rosemary Clooney's 'Mambo Italiano' (1955). One of Miller's biggest successes was with the impudent 'I Saw Mommy Kissing Santa Claus' by the 12-year-old Jimmy Boyd in 1953, and he produced the ultra-novelty 'Too Old to Catch the Mustard' (Marlene Dietrich and Rosemary Clooney together), 'Singing the Blues' (Guy Mitchell) and 'Whatever Will Be, Will Be' (Doris Day).

Mitch Miller was creating hits for the new boys on the block – indeed, he was creating the new boys on the block and so Sinatra must have felt vulnerable, especially when he heard Tony Bennett sing. Frankie Laine was less of a threat: Bob Hope remarked, 'No wonder Frankie Laine is doing well. The public has never seen a foghorn with lips before.'

Johnnie Ray's highly emotional 'Cry' (1952) caused a sensation. It was a huge influence on Elvis Presley and Ray's lack of inhibition paved the way for rock'n'roll. Frank and Ava saw Johnnie Ray at the Copa but Frank disliked him because he had been dating Ava. However, Ray was gay and had been arrested for soliciting in Detroit in 1951. Years later, in 1966, Sinatra asked Ray to record for his Reprise label and had the satisfaction of shelving his recordings because, he said, they weren't good enough. In retaliation, Johnnie Ray destroyed all his Sinatra albums.

Although 'Cry' was seen as a precursor to rock'n'roll, Mitch Miller himself frowned upon rock'n'roll and is now often cast the villain of the story – the industry man who held out against it. He told *Melody Maker* in 1957, 'Rock'n'roll is the glorification of monotony. A certain element of juveniles accepts almost any form of it, even the lowest and the most distasteful, because everybody else in their group does.' Frank could have said that.

Miller's response to the advent of rock'n'roll was to make an international star from a new ballad singer, Johnny Mathis, and he encouraged an arranger, Ray Conniff, to make his own easy listening albums.

Johnny Mathis was a good-looking athlete who became an unlikely star in both his own eyes and Sinatra's. He had done very well at the Blue Angel in New York in 1956 and Mitch Miller saw his potential. Mathis said, 'People told me that I sang too high and I sounded like a girl. I thought it was a horrible thing that God had given me, this strange voice.' But many found his bleating vibrato attractive. Also, because some teeth on one side were missing, he sang with a twisted mouth. Besides Ray Conniff's and Mitch Miller's support, he had a supreme accompanist in Bart Howard. Mathis said he was 'the kindest, nicest man with nothing in his mind except he wanted me to sing the best music I could.' When asked about Mathis, Sinatra scorned him as he would Presley; he never regarded him as a threat in the way that Bobby Darin was.

As a recording manager and record producer, Mitch Miller nurtured the talents of some of the biggest names in American music and made the Columbia label the biggest label in the country. For several years in the 1950s, he was the most important figure in the record industry and many younger talents followed his example and learnt how to produce records.

When the jazz pianist Erroll Garner recorded 'On the Street Where You Live', he played it to Frank over the phone. 'Wonderful,' said Frank, 'Whose orchestra is that?' Erroll said, 'Mitch Miller.' Frank put the phone down. Years later, Mitch Miller rang into Frank in Las

Vegas. He extended his hand and said, 'Let bygones be bygones.' 'Fuck you,' said Frank and walked on.

In the first months of 1951 *The Frank Sinatra Show* continued on its weekly way without much controversy. The guests included Perry Como, Frankie Laine, Peggy Lee, Rudy Vallée and Basil Rathbone. In place of a live appearance by Bing Crosby, Frank talked to a cardboard cutout of 'The Groaner'.

A tall, busty blonde, Dagmar, appeared regularly for so-called comic relief. Dagmar wasn't her real name – she was born Virginia Ruth Egnor in 1921 and she was asked to read out doggerel laced with innuendo. When Jayne Mansfield saw her, she said, quite brilliantly, 'This town isn't big enough for the four of us.' One famed review said, 'Last night Dagmar fell face downwards and rocked herself to sleep trying to get up.' Introducing her on stage, Frank said, 'Watch out in the front row. If she takes a bow, you'll get crushed.'

In one typical sketch, an up-and-coming TV celebrity, Jackie Gleason, sold Frank his hunting lodge sight unseen for $5,000, and they invited June Hutton and the Heathertones to join them for the weekend. When Frank and the girls wanted something to eat, they got a ready-to-cook Jackie Gleason; later, Frank Sinatra has his head mounted on a trophy. This is comedy? Once, Jackie Gleason refused to appear because Frank had missed rehearsals, but Frank was by now becoming a confident TV performer. He was also the guest of Milton Berle and Jack Benny.

On 1 March 1951 Frank was interviewed by a Senate committee at the Rockefeller Centre in New York at 4am, in order to retain his privacy. He said he knew no one in the Mafia. Joseph Nellis, a lawyer who questioned him, said that Frank was let off 'even though I recognised the inconsistencies in Sinatra's testimony and knew he was lying.' So why didn't he point them out at the time?

Mitch Miller was doing his best to build bridges with Frank. They were on mutually happy ground with the new Rodgers and Hammerstein musical, *The King and I*. Some years earlier Oscar Hammerstein had asked Jerome Kern what sort of music he would be writing for a musical about the 13th century Italian explorer, Marco Polo. Without missing a beat, Kern said, 'It'll be good Jewish music as usual.' In other words, the fact that *The King and I* was set in Siam wouldn't make much difference to the score.

In the Broadway musical Anna (Gertrude Lawrence) greeted the young sweethearts and gave them advice, 'Hello Young Lovers', although the King (Yul Brynner) was less sure. Frank treated the song like a western waltz and is at his best on the knowing phrase, 'I've been in love like you.' In 1963, this song was parodied in the TV show, *That Was The Week That Was* as 'Hello young lovers, you're under arrest.' Frank sang about conquering fears in 'I Whistle a Happy Tune', which contains a rare example of Sinatra whistling, and there was the poignant lament about forbidden love, 'We Kiss in a Shadow'.

The MGM Theatre of the Air told the songwriter Jack Wolf that they wanted something similar to 'Take My Love' and so Joel Herron wrote the melody for 'I'm a Fool to Want You'. Wolf wrote the lyric and took it to Sinatra's publishing company. Sinatra liked the song but wanted to change some of the words. Exactly what Sinatra contributed for his writing credit isn't known but he regarded the song as reflecting his challenging relationship with Ava Gardner. It is like an open letter to her and has similarities to Billie Holiday's 'Don't Explain'.

Axel Stordahl made the recording even more mournful by adding a choir for the final chorus. Sinatra left the studio in tears. The song was immediately covered by Billy Eckstine and although Frank's record did well, there were split sales. The *Sunday Times* reviewer, Derek Jewell called it, 'the darkest of songs and perhaps the greatest arrangement Stordahl ever did.'

In April 1951 Frank was back at the Paramount with the singer Eileen Barton and Dagmar. He was making jokes about the new idol of the bobbysoxers, Johnnie Ray, mocking his lachrymose style. When he sang the line, 'When I think of Ava, I no longer cry', Dagmar came out and smothered him with kisses. It's all show business; Sinatra could hardly complain of press intrusion when he was actively encouraging it.

The accompanying film was *My Forbidden Past* with Ava Gardner playing a woman who wanted to break up Robert Mitchum's marriage. It seemed that Frank couldn't escape from her. As Frank was appearing with Dagmar on stage and on TV, Mitch Miller wanted Frank to record with her, hence the infamous 'Mama Will Bark'. This was, effectively, a conversation between two dogs, which includes the line,: 'I swear I shall never see, A canine as lovely as thee.' Frank contributed a couple of yips, 'hot dog, woof!', the others coming from impressionist, Donald Baine. Going from the sublime to the cor blimey, 'Mama Will Bark' was the B-side of 'I'm a Fool To Want You'. Frank would call this his worst record and blamed Mitch Miller for it, but he was a willing participant and what's more, he had previously worked with Dagmar on stage and TV. Indeed, there is a photograph from the session and he looks pretty happy next to Dagmar. Well, who wouldn't be?

The casting of Ava Gardner as the woman who destroyed Robert Mitchum had been Howard Hughes' idea, so he was prepared to pay thousands of dollars for a vindictive ruse, but we all know he was nuts anyway. He didn't want Ava associating with Sinatra or Mitchum and he did want to marry her himself, besides having a relationship with Jean Peters whom he married in 1957.

Ava had encouraged him from time to time. Hughes had taken her up in his plane and put the plane on automatic pilot so that they could be members of the mile high club (according to Ava). He had bought her a house on Sunset Boulevard and even a Beverly Hills restaurant so that they could eat there undisturbed.

Hughes had spies on Ava and Frank, noting their quarrels and clocking their nights apart. Although he was delighted that they were fighting, he couldn't separate them. He would lecture her about Frank's promiscuity and when he sent her a gold bracelet and necklace, she threw them out of the window to show Frank that Howard Hughes meant nothing to her.

At the end of May, Nancy told the press that she would give Frank a divorce: 'This is what Frank wanted and I've said yes. I refused him a divorce for a long time because I thought he would come back home.' She was owed $40,000 from their separation settlement, but Frank didn't have the money. In addition, he owed $100,000 in back taxes. Oddly enough, Frank's children, who strongly supported their mother, couldn't dislike Ava. Young Nancy said, 'Ava was earthy and gorgeous and funky and fun, all in one. She wasn't afraid to get down in the dirt and dig up flowers or put on grubby clothes.'

The simplest and quickest way to obtain a divorce was in Nevada, which required six weeks residency. Frank thought he would tie it in with appearances at the Riverside Inn and Casino in Reno. As it happens, his first casino booking in Nevada.

In September he played Las Vegas for the first time, headlining the Painted Desert Room in Moe Dalitz's Desert Inn, while Rosemary Clooney was at the Thunderbird. Frank opened with some rude remark about her. Like most singers, Frank would travel with a pianist and the musicians at the various venues would play the written arrangements. His pianist was Graham Forbes but Forbes' wife didn't like him being on the road and wanted him to quit.

While Frank was playing the main venue, a pianist, Bill Miller, was playing in the Sky Room. Jimmy Van Heusen heard him play 'Polka Dots and Moonbeams' and recommended him to Sinatra. Sinatra's opening words were, 'How would you like to work with me, kid?' even though Miller was a year older. Almost from the start, Sinatra was calling him

'Moonface' or 'Suntan Charlie' because his skin was so white. Miller was to play for Sinatra from 1951 to 1978, then there was the inevitable rift, but he was back in 1985 until the end. To have lasted that long with Sinatra is a considerable achievement, but the trick is to play with him and not drink with him.

Graham Forbes, who came from Brooklyn, spent many years playing the clubs around Long Island and he enjoyed his brief time with Sinatra. The rule was simple: 'He told me, "When I run out of gas, you be there." I worked with Roy Hamilton too so I worked with the best white singer and the best black singer.'

Frank and Nancy Sinatra were granted their divorce on 31 October 1951 with Nancy and the children having a strong claim on his assets. The columnist Louella Parsons, being a staunch Catholic, had only contempt for Sinatra. Frank and Ava immediately applied for a marriage licence. The day before they were to be married, Ava received a letter from a girl saying that she was having an affair with Frank and giving intimate details about his anatomy. She turned out to be a hooker and had almost certainly been set up by Howard Hughes.

It didn't stop the wedding which took place on 7 November 1951 at the home of Manie Sacks' brother in Philadelphia with Axel Stordahl as best man. They hoped this would keep it quiet but the press soon found out. They had their honeymoon in Havana. Frank's parents hadn't spoken to him for two years as they had sided with Nancy and the children, but now they met Ava and were very impressed. Dolly and Ava saw their similarities – they were restless and easily bored; they talked dirty and they liked to tell it how it was; and they loved Frank.

Frank didn't record many tracks in the last half of 1951 but he did reunite with Harry James and his Orchestra, whose arranger was Ray Conniff. They recorded a superfast dance tune, 'Castle Rock', and perhaps Harry James was playing so well to show Frank what he was missing, although James later said that it was 'the worst thing that either of us had recorded.' Johnny Hodges had first recorded the 12-bar blues, 'Castle Rock' as an instrumental and now it had words from Ervin Drake, who later wrote 'It Was a Very Good Year'. At the end of his vocal, Sinatra shouts, 'Go get 'em, Harry, for old times' sake' and Sinatra sounds restrained by comparison. The lyrics are a portent for rock'n'roll:

'I met her dancing to the Castle Rock,
I held her tight and danced around the clock
We rocked to romance to the Castle Rock.'

They also recorded Jack Wolf's 'Farewell, Farewell to Love' and a beautiful ballad associated with Rudy Vallée, 'Deep Night'. It was a good session and 'Castle Rock' was Frank's final hit of 1951.

Frank recorded a duet with the actress Shelley Winters of 'A Good Man Is Hard to Find' with a Trad Jazz backing. Winters had a decent voice and had the potential to be a good blues singer. There are plenty of asides with Frank saying, 'Keep a smile on your face and your big mouth shut' – the way he should have handled the press.

'A Good Man Is Hard to Find' was featured in the film, *Meet Danny Wilson*, which featured Frank, Shelley, and Raymond Burr. It was based on a short story by Harold Robbins and the screenplay was written by a B-movie actor, Don McGuire, whom Frank had met on the set of *Double Dynamite*. The film was about the rise and fall of a brash young singer with a temper, Danny Wilson, and Sinatra didn't mind the parallels with his own life as he gave McGuire some help with the script. Indeed, there are so many parallels to Frank's life that you expect Ava Gardner to pop up in the last reel. Frank commented, 'I wish my life was as exciting as Danny Wilson's.'

The songs were great: 'All of Me', 'I've Got A Crush on You', 'She's Funny That Way',

'When You're Smiling' and 'That Old Black Magic'. When Frank sang 'Lonesome Man Blues' with an harmonica in jail, his pianist remarked, 'Your finest hour.' 'A Good Man Is Hard to Find' worked well on film and was Shelley really pretending to squeeze his balls at the end of the song? However, the song was about two people not getting along and Frank and Shelley didn't connect, although he coached her with her vocals.

There was a hospital scene where Frank Sinatra was to say, 'I'll have a cup of coffee and leave you two lovebirds alone' but instead he said, 'I'll have a cup of Jack Daniel's' and on a second take, 'I'm going to pull that blonde broad's hair out by its black roots.' Winters hit him with a bedpan and they both stormed off the set. Nancy was asked to intercede, telling Frank that if he didn't go back he would lose his fee for the movie and his family could be evicted.

Because of his divorce, Sinatra was unpopular with the public and the film flopped but Don McGuire remained his friend. When McGuire wrote *Three Ring Circus* for Dean Martin and Jerry Lewis, Martin wasn't impressed as he thought he had been relegated to a supporting role.

Frank was not getting many movie offers. He wanted to be a book-keeper for the Mob in *The Brothers Rico* and he failed in securing another tough guy role, *Knock on any Door*, which went to John Derek who played alongside Humphrey Bogart. The film had the famed byline, 'Live fast, die young and leave a good looking corpse.' He fancied George Bernard Shaw's *Androcles and the Lion* but he was better out of it. It transpired that Harpo Marx was so out of his depth that the producers had to start again. A proposed animation of *Finian's Rainbow* was never made, although he and Louis Armstrong did work on two songs, 'Lonesome Man Blues' and 'Ad Lib Blues'. Frank always wanted to make an album with Armstrong but it never happened. He liked to say, 'Louis Armstrong is a credit to his race – the human race.'

After the summer break, the second series of *The Frank Sinatra Show* for CBS started at 8pm on 9 October 1951, broadcast live and sponsored by Ekco household products. Frank was directly running against Milton Berle's *Texaco Star Theatre* and although he booked Perry Como and Frankie Laine for the first show, Berle had Tony Bennett and Rosemary Clooney, a tricky choice for viewers in the days before VCRs. The cigar-chomping Berle had twice as many viewers as Sinatra and continued to do so throughout the season. Milton Berle joked in one programme, 'My next guest has never been seen on television. Last week she was on Frank Sinatra's show.'

Maybe it wasn't star power: maybe the great American public didn't want someone with loose morals in their living room. The TV shows have been preserved and licensing clips has proved a bonanza for his family after his death.

In one episode, he and Jackie Gleason played private detectives trying to recover some stolen money. When the props failed, they ad libbed brilliantly. Frank and Jack Benny worked well together both on Frank's show and in a reciprocal spot on Benny's. Just as an aside, Frank refers to a Rat Pack which beat up people. The show moved from New York to LA in November and the guest list after that date was not as strong as it could have been but included the Andrews Sisters and June Hutton, now married to his arranger, Axel Stordahl.

Frank finished his radio series *Meet Frank Sinatra* in June 1951 and from now on, he would only make guest appearances on radio. On a Christmas show hosted by Bob Hope, he and Bing sang 'Silent Night' together.

Frank's problems with the press continued. His adversary, Lee Mortimer, made damning references about Sinatra in an article for the Mercury magazine, called *Gangsters in the Nightclubs*. Frank nearly ran over a photographer and shouted, "Next time I'll kill you!"

When Frank heard he had been given the Sour Apple award by the Hollywood Women's Press Club, he threatened to rip off Louella Parsons' head and shove it up her ass, thereby living up to the citation. When Doris Day was given a similar award, she realised where she was going wrong and changed her attitude.

On 12 December 1951, his 36th birthday, Frank gave two performances at Wiesbaden, for US army personnel. Frank and Ava were in a friendly mood and they were photographed with customs staff and even talked to reporters.

Then Frank and Ava flew to London for a midnight charity performance for the National Playing Fields Association. The concert also featured Tony Curtis, Janet Leigh and Orson Welles. The intention was to include a tribute to the songwriter Jimmy McHugh at which Janet Leigh with the Tiller Girls would sing 'When My Sugar Walks Down the Street' and 'On The Sunny Side of the Street'; Rhonda Fleming would do 'I Can't Give You Anything But Love, Baby' and 'Comin' In on a Wing And A Prayer'; and Frank would finish with 'I Couldn't Sleep a Wink Last Night'.

At rehearsal, Frank was in a foul mood as he listened to the orchestra. He said, 'That's nice, but what was it, boys?' He ended up singing 'Soliloquy' from *Carousel* with Jimmy Van Heusen on the piano. He shouted at the press and it was not a happy time. Their suite was burgled and Ava had her jewellery stolen. Still, the concert itself did raise $50,000 for charity.

At the start of 1952, Frank was on his own as Ava was in Kenya making *The Snows of Kilimanjaro* with Gregory Peck. He was paranoid, thinking that she and Gregory were getting it on. His agent, Lew Wasserman, at MCA had dropped him as he was no longer earning enough. His film, *Meet Danny Wilson*, opened – and closed. A headline in the New York World Telegram was *Gone On Frankie in '42; Gone in '52*. The feature said the difference between his audiences now and ten years ago was that ten years ago there was one.

Frank had the embarrassment of being the live attraction at the Paramount when they were showing *Meet Danny Wilson*. Mel Tormé was in the audience and later commented, 'I thought he couldn't sink any lower than that.' Oh, but he could. The audience jeered him at a home show in Hoboken and only 150 people turned up in Chicago when he appeared at Chez Paree, a venue which held 1,200 and was owned by the Fischettis. After playing a leaky tent at a fair in Hawaii, he must have wondered what was coming next.

His radio series had finished in 1951 and his TV series staggered on until in June 1952 despite poor ratings. Frank was singing well and the arrangements were good but the comedy was too forced. It was the turmoil in Frank's personal life that had caused the ratings to fall. Frank had become a pariah. The sponsors were no longer interested in supporting the programme, especially at $40,000 a programme.

Among the guests on his TV series in 1952 were the Three Stooges (playing his butlers), Louis Armstrong (performing that 'Lonesome Man Blues'), Dick Haymes, James Mason, Zsa Zsa Gabor, Yma Sumac, Liberace, Victor Borge and the Andrews Sisters. Well, that line-up would have me hooked. When Frank sang his Dorsey success, 'Oh, Look At Me Now", he added a new line, 'You're in trouble, friends, when Ava starts to look like Marjorie Main', a reference to the character actress who played Ma Kettle.

Columbia Records had loaned Sinatra $100,000 to pay his taxes. The only way they would get it back was through some hits and they weren't coming. Because of Mitch Miller, he was avoiding the studio whenever he could, but there were a few gems like 'I Could Write a Book' from *Pal Joey*, 'The Birth of the Blues' and an excellent ballad, 'My Girl', which could be mistaken for one of his Capitol recordings. There was attractive scat singing at the start of 'Don't Ever Be Afraid to Go Home', but then there's lamentable lament 'Feet of Clay'. The Italian ballad 'Luna Rossa' ('Blushing Moon') is okay and Mitch Miller was especially pleased with 'Azure-Te' ('Paris Blues') and for good reason.

Sinatra was horrified when Mitch Miller wanted to use a washboard on 'Tennessee Newsboy (The Newsboy Blues)', which was written by Percy Faith. It is a country song with slap bass and steel guitar and at the end of the take, Mitch Miller congratulated Speedy West for his pedal steel playing, ignoring Frank completely. It's a good track, like early Bill Haley and the same applies to 'Bim Bam Baby' which uses jive talk: 'Run your flim flam fingers through my greasy hair'. Some good stuff, but no hits.

In a telling interview, Frank Sinatra told Nat Hentoff for *Down Beat*: 'We've got to convince the accepted songwriters to come out of hiding and write again. The way things are now; they feel like they're wasting their time. Another way is to record and revive more of the standards like 'The Birth of the Blues'. That way we can at least balance the hokey tunes. It's murder now. Eventually the people who have something to say musically will be the ones who survive.' In other words, he was in for the duration – he wasn't going anywhere.

In September 1952 Frank made his last record for Columbia in a split session with Mindy Carson in New York. It was called, appropriately enough, 'Why Try to Change Me Now' and it was first song of note by Cy Coleman. The song was arranged by Percy Faith and according to Coleman, Sinatra improved the melody. There was immense confidence in the way he sang, 'I was always your clown' and the lyric did anticipate 'My Way'. One line is very Sinatra: 'I've got some habits even I can't explain.' Mitch Miller loved the record and at the end, he flicked the intercom and said, 'That's it, Frank.' It had been his last recording for Columbia and also the last track he would cut in New York for 10 years. In December 1952, *Billboard* reported that Frank was leaving Columbia after a long running feud with Mitch Miller over material.

And wouldn't this make an extraordinary scene in a film biography: when Frank was unable to get any decent work, he asked Richard Burton to read *Hamlet* with him. 'He was going to make a comeback thrugh the classics,' records Burton in his diaries, 'and he would show the motherfuckers.'

In October, Frank and Ava had a huge bust-up in Los Angeles. Frank yelled, 'If you want me, I'll be in Palm Springs fucking Lana Turner.' Frank drove to Palm Springs, which took four hours. He was known to drive fast, but somehow Ava was there first. She found Lana and her business manager Ben Cole eating fried chicken. Ava joined them and then Frank arrived and went berserk. The police were called and Ben went back in the house to retrieve the chicken as nothing was going to spoil his dinner. That's the most likely story – other versions say Frank caught Ava and Lana in bed together. Both events could have happened – we are after all dealing with a marriage as dramatic as the Burtons. Whatever. Six days later, on 27 October 1952, Earl Wilson wrote a column that read like a Want Ad, 'Frankie ready to surrender, wants Ava back, any terms' and it worked.

Frank and Ava celebrated their first wedding anniversary on 7 November. It was Ava's third marriage and the first time she had gone a full year. And what did they do? They sailed to Africa.

Ava Gardner was starring in the jungle drama *Mogambo* with Clark Gable and Grace Kelly and directed by John Ford. It was a lavish remake of a 1931 film Gable had made called *Red Dust* with Ava in Jean Harlow's role. At a party at the British High Commission in Nairobi, John Ford asked Ava what she saw in that 120 pound runt and her reply has made dictionaries of quotations: She said, 'Well, there's only 10 pounds of Frankie but there's 110 pounds of cock.'

There might be some truth in this as Sinatra's valet George Jacobs revealed that he wore special underwear to keep it in check, and he certainly asked his girlfriends if they would like to see 'Big Frankie'. Oddly enough, Elvis would ask girls if they would like to see 'Little Elvis'. On the set, Ava and Grace were once walking past the African extras. Ava walked up to a well-built African, undid his loincloth and said, 'Frank's is bigger.' So we have enough evidence to say that it was.

Perhaps through boredom, Ava was provocative. She bathed nude in front of the extras and when Ford told her off, she walked naked through the camp. On the other hand, John Ford had the measure of Frank. He told him to cook them all a spaghetti dinner if he wanted to stay on the set.

Despite the A-list cast and director, *Mogambo* seems stilted today and the animals had the best roles as they were not lumbered with the dialogue. The costumes were ridiculous as both Ava and Grace looked like Hollywood beauties exquisitely made up without a hair out of place in designer clothes and yet here they are in the middle of the jungle. Ava received an Oscar nomination for Best Actress and Grace for Best Supporting Actress. As an indication as to how bad the acting is, Donald Sinden as Kelly's husband looks like he is acting normally. *Mogambo* which was filmed in colour with some remarkable scenery and sunsets was nevertheless a tedious film by John Ford's standards, Still, Ava won an Oscar, Grace received a nomination and Clark Gable's career had been revived.

Sinatra was there because he was at a loose end and had little work. He had even asked the William Morris Agency to take him on and they would arrange a charm offensive in which he would apologise to the press.

He did however return home at the end of November to play the French Casino in New York and then open a new Las Vegas casino, the Sands, which was now managed by his friend from the Copa, Jack Entratter. For once, he was working with Ray Sinatra. Gambling itself was second nature to Sinatra, which came from growing up with Dolly.

While Frank was away, Ava left Nairobi for a few days and, unknown to Frank, had an abortion in Wimbledon, though the press said it was 'a tropical infection'. She wrote in her autobiography, 'Unless you are prepared to devote practically all your time to raise your child in its early years, it is unfair to the baby.'

Frank returned for Christmas and arranged a special show for the cast and crew where John Ford recited ''Twas the Night Before Christmas'. Back home, George and Gracie Burns invited the Sinatra family over to their home and gave them all presents.

Despite his marriage, perhaps because of it, Frank Sinatra was at his lowest point. There was no radio, no TV, no films, no records and only a few live appearances. Frank was losing his original fan base as the bobbysoxers were growing up and the new ones wanted new idols. Frank was depressed when he passed a theatre with a huge crowd going in to see Eddie Fisher, a protégé of Manie Sacks.

1952 was a year in which Frank Sinatra's career was going nowhere. That was about to change. 1953 was the year in which Frank's career went from here to eternity.

CHAPTER 8

From here to eternity

Beverly Sills: *'What do you get out of insulting people?'*
Frank Sinatra: *'Satisfaction.'*

I. Making Arrangements

We have already seen how Frank Sinatra owed a considerable proportion of his success to the skills of his arrangers: Axel Stordahl, in particular, but also Sy Oliver and George Siravo. In this chapter, Frank joins Capitol Records and nearly all his records for the next seven years, his classic years, were the work of three men: Nelson Riddle and Billy May, starting in 1953, and Gordon Jenkins from 1957. Sinatra was well aware of his debt to them and he frequently credited their work in his stage introductions. He referred to Nelson Riddle as 'Maestro'.

In summary, Nelson Riddle is the maestro, the most important and most productive of the three, being primarily responsible for creating Sinatra's swingin' persona. Billy May is famed for brash, often humorous, big band performances, while Gordon Jenkins emphasised Sinatra's sentimental side with banks of strings. In reality, the lines between them are blurred as they could work in each other's territory but that is broadly correct.

Nelson Smock Riddle Jr was born in the small town of Oradell, New Jersey on 1 June 1921 but the family soon moved to nearby Ridgewood. His father, also Nelson Riddle, was a sign painter and commercial artist of Dutch parentage, while his mother, Albertine claimed to be related to Spanish monarchy and felt she had married beneath herself. She was a domineering woman who had had six miscarriages before Nelson which explains why she doted on him, even smothered him. Whatever. It left Nelson with an inferiority complex.

With family encouragement, Nelson took up the piano and switched to the trombone when he was 14. After graduation he played trombone in local dance bands, having his first taste of success in Charlie Spivak's orchestra. He studied orchestration and had a short time in Tommy Dorsey's orchestra before being drafted. While in the army, he married a pretty waitress from Los Angeles, Doreen Moran, but in 1946 he had an accident with a garage door that knocked out his front teeth. Realising that he would never be able to play the trombone again he determined to become a professional arranger and hopefully a composer too. He arranged NBC's radio shows in Hollywood. The following year Nelson, who drank too much, hit a tree while driving home, wrecking his car and breaking several ribs. Sinatra recalled that the first time he met the accident-prone Riddle, he was on crutches.

The bandleader Les Baxter often commissioned others to write arrangements for him, including Albert Harris and Pete Rugolo, although he would take the credit. Indeed, he was a con artist. He was a poor conductor and his musicians would tell new members, 'Don't look at Les, just play it.' There was a saying within the band, 'The less Baxter, the better.' Baxter got where he was by being a good front man for radio, TV and concert appearances.

As well as making his own orchestral records, Capitol asked him to write and conduct arrangements for other performers. No problem, said Les, who immediately hired someone to do the work for him. This happened in 1950 when Nelson Riddle arranged 'Mona Lisa' for Nat 'King' Cole at Capitol Records, his sublime orchestration being almost as beautiful as the painting.

Nat 'King' Cole was already recognised as a jazz pianist but now he was hailed as a great singer, almost by accident. 'Mona Lisa' became an international hit and Cole was given another song 'Too Young', although at 34, he was too old to be singing 'They try to tell me I'm too young.' It was another ghosted arrangement bearing Les Baxter's name and another worldwide hit.

One day Nat was recording one of Nelson's arrangements and he had a technical question. Les Baxter was flummoxed and Nat realised that it wasn't his work at all. Lee Gillette, who was producing the session, told him to ask Nelson. Later in the year, another Nat 'King' Cole winner, 'Unforgettable' was released and this time Nelson Riddle's name was on the label. The arrangement was based on the piano-vibes-guitar sound of George Shearing and Shearing, a delightful man, took it as a great compliment. He told me, 'I didn't work with Nat until 'Let There Be Love' in 1961 but everyone assumed I'd been working with him for years.'

Nelson Riddle was made a musical director at Capitol and in 1952 he recorded a million seller, 'Blacksmith Blues' with Ella Mae Morse. He wrote scores of scores for Margaret Whiting, Dick Haymes and Al Martino and he showed his flair for comedy with several novelties for Jerry Lewis – Billy May did some of them too.

In 1953 Nelson was asked to work with Frank Sinatra, and Nelson commented, 'Most of our best numbers are in the tempo of the heartbeat. That's the tempo that strikes people the easiest because they are moving to that pace all their waking hours.'

Nelson Riddle rarely told anyone he was too busy; he would write for Nat King' Cole and anyone else that Capitol wanted. Some books and articles depict him as a recluse but with that workload he would have had to be. He once wrote a note to Ella Mae Morse, ending 'My ashtray runneth over!'

Billy May was of the same opinion, saying in 1992. 'Nelson Riddle and I agreed that making a living as an arranger, you couldn't afford to turn down any work. Some of it was interesting and some of it was quickly forgotten – crap!'

True, but most of the work with Sinatra was inspirational, bringing out the best in everyone. Sinatra recorded over 300 tracks for Capitol and there are few that lack merit. Two-thirds of them were arranged by Nelson Riddle.

Edward William May Jr was born in Pittsburgh, Pennsylvania on 10 November 1916. He played the tuba in his high school band. He became intrigued by the way that the instruments blended together, and realised that he wanted to be an arranger. When he was 17, he was playing with a local band, Gene Olsen's Polish-American Orchestra, but he aimed for the famed big bands. When Charlie Barnet came to town, he asked him if he could submit arrangements and soon he was both playing trumpet and writing arrangements for him.

In 1939 he wrote a fiery, hot-headed arrangement for a British tune, Ray Noble's 'Cherokee'. It was not only a hit for Barnet, it became his signature tune. May worked for Barnet for another year and then moved to Glenn Miller and his Orchestra. He created the horn line for 'Serenade in Blue' and wrote 'Boom Shot' with him. When May was divorced in 1954, he allowed his wife to keep the royalties from his time with Glenn Miller. This backfired when he found that Universal was making *The Glenn Miller Story*. He also assisted John Scott Trotter with arrangements for Bing Crosby.

After a short time with Les Brown, Billy May became part of the LA session scene and then he joined Capitol, employed by Alan Livingston as a staff arranger. Alan Livingston was keen on creating records for children and they worked on the series of Sparky's Magic Piano and Bozo the Clown. Most famous of all, May arranged Mel Blanc's 'I Tawt I Saw A Puddy Tat' and he orchestrated the dance instruction series with Arthur Murray. His comedy came to the fore in a series of brilliant parodies for Stan Freberg, which are funnier than any of his records with Jerry Lewis. They mocked Elvis Presley, Johnnie Ray and Harry Belafonte and there was a blisteringly funny attack on *The Lawrence Welk Show*. Additionally, he wrote for the extreme vocal range of Yma Sumac, said to be five octaves, which would be a challenge for any arranger.

Billy May formed his own band in 1951 but the big band era had passed and this was largely for studio work. In 1952 he had his own US hit with a unique 'slurping saxes' arrangement of 'Charmaine', but Mantovani took the main honours with his equally distinctive cascading strings. Billy followed it with an album, *Sorta May*. He was a forceful, over-the-top character who drank and ate heavily. His music was similarly to excess. He liked saying, 'There'll be no drinking off the job.'

Although Billy May became famous for his brisk tempos and his slurping saxes, he could be a problem for Capitol. He would turn up for the sessions in old pullovers and tennis shoes with a cigarette in one hand, a vodka in the other and the arrangements, written at the last minute, under his arm. He had an unlikely private life too: his wife married his manager while he married his manager's ex-wife.

By 1956 Billy May's energetic, horn-based sound had become so familiar that it could be parodied by Johnny Dankworth on his hit single, 'Experiments With Mice'. Sinatra was naturally drawn to such a boisterous, fun-loving character while May saw how he could bring out Sinatra's confidence and humour in his arrangements. Billy May and Nelson Riddle could mimic each other and one of May's compositions in 1958 was called 'Solving the Riddle'.

Gordon Hill Jenkins was born in Webster Groves, Missouri on 12 May 1910, the son of a cinema organist. While still a child, he would sometimes play the organ for his father. During Prohibition, he was playing piano in a St. Louis speakeasy. He joined Isham Jones's band as a pianist and was soon writing arrangements for them. In the mid-1930s, he was managing Woody Herman's band and writing arrangements for Paul Whiteman, Benny Goodman, and Andre Kostelanetz. He married in 1931 and had three children, and after they divorced, he married the singer, Beverly Mahr.

In 1938 he worked for Paramount Pictures and became a music director for NBC in Hollywood. In 1944, he worked on Dick Haymes' radio show and he had a hit record, 'San Fernando Valley' under his own name. In 1945, he became a staff conductor for Decca Records and had his own hits with 'Maybe You'll Be There' and 'My Foolish Heart'. He conducted for Dick Haymes ('Little White Lies'), Ella Fitzgerald ('Black Coffee'), Louis Armstrong ('Blueberry Hill') and Billie Holiday ('God Bless the Child'.). When he stood in front of an orchestra, about to conduct for Louis Armstrong, he told the musicians, 'This is the greatest moment of my life.'

Gordon Jenkins saw how to make a folk group from Greenwich Village, the Weavers, commercially successful, which was as much to their surprise as anyone else's. The blending of their folk harmonies with an orchestra was enormously successful and meant that a Leadbelly song, 'Goodnight Irene', reached the top of the US charts.

Gordon Jenkins and his Orchestra performed his New York suite, 'Manhattan Tower' on *The Ed Sullivan Show* and his 'Crescent City Blues' was pillaged by Johnny Cash for

'Folsom Prison Blues'. He loved string-heavy, semi-classical orchestrations although many of them sound lush and syrupy today. 'I was never a great fan of Gordon Jenkins,' said Bill Miller, 'but he did some nice things. I have played enough of his rhythm parts to know that he wasn't a complete musician but he developed a trademark with those high strings.'

Much more than Nelson Riddle and Billy May, Gordon Jenkins was a songwriter, usually writing both words and lyrics. In 1945 Frank recorded 'Homesick, That's All'. He often put his thoughts on life into his songs and these philosophical musings resonated with Sinatra. However, he was to have his run-ins with Sinatra as he was tough and forthright and not someone who could be easily intimidated.

As we shall see, Frank Sinatra was sorry to lose touch with Axel Stordahl but he realised that Nelson Riddle, Billy May and Gordon Jenkins were working wonders on his behalf. One great album followed another and despite the advent of rock'n'roll, Sinatra was in his prime. Frank Sinatra Jr recalled, 'There was a tremendous level of excitement every time he recorded. Everyone knew that they were making the best records around. How could they miss? They had the best singer, the best arrangers, the best musicians, the best engineers and the best studio in town.'

Sinatra felt that he could get his best performances with an audience, and so there was often a small coterie of friends and admirers at the sessions, and none of the arrangers objected to this. 'Attending recording sessions at Capitol was like going to a concert today,' said his daughter Nancy, 'It was the hottest ticket in town, it was fantastic. It was great for him to have a small audience in the room and everyone as a result of that did their best. There was magic in those studios and in that building.'

One arranger who might have been great for Sinatra was Pete Rugolo but he resisted the call, saying, 'I got to be a buddy of Frank's. I kept company with him, especially during his bad year. He was always after me to write an arrangement for him and I never did it. He was my favourite singer and I thought 'Suppose I do something and he doesn't like it?''

II. Day In–Day Out, 1953

Things weren't looking good for Frank Sinatra at the start of 1953. He later said, 'I was a has-been, sitting by a telephone that wouldn't ring. My friends had grown invisible when the music stopped. I was finding out how tough it was to borrow money when you're all washed up.' Nothing much was happening but as he was no longer confined to New York and Los Angeles through TV or film commitments he could work elsewhere. Frank went on the road with a small group, using arrangements from George Siravo.

Early in 1953 the producer Harry Cohn was after Marlene Dietrich to star in the film of the Broadway success, *Pal Joey*. 'Bewitched, Bothered and Bewildered' would have been perfect for her and she wanted Frank to co-star. Cohn felt that the fans might stay away and suggested Jack Lemmon. Dietrich considered him a lemon and the film was off. At the same time, Dietrich wanted Jean Louis Berthault who was under contract to Columbia to design her gowns for Las Vegas. Cohn said no, but Dietrich spoke to the Mafia boss, Frank Costello who reminded Harry Cohn that he had growing children. She got Jean Louis.

The Mafia had its interests in the entertainment business. Al Martino, who had hit success in 1952 with his first record 'Here in My Heart', commented, 'When I first started I had a manager and he was approached by some underworld figures in New York City. He was forced to sell my contract to them, and from then on I never knew where my salary was going. It was being channelled into other accounts. When I fired them, there was some physical harm, so I decided to flee the country and I came to Great Britain. That cloud lived over my head for seven years. I pursued that role in *The Godfather* because I thought it paralleled my life. Sinatra thought it was his life, but not really. It was mine. (Laughs)'

In 1953 Peter Lawford met Ava Gardner and her sister at Luau in Beverly Hills for drinks. When it was reported by Louella Parsons, Frank called him and said, 'Do you want your legs broken?' His manager, Milton Ebbins told Frank he was there as well and it was only for drinks. Frank didn't speak to Peter Lawford for five years. Peter tried to repair the damage but it didn't work. Then Frank thought he would like to be a pal of the future President...

In February 1953 Frank Sinatra came to the UK to arrange some touring dates and even gave a friendly interview to Tony Hall for the *New Musical Express*. He was given a song, 'My One and Only Love', written by British publisher Robert Mellin. He said, 'For you, Bob, I'll do it'" which was patronising as it was a good song. He was true to his word, recording it in May 1953, but it was a strange business. Guy Wood had originally written it as 'Music From Beyond the Moon' with Jack Lawrence. Mellin had simply reused the melody and the first Guy Wood knew about it was when Frank's record was released.

Manie Sacks had wanted to sign Frank to RCA but his new bosses said no: Sinatra was trouble and he no longer was selling. Alan Livingston, encouraged by his deputy the jazz writer Dave Dexter, wanted him for Capitol and he signed with the label at Lucy's Restaurant in Hollywood on 14 March 1953. It was a one year contract with six options for Capitol to renew, effectively a seven year contract and Sinatra would receive a 5% royalty on his releases, although the recording costs would be deducted first. Outside of Livingston and Dexter, the Capitol team was unimpressed but Livingston told them, 'I can only judge talent and Frank is the best singer in the world.'

Dave Dexter was the obvious choice for Frank's producer but Frank wouldn't have this as he had taken exception to something Dexter had written some years back. Voyle Gilmore was appointed Sinatra's producer and Livingston wanted him to work with Nelson Riddle. At the time, Nat 'King' Cole was in the Top 10 with Nelson's sublime arrangement for 'Pretend'. Gilmore wanted to try Sinatra with Billy May's humorous arrangements. Normally Capitol preferred to develop new talent and they knew it would be a challenge to get Frank selling again. It wasn't as though his music was unfashionable. The general public thought he was a great singer and liked his songs, but they didn't like Frank Sinatra as a person, so he wasn't selling anymore.

Frank wanted to stay with Axel Stordahl and, knowing that Sinatra could be awkward, Voyle Gilmore said, 'Okay, we'll have one session with Axel and see how it goes.' That first Capitol session took place at the KHJ radio studio in Hollywood as Capitol's own studios in that big round tower were not yet ready. The first track, 'Lean Baby' had been an instrumental piece written by Billy May. May had used the term as a dance instruction – Lean forwards, Lean back – but the lyricist, Roy Alfred thought it could apply to a skinny girl. In a sense Sinatra was mocking his own image ('The feeling is nice, My arms can go round twice') and the playoff suggested that Frank had been listening to some R&B. It was a promising start.

The second song was a British composition, 'I'm Walking Behind You', a song of lost love where the singer was walking behind his intended on her wedding day. Sinatra gave a fine bur restrained performance and, much to Sinatra's chagrin, the best-selling version came from Eddie Fisher on RCA.

The songwriter Johnny Mercer had been one of Capitol's founders but there was no compulsion to perform his songs. He and his co-owners had done a remarkable job, creating a company that could rival the giants – Columbia, RCA Victor and Decca – and they were now planning their highly lucrative exit. In a shock move to the industry, in January 1955, the British company EMI paid $8m for Capitol Records and so from that date, Sinatra was then effectively working for a British company.

Frank thought that Johnny Mercer was among America's greatest lyricists and he recorded a fine version of 'Day In – Day Out' from the revue, *Lew Leslie's Blackbirds Of 1939*, a Broadway show featuring Lena Horne. It is among Stordahl's best arrangements with the 'pounding becomes' suggesting the ringing of an alarm clock, and it is more reflective than Frank's swinging version in 1958. The fourth song was 'Don't Make a Beggar of Me', a weak song that sounds as it was written to follow Guy Mitchell's hit 'A Beggar in Love'.

Frank Sinatra had been most impressed with *From Here to Eternity,* an 800-page novel written by James Jones in 1951 about an army barracks in Hawaii just before the Pearl Harbour attack by the Japanese. James Jones had served in conflict and his novel had an authenticity which was lacking in many other works from the period. It was a tough book about the brutality of army life and the destruction of individual personalities in a regiment. The novel incorporated prostitution, sadism and buggery as well as strong language and with the highly moral screen codes of the time, it seemed an unlikely film subject. Indeed, the efforts to turn it into a film would be worthy of a film in itself.

Harry Cohn, who was born in 1891, had been involved with films since the silent movies and Columbia Pictures made money every year during his 30 year reign. He and his brother Jack constantly disagreed and each tried to undermine the other. Somehow, Columbia flourished and Harry got the top job. The major companies were MGM, Paramount, Universal, Warner Brothers and 20th Century Fox with Columbia and RKO regarded as minor studios by comparison. They couldn't pay the huge salaries of the majors and were called 'The home of falling stars' by their rivals.

Although Harry was a brilliant businessman, he was brash and abrasive and he loved his reputation as 'the most hated man in Hollywood'. By industry standards, he was an honest man and he did not deal with gangsters. However, he had met Mussolini in the 1930s and seen how nobody could barge into his office because the door could only be opened with a switch. He copied that and also the dictator's raised desk so that he could look down on everyone and stare at them with his intense blue eyes. From time to time two blue eyes stared back at him.

Cohn's insults were legendary. When he turned down Peter Falk for a role, he said, 'For the same money, I can get an actor with two eyes.' John Wayne was furious when he found that Cohn had told other producers that he was a drunk and troublemaker and he refused to work for Columbia again.

But Cohn did appreciate those who answered back. He said to one of his screenwriters, Jo Swerling, 'Your wife drove into my Rolls-Royce in the parking lot' to which Swerling replied, 'She must have thought you were in it.' However, one drunken actor, Warren Hymer, went too far. While Cohn was yelling at him, Hymer unzipped and urinated over Cohn's desk. He never worked for Columbia again and the desk was replaced.

When Cohn saw the rushes for a film based on the Arabian Nights, he called the management team together. He yelled, 'I pay you college men thousands of dollars to know something and all I get is ignorance. Tell me, when does this picture take place?'

'About 1200 AD.'

'Exactly,' said Cohn, 'I never went to college like you sons of bitches but I do know that nobody in 1200 AD said "Yes siree!"'

'They don't,' was the reply, 'They're saying, "Yes, sire".'

In the early 50s, the major film companies were in turmoil. They did not see television as a friend but a threat. They feared that the public would stay at home and ignore their productions so a series of gimmicks emerged, Cinerama, CinemaScope and VistaVision, but the most controversial was 3-D. The novelty of 3-D would soon pass (although it has returned in recent years) as the glasses were irritating and gave headaches. Columbia was not one of the giant studios but Harry Cohn was the first to seize the initiative by creating 'made-for-TV' films and by selling back catalogue to the TV networks, all through a new subsidiary, Screen Gems. He also believed that if you had a great product, the public would come to see it no matter what. In 1953 that product would be *From Here To Eternity*. He was sure that this could be a major film and he didn't want any slip-ups.

Through one character, the likeable and high-spirited Maggio, in *From Here to Eternity*, James Jones dealt with the difficulties that Italian-Americans had when fitting into society. Maggio was a decent but stubborn, fun-loving soldier from Brooklyn. He received some setbacks and paid for it with his life. When Frank heard that Harry Cohn was producing a film version for Columbia, he wanted to be Maggio. Cohn was reluctant even to give him a screen test because he was trouble and his very name might turn cinemagoers away. More than anything, he disliked Sinatra's arrogance and he told him, 'This is an actor's part, not a crooner's.'

The film was to be directed by Fred Zinnemann, who had had a major success with the western, *High Noon*, starring Gary Cooper and Grace Kelly. *From Here to Eternity* was to be an expensive production but Zinnemann was insisting on black and white as, like many directors of the day, he thought that colour would trivialise the drama.

Every actor with any talent wanted to be in *From Here to Eternity* and the film could have been shot with several potential casts. Ronald Reagan, Walter Matthau and Jack Warden were all considered for the philandering Captain. At one stage, the role was assigned to Edmond O'Brien but everyone really wanted Burt Lancaster. Burt had his own production deals and didn't want to be an actor for hire. However, he owed Hal Wallis a film for which he would earn $120,000. Wallis hadn't decided what that film would be and he sold the contract to Columbia for $150,000, so they now had Burt Lancaster for the role.

Aldo DaRé had been groomed for stardom by Harry Cohn and had had a success as Aldo Ray with Judy Holliday in *The Marrying Kind* (1952). He sent the extravert actor on a very successful tour of personal appearances but Ray clocked up the expenses, so much so that Cohn presented him with his wages one week – just 24 cents. Cohn promised him the role of the conscience-stricken Robert E Lee Prewitt in *From Here to Eternity* but Zinnemann insisted on Montgomery Clift, a great looking guy and part of the new school of Method actors. Instead, Ray was loaned out to other studios and he faced suspension rather than act in films he considered inferior. He became estranged from Cohn but from the late 1950s onwards he appeared in many films.

Prewitt was a bugler who had blinded a friend in a boxing match and didn't want to fight again. Transferred to Hawaii, the Captain wanted him to fight and when he refused, he got 'the treatment'. Prewitt accepted the bullying because he would feel even worse if he did fight. For the role, Montgomery Clift shaved his chest as he felt that chest hair was a sign of virility and Prewitt's bravery had to be hidden.

Because of his training, Clift was intensely into his role with long pauses and speaking in off-beat rhythms. Clift told Sinatra, 'Good dialogue is never enough to explain all the infinite gradations of character.' This increased his edginess and when he said, 'I know where I stand. A man don't go his own way – he's nothing', it sounded like the real life Sinatra. The surprise was that Sinatra wasn't after this role.

Sinatra kept sending Cohn telegrams signed 'Maggio' and insisting on a test. Ava even asked Harry's wife, Jean, to persuade Harry to give him the role. Sinatra offered to work for $1,000 a week, and that might have appealed to Cohn the most. It is thought that this is the time that Harry Cohn found a horse's head at the end of his bed, but Mafia involvement is unlikely. Surely if the Mafia was lobbying for Sinatra, they would have secured him the prime role of Prewitt, and surely Prewitt's 'If a man don't go his own way, he's nothing' is pure Sinatra.

Actually, Harry Cohn, his fellow producer Buddy Adler and Fred Zinnemann were all agreed upon Eli Wallach for Maggio. He had been informed that the role was his but at the same time he was offered a Broadway part in Tennessee Williams' *Camino Real*. He chose that role so his good fortune was also Sinatra's good fortune. Simple as that.

Or was it? There were other actors who could have played the role and Cohn hated Sinatra, referring to him as a 'guinea greaseball wop'. Gianni Russo, the stepson of Frank Costello, knew the major participants. He says, 'I am sure that was no Mafia involvement. Harry Cohn was the ugliest man in the world and he wanted to screw Ava Gardner. She knew how much Frank wanted that part and she promised Harry Cohn a weekend in Acapulco. Frank was furious when he found out. That's worse than the Mafia getting you the role. Harry Cohn's wife was a nice Jewish lady who knew that her husband wanted to screw Ava Gardner and she let him go.'

Ernest Borgnine had read the book and didn't mind being cast as the bad guy, Fatso: indeed, James Jones was most impressed with his casting, telling him, 'You're absolutely the son of a bitch I was writing about.'

When Borgnine heard Sinatra was in the cast, he was sure there would be some songs somewhere. As it was, the only musical moment for Sinatra is a brief acappella 'Chattanooga Choo Choo', but the country singer Merle Travis performs 'Re-enlistment Blues' with some soldiers.

Borgnine was similarly surprised to find that Sinatra was a seriously good actor. In the film, he had to smash Sinatra's skull but after the scene had been filmed, the censors decided that the scene was too strong and we just see Fatso pick up the baton. Frank looked at him in the first take and said, 'My god, he's ten feet tall', which must have been very funny.

Burt Lancaster commented, 'Sinatra's fervour, anger and bitterness had something to do with the character of Maggio, but also with what he had gone through in recent years: a sense of defeat, and the whole world crashing in on him.' In other words, Frank didn't have to do much acting: he was playing a version of himself.

For its time the book was crude and violent and the talk in Hollywood was 'Why would Harry Cohn buy a dirty book like *From Here To Eternity*?' The jokey answer was, 'Because he thinks everybody talks like that.' Cohn paid $82,000 for the book and he asked James Jones to write the first screenplay, though this proved impractical. Dan Taradash saw a way around the problems and also saw how to placate the army. Cohn wanted to use army premises but for that to happen, changes needed to be made. In the novel, the corrupt captain was promoted to a major; in the screenplay, he accepted his actions and resigned. This version of the script was approved in the Pentagon and permission was given to film at Scofield Barracks in Hawaii.

The brothel in the novel became a drinking club where the soldiers merely chat to the girls and sip Coca-Colas. A contract player with Columbia, Donna Reed was Cohn's choice for the 'hostess' but Zinnemann favoured Julie Harris, who had been in his film, *Member of the Wedding*. Cohn said no, she was a 'child frightener' and so Donna Reed it was. When she was nominated for an Oscar for Best Supporting Actress, Harry Cohn mounted a publicity campaign on her behalf. She did win but because Cohn thought she was ungrateful, he then cast her in cheap westerns. She stopped making films in 1955 and concentrated on TV.

Harry Cohn had wanted Joan Crawford as the Captain's wife who was sleeping around but she didn't care for the script and an agent suggested Deborah Kerr. Cohn thought it was a terrible idea as she invariably played prim British ladies. However, he was persuaded that this would add an element of surprise to the film and agreed.

The film is famous for Burt Lancaster and Deborah Kerr rolling over romantically in the surf. Even though not much is shown, the effect is erotic, but the scene is short as they then have an argument. The censors insisted that Deborah Kerr had to wear a skirt over her bathing suit. The site of their lovemaking has become a tourist attraction.

Of course Sinatra was trouble. Just before filming, Sinatra was with union organiser Benny Macri at the Desert Inn in Vegas. He wanted to see Ray Sinatra at some other casino. He drove a Cadillac at 100 mph and nearly hit the sheriff Glen Jones. Sinatra jumped out of his car and called Jones a motherfucker – he should have been arrested. Later, Glen Jones was in the cocktail lounge at the Desert Inn and Benny Macri went over and apologised for Sinatra. Jones said, 'Don't worry about it.'

Even though Sinatra wanted the part so much, he was no model actor and caused problems by drinking too much. Even on the first day when flying to Hawaii, he and Montgomery Clift got drunk. The media were waiting but somehow they muddled through the press conference. Sometimes Burt Lancaster and Deborah Kerr would see Sinatra and Clift to bed and then go to Zinneman's apartment for dinner. Sinatra was missing Ava and he could rarely contact her in Spain because of poor communications. One day though he got Clift sober enough for a shoot. Although he loathed another Method actor, Marlon Brando, he didn't mind Clift, especially as he didn't want multiple takes like Brando. Clift gave Sinatra advice, telling him, 'Don't overdo the death scene. It should be like snow falling.'

In the scene in front of the officers' barracks, Cohn said that the drunken Clift and Sinatra should play the scene standing up but it flowed better when they were sitting. Someone told this to Harry Cohn who was at the Royal Hawaiian Hotel with an air force general. As they were filming, Cohn and the general drove up and Cohn said to Zinnemann, 'You shoot it the way I told you or I will shut down this picture.'

Cohn was so impressed with the results that he lent his name to trade ads for the film. *From Here to Eternity* cost $2.4m but within two years, it had grossed $80m, the biggest moneymaker in Columbia's history. The film won eight Oscars, tying with the record held by *Gone with the Wind*. No one was more pleased than Harry Cohn. He had shown the industry that a black and white film with no gimmicks could still do big business.

George Reeves played Sgt Stark. He had been in *Gone with the Wind* and was about to become a TV star as Superman. From then on, everybody shouted, 'Here's Superman', when they saw him. He got so depressed that he killed himself in 1959.

Sinatra had had a brief session with Nelson Riddle when he came in to do a song at the end of a session. Nelson had written an arrangement for 'Wrap Your Troubles in Dreams' but Sinatra didn't like it and the version was never released. He told Nelson, "When you're writing, write a fill for me when I'm through singing, but don't have a concerto behind my voice."

On 30 April 1953 Sinatra had another session with Nelson in Los Angeles and this time Nelson knew what was wanted. Oddly enough, the session was going to be with Billy May but as Billy May was on the road, Nelson took his place. The tracks have always been issued as 'Frank Sinatra with Billy May and his Orchestra', although Billy May was nowhere to be seen.

The first song was a brilliant, life-energising performance of 'I've Got the World on a String', a song that Sinatra had been performing in concert. It had a stunning crescendo opening and Sinatra and Riddle were working well together. Next came a ballad 'Don't Worry 'Bout Me', a song popularised by Hal Kemp in 1939 but also recorded by Cab Calloway and Count Basie. It is among Sinatra's greatest recordings. However, he didn't include the introductory verse which he would sometimes sing in concert. This was followed by a delightful ballad from the 1923 show, *Little Jessie James*, 'I Love You'. Sinatra sang, 'I love you is all that I can say' and then repeated it 10 times. Finally, there was 'South of the Border' with Sinatra swinging harder than ever before. This arrangement was unlike Nelson Riddle as he was aping Billy May.

On 2 May he was back with Nelson for a pleasant ballad, 'Anytime, Anywhere', 'My One and Only Love' (fancy starting a song with the words, 'The very thought of you'), 'I Can Read Between the Lines' (a neat song about an impending breakup) and a song to promote *From Here To Eternity* featuring a lyric penned by Robert Wells to fit the melody heard on the film's credits. It was published by his own Barton music and at the end of the take, Sinatra says, 'Bob, is that all right?' Alan Livingston thought this was an excellent idea and from then on, he would be looking for title songs that Sinatra could record.

Before Frank Sinatra came to the UK, he was to give a few concerts in Italy, Belgium, Denmark, Sweden and Norway, but there were many problems. In Naples, tickets were sold on the grounds that this was a concert by Frank and Ava. Just 4,000 turned up to see him in the 15,000 capacity Folkparken in Malmö. The promoters refused to meet his whole fee and so Frank, in a fit of pique, only performed for 30 minutes as that was all they had paid for. While that was understandable, it was unfair to the 4,000 who had paid for a full show. Further dates in Sweden and Norway were cancelled.

Melody Maker published a critical feature about the concerts or lack of them, which did not bode well for the UK. The paper said, 'Frank has been a flop in Denmark and Sweden and tonight when I called the hotel, I was told he was ill and gone to bed.' *New Musical Express* carried Frank's side of the story. He hadn't been prepared for Malmö being an outside concert in the rain and cold. He commented, 'The audience was wrapped in blankets and rugs while I wore a thin, Palm Beach suit. No one told me that it was going to be an open air event.' When someone brought him a cup of hot tea, which was not to his liking, he remarked, 'Crosby must have made this.'

From June to August 1953 Frank Sinatra was in the UK for a variety tour of Moss Empires with his pianist Bill Miller and backed by Billy Ternent and his Orchestra. It is Sinatra's one and only comprehensive UK tour. He was playing a week's variety in each of four cities: Bristol, Birmingham, Glasgow and Liverpool as well as making some one-off appearances. He had Ava with him from time to time as she filming *Knights of the Round Table* in England with Robert Taylor and Stanley Baker. Ava was staying out of America for tax reasons. It would have cost her $150,000 to return to the US early.

When Frank Sinatra had first came to the UK in 1950, he'd read British newspapers and periodicals and was intrigued by *Radio Times*. Every household had a copy and years before Dr Hook wanted to be on the cover of *Rolling Stone*, Frank Sinatra wanted to be on the cover of *Radio Times*.

Frank Sinatra agreed to a radio broadcast with the prestigious BBC while he was in the UK. The BBC didn't pay big money but Sinatra was prepared to donate his fee to charity. Once again, he favoured the National Playing Fields Association, not because he knew much about playing fields but because its president was the Duke of Edinburgh – and Frank was a sucker for the one thing America hadn't got: a Royal Family.

So Frank's agent, John Harding, negotiated for him to appear on the Light Programme with the BBC Show Band Orchestra conducted by Cyril Stapleton. His fee would only be 50 guineas provided he got his way over something else. On April 5, the BBC's Variety Booking Manager told his superiors that Frank had a stiplulation on which the whole show stood or fell: he wanted the front cover of the *Radio Times*.'

Such a request was unprecedented at the BBC, but normally no one in their right mind would argue with Sinatra. However, Sinatra reckoned without the BBC's protocol and its inflexible rules that were not made to be broken. Frank Sinatra was told no, he could not be guaranteed the cover of *Radio Times* as that would compromise its editor. It was hoped that Frank would appreciate the impossibility of his request. There was little chance of that.

However, there was a let out in the shape of Her Majesty. The Coronation was taking place in June and it would coincide with Frank's début on the BBC. The Queen would very definitely be the cover story for the *Radio Times* and even Frank Sinatra could appreciate that. In the event, Frank capitulated and the *Radio Times* wrote a feature about him for its inside pages. Frank was so happy with the programme that he agreed to another Show Band Show and this time the BBC paid him an unprecedented 75 guineas, a win/win situation all round. Over two appearances, Frank performed 'The Birth of the Blues', 'Ol' Man River', 'I'm Walking Behind You', 'I've Got the World on a String', 'Day In – Day Out' and 'London by Night'.

Frank recorded an interview with David Jacobs for Radio Luxembourg, which went fine as Jacobs had stuck to the rules: 'He said that if I mentioned Ava Gardner, he would push the microphone down my throat.' He told another reporter that he was going to send Bing a postcard from the Chamber of Horrors.

Sinatra's first appearance was at the Tooting Granada. It was the first live show in that cinema and it had not been well publicised. The Granada TV producer, Johnnie Hamp, recalls, 'When I first got a job with Granada it wasn't with the television company but with Granada Theatres. I was the assistant manager at the Granada in Tooting which was a big cinema in London. Their very first one night stand was by my idol, Frank Sinatra. I had to go and meet him and I mixed the sound for him and I was really chuffed. The cinema held 3,600 people and only 150 turned up, which is impossible to believe these days. Sinatra walked out and did his first number, 'I've Got the World on a String', and he said to the audience, "Why don't you all come down the front?" There were a few up in the circle. They sat around him and he said, "What do you want me to sing?" and he did some requests including 'Nancy' and it was the best concert I ever saw him do.'

The shows at other venues were better attended but were not full houses. The Eurovision songwriter, Bill Martin, was at the Glasgow Empire: 'I saw Frank Sinatra when he, comparatively speaking, was down and out. He had lost his way as Frankie Laine, Johnnie Ray and Guy Mitchell had taken over, and it was just before he made his big comeback with the war film, *From Here to Eternity*. He'd committed himself to a tour of Great Britain and the theatre, which seated 2,000, was half-empty. He was as skinny as the microphone. His voice was at its best, but there was a big black crack painted on the floor on the stage. He walked on and jumped over the crack and said, 'You nearly lost me there' but he didn't have the timing for jokes. Sinatra was singing very tortured, very slow ballads, all aimed at Ava Gardner, who wasn't there. I especially remember him singing 'Try A Little Tenderness'. Bing Crosby had recorded an excellent version but Frank took the song to another level, and the Empire crowd loved it.'

Melody Maker changed its stance with the headline, *Sinatra Scores a Triumph!* Frank commented on his continental gigs by saying, 'Things are a little different over there. You see, there was that little difference of the language barrier.' In the UK, Frank could joke with the audience. When several people shouted out requests at one venue, he said, 'What do you think this is? An auction?' When somebody requested 'Bim Bam Baby', he said,'There's one thing wrong with that record. Columbia put a hole in the middle of it.'

Frank had been booked into the Prince of Wales hotel in Southport but the receptionist had not recognised him. He said, 'If you don't know my name, I'm off.' He had met the local golf pro Bob Halsall in Monte Carlo and he asked him to sort another hotel, so Bob arranged a suite at the Palace. They played golf on the Tuesday and asked by the *Southport Guardian* how he pronounced his wife's name, he said, 'Just think of the word braver and then say Ava.'

Frank and Bob went round the Royal Birkdale, playing for £25 a hole with Bob conceding a couple of strokes on each hole. They came out even and Sinatra challenged him to a singing contest at 2am. He told the barmaid to be the judge and Bob sang 'How Deep is the Ocean' and Frank 'Night and Day'. When the barmaid picked Frank, he said, 'Bob, stick to your golf.'

His driver for the north-west was Ginger McCain, subsequent trainer of Red Rum, who wrote in his autobiography: 'I had to drive him from Southport to Blackpool every day for a week. He was a little rabbit of a man. I wouldn't give you tuppence for him. He was supposed to a big star but Red Rum knocked him into a cocked hat.'

Dorothy Webster, who worked at the Liverpool Empire, recalled, 'On the opening night, he said that he needed some tea without milk and with lemons. We didn't have any lemons backstage and so he had to have it black. The next day I bought some lemons and he had tea with lemons for the rest of the week.'

The future DJ of the Cavern, Bob Wooler, was at the Liverpool Empire: 'I saw Frank Sinatra in 1953 and I paid 3/6d for my ticket – and threepence for the programme. Relatively speaking, he was on the skids. All the bobbysoxers had been screaming for him at the Paramount in New York and now nothing was happening. I saw him on Tuesday at the Empire in a half-empty house, and in the interval, I moved to a seat in the front stalls. I'm glad I did because Sinatra did the whole of the second half with Bill Miller at the piano and the orchestra on stage. I remember him going into the wings and coming out with a cup of tea and saying, 'It's tea, I can assure you.' Sinatra gave a very good concert, and then *From Here to Eternity* came along and re-established him as a major star. Pavarotti said that Sinatra was the Mozart of singers, which is a good way of expressing a truism.'

On Sunday 26 July, Frank played two houses a night at the Blackpool Opera House. The three main theatres in Blackpool had the same management and their output was piped into an underground room where a technician would listen for faults and go to the appropriate theatre to correct them. A doctor from Leeds asked if he could place a reel-to-reel tape recorder next to the speaker for Sinatra's show and against all the odds, he got a near perfect recording. Its quality is far superior to the tapes of the early Elvis stage shows or the Beatles at the Star-Club in Hamburg.

So, unknown to Frank Sinatra, a concert at Opera House, Blackpool was recorded, surfacing on CD much later. As well as performing 13 songs during his 50 minute appearance, Sinatra joked about the English weather ('I got a parka made in Alaska and had it sent down here'), our passion for tea ('Don't you put anything in it?') and the decline in his career ('They didn't put the hole in the middle of this record.').

He parodied Bing Crosby with a spoof lyric called 'Ol' Man Crosby' and also made jokes about Frankie Laine, Billy Daniels, Perry Como and the British heart-throb, Donald Peers. He sang,

'He don't wear bowties of silk or cotton
And though I wears them, I still got nuttin'

But that ol' man Crosby, he goes on singing along.
Donald Peers and me, we sweat and strain
Throats all aching and wracked with pain.'

Indeed, Sinatra had commendably found out what was happening in the UK. At another show, he described Ruby Murray as 'the girl who has made a fortune out of laryngitis'.

Sinatra was playful throughout the whole performance announcing that his next record would be called 'I'm Gonna Put a Bar in the Back of my Car and Drive Myself to Drink' and he said, full of fun, 'Oh, it's a happy night.' He asked, "Do you think I look a little like Guy Mitchell?" and said, "Anybody want the paint burned off their car, give me a call and I'll be happy to do it." He impersonated Churchill by saying to Billy Ternent, 'Get your money, wash up and get out of here.' He added, 'That was Charlie Churchill, a distant nephew.' No wonder the audience was sometimes bemused.

He mentioned Ava obliquely by referring to 'Show Boat starring you know who' and quickly added, 'I'm a big Joe E Brown fan.' He praised the 15-piece orchestra 'mortgaged and led by the little giant', Billy Ternent. Unprofessionally but entertainingly, Sinatra commented that they are far superior to the orchestra on his last visit, led by 'Wolfie Phillips'. He blamed a Mr Lopez for the mistakes in the printed programme.

Sinatra is on top form as he performed 'You Go to My Head', 'That Old Black Magic', an utterly delightful 'Sweet Lorraine', a sublime 'One for My Baby', and 'When You're Smiling' with scat singing. He added, 'Do you think I sound a little like Guy Mitchell? I wish I knew 'She Wore Red Feathers'.' He previewed two songs he had recorded with Nelson Riddle, 'Don't Worry 'Bout Me' and 'I've Got the World on a String'. At one point he said, "I may set fire to this joint, I don't know". Maybe the maintenance man was needed after all.

A concert at Caird Hall, Dundee was banned by the local watch committee as it was to take place on a Sunday and he cancelled dates in Hammersmith and Coventry because of film commitments. Frank placed a goodbye note in the *NME*: 'I shall cherish the thought of the very friendly manner in which I was treated by everyone I met up and down your country.' Despite that, he didn't perform in the UK again until 1962.

Frank told the *NME* that he was going to make *Brigadoon* with Cyd Charisse and Gene Kelly but it never happened. There had been plans to make *St Louis Woman* with Ava Gardner but although that looked viable on paper, the studio realised that it would be a nightmare to film. Ava was now filming *Ride, Vaquero!* in Utah and, according to her autobiography, was having sex both the stuntman and the director, who happened to be Mia Farrow's father, John.

Oddly enough the British entertainer Max Bygraves caught Frank Sinatra in cabaret in the US in the early part of 1953 and he wrote a song about Frank's small audience for his LP, *Maximemories*, in 1981.

In August 1953 Sinatra was booked to appear alongside his new film, *From Here to Eternity* at the Capitol Theatre in New York. He called Axel Stordahl: 'Axel, we're leaving on Sunday for New York.'

'Gee, Frank, I can't. I've begun this TV show with Eddie Fisher.'

'Apparently, you didn't hear what I said. We're leaving Sunday for New York. We're going to be at the Capitol Theatre.'

'I can't do that, Frank. I've got a contract.'

Sinatra thought that Eddie Fisher was a decent guy with little talent so Stordahl was wasting his time. Frank slammed down the phone and he and Axel didn't speak again until 1961.

From Here to Eternity was released to excellent reviews and very good audiences and, indeed, it became Columbia's highest grossing picture up to that point. Sinatra was back to standing room only at the 500 Club in Atlantic City in September. He included the song, 'From Here to Eternity' in his act and when Eddie Fisher caught him at the Riviera in New Jersey, he told the press that Sinatra was electrifying. Frank wouldn't have done the same for him. Frank didn't have a good word to say about Ava directing the 'kick' in 'I Get a Kick Out of You' at her. Strange man.

By way of contrast, Dick Haymes and Mickey Rooney's MGM musical, *All Ashore*, with arrangements from Nelson Riddle, was washed up. It was a pale imitation of *On the Town*, but okay in its own right. The press thought Haymes should be deported and the public still regarded him as a draft dodger. He was in debt, owing taxes and child support, and the Sands in Vegas booked him at a knockdown price. While he was there, he married the acclaimed dancer and actress, Rita Hayworth in the Gold Room but that proved to be a disaster too.

Rita Hayworth had her own problems. She had married Orson Welles in 1943 but they were soon divorced. She took up with the Aga Khan's son, Aly, whom she married in 1949. She lived for two years as his princess but she was fleeced of her earnings and when she returned to Hollywood two years later she was broke and had to beg Columbia's studio head, Harry Cohn for work. He had been insulted when she had walked away from her Hollywood life, but he did approve of her breakup with Orson Welles, whom he loathed. 'All's well that ends Welles,' he would say.

In 1953 Rita Hayworth had only married Dick Haymes as a favour to prevent him being deported, but Haymes didn't see it that way. He thought that producing Hayworth's movies might be a road to success. They were soon fighting and when Haymes hit her in public at the Coconut Grove in Los Angeles, she was in hospital for several days. They divorced in 1955 and Rita then married the producer, James Hill, who made *Separate Tables* with her. However, he would insult her in public and they divorced in 1961,

Following the success of *From Here To Eternity*, Sinatra was now the good guy and as Mitch Miller joked, 'By getting stomped to death in that movie, he had done a public penance.' *From Here to Eternity* also did well in the UK, although the politician Michael Foot, then a film reviewer, called it 'pro-American propaganda'.

Frank and Ava attended the opening of *Mogambo* at Radio City in New York, but they had a row and were not at the Hollywood première the following day. On 27 October, Frank and Ava announced their separation although they would reconcile and break up several times before their divorce in 1957.

No one knows what Frank and Ava got up to on 28 October but the following day Frank appeared before the Nevada Tax Commission about his wish to purchase a 2% interest in the Sands. It was the most rewarding $50,000 he ever spent.

When he opened in the new Copa Room at the Sands, he said, 'Welcome to my room.' This time Frank was working with George Siravo's arrangements for eight musicians and performing standards with a breezy, easy confidence. Voyle Gilmore saw him at the Sands and wanted to record the set for an album, hence the 10 inch Capitol LP, *Songs for Young Lovers*. It had eight songs and only lasted 20 minutes but it set the path for the new Sinatra. Because he was performing in Vegas, his act had been aimed at an older set and this album showed that he was leaving the bobbysoxers behind. The novelty songs like 'The Hucklebuck' which he might sing at the Paramount were dropped for night clubs.

With Nelson Riddle filling out the arrangements for more musicians, the tracks were recorded in November. The opening song was 'My Funny Valentine', written by Richard Rodgers and Lorenz Hart for the Broadway show, *Babes in Arms* (1937), but arguably Hart was writing about himself. He was paranoid about his looks, his short stature and his homosexuality. There was a wonderful moment when Sinatra realised that the girl's faults were what he appreciated and he changed key as he sang, 'Don't change a hair for me', and whoever got more out of the word 'unphotographable' than Frank Sinatra? This wonderful recording was matched by one around the same time by the jazz trumpeter, Chet Baker. Frank stayed with Rodgers and Hart for a second song, 'Little Girl Blue' from the 1935 extravaganza, *Jumbo*, and again sublimely recorded.

In 1937, Fred Astaire had played an American in London for the film, *A Damsel in Distress*, and the Gershwins wanted to write a song about the city, hence 'A Foggy Day (In London Town)'. Ira thought of pea-soupers and swirling mists, which, following legislation, are no more. Unusually for a travelogue song, Ira makes the city dreary until the girl comes along and it's hard to imagine Frank going round the British Museum. The song begins with a slow introduction and then has a very hip arrangement with Sinatra going 'shining, shining, shining, shining, shining everywhere'. Ira didn't care for the way he had changed 'with alarm' to 'with much alarm'. Another of the Gershwins' songs, 'They Can't Take That Away from Me', came from the 1937 film, *Shall We Dance*, and Fred sang it to Ginger when they took a ferry boat ride to Hoboken. Frank gave a delightful performance well in keeping with Nelson's lighthearted arrangement.

Cole Porter's 'I Get a Kick out of You' made its first appearance in the 1934 Broadway musical, *Anything Goes*, and it was regarded as daring for its reference to sniffing cocaine: again, showing the difference between show tunes and pop tunes. The song is famed for its remarkable multiple rhyme, '*Fly*ing too *high* with some *guy* in the *sky* / Is *my* *i*dea of nothing to do' although Sinatra spoils it by singing 'gal' instead of 'guy'. This was one of Sinatra's all-time favourite arrangements and he would always credit Nelson Riddle, though George Siravo was the instigator.

The only song that Nelson Riddle brought to the project from scratch was 'Like Someone in Love', written by Johnny Burke and Jimmy Van Heusen for the 1944 film, *Belle Of The Yukon*. It had been a B-side for Bing Crosby. That solo flute is typically Riddle touch. Björk put the song on her album *Debut* in 1993.

The one song on the LP which Frank had recorded before was 'Violets for your Furs', here enhanced by Felix Slatkin's violin. The eighth song was 'The Girl Next Door' from the Judy Garland film, *Meet Me in St Louis* (1944). It works despite the jarring line, 'I live at 5135 Kensington Avenue and she lives at 5133.'

As well as album tracks, Nelson Riddle arranged an odd assortment of songs for songs for Frank including 'Young at Heart', which became a hit in 1954; another British song from Robert Mellin, 'Rain (Falling from the Skies)' with the strings replicating rainfall; 'Why Should I Cry over You' which was taken more seriously by Nat 'King' Cole; 'Take a Chance' with its reference to Donald Duck; and the innuendo-laden 'Ya Better Stop'. 'I'm just about to blow my top, Ya Better stop,' sings Frank, perhaps the reason it was never issued until 1978. That track contains a parody of a fade-out ending: 'Here now, this is not going to be another one those fadeaway records. Get your grimy hand off that dial, man.'

In October 1953 Frank returned to radio, playing a private eye in the series, *The Rocky Fortune Show*, which ran for 26 half-hour episodes. They were intended as comedy shows but they were very silly without having, say, the inventiveness of *The Goon Show*. The best is *The Plot to Murder Santa Claus* in which Sinatra wanted to buy his girlfriend a mink toothbrush. This episode kicked off with Frank's most irritating habit – deliberately misspelling words, here 'elf spelt o-a-f'.

Concurrently, Frank appeared in his final radio series, *To be Perfectly Frank*, sponsored by a shampoo company, the irony not being lost on Frank, who was usually not around when his hair was shampooed. These were two 15 minute shows a week in which he was spinning records, both his own and some favourite artists, with one original performance per show. Among the records was one by the British bandleader Wally Stott, no doubt picked up on his travels.

Frank performed with a small group, billed as the Sinatra Symphonette and led by Bill Miller. When he suggested a duet to Jimmy Durante, Durante replied, 'Don't you think that's a little ambitious?' When singing 'Yes Indeed!' with Sy Oliver, he said it was 'groovy like a movie'. The songs included 'I Can't Believe that You're in Love with Me' and' Wrap Your Troubles in Dreams'.

But there were still down days, mostly related to Ava. On 18 November, Frank cut his wrists while staying at Jimmy Van Heusen's apartment in New York. Van Heusen took him to the Mount Sinai Hospital and tried to keep the incident out of the papers. Was it serious or merely a ploy? If the latter, then it was a drastic one. Incidents like this are piling up, suggesting some sort of mental instability and maybe this was another reason behind him not serving in the army.

On Christmas Eve Frank did a broadcast with Bob Hope, Frank said he was buying 12 sets of cufflinks for the crew of his film. He forgot to do it last year 'and for the rest of the picture, it looked like I was walking around in Sydney Greenstreet's skin.' This got a big laugh as Greenstreet was a large, fearsome actor and Frank delivered the joke just in time as Greenstreet died three weeks later. In reality, Frank's gifts were likely to offend: he bought a pair of binoculars and chopped it in half, sending them to Sammy Davis and Jilly Rizzo who had both lost an eye with a note that 'You guys should get together.' Bing was equally tactless as every year he sent a cufflink to the one-armed trumpeter, Wingy Manone.

When Frank cracked a good joke, Bob Hope said, 'Don't get too many laughs, I can always finish this show with Eddie Fisher.' Sinatra retorted, 'You deserve it.'

1953 had started off shakily but it had been a brilliant year for Frank Sinatra. He said, 'I changed record companies, changed attorneys, changed accountants, changed picture companies and changed my clothes, and just went right back to work again.' Frank was back on top.

CHAPTER 9

Call me irresponsible

'My dream was to become Frank Sinatra. I loved his phrasing, especially when he was very young and pure. He grew into a fabulous jazz singer and I used to fantasise about having a lifestyle like his – carrying on in Hollywood and becoming a movie star. Every woman in America wanted to go to bed with Frank Sinatra. He was the king I longed to be. My greatest dream was to satisfy as many women as Sinatra. He was the heavyweight champ, the absolute.'

Marvin Gaye

I. I've Heard That Song Before

When I was talking to Jimmy Webb about working with Frank Sinatra, he made the observation, 'I had the pleasure of his company many times and he treated me extremely well. I think he respected songwriters more than anybody else in the world.' That seems correct – Sinatra fell out with people right, left and centre but he did appreciate songwriters. He only dabbled in songwriting himself but he had a strong sense of what worked and what didn't work in the songs he heard. He was grateful to the songwriters, often acknowledging them in concert.

The name of the lyricist Sammy Cahn has already occurred several times, writing a song here and a song there, but he came into his own with Frank Sinatra during the Capitol years. Sinatra was to record 88 of his songs, more than any other songwriter, yet compared to Cole Porter or Irving Berlin, Sammy Cahn was relatively unknown. Just who was this man and how did his work come to have such a hold on Sinatra? He told me that Sinatra never turned down any of his songs, which is an exaggeration, but only a little one, really said to emphasise that he and Sinatra were hand in glove.

Having been nominated for 26 Oscars and winning four, Sammy Cahn is a strong contender for the lyricist of the 20th century and I was fortunate to interview him when he came to London in 1987 to present his anecdotal show, *Words and Music*, at the Duke of York's. The two hours that I spent with him represent two of the best hours of my life.

Samuel Cohen, as he was then, was born to an immigrant family from Galicia, Spain, in the poverty-stricken Lower East Side of New York on 18 June 1913. His father owned a small restaurant and, like so many of the pre-rock'n'roll songwriters, he came from Jewish stock. He learned the violin as a child and was to play in a few little local orchestras and dance bands. He was adept on other instruments but he doubted that he was good enough professionally. When he was 16, he wrote his first song, 'Like Niagara Falls, I'm Falling for You', so the wordplay was already in place.

Sammy befriended the pianist Saul Kaplan, who was training to be an accountant, and they started to write together. A friend of a friend put them in touch with the bandleader Jimmie Lunceford and in 1935 they wrote 'Rhythm Is Our Business', which became both a hit single and Lunceford's signature tune. It was also recorded by Wingy Manone, so the team was off to a good start. They had a Top 10 single in February 1936 with 'Rhythm in my Nursery Rhymes' which was recorded by both Lunceford and Tommy Dorsey.

According to Sammy Cahn, 'The Jimmie Lunceford band was for me the single best band, and I say this with the knowledge that there was also Chick Webb, Count Basie and Duke Ellington. Jimmie Lunceford's was the single best band, both to watch and to listen to. It had Sy Oliver's arrangements; Tommy Dorsey had been bright enough to take Sy Oliver, an incredibly talented man, away from Jimmie Lunceford. The Sy Oliver arrangements had a vast, vast effect on the Tommy Dorsey Orchestra. His work was just priceless.'

Now calling himself Sammy Kahn, Sammy decided that Kahn and Kaplan sounded more like tailors than a songwriting team (admittedly, Lunceford had got his name onto the credits as well) and so they became Cahn and Chaplin. Cahn had a strong sense of humour and he wrote special material for cabaret shows for resorts in the Catskill Mountains, where Jewish businessmen and their families often went on holiday. In particular, he was writing both original material and parodies of current favourites for Dolores Reed, Bob Hope's wife for nearly 70 years.

In September 1936, Cahn and Chaplin had a major success with 'Until the Real Thing Comes Along', which was recorded by Andy Kirk and his 12 Clouds of Joy, Fats Waller and the Ink Spots. Louis Armstrong sang their 'Shoe Shine Boy' in the revue, *Connie's Hot Chocolates* at the Cotton Club, and this song was recorded by Bing Crosby, Wingy Manone, the Mills Brothers and Duke Ellington. As Ella Fitzgerald and the Casa Loma Orchestra were also recording their songs, this was a hot team.

The Jewish songwriters were always adapting music and chants they heard in the synagogues (which is still apparent today, *vide* Leonard Cohen). In 1938 they had a No.1 single with 'Bei Mir Bist Du Schön ('To Me, You Are Beautiful') recorded by the close harmony group, the Andrews Sisters. It was featured in the film, *Love, Honour and Behave*, which prompted Cahn and Chaplin to go to Hollywood and write for the movies.

Soon, however, they split up but remained friends. Chaplin's accountancy side was taking over as he became involved with the production of many famous films including *West Side Story* (1961). Cahn could, and would, write with anyone but he wanted another regular partner and found him in Jule Styne, who, oddly enough, was British. He had been born Julius K Stein in London on New Year's Eve 1905. His family moved to Chicago when he was eight. He became an accomplished pianist who could have had a fine career on the concert platform, but for one thing. His hands were too small which meant he didn't have the range of other pianists. Not to worry, he wrote a hit for Cliff Edwards in 1927 and he became a vocal coach for Hollywood musicals. He wrote 'I Don't Want to Walk Without You' with Frank Loesser for Helen Forrest to sing with Harry James and his Orchestra, but once he started writing with Sammy Cahn, they both realised that they had the basis for a strong working partnership. They had an entrée into Frank Sinatra's world and they wrote many songs for him including 'Saturday Night (Is The Loneliest Night of the Week)' (1945), 'I Fall in Love Too Easily' and 'Five Minutes More' (both 1946), and 'Time After Time' (1947). In 1948 they wrote one of the biggest hits of the era, 'It's Magic', which was famously sung by Doris Day in *Romance on the High Seas* (great title!) and also recorded by Dick Haymes, Gordon MacRae, Tony Martin and Sarah Vaughan.

In 1943 Jule Styne played him a new melody and Sammy Cahn listened and said, 'Seems to me I've heard that song before.' Styne said, 'What are you? A tune detective?' The resulting creation, 'I've Heard That Song Before' proved a major success for Harry James and his Orchestra with Helen Forrest.

In a way, their success was also their downfall. In 1947 they wrote a Broadway smash, *High Button Shoes*, a musical comedy which starred Phil Silvers and involved knockabout clowning. The public loved it and Styne wanted to stay with Broadway, while Cahn preferred the movies. Styne wrote *Gentlemen Prefer Blondes* with Leo Robin, *Gypsy* with a young Stephen Sondheim and *Funny Girl* with Bob Merrill, which included 'People' and made a major star of Barbra Streisand. Cahn and Styne still collaborated from time to time – 'Three Coins in the Fountain' (1954) being a notable example – but rarely wrote for Sinatra. As will be revealed, Styne foolishly upset Sinatra – he should have seen it coming – and Sinatra said he would never record another of his songs.

Cahn and Styne were never exclusively writing with each other anyway. Cahn wrote the touching 'I Should Care' (1945) with the bandleaders, Axel Stordahl and Paul Weston and 'Teach Me Tonight' with Gene DePaul. He wrote with the Russian composer Nichos Brodszky on 'Because You're Mine' and 'Be My Love' (both Mario Lanza) and 'I'll Never Stop Loving You' (Slim Whitman, Doris Day), but the strain of working with Brodszky meant that he didn't want to do it too often.

Most songwriters put their songs on demonstrations discs and leave it to the publishers to find the performers. Whenever possible, Sammy Cahn wanted to audition the songs himself for the potential recipients. 'To me, the greatest thrill of songwriting is the demonstration of the completed song. I always liked to do it myself. I would stand right in front of Sinatra and I would sing it to him. It was an amazing thing to be doing. When I sang to one singer,

And when we kiss that isn't thunder, dear,
It's only my poor heart you hear
And it's applause,
Because you're mine.'

he said, "How do you say 'Thunder, dear'?", but there was none of that with Sinatra. "Weatherwise, it's such a lovely day" – he knew instinctively how to do it. It was very easy to write for Sinatra.'

Cahn's third major partnership was with Jimmy Van Heusen. The songwriter got his break in 1938 when the bandleader Jimmy Dorsey recorded 'It's the Dreamer in Me'. A few months later, his atmospheric ballad, 'Deep in a Dream', was recorded by Artie Shaw and his Orchestra.

Van Heusen has already played a significant part in Sinatra's story, befriending him in his early years and writing songs for him and Bing Crosby, mostly with Johnny Burke including the glorious 'Moonlight Becomes You' and the wittiest of all children's songs, 'Swinging on a Star'. 'I worked differently from Johnny Burke,' said Cahn, 'I start at the top and I don't know where the lyric is going. Johnny Burke used to start from the bottom – he had his key idea and he would work backwards from that.'

Writing a Broadway show is always a risk and Burke and Van Heusen not only wrote but also produced *Carnival in Flanders* (1953) starring John Raitt, father of Bonnie. Even the inclusion of 'Here's That Rainy Day' didn't save it and the show folded within a week. Everybody was blaming everybody else and Burke fell ill and felt he would never write again. He did – contributing a brilliant lyric for Erroll Garner's 'Misty' and, with Van Heusen, adding songs to the film version of the operetta, *The Vagabond King* (1956), starring Kathryn Grayson – but he had had enough. He died in 1964 following a long illness.

Besides all the songs for Sinatra, Cahn and Van Heusen wrote the score for the Julie Andrews film, *Thoroughly Modern Millie*, in 1967 and the following year, the title song for *Star!*, which starred Andrews playing Gertrude Lawrence and was produced by Saul Chaplin. Marilyn Monroe's film, *Let's Make Love*, had a troubled history but there was nothing wrong with their score which included 'Incurably Romantic' sung by Frankie Vaughan.

In 1945 Sammy Cahn married a Goldwyn girl Gloria Delson and they had two children, a boy and a girl, but were divorced in 1964. He strove to be one of the Rat Pack but he wasn't in that league. With his high forehead and his thin moustache he looked like a Groucho Marx tribute act and, taking his cue from Groucho, he enhanced his popularity by being funny. He was happy to parody his own songs as well as others, often writing special material for charity events. We will come across some of his special lyrics for Sinatra (they should all be gathered for a book) but how about these for Dean Martin:

'The girl that I marry will have to be, A nympho who owns a distillery.'
'You made me love you, You woke me up to do it.'
'I didn't know what time it was, I drank my watch.'
'I looked under Jordan and what did I see? Mrs Jordan.'

Sammy Cahn's singing voice was rudimentary, but he was a splendid raconteur with a flair for self-promotion, whether on stage, on TV (with Michael Parkinson) or in print (his autobiography). He loved telling his carefully-honed anecdotes and many of them stood up to repetition. Sammy Cahn died in his 80th year on 15th January 1993 and I can imagine that his idea of heaven would be talking, endlessly talking, about his songs and, of course, writing new ones.

II. Day In–Day Out, 1954–1956

The press release for *From Here to Eternity* referred to the film being Frank Sinatra's comeback. Frank was so incensed that he stormed into the studio's publicity department and said to the manager, 'What comeback? I've never been away.' Who was he kidding? *From Here to Eternity* turned his career around. *From Here to Eternity* was a huge critical and commercial hit, the most successful film Columbia had ever had.

The film was nominated for 13 Oscars and Frank was up for Best Supporting Actor. On 25 March 1954, the Oscar ceremony was televised for the first time with Bob Hope as compère and an audience of 43 million. Hope's jibe, 'There's money in popcorn', rings true today. The tension between television and cinema is evident throughout his introductory remarks and he comments, 'Television – that's where movies go when they die.' Unlike today, where they don't emphasise that most participants are going to lose, he told the viewers that they would see, 'great understanding, great sportsmanship and great acting'.

From Here to Eternity won eight Oscars and could have won more. Montgomery Clift deserved to win Best Actor but possibly his Method acting was too radical for some of the Academy and the award went to William Holden in *Stalag 17*. Holden made the shortest acceptance speech in Oscar history simply saying 'Thank you'. It was touch-and-go for Frank as well as he was up against Jack Palance in *Shane*, but win he did and he rushed to the podium to grab the statuette, given to him by Mercedes McCambridge, before they could change their minds. On the way out, he was stopped in the street for carrying his Oscar when the police mistook him for a burglar. Also, shortly after the ceremony, Ernest Borgnine was pulled over by a traffic cop who said, 'You're the son of a bitch who killed Frank Sinatra.'

Frank though was never content. Having to sit through the contenders for Best Song without singing a note himself, he commented, 'They're doing a lot of songs here tonight, but nobody asked me.' Still, Frank was hardly best suited for 'Secret Love', but perhaps he fancied 'That's Amore', which Dean had stubbornly refused to sing at the ceremony. Ava Gardner, who was in Spain with a bullfighter, lost the Best Actress award for *Mogambo* to Audrey Hepburn in *Roman Holiday*. Similarly, Grace Kelly, nominated for Best Supporting Actress in *Mogambo*, lost to Donna Reed in *From Here to Eternity*.

Prior to *From Here to Eternity*, Frank had been seeing a psychiatrist for the first time. Dr Ralph Greenson had written learned papers on the problems of the rich and famous and Sinatra wanted him to put his life into perspective. After seeing Sinatra win the Oscar on TV, Greenson said to his wife, 'We'll never see him again', a very telling remark, and he was right.

Frank had been plugging the film at every opportunity. Every week he found a new gag to slip into the script of his weekly radio programme, *The Rocky Fortune Show*. Despite such actors as Raymond Burr, the scripts were feeble and the titles included *Too Many Husbands, Actuary Friend, Rocket to the Moon* and *Witness to a Will*. By April, Sinatra was relieved to be free of the show. He had better things to do.

His other radio series, *To be Perfectly Frank*, lasted until June. Mostly he was playing his own records ('Young at Heart', 'From Here to Eternity', 'Three Coins in the Fountain') but the live performances included ''S Wonderful (Frank Crumit, 1928), 'If I Could be With You', (Louis Armstrong, 1930), 'Under a Blanket of Blue' (Casa Loma Orchestra, 1933), 'Don't Blame Me' (Ethel Waters, 1933) and 'Love is Just Around the Corner' (Bing Crosby, 1935).

As luck would have it, Frank was a guest on Bing Crosby's programme on either side of his Oscar success and there was much gentle ribbing. Would he have pulled out of the second appearance had he lost? They duet on 'Among My Souvenirs', 'As Time Goes By' and 'There's a Long Long Trail', a 1916 song which was dipping back into Bing's past rather than Frank's. There was a rather silly radio interview about the Oscar ceremony with Louella Parsons but it was self-evident that the interview was scripted. Similarly, in June 1954, he turned his appearance as the guest celebrity on *What's My Line* into a plug for his latest film, *Young at Heart*. His celebrity status was further enhanced when he became the subject of *This is Your Life* in October 1954. This must have been nerve-wracking as he had no advance notice as to who was going to appear and what they were going to say, but he knew the producers didn't want controversy.

The song Frank had recorded to plug *From Here to Eternity* was never strong enough to be a hit single. Much better was 'Young at Heart', written by Carolyn Leigh and Johnny Richards, which gave Sinatra his first chart-topper since 1947 and provided his first gold disc as a solo artist. The song had been written for Nat 'King' Cole but Cole turned it down, perhaps feeling that he was recording too many songs about being youthful. Nelson Riddle didn't hide its history, telling Sinatra, 'It's a good song but nobody wants to do it.' 'Let's do it,' said Sinatra, but after completing the recording, he didn't even wait to hear the playback. In 1975 the song was used to brilliant effect in the Woody Allen film about the Communist witch hunts of the 1950s, *The Front*.

While 'Young At Heart' was climbing to No.2 on the singles chart, his first Capitol, album, *Songs for Young Lovers*, was Sinatra's biggest album in five years, selling 150,000 copies from its release in February to the end of June. Artie Volando, who had given Frank 'Young At Heart', received two cashmere jackets which were inscribed 'To Artie Volando, From Frank Sinatra'. Frank felt less affectionate about the song in concert, sometimes singing in Vegas, "Fairy tales can come true, It can happen to you, If you're young and hard."

The film *Three Coins in the Fountain* had a predictable plot and the title says it all. Three American girls throw money into the Trevi Fountain in Rome and wish for love and along come three handsome Italians. The Trevi Fountain was used for spectacular effect when the statuesque Anita Ekberg cavorted in it during *La Dolce Vita* (1959), the Vatican condemning the film as immoral. *Three Coins in the Fountain* was a much blander affair.

The producer Sol Siegel asked Sammy Cahn and Jule Styne for a theme song, prompting one of Cahn's best anecdotes: 'You ask which comes first, the words or the music? I will tell you, the phone call.' Because of studio deals, Cahn said that when you hear 'Make it mine, make it mine, make it mine', 'Remember that only one-third of the song is mine.'

It's a wonderful yarn, but not strictly correct. Sol Siegel thought that the film, then called *We Believe in Love*, was too sentimental and might flop, even though it was a new wide screen CinemaScope production. Styne told Siegel that that *Three Coins in the Fountain* would be a better title. Siegel thought that 'love' in the title was a selling point, but he asked, 'Can you write a song called 'Three Coins in the Fountain'?' 'It's a hell of a lot easier than 'We Believe in Love',' said Cahn.

Cahn told me, 'We never saw the rushes, we never saw the script. All we had was three girls going to Rome and throwing coins in the fountain.' That was enough as within an hour they had the song. Although it was for a girl singer, Styne told Siegel, 'Get Frank.' Frank was recording the following Monday (1 March 1954) and they asked Nelson Riddle to write an arrangement quickly and add it to the session. Although Frank's version was on the soundtrack and a substantial hit, it was the Four Aces who took the song to the top of US charts. The song won an Oscar at the 1954 ceremony, beating 'Count Your Blessings' and 'The Man that Got Away'. Frank did record the latter as 'The Gal that Got Away' after asking Ira Gershwin to amend his lyric.

On that same day Frank cut a majestic, slow version of 'Day In – Day Out'. In 1958 he recorded a swing version with Billy May; both worked equally well. He sang 'Last Night When We Were Young', which Harold Arlen considered his strongest melody and it was enhanced with a reflective lyric from Yip Harburg. Back in 1935, George Gershwin had told Arlen to forget about the song, that it was too good for public acceptance, but he didn't bank on Frank coming along. Indeed, the fact that Frank liked a song is often the key ingredient in it becoming a standard. 'Last Night When We Were Young' is sung slowly and passionately and Alec Wilder called it 'a most remarkable and beautiful song'.

In April, Frank recorded the title song of a new musical, *The Sea Song*, which sank without trace, so much so that Frank's recording was shelved. Cole Porter's 'Just One of Those Things' was to be featured in *Young at Heart*. When Cole Porter had been looking for a three syllable word to describe 'wings', a friend suggested 'gossamer', a word that enhanced the song as surely as the 'huckleberry' in 'Moon River', although 'a trip to the moon on gossamer wings' now sounds like an ad for Durex. Note how Frank is so playful on this recording, having fun with the sibilant 's'. There is a slurring of the title line in the coolly confident 'I'm Gonna Sit Right Down and Write Myself a Letter', a song associated with Fats Waller. There was a leisurely 'All of Me', a playful 'Jeepers Creepers', the gospel feel of 'Get Happy' and the glorious 'Taking a Chance on Love', from the 1943 film, *Cabin in the Sky*. 'Here I slip again about to take that trip again' sounds like one of Frank's hip additions but is in the original. These tracks formed the basis of his second 10-inch album for Capitol, *Swing Easy*. It was an easy-going up tempo collection with Nelson Riddle's arrangements including plenty of vibes and no strings, almost a tribute to a favourite musician of theirs, Red Norvo.

Early in 1954 Frank had asked Jule Styne to move into his apartment with him. He said, 'If you don't stay with me, I will kill myself.' Jule didn't mind as he could write anywhere, and what's more he had now unparalleled access as a songwriter to Frank Sinatra.

Sammy Cahn recalled, 'Jule Styne used to limber up with two songs, a Viennese waltz and a tango. He said to me one day, "Frank wants a Christmas song." I said, "A Christmas song after 'White Christmas'. What's the point? We're not writing a Christmas song." He said, "Don't you understand – Frank WANTS a Christmas song." I said, "Slow down that Viennese waltz" and then we had (Sings)

'It's that time of year

When the world falls in love'
So 'The Viennese Waltz' became 'The Christmas Waltz'.'

Frank and Jule stayed together for nine months and then Frank suddenly said, 'I'm over Ava, so you can leave.' That was fine but Jule made one big mistake. *Esquire* magazine wanted to write a feature about his songs and, as songwriters don't often get asked for big interviews, he said okay. When asked about living with Sinatra, he said that he had been living in a shrine to Ava Gardner. Her photographs were everywhere. One night Sinatra tore up a large photograph of her and they spent the next hour pasting it back together.

The reporter couldn't believe his luck; a story about Styne's songwriting was swapped for one about living with Sinatra. When it was published, Sinatra wouldn't even lower himself to call Styne. He telephoned Sammy Cahn and said, 'I am never going to record any more of Jule's songs. If you want to write for me, you write with Jimmy Van Heusen from now on.' And that's what happened.

Because Sinatra was an Oscar winner, admittedly in a supporting role, he was hot property and despite his reputation, the studios wanted him. *From Here to Eternity* had been a one-off deal for Columbia and so he could go wherever he wanted. Columbia did consider *Pal Joey* but Harry Cohn didn't want any more trouble with Sinatra. John Huston considered Frank Sinatra for a film version of the stage hit, *Mister Roberts*, but went with Jack Lemmon as Sinatra looked too old.

Over the next two years, there were several projects which never came off. Twentieth Century Fox had plans to star Marilyn Monroe with Frank Sinatra in a remake of *Coney Island* (1943), now called *Pink Tights*. The score was to be written by Sammy Cahn and Jule Styne. When Monroe didn't show for rehearsals, she was replaced by Sheree North and then the project was abandoned with Sinatra being paid off. Gene Kelly wanted Frank for *It's Always Fair Weather*, but Frank said no, he was not going wear a sailor suit again.

The most tantalising miss has to be *On the Waterfront*, a story of union corruption set in Hoboken and ideal for Frank, excepting that, again, he looked too old. Age apart, it would have been a perfect film to follow *From Here to Eternity*.

The film was produced by Sam Spiegel, one of Hollywood's great bullshitters. When he fled from the Nazis in 1933, he left behind scores of bounced cheques. He produced relatively minor films until he hit the big time with *The African Queen* in 1952. There was a Hollywood phrase, 'To be Spiegeled' which meant to be conned by the smooth-talking producer. Spiegel wanted to keep his options open so he promised the lead to both Marlon Brando and Frank Sinatra. In truth, he wanted Brando but he feared that Brando would refuse to work with the director Elia Kazan. Kazan had founded the Actors' Studio, which had introduced Method acting of which Brando was the most successful student. Since then, Kazan had testified to the House Un-American Activities Committee and identified fellow workers as Communists. Brando had been appalled by his behaviour. If Brando said no, then the role was Frank's.

Although Kazan had worked with Brando on *A Streetcar Named Desire*, he favored Sinatra as he knew the area and would be easier to work with (that's saying something). In a Hollywood coffee shop, Spiegel told Brando that acting was one thing and politics is another and that he had to separate them. He called Kazan and invited him to join them. Brando was unsure but he needed the cash as he was paying for four sessions a week with a psychoanalyst. He said yes and Sinatra was passed over.

Sinatra was furious. He complained to the William Morris agency and said he intended to sue. They advised against it: 'Do you want the world to know that Hollywood doesn't want you?' Sinatra was unwavering and said he was suing for $500,000 damages, which was ridiculous as Brando was only paid $125,000. The matter was settled out of court in 1959, which shows how these things can rumble on.

Brando's performance in *On the Waterfront* was electrifying, although it has its detractors, one of them being Sinatra. At the 1954 Academy Awards, *On the Waterfront* won Best Picture, Best Director and Best Actor and four more Oscars. Sinatra would never forget that Brando had taken his role. He thought Method acting was a con and that he himself was a natural: he had had the best training of all as 'A singer is essentially an actor', which was something he often said. *On the Waterfront* is one of those occasions where I wish there could have been two versions, rather like records, one starring Marlon Brando and one starring Frank Sinatra.

Not to worry because Sinatra did make two films in 1954, both of them having merit. *Suddenly* is like a prototype of the TV movie. It was a tense, cheaply made drama that only lasted 76 minutes. It was made by a British director, Lewis Allen, who had been an apprentice with Paramount and had a talent for making taut, suspense films of which *Suddenly* was one. Sinatra, in a role that had been written for Montgomery Clift, arrives in a town called Suddenly, the name harking back to its wild west days. The President's train is scheduled to stop at 5pm – a touch of *High Noon* here – and Sinatra and his gang are planning to assassinate him. A grandfather, mother and son are held hostage as the gang set up their equipment. Their house was on a small hill and offered a perfect view of the railway station.

We have no idea why the killer wanted to kill the President, presumably Eisenhower. He was a psychopath, hired for money and he was surprisingly talkative for a hit man. He didn't know why his employer wanted him killed and he didn't think anything would change if he succeeded, but 'Because of the gun, you'll remember me as long as you live.' Just before the train arrived, he said, 'Let's go to work', a phrase taken up by *Reservoir Dogs*. The film lacked suspense because we know the President will not be killed.

There were many anomalies in the script. Why did Sinatra want the repairman to fix the TV, and how did he expect to escape? Why did Sinatra keep his hat on at all times? (Well, I think we know the answer to that one.) *Suddenly* was a critical success but the public was not interested in Sinatra as a hit man. With one exception. Lee Harvey Oswald watched *Suddenly* shortly before he killed Kennedy. As a result, Sinatra felt that the film should not be in the public domain and it was withdrawn for many years.

Frank's favourite actor was Humphrey Bogart. He often played Bogie-styled roles, typically in *Von Ryan's Express* (1965), *The Detective* (1968) and the two Tony Rome films, where Tony Rome is effectively Sam Spade with a weaker script. For *A Hole in the Head* (1959) he possessed a lightness of touch which wouldn't have worked with Bogart. Frank goes for the full Bogie in *Suddenly*, which can be compared to Bogart's role in *The Petrified Forest* (1936).

Warner Brothers had plans to remake an earlier film of theirs, a romantic comedy, *Four Daughters* (1938), which featured the Lane Sisters but the key role had gone to John Garfield as a musician set back by the Depression. This time there were going to be three daughters, one of them being Doris Day. She didn't like the first choice of director, Michael Curtiz, having clashed with him during *Romance on the High Seas*. The producer, Hal Roach suggested Gordon Douglas, an experienced actor and director who was regarded as a safe pair of hands. Douglas always wore a baseball cap on set and would turn it back to front when he wanted the cameras to roll, thereby being 20 years ahead of fashion trends.

John Garfield's role was offered to Frank Sinatra. He was in two minds: he had worked with Doris Day on *Your Hit Parade* for several months and their egos had collided on several occasions, but he respected her talent. More significantly, he loathed her husband, Marty

Melcher, sensing that he was a crook and a fraud. At an early meeting to discuss the project, Sinatra held up a newspaper rather than look at him. The film was to be made by Melcher's production company, Arwin, for Warner Brothers and Sinatra would only make the film if he and Melcher would never be on the set together. In this regard, Sinatra's instincts were correct. The fact that Day accepted it suggests that she was suspicious of him too. However, Sinatra was friendly with far deadlier people than Marty Melcher, who was simply a con man.

The idea was to call the film *Young at Heart* after Sinatra's hit song but Melcher wanted Day to sing the song on the opening and closing credits. Sinatra took that as an insult. He wanted top billing and not shared billing which suggests that the success of *From Here to Eternity* had gone to his head. Ultimately they shared top billing, which was after all a selling point and although the film was called *Young at Heart*, the song had nothing to do with the plot. It is an unlikely story – why would three attractive unmarried women in their thirties be living at home being bossed around by their aunt?

As the story had been updated, Barney Sloan (Sinatra) had no reason for being so grouchy. He didn't appear in the first half hour of the film and his entrance was superb. He called at the house and was shown, back to the camera, on the doorstep. When he turned around, he looked like Tom Waits. Sinatra was good in this crumpled and careworn role which had been written to accommodate him: he says that he became Barney Sloan as he wanted to change his Italian name. There is one of his favourite quirks: the misspelling – 'D E D, dead'.

Doris Day – a daytime person – wanted to start filming early while Sinatra wanted to start at noon. Sinatra felt that the chief cameraman, Charles Lang, was too slow despite being one of Hollywood's finest craftsmen. Sinatra had him replaced by Ted McCord, another leading figure. The delays were often down to Sinatra himself. He might have been on a bender the night before and kept the crew waiting. Doris Day determined never to work with him again.

Young At Heart was unusual in that it began as a romantic comedy and then became much darker. Day's character thought she was in love with the successful composer, Gig Young, but she realised that she cared for the pianist and failed songwriter, played by Frank Sinatra. In the original film, John Garfield died but Sinatra announced that he was not dying on screen again and the script was amended. He has completed his song, 'You My Love', by the end of the film and this pseudo-concerto by Jimmy Van Heusen and Mack Gordon was a hit single for the real life Sinatra.

Gig Young was very good as the loser. You may wonder why he was there for Christmas as he has lost out, but on the other hand, the best scenes are when he is around. Anyway, don't look for logic as the plot is full of absurdities. Why did Laurie (Doris Day) give up her man at the altar and then shack up with grumpy ol' Barney with whom she has nothing in common? Of course, grumpy men are as entitled to partners as much as anyone else but surely not with Doris Day? It was bad casting.

Although they were acting, there was something of the real Doris Day and Frank Sinatra in their performances. She was Doris Daytime while Frank was for the dark. They had had disagreements on radio programmes and indeed, Day was never a part of Sinatra's world. When she was offered Vegas, she said that she would only do afternoon shows. They could have acted better in *Young At Heart*. Doris Day was wholly convincing in her next film, *Love Me or Love Me* where she had to be a gangster's moll but left to her own devices she preferred the sunshine persona.

The veteran actress Ethel Barrymore (Aunt Jessie) was in poor health and felt sure she was going to die making the film. She made one more film, *Johnny Trouble*, and died in 1959. On 15 August 1954, the crew threw a 75th birthday party for her and Doris Day burst into tears when she saw her in pain. A technician threw a box of tissues at Doris and hit her in the face. Frank laid into him.

In 1958, there was a TV testimonial to Ethel Barrymore. Sammy Cahn recalls, 'She had an incredible face, and Sinatra's face and hers would look great together. I said, "It would be marvellous if you sang 'I've Grown Accustomed to Her Face', so why don't you call Alan Jay Lerner and ask him to write a special lyric for you." He called Alan and he said, "C'mon, Frank, don't bother me with this. Let Sammy do it." So that's what I did and I rather like: (Sings)

"You're all the lovely things I've known
And that is why I've grown
Accustomed to your face."'

Given Frank Sinatra's behaviour it is surprising that Gordon Douglas would want to work with him again but his name continually appears in this story. Indeed, Sinatra later had a major production partnership with Warner Brothers so he hadn't burnt his bridges.

Doris Day's next film was a biopic of the entertainer Ruth Etting. Frank, in his usual tactful manner, told the producers that she was wrong for the role and they should choose Ava Gardner instead. The film, *Love Me or Leave Me*, was one of Day's career highlights. When Frank was impressed by Judy Garland and James Mason in *A Star Is Born*, he sent George Cukor a telegram. 'You're the goddamnest director that ever was, is, and will be. Don't you dare ever die, we need you.' I presume that was a plea for work, but he didn't get any.

Young At Heart came out the same year as *On the Waterfront* and looks like a fairy tale by comparison but the saving grace is the score. Most of the songs are standards and Sinatra insisted on singing without plot interruption. There is a voice-and-piano version of 'Someone to Watch over Me' (Sinatra's hands are shielded from the camera as somebody else is playing), 'Just one of Those Things' (with Nat 'King' Cole styled arrangement) and 'One for My Baby'. Frank recorded 'Someone to Watch over Me' and it is an immaculate performance with a great string arrangement from Nelson Riddle.

Frank was occasionally willing to admit to a mistake. Rosemary Clooney had a No.1 hit with 'Hey There' from *The Pajama Game*, produced by Mitch Miller. When Frank met the composer Richard Adler at a party, he said to him, 'I'm the schmuck who turned down 'Hey There'.'

He indulged in some good-natured banter on *The Amos'n'Andy Music Hall*. Frank, Bing, Bob Hope and Judy Garland combined forces for rewritten versions of 'Thanks for the Memory' and 'You're the Top'. The three men eventually decided that Garland is the top, with Frank singing to Bing:

'You're the top, you're the head canary,
You're the top, though your head ain't hairy.'

These guys were far more obsessed about hair loss than their audience.

In November 1954 Frank Sinatra took part, indeed, instigated an event which was outlandish even by his standards. His friend, the baseball star, Joe DiMaggio, had married Marilyn Monroe in January 1954. Eight months later, they had a huge public argument after the skirt-blowing scene in *The Seven Year Itch* and Marilyn filed for divorce. Joe, Frank and two friends were dining in a restaurant and Joe said that a private detective had been following Marilyn around and she was having an affair, probably a lesbian one. They decided that they would go round to where Marilyn was living and confront her. Off they went, pretty loaded, and they parked round the corner. The private detective pointed out the house and they bashed down the door. It was the wrong address. It belonged to an elderly lady who lived alone and she wondered what these brawny men were doing in her bedroom. This became known as the Wrong Door Incident but it wasn't made public until 1957. Evidence was obtained under oath but because there were conflicting reports, Frank emerged unscathed. It was typical of the silly incidents that Frank got involved with.

A recent biography by Lois Banner, *Marilyn: The Passion and the Paradox*, throws new light on his incident. According to the author, the private investigator, Bernie Spindel, deliberately gave Sinatra and Co the wrong address, fearing what might happen, though that might have made it a whole lot worse (and it did). Marilyn was staying with Hal and Sheila Schaefer, Banner cites Hal, her voice coach, and not Sheila as Marilyn's lover.

When *The Seven Year Itch* was released, Frank acquired his own copy and he would show it to his friends. They would marvel at the freeze frame facility and, nearly 40 years before Sharon Stone in *Basic Instinct*, they would argue over whether you could see Marilyn Monroe's most intimate part.

During that year, Frank had a public argument with the photographer Jim Byron who hadn't recognised that he had Judy Garland with him at the Crescendo on Sunset Strip. Another time he fell out with his agent, Irving 'Swifty' Lazar, the nickname coming from Bogie. Frank paid someone to break into his house and brick up his built-in wardrobe. Swifty was not a man to fall out with; it was said that everybody in Hollywood had two agents – their own and Swifty. He had legendary chutzpah and he was a dealmaker. He even put the Frost/Nixon deal together.

When Frank wanted to entertain troops stationed in Korea, he was told that he couldn't because of his Communist sympathies. He appealed on the grounds that he was 'about as communistic as the Pope'. He still couldn't go.

Bing Crosby, now over 50, acted against type in *The Country Girl* by playing an alcoholic. He was nominated for an Oscar but didn't get it, though Grace Kelly did get one for the same film. *The Country Girl* was based on a Broadway play by Clifford Odets, who had been in trouble with McCarthy but had admitted he had made mistakes. The Los Angeles Times said, 'If there is a surprise in this film, it is doubtless the maturing of this bland little man, the Old Groaner, into an actor.' Bing only played a handful of dramatic roles after this, so we can assume that he didn't care for it much. He would go back to playing Bing. He made *White Christmas*, the biggest of all Irving Berlin's musical films and the most successful film of the year.

In January 1955 Frank Sinatra took his daughter, Nancy, then 14, with him to Australia where he performed some successful concert dates. However, it didn't stop him romancing – Nancy discovered ladies' underwear in his hotel room.

Sinatra had been quick to spot the potential of the album, first as a collection of 78 rpm records and then as a 10-inch LP. Now he wanted to make a 12-inch album and although it was possible to fit as many as 16 songs onto an LP, singers were soon discouraged from doing that! The result was *In the Wee Small Hours of the Morning*, recorded in February 1955 and released in May. This No.2 album was on the US charts for 33 weeks and endures as one of the greatest albums of all time. It was also available as two 10-inch albums, the world's first double-album and probably the world's first concept album. (This depends on how you view such terms: strictly speaking, a collection of Christmas songs is a concept album.)

And the concept is – a man can't leave his home or the bar because he is haunted by the memories of a lost love affair: in other words, the LP is a letter to Ava. It has a *film noir* cover and Tom Waits commented, 'The cigarette and the tie undone and the late-night poet on the microphone was what captured me at first. When I was a teenager, it was a rebellion against rock'n'roll to listen to Frank Sinatra. So when I went through my parents' record collection, that's what I pulled out.' Waits later called an album, *Frank's Wild Years*, and he has covered 'Young At Heart'.

According to the sleeve note, 'Standing in front of the mike with his hands nearly always jammed into his pockets, his shoulders hunched a little forward, he sang. And as he sang, he created the loneliest early-morning mood in the world.' It is music to break your heart.

Toni Tennille recalled, 'When I was 13 my dad brought home *In the Wee Small Hours*. No one did these achingly beautiful ballads like Sinatra. I would go upstairs to my bedroom with a box of doughnuts, shut the door, put the record on and weep. I was 13, my hormones were going nuts, and nobody understood me except Frank Sinatra.'

The British country singer Hank Wangford recalls, 'I drove right across America with my son who was relocating from New York. After 16 years in New York, he was going to live in California and his marriage was breaking up as it happens. We went through Death Valley and our brakes melted. We had to wait for them to solidify and then we crawled out of Death Valley. That night we were driving up this mountain and we had Sinatra on with *In the Wee Small Hours of the Morning*. It sounded fantastic and I heard every fantastic note of that record in the silence of Death Valley. There are fantastic orchestrations from Nelson Riddle, and Frank's timing is breathtaking. You just know that he sang every note live with the orchestra.'

Frank wanted to record low-key songs of lost love with a small group, five musicians with Bill Miller on piano and Paul Smith on celesta, and he told Nelson, 'I want the songs to sound unrehearsed' which was a difficult assignment. By sheer good fortune, the songwriter Dave Mann pitched Frank a new song, 'In the Wee Small Hours of the Morning', which Frank chose for the title song as it set the mood. It evoked loneliness and sadness, but it was sensual too, rather like 'One for My Baby'. Listeners would identify with the mood and women would want to be with him.

Even though the songs were of the same tempo and theme, the order was all important. The second track was Duke Ellington's majestic 'Mood Indigo' (1931). As the lyric says, this is a 'lay me down and die' song and Frank's vocal included a resigned 'no, no, no, no, no, no, no, no, no, no'. This was followed by the riddle of 'Glad to be Unhappy' where the singer revels in his unhappiness. It was a little-known song from Rodgers and Hart's Broadway show, *On Your Toes* (1936) and later revived by the Mamas and the Papas.

There is a similar conundrum in Hoagy Carmichael's 'I Get Along without You Very Well'. A student at Indiana University had passed a poem called 'I Get Along without You Very Well' to Hoagy Carmichael. He kept it for some time and then, in 1939, he wrote a beautiful melody. He needed to contact the writer and after a long search, Jane Brown Thompson was found. She was told that the song would be introduced on radio by Dick Powell. Sadly, she died the night before the broadcast. The song was a success for Jimmy Dorsey and his Orchestra. It is easy to see why the bitter-sweet words were so appealing to Hoagy Carmichael: the singer states that he doesn't miss his partner but everything he does makes it clear that he does; the same idea as 10cc's 'I'm Not In Love'.

This was followed by an early Jimmy Van Heusen song, 'Deep in a Dream', where Frank awakes from his daydream with a cigarette burn, the antithesis of Peggy Lee's 'Don't Smoke in Bed'.

'I See Your Face before Me', came from the Broadway musical, *Between the Devil* (1937) and had been sung by Evelyn Laye. It was a haunting song of unrequited love and Riddle cited it amongst his favourites. The lyricist Howard Deitz worked as Vice-President of Publicity at MGM and had been responsible for the roaring lion. Because he was writing musicals he was often late for work and was chided for it. He responded, 'But I go home early.' He once invited Greta Garbo for dinner on the following Monday and she said, 'But I don't know if I'll be hungry.'

'Can't We Be Friends' came from the 1929 Broadway revue, *The Little Show*. It sounds at times like Frank is singing about Ava, and then there's 'When Your Lover Has Gone', which Frank had sung on V-Disc. It comes from Jimmy Cagney's *Blonde Crazy* (1931) and has a beautiful string arrangement. Elvis Costello said, 'He seemed to turn his then rare vocal frailty into an asset.'

Side 2 opened with Cole Porter's 'What Is This Thing Called Love' taken as a reflective ballad. Originally Frank had thought of doing a four minute version but in the end, he sang eight lines and it was taken so slowly that it lasts two and a half minutes. After the final take, Frank shouted, 'Nelson, you're a gas!' 'Last Night When We Were Young' was recorded earlier but fits in perfectly, and was followed by Alec Wilder's 'I'll Be Around' with a rhythm section and celesta. Frank's deep final notes are mesmerising. This is followed by Harold Arlen's 'Ill Wind' from the *Cotton Club Parade* (1934). Frank's melancholy performance was enhanced by a trumpet solo from Harry Edison.

Two more Rodgers and Hart songs follow: 'It Never Entered My Mind' with its witty take on loneliness ('Now I even have to scratch my back myself') and 'Dancing on the Ceiling', again with a small group with celesta and piano. Elvis Costello said, that Frank adds 'a crucial 'all' to 'all through the night' and he drags it out to give it a sense of longing.' 'I'll Never Be the Same' was a 1932 song that was a hit for Paul Whiteman with Mildred Bailey and the album ended with Frank reviving his own 'This Love of Mine', a very good ending to a brilliant album.

Frank recorded the theme song of his next film, *Not as a Stranger*, the title coming from the book of Job. This song pre-empts the theme of 'Strangers in the Night', a song that Sinatra loathed – but at least that song was memorable.

As Morton Thompson's novel *Not as a Stranger* ran to 950 pages, the producer and director Stanley Kramer has to be applauded for reducing it to a feature-length film. The main role was going to be played by Montgomery Clift but when he became unavailable, Kramer signed Robert Mitchum as the wayward doctor. Sinatra was one of several medical students who are surely the oldest medical class in the world. He looked vulnerable next to the placid and immovable Mitchum, who was at his best behind the surgeon's mask. With the thought of instilling some realism, dummies were placed around the set so that actors could practice mock operations when they weren't on camera.

With the actors including Robert Mitchum, Frank Sinatra, Broderick Crawford and Lee Marvin, it was not so much a cast as a day out at the brewery. In 1952 Crawford had been drunk on the set of the western, *Lone Star*, and didn't know his lines. 'What about the townsfolk?" asked Clark Gable. 'Fuck the people' said Broderick, a take that sadly remained on the cutting room floor.

After one drinking session, Broderick Crawford tore off Sinatra's wig and forced him to eat some of it. Another wig had to be made quickly as this one could not be salvaged. The boozers wrecked Sinatra's dressing room after a binge and a drunken Sinatra fell asleep on an operating table, fortunately not at a time when an actor was about to practise an operation. Sinatra gave Mitchum a cure for resolving a hangover.

Mitchum said that Sinatra would fight anyone over anything and once when Mitchum was reading a newspaper, he set fire to it. Mitchum called him 'Mother' and sent him a Mother's Day card. In return Frank sent him a photo he had taken of Mitchum in his shorts over which he wrote, 'I've seen some big cocks, but this is ridiculous. Love, Francis Albert'.

This should have been a good film as Kramer had produced the classic western, *High Noon* and the controversial biker epic, *The Wild One*, with Marlon Brando, but this time he was both producer and director and the main character, Robert Mitchum, was woefully miscast. (You could argue that Mitchum was always miscast.) It was terrible but the public bought into medical dramas and this was Mitchum's biggest success to date. Frank picked up some plaudits with *Hollywood Reporter* commenting, 'Sinatra, who seems to become a better actor with each successive part, is simply terrific.'

On 7 March 1955 Frank was back at the Capitol studios, but with a difference. He referred to this, somewhat disparagingly, as his rock'n'roll session. He did four songs backed by Big Dave Cavanaugh and the Nuggets, and he was happy with Dave's musicianship as a couple of years later, he was producing him for Capitol.

It wasn't really rock'n'roll but it was more contemporary than his usual offerings. They started gently with 'If I Had Three Wishes', a silly song in that his second and third wishes are that the first comes true. Still, it might suit a pantomime somewhere. They there was the gently swinging 'How Could You Do a Thing Like That', which gives the musicians a chance to shine. The surprise was 'Two Hearts. Two Kisses', originally recorded by Otis Williams and the Charms and a US hit for Pat Boone in April 1955. The rhymes must have made Frank wince ('I have plenty of lovin' / Your kiss is hotter than an oven') but this was Frank Sinatra doo-wopper. 'From The Bottom to the Top', was rock'n'roll by numbers but there were piano triplets and Frank did sing, 'I will try at one o'clock, two o'clock, three o'clock, four o'clock.'

A couple of weeks later Frank was back in the studio to cover 'Learnin' the Blues', a hit in Philadelphia for Joe Valino, who also recorded the original version of 'The Garden of Eden', a No.1 UK hit for Frankie Vaughan. It was an up-tempo saloon song and Nelson Riddle has the whole trumpet section blaring out. Frank and Nelson knew this was a big song and they had to knock the hapless Valino out of the way. They took 31 takes to perfect it and recorded nothing else that day. It was worth it. It was Frank's only US No.1 while he was at Capitol.

Although his Capitol records were selling well, Frank felt that they could sell better and he blamed Mitch Miller and Columbia for this. Time and again, Columbia would be repacking his old material and releasing it in competition. He wanted to forget about anything produced by Mitch whom he saw as the Devil incarnate. He would criticise him on stage and also throw barbs at the Hollywood columnist Dorothy Kilgallen who was forever writing about his indiscretions. He called her 'the chinless wonder' and things came to head in February 1956 when she wrote *The Real Frank Sinatra Story* over a week in the *Los Angeles Examiner*. Frank was so furious that he sent her a tombstone with her name engraved on it.

He had brought a lot of it upon himself. He was forever seen escorting beautiful stars. He had relations with Judy Garland, Dinah Shore, Kim Novak, Vanessa Brown (who had played Monroe's part in the original Broadway production *of The Seven Year Itch*) and Mona Freeman (a starlet whose measurements were identical to the Venus de Milo, plus arms). It was rumoured that when Elizabeth Taylor had found herself pregnant by him, Frank paid for the abortion.

On 30 March 1955 he attended the Academy Awards where it was his duty to present the Oscar for Best Supporting Actress. It went to Eve Marie Saint for *On the Waterfront*. She was eight months pregnant and laughed, gasping, 'I think I may have the baby right here.'

In June the very British entertainer, Noël Coward, was booked for four weeks at the

Desert Inn in Las Vegas. It was great money – $160,000 for a month's work – and Coward wrote to a friend, 'Las Vegas was rather a dangerous challenge and has turned out to be successful beyond my wildest dreams.'

Frank loved Noël Coward's wit and he arranged an outing for his close friends. He chartered a plane to Vegas and they would eat caviar and drink champagne, see Noël's show and some others, and stay for three nights in their own apartments. It was an act of immense friendship and generosity as Sinatra would meet all the bills, apart from the gambling losses. The guests included David Niven, Humphrey Bogart and his partner Lauren Bacall, Judy Garland and her husband Sid Luft, Joan Fontaine, Rosemary Clooney, Angie Dickinson and the comedian Ernie Kovacs.

In Holmby Hills, Humphrey Bogart assembled an anti-Hollywood, non-conformist group of loose-living, hard drinking celebrities who included David Niven, Judy Garland, Nathaniel Benchley, Frank Sinatra and Jimmy Van Heusen. Some nights they might just play charades but generally the outrageous behaviour would include some hookers for the men. The secrets stayed within the group. There was no commercial or political reason for its existence but they had supported the Democrat Adlai Stevenson, the Governor of Illinois, when he stood for President in 1952.

Most of the Holmby Hills gang were in Frank's party in Vegas and on the final day, Lauren Bacall surveyed them and said, 'You look like a goddamn rat pack.' A week late they gave Frank a testimonial dinner. There was a package from Jack Entratter for everyone. Inside each one was a live white rat. The idea of the Rat Pack had been born, though with Frank, the group was exploited for commercial gain.

Frank Sinatra met Joan Collins at a Hollywood party and he kept twanging the elastic on the top of her shoulder. Joan Collins said, 'You're like some Mafia gangster from *Guys and Dolls*,' to which Humphrey Bogart retorted, 'Don't you ever speak like that to a pal of mine.'

In July 1955 Walt Disney opened his first Disneyland theme park in Anaheim, California. He took his children to the preview, along with Sammy Davis. Tina was not allowed on the car ride as she was too small. To compensate Frank gave her a battery powered Thunderbird Junior for Christmas. Both Nancy and Tina received extravagant birthday and Christmas gifts, but Frank Jr never fared as well. There doesn't appear to be any malice in this – just Frank not connecting with his brain.

More than any other studio, MGM was geared to making lavish musicals. The producer, Sam Goldwyn paid $1m for the rights to film the Broadway smash, *Guys and Dolls*, based on Damon Runyon's lowlife characters and set in the Prohibition era in New York. He had Frank Sinatra for Nathan Detroit, so what could possibly go wrong?

At first Gene Kelly was in the frame. Goldwyn wanted him for Sky Masterson but he couldn't break free of *It's Always Fair Weather* where he was both acting and choreographing the dance sequences.

Then Sam Goldwyn had an idea: what if he signed the hottest star of the moment, Marlon Brando? The director, Joe Mankiewicz, said, 'Do you know if he can dance or sing?' Good question, but Goldwyn said it didn't matter: the public would pay good money to see Brando in a musical. There would be tremendous publicity.

The answer to both of Mankiewicz's questions was no and it was obvious that the publicity would be lost if Brando mimed to somebody else's voice. Amazingly, and this is hard to credit, Brando was given the key role of Sky Masterson (a gambler where the sky's the limit) while Sinatra, the best popular singer in the world, was relegated to Nathan Detroit. Mankiewicz, although a highly experienced director, was in way over his head.

As with *On the Waterfront*, Brando needed the money. This time he had foolishly bought some cattle and it was all going wrong. He was offered $200,000, a mammoth fee for the time. He had some provisos, principally over Frank Sinatra's role. He feared that Sinatra could steal the film and his insecurity was revealed in a letter to Mankiewicz where he said that Nathan Detroit was a one joke character so the less he did the better. Nathan's role was less prominent than in the stage musical and that could be the reason.

Goldwyn wanted Betty Grable for Miss Adelaide, but Mankiewicz said it would be directing a pair of tits. Marilyn Monroe was similarly dismissed. In truth, Mankiewicz had never directed a lavish musical and he thought it would be easier to have as many of the New York leads as possible. This didn't work out but he did secure Stubby Kaye for Nicely-Nicely who stole the film from both Brando and Sinatra with a glorious song about crapshooting your way through the Pearly Gates, 'Sit Down, You're Rockin' the Boat'.

Jerry Wayne, who was in that Broadway production, said, 'In my opinion, it is the best of all the musical scores, such clever lyrics and such wonderful tunes. The film was terribly miscast as Sam Goldwyn was the producer and he went with what he thought were surefire names. Why he thought he needed them when the show itself was internationally so successful, I don't know. Sinatra played Sam Levene's part and he was all wrong for it and Marlon Brando played the part I played and he was all wrong for it *and* he couldn't sing. It was a bad film.'

Mankiewicz wrote the screenplay but unfortunately his ingenuousness showed as it was too slow and too wordy. However, he retained the opening ballet, a fantastic conglomeration of pickpockets, prostitutes, con men and hoodwinked tourists. Who knows why but he told Frank Loesser that some of his songs would not work on screen. Loesser dutifully gave him a romantic ballad, 'A Woman in Love' for Brando and a love song, 'Adelaide' for Sinatra. More resentfulness followed when Sinatra realised that Brando had been given a major popular song.

Frank felt that the film called for little research on his part. He knew the characters, he knew the location, and he knew how to drink and gamble. All he had to do was to turn up and say his lines, sing his songs and dance a little and then collect his money.

On the first day of rehearsals, Marlon Brando approached Frank, 'Frank, I've never done anything like before, and I was wondering if I could come to your dressing room and we could just run through the dialogue together.'

Still smarting over *On the Waterfront*, Frank responded, 'Don't give me any of that Actors' Studio bullshit' and the battle lines were drawn.

Take the first scene, which was shot at Mindy's, the studio's version of Lindy's Delicatessen in New York. Sinatra had to eat cheesecake while Brando talked. He would stumble over his lines or he would try them in different ways. This was the first scene and they were up to Take 34. Bear in mind that Sinatra's favourite words were 'Jack Daniel's' and his least favourite, 'Take 2'.

Frank said, patiently and quietly, 'I'm doing this scene just once more. You see this cheesecake. You're going to get it all if you don't do it right.'

Brando paused and smirked. He knew he had needled Frank. Frank said, 'I give up' and went to his dressing room. The next morning Mankiewicz asked them to return to the scene. Frank said, 'These fucking New York actors! How much cheesecake do you think I can eat?'

Fortunately they finished the scene without further incident, but thereafter nearly every scene with them was fraught with tension. Sinatra who was used to learning lyrics just learnt his lines and said them, while Brando was repeatedly changing dialogue. He put in his trademark hums and haws and soon Sinatra was referring to him as Mumbles. In retaliation,

Brando called him Baldie and when he publicised the film on *The Ed Sullivan Show*, he said, 'Frank is the kind of guy who, when he dies, goes to Heaven and gives God a hard time for making him bald.'

One scene clocked up 135 takes, nearly all down to Brando. Sinatra told him, 'I don't buy this take and retake jazz. The key to good acting on the screen is spontaneity – and that's something you lose a little with each take.' Asked to join the other actors for a scene, Sinatra told Mankiewicz, 'Don't put me in the game, coach, until Mumbles is through rehearsing.' Sinatra was amused by Brando's increasing weight and thought he might end a scene considerably heavier than when he started. At one point in the film, Sinatra stepped on the scales and was 124 pounds: Brando was 210.

Of course Sinatra was furious that the Sky Masterson role had gone to Mumbles but it was hard to say no to Sam Goldwyn even if you were Frank Sinatra. Brando made a singing fool of himself on a key song, 'Luck Be a Lady', a song that Sinatra could have performed better in his sleep. As the *New Yorker* said, 'Brando sang through an unyielding set of sinuses.' Frank was happy that Brando was doing so badly but he didn't want to be in a turkey. Not only was Brando singing flatly and badly: his speech was equally irritating.

Believing that the best defence was attack, Brando complained about Sinatra's singing. He told Mankiewicz: 'He's supposed to sing with a Bronx accent, to clown it up, but he's singing like a romantic lead. We can't have two romantic leads in the same film.' Mankiewicz refused to intervene; far better to have someone singing some of the songs decently. Then that hothead Frank Loesser, visiting the set, stirred it up. He told the equally hotheaded Sinatra how he wanted his lyrics phrased. They never spoke again.

There was tension backstage as well. Right from the start, Brando started screwing the chorus girls. Sinatra was so competitive that he knew he would have bed more than Brando.

One of the most curious scenes was when Brando gave Jean Simmons several Malibus (coconut milk, Bacardi and pineapple) on a trip to Havana. This is date rape and certainly not something the hero of a movie would do today. Fortunately, the scene ended with a fight and Brando being gallant.

Once the filming ended, the producers would find out if 'Brando Sings!' would bring in the punters. Brando threw another wobbly: he didn't want to promote the film. He had to be bribed with a new Thunderbird. The New York première went very well with fans 20 deep in the rain and both Brando and Sinatra being mobbed. Brando even appeared in a TV special from the Sahara in Las Vegas, but when he was asked to attend the opening Japan, he said, 'I've done enough for that Thunderbird.'

The film lasted 150 minutes, seemingly longer because of Brando's incompetence, and the *New Yorker* commented, 'Sam, you made the film too long'. Capitol would not allow Frank to appear on a soundtrack album for Decca, so the LP was scrapped and the public could not buy Marlon Brando singing 'A Woman in Love'. Thank you very much, said Frankie Laine, who scored an international hit with the song, produced by Mitch Miller.

Goldwyn had spent $5.5m on *Guys and Dolls* and he was hoping for a cash bonanza of $50m. But it did well, only being outgrossed by James Dean in *Giant*. *Guys and Dolls* made $13m gross and so the film made money but it could have been so much better. I'd have kept Frank Sinatra as Nathan Detroit but given him a couple more songs and I would have replaced Brando with Dean Martin, who would have been perfect for Sky Masterson.

When Mongomery Clift went to see *Guys and Dolls*, he told Brando that he had punched the glass in the display case. 'Why did you do that?' said Brando. 'Because all I'd been watching was your big, big, big, fat arse,' said Clift. Many years later, Tony Bennett told Frank Sinatra, 'You know, I liked *Guys and Dolls*, Frank.' Frank retorted, 'Go back to San

Francisco and look for your heart.'

In a sense, Goldwyn was ahead of the pack as a few years later there was a craze for putting non-singers in musicals: Rex Harrison in *My Fair Lady*, Lee Marvin in *Paint Your Wagon*, Peter O'Toole in *Man Of La Mancha* and Richard Harris in *Camelot*, although Harris made that work for him. Not to mention Pierce Brosnan in *Mamma Mia!* Even Sam Goldwyn would have had doubts about that.

In late July 1955, Sinatra was back at Capitol recording another hit song, this time by Sammy Cahn with Frank Reardon, the bouncy 'Same Old Saturday Night'. A bored man was going to the cinema alone, drinking coffee and reading the Sunday papers, but his routine changed when he found his girl, precisely the same theme as Abba's 'The Day Before You Came'. On the same day he recorded his worst song ever, 'Fairy Tale', written by Alan Livingston's brother, Jerry. The gusts in Nelson Riddle's arrangement heralded the genie appearing. Surely he would rather be recording rock'n'roll.

As 'Our Love Is Here to Stay' was the last song written by George Gershwin; he, unlike love, was not here to stay. It appeared in MGM's first Technicolor release, *Goldywn Follies* (1938) and was reprieved by Gene Kelly for *An American in Paris* (1950). It was a beautiful arrangement by Nelson Riddle featuring a muted trumpet, causing Nelson to remark, 'Frank used to sound like a violin and now he's a fine cello.' The song was revived by Harry Connick Jr for *When Harry Met Sally* (1989) and recent versions have emanated from Rod Stewart, Natalie Cole and Smokey Robinson.

'You'll Get Yours', recorded in 1955, was a wacky Jimmy Van Heusen and Dok Sandford song, about a girl getting her comeuppance. This minor hit for Frank Sinatra was hardly heard in the UK as it was banned by the BBC. The Corporation decreed that the song could be performed live, providing this reference to God was amended:

Just like Eve who tricked old Adam
She had to play the cost
A great voice boomed and said "Madam,
Get lost."'

On the same day Frank recorded a classic '(Love is) The Tender Trap', one of the most commercial Cahn/Van Heusen songs with a terrific arrangement from Nelson Riddle. Its theme, a very 1950s one, is that if you want sex, get married. Sinatra heard the arrangement and said, 'Did you hear how high the note is for the last 'love' in the song? How can you expect me to hit such a note?' Sammy Cahn responded, 'Because you're Frank Sinatra' which was the perfect response. Frank hit the high F on the word 'love' with ease. The song was cloned by Bobby Darin for 'That's the Way Love Is'.

The MGM film, *The Tender Trap*, based on a Broadway hit, had an arresting start. Frank is performing the title song jauntily as he walks towards the camera. The song, which was published by Sinatra's Barton music, was heard five times in the film. Sinatra played a 35-year-old theatrical agent in New York leading a happy-go-lucky bachelor life. Frank's views on love and marriage were shattered on meeting Debbie Reynolds. She said to him, 'You're even attractive in an off beat, beat-up sort of way.' The chemistry between them is so good that they should have done more together. He gave her some advice when her character was singing, 'You can't throw a song like that away, you've got to have some warmth.' During the making of the film, Debbie became engaged to Eddie Fisher and he told her, 'Never marry a singer.' The film now seems very sexist and out of date but many 1950s films are like that.

In October 1955 Manie Sacks persuaded Frank agreed to participate in a live TV play, *Our Town*, written by Thornton Wilder and featuring Paul Newman and Eve Marie Saint.

He played the singing stage manager and Sammy Cahn and Jimmy Van Heusen wrote two songs for the project including the title song, which can be seen the precursor of his concept album, *Watertown* (1970). 'Love and Marriage' was also like 'The Tender Trap, Part 2', and both were in the charts at the same time. It's hard to tell how seriously Frank took the song as his whole life was demonstrating that you can have one without the other. It had a lively arrangement with tubas and there is a wonderful moment when the band shouts, 'You can't have none', reminding us of the Dorsey days. Later, it was the theme song for the 1980s sitcom *Married...With Children.*

Sammy Cahn recalled demonstrating the songs to Sinatra: 'He had his thumb on his lower lip, just kneading the lip and listening. He heard all the songs, every song, and then he looked at me and nodded. He's not too demonstrative and it was the most incredible experience. *Our Town* went on the air in Los Angeles at 6pm, to be shown in New York simultaneously at 9pm, and it was a 90 minute broadcast, live, with Nelson Riddle and his Orchestra. Nelson was a block away, watching the monitor and conducting. Sinatra was singing for the angels that night, he has never sung better in his life He was just incredible, and I won an Emmy for 'Love and Marriage'.'

Our Town was never seen again or sold abroad as it was not recorded. Frank said that the TV producers were idiots and that he could have made a movie in that time.

The sports writer, Jimmy Cannon, recommended a novel, *The Man with the Golden Arm*, to Sinatra. He saw its potential and wanted to play the lead role. He found out that another actor John Garfield had bought the property for himself but he had died and the rights could be purchased. When he learnt that Mumbles was chasing the property, he was determined to get there first. The film about a jazz drummer with a heroin addiction was uncompromising material for 1955 and the producer and director, Otto Preminger, knew that he would have to defy the Motion Picture Association of America who disapproved of drug use in most films, no matter what the rating. Actually, there were a few films about drug addiction around at the time – *A Hatful of Rain* being one – but this was a film with a star cast and the potential of full promotion.

Sinatra knew that he would have to look convincing as a jazz drummer and he had coaching from Shelly Manne, who proclaimed that Frank had 'a definite feel for it'. The film, although set in Chicago, was completely shot on a sound stage. The set added to the claustrophobia and the film was enhanced by a brassy, jazzy score from Elmer Bernstein and superb credit titles from Saul Bass. The musicians came largely from the team for *The Wild One* – Bob Cooper, Bud Shank and Milt Bernhart. Sinatra is brilliant throughout, doing the cold turkey scene in a single take, and Sammy Davis, for one, was immensely impressed.

This was the first major film to feature Kim Novak. She was the daughter of a Polish railway worker. She had been a salesgirl in Chicago and then chosen to be Miss Deep Freeze for a national promotion for fridges. (Sometimes there's no need to write the jokes.) She was being groomed for stardom by Harry Cohn. Her acting skills weren't great but she had a winsome smile and such a good figure that usually she went braless.

Harry Cohn was able to hire Novak out to Otto Preminger for $100,000, although she only received $750 a week. She did okay in *The Man with the Golden Arm* even though a better actress would have made more of the role. Sinatra offered to 'coach her' and didn't mind multiple takes while she was around. Wonder why.

The film was an accurate portrayal of drug addiction, although surely there was more than one dealer in the whole of Chicago. The ending could have been stronger: nobody knew that Sinatra's wife could really walk so she could have committed the perfect crime.

The film was rushed out in the hope that Sinatra could pick up an Oscar for Best Actor.

He didn't fancy his own chances as he felt that the theme would put off many Academy voters, but Noël Coward sent Sinatra a note of praise suggesting he should now make *The Man with the Plastic Prick*. At the Oscar ceremony, Jerry Lewis said to Ernest Borgnine, who was up for *Marty*, 'Tracy's already won, Cagney's won, Frank's won and James Dean is dead. I'll bet you $1.98 that you're going to win.' As Borgnine went on stage to collect the award from Grace Kelly, he put $1.98 into Lewis's hands. Frank commented, 'He won me one, he lost me one.'

The BBC decided that it did not want to publicise such a film and so the title was banned. When Billy May and his Orchestra released the theme from the film, they called it 'Main Title' to escape the ban, though surely 'main' might have been short for 'mainlining', and it became a Top 10 single. DJs were instructed not to say where the main title came from. Cover versions from Eddie Calvert and the Ted Heath Orchestra were banned as they still referred to the film's title. The Salford poet, John Cooper Clarke, recalled the film, 'All films about drugs have to say how terrible they are, but when I saw *The Man with the Golden Arm*, I thought those drugs must be fantastic if he's going to all this trouble to get them.'

Again, in 1956, there were many projects which didn't get under way. Frank and Bogie wanted to make a heist movie, *Underworld USA*, but Bogart had developed cancer of the oesophagus. Two films with Sammy Davis, *The Jazz Train* and *The Harold Arlen Story* never materialised but Frank did almost star in *Carousel* as Barry Bigelow. He wasn't too sure about the role, feeling that it needed someone who was big and burly, but he was offered $150,000 and looked fine in the wardrobe tests. When he turned up for the first day of shooting in Booth Bay Harbour, Maine on 20 August 1956, he learnt that Fox was shooting the film in their standard process and their new CinemaScope '55. Sinatra said that he wasn't going to make two films for the price of one and walked out. He was replaced by the big and burly Gordon MacRae. He wanted to play the part and was ideally cast. Frank was sued over this and the matter was settled out of court by him agreeing to make *Can Can*. After a few days' shooting, the producers decided to only make *Carousel* in CinemaScope '55 so what was all the fuss about? In retrospect, it looks as though Frank was still uncomfortable about the role and this gave him an escape route.

Sinatra was friendly with MacRae and didn't mind him taking his role. At a charity ball, Jack Warner had bid $1,000 for Gordon MacRae to sing and John Wayne had bid $2,000 for him not to. Frank felt that John Wayne had insulted his friend and made a point of saying so.

Frank Sinatra had made a deal with United Artists through his own company Kent to make six films over five years, one of them to be directed by Frank himself. It was a good idea to have him producing as well as appearing because it kept him busy between takes, but it created further tensions as Frank was employing the very men who were directing him. Such a relationship worked fine for many stars but it was likely to be problematical with the volatile Sinatra.

The first project was a western *Johnny Concho* with Frank and Hank Sanicola as producers and Don McGuire as writer and director. As a producer, Frank was able to dictate that the shooting (in both senses) would take place late in the day and that it had to be fast (in both senses). He took lessons in gunplay from Gary Cooper and the schedule couldn't overrun as he was committed to making *High Society*. So Frank was as demanding as Johnny Concho himself.

The film was based on a western from 1954, *The Man Who Owned the Town*, written by David P Harmon and starring Leslie Nielsen, for the TV series, *Studio One in Hollywood*. Frank had planned to make one of his girlfriends, 32-year-old Gloria Vanderbilt, the lead actress. As the surname implies, she was excessively wealthy, but she was a limited actress and he had to replace her with Phyllis Kirk. Vanderbilt had already been married to an abusive agent and to the conductor Leopold Stokowski and in August 1956, she married the director, Sidney Lumet. More successfully, Frank asked Nelson Riddle to score the film, his first, thus establishing a secondary career path for him.

Today, *Johnny Concho* would be called a psychological western. It was set in Cripple Creek, Arizona in 1875 and Frank in the title role was playing the bad guy. Everybody feared his brother and he used this to his advantage to intimidate the townsfolk. When they played poker with him, Johnny Concho merely said he had a winning hand and took the money. There were inconsistencies in the plot: how did anyone know for certain that his brother, Red, has been killed? The sheriff had a special holster to enable him to draw faster, so why didn't the gunslingers have it as well? Still, they were interesting characters in difficult situations and it worked fine.

Although some critics thought Sinatra uneasy in the title role, he was nevertheless convincing, but he disliked riding horses. The story could have been improved if Johnny Concho had shot the gunman rather than the townsfolk doing the job for him, but the film did make strong points about conscience and duty. Although a cheapo-cheapo production, *Johnny Concho* was a good film and it could be remade successfully today.

Sinatra was heard singing 'Wait for Me (Theme from *Johnny Concho*)', which was written and orchestrated by Nelson Riddle. The female singer (Loulie Jean Norman) warbling along beside him is given a few lines of her own. Such an effect was first heard in Frankie Laine's 'Girl in the Wood' (1953) and later in John Leyton's 'Johnny Remember Me' (1961). It was a prototype for Ennio Morricone. Incidentally, Norman was also a high voice on the Tokens' The Lion Sleeps Tonight' and on the original *Star Trek* theme.

Being someone who liked to fill his diary, in December 1955, Frank Sinatra had a brief cameo in the MGM film, *Meet Me in Las Vegas*, directed by Joe Pasternak and starring Dan Dailey and Cyd Charisse. The film was partly shot at the Sands and Frank is shown winning on a slot machine, precisely what he was doing as one of the owners.

Spare a thought for Dick Haymes. For once, he had struck lucky – a record deal with Capitol. He was to make two albums for them, *Rain Or Shine* (1955) and *Moondreams* (1957) with arrangements from Johnny Mandel and Ian Bernard, but his time has past and they didn't sell.

In January 1956 Frank Sinatra recorded the most influential album of his career, *Songs for Swingin' Lovers!* Even the title has been much parodied including Peter Sellers' *Songs for Swingin' Sellers!* (1959) and Allan Sherman's *For Swingin' Livers Only!* (1965). It was the culmination of his time with Nelson Riddle – it was though he had been taking a rocket ship to the moon and was now walking on the craters in the most relaxed, carefree and confident manner. Another musical revolution was taking place in the early months of 1956 with the commercial success of Elvis Presley and 'Heartbreak Hotel'. *Songs for Swingin' Lovers!* was less radical but it was just as game-changing – Frank Sinatra and Nelson Riddle with producer,Voyle Gilmore, had developed a new hip way to perform standards.

All the songs were recorded between 9 and 16 January 1956 and oddly enough, they were the last songs that Sinatra recorded at the radio station KHJ as Capitol's new recording studio was then open for business, the final song being appropriately enough, 'We'll Be Together Again'. This time there were 14 songs, most of them dating from Sinatra's formative years. The album opened sparklingly and joyously with 'You Make Me Feel So Young' from the 1946 film, *Three Little Girls in Blue*. Sinatra twinkled as he sang 'in-div-id-u-al' or 'r-r-r-r-running'. In 2013 the performer Curtis Stigers said, 'I love 'You Make Me So Feel Young'. As I get older and am recently divorced, I am thinking about love again and that song really evokes that. It has that feeling of spring and falling in love.'

The success of Al Jolson in the first 'talkie', *The Jazz Singer*, in 1927 had prompted other films based around musical personalities. Paul Whiteman and his Orchestra with their vocalist Bing Crosby were featured in the 1930 musical, *King Of Jazz*, which was also in colour and featured a cartoon section. Talk about doing everything at once! The wonderful score included George Gershwin's *Rhapsody in Blue* and three classic songs – 'Happy Feet', 'Mississippi Mud' and 'It Happened in Monterey'. Not many artists were singing 'It Happened in Monterey' in the 1950s but Sinatra knew it was worth reviving. Note the looseness of his phrasing in the second chorus.

The third song, 'You're Getting to Be a Habit with Me', was a Harry Warren and Al Dubin song from *Forty-Second Street* (1932). Bebe Daniels sang it on celluloid and then Bing put it on record. It is a song about addiction, similar in that way to 'I Get a Kick Out of You' and contains the questionable line, 'I couldn't do without my supply.'

'You Brought a New Kind of Love to Me' was sung by Maurice Chevalier in the film, *The Big Pond* (1930) and was a hit record for Bing Crosby with Paul Whiteman and his Orchestra. Nelson Riddle wrote a stunning instrumental break for brass and strings.

In 1937 the film producer Hal Wallis told Johnny Mercer and Richard Whiting that he wanted a tune which could be reprised with several different lyrics in *Ready, Willing and Able*. Mercer thought he would find this difficult and Whiting for a joke gave him a copy of Webster's Dictionary. That led to him writing about someone who was tongue-tied and couldn't find the right words, calling it 'Too Marvellous for Words' and even including a reference to Webster's Dictionary. It was a No.1 for Bing Crosby with Jimmy Dorsey and his Orchestra. As Sinatra loved crossword puzzles, this lyric had a particular appeal for him. It was a stupendous, striking and stunning song from Sinatra – in fact, too marvellous for words.

There was a change of mood for the sultry 'Old Devil Moon' from *Finian's Rainbow* (1947). It was another superlative performance and a fine contrast for the album, after which Side 1 closed with 'Pennies from Heaven'. Songs about money were ten a penny after the Depression and this was a chart-topper for ten weeks, best known by Bing Crosby with Jimmy Dorsey and his Orchestra. It was also the title song of a film starring Bing and Louis Armstrong. Frank's version opened with strings and moved into Harry 'Sweets' Edison's trumpet. His contribution was as crucial as Sinatra's. Again, Sinatra was playing around with his s's again in 'sunshine and flowers'. There was an equally colourful reading from Louis Prima who changed the line to 'sunshine and ravioli'. 'Pennies from Heaven' became the title song of Dennis Potter's celebrated TV serial about a sheet music salesman and a parody, 'Benny's From Heaven', has been recorded by Eddie Jefferson and James Moody.

If Side 1 was brilliant, Side 2 was even better, opening with the most famous of all the Cole Porter songs associated with Frank Sinatra, 'I Got You Under My Skin'. Sinatra had suggested this song at the last minute and Nelson had stayed up to write the pulsating arrangement. He was inspired by what he had heard on Stan Kenton's '23 Degrees North, 82 Degrees West' (1952) and he asked Kenton's trombonist, Milt Bernhardt, to join them. His fierce, exciting contribution, which was partly improvised, is the best known trombone solo in the world. The musicians applauded when Berhhardt played and even the unflappable Nelson said, 'How about that!' Sinatra was so impressed that he asked Milt to join them in the control room for the playback.

As for the song itself, in 1936 Cole Porter had heard a French song, 'Mon Homme', and was captivated by its opening line, 'Je l'ai tellement dans le peau', which translates as 'I've got him so much under my skin'. He set about using the phrase himself and 'I've Got

You Under My Skin' is a typical Cole Porter song, full of sensuality and innuendo. It was performed in the film, *Born to Dance*, by Virginia Bruce, but it was Fanny Brice who made the song popular. Sinatra is very respectful to Cole Porter's lyric although he has fun with the phrase, 'how it yells'.

This record got under nearly everybody's skin. Elvis Costello recalls that one of his first words was 'skin' and he would keep requesting that record. He has said, 'The greatest moment in popular music is when Frank goes 'Don't you know, little fool' after the trombone solo.' But the song does have its detractors: Michael Gray in *The Bob Dylan Encyclopedia* thought that 'Use your mentality, wake up to reality' was awful songwriting.

The songwriter Bill Martin said, 'My all-time favourite lyric is Cole Porter's 'I've Got You Under My Skin'. It is a song that gets you if you are truly in love with somebody. You would walk across coals for them and sacrifice anything, come what may, as the song says. Frank Sinatra's recording with Nelson Riddle builds up like you wouldn't believe: it is a fabulous arrangement. What could be better than having Frank Sinatra, Nelson Riddle and Cole Porter on the same record, and this is their finest hour.'

Johnny Mercer had the idea for 'I Thought About You' while he was travelling on a train, hence the reference in the lyric. He wrote the words in 1939 shortly after his songwriting partner Richard Whiting had died and it was the first song he wrote with Jimmy Van Heusen. The first version by Mildred Bailey with Benny Goodman and his Orchestra was quite playful, but Billie Holiday added melancholy in 1954. Sinatra started the song as a solo ballad but the tempo quickened and the arrangement built magnificently. It's a great lyric and by the end Sinatra was realising that everything reminds him of her.

'We'll Be Together Again' was typical of the songs written at the end of the war, this one being unusual as the lyric came from another singer, Frankie Laine. The music was written by Carl Fischer, who had been Frankie Laine's conductor and who had recently died. Again, Harry Edison added a poignant trumpet solo.

Writing truly witty songs is very difficult but Gus Kahn and Walter Donaldson pulled it off with the highly engaging 'Makin' Whoopee', which was sung by Eddie Cantor in the stage revue, *Whoopee*, in 1928. Both Sinatra and Riddle appreciated how they could make the song even more humorous and Sinatra added little touches like 'The cat's so willing'.

'Swingin' Down the Lane' was a perfect song title for *Songs for Swingin' Lovers!* and had been successful for its composer, the bandleader Isham Jones, in 1923. This time there were two trumpet soloists in Conrad Guzzo and Harry Edison and they playfully chased each other.

In 1934 Cole Porter's title song for his show, *Anything Goes*, was daring, even making a reference to D H Lawrence's *Lady Chatterley's Lover* with 'four-letter words'. It was been a *tour de force* for Ethel Merman on stage and then recorded by Paul Whiteman and the Dorsey Brothers. Most singers would take the arrangement up to a top note, but Nelson had Frank go to a low E, doing something similar on the final track, 'How About You'. There was a post-modern touch where Sinatra referred to making an LP with 'May I say before this record spins to a close, Anything goes.'

In 1954 Ethel Merman received $50,000 for two appearances on *The Colgate Comedy Hour*, much more than she would earn on Broadway. One was a one-hour production of *Anything Goes* with Sinatra as Billy Crocker, Bert Lahr as Moonface Martin and herself as Reno Sweeney. With only an hour to play with, the narrative section of the show was trimmed to a minimum. It marks the only time Frank performed in a Broadway musical, albeit on radio, and his role had been played on film by Bing Crosby, also with Merman, in 1936.

Merman has another link with Sinatra. Ernest Borgnine, who had beaten up Frank in *From Here to Eternity*, was a heavy in real life having attacked his wives, Rhoda Kemins and Katy Jurado. Ernest and Ethel met in 1963 and they married in June 1964 in front of 500 guests. Merman was appalled to find that her so-called honeymoon was a junket in the Far East to promote Borgnine's latest film and he was also having a relationship with his maid. She moved out in August, having been married for 38 days. The marriage became a showbiz joke and Merman hated being a figure of fun.

There is another cross-reference in Burton Lane and Ralph Freed's 'How About You' with the line, 'I like a Gershwin tune', although there are none on this album. Again, this is an amusing reworking of the song and here Sinatra referred to 'James Durante's looks'. Both Joni James and Bertice Reading alluded to Sinatra's looks as did Rosemary Clooney when she sang it with Bing.

'Memories of You' was recorded for *Songs for Swinging Lovers!* but not issued at the time. It had been written by the black musician, Eubie Blake, for the revue, *Lew Leslie's Blackbirds Of 1930*. Louis Armstrong recorded it with Lionel Hampton playing vibes for the first time in his life – the vibes happened to be in the studio – and it worked. The song was also successful for the Casa Loma Orchestra. There were celebrations when Eubie Blake reached 100 in 1983, but nobody had checked the information. In reality, he died later that year, aged 96.

At the sessions, Sinatra also cut the single 'Flowers Mean Forgiveness', a US Top 40 single, but sounding feeble after 'Love and Marriage and 'The Tender Trap'. It sounds like an ad for Interflora.

You can make a good case for *Songs for Swingin' Lovers!* being the first concept album but there was a touch of the last chance saloon about it. Sinatra is demonstrating how good and vibrant these old standards are, just before the rock revolution took over. Sinatra based much of his subsequent career around this album and indeed, Bobby Darin took the same stance for a younger generation. The LP made No.2 on the US album chart and was the first LP to sell sufficiently to get onto the singles chart in the UK, although the notion of merging LPs with singles was soon dropped. Despite the meteoric rise of Elvis Presley, Frank Sinatra was the Top Male Vocalist in *Playboy* every year from 1957 to 1966, also revealing that Frank did have a loyal male following.

If Sinatra's life equated with vintage wine (cue for song), 1956 would be the connoisseur's choice as that was the year that he also made the film, *High Society*.

Born in Philadelphia in 1928, Grace Kelly was a Hitchcock blonde, a Hollywood beauty, who had turned down Bing Crosby and William Holden and had dated Frank Sinatra, David Niven, Ray Milland, Gary Cooper, Clark Gable, the designer Oleg Cassini and probably Spencer Tracy.

Prince Rainier III of Monaco was the last heir of the Grimaldi family. If he produced no children, the tiny principality of Monaco, which was smaller than Hyde Park, was destined to become French. He was going to marry the French actress, Gisele Pascal but she failed the fertility tests. Strangely enough, she later had a family.

The tycoon Aristotle Onassis had arranged for Prince Rainier to meet Marilyn Monroe but the prince didn't care for this showgirl, preferring Grace Kelly, whom he met in spring 1955. They became engaged in December and Kelly wore his ring when making *High Society* rather than a prop. They would be married in 1956 but first she would complete *High Society*. It was the best exit ever made by a Hollywood star, a real life *Philadelphia Story*.

Grace didn't make any more films but she still associated with her old friends. The biopic *Grace of Monaco* (2014) was about Alfred Hitchcock's proposal for her to star in

Marnie (1962), but even though an Oscar-winning star (Nicole Kidman) was playing another one, the film had no saving graces.

That most swellegant of films, *High Society*, was made by MGM with Sol Siegel producing and Charles Walters directing. It was a musical update of the Broadway play and film, *The Philadelphia Story*, and in a way the casting was wrong. Grace Kelly was no Katherine Hepburn and Bing Crosby was too old to play Grace Kelly's boyfriend. Indeed, Kelly had come in as a replacement for Elizabeth Taylor. Even Frank Sinatra said, 'I couldn't figure how they could cast a 53 year old balding little man to romance the gorgeous Grace Kelly with me at 40 given the supporting role. Maybe it was jealousy on my part because I really fancied the gal.' Bing got the gal in the end, perhaps because he had been more considerate.

The miscasting didn't matter because the songs were so right. The major plus was a scintillating score by Cole Porter, a combination of old and new material. There wasn't any big production number but each song worked fine in its setting with arrangements from Conrad Salinger and Nelson Riddle.

Cole Porter considered 'I Love You Samantha' to be the best song in the film but he was delighted by the success of 'True Love', a hokey ballad sung romantically at sea with Bing in a captain's hat playing an accordion and Grace Kelly harmonising. Cole's publisher described it as 'a simple, beautiful tasteful composition worthy of Franz Schubert'. It was a major international hit. When Sinatra sings 'Mind If I Make Love to You', Grace keeps her mouth shut.

Cole Porter had never won an Oscar and so when 'True Love' was nominated, he hired the publicist, Stanley Musgrove to push the song forward. Hard luck, Cole, Alan Livingston's brother, Jay, had written 'Whatever Will Be, Will Be' for Doris Day to sing in Alfred Hitchcock's *The Man Who Knew too Much*. When Hitch first heard it, he said, 'I told you I didn't know what kind of a song I wanted, but that's the kind of song I wanted.'

Bing and Frank had a good relationship, both on and off set. They both liked to work fast, though Bing would often say, 'Would you like that again?' Because Frank was hyper and Bing laidback, they nicknamed each other Dexedrine and Nembutal. Their chemistry on 'Well, Did You Evah!' is exhilarating and it is a great movie sequence with several digs at their real life personas – Bing's 'ba ba ba boom' is met with 'Don't dig that kind of crooning, chum.' The song had originally been a male/female duet from *Du Barry Was a Lady* (1939).

Frank was oddly cast as a reporter for *Spy* magazine looking for sleaze. He and Celeste Holm had to work hard to coordinate their vocals on 'Who Wants to Be a Millionaire' with dance steps, but the effort was well worthwhile, a highlight in a film full of highlights. The duet was not re-recorded for the soundtrack album and so would be perplexing if someone heard it as audio for the first time. Celeste sang into one of the wedding gifts, a silver urn, to create an echo effect but just heard aurally, it sounded odd. Sinatra was given 'You're Sensational', a decent romantic song and a hit single but nowhere near as strong as Bing's 'I Love You, Samantha'.

There is a bonus with Louis Armstrong commenting on the action from time to time – 'End of song, beginning of story' – and again there was another brilliant duet, this time with Louis and Bing for 'Now You Has Jazz'. It's hard to imagine Frank pulling this one off with such ease.

The cast were very relaxed in each other's company and Frank always called Grace Kelly 'Gracie'. When Prince Rainier was on the set with another visitor, David Niven, they had both had a few drinks. 'Tell me, David,' said Rainer, 'Out of all your conquests, who was the best lover?'

'Oh, your grace, I couldn't possibly be so indiscreet.'

'Come on, David, it is just between you and me.'

'All right,' said David Niven, 'I will tell you. It was Grace.'

'Grace!'

'Yes, Gracie Fields, she was magnificent.'

Some years later, Frank Sinatra said to Prince Rainier, 'You know, Grace got a platinum record before I did.' 'Worse still for you,' said the prince, 'she got it with Crosby.'

The big new recording studio at Capitol's circular building was ready and open for business on 22 February 1956. That the first session should be by Frank Sinatra was predictable, but not its contents.

Frank had been intrigued by some poems written by Norman Sickel, each of which featured a colour and he thought of asking composers to create musical settings for those colours. The result was an instrumental album, *Tone Poems of Colour*, featuring a 50 piece orchestra conducted by Sinatra with some encouragement from Felix Slatkin. Overall, it sounded like 1950s soundtrack music and was never going to sell. Capitol knew that; they were indulging Sinatra. At the same time, the project was a good way to test the new equipment. Sinatra was allowed to issue it through his own Essex imprint, which was distributed by Capitol. At the time this was considered to be some tax loss scheme dreamed up by his accountant, but it was the first stirrings that Frank wanted his own record company.

Elmer Bernstein's 'Silver' could have come from *The Man with the Golden Arm*, Nelson Riddle's 'Orange' is inspired by Richard Rodgers, and André Previn's 'Red' is like a war soundtrack. Sinatra's first work with Gordon Jenkins was 'Green', which opened with one finger piano from Bill Miller. Victor Young's 'White' was chosen by Peter Sellers as one of his *Desert Island Discs*. The other composers are Jeff Alexander, Alec Wilder and Billy May. But just what was the point of the album? Why would anyone want to hear a colour in musical terms?

Sinatra's first vocal performance at the Capitol Tower followed on 8 March 1956. Nelson Riddle was the arranger and they were working with the Hollywood String Quartet, led by Felix Slatkin, and a few additional instruments. In the main, they were cutting the songs that would form Frank's next album, the intimate *Close To You*, although the first song, 'If It's the Last Thing I Do', a success for Tommy Dorsey and Jack Leonard in 1937, was held in the vaults for many years.

'Don't Like Goodbyes', written by Harold Arlen with Truman Capote, came from the 1954 Broadway musical, *House Of Flowers*, starring Pearl Bailey and Diahann Carroll about a fight between two brothels on a West Indian island. This five minute song had an intriguing lyrics as Frank was leaving his friends for 'another love, a different kind', but context, it would seem, is everything..

In 1934 the lyricist Johnny Mercer was writing to his wife, Ginger, and realised he had forgotten to say something. He wrote a P S and this led to the song, 'P S I Love You'. I rather believe that Ginger would have overlooked this after hearing, 'I burned a hole in the dining room table.' It's a wry song about living a bachelor life for a while. The fourth song was a British composition, 'Love Locked Out' by Ray Noble, which had been a success for Noble's orchestra with Al Bowlly in 1933. It's a strong performance of a quirky song.

Frank was back a month later for 'I've Had My Moments' from an all-star caper *Hollywood Party* (1934), the song having a delightful lyric that was both modest and boastful. 'Blame It on My Youth', a jazz standard from 1934, was a classic performance of a classic song, and a few months later, in the same studio, Nat 'King' Cole recorded another definitive version, this time for his *After Midnight* album. 'It Could Happen to You' came from the 1946 film, *And the Angels Sing*, and it had been recorded by Jo Stafford and by Bing Crosby. 'With Every Breath I Take' was another song associated with Crosby, who performed it in the film, *Here is My Heart* (1934). In retrospect, it's remarkable how many Crosby songs Sinatra recorded, but Crosby had been given the best songs of the day. Also recorded was'The End of a Love Affair', a saloon song regarding love and loss, featuring an invocative Sinatra vocal enhanced by Harry Edison's trumpet

There was no rush to complete the *Close to You* album because *Songs for Swingin' Lovers!* was still selling so well. Frank didn't complete this until 1 October 1956 when he added three fine performances: a new recording of 'I Couldn't Sleep a Wink Last Night' with a stunning clarinet break from Mahlon Clark; a wistful romantic ballad associated with Bing Crosby, 'It's Easy to Remember'; and the title track with beautiful violin playing from Felix Slatkin. Studio conversation shows how intense Frank was about getting this track right. It was, when all is said and done, a remarkably low-key start for a low-key album of love songs (but not of love lost) yet it contained some of his finest work. The advertising strapline said it was Sinatra 'in his most intimate mikeside manner'. *Close to You* would never be a crowd-pleaser like *Songs for Swingin' Lovers!* but it was a US Top 10 album. Nelson Riddle was never sure that the structure of popular songs lent itself to a string quartet, albeit with additional instruments. Ever the diplomat, if he was asked about the album, he would say, 'Sinatra liked it!'

Frank often had guests in the studio and he allowed his children to attend sessions. Frank Sinatra Jr recalled, 'There was a tremendous level of excitement every time he recorded. Everyone knew that they were making the best records around. How could they miss? They had the best singer, the best arrangers, the best musicians, the best engineers and the best studio in town?' His sister Nancy added, 'Attending recording sessions at Capitol was like going to a concert today – it was the hottest ticket that you could get your hands on; it was fantastic. It was great for him to have a small audience in the room and everybody as a result of that did their best. There was magic in that building."

Sinatra recorded the sublime '(How Little It Matters) How Little We Know' with its intriguingly philosophical lyric about the depth of our knowledge. Just before a take is called, Frank shouted, "Bartender!" but he also commented, 'You can't cheat with notes. You've got to sing them.' This leads to a deep final note. This song by Carolyn Leigh (writer of 'Young at Heart') and Phil Springer was broadcast without complaint in the US. The BBC objected to the interpretation that could be placed on the line, 'What chemical forces flow from lover to lover' and banned it. Not to mention 'That sudden explosion when two tingles intermingle.'

On a lighthearted radio programme in 1949 called *The Flop Parade*, Bing Crosby and Ethel Merman sang a Jimmy Van Heusen novelty, 'There's a Flaw in My Flue' in which a ruined fireplace was a metaphor for a broken romance. It included such lines as 'Your lovely face in my fireplace' and 'Smoke gets in my nose'. Frank and Nelson recorded this as a straight romantic song for a joke, not intending it for release, but to make the Capitol executives think that they were losing the plot. This wasn't the only unlikely use of Capitol's facilities. Sinatra arranged an 11.30pm session at short notice with Nelson Riddle simply because he wanted to serenade Kim Novak (well, let's be tactful).

As with Columbia, Sinatra found that he had to record what he called 'kiddie pop' from time to time. In April 1956 he recorded a commercial but lightweight song, 'Five Hundred Guys' – '500 guys have 1,000 eyes for my baby' After finishing the song, Sinatra took the chart from the music stand and dropped it on the floor. He was right.

Rather better was 'Hey! Jealous Lover', a curious song in which the singer was accused of infidelity and blamed the girl instead, which was an implausible argument. On stage in

Seattle, Sinatra said, 'I absolutely and unequivocally detest this song.' So it wasn't just Mitch Miller then, and as it happens, the song was written by Sammy Cahn. Still, it made the Top 10 and was on the charts for five months.

Twentyfour-year-old Carroll Coates wrote the lyric for 'No One Ever Tells You' with an arranger for Harry James, Hubbard Atwood, the words evolving from a lost love affair. Their publisher Sam Weiss, known as Sad Sam as he was always reading obituaries, passed it to Frank who said he would record it the following night. Nelson Riddle wrote a quick arrangement and unusually Sinatra sang the song several times in order to get a bluesy rasp in his voice. It was recorded for a single but Sinatra put it on his next album, *A Swingin' Affair* as he wanted to save 'The Lady Is a Tramp' for something else. It was the only new song on that album but it fitted in okay. Later, Carroll Coates expanded his lyric for a new version by Rebecca Parris.

The film producer and director, Stanley Kramer, had plans to make a film based on C S Forester's novel, *The Gun*, a historical war drama set in Spain. The film was to be called *The Pride and the Passion*, which was an apt title for both the characters and the actors who were playing them. Kramer had the funding so that no expense would be spared and he wanted to attract the biggest stars. He secured a British actor based in Hollywood, Cary Grant, without much trouble, and he wanted Marlon Brando for the Spanish guerilla leader. Brando turned it down, saying that the script was badly written. This is possible as the scriptwriters, Edward and Enda Anhalt, were getting divorced and had to be forced to complete the project.

Kramer rightly thought that Frank Sinatra and Ava Gardner would be a marvellous publicity coup but Ava Gardner said no. She was going to make another film in Spain. One of the reasons why Frank agreed to a location shoot was because he would be able to visit Ava. The main reason was his fee: a whopping $250,000. Yet another could be the new leading lady, the fiery Italian sex goddess, Sophia Loren, in her first American film.

In normal circumstances, Frank would have turned the film down. He didn't like being away from home or Vegas, and he was appallingly miscast. How did Stanley Kramer convince him to play a Spanish peasant with no dress sense and a bad wig? Cary Grant also thought he was miscast but his plight was nothing like Sinatra's. As well as the stars, there was a huge supporting cast with 9,000 extras (thousands of them in the final battle) and over 1,500 livestock, not to mention the huge (fibreglass) gun, which was the true star of the film and didn't have to say any of the deplorable lines.

Kramer had to obtain General Franco's permission to make the film. He asked to see the script and was concerned that the British were coming to the rescue. The ending is so confusing that amendments had to be made. Also Franco insisted that the roads made by the film crew should be permanent.

The filming began in Segovia in April 1956. Kramer had another problem: both Cary Grant and Frank Sinatra were smitten with Sophia Loren. Frank gained the upper hand by mockery. As he was several years younger than Grant, he called him Mother to needle him and also to imply he was gay. Loren had heard how moody and difficult Sinatra could be but at first they got on well and he introduced her to Ella Fitzgerald's albums, which she loved.

The Pride and the Passion was set in 1810. Napoleon had conquered Spain and his troops had abandoned a cannon, the biggest in use anywhere. The English led by Cary Grant set out to retrieve it and he encountered Sinatra as a guerilla leader, lumbered with a strange hairpiece and even stranger accent. To his credit, Sinatra pulled it off, just about. The plan was to shift the gun 200 miles to the French stronghold at Avila and then blow the walls apart, demolishing the French in the process. When Sinatra died, Cary Grant laid him by the statue of St Teresa.

Both Grant and Sinatra were keen at first. Possibly to impress Loren, they eschewed stuntmen and performed the dangerous jumping out of the burning wagon themselves. Loren was less fortunate: a mine exploded close to her face and she was momentarily blinded. You may wonder what Loren was doing in the film anyway; she was often the only woman around, and just what was the point of her rushing into battle without a weapon?

At first Kramer was happy with Sinatra. He once said, 'If Sinatra really prepared for a role, he'd be the greatest actor in the world.' But his mind was on other things. He had had his own Ford Thunderbird shipped to Spain but he had nowhere to go. Ava didn't want to see him as she preferred the company of a young Italian actor Walter Chiari, a bullfighter and some black jazz musicians. All this and Ava was supposed to be filming.

There is a scene in *The Pride and the Passion* where Frank Sinatra watches Cary Grant watching Sophia Loren dance, which says it all. Then, when Loren says to Sinatra, 'You're jealous of him because he can fire the cannon and you can't', you realise that there is not much different between fact and fiction.

Sinatra was bored stiff, writing home and marking all his envelopes, 'Franco is a fink.' He was liable to crack at any minute. When Loren turned Sinatra down, she screamed that he was 'an Italian son of a bitch'. Frank had had enough and said he was leaving the production. Kramer could have kept him against his will but he knew the shooting would be easier without him. He agreed to shoot some of Sinatra's remaining lines together and let him go, the rest of the cast acquiescing because of the tension. Sinatra left after seven weeks shooting, leaving Cary Grant and Loren to act some of their scenes to a coat on a hanger. Later, he did a week in Los Angeles with them in post-production.

Strangely enough, this ragtag film worked out okay both commercially and critically, despite the confusing ending: the Spanish won, I think. Meanwhile, Sophia Loren's boyfriend, Carlo Ponti, realised that Cary Grant was obsessed by Loren and he quickly married her.

When *Johnny Concho* was released in July 1956, Frank was to promote it with two weeks at the Paramount with the Dorsey Brothers. The big band era had finished and the brothers had come to an uneasy truce. After three days Frank went on the razzle with Spencer Tracy. They got to 5am and Spencer said, 'Oh, the hell with it, we'll have another one and you'll be there on time.' Frank pulled out with, ahem, laryngitis. Spencer and Frank also went to the new Broadway sensation, *My Fair Lady*. They went backstage and Spencer said to Rex Harrison, 'You made the little wop cry.'

During Frank's brief stint at the Paramount, he met Tony Bennett for the first time. He had had a few hits and was about to host the summer replacement show for Perry Como. Frank advised him, 'Stay away from cheap songs and the rest will follow.' Bennett did record some plonkers but his overall level of good to bad has to be higher than Frank's.

One of the big films of the year was the epic *Around the World in 80 Days*. David Niven played the star role in Mike Todd's epic film, which was shot in his new Todd-AO widescreen process. It was the world's most expensive travelogue, employing 70,000 extras, and in each destination there were star cameos. David Niven came across Marlene Dietrich, a dancer, and George Raft, a knife-throwing bouncer, in a saloon in San Francisco and when the piano player faces the camera, it is Frank Sinatra. Dietrich said, 'That was a wonderful film because it gave me the chance to work with Frank Sinatra – he played the part of my pianist. He's my very favourite American singer and he and I have a lot in common. Frank doesn't like all those so-and-so journalists poking their noses into his affairs. That's why he always appears to be tough. In reality, he's a gentle, gentleman.'

The sessions for the next album, *A Swingin' Affair*, took place in November, a highly confident and energetic 15-track LP of up-tempo songs, arranged by Nelson Riddle and produced by Voyle Gilmore, and the ideal companion to *Songs for Swingin' Lovers*. Some might have thought that Frank was treading water by returning to 'Night and Day', but the new dynamic arrangement was the perfect opening track and is his best-known recording of the song. It's a wonderful example of Frank knowing how to tell a story and he phrased in the way that he spoke for a natural feel, and a lot of singers didn't do that. This is followed by a swinging arrangement of 'I Got Plenty o' Nuttin' from *Porgy and Bess*, and the song has been taken away from its normal semi-operatic style.

Lorenz Hart's pithy lyric, 'I Wish I Were in Love Again' from *Babes in Arms* (1937) was a refreshingly honest song about a relationship with references to flying plates and black eyes, plus the totally off-the-wall allusion to 'the faint aroma of performing seals'. 'I Guess I'll Have to Change My Plans', a hit in 1932 for Rudy Vallée, contained the equally bizarre line, 'Why did I buy those blue pyjamas?'

Fred Astaire had sung the Gershwins' song, 'Nice Work If You Can Get It' in *A Damsel in Distress* in 1937, the same year it was recorded by Billie Holiday. The great lyric needed the introductory verse to explain why love was like work but Sinatra didn't sing it. When Frank sang the song on TV with Peggy Lee, he told her, 'You're looking at me strangely.'

The lyricist of 'Stars Fell on Alabama' calls the state a 'fairyland', not a term that many would use. The flutes at the start suggested fallen stars. This is a brilliant performance by Sinatra as he extended and slurred words and provided two different readings of 'My heart beats like a hammer' and added 'Stars fractured 'bama'.

'I Won't Dance' was sung and danced by Fred Astaire and Ginger Rogers in *Roberta* (1935). Ginger was underrated – she did all the same steps as Fred Astaire and did them backwards. This record marks the début of Sinatra's pet phrase 'Ring-a-ding-ding'. The lyric referred to the Continental, an outmoded dance, and had the ingenious line, 'Heaven rest us, I'm not asbestos', but then it should be a great song as it has five wonderful writers on the credit: Oscar Hammerstein, Jerome Kern, Otto Harbach, Jimmy McHugh and Dorothy Fields.

The mock spiritual, 'Lonesome Road', opened the second side of the LP. This had been made popular by Gene Austin in 1928 and had a good blues feel – if only Sinatra had recorded more songs like this. Then came 'At Long Last Love' written by Cole Porter for *You Never Know* (1938), and performed in the show by the torch diva, Libby Holman. According to legend and to Porter himself, he wrote the song while waiting for an ambulance, 'When this horse fell on me, I was too stunned to be conscious of great pain, but until help came along, I worked on the lyrics of a song called 'At Long Last Love'.' Sinatra revelled in a local reference, 'Is it Granada I see or only Asbury Park?'

Another Cole Porter song followed: 'You'd Be So Nice to Come Home to', which had been a hit for Dinah Shore. 'From This Moment On' was written by Cole Porter for *Out of This World* (1950), which became the film, *Kiss Me Kate* (1953). It is a beautiful love song and a minor classic, and the phrase, 'whoop-dee-doo songs' was in Porter's original. Frank's voice is matched by a solo trumpet on Duke Ellington's 'I Got It Bad and That Ain't Good', one of several great versions of this song, others including Ella Fitzgerald, Louis Armstrong and Nina Simone.

'If I Had You' is normally performed as a ballad, so it is good to hear this swinging arrangement, despite the song having a totally unrealistic lyric. The album closed with a revival of 'Oh, Look at Me Now' which Frank had sung with Dorsey in 1941.

The track that Sinatra held back from *A Swingin' Affair*, 'The Lady Is a Tramp', had been written by Richard Rodgers and Lorenz Hart for the Broadway show, *Babes In Arms* (1937), but the song had been relegated to background music in the film version two years later. MGM featured it in *Words and Music* (1948) an almost fictional biopic about the two composers. MGM's performance was by the black artist Lena Horne in a standalone sequence which could be removed for cinemas in the south. Prior to Sinatra, the song was usually performed by females. More than any other song, this one summed up Sinatra with his hat on his head and raincoat over the shoulder. In actuality he turned up late for the session in black suit, black shirt and white tie, looking like a gangster. He told the band that they had had enough time to prepare so 'No fooling!'

It is not so much a passionate lyric as a clever, cynical one. It is a list song where the lyrics concentrate on the low behaviour of high society. ('She goes to Harlem in ermine and pearls' – is this why Luther Vandross was later chosen as Sinatra's duet performer for this song?) The original lyrics are dated – who cares if someone dines before eight – and why is California said to be cold and damp? The song is often updated – Sinatra had added the sharpies and frauds and Buddy Greco added the Cold War for his hit single of 1960. Frank tended to stick with the original words but added mild swearing: 'She's broke, what the hell?' Calling a lady a tramp also anticipates the Rat Pack. Sinatra gave a wonderful performance but there were much looser versions (perhaps too loose) in the years to come.

Three days after this session, on 29 November 1956, Tommy Dorsey died from asphyxiation, an unlikely end from someone so keen on breath control. Frank was asked if he would contribute to a TV obituary but he declined, feeling he would be a hypocrite if he were to praise him. Clearly, they had caught Sinatra on the wrong day. The best tribute of all was the music they had made together.

In August 1955, with *Time* magazine featuring Frank Sinatra on its cover, the strapline called him 'the hottest item in show business today'. Admittedly it was written just a few months before Elvis Presley changed popular music but it held true. However, despite best-selling albums and box office success, Sinatra had only had one Top 20 single in 1956 when 'Hey, Jealous Lover' made No.6. In December 1956, he recorded 'Can I Steal a Little Love' from the film *Pretty Baby*. It was in the same vein as 'Hey, Jealous Lover' and was close to rock'n'roll. The lyrics included 'Coo me, woo me, turtle dove' and 'Why do I dig you like I do?' Still it had its moments. Frank sang the title line like Dean Martin at one stage and he ended with 'Can I grab a little love?' He recorded 'Your Love for Me', on the same day, an okay ballad that Hank Sanicola wanted him to record.

Capitol had some impressive jazz and MOR (middle of the road) artists on their books but not Ella Fitzgerald who had signed with Norman Granz to the Verve label. As Granz did not get on with Sinatra, there were relatively few tie-ups for the foremost interpreters of the popular songs – Ella and Frank – outside of a few concerts and TV appearances. They could have made some stunning albums together.

In 1956 Ella Fitzgerald began her legendary *Songbook* series of albums for Verve, beginning with Cole Porter. She took a different approach from Sinatra by concentrating on one songwriter after another, while Frank tended to make albums which reflected a mood and would also indulge himself with lesser-known songwriters. However, the general principle was the same: to reflect the Great American Songbook in all its glory – although it did not yet have that name. Verve often used Capitol's studios in Los Angeles and Ella's albums devoted to Jerome Kern and the Gershwins were arranged and conducted by Nelson Riddle. It's tough to compare Frank with Ella as they could both be superlative, but on the whole Ella is excellent with a small group but not as powerful as Sinatra when the brass is blasting away. To give credit where it's due. Oscar Peterson started the songbook series with *Oscar Peterson Plays Cole Porter* (1951) and *Oscar Peterson Plays George Gershwin* (1952).

As has been pointed out, Frank was working for the British as they had bought the controlling share in Capitol Records. As well as being a sound investment in view of their rosters of artists, EMI wanted to create some links between Britain and America, and expected Capitol to be releasing its products almost as a matter of course. Capitol resisted strongly and things would come to a head when the Beatles started having worldwide success, but not in America, during 1963.

Frank meets Queen Elizabeth II at the British premiere of *Me and the Colonel*, 1958.

Long before Beatlemania, note this crowd for Frank outside the London Palladium in 1950.

Frank at Sunshine Home for the Blind, Northwood, London in 1962 was asked, 'What colour is the wind?'

Frank and daughter Nancy attend a film premiere in Hollywood, 1955.

'You married the wrong guy, honey'. Frank and Princess Grace in London, 1970.

Frank as Danny Ocean gives Patrice Wymore the key to his room in *Ocean's 11*, 1960.

A rare shot of Frank conducting, 1962.

Frank at the Royal Festival Hall, 1978.

Sweatshirt with Ol' Blue Eyes is Back – and he was, 1973.

Handbill from 1953.

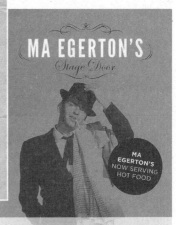

In 1953 Frank visited Ma Egerton's, which is behind the Liverpool Empire. In 2015, the visit is still used to promote their pizzas.

Frank honoured by the US postal service, 2008.

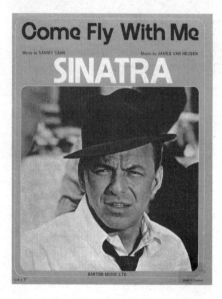

CHAPTER 10

Game changers

'There are three questions about Frank Sinatra that no one can ever answer at any given time. What is he like? Where is he now? Will he show up tonight?'

Sammy Cahn

I. The Young Pretenders

The path from Frank Sinatra to Elvis Presley to the Beatles seems logical today, but at the time it was nothing of the sort. Rock'n'roll is so much a part of our culture that it is hard to imagine how cutting edge it was and how despised it was in the 50s by people, well, in their fifties. Culturally, nothing before or since has divided the population more than the advent of Elvis Presley in 1956. The American sociologist, Vance Packard, the author of *The Hidden Persuaders*, said, 'Rock'n'roll might be summed up as monotony tinged with hysteria.'

One of the great classical conductors, Sir Malcolm Sargent, said in September 1956, 'The amazing thing about rock'n'roll is that the youngsters who go into such ecstasies sincerely believe that there is something new and wonderful about the music. There is nothing new or wonderful about it. Rock'n'roll has been played in the jungle for centuries. It is nothing more than an exhibition of primitive tom-tom thumping.'

Even Peter Potter, the chairman of the American original of *Juke Box Jury*, told *Billboard* in March 1955, 'All rhythm and blues records are dirty and are as bad for kids as dope.' Notwithstanding that remark, Peter Potter appeared the following year in the rock'n'roll film, *The Girl Can't Help It*, and introduced Eddie Cochran doing 'Twenty Flight Rock'.

When moral outrage is at hand, it is easy for reporters to persuade clergymen to state their views. Still, the Methodist minister, Lord Soper, spoke for millions when he said, 'I can't understand how intelligent people can derive any sort of satisfaction from something which is emotionally embarrassing and intellectually ridiculous. I heard one songwriter say that his song said as much as a Shakespeare sonnet. That is what I call invincible ignorance.'

In 1957 the listeners of Peking Radio were told of this phenomenon: 'Those who dance to the musical beat must not only roll with force but must also scream like pigs and cry like cats. In addition, flirting goes on while dancing. When a man dances with his partner, he can hold her in any way he likes. He can also pull or push the girl back and forth, and even turn her upside down.'

For over 50 years *The Uses of Literacy* by the Yorkshire sociologist, Richard Hoggart, has been a key text for studying social behaviour. His book offers an excellent study as to why people read what they read but when it comes to the youth of the day, he sees red and goes into a rant. He loathes the so-called Juke Box Boys and blames them for the Americanisation – rather than the Africanisation – of our culture.

This anti-Americanism can also be seen in this review of 'Ain't That a Shame' (no doubt the 'ain't' would appall Hoggart) in the *NME*: 'Now across the Atlantic to meet Fats Domino and without being sarcastic, may I say that we could have almost saved ourselves the journey, for this disc is, in my opinion, of very poor quality. Personally, I feel that no studio in this country would allow it to go into the record shops, but do not forget that this disc was made for the American public.'

The *NME* called Frankie Lymon and the Teenagers, 'Why Do Fools Fall in Love' 'an inspiration to all writers of rubbish.' Bruce Charlton in *Hit Parade* said, 'Chuck Berry's 'Johnny B Goode' may have climbed high in the States, but it leaves me cold. It's an uninspiring, monotonous rock riff.'

The irony is that the first rock'n'roll star, Bill Haley, looked as old as Frank Sinatra and was as benign as a scoutmaster. The main contempt was directed at Elvis Presley. The songwriter Billy Rose, who wrote 'Happy Days and Lonely Nights' and 'I Found a Million Dollar Baby', speaking to Congress about corruption in the record industry, said, 'Not only are most of his songs junk, but in many cases they are obscene junk, pretty much on a level with dirty comic magazines. It's this current climate that makes Elvis Presley and his animal posturings possible. It used to be people like Al Jolson, Eddie Cantor and Nora Bayes who were the big salesmen (sic) of song. Now it's a set of untalented twitchers and twisters whose appeal is largely to the zoot suiter and the juvenile department.'

As Presley often recorded standards, Rose might have been biting the hand that would feed him, but several old-time songwriters had no interest in the new music. When Presley recorded 'White Christmas' in 1957, Irving Berlin was so appalled that he had his staff call American radio stations and beg them not to play it. In 1961 Richard Rodgers was horrified at the up-tempo doo-wop treatment of his romantic ballad, 'Blue Moon', by the Marcels and even when the record was topping the US charts and thereby making him a tidy sum, he was condemning it. A notable exception was Johnny Mercer who entered into the spirit of new music and wrote Pat Boone's 'Bernadine'.

Al Hoffman, who wrote 'Hot Diggity' and 'I Apologise' with his partner Dick Manning, told the *NME*: "We always try to adapt our numbers to current trends, but we're not rock'n'roll writers. We just can't write that badly."

Bing Crosby told the same committee as Billy Rose: 'It galls me exceedingly to see so much trash on our airwaves and TV screens while the work of talented, dedicated songwriters is crowded out of the picture. A healthier balance should be maintained for the benefit of youngsters who follow these trends so religiously.'

Nat 'King' Cole responded in jokey fashion by including 'Mr Cole Won't Rock'n'Roll' in his club act. Cole's wife, Maria, made an accurate statement to Congress about the music's development from black American culture.

Even more vocal than Bing Crosby was Frank Sinatra, who condemned the new music, and Presley, at every opportunity. He said of Presley, 'His kind of music is deplorable, a rancid-smelling aphrodisiac.' He told *Life* in 1957 that rock'n'roll smelt 'phony and false'. Keen not to appear as an old fogey, Sinatra said that he did like some new trends: he loved calypso and thought Harry Belafonte was 'a wonderful performer'.

In 1958 Frank wrote a feature for the US magazine, *Western World*. No doubt it was ghosted, but it accurately conveyed his views. Sinatra said, 'My only deep sorrow is the unrelenting insistence of recording and motion picture companies upon purveying the most brutal, ugly, degenerate, vicious form of expression it has been my displeasure to hear and naturally, I'm referring to the bulk of rock'n'roll.'

And just why don't you like it, Frank? 'It fosters almost totally negative and destructive reactions in young people. It is sung, played and written for the most part by cretinous goons and by means of its almost imbecilic reiterations and sly, lewd – in plain fact – dirty lyrics, it manages to be the martial music of every sideburned delinquent on the face of the earth."

Could this be the same Frank Sinatra who staged a homecoming show for Elvis Presley in 1960 and recorded 'Ev'rybody's Twistin'' in 1962? Afraid so, but he never really changed his views. He regarded Presley as another Mr Mumbles and he made offensive jokes about him. Presley wouldn't be drawn into the argument, instead saying of Sinatra, 'I admire the man. He has a right to say what he wants to say. He is a great success and a fine actor.' He did however nominate Dean as his favourite singer and maybe this was to needle Frank, who knows? As well as disliking the music, Frank was finding it harder to sell his own records and, for the first time in his life, Frank was being seen as one of the oldies.

Jackie Gleason said, 'Elvis Presley can't last. I tell you flatly, he can't last', at the same time he was booking Presley to appear on national TV with the Dorsey Brothers. Charles Laughton, who was replacing the host, introduced Elvis Presley on *The Ed Sullivan Show* with what seemed like contempt. They were not alone. *The Times* said on 15 September 1956, 'Elvis Presley's first appearances on television were disliked by so many viewers that his subsequent career in the medium seems doubtful.' That's twisted thinking because there were millions who loved him.

A Californian police officer commented; 'If he did that in the street, we'd arrest him', but then if Charles Laughton had recited speeches from *King Lear* in the street, he would also have been arrested.

The UK bandleader Cyril Stapleton informed the *Daily Express* readers in May 1956 that 'Elvis Presley's record of 'Heartbreak Hotel' should be appearing in the best sellers soon – despite the fact that you can't understand a word he's singing about.' Whatever else, nobody today would complain about Presley's diction on 'Heartbreak Hotel' today as times have changed so much and there is no trouble in understanding him at all.

The show business writer, Dick Tatham, was to write a biography of Elvis Presley but he had this to say in *Record Mirror* in 1956: 'The incomparably incomprehensible Mr Presley realises, for example, that 'Heartbreak Hotel' called by any other name would sound just as ear-catching. He is probably aware that the lyrics are so inane, it doesn't matter whether you hear them or not.'

Back in the *Daily Express*, another bandleader, Ted Heath, didn't think that rock'n'roll would catch on in Britain. 'It's primarily music for coloured folk played by coloured bands. It includes a great deal of jumping up and down and crazy antics, which I do not feel would be acceptable here.' He thought that people who liked beat music were to be pitied.

Patrick Doncaster wrote a feature for the *Daily Mirror* in August 1956 called *Do We Want This Shockin' Rockin'?* He clearly didn't as he said that 'the rhythm is about as musical as the flushing of a sewer.' Doncaster interviewed Ed Sullivan, who unexpectedly, downplayed Presley's appeal: 'I'd been told this guy was disrupting the morals of kids, that his whole appeal was sensual, but all I saw was a pale carbon copy of Johnnie Ray.'

Here's *Melody Maker's* review of Elvis Presley's first album, *Rock'n'Roll*; with the reviewer contrasting Presley with a gospel singer: 'I have listened to these pieces with an increasing horror. They certainly didn't remind me of the excellent Rosetta Tharpe, but I had in mind one cold night on a friend's farm when one of the cows became entangled in some barbed wire and we had to wade through the mud to try and extricate the suffering animal.'

Even Ray Charles was unimpressed: 'Here was a white kid that could rock'n'roll or rhythm'n'blues or whatever you want to call it, and the girls would swoon over him. Black people have been going out shaking their behinds for centuries. What the hell's unusual about that? I think all that stuff about saying he's the King – that's a piece of bunk.'

Lord Auckland told the House of Lords of his research: 'I have seen at least two cinema managers. One has told me that British comedies attract approximately 70% of his clientèle. The other week he showed, because he was forced to show it by his circuit, one of these rock'n'roll films, with Elvis Presley or some such star; and after the cinema showing some of his regular patrons went to him and said, 'Why the blazes do you show this kind of stuff here? I have been patronising this cinema for many years and I shall think twice about coming again.' He had to reply that his circuit ordered that he should show this film. Here, I think, is a case where circuits should arrange for a local polls to be taken, so that the right kind of film is shown in the area.'

Here is *The Times* on Elvis Presley's first film, the western *Love Me Tender*: 'Elvis Presley has a small mouth which can fall easily into a pout of sulkiness. He sings with a kind of outside mandolin, with jerks that suggest a species of St Vitus's dance and breathlessness natural to the end of a cross-country race. There is some attempt to keep his style down to the 1860s but it has a way of escaping and certainly the ecstatic moans set up by the muslin-dressed maidens at the county fair whenever he waggles his knees indicate that time has somehow slipped forward a matter of 90 years or so.'

At least Sinatra did try to comprehend what was going on. His valet, George Jacobs, said, 'Mr S hated Elvis so much that he'd sit in the den all by himself at the music console and listen to every new track over and over, 'Don't Be Cruel', 'All Shook Up', 'Teddy Bear'. He was trying to figure out just what this new stuff was, both artistically (though he'd never concede it was art) and culturally (though he'd never concede it was culture). Why was the public digging this stuff? What did it have? What was the hook?'

Of course he would see parallels to the frenzy over his appearances at the Paramount in 1940s. The sociologist Camille Paglia said of Presley, but it could just as easily been about Sinatra, 'You see the reality of sex, of male lust, and of woman being aroused by male lust.'

The *Toronto Daily Star* thought, 'One rock'n'roll ballad sounded just like the other, and the basic theme and appeal were sex, which Elvis lays on with the subtlety of a bulldozer in mating season.'

The US TV host Steve Allen condemned rock'n'roll for its moral degeneracy and read out the lyrics of 'Be Bop a Lula' to get laughs and yet he had Presley on his show to boost his ratings.

The evangelist Billy Graham was horrified by Presley's contortions and said, 'I wouldn't let my daughter walk across the street to see Elvis Presley.' Yet he modified his stance as in 1964 he famously watched television on a Sunday for the first time in his life to see the Beatles on *The Ed Sullivan Show*.

Jazz trumpeter Humphrey Lyttelton told *Melody Maker* in June 1959; 'How do you go about combatting boredom, disillusionment, conformity or whatever it is you're kicking against? By championing and claiming as your own a music which for monotony, emptiness and drab uniformity is unrivalled in the history of popular music.'

In February 1959 the *Daily Mail* was not impressed. 'Good music will never return because the younger generation are not being educated up to it.'

In 1960 the British bandleader Jack Payne was in trouble for a parody of Guy Mitchell's 'Rock-A-Billy' in his column in the *Sunday Pictorial* as the publishers alleged a breach of copyright. There was this wonderful exchange in court:

Jack Payne: 'The rock rhythm has unfortunately become very popular in recent years, but I feel it is on the wane now.'

His Lordship, Mr Justice McNair: 'Is there anything worse coming?'

Jack Payne: 'I hope not. I think it is going to quieten down.'

Rock'n'roll did put many of the crooners out of business as they became yesterday's news. Frank and Dean were able to override that because they had created, largely by accident, the Rat Pack, which developed its own momentum.

As Danny and the Juniors sang, 'Rock'n'Roll Is Here to Stay' and Frank Sinatra had to live with it. Paul Anka said that he called it 'funny music' and Frank never really got it. As the years went by he would despair about the quality of rock'n'roll (and then rock) lyrics. When he complained to Mia Farrow once too often about the appalling lyrics in the songs she liked, she replied, 'Dooby dooby do.' When Frank met Ahmet Ertegun, the founder of Atlantic Records in 1983, he said, 'You ruined music with your rock'n'roll. It's your fault what's happened to the music business.' Bono, who knew Frank said, 'Frank never did like rock'n' roll, and he's not crazy about guys wearing earrings either, but he doesn't hold it against me.'

Sinatra never withdrew or apologised for his remarks, but in the end he had to follow the trends and have some rock elements in his work, but throughout it all, he still was, very definitely, himself..

Sinatra saw Presley as doing something different to himself and so he never felt threatened by his music. He was much more wary about a fellow Italian-American from New York, Bobby Darin, who was 20 years younger than himself and at times seemed like a mirror image.

Darin had started as a rock'n'roll singer with hits like 'Splish Splash' and 'Queen of the Hop' but he soon showed that he had much wider intentions. In 1959 he recorded a big band version of 'Mack the Knife' which became a transatlantic No.1 and followed it with an equally awesome 'Beyond the Sea', which was Charles Trenet's 'La Mer', and neither song had been given such a swinging arrangement before. These were the best records that Sinatra never made. Apparently, Buddy Greco had confided to Darin that he was going to swing 'Mackie' and Darin, valuing a hit more than a friend, beat him to it.

George Burns was the first of the old brigade to extend the hand of friendship. He invited him to be his opening act at Harrah's in Lake Tahoe. They worked together very well and he treated him like a son. One night Darin lost $1,600 gambling and Burns refused to shake his hand on stage the next day. Burns explained why to the audience and Darin had promptly learnt a lesson. They remained friends with Burns dropping in on a Darin session to add ho-ho's on the Gershwins' 'They All Laughed'. Darin recorded albums of standards (*That's All, Love Swings*) and even recorded an album with Johnny Mercer, *Two of a Kind*. The Frank Sinatra influence is particularly evident on *Darin at the Copa* (1960), though some of Dean is in there too.

Sinatra picked up his first Grammys in 1959 for *Come Dance with Me!* but the world was changing. The record of the year, that is, the key single was not Frank Sinatra's 'High Hopes' but Bobby Darin's 'Mack The Knife' and the Best New Artist was Bobby Darin (beating Johnny Restivo and Edd Byrnes, I kid you not).

Darin became the youngest act to headline at the Sands and he was bringing in a younger audience, but just like Frank, he overstepped his mark. In November 1959 he said that he hoped 'to surpass Sinatra in everything he's done' (thereby implying Frank was a spent force) and he added, 'If I'm great now, think what I'll be like when I'm Sinatra's age.'

The press asked Sinatra, 'What do you think of Bobby Darin?' and he replied, 'I sing in saloons. Bobby Darin does my prom dates.' Darin retorted, 'I'm only too happy to play his prom dates... until graduation.' The jazz magazine, *Down Beat*, concluded, 'Darin can sing and Darin can swing. He may even be the heir apparent to Sinatra's mantle. If Darin can become the next big thing among our teenagers, perhaps all is not lost.'

Sinatra and Darin had much in common. They were both arrogant (Billy May who could tolerate Sinatra didn't like Darin), wore tuxedos, liked beautiful women, wanted to be considered as serious actors, courted politics (Darin wanted to stand for Congress until he learnt his sister was his mother and the scandal might be revealed), admired the same songwriters and worried about hair loss. They both could explode for no reason. Before Darin left Hollywood for the Copa, Nancy Sinatra and Tommy Sands threw a good luck party. As they had failed to invite a particular friend, Darin said, 'This party isn't for me' and walked out.

Bobby Darin was a chameleon with a far wider range than Sinatra – rock'n'roll ('Bullmoose' with Neil Sedaka), country ('Eighteen Yellow Roses') and folk ('If I Were A Carpenter'). Frank said to Darin, 'I wouldn't be caught dead singing 'Splish Splash'', but by 1960, Darin felt the same way himself.

The answer to Darin's question, 'If I'm great now, what I'll be like when I'm Sinatra's age?" was sadly, 'Dead'. Darin knew he had an impaired heart through having rheumatic fever as a child and he died in 1973. In 1984 Sinatra recorded 'Mack the Knife' and, with rare modesty, commented, 'Ol' Blue Eyes can add nothing new.'

II. Day In–Day Out, 1957–1959

Frank Sinatra started 1957 with a short season at the Copa in New York, made even shorter by the death of Humphrey Bogart on 14 January. Sinatra took time out as he was distraught at the loss of his friend but he didn't attend his funeral.

Frank was to return to Australia for concert dates but he didn't want to go. When he got to Honolulu to catch a Qantas flight he found that there were seats for himself and Hank Sanicola but not one for Jimmy Van Heusen. He was so mad that he returned to Los Angeles. The tour was cancelled and the ticket money had to be refunded. Frank had to compensate the promoter, Lee Gordon, and pay the musicians for lost earnings. It was ridiculous behaviour and, not for the last time, the Australian press called him Cranky Franky.

In 1940 the Broadway musical *Pal Joey* had been adapted for the stage from stories in the *New Yorker* by John O'Hara with music from Richard Rodgers and Lorenz Hart. Hart, a heavy drinker, was ejected on the opening night for singing along with the performers. He disappeared into the night without a coat and his health never recovered. His final words were 'What have I lived for?' but his legacy continues to this day.

That incident notwithstanding, *Pal Joey* was a controversial production as the leading man, Joey Evans, played by Gene Kelly, was a self-serving nightclub entertainer who wanted everything his own way. It was set amongst among strip clubs and lowlife bars and the *New York Times* asked, "Can you draw sweet water from a foul well?" Most of the critics and a lot of the public thought no. Columbia had wanted to film it in 1944 with Kelly and Rita Hayworth (as the younger girl). However, they couldn't agree terms with MGM for Kelly's services and although they considered making it with Cary Grant or James Cagney, the project was shelved.

The Broadway production had lasted a year and it was revived with greater success in 1952 with Harold Lang in the title role. The filming of *Pal Joey* had been under consideration for years. Harry Cohn wanted to film the musical with the improbable casting of Marlon Brando and Mae West, but Mae West wanted the ending changed as she would not play someone who lost her man. Marlene Dietrich was another exotic choice but when Harry Cohn thought of Frank Sinatra and Rita Hayworth (as the older girl), everything fell into place.

Or it should have done. Frank naturally was perfect casting for a nightclub hustler and ladies man and as he wanted to play the role, this should have been a highlight of his career. He is cast alongside Rita Hayworth (whose songs were sung by Jo Ann Greer) and by Kim Novak (sung by Trudi Erwin). In addition, Sinatra's piano playing was ghosted by Bill Miller.

It was a commercial cast as Novak was a rising star, who had done well in *Picnic*. Sinatra suggested the design for the posters which pictured him between the two women. He said, 'People will think, "Gee, I'd like to be that fella. What a sandwich."'

Sinatra's agent, Abe Lastfogel, had negotiated a very favourable deal with Harry Cohn-$125,000 plus 25% of the profits – so Sinatra had every incentive to make a good film. One reason for the good terms was because Cohn had been persuaded to make *The Bridge On The River Kwai* and he had realised that there were no women in it, which might reduce its potential. Hence, he pinned his hopes on *Pal Joey*.

For all that, there is little on-screen chemistry or eroticism between Sinatra and his leading ladies. Indeed, his best scene are often when Sinatra is singing on his own ('I Didn't Know What Time It Was' 'My Funny Valentine', 'I Could Write a Book' and the glorious 'The Lady Is a Tramp') or when he is playing with his dog, although who feeds a dog bagels and coffee? Maybe it was the coffee – the dog, Snuffy, gives the most spirited performance in the film.

Being Sinatra, we are meant to sympathise with this character, and if that were so, nobody would have an opening scene like *Pal Joey* today. A squad car pulls into a train station and Sinatra gets out, flanked by two cops. He is a singer caught in a hotel room with the mayor's daughter who is possibly under age but he is not charged. Instead he is put on a train and sent to another state. We are supposed to see Pal Joey as a lovable rogue.

The film was set amongst the sleazy strip clubs of Barbary Coast, but the director, George Sidney, was keener on travelogue shots of San Francisco. 'Zip' although well performed by Rita Hayworth, loses its bite. There were too many hands on the wheel: the Broadway play had many of its scenes changed and although the score was still by Richard Rodgers and Lorenz Hart, several songs were replaced with ones from other musicals. By its very nature, a musical is irrational as the characters suddenly burst into song, and there's no logic behind anyone's behaviour in this film.

John O'Hara said that Pal Joey was no longer like his creation. In fact, Sinatra was, more or less, playing himself. Certainly Pal Joey's *bon mots* sound like Sinatra's own philosophy: 'Treat a dame like a lady and a lady like a dame.' At one point, Sinatra says, 'She's not my type' and the club manager retorts, 'They're all your type.' Sinatra enjoyed wearing his suit so much that he didn't want to put a coat over it, hence the iconic look of Sinatra with the coat over the shoulder. Once again, Frank did his misspelling routine: o-r-f spells off, m-o-n-y money and k-l-a-s-y classy.

Frank was working on his Rat Pack lingo. He said that he would land on his francis and commented that a gal had 'a fine woofer and tweeter', an early hi-fi joke. Frank did a trailer to promote the film in which he explains the terms 'gasser' and 'mouse'. The Rat Pack speech was a mixture of jazz talk, phrases from the chitlin circuit, some phrases from Sammy Davis and some that Peter had picked up from Californian surfers. When they met, the general greeting was 'How's your clyde?', a sexual reference.

Frank attended the opening of *Pal Joey* with Bogart's widow, Lauren Bacall, who must have thought that Bogie could have played the role. The film did moderately well at the box office and made its profit from TV sales. The LP went to No.2 on the US album chart and Frank won a Golden Globe as the Best Actor in a Musical.

Both sides of Frank's next single, 'Crazy Love' and 'So Long My Love', made the US charts, albeit getting no higher than No.60. 'Crazy Love' was a decent enough dance tune written by Sammy Cahn with Phil Tuminello, who had penned the music for the rock'n'roll film, *Rock Pretty Baby*, while Sammy wrote 'So Long My Love', a fast and furious swinger with some madcap lyrics, 'Give me my chapeau, I've got git-go.'

As Frank had confidence in Voyle Gilmore, he told him to pick the song for the next single. He picked 'Witchcraft', a wonderful fusion of Carolyn Leigh's lyric and Cy Coleman's music. To this was added Nelson Riddle's ingenious score with Sinatra's finger clicks being part of that arrangement. 'Witchcraft' was a US Top 20 single, but it does sound fairly tame compared to how Sinatra played with the song in later years.

Not only was this recorded on 20 May 1957 but also Joe Bushkin's 'Something Wonderful Happens in Summer', the big band sound of 'Tell Her You Love Her' and a 'what's good for the goose' song, 'You're Cheatin' Yourself (If You're Cheatin' on Me)'.

Peggy Lee recorded an album of standards for Capitol, *The Man I Love*, with arrangements by Nelson Riddle and conducted by Frank Sinatra. The title song, written by the Gershwin brothers, had been written for the Broadway show, *Lady Be Good!* in 1924 but it had been dropped after a week. It was then dropped from *Strike Up the Band* (1927) and *Rosalie* (1928) before the music publisher pushed it as a stand alone song. It became a hit for Sophie Tucker and Marion Harris and, in 1947, was the title song and the theme for an Ida Lupino film. Peggy Lee's bluesy and highly romantic performance took it to a new level. The music critic Wilfrid Mellers called it 'the most moving pop song of our time'.

The Man I Love was a beautiful collection of breathy ballads including 'My Heart Stood Still', 'Happiness Is a Thing Called Joe' and Sammy Cahn's 'Please Be Kind', which was intended for a younger singer, but the 12 songs could just as easily have been sung by Frank. Indeed, Frank had chosen them for Peggy's album. The most famous track is 'The Folks Who Live on the Hill', a wonderful hymn to domesticity with some stunning rhymes notably 'verandah' and 'command a'. Its theme contrasts with Peggy Lee's subsequent success, 'Is That All There Is'. It became one of Peggy Lee's favourite songs and an in-concert favourite. Only two castaways (the comedian Ken Dodd and the golfer Peter Alliss) have chosen this as a Desert Island Disc, which is surprisingly low in view of its sentiments.

It has been said that the album cover shows Peggy in the arms of Frank Sinatra, but the man with his back to the camera was her current husband, the actor Dewey Martin. At Frank's instigation, menthol was sprayed into her eyes to give a misty look.

In May 1957 Frank was soaring up the Billboard album charts with *A Swingin' Affair*, (Frank's title, as it happens) which reached No.2, but his mind was on his next project, *Where Are You?*, his first to be recorded in stereo and arranged and conducted by Gordon Jenkins, who had moved from Decca. It was an album of polished ballads, beautifully sung, with a pensive mood continuing throughout the LP.

The album opened with the title song, a little known work from a long forgotten film, *Top of the Town* (1936). When Sinatra sang, 'Where is my happy ending?', you might think it was a song about his relationship with Ava, talking of which, he revived his own 'I'm a Fool to Want You', drawing his performance out for nearly five minutes.

There was a stunning version of the French ballad, 'Les Feuilles Mortes (Dead Leaves)', now with an English lyric, 'Autumn Leaves', by Johnny Mercer. It had recently been a hit for the pianist Roger Williams, who duplicated the falling leaves with descending notes. Nat 'King' Cole had sung it on the soundtrack of the thriller *Autumn Leaves* (1956), starring Joan Crawford. After writing the lyric, Mercer said it was easier to write love songs in French because there are 51 rhymes for 'amour' but only five for 'love'. 'There's No You' sounded as though the writers had been commissioned to write another 'Autumn Leaves''

Leonard Bernstein's 'Lonely Town' had been dropped from the film of *On the Town*, which was a pity because the song belonged to Frank's character but it was too sombre for the mood of the film. Frank nursed a grudge over this as he loved the song and this recording featured an exquisite arrangement with horns and strings. Both Frank and Gordon Jenkins called this the best performance on the album. The album had many delights including Alec Wilder's 'Where Is The One' and a blues song associated with Bessie Smith, 'Baby, Won't You Please Come Home', which was transformed into a stunning romantic ballad.

'Laura' began with a stunning minute of strings before Frank sang and then he gave one of the greatest performances of his life. The music had been written for *Laura* (1944), a film about a detective investigating a murder. David Raksin composed the melody the day that his own wife left him and then Johnny Mercer added the lyric. Cole Porter said that this is the one song he wished he'd written.

Because of the necessity for wider grooves, the new stereo recording permitted less playing time for the LP and so one track was dropped, namely, 'I Cover the Waterfront'. The evocative title had been used in 1932 for a novel about a boatman smuggling Chinese immigrants, wrapped in shark skins, into the US. The book was filmed with Claudette Colbert and Ben Lyon. The song, which had been recorded by Billie Holiday and Louis Armstrong, sounded mysterious even without knowing the story. It's really a girl's song but Frank was waiting for his love to return in a setting that had French horns representing the sound of a foghorn.

Because of his excessive spending, Sinatra's finances went up and down but he still gave Nancy a pink Thunderbird with a detachable hard top wrapped with a huge red bow for her 17th birthday. Tina, however, had not inherited her father's spending genes. She was saving money from a young age and Frank would call her 'Miss Moneybags' and ask for a loan.

In July 1957 Frank also recorded seasonal songs with Gordon Jenkins for an album, *A Jolly Christmas*. Sinatra never fully cracked the Christmas market; there was not a perennial Sinatra standard like Bing's 'White Christmas' or Nat's 'The Christmas Song'. He recorded carols with a choir, a string-laden 'The First Noel', 'I'll Be Home For Christmas' (with a choir humming 'Silent Night' at the start), the 'Rag Mop' arrangement of J-I-N-G-L-E B-E-double L-S and his own 'Mistletoe and Holly' ('Oh by gosh by golly / It's time for mistletoe and holly' – can't you just see Frank sitting down to write that?). In 1995 the producer Phil Ramone merged his version of 'The Christmas Song' with Nat 'King' Cole's for a surprisingly convincing duet.

When Charlie Morrison, the owner of the Mocambo club in Los Angeles, died, his widow Mary had many debts. It seemed likely that the club would close and she would be bankrupt. In order to help out, Frank Sinatra came to the club with Nelson Riddle for a two week residency, all bills paid. It was typical of Frank's generosity to his friends.

Frank wanted to help the nightclub comic, Joe E Lewis, by filming his life story. In the 1910s Joe E Lewis was a nightclub entertainer who had made his name as the partner of Johnny Black, who had written 'Paper Doll' (1915) and 'Dardanella' (1919). When Black died in 1936, five different people claimed the right to his estate, the sure sign that someone had led a full if rather complicated life. Joe and Johnny didn't last very long as a duo and Joe went solo. One of his key numbers was 'Chicago'.

In 1927 Joe was performing regularly in Chicago, but he switched clubs, thereby incurring the wrath of Jack 'Machine Gun' McGurn. His nickname should have indicated that trouble was afoot. Joe was beaten up and his throat was severely damaged.

Only three months after he was attacked, Sophie Tucker introduced him at a benefit show which featured Al Jolson and Tom Mix. Joe was given $14,000 of which he used $3,000 to settle his medical bills. The rest he used to promote a boxing match with Jack Dempsey. He returned to the circuit as a night club comic and W C Fields told him, 'If at first you don't succeed, try again. Then quit. No sense in being a damn fool about it.' Joe became a truly successful comedian and developed a drunk act, which Dean copied.

The film, *The Joker is Wild*, was made through Frank's company, Bristol Productions, and directed by Charles Vidor. The film co-starred Mitzi Gaynor (excellent as Joe's wife), Eddie Albert, Jackie Coogan and Hank Henry with the veteran entertainer Sophie Tucker playing herself. Sinatra made no attempt to sound like Lewis and when he sang 'I Cried for You' at the start of the film, he was simply being Sinatra. Joe E Lewis said, 'Frankie enjoyed playing my life more than I enjoyed living it.'

There was one new song written for the film and it was a beauty: Sammy Cahn and Jimmy Van Heusen's 'All the Way' – which, with a touch of overkill, is heard seven times. On the other hand, 'Chicago' is only heard instrumentally. There was a plan to release a soundtrack album which would feature the jazzy score through another of Sinatra's companies, Essex, but Capitol wouldn't play ball.

Sammy Cahn had told Jimmy Van Heusen, 'They'll never call the film *The Joker is Wild* as it sounds too much like a poker game. Let's think of a song that they can use for the title instead.' As a result, Cahn and Van Heusen came up with 'All the Way', which was to establish a big, dramatic point. As Cahn said, 'When Joe E Lewis was young, he was a singer and we gave him some big notes. (Sings) "When somebody loves you, / It's no good unless she loves you…" Big notes. "All the way". Later in the film the boy's in Chicago and the hoodlums cut his throat and leave him to die. He recovers and he tries to sing again but this time he can't get the big notes. He realises that he is never going to hit those notes again and he becomes a singing comedian. That's the power of that song; it was written for dramatic effect. They still called the film, *The Joker Is Wild*, though.'

It is for sure that 13 August 1957 was one of the greatest days ever in a recording studio. Frank put down two of the songs from *Pal Joey*, 'I Could Write a Book' and 'Bewitched', which was given to Rita Hayworth in the film, and then two songs from *The Joker is Wild*, 'All the Way' with its wonderful final note and 'Chicago' with its Dixieland arrangement. 'Chicago' was written by Fred Fisher in 1922 but Frank didn't update the lyric – 'The town that Billy Sunday couldn't shut down' meant nothing at the time. And also, just what is a 'toddling town'? Still, it's a brilliant performance and you can tell that Sinatra was smiling throughout the song. He rounded off the day with that Rodgers and Hart song about a romantic honeymoon, 'There's a Small Hotel', amending the lyric to 'When the steeple bell, says ring-a-ding, sleep well.'

A single which combined 'All the Way' with 'Chicago' only went to No.15 in the US but remained on the listings for 30 weeks. In the UK 'All the Way' reached No.3 and was on the charts for 20 weeks.

Although Mob films are big business today, this was considered a drawback in the 1950s and the brutality went against it at the box office. The song won an Oscar for Best Song beating 'An Affair to Remember' (Vic Damone), 'April Love' (Pat Boone) 'Tammy' (Debbie Reynolds) and 'Wild is the Wind' (Johnny Mathis).

Over at the Sands, Frank Sinatra and Joe E Lewis did a sketch in which they mocked Shakespeare. Frank read it straight and Joe did his take on it. They remained good friends, and when having a meal, Joe ordered something from the sweet trolley. Frank said, 'Joe, you're not supposed to eat that, you're diabetic' 'Don't worry about me,' replied Joe, 'I'm very calorie conscious. I won't even shake hands with Sugar Ray Robinson.'

Relations between Frank and Ava had completely cooled and she established six weeks residency in Nevada so that she could divorce him. She told the press that it was 'on the usual grounds, mental cruelty' Usual? Usual for her? Although she had several more relationships and fascinated Ernest Hemingway and Robert Graves, Ava never married again; once you've had the best…

Frank still had a statue of Ava in his garden. Didn't he think that his future partners might be intimidated by this? To be fair, this was a statue made by Assen Peikove for Ava's film, *The Barefoot Contessa*, and I suppose it had to go somewhere.

Frank always had a roving eye and there are numerous incidents, often with a comic touch. When Kay Kendall admired Frank Sinatra's shirt at a party, her partner Rex Harrison slapped him, assuming that they had been up to hanky-panky. The playwright Terence Rattigan pulled them apart. An actress Gloria Rhodes wanted Frank's approval for a memoir of her Hollywood life. It was her Joe E Lewis moment. The book never came out and she never made another film.

When Frank was at the Sands with Dean, he shouted to one of the showgirls, 'Hey blondie, come over here and join us.' She kept on walking on as they were being obnoxious. She was Barbara Blakeley, who in 1959 married Zeppo (Herbert) Marx, the straight man in the comedy partnership. Many years later, she became Barbara Sinatra. Zeppo and Barbara lived in Rancho Mirage in Palm Springs and had Frank as a neighbour. Zeppo owned a talent agency and the Marx Brothers were his most difficult clients.

While at the Sands, Frank practiced throwing custard pies with the comedian Joey Bishop. He wanted to perfect his slapstick as his daughter Tina loved *The Soupy Sales Show* and he had agreed to appear on it. When the teenage show, *American Bandstand*, started in August 1957, Frank Sinatra sent a congratulatory telegram to the programme. If this seems out of character, remember that he was negotiating for his own series with ABC.

After four years at Capitol, Frank Sinatra got to work with Billy May and during the summer, they discussed the songs and the arrangements for their first album together, *Come Fly with Me*. For all that, every session with Billy May was wacky and hairy as so little was ready beforehand, but once he got going, Billy May was the fastest orchestrator in Hollywood. The theme of the album was perfect. Air travel was becoming less expensive and opening up the world. Many Americans had never left their continent – and Frank himself hadn't travelled far. Here was an album telling of the delights that lay ahead.

Overall, *Come Fly with Me* was an album of standards but the title song was newly written by Sammy Cahn and Jimmy Van Heusen. The plane was preparing for takeoff during the introduction and as it soared into the air, Frank sang the title line. The song was inviting you to make the best of your opportunities, although it was also another wedding song ('perfect for a flying honeymoon, they say'). It was also ideal for the mile high club. At the end of a perfect take, Sammy said to Frank, 'When you do it in Vegas, sing "exotic booze" instead of "exotic views".' Frank said, 'Let's do it again.' Cahn was wary of the 'exotic booze' being used as he thought the record might be banned. In cabaret, Sinatra added his own annotations; 'Just say the word and we'll take our birds down to Acapulco Bay' being one of them. It was a wonderful start to the album and Frank won a Grammy for the best solo vocal performance of 1957. The song has become a standard in its own right – indeed, it is now the best known song in the collection and has the dubious distinction of being a karaoke favourite.

Frank had other songs based around flying such as 'Let's Get Away from it All', a shorter version than the one he had recorded with Tommy Dorsey and another song from Cahn and Van Heusen, 'It's Nice to Go Trav'ling', a list song which needed a stronger melody. In the lyric, Frank is singing about going home, but home to him is New York, where most people would go travelling. His final comment is 'Make a pizza', so how American can you get?

Many of the top MOR singers had recorded 'Around the World' the theme song from *Around the World in 80 Days*, except Frank who was in the film. Now Frank took it as a straight romantic waltz but the singer in the song hasn't been searching very far: County

Down, Paris, London and New York. Billy May later commented, 'That's a beautiful tune and Frank sang the shit out of it.'

All the other songs on the album referred to specific places. There is the beautiful and melancholy 'Autumn in New York' and a reprise for a favourite song, 'London by Night' ('Most people say they love London by day, But I love London by night.'). Glowing cigarettes were seen as a romantic image – how times change. There are delicate versions of 'April in Paris' and 'Moonlight in Vermont', which is written in blank verse. His 'Blue Hawaii' is less Hawaiian sounding than Bing Crosby's hit recording. Elvis Presley was shortly to record the song with much echo, but of the famed standard singers, only Andy Williams used echo to any extent.

Some of the big band effects on the glorious 'Brazil' had been written specifically to demonstrate the new stereo sound, so this track was perfect for showrooms around the world. The exciting samba had been written in 1939 although it wasn't given an English lyric until the Walt Disney cartoon, *Saludos Amigos* three years later. The track ends with Frank's summary on the country, 'Brazil, man, it's old.'

Frank was happy to record songs with Billy May that didn't have too much value if they could have fun with them, a good example being 'Isle of Capri'. It is performed with great panache with the saxophones copying the sound that May had created for Glenn Miller. Frank has fun with the lyrics – 'She wore a lovely meatball on her finger' – and there's a plug for the Hollywood restaurant, Villa Capri.

Rudyard Kipling had written 'On the Road to Mandalay' for his *Barrack Room Ballads* in 1892 and a melody by Oley Speakes was added 15 years later. In 1957 Billy May was working on the comedy programme, *The Stan Freberg Show* and this arrangement seemed an extension of that. Frank loved the gong and he told the percussionist, 'Let's hear the gong, let the mother ring.' Billy May had intended to keep the arrangement going after the gong but Sinatra threw his coat over his shoulder and was already walking out of the studio. It gave Side One of the album an abrupt end: that is if you bought the album in America. The Kipling Estate objected to the recording and, with the copyright laws being different in the UK, they were able to get the track banned. EMI replaced the errant song with 'Chicago' which fitted beautifully. Frank said, 'This is an unusual version of 'On the Road to Mandalay'. It's comedic, it swings, it jumps.' And it swung and jumped even more in concert with Frank often adding, 'Come you back, you mother soldier.'

In October 1957 Frank was a guest on *The Edsel Show*, a classic TV broadcast hosted by Bing Crosby. On the show, he sang 'September Song' with Bing Crosby and 'The Birth of the Blues' with Louis Armstrong. 'B-l-u-z, blues,' said Frank and he copied Armstrong's voice at its conclusion. When Rosemary Clooney sang to Frank, he made faces at her, and Bob Hope interrupted when he sang 'The Road to Morocco' with Bing. It was superstars being daft but it's fun.

At the same time, Frank had started his second TV series for ABC, *The Frank Sinatra Show*, a curious combination of 21 one-hour programmes, sponsored by Bulova, and 10 thirty-minute dramas, sponsored by Timex. He was reluctant to rehearse: indeed, why learn your lines when there is a teleprompter to hand? This nonchalance was to be the show's downfall and he should have heeded Bob Hope's telling gag on the first programme, 'Frank, you just can't plunge into television without some preparation.' *Variety* called the series 'a flop, ratings and otherwise' and *TV Guide* said it was 'one of the biggest and most expensive disappointments of the current season.'

It wasn't all bad as there were many fine performances recorded by Frank with Nelson Riddle's orchestra at the El Capitan Theatre in Hollywood. He sang with Peggy Lee on

'Nice Work If You Can Get It' and 'Love Is Here to Stay' and joined the McGuire Sisters for 'Something's Gotta Give'. His daughter Nancy, now 14, appeared with her friends Jane and Belinda as part of the Tri-Tones vocal group to join him for 'Side by Side'. He and Dean were equally casual (you might say indifferent) on a medley of their hits and it looked as though the script simply told them to leer at girls. This laidback approach worked for Dean but it was wrong for Sinatra. His closing line was always 'Goodnight and sleep warm', the latter part of the phrase later providing a title for a Dean Martin album.

The first drama, screened on 25 October, was *The Hogan Man* with Frank as a cab driver adopting two war orphans. A fortnight later came *The Brownstone Incident* with Frank and Cloris Leachman wondering whether to move from the big city. In *Take Me to Hollywood*, Frank played a talent scout who discovered an actress (Christine White) and fell in love with her.

The tradition was building for stars to make Christmas shows with their families but that was hardly practicable for Frank, now a single man again, so he had Bing join him instead. This should have been easy-peasy, but Bing preferred to record his songs first and then mime them and he also preferred to work mornings. Neither would give way and so their duets were solo performances segued together, thereby creating additional work for Nelson Riddle.

Frank's agent had managed to secure a massive fee for his television shows, even $3m was reported. Whatever it was, it was large. Sometime later, Frank was stung with a huge bill from the IRS and he told Joe Kennedy about it. Old man Kennedy showed how to circumvent tax and he paid $65,000 instead of $1m.

Frank ended the year with a few one-off tracks with Nelson Riddle, including a new version of Ken Lane's song, 'Everybody Loves Somebody', but it was Dean who would hit paydirt with this one, admittedly on Frank's record label, Reprise, in 1964. Frank also recorded a brilliant version of the Sammy Cahn and Jule Styne song, 'Time After Time'. Jule Styne tried to regain Sinatra's favour by taking space in *Variety* to say, 'Only your voice and complete musicianship has made it possible to defeat rock'n'roll.' Well, I don't think rock'n'roll had been defeated. Still, his *Where Are You?* album was high on the LP charts and had climbed to No.3.

Although Frank had been making popular albums, he was not as successful as Nat 'King' Cole. In 1957 Gordon Jenkins had arranged and conducted *Love Is the Thing* for Cole and the album topped the US charts and remained on the listings for over a year. *Come Fly with Me* was released in January 1958 and at last Sinatra had a major, major album. It topped the charts for five weeks (his first No.1 album since 1946), and stayed on the listings for 71 weeks.

Kim Novak who was one of Sinatra's part-time girl friends made a film *Jeanne Eagels* in 1957. Jeff Chandler got $200,000 but Novak who received much less made the bigger impression. Sinatra told her to go to his agent, William Morris, and sort out new terms. Harry Cohn, who called Novak 'the fat Polack', was furious with Sinatra as this was none of his business.

Sammy Davis was experiencing a major setback that had nothing to do with his artistic abilities. Harry Cohn was furious when Sammy had started dating Kim Novak. 'Harry Belafonte, I could understand,' he argued, 'but Sammy Davis, no!' Cohn told Sammy to back off or he would lose his other eye. Rather than ride the bad publicity, they knew they had to part and Sammy Davis, in a move which indicated how threatening this was, married a black chorus girl, Loray White, whom he scarcely knew. The marriage only lasted a few months.

Harry Cohn was so devastated by this news that he suffered severe chest pains, possibly made worse by swallowing more pills for his heart condition that he should have done. He died in 1958 and there was a huge attendance for his funeral, prompting Red Skelton's infamous remark, 'Give the people what they want and they'll turn out of it.'

Very soon Davis would be chasing another white girl, the Swedish actress, May Britt, who had been discovered by Carlo Ponti in 1952. She came to the US for *War and Peace* in 1956, which was co-produced by Ponti and then made *The Young Lions* with Dino for Twentieth-Century Fox in 1958.

The Young Lions, which was based on a dramatic novel by Irwin Shaw, was Dean Martin's *From Here to Eternity*; it was a bigger challenge although Dino took everything in his stride. Frank had played serious roles before *From Here to Eternity* but Dean hadn't although the director Edward Dmytryk, one of the Hollywood Ten and known for *Farewell My Lovely* (1944), had faith in him. He said, 'I knew Dean could rise to the occasion as he had that ethnic working-class background which gave him a real toughness. He was also a real pro. I mean, after working with Jerry Lewis, why would be he afraid to stand up to Marlon Brando and Montgomery Clift?' Sammy Cahn added to his confidence, 'Dean, don't you know they'd give up everything to be able to do what you do.'

Dean would have been as aggravated as Sinatra if Brando was going for take after take, but fortunately Brando was feeling lazy. He didn't bother to learn the script and he pinned his lines on the backs of other actors. But being Brando, he still managed to impress in his role as a German officer. Frank Sinatra had been offered the role first but when he saw Brando was involved, he declined and in any event, he had proved his worth in *From Here to Eternity*. The role had then been offered to Tony Randall but he had been so bad in his first film, *Oh, Men! Oh, Women!*, that Dmytryk changed his mind. Dean took the role for $20,000. In the film, Dean's character had to kill Brando and he remarked, 'All I ever killed in my other movies was time.'

In 1956 Montgomery Clift had had a car crash which scarred his face and damaged him psychologically. He continued acting because that's what he did, but he had lost his confidence and was pilled up. However, he warmed to Dean whose records he loved as much as Frank and Ella's. He helped Dean with his lines and Dean called him Spider because of his twitches and generally took care of him when he was out of it.

The role wasn't much of a stretch for Dean Martin as he played a Broadway star who was a playboy and who becomes a hero after being conscripted by going after the sniper who has shot Clift. 'Hell,' he said, 'I just played myself, a likeable coward.' The main thing that bugged Dean was the location – he didn't like shooting in Paris. Unusually for him, he spent a few hours in the Louvre, saying in typical Dino fashion, 'I had a guy once who did my house in two days. He was a better painter than those guys.'

While the crew was at the Hôtel Prince de Galles in Paris, Dean Martin stood up to greet a visitor and somehow the tablecloth went with him and a teapot landed in Marlon Brando's lap. Everyone was laughing hysterically as Brando dropped his trousers and doused himself with a soda siphon. These days the headline would be "Brando scalds balls at the Prince de Galles'.

1958 was a magnificent year musically for Dean Martin as he scored two of his biggest hits with 'Return to Me', sung in both English and Italian, and 'Volare', an English version of Domenico Modugno's entry for the Eurovision Song Contest. Either song would have been ideal for Frank, although Dean, despite his change of name, was more open about his Italian roots. During the late 1950s, many great popular songs were coming from Italy and Frank, by and large, ignored them.

The Young Lions was a box office hit and could have established Dean as a serious actor, but he had a lackadaisical approach to films and, indeed, to everything. He knew he wasn't a musical genius like Sinatra – nobody would call him 'The Voice' – but he couldn't care less.

Dean's views of rock'n'roll were as cutting as Frank's and when they appeared on the TV variety show, *Club Oasis*, they performed a parody of 'Jailhouse Rock'. This was one of Sinatra's more spirited TV performances as *The Frank Sinatra Show* lurched to its inevitable cancellation. The producers must have known that Sinatra was ambling through his performances and yet what do they do? Hire Robert Mitchum as a guest star. One sketch had Frank performing at a high school prom while the students wanted a rock'n'roll star.

The tension mounted when Shirley Jones was a guest star in February. She was a fine singer who had starred in the film versions of *Carousel* and *Oklahoma!* and she was slated to sing 'If I Loved You' with Frank. Nelson Riddle asked her what key she wanted. She said she didn't know, she just did it, and Nelson was furious: 'How could you come on a show and not know what key you sing in?' Shirley Jones was distraught and Frank put his arm round her and said, 'Don't worry, Nelson, we'll work it out.'

The Frank Sinatra Show had the potential to be a groundbreaking series but it was hampered by feeble scripts and a star with no intention of putting himself out. All the sadder then that his guests were fine performers who were well suited to working with Frank. His duet partners included Dinah Shore, Eydie Gormé and, with a tribute to Tommy Dorsey, Jo Stafford (who was on the verge of retiring as she had no taste for stardom). Frank sang 'You're the Top' with Ethel Merman and 'Moonlight in Vermont' and 'I May Be Wrong' with Ella Fitzgerald. Frank had a fondness for 'Them There Eyes', which he sang separately with both Natalie Wood and the British actress Jeannie Carson. On 14 February, he intended to sing 'My Funny Valentine' to his daughter Tina but she had stage fright, and Nancy stepped in. He and Sammy performed 'Me and My Shadow', something they would repeat with greater success later, and he always loved working with Louis Prima and Keely Smith. The only bow to the contemporary scene was Eddie Fisher and he also invited the musical satirists, Spike Jones and Stan Freberg. The dramas included *Time to Cry* with Anne Bancroft and Lloyd Bridges, *The Man on the Stairs* with Michael Rennie and *Face of Fear* with Glynis Johns.

Viewers turning on for a new Sinatra show were soon disappointed as new shows were dropped for repeats and in July 1958, *The Frank Sinatra Show* was replaced by the world's worst game show, *E S P*, hosted by Vincent Price. All the contestants claimed to have E S P, but whole thing was exposed as a scam and the programme was cancelled after three episodes. Sadly, Vincent Price, like the contestants, had no E S P, but his instincts should have told him that this was as ridiculous as *The Fly*.

The film producer Frank Ross who had made *The House I Live In* asked Frank to appear in an adaptation of a novel by Joe David Brown about racial intolerance, *Kings Go Forth*. Dorothy Dandridge was going to play Monique, a girl from a mixed marriage, but the role went to Natalie Wood, who was admittedly from a mixed marriage (Russian and French!) but was totally wrong for this role. Indeed, Frank referred to her as the 'black Russian'.

Kings Go Forth was set in St Tropez towards the end of the war when the American forces were fighting the Germans only a few hours from the Riviera. They could make occasional forays into enemy lines and enjoy themselves the rest of the time. Frank had the same idea, thinking that if he had to be on location, this was as good as anywhere.

The black and white filming was effective but the director Delmer Daves treated it like a play with too much talk and no excitement. After all, the rivals (Frank Sinatra, 42, and Tony Curtis, 32) for the girl's hand (Natalie Wood, 19) have to depend on each other for their lives. We don't however know how old Frank Sinatra was supposed to be. The film ended with Curtis dying and Sinatra losing his arm and being reunited with Wood.

The film suffered from too many close-ups, that is, when the stars were there. Tony Curtis arrived late because his previous film had overrun. Frank returned to the States when Manie Sacks was dying and saw him in hospital. Natalie Wood took time off to marry Robert Wagner. As a result, several scenes were shot with doubles and sometimes, the real actor was substituted later.

Kings Go Forth had poor reviews and fared badly on general release. The music was by Elmer Bernstein but the title song, with lyrics from Sammy Cahn, was inconsequential and didn't help promotion. Sample line: 'Was Paris always there? I didn't know or care.' Pronouncing her name 'Mo-neek-er' lost potential sales to all the Moniques out there. Sinatra did include the song in his cabaret act for a short while but then dropped it for good.

Frank Sinatra and Tony Curtis did become good friends, although Curtis's claims that he was a member of the Rat Pack were fanciful. Shortly after making this film, Frank invited Nat 'King' Cole and Tony Curtis round to see his electric train set with several engines and a large landscape. Lauren Bacall was at the house, making them all a meal. The three men became engrossed in the trains and Bacall told them they had to eat. When she handed Frank his plate, he turned it upside down.

In March 1958, Frank did propose to Lauren Bacall who said that she would think it over. When she told the press that it might happen, Frank immediately declared that the wedding was off. Indeed, he didn't so much as speak to her for six years. Bacall later said, 'It would never have worked because he'd be cheating on me in five minutes. That's what he always did.' In 1961 Lauren Bacall married the actor Jason Robards Jr, a marriage that lasted eight years.

Considering that Dean Martin, Nat 'King' Cole, Peggy Lee and Jo Stafford were all signed to Capitol, it is surprising that Frank didn't record duets during his seven years with the label. Apart from some soundtrack items, his only duets for Capitol were two songs with Keely Smith, recorded in March 1958. 'How Are Ya Fixed for Love' and 'Nothing in Common' were cheerful compositions from Sammy Cahn and Jimmy Van Heusen with arrangements by Billy May. At the same session, he cut another Cahn and Van Heusen song, 'Same Old Song and Dance' about a fella 'winding up No.1 on the all-time losers chart'. He finished the session with 'Here Goes', words and music by Cahn and a catchy vaudeville romp. Capitol misfiled 'Here Goes' which meant it was lost for years.

Sinatra loved the on-stage banter between the irrepressible Louis Prima and his wife, Keely Smith. He played an older man desperate for her attention. She sang ballads beautifully and he would try to break her down. They were in their element in Las Vegas lounges but even though they were offered a TV series, they realised that they were too jokey and vulgar for a mass audience, although it would seem tame today. It contained an element of truth as Prima was always on the lookout for potential conquests. Once he caught his wife (he had several) having sex with a casino dealer in a dressing room. He sneaked up on them, tickled the guy's scrotum and then punched him out. Sinatra and Smith did have an on-off affair for some years.

Frank and Nelson decided to work on another album of lost love songs, which must have been difficult for Nelson as he had to write the arrangements in tragic circumstances. His six-month-old child had died from bronchial asthma and his mother, who had been critically ill, died. Although Nelson wrote all the arrangements, some of the tracks were conducted by Felix Slatkin, and Dave Cavanaugh had come in as Sinatra's producer as Voyle Gilmore was retiring. The session employed a huge string orchestra, and the guitarist Al Viola commented, 'We had so many musicians that when I got to the first date, I thought it was a union meeting.' Sinatra said on a few occasions that *Only the Lonely* was the favourite of his albums. It topped the US album charts for five weeks and spent over two years on the listings.

Just as they would write title songs for films, Sammy Cahn and Jimmy Van Heusen enjoyed creating the title songs for Sinatra's albums, and they were spectacularly good at it. 'Only the Lonely' was a beautiful mood piece with an excellent lyric and a deliberately minimalist melody. The title was taken up by Roy Orbison in 1960, although his song was initially marketed as 'Only the Lonely (Know How I Feel)'. When Sinatra first recorded the song on 5 May 1958, he realised that he was in poor voice. He went home to Palm Springs and returned to the Capitol studios at the end of the month.

For the first time, Sinatra recorded Matt Dennis's song, 'Angel Eyes', which was written in 1953. It is an ingenious song in which the lyrics break out of metre to show that the singer is cracking up. Ella Fitzgerald, who sang it with the Count Basie band in 1956, has called it her all-time favourite song.

Another despondent song, 'Willow Weep for Me', was a rarity for pre-war popular music: a song completely written by a female composer. Ann Ronell had been encouraged to write by George Gershwin and as she loved the beauty of willow trees, she wrote 'Willow Weep for Me'. She took it to Irving Berlin's publishing company where it was recommended to Berlin himself. He loved the song but didn't like the dedication to George Gershwin. It was a hit in 1932 for Paul Whiteman and then in 1964 for Chad and Jeremy. Ann Ronell was a versatile writer as she also composed 'Who's Afraid of the Big Bad Wolf'.

Inspired by the book title, 'Gone with the Wind' had been a US chart-topper for bandleader Horance Heidt in 1937 and there had been moody revivals from Johnny Hodges and Mel Tormé. It suited the album but it was not Frank's strongest song.

Nelson Riddle had arranged Gordon Jenkins' song, 'Goodbye', which was Benny Goodman's closing theme. Taking a line from a Scottish folk song ('You take the high road and I'll take the low') deflected the drama but it was a fine record.

Sinatra's only recording of Harold Arlen and Johnny Mercer's 'Blues in the Night' was for *Only the Lonely*. It was written for the 1941 film of the same name. Arlen had the melody first and when he looked through Mercer's notes, he noticed that the lyricist had deleted 'My mama done tol' me when I was in knee pants'. Arlen declared, 'That's it, that's what we want' and a standard was completed. At the start, the arrangement echoed Stravinsky and as well as Sinatra whistling, the track featured Harry Edison's muted trumpet. There were echoes of Debussy in the arrangement of 'Ebb Tide', the only song on the album where Frank got the girl.

A similar comment had inspired 'What's New' as Bing's brother, Larry Crosby, had said to the lyricist, Bob Haggart, 'Your lyrics are very poetic. Couldn't you write something more conversational like 'What's new?' or 'How's things?'' Billie Holiday recorded the song in 1955 and Sinatra's version featured Ray Sims on trombone. Sims was strongly featured on another sad ballad, 'It's a Lonesome Old Town', which had been written in 1930.

Despite Sinatra's embargo on new Jule Styne songs, he did revive one he had written with Sammy Cahn, the brilliant 'Guess I'll Hang My Tears Out to Dry' in which the singer was making jokes to disguise his pain. There were two songs that Sinatra had recorded before, Rodgers and Hart's 'Spring Is Here' and Arlen and Mercer's 'One for My Baby'. It turned out that Sinatra recorded two distinct versions of 'One for My Baby' in June 1958. At the end of one session, he had a runthrough with just Bill Miller on piano and it happened to be recorded. It was stunning. You can imagine Sinatra in the studio with all the lights off apart from a soft spot on himself. The next day he recorded it with an orchestra, a magical performance which showed his skill as both a singer and actor. He sounded like someone at the end of his tether and it closed the album.

There was one song that had been tried but discarded – Billy Strayhorn's 'Lush Life'. Duke Ellington and his Orchestra were the first to play it and then Nat 'King' Cole recorded it in 1949, but only for a B-side. It was recorded by Harry James (four times), Carmen McRae (1956), Sarah Vaughan (1956) and Ella Fitzgerald (1957). John Coltrane gave it a 14 minute workout in 1958, but his famed version is a shorter one with the singer Johnny Hartman in 1963. This is a very difficult song to sing as it decried romance whilst hiding a broken heart. Nelson Riddle had the idea of an out-of-tune piano playing ragtime but the arrangement fell apart in the studio. Sinatra said, 'Hold it. It's not only tough enough the way it is, but he's got some flies in there', implying that some additional notes were being played, Riddle could have fixed it but Felix Slatkin was conducting. Frank said, 'I'll leave it to Nat Cole.' It's a shame because Sinatra could have recorded a great version of this song. There is a very poignant version from Sammy Davis in which he rose to the challenge.

One song that had never made it to the studio was 'Warm And Tender', an early composition by Burt Bacharach and Hal David. Bacharach was Marlene Dietrich's MD. She thought that the song was ideal for Frank but nobody told Sinatra what to do especially an assertive German broad. The song was recorded by Johnny Mathis and sung in the film, *Lizzie*.

When *Only the Lonely* topped the album charts in 1958, Frank must have been doubly pleased as he displaced *Sing Along with Mitch* by Mitch Miller and the Gang. It was an astonishing achievement for such a bleak and desperate album, especially when it contrasted with Mitch Miller's good-natured bonhomie. Sinatra said, 'This is the greatest blues album ever made. This album should be available in drugstores by prescription only' – and he probably wasn't joking. Linda Ronstadt loved the album so much that it heralded a change in her career.

1958 was the first year of the Grammys, the list of contenders suggesting that rock'n'roll was of a lower order. Perry Como and Ella Fitzgerald won the best vocal performances and *Only the Lonely*, the best album cover: it depicted Sinatra as a sad clown. Maybe it was a split vote as there were two Sinatra nominations ('Come Fly with Me', 'Witchcraft') that enabled Perry Como to win with the pleasant but inferior 'Catch a Falling Star'. Whatever, his date Sandra Gill no doubt had to endure the grumpy Sinatra. Frank commented, 'I should be grateful that Elvis didn't win anything.'

Princess Grace suggested a charity gala for the première of *Kings Go Forth* at the Monaco Sporting Club in Monte Carlo. It was arranged for 7 July 1958 and Frank would perform with an orchestra. He didn't want to bring musicians from America and he thought the best solution would be to hire 25-year-old Quincy Jones who was working for Eddie Barclay's record company in Paris. It was a daunting task as he had not worked with over 50 musicians before, but Frank simply said, 'You've heard the records, you know what to do.' His only comments at the rehearsal were of the order of 'a little faster' and 'That's in the pocket.' The première itself was a great success. Frank declared the show 'koo-koo', shook Quincy's hand, said 'Nice job, Q', and left. Quincy Jones was to work with him again in 1962 and then in later years.

One of the most successful films of 1958 was *Gigi*, a feelgood MGM musical based on Colette's story of a young Parisian girl (Leslie Caron) and her love for Gaston (Louis Jourdan) with scene stealing performances from Maurice Chevalier and Hermione Gingold. Ah yes, I remember it well.

Frank was intending to star for Twentieth-Century Fox in *Can-Can*, which in marketing terms was *Son of Gigi*. As if to illustrate what a small world it was, Frank was first to appear in *Some Came Running*, directed by Vincent Minnelli at MGM, the combination that had made *Gigi*. The film was based on a novel written by James Jones as his follow-up to *From Here to Eternity*. At the American première for *Kings Go Forth*, Dean, who had skimmed through the book, had suggested himself to Frank for the alcoholic gambler, and Frank persuaded Minnelli to take him. Although excessive drinking took place on and off screen, they proved to be very good together. Frank recommended Shirley MacLaine, whom he had seen on TV and been impressed.

Dean was doing great musically and at the Sands but he desperately needed a hit film. Freed from Jerry Lewis, he had turned down the male lead in film of *The Pajama Game* with Doris Day. Instead he took *Ten Thousand Bedrooms* which had flopped but it was hardly his fault. He had been matched with Anna Maria Aberghetti who had a clean cut image and was wrong for Dean. He received great reviews for *The Young Lions* but it wasn't a commercial hit.

Shirley MacLaine had very good chemistry with Sinatra and Martin – they certainly would have admired her legs – but she is very much an acquired taste, generally playing characters that are shrill and irritating. With her jangling bracelets and bunny purse, she is especially annoying in *Some Came Running*, the worst moment coming when she joins the Hi-Los for a drunken 'After You've Gone'. Still, Frank did his best for Shirley, having the ending changed to make her part more dramatic. He told the director, 'Let the kid get in the way of the bullet. That'll make the audience feel sorry for her. She might get a nomination out of it.' It resulted in her first Oscar nomination as well as one for Martha Hyer. However, his seduction scene with Shirley was shot incredibly quickly as Frank wanted to see Minnelli's former wife, Judy Garland in Las Vegas.

The film was largely shot in location in Madison, Indiana and very often fans would be disturbing the shoot. When a female fan rushed at Frank on the set and hugged him, he said, 'I feel dirty. I must have a shower.'

To make it worse, the production was delayed because Vincent Minnelli was so fastidious. Sinatra was mad when Minnelli wanted to move a ferris wheel and he said, 'No more multiple takes.' When the schedule was overrunning, Frank did his usual trick of tearing pages out of the script. Dean was more passive, commenting, 'As Bama, I sit around most of the time playing cards with Frank. When the director yells "Cut!", what do I do? I sit around playing cards with Frank.' When gambling with Dean, Frank comments, 'Ain't that a kick in the head?', more Rat Pack jive. In what would be seen as politically incorrect now, Dean has to refer to the various girls in the movie as tramps, broads and pigs. Incidentally, when Frank falls out with a schoolteacher in the film, does he really say, 'You will never get a chance to fuck me again.' Of course he doesn't but it sure sounds like it. At a guess, he's really saying 'flunk'.

Some Came Running was a commercial hit, especially in Europe. The music was by Elmer Bernstein, but Sammy Cahn and Jimmy Van Heusen had written 'To Love and Be Loved", sung in the film by the Hi-Los in a night club sequence. Frank recorded the song with Nelson Riddle as a single to promote the film. It's a typical ballad of the period, but it includes a reference to the moon race. This cut across the Hi-Los who were hoping for a hit single themselves, but that's show business. Frank liked the Hi-Los and joined them on TV for a harmony version of 'I'll Never Smile Again'.

On the same session, he recorded another Cahn and Van Heusen song, 'I Couldn't Care Less', which could easily have been a successful single but *Entertainment Weekly* wrote, 'That song embraces moral exhaustion, banked arrogance, and translucent romantic regret.' Was that why it wasn't released until 1973?

Twentieth Century-Fox thought they would ensnare cinemagoers with another lavish French musical, *Can-Can*, Cole Porter's long running, Broadway success from 1953/5. The librettist Abe Burrows wrote to Cole Porter in 1952: 'Our hero is going to fall in love with the girl and he is going to be astounded by the fact. I should think it would be a good idea if the lyrics could contain, in addition to the hero's happiness, something about the fact that he is surprised by all this. This is a fellow who never thought he would fall in love with a woman, never thought he was capable of emotions like that. He was sure that his only interest was the law. Consequently, when love hits this man, his reactions will be slightly atomic. He'll be frightened, happy, chilled, warmed, ecstatic, puzzled, upset, shocked, and delighted.'

As a result Cole Porter wrote 'C'est Magnifique' and its critical reception caused him to remark: 'When I tried to write a typical French popular song, it was dismissed by the critics. It's rather nice to find that it has at last become a typical French popular song.' He was, however, irritated that the French authorities had not praised his hymn to the city, 'I Love Paris'.

Can-Can was planned as a lavish film, shot in Todd-AO and Technicolor and directed by Walter Lang, who had been making films since 1927 and had directed *The King and I* (1956). Set in Montmartre in the 1890s with many scenes in the Café Bel du Paradis, the plot concerned a young and inexperienced judge who has to determine whether a scandalous dance performed at the club should be declared illegal.

Frank Sinatra was in the frame from the start as François Durnais, a French lawyer defending the dance, but Cary Grant turned down the role of the newly appointed judge as he had had enough of working with Sinatra. In his place came Louis Jourdan from *Gigi* with Maurice Chevalier overdoing the charm as the retiree. Marilyn Monroe was to play the owner of the Café Bel du Paradis, but she received a better offer – to star in *Some Like It Hot* for Billy Wilder. She was replaced by Shirley MacLaine as strident as ever. It is hard to believe that anyone would want to date her, let alone fight over her.

In its time, the can-can had been a very controversial dance in Paris, really because the dancers wore open crotch knickers as well as displaying their derrières. Such smutty entertainment was clearly not permissible on Broadway and even less so in a mainstream, commercial film, so the script seemed weak because you are left wondering what the fuss was about. The fact that the film was 'Certificate U' indicated the blandness.. Why was it a no can-can do? Oddly enough, the long Adam and Eve ballet sequence staged by Hermes Pan, who was associated with Fred Astaire, seemed far more daring and yet no one in the film blinked an eye. Indeed, the French authorities should have been concerned with the knife-throwing act where the stooges (including Sinatra's character) were in considerable danger.

Psychologists could have a field day discussing Cole Porter's involvement in *Can-Can*. Here was a man who had lost the use of his legs writing about leggy dancers. With no disrespect to Cole Porter, the dancing is weakened by not using Offenbach's original 'Can-Can' for the dance.

There were numerous attempts to get the score right and songs were imported from other Porter musicals and others dropped. Because of the film's length, even Maurice Chevalier's 'I Love Paris' was deleted for some countries. The memorable songs include 'Let's Do It', which should have been more of a production number, 'Just One of Those Things' (with a great introduction from Chevalier) and 'You Do Something to Me'. The lesser-known 'Live and Let Live' works particularly well because Jourdan and Chevalier are so engaging.

Sinatra suggested that his current girlfriend, Juliet Prowse be brought into the film as a chorus girl and they perform a sultry 'It's All Right with Me'. It is a highlight but not a perfect take: Frank takes out his cigarette case the wrong way round and Prowse makes two attempts at blowing out the match. Frank must have said, 'That's a wrap.'

Richard Rodgers said of the song, 'To describe a tune in terms of its attractiveness is almost impossible, but this one with its criss-crossing of minor to major and the insistence of its rhythm, makes it just about irresistible. With this song Cole Porter was never better, and there is no higher praise.'

The song tells of a brief but passionate affair and Cole Porter's instruction was 'You should cry when you sing it.' The song had a connection with reality as Prowse became one of Sinatra's on-and-off girlfriends (perhaps literally) and they were engaged for six weeks. In his autobiography, Paul Anka says that she wasn't right for Sinatra as she was 'ballsy and aggressive'.

In the film, Juliet Prowse was fine, but Shirley MacLaine was capable of ruining any Sinatra performance, especially 'Let's Do It'. Cole Porter loved this song, being especially pleased that he had beaten the censors. He had expected it to be banned when he added to the score of *Wake Up and Dream* (1929) in London, but instead the Lord Chamberlain congratulated on his knowledge of zoology. ('Some courageous kangaroos do it').

Frank is referred to as François throughout and he is wisecracking Rat Pack mode, even saying 'Ring-a-ding-ding', a curious phrase for the 1890s and sounding rather like Leslie Phillips. One scene required Shirley MacLaine to burst into Sinatra's office and find him in a wardrobe. Instead she opened the door and was greeted by his back and he said, 'Sorry, this is the men's room' instead of 'Go ahead, shoot me.' At the end of the film, Shirley MacLaine chose Sinatra but as Louis Jourdan remarked, 'It's hard to argue with anyone who can sing like that.'

The film received unexpected publicity when the Russian premier, Nikita Khrushchev visited the set on 19 September. Frank had to explain the plot, telling him, 'The movie is about a bunch of pretty girls and the fellows who like pretty girls.' Caught in a rare smiling moment with the dancers, Khrushchev said, 'This is what you call freedom but it's only freedom for the girls to show their backsides. It's capitalism that makes the girls that way.' It's fortunate that his itinerary didn't include Vegas and maybe there was a touch of envy in his remarks.

The next day Khrushchev, acting rather like the judge, called the film 'lascivious, disgusting and immoral', but it should be noted that he hadn't rushed away. The publicity people missed a coup. They should have put Khrushchev's condemnation on the posters and scored a major success. Still, *Can-Can* was a popular film with a personality of its own and not just a *Son of Gigi*. Back home, Khrushchev told his associates that Russia didn't need to lift a finger as America would bury itself.

It was mooted that Frank might make another film with a Cole Porter score, *Paris by Night*, co-starring with Brigitte Bardot, directed by Roger Vadim and produced by Raoul Levy. Frank would play an American gambler who meets a great looking girl in Paris and wants to make her a star. Vadim and Levy met Sinatra at the Fontainebleau Hotel in Miami where he was sharing his suite with two curvaceous redheads. They went for a meal and then heard Ella Fitzgerald sing. Sinatra agreed to $250,000 plus 40% of the profits as co-producer and another 6% for being the star. Part of the marketing plan was a *Playboy* pictorial of Bardot and Sinatra together. Levy picked up the wife of a boxing champ and quickly realised he had to leave town fast. They met again in Chicago but Frank had cooled, 'I've done the location bit and there are too many idiots standing around watching.' Vadim and Levy tried to interest Danny Kaye in the project but that didn't work out either. Possibly Sinatra had guessed that the American interest in Brigitte Bardot would decline quickly, but no doubt

Playboy was disappointed. Still, they did get Nancy Sinatra many years later.

Some Like It Hot had gone through many potential casts. It had started with Bob Hope, Danny Kaye and Mitzi Gaynor in the frame, but then settled on Frank Sinatra, Tony Perkins and Marilyn Monroe. Then Tony Perkins was swapped for Tony Curtis. The director Billy Wilder, after pitching it to Sinatra in Palm Springs, could sense that he wasn't too keen. Wilder told Curtis, 'He'd have to dress as a woman every day and I can't see him doing that.' When Frank didn't meet Wilder for a restaurant date in Beverly Hills, Wilder forgot about him and went with the winning combination of Jack Lemmon, Tony Curtis and Marilyn Monroe. Other films that might have been different were *Gypsy* with Barbra Streisand and *South Pacific* with Doris Day.

On 27 September 1958, Frank returned to London to host a gala première of *Me and the Colonel* starring Danny Kaye and attended by the Queen. The newspapers were saying that he was romantically entangled with Lady Adelle Beatty, but he said from the stage, 'I'm in London solely for the charity showing of tonight's film and to introduce the cast. I did not come here to get married.' However, Ava did return his wedding ring, saying 'Give that to your English lady.' When Adelle married the film director Stanley Donen in 1960, Frank sent her a telegram which said, 'How could you?'

Frank was introduced on stage by David Jacobs and in the minutes beforehand, Jacobs was sitting down waiting to be called and Sinatra was walking around like a penguin. Jacobs offered him a seat but Sinatra declined, saying, 'I know my voice is good order, but when I go out on stage, I don't want to be in a creased suit like you.'

Sinatra and his manager Hank Sanicola had written a novelty song, 'Mr Success' that they thought could be a single. It wasn't much of a song ('Put your head on my chest, And I'm Mr Success') but it was strikingly arranged by Nelson Riddle. 'Mr Success' made the US Top 50 and the UK Top 30 though it might have been better to have gone with a song from *Can-Can* instead.

Frank asked Alan and Marilyn Bergman to write a song around his closing phrase on TV, 'Goodnight and sleep warm'. They wrote a gentle, romantic lullaby which he now recorded as well as a superb 'Where or When' featuring Bill Miller on piano but which wasn't released until 1978.

Frank and Dean never cut duets while they were at Capitol, but Frank did select the songs for one of Dean's albums, *Sleep Warm*, which was arranged by Nelson Riddle and conducted by Frank himself. All the songs were about dreaming and indeed, Frank could have made this album himself – in his sleep. There is naturally 'Sleep Warm', which captures Dean's romantic persona. The selection of songs could be done in a couple of minutes with a computer today but Frank and Dean had to do some lateral thinking to come up 'Dream', 'Dream a Little Dream of Me', 'Wrap Your Troubles in Dreams', 'All I Do Is Dream Of You' and 'Hit The Road to Dreamland' on which Dean already sounds asleep (so the album has worked for him). There is a lightly swinging 'Sleepy Time Gal' with a jazz piano break and the fun of 'Cuddle Up a Little Closer', but mostly it's thank you and goodnight.

Frank tried to keep it quiet that he was dating Dixie Evans, 40-26-34, a stripper and a Marilyn Monroe lookalike and devotee. Her routines were inspired by Monroe's films. She draped herself over a producer's chair wearing only a G-string as the musicians played 'You Must Have Been a Beautiful Baby', waltzed across the stage with a dummy of Laurence Olivier in tribute to *The Prince and the Showgirl* (1957), and sang 'You Made Me Love You' to a photograph of Elvis Presley. In 1958 Marilyn Monroe threatened her with a lawsuit, but the dispute was resolved without going to court after Dixie agreed to restructure her act if not her body.

It didn't matter as Dixie Evans had become the best known stripper in the US. Frank attended one of her shows and was soon between the sheets. In the wake of his divorce from the real Marilyn, Joe DiMaggio asked Frank to arrange a meeting with Dixie, and she gave him a private performance of the number that satirised their relationship.

'Why shouldn't I cry,
Joe, you walked out and left me flat,
So now you're gone and I'm all alone,
Thank heavens you left your bat.'

Frank's first album with Billy May, *Come Fly with Me*, had been very successful and was encouraging other singers to indulge in similar musical trips. Bing Crosby and Rosemary Clooney even booked Billy May for their flights on *Fancy Meeting You Here* (1958) and later *That Travellin' Two Beat* (1965). Similarly Mel Tormé made an album of South American songs with May, *¡Olé Tormé! (1959)*.

Frank Sinatra's second album with May was a much looser concept, the high energy *Come Dance with Me!*, which could perm any 12 of several thousand titles. Sammy Cahn said that he didn't know what to write as Irving Berlin had covered all the bases. Rather than leave things completely to the last minute, Billy May had some charts written for him by Heinie Beau.

The first session on 9 December 1958 found Billy May swinging like mad on 'Just In Time' (from the 1956 Broadway musical, *Bells Are Ringing*, a show about a telephonist) and 'Something's Gotta Give' (written for Fred Astaire in 1955 but associated with Sammy Davis) as well as Frank's fourth recording of 'This Song Is You', but this time up-tempo and brassy. Frank was loving it, shouting out 'Aw, let's tear it up' in 'Something's Gotta Give' but when Frank turned up for more recordings on 12 December, he said, 'Aw, the hell with it. It's my birthday – let's go to my house and party.' Officially, Capitol was told that Frank had a throat infection and the rest of the album was rearranged for 22/23 December.

Frank was reunited with 'Day In – Day Out', but this time he took his vocal into the stratosphere so that he sounds like he is madly, deliriously in love. The song builds in passion and the first time you hear it at least, Billy May's arrangement is full of surprises and praise too for the musicians in his 20 piece orchestra especially the drummer Alvin Stoller.

The critics didn't care for *Kismet* when it opened on Broadway in 1953, but because of a newspaper strike, the reviews were deferred and the show became a smash. The melodies were based on various works of the classical composer Alexander Borodin; 'Baubles, Bangles and Beads' was presented with a string quartet. When the tune was given a sparkling, up tempo arrangement by the Kirby Stone Four, it was banned by the BBC which felt an obligation to the composer who had died in 1887. Sinatra had a fabulous swinging arrangement and he is so keen to attack the words that he returns early after the instrumental break.

'Dancing in the Dark' from the Broadway show, *The Band Wagon*, in 1931 was associated with Bing Crosby but now we had a new, high energy arrangement which swung like mad. May's tricks didn't always work: 'Saturday Night Is the Loneliest Night of the Week', which Sinatra first recorded in 1944, didn't suit the up tempo treatment. Frank's version of 'Too Close For Comfort' was not as dynamic as Sammy Davis's but this might be because it is Heinie Beau's arrangement and not Billy May's.

One of Fred and Ginger's classic dance sequences is 'Cheek to Cheek', written by Irving Berlin for the film *Top Hat* (1935), but it had been difficult to complete because Ginger's ostrich feathers would make Fred sneeze. It was a very clever composition in which the singer goes from verse to chorus on the word 'Heaven' and Sinatra was able to take such vocal gymnastics in his stride. 'I Could Have Danced All Night' from *My Fair Lady* could have been a major success but Frank overdoes the Sinatraisms, for example, by dropping 'I' from the title. He sounds more like a Sinatra imitator than Sinatra.

The same can be said of Sammy Cahn and Jimmy Van Heusen's 'Come Dance with Me' with its 'Hey there, cutes, put on your Basie boots' and 'What kookoo things I'll be saying'. Good fun but the title song shouldn't be the weakest track on an album. Their second song, 'The Last Dance' is much better and brings the LP to a perfect conclusion, conveying the feeling that the band and the album is winding down after a night of spirited playing.

Frank returned after Christmas for some singles with Nelson Riddle. The hit song from the session was 'French Foreign Legion', a ridiculous song helped by a ring-a-ding-ding vocal from Frank and a fun arrangement from Nelson Riddle, but the line 'Think about that uniform with all its charms' is just crazy.

Sammy and Jimmy had written the title song for *They Came to Cordura*, a western starring Gary Cooper, Rita Hayworth and Tab Hunter. The song promoted the film but it gave the plot away, although that depends on knowing whose voice Frank was representing. The title was awkward and the song represents writing by rote.

'All My Tomorrows' is an underrated Cahn and Van Heusen ballad. Sammy Cahn recalled, 'I knew Bob Dylan because I had inducted him into the Songwriters Hall Of Fame. He said to me, "I've done one of your songs." I said, "YOU have done one of MY songs?" He said, "Yes" and I expected him to say something like 'Teach Me Tonight', but he said, "It's 'All My Tomorrows'." Frank did it for *A Hole in the Head* and it's since been recorded by Pia Zadora with the London Philharmonic. It illustrates Jimmy Van Heusen's maxim, "Write the best song you know how and don't worry about it."'

Frank Capra, a chemical engineer who became the famed feelgood director of *Mr Smith Goes to Washington* (1939) and *It's a Wonderful Life* (1947), saw another patch of blue sky in the Broadway success, *A Hole in the Head* by Arnold Schulman. He asked Schulman to change his story from a Jewish family to an Italian-American one and to create an upbeat ending. Schulman had some misgivings but he did as requested. Sinatra liked the story and he and Capra formed a production company, SinCap, which went into partnership with United Artists. However, much of the play's original structure was retained as Sinatra is wisecracking as much as Jackie Mason. In a curious piece of casting, Edward G Robinson is Frank's elder brother and the noted tough guy is playing for laughs and doing it well.

In the film, Frank runs a beach hotel in Miami but he is not a good businessman and he doesn't want to be tied down by his girlfriend, Carolyn Jones. His ambition is to build Disneyland in Miami (this predated Orlando) but he's facing eviction. He was very comfortable when acting with the young boy, Eddie Hodges, and together they performed 'High Hopes'. The song neatly tied up Capra's philosophy: do good things, have good thoughts and lead a good life and all will be well. It's another way of saying 'Ac-Cent-Tchu-Ate The Positive'.

Sammy Cahn had a rhyming bonanza when he wrote 'High Hopes', 'The song is very infectious and people love to sing it. Originally I only had the title phrase. "High hopes, High hopes, High apple pie in the sky hopes", and then Van Heusen came back with some music. I said, "Maybe we should write this from the viewpoint of the animals." I had made a *faux pas* as he had written the best animal song ever in 'Swinging on a Star'. I looked around and I saw a stream of ants. I said, "No, I don't mean animals. I mean insects. Those ants have a sense of fulfilment, going up and down all day. A fella gets a sock on the jaw and as he falls to the ground, a stream of ants goes past his nose." What makes the song funny for me is that I have never seen an ant near a rubber tree plant, but when you say,

'Just what makes that little ol' ant

Think he'll move a...'

It can't be anything but "rubber tree plant". You can't say "acacia" because the architecture of the song calls for "rubber tree plant." When we sang the song to Sinatra, he laughed, and the song became a smash, smash hit.'

'High Hopes' is a strange single as Sinatra delivers the verse rather flatly, so much so that it must be deliberate. The single credits Frank Sinatra and Eddie Hodges 'with a bunch of kids'. Not so as Nelson preferred to use adult females. The other song on the session was 'Love Looks So Well on You' a poor man's 'Stardust'. Sinatra, Riddle, Cahn and Van Heusen missed a trick here. When 'High Hopes' did so well and won an Oscar for Best Song, they should have made the definitive children's album. Sammy Cahn was competing with himself at the Oscars as Johnny Mathis sang the title song from *The Best of Everything*, but it wasn't an inspiring field.

Capra got a strong performance out of Sinatra but they were friends and he knew how to handle him. He said, 'Sinatra is a great singer and he knows it. Sinatra is also a great actor, and he knows that too, but he cannot bewitch an audience of dispassionate cameramen, soundmen, script girls, makeup people, and deadpan electricians who have seen it all before. If directors keep him busy, he maintains an easy truce, for having started something, Sinatra's next goal is to finish it – but fast. He bores easily; he can't sit still or be alone and he must be where the action is.'

When it came to lost causes, Capra had more than most film directors. After *A Hole in the Head*, Capra wanted to make a film about St Paul, but neither Frank nor Jimmy Cagney thought they were right for the job. Frank as St Paul would have been as miscast as John Wayne as the centurion at the foot of the cross in *The Greatest Story Ever Told*. When he had to say, 'This truly was the Son of God', the director George Stevens said, 'No, John, saw it with awe.' Wayne responded with 'Aw, this truly was the Son of God.'

Capra moved over to a comedy about a monk, *Brother Bertram*, and this time both Frank and Elvis Presley turned it down. Capra then floated *The Jimmy Durante Story*, which was to feature Frank, Bing and Dean, with Frank as his manager and former vaudeville partner, Lou Clayton. Although Frank mentioned this on a TV special, nothing came of it. Mind you, Dean was scheduled to play Durante and having had a nose job, he can't have relished having a large hooter again.

There were plenty of non-Capra proposals which were rejected. Frank wouldn't play a gangster who had his life turned around by Bing Crosby playing a priest, in *Say One for Me*. Although *Manolette* might have reunited him with Ava, he declined the role of a Spanish bullfighter as the so-called sport was unpopular with the American public.

Frank did think that Spencer Tracy and he could play son and father in *Exodus*, but Tracy declared that he couldn't lose enough weight for Sinatra to carry him in a crucial scene at the end. Also, Frank, Fred Astaire and Jack Benny agreed to cameo appearances in *Let's Make Love*, which starred Marilyn Monroe, Yves Montand and Frankie Vaughan. The film was becoming a disaster and it was hoped that the cameos could turn it round but their schedules couldn't tally and the cameos went to Bing Crosby, Gene Kelly and Milton Berle instead. It made no difference – the film was a dog, though not without its moments.

As a business venture, Sinatra and Peter Lawford bought Puccini's restaurant in Beverly Hills and put Chicken George Raft on the menu. It became a Rat Pack haunt but Sinatra gave up his ownership once he had started his own record label, Reprise. It is unlikely that Peter put money into the project; his in-law's name was enough.

Come Dance with Me! was issued at the end of January 1959 and climbed to No.2 on the US album chart, not being able to dislodge Henry Mancini's soundtrack recordings from

Peter Gunn, which had a 10-week stay at the top. Still, *Come Dance with Me!* remained on the listings for 140 weeks. *Come Dance With Me!* sold so well in the UK that it clambered to No.30 on the singles chart. The album won Grammys for Album of the Year and Best Male Vocal Performance and Billy May won another for his arrangements. A special award was given to Dave Cavanaugh for his 'Artists & Repertoire Contribution' as the Committee was not yet sure how to honour production.

The image of Frank Sinatra as the perpetual swinger was lightly mocked by Peter Sellers on his album, *Songs for Swingin' Sellers*. Sellers wanted to ape Sinatra with a song called 'You Keep Me Swingin'' and he asked his producer, George Martin, to find someone who could sing the song like Sinatra and he could use it as a blueprint for his own vocal. George Martin found Matt Monro and when he heard Matt's version, Sellers said, 'I can't beat this guy. Let's use this.' Monro appeared under the name of Fred Flange and the newspapers wondered who it really was, perhaps even Frank himself. When his identity was revealed, Monro's career took off and he was soon having hits of his own, eventually recording in the same studio as Frank and making a BBC-TV special with Nelson Riddle in 1967.

While Sinatra was promoting one album, he was usually making another. His next project was his second album with Gordon Jenkins, *No One Cares*. It was in the same melancholy vein as *Where Are You?*: songs of lost love, heavily scored with strings. The spiralling strings are beautifully showcased on a revival of Russ Columbo's 'Just Friends' (1932). Frank Sinatra said that he wanted to make the saddest imaginable album, and he succeeded.

In 1869 Tchaikovsky wrote music for a poem of Goethe's 'Nur wer die Sehnsucht kennt (None But the Weary Heart)', though it was now given a new English lyric, 'None But the Lonely Heart', and it was recorded by Sinatra with a full orchestral arrangement. As you might expect, it was banned by the BBC for being disrespectful to the classics.

In 1953 the musical, *Carnival In Flanders*, starring John Raitt and Dolores Gray only lasted six performances on Broadway, but Sinatra saw the potential of 'Here's That Rainy Day' and gave an effortless performance of a difficult song. Listen to his beautiful phrasing on 'That rainy day is here.' The show was partly financed by the songwriters Jimmy Van Heusen and Johnny Burke (plus Bing Crosby), so they must have been gratified to see this emerging from the rubble. Sinatra's voice is equally fantastic on 'Cottage for Sale', associated with Billy Eckstine in 1945, and his low, final note is almost a growl.

Ira Gershwin gave Frank some amended lyrics for his list song, 'I Can't Get Started', a number associated with Bunny Berigan (1937), including 'Superman turns out to be a flash in the pan' and references to meeting President Roosevelt and Queen Elizabeth II. The song usually has a comic interpretation but not on this album. On a similarly personal note, Frank loved Alec Wilder's song, 'Where Do You Go' as it defined his relationship with Ava.

The liner note from Ralph J Gleason said, 'If I had my way, I would have Frank Sinatra record every song I have ever liked. I wouldn't care how he did it, with what accompaniments, with what interpretations or changes in tempo, I know I would like it. The fact that Capitol is gradually, though its series of Sinatra recordings accomplishing this for me, I count this as one of the great blessings of the decade.'

My sentiments entirely but this being the case, I do wish Frank hadn't spent so much of his time remaking songs he had recorded before, although in this case, they hadn't been recorded better. His 'Stormy Weather' had a stunning moment when very quietly and dignified, he murmured 'Just can't get my old self together'. Because of the stereo grooves, only 11 tracks would fit onto the album and a brooding version of 'The One I Love (Belongs to Somebody Else)' was recorded but dropped. A nod to his version of 'Stormy Weather' was the centerpiece of Cake's 1996 record, 'Frank Sinatra', which was included on the soundtrack for *The Sopranos*.

Alan Livingston had left Capitol, and Sinatra had fallen out with Glenn Wallichs, the chairman at Capitol. He wanted a deal to allow his own company Essex to make his records and Capitol to distribute them. Wallichs refused, not least because the other Capitol stars would want a similar deal. The only bargaining tool open to Sinatra was not to record. He only broke it in 1959 for the *Can Can* soundtrack.

In March 1959 Sinatra returned to Australia, this time working with Red Norvo's Quintet. He enjoyed working with a small group and the performances were loose and jazzy. He wanted to make an album with Norvo and another with George Shearing but he did not want to give Capitol his suggestions. Quite fortuitously, Dinah Shore made her own album with Red Norvo, *Dinah Sings Blues with Red*, in 1960. In 1997 an album of one concert, *Live in Australia*, was issued by the jazz label, Blue Note. The release also featured Frank backed by a local big band on three numbers.

Inspired by the runaway success of *The Bridge on the River Kwai*, Sinatra signed up to the new John Sturges film, a war film set in Burma, *Never So Few*. The title sounded Churchillian, but the poster said, 'Kiss by kiss the time ran out and never so few were the moments left for love!'

Sturges had had a run of commercial and critical hits including *Bad Day at Black Rock* (1955), *Gunfight at the OK Corral* (1957) and *The Old Man and the Sea* (1958). He had almost cast Frank Sinatra as Doc Holliday in *Gunfight at the OK Corral* but went with Kirk Douglas instead. With his experience, he should have been able to contain Sinatra. Not so. Looking back on the movie, he said, 'Frank almost ran the picture. He had his best friends in the film and Sammy was supposed to have been in it. I've no idea where Dean was at the time.' The supporting cast included Peter Lawford, Charles Bronson and Gina Lollabrigida, whom Frank called 'GinaGetalittlebitofher, though not to her face.

For once the Sinatra charm did not work on Lollabrigida, who simply thought that he had one thing in mind. Frank told her that Dolly used to put garlic around his neck whenever he had a chill and as a result, he hated it. When she had to do a romantic scene with him, she ate a bulb of garlic beforehand just to spite him.

When Frank wanted to hire Sammy Davis, he was told that there were no black GIs in the Burma campaign. Frank said, 'Now there are' and Sammy came aboard for $75,000. In February 1959, Sammy made a nightclub appearance in which he said of Sinatra, 'Talent is not an excuse for bad manners. It does not give you the right to step on people and treat them rotten.' He added that he had replaced Sinatra as the country's No.1 popular singer.

Oh dear, dear. When Sinatra was told, he went into a rage and refused to speak to Sammy. As Frank had recently made it up with Peter Lawford, Sammy asked him to plead on his behalf. No joy. Peter Lawford was working on *Never So Few* on a reduced salary and he was so in awe of Sinatra that his new daughter was called Victoria Francis. He and Sammy had realised the No.1 rule of the Rat Pack: total obeisance to their leader. Frank called Peter the 'brother in Lawford': a good joke but a constant reminder of why he was tolerated.

Sammy had been replaced by Sturges' recommendation, Steve McQueen. McQueen was previously known as a TV actor but after *Never So Few*, he was offered *The Magnificent Seven* and stardom beckoned. However, *Never So Few* cost $3.5m to make and had a net loss of $1.15m.

Steve McQueen responded well to Sinatra and Peter Lawford's clowning. When they put a firecracker in his ammunition belt, he was blown out of his chair. McQueen fired blanks at them and they all laughed. Frank commented, 'Steve had a 'fuck you' attitude that I liked.' For the film, Sinatra had his own mini-Rat Pack with Lawford, McQueen and

Bronson. There was an accident on set when a gun was fired too close to Sinatra's head and damaged his cornea but the matter was resolved satisfactorily.

Sinatra was in control. When a member of the crew told a negative story about him, it got back to Frank. Frank beat him up and had him thrown off the set. Then he got rid of the person who had told him: 'Can't stand snitches,' he said.

Frank Sinatra, first seen with a beard, is leading a band of GIs and guerillas fighting the Japanese. Despite its implausible plot the *LA Examiner* said, "Sinatra is in his element, swinging with the plot from tough soldier to teasing lover, and tossing off smart dialogue in that casual, underplayed way of his." Er, yes, that means lazy, I think. There is a moment where Frank cuts across another actor's lines in a hospital sequence, a sign that that he had done his take and was moving on.

Never So Few debated some of the moral questions of war, particularly when Sinatra's character shot one of his own men because there was no doctor or appropriate medication around. The film had the potential to be better than it was. At the time, the film was criticised for too much swearing though nobody would notice it today.

In the end, Frank and Sammy made up and got together in May for a charity gala at the Moulin Rouge in Hollywood which raised $100,000. It was a rare treat for Sammy Cahn, a frustrated performer, who found himself on stage with Frank, Dean and Sammy.

When Frank returned to the Sands, his special guest was Marilyn Monroe. He wanted to make love to her on the roof but he had to plan the tryst. Strange but true, this memo from Jack Entratter to the security staff gave him permission: 'Please be advised that Mr Frank Sinatra is permitted 24 hour access to the roof of the Sands Hotel. Mr Sinatra will use his own discretion in choosing to entertain any guest on those premises. Thank you.'

More seriously, the Mafia connections were mounting up. Born in Chicago in 1908, Sam Giancana had been in trouble from the start, serving a year for violence and car theft when he was 15. He became a superb getaway driver and was soon working up the ranks of Al Capone's organization, becoming Capone's favoured driver. He was questioned about three murders before he was 20 and in one case, when he was arrested, the prosecution witness was murdered. He was deemed too much of a psychopath to serve in the war. By the time, Sinatra knew him, he was said to have killed over 200 men. He had inherited Capone's title of Public Enemy No.1. Like many mobsters, he enjoyed the night life in Vegas and Frank loved to talk to him, though at different times Frank said he didn't know him, that he was a passing acquaintance and that he was a good buddy – it depended on whom he was talking to. Ava just said that she hated him. Frank gave him a sapphire ring for friendship and no doubt added him to the Christmas card list. Giancana offered Sinatra advice, which he ignored: don't get hot-headed, don't pick fights and take it easy.

In 1958 Lana Turner made national headlines when her daughter, Cheryl Crane, stabbed her boyfriend, Johnny Stompanato, to death. He was an underworld thug. The killing was pronounced justifiable homicide as Cheryl believed her mother's life was under threat. Lana Turner returned to the screen with *Imitation of Life* in 1959, which became a big hit. Frank sent her a clock in the shape of a globe. The note said, 'You're back on top of the world.' Frank gave Cheryl a record player with a host of albums, thereby testifying to the healing powers of music. Sinatra never liked Turner's former husband and Cheryl's father, the restaurant owner Stephen Crane, calling him a gigolo. Once they fought in public, but they made up for Cheryl's 21st party in 1964.

Because Frank was refusing to record and the label wanted to save *No One Cares* for the autumn, Capitol issued a compilation, *Look to Your Heart*, in June and marketed it as a new collection. It made No.8 on the US album chart, which was commendable for a compilation.

Frank's album with Gordon Jenkins, *No One Cares*, was released in August 1959. It went to No.2 on the US album chart and remained on the listings for 73 weeks. This was exceptionally good for such a morose and introspective album and it showed that the general public could appreciate quality.

However, Frank had fallen completely out of love with Capitol. He had decided that he was being ripped off. He wanted a better deal for himself with Capitol and he refused to record unless his demands were satisfied. Alan Livingston, who had returned to Capitol, was asked to sort out the mess and get him recording again. Frank said, 'I don't want to talk to you. I'm gonna burn down the round building.' Alan Livingston resolved the stalemate. If Frank made five more albums for the label, then Capitol would cancel his contract and he could do what he liked. Okay, said Frank and Reprise Records was born.

On 19 October 1959 when Sinatra made *The Frank Sinatra Show* for Timex, he rolled up his sleeve to show six watches. His guest artist, Dean was keen for his own free advertising as he revealed the bottom of his shoes to show, 'Eat At Dino's', an ad for Dino's Lodge, a restaurant he had opened in Los Angeles. Sinatra performed 'High Hopes' with a gang of 40 kids, added a scat ending to 'Just One of Those Things' and sang a lively, fun-packed version of 'The Lady is a Tramp' with Bill Miller on piano. The in-jokes were mounting up; if you weren't clued into Sinatra, he might as well be performing in a foreign language.

A week later Frank was a guest on *The Bing Crosby Oldsmobile TV Show* and they both performed with Louis Armstrong and Peggy Lee on 'I'm Glad I'm Not Young Anymore' and 'Now You Has Jazz'. Bing and Peggy sang Cahn and Van Heusen's 'Too Neat to Be a Beatnik, Too Round to be a Square'. Frank, Dean and Bing performed 'Together Wherever We Go' with new lyrics referring to Elvis and the Everly Brothers, so the contemporary trends rattled them. They were then joined by Jimmy Durante and Dean's impersonation of Durante proved uncannily accurate. With George Shearing and Mitzi Gaynor on the guest list, this show is a candidate for TV's greatest variety show.

There was another Frank Sinatra special at Christmas on which Frank worked with Red Norvo and his combo. The guest stars included Hermione Gingold and Peter Lawford, who perform 'Comes Love' together. Frank and Juliet Prowse reprised 'It's All Right with Me' from *Can-Can*.

Frank heard that Norman Granz wanted to sell his jazz label, Verve, whose main artist was Ella Fitzgerald. He was furious when Granz went to MGM instead, but he couldn't match their $3m offer. He did however meet Mo Ostin, the chief accountant at Verve, and took him on board for his own project. As they drove past the Capitol Tower one day, Frank said, 'I helped build that. Now let's build one of our own.'

Because Frank and Norman Granz disliked each other, he was not allowed to make an album with Ella, which could have been audio heaven. Their few televisions appearances together hint at what we were missing.

Frank would call his label, Reprise, which he pronounced Re-preez not Re-prize. You can hear him sing the word in 'April in Paris'. It was an ideal name for a label focusing on established artists and reworking standards, although Reprise came to be much more than that. He also chose the name because he wanted a reprisal against Capitol.

CHAPTER 11

Election year

'What did you say your name was?'
Dean Martin to John F Kennedy, 1960

I. Ambassador for Pussy

The accepted view is that before Kennedy's assassination in November 1963, the youthful and dynamic politician was changing the world with his presidency and so the world lost a great leader. Maybe. But behind the scenes, the picture was very different. Although Kennedy was photogenic and convincing, he was deeply flawed and the way he had obtained his presidency was, to say the least, questionable. Frank Sinatra was fascinated by the power and celebrity of John F Kennedy and the association between them forms a significant part of each other's story.

The links between the Irish-Catholic family, the Kennedys, and America began when the immigrants John and Bridget Kennedy fled the potato famine and started farming around Boston. Nearly all immigrants faced hardship but the Kennedys were always full of initiative. President Kennedy's grandfather was said to have electrified the city of Boston and robbed nearly everyone by overcharging. The pivotal figure here is his son, Joe Kennedy, who was born in Boston in 6 September 1888. He was a tall, well-built man with sparkling blue eyes who was always smiling – in public at least. He was well educated, spending time at Harvard and becoming a bank president when only 25. In 1914, he married the daughter of the Mayor of Boston, Rose Elizabeth Fitzgerald and they were to have nine children.

Joe was a skilled negotiator who could make things happen. He knew the importance of timing and perhaps more significantly, how to obtain and use insider information. His first big move was to raise money to purchase the troubled Columbia Trust Bank. He resolved its problems and became wealthy. He made additional income for himself through the stock market, selling commodities and dealing in properties. During the First World War, Kennedy arranged transportation for the warships and as a result, he befriended Franklin Roosevelt, a Democrat and the Assistant Secretary to the Navy.

Many believe that Kennedy increased his fortune by selling bootleg liquor during Prohibition and thus establishing links with organised crime. Certainly, after Prohibition, he secured a deal for importing Scotch whisky into America. As he always wanted to be in control he drank very little himself and offered all of his sons $1,000 if they did not touch alcohol before they were 21.

Joe was a womaniser, having a long affair with the actress Gloria Swanson. She was glamour personified but also a businesswoman for whom he financed some of her films. Joe encouraged his sons to think the same way: grab what you can but do it discreetly and don't embarrass your wife in public. His mixture of politics, organised crime and celebrity was repeated with his son, John F Kennedy.

Joe Kennedy was as dangerous as any Mafia boss but he smiled a lot and seemed very friendly. He had respectability on his side and was far more devious and conniving. It is said that he amassed a vast fortune by selling short during the stock market crash.

It was also a good time to invest in films. The new 'talkies' thrived during the Depression, the slogan being 'Forget your troubles and see a movie.' Joe Kennedy had bought some film studios, including RKO, and so he needed a chain of cinemas to show the films. He made an offer to Alexander Pantages who owned several hundred movie theatres. Pantages refused to sell and a few weeks later, he was arrested for rape and found guilty. His reputation was ruined. He sold his cinemas to Kennedy for a knockdown price of $3.5m. He was found not guilty at a second trial. The whole thing was probably set up by Kennedy to get what he wanted. One of Kennedy's business rival, Howard Hughes, established himself by making *Hell's Angels* (1930), which launched Jean Harlow. Howard Hughes and Joe Kennedy loathed each other and the last thing Hughes wanted was a 'Mick' for President.

In 1932 Kennedy supported Roosevelt for President and he was made chairman of the US Securities and Exchange Commission. He changed the rules so that a number of sharp practices including insider dealing became illegal. When a friend asked Roosevelt why he had appointed a crook, he said, 'It takes one to know one.' In 1935 he took over the Maritime Commission.

Kennedy's children could see that their father was fiercely competitive; he would tell them that life was about winning. The ultimate goal was the presidency, but it had never been won by a Catholic. The American public was wary of having a president whose strings might be pulled by the Pope. Not that it would have been a problem with Joe Kennedy as he would have been pulling the Pope's strings.

In 1938 Roosevelt sent Kennedy to London and he became the Ambassador to the UK, the irony of an Irishman holding this position not being lost on the British. He enjoyed mixing in London society and it was a wonderful opportunity for more wheeling and dealing. However, with war on the horizon. Kennedy made some decidedly undiplomatic remarks for a diplomat. He told his acquaintances that Hitler was right to be critical of the Jews but he was wrong to exterminate them, adding, 'Well, they brought it on themselves.'

Kennedy wanted appeasement with Hitler and he tried to secure an understanding between America and Germany. In 1940 he commented publicly that 'Democracy is finished in England.' The MP Josiah Wedgwood commented, 'We have a rich man, untrained in diplomacy, unlearned in history and politics who is a great publicity seeker and whose ambition is apparently to be the first Catholic president of the US.' Spot on.

That was it. The backlash against Kennedy was so severe that Roosevelt demanded his resignation. Kennedy knew that he could never stand for the presidency. He pinned his hopes on his first son, also called Joe. He would be groomed for the job but he was reported missing after a bombing raid in 1944 and never returned.

Then Joe favoured his second son, John Fitzgerald Kennedy, known as Jack, who was born in Brookline, Massachusetts on 29 May 1917. He had graduated from Harvard and he had joined the US Navy during the war despite chronic back problems. He commanded a patrol torpedo boat, PT-109. He showed immense bravery by saving others without thinking of himself when his boat was rammed by a Japanese destroyer, though how the boat didn't see the destroyer coming is a mystery. Kennedy was awarded a Purple Heart. Such was the magic of the Kennedys that Jimmy Dean had a US Top 10 single with the story of 'PT-109' in 1962.

Writers have talked about the Kennedy curse. Certainly the family had its share of misfortune but there were so many of them that are a few troubles were inevitable. Joe and

Rose's third child, Rosemary, had radical surgery, a lobotomy, in 1941 which left her unable to look after herself. She was placed in a home and Joe Kennedy did not allow her name to be uttered in their home at Hyannis Port, Massachusetts. Against the odds, she survived until 2005.

Patricia Kennedy, known as Pat, was born in 1924 and she dated Senator Joe McCarthy, who was a friend of Joe's. In the early 1950s, McCarthy was responsible for the Communist witch-hunts and this time Joe realised that he had better distance himself from this politician. However, Joe did not approve of Pat's relationship with Peter Lawford. He didn't mind her marrying an Englishman but this was an Englishman without money and a Protestant to boot. He thought Lawford was marrying her for her wealth, which was probably true. When they married in 1954, Joe Kennedy was worth over $200bn and was one of the ten richest people in America.

John F Kennedy became a representative in the House of Congress in 1947 and was a senator for Massachusetts in 1952. In 1953 he married Jacqueline Bouvier, born 1929, in New York, a golden couple if there was one. Their first child was stillborn in 1956 but Caroline followed in 1957.

Adlai Stevenson had sought the Democratic nomination for the presidency in 1952 and 1956, but had been defeated by Eisenhower. 'Madly for Adlai' hadn't worked. Bobby Kennedy, who became his brother's campaign manager, said, 'OK, let's go to work on the next one.' Eisenhower was President from 1953 to 1961 – there was talk of an Eisenhower doll: you wind it up and it does nothing for years. In December 1957, Jack Kennedy's face was on the cover of *Time* magazine, which kickstarted his presidential campaign: how did he make the cover? We don't know for sure but Joe Kennedy would say it was $75,000 well spent.

In 1959 when Adlai Stevenson decided to stand a third time for the Democratic nomination, Joe urged his son to push forward and challenge him. Jack knew that it would look bad for him if it appeared that his father was all but running for the Democratic nomination, and so he instructed him to act behind the scenes: calling in favours, fundraising and building alliances. Although he did not like it, Joe Kennedy could appreciate the logic of this.

The presentation of politics was dramatically changing as America was entering the TV age. In 1950 just 10% of Americans had TV sets and in 1960, it had risen to 90%. Vast funds were needed for advertising and gala dinners and balls with celebrities at $100 a plate helped.

At the Democratic Convention in Los Angeles, Jack floated the concept of a New Frontier which would cover 'uncharted areas of science and space, unsolved problems of peace and war, unconquered pockets of ignorance and prejudice.' The implication was that Kennedy would not only sort out today's problems (civil rights, the space race, social revolutions), he would also be determining the future of mankind. Powerful stuff, yet Jack Kennedy read James Bond books for relaxation.

Joe Kennedy wanted to get his son into the White House, but first he had to win the Democratic nomination. Joe said to him, 'Jack, just how many votes do you need to win? I'm not paying for a landslide.' During the campaign, Bob Hope made a pointed joke which must have hit home: 'The Senator's victory in Wisconsin is a victory for democracy. It proves that a millionaire has just as good a chance as anybody else.'

Anti-Catholic feelings were high in some states and Joe needed a man with union connections who could be persuaded to help him. That man was Sam Giancana. At the time, Giancana was furious that Desi Arnaz had made a TV series about the Mafia, *The*

Untouchables, and he wanted Arnaz killed. This was a close call, but he decided against it as his death might then make the series look like the truth.

Joe Kennedy knew better than to deal with Giancana directly, but he knew a man who would – Frank Sinatra – who was keen to ingratiate himself into both the Kennedy and the Giancana circles, a very dangerous game. Joe asked Sinatra to persuade Giancana to arrange the votes that would swing the election. 'Oh yes,' said old man Kennedy, 'If he can pull the primary, there won't be any more talk of going after the Mafia.'

Sinatra did not like Joe Kennedy, but then who did? Joe told him that supporting the Kennedys would be the best investment he could possibly make. Sinatra nursed dreams of becoming an American ambassador. Jack Kennedy would joke privately that he could become ambassador for pussy.

With all this to play for, Sinatra saw Giancana on the golf course so that their conversation could not be easily bugged. Everything had to be secret as the anti-Catholic sentiment would increase if illegal arrangements were discovered, as indeed, Kennedy would then be out of the presidential race. Giancana said yes and as a result, JFK won West Virginia. Another Mobster, Skinny D'Amato, the owner of the 500 Club in Atlantic City, was able to persuade the local sheriffs and the coal miners' unions to deliver 120,000 votes. Kennedy secured the Democratic nomination by a narrow margin and then was up against the Republican, Richard Nixon, for the Presidency.

One of Robert Harris's novels, *Fatherland*, is about Joe Kennedy becoming President instead of his son and having to deal with Hitler in the 1960s. Both events could have happened.

II. Day In–Day Out, 1960

It was Peter Lawford's idea.

Only it wasn't.

A petrol pump attendant Richard Breen had a good idea for a film. During the war, Breen had dismantled radio equipment in Germany and he longed to do something exciting again. In his imagination, he created *Ocean's 11*. Some years after their wartime exploits, 11 former servicemen reunite under the leadership of Danny Ocean. They are bored by their civilian jobs and so they meticulously plan to rob several Las Vegas casinos at midnight on New Year's Eve. Breen discussed the plot with Gilbert Kay, an assistant director who worked on the TV western series, *The Range Rider* and *The Gene Autry Show*, and they showed their ideas to Billy Wilder, the director of *Some Like It Hot*. He made some few good suggestions which they took on board, but he decided against it and, in 1955, Kay pitched it to Peter Lawford, telling Lawford that he wanted to direct it himself.

Peter Lawford thought that it had great potential and that he could star in it with William Holden. He and his wife Pat each put $5,000 into the project. The Lawfords gave Kay $10,000 for the rights, a decent price as it might generate no interest whatsoever, but the Lawfords had a good feeling about it and *Ocean's 11* was now their property. They knew that the script needed some work as neither Breen nor Kay had been to Vegas.

Sinatra wanted to make a film with his group of friends, not yet called the Rat Pack, but often referred to as the Summit or the Clan, a curious name with Sammy Davis in the group. *Guys and Dolls* would have been perfect – funny, musical, full of colourful characters – but such casting would have distracted from the musical itself. No, a film had to be something less structured that the group could have fun with.

When Peter Lawford told Frank Sinatra of *Ocean's 11*, he was immediately intrigued and offered to purchase it. The Lawfords received $20,000 for the story and 16% of the gross receipts. They were to make $500,000 from a $10,000 investment –that's life, and Gilbert Kay could do nothing about it. Sinatra, who didn't want to jeopardise a box office smash, saw Lawford in one of the supporting roles, not as one of the leads.

Sinatra wanted his own man to direct the film and he picked 64 year old Lewis Milestone, who had made *All Quiet on the Western Front* (1930), *The Front Page* (1931), *Of Mice and Men* (1940) and *Kangaroo* (1952) with Peter Lawford. He was winding down and taking whatever he was offered, which were some episodes of the TV western, *Have Gun – Will Travel* and a Korean war film, *Pork Chop Hill* with Gregory Peck. As far as Sinatra was concerned, Milestone had one huge plus in his favour – unlike most Hollywood directors, he didn't like shooting until 1pm.

But could *Ocean's 11* ever be made? It needed the cooperation of five casinos which would all appear vulnerable to robbery. The plan was for Ocean's 11 to cause a blackout in Vegas and then short-circuit the emergency lighting thus causing the money vaults to open. The police chief for Las Vegas was asked to approve the script for accuracy. Although the film wouldn't expose their real security systems it was close enough and might have given some criminals ideas. Indeed, when Dean Martin was offered the film, he said to Frank, 'To hell with the script, let's pull the job.'

At the end of the 1950s the casinos were in trouble. One complex had shut down and there were a dozen hotels with 2,500 rooms that were not always occupied, especially in winter. It was freezing at Christmas and who except dedicated gamblers would want to go there? The house of cards was in danger of falling down. A film like this, if shot in the off season, could provide much needed free publicity. Frank and Dean both had financial interests in Vegas casinos and so this was to their benefit as well. They could get their own casinos to take part and then persuade their associates who owned the others. As a result, the Sands, the Desert Inn, the Flamingo, the Sahara and the Riviera, all of which were on Route 91, agreed to take part. It is doubtful if anyone other than Frank Sinatra could have put this together. Oddly enough, the main resistance came from the Clark County authorities who did not want their garbage truck to be used for transporting the loot.

Frank Sinatra sold the project to Warners. He was paid $30,000 plus 16% of the gross receipts for the story as well as $200,000 to play Danny Ocean. Dean would receive $150,000 and Sammy $125,000. Until March 1960, the Moulin Rouge was the only casino which permitted black customers and anyway, it was not one of the chosen five. Otherwise, black people were only allowed in the casinos as performers, so Sammy had a demeaning role in the film outside the casinos as a garbage collector.

The body of the cast came from Frank's social circle – Angie Dickinson, Richard Conte, Cesar Romero, Joey Bishop, Red Skelton, George Raft and Shirley MacLaine. Considering that the script called for a gang of war heroes, they have an unlikely jokey, wisecracking, playboy way of pulling the job. Steve McQueen turned down a role because he didn't want to be seen as one of Sinatra's flunkeys. There were bit parts from stars who happened to be in Vegas but Louis Prima and Keely Smith were only seen performing in long shot.

The casinos were told to retain their Christmas and New Year decorations and the filming took place from 26 January to 16 February 1960, normally the lowest point in the Vegas year. The casinos would open as usual and although Joey Bishop had been booked in as the main attraction at the Sands, Jack Entratter suggested that they turned it into a Summit performance with Frank, Dean, Sammy, Peter and Joey performing together every night after the shooting had finished. Milestone should have said no to this millstone as they were in Vegas to make a film but he was Sinatra's man. Sinatra would stand next to Milestone and make suggestions while he was shooting so he was directing by proxy. Milestone didn't seem to mind.

From an historical perspective, it's unfortunate that the five man Sands shows weren't filmed in their own right as they were never to be repeated. In addition, Sinatra and some of the others found time to film guest appearances for a Vegas sequence in *Pepe*, a lavish new film in the style of *Around the World in 80 Days*.and featuring Cantinflas from that film, searching for his horse. Frank gave him a crash course in gambling.

On 7 February, the presidential candidate, John F Kennedy, came to the Copa Room and the casino gave him $1m for his fund. The Rat Pack called him 'Chicky baby' and during the show, Dean Martin took Sammy Davis in his arms and told JFK that this was an award from the National Association for the Advancement of Coloured People. Everybody laughed – today they would do no such thing.

They all performed a personalised 'High Hopes'. Sammy Cahn: 'When we had to write a campaign song, the word 'Kennedy' didn't fit into 'High Hopes', although the title was right. Van Heusen said, "All right, Big Mouth, what are you going to do now?" I said, "There's always a way. Supposing we spell it. Remember 'H-A-double R- I-G-A-N spells Harrigan." He said, "We're trying to elect Kennedy." I said, "I know who we're trying to elect but listen to this." I had, "Just what makes that little ol' ant…" and it became,

"K-E-double N-E-D-Y,
Jack's the nation's favourite guy.
Everyone wants to back Jack,
Jack is on the right track."'

That's the great fun of writing special lyrics.' The funniest line was 'Oops, there goes the opposition, kerplop!'

Frank was with his girlfriend, Juliet Prowse, but he had time to introduce Kennedy to Judy Campbell. She had been Frank's girlfriend but she stopped having sex with him 'because of his kinky taste' (according to her memoir) and she was now dating Sam Giancana, so we have a presidential link to the Mafia. Most people left Vegas considerably lighter than when they arrived but JFK left with $1m and a new girlfriend.

The principals for *Ocean's 11* had a schedule of acting in the afternoon, taking a sauna with gin fizzes, performing two shows in the evening at 8pm and midnight, late night drinking and sleeping through the morning, perhaps with a showgirl to hand. Filming rarely started before 2.30pm and Milestone had to make do with whomever would turn up. Then he would concentrate on the ones who were sober. This is why there are few scenes with the five key players together and why a fair proportion of the script sounds improvised. Frank as usual wanted the first good take to be the only take, saying at one point to Milestone, 'You want two takes? Print it twice!' With such a ridiculous schedule and Milestone having to wrap up at 6pm, the momentum of the plot was lost.

Dean's character like Dean himself was indifferent throughout the film, which led to a curious scene where he encountered Shirley MacLaine, acting way over the top as a drunken reveller. It must have reminded Dean of his times with Jerry Lewis; nevertheless he could make it work. Throughout the filming, Dean was suffering from a hernia and he had surgery when the film was complete.

It wasn't so much about making a movie as having a party. After filming in Las Vegas, the cast and crew returned to Los Angeles and shot the hotel room sequences on the Warners lot with everything wrapped up by the end of March. The original intention had been for Ocean's 11 to get away with the heist but for them to die when their plane crashes, but this was deemed too downbeat. Instead, Richard Conte's character died and the team decided to smuggle the money out of Vegas in his coffin, not knowing that his widow is set on cremation, and so everything went up in smoke. Either way, neither ending was appropriate for what was a daft caper movie.

With three fine singers in leading roles, there should have been more songs. Sinatra didn't sing at all, but Dean as a lounge singer performed the jaunty 'Ain't That a Kick in the Head', both alone at the piano and with Red Norvo's combo. Sammy Davis is given the bluesy 'Eee-O-Eleven', the title being a reference to throwing a 5 and 6 and then joining the dots. Both songs were by Sammy Cahn and Jimmy Van Heusen and a previous success, 'The Tender Trap', is heard in a stripper sequence.

The credits by Saul Bass were tremendous but the first part of the movie was slow and the cast not very engaging. We don't see the best character, the manipulative Duke Santos, played by Cesar Romero, until late in the production. The colour photography by William Daniels was fine – but was he working to his own agenda by making Vegas appear a hellhole? One of the most unlikely scenes, presumably improvised, was when the lead actors talk about what they would do if they were in the White House. Lawford says, perhaps without any prior knowledge, 'Think I'll buy me some votes and go into politics.' There was plenty of cool Rat Pack lingo, the best line coming from the dying Richard Conte who asked, 'Is it the Big Casino?'

Frank, again dishing out favours, asked Patrice Wymore, the widow of the recently deceased Errol Flynn, to be in charge of publicity. She had had a minor role in the film itself and she did a fine job of promoting it. The film premièred at the Fremont Theatre, Las Vegas on 13 August 1960 and, for all its faults or perhaps because of them, it did extremely well commercially. Audiences loved it and many immediately booked holidays in Vegas. *Ocean's 11* sold the city better than any travelogue or advertisement.

The reviews were mixed – the film was criticised for praising lecherous, middle-aged playboys, endlessly smoking and drinking. *The New York Times* said that it provided 'a surprisingly nonchalant and flippant attitude towards crime' which was in keeping with Frank's own personality. Frank couldn't care less what the critics thought, saying, 'Of course it's not a great movie. We're not setting out to make *Hamlet* or *Gone with the Wind*.' Still, *Ocean's 11* was nominated for the Best Comedy by the Writers Guild.

Ocean's 11 was a huge publicity bonanza for Las Vegas and the casinos became cash cows. The Rat Pack had saved Vegas. Lewis Milestone, for all the handicaps, had done well and considering his next film, his last, was Marlon Brando, Trevor Howard and Richard Harris in *Mutiny on the Bounty*, he must have looked back on *Ocean's 11* as a walk in the park.

On 15 February 1960 Frank presented another of his TV specials, this time hosting *Here's to the Ladies* in which he was joined by Lena Horne for a tribute to Harold Arlen, the opera singer Mary Costa, the pianist Barbara Heller, and Juliet Prowse, who paid a tribute to Frank by ballet dancing to 'My Funny Valentine' and by changing 'Come Dance with Me' into 'Come Cha-Cha-Cha with Me'. The programme is best remembered for his toadying interview with Eleanor Roosevelt in which she recited the lyrics of 'High Hopes' – it all helped in election year.

At Fontainebleau in Miami, a girl on a high ledge threatened to jump if she didn't meet Frank Sinatra. Joey Bishop went to his suite and found Frank and Juliet Prowse together. He persuaded Frank to get up and present the girl with some flowers, a signed photograph and tickets for the next show. She didn't jump.

The Execution of Private Slovik was a book written by William Bradford Huie in 1954 about the only soldier to be shot for desertion since the Civil War. Dwight Eisenhower, then US army chief of staff, had agreed his execution. It was a controversial, not to say dangerous, subject for a film. Frank wanted to produce and direct the film version with Steve McQueen in the title role and he hired Alfred Maltz, who had been on the Hollywood blacklist for communist sympathies and was now in Mexico. Frank for once was not being awkward as he knew Maltz, who had written the script for his Oscar-winning short, *The House I Live In*. There was a right wing backlash against this. John Wayne and Ward Bond publicly criticised Frank for hiring him.

Joe Kennedy was furious with Sinatra: how could someone who was associated with his son be so disloyal? He told Frank, 'It's either Maltz or us.' Sinatra dropped the subject, paying Maltz in full. In 1970, Frank sold the options and it was made into a TV movie with Martin Sheen.

Elvis Presley was discharged from the US army in March 1960 and one way to promote his first new single for 18 months could be via *The Ed Sullivan Show*. However, Frank's TV ratings needed a boost and Timex suggested that he should swallow his pride and make an offer to Colonel Parker. Presley knew that Sinatra hadn't changed his views but both could see that such a combination made good commercial sense. Hence, a special edition of *The Frank Sinatra Show* called *Welcome Home, Elvis,* which was taped at the Hotel Fontainebleau in Miami and broadcast on 12 May 1960. The stars had their own spots and they also swapped songs with Frank singing 'Love Me Tender' and Elvis 'Witchcraft', both looking uncomfortable. Frank relayed to Elvis what he has missed while he had been away, which turned out to be his *Only the Lonely* LP and Sammy Davis in *Porgy and Bess*. Peter Lawford, Joey Bishop and Nancy Sinatra contributed to the show with Nelson Riddle conducting, but the show didn't sparkle in the way that it should have done. Someone should have filmed the backstage moment when Joey Bishop asked Elvis for his autograph and Colonel Parker charged $1. Still, the show grabbed 40% of the audience, Frank's highest ever rating.

During the show Frank said, 'Glad to see the Army hasn't changed you, Elvis', when it must have been obvious to everybody else that it had. When Elvis eyed Nancy, Frank said, 'She's spoken for.'

In June 1960 Dean was celebrating his 43rd birthday and he talked to Frank about the Cal-Neva Lodge, which was advertised as 'Heaven in the High Sierra'. Frank had 25% of the stock. Dean had bought 7% but he hadn't known that Giancana had a large stake. Unlike Frank, Dean realised that this could have repercussions on his career and he was thinking of getting out. A few months later, another Mob boss, Lucky told Dean that he was seriously ill but he wanted Dean to play him in a film of his life. Dean wasn't keen on that either and fortunately for Dean, the not so Lucky Luciano died before the talks got too far.

In March and April 1960 Frank had returned to Capitol for sessions with Nelson Riddle which resulted in the album, *Nice 'n' Easy*, an LP of no real theme, just a collection of excellent, mid-tempo numbers, most of which he had sung before. The title track was written by Lew Spence with Alan and Marilyn Bergman. Lew Spence had played the song to Sinatra when he was making *Ocean's 11*, but he wasn't impressed, possibly because he didn't do anything Nice 'n' Easy. Now if only the song was called 'Impetuousity', he'd have been listening. Hank Sanicola told him that he was wrong: this was excellent material and perfect for him. The recording ended with a humorous coda from Frank, and there are other takes with off-colour codas instead. Frank performed the song in concert with a glass of Jack Daniel's and the band would never know how he would end it. It was a chart hit in both Britain and America.

The original intention had been to call the album, *The Nearness of You*, and Frank did record a superb version of this Hoagy Carmichael standard which was not used on the LP. The standards that did make the cut included 'That Old Feeling', 'How Deep Is the Ocean'. 'Fools Rush In' and 'Try a Little Tenderness'. Note how low Frank's last note was on 'You

Got to My Head' and marvel at the mix of Frank's voice and Felix Slatkin's violin on 'She's Funny That Way'. The album may have lacked the theme of his others but it was a superb work released in August 1960 and topping the US album charts for 9 weeks and becoming the biggest selling album of Sinatra's career.

The bass trombone on 'How Deep Is The Ocean' was played by George Roberts who was featured in many of Nelson Riddle's arrangements. Usually for the instrument, he played throughout 'Days Of Wine And Roses' (1964) and he did record two solo albums, *Meet Mr Roberts* and *Bottoms Up*, in 1960. His instrument was combined with Tommy Johnson's tuba for the notes when the shark made its first appearance in *Jaws* (1975).

Frank recorded 'River Stay 'Way from My Door', a curious song about someone worried about flooding but being philosophical about it. Harry Woods had written the song in 1931 and it had been successful for the Boswell Sisters and Paul Robeson. Sinatra's intentions were written all over this. He said to Nelson Riddle, 'Let's show Bobby Darin who the boss is.' It sounded like a companion to 'Beyond the Sea', but it didn't fare as well making the UK Top 20 but only No.82 in the US.

Not to be outdone, Buddy Greco took Sinatra's signature song, 'The Lady Is a Tramp' and gave it a smart new finger-snapping treatment that became a best-selling single. He said, 'I was working in a little place in Chicago and my brother was really the singer in the band and he got laryngitis one night. I've always been a rebel, whether it's been in my personal life, musically or whatever, and I thought, "What can I do that is really catchy that Sinatra or nobody else has done? I know what I'll do. I'll take the first couple of lines and go, 'That's why, that's why, the lady, That's why, that's why, the lady is a tramp.'" It caught on. Through the years when I went to see Sinatra and Sammy and Lena and Tony and they knew I was in the audience, they would go "That's why, that's why, the lady" as a tribute to me, which was very nice.'

Frank had to come to terms with rock'n'roll when his daughter Nancy started dating Tommy Sands. Tommy Sands had been born in Chicago in 1937 and he came to popularity with his appearance as a rock'n'roll star in a TV play, *The Singin' Idol*, in 1957 which led to a US No.2 with 'Teen-Age Crush', on Capitol, when the word was so new it was written like that. Sands had further hits with 'Goin' Steady' (1957) and 'Sing Boy Sing', the title song from a movie in which he'd starred. When a writer for the *New York Herald Tribune* in August 1958 suggested to Tommy Sands that any teenager would gladly change places with him, he replied with unexpected candour: 'I suppose you're right but they are not with me when I get up in the morning and face that terrible insecurity. I look in the mirror and say to myself, "You aren't the greatest actor or singer in the world. What are you? Nothing."'

Tommy Sands drifted along the Bobby Darin trail with 'Sinner Man' and he worked with Nelson Riddle on the ballad albums, *When I'm Thinkin' of You* (1959) and *Dream with Me* (1960). He told me, 'I met Nancy Sinatra about 1960. She came to a concert of mine at the Coconut Grove in Los Angeles and a friend of mine was with her that night. He brought her back to introduce her to me and it was love at first sight for both of us.'

Tommy Sands and Nancy Sinatra were married in September 1960 and Frank gave Nancy away. He made his début in Las Vegas at the Sands, leading to the album, *Sands at the Sands* (1960), but what did Frank make of his records? 'Well, he was always so nice to me; he was a great father-in-law. He was non-intrusive and didn't butt into our business and he didn't tell me how to do things. I can't say enough good things about him. I liked him a lot. Frankly it didn't interest me whether he liked my records or not. I wanted him to like me and I know I liked him. That was what was important.'

In August 1960 Sinatra had further recording sessions with Nelson Riddle at Capitol for an album which would be called *Sinatra's Swingin' Session!!!* Although Frank was recording for Capitol under sufferance, he was on fine form, but he had decided that he was only going to give Capitol the bare minimum. Instead of reprising verses and choruses, Frank would only go through each song once, hence the 12-track album only lasted 26 minutes. The producer, Dave Cavanaugh, could not stop him because he was not technically violating his contract and anyway, Frank would have enjoyed the opportunity to walk out. It wouldn't have occurred to Sinatra, but should have done, that the real losers were the very fans who bought his records.

Still, there was plenty to enjoy on *Sinatra's Swingin' Session!!!* Nelson Riddle had written imaginative arrangements and Sinatra was in fine, if abbreviated, form. The album was very fast, very jazzy and very swinging and even the ballads bounced along. Just take the opening cut, 'When You're Smiling', where Sinatra throws in a terrific impersonation of Louis Prima. There was a beautiful version of Irving Berlin's 'Always' and Sinatra later said, 'When a man writes a song and says, "Not for just an hour, not for just a day, not for just a year, but always", that's as simple and as pure as anybody can write.' Frank rang Nelson Riddle one afternoon at 3pm and said, 'I want to do 'Blue Moon' tonight.' Nelson wrote a fine arrangement in a couple of hours and they recorded it that evening.

As well as the album tracks, Sinatra recorded two songs from Lew Spence and the Bergmans. 'Sentimental Baby' was a deliberate but successful attempt to write a song in the Dorsey tradition. The other was the hit single, 'Old MacDonald', of which the jazz critic Gene Lees said, "'Old MacDonald' told us that Sinatra was a man of great arrogance. It said, "I'm so big and I'm so great that I can make a hit out of anything, even something as lousy as 'Old MacDonald'."' I disagree. It was another attempt by Sinatra to emulate Bobby Darin. In March 1960, Darin had made the charts with a swinging, swaggering 'Clementine', the Huckleberry Hound song, and Sinatra wanted to take another children's song and have some of Darin's success. Nelson was up to the challenge but he was going to start with an orchestral introduction. 'No, no,' said Sinatra, 'just the rhythm section.' Nelson was a little nonplussed but he had to concede that Sinatra was right. 'Old MacDonald' was a record to make people laugh – and it worked, except for Gene Lees. Around the same time, Bo Diddley reworked 'Ol' MacDonald' as 'Hey! Bo Diddley'.

One of the oddest songs that Sinatra recorded was 'Hidden Persuasion', written by the sociologist Wainwright Churchill but perhaps Frank was thinking of Dean when he came to the line, 'Your charming indifference is but a disguise'.

Throughout the year, Frank had been campaigning for John F Kennedy. Kennedy did spend a little time with Sinatra in Palm Springs when Jackie was away. According to Richard Burton's diaries, 'The place was like a whorehouse with Kennedy as chief customer. Christ, the chances those fellers took.'

Sinatra did whatever he could to help. Off his own bat, he asked a private investigator to check Nixon's activities, obtaining evidence that he was seeing a psychiatrist. He gave the report to Joe Kennedy who sat on it. If the Kennedys were to throw dirt at Nixon, there was a lot worse that Nixon could throw at them.

When Frank and Sammy appeared at the Democratic National Convention together, they sang 'Star Spangled Banner' and as some delegates booed Sammy, the delegates were not as democratic as their name suggested.

An even bigger problem was mounting. Sammy had fallen in love with the beautiful Swedish actress May Britt, who had been discovered by Carlo Ponti in 1952. She had come to the US for *War and Peace* in 1956 and she had appeared with Dean Martin in *The Young Lions*. Dino had tried to hit on her but for once, his Latin charm didn't work as she didn't believe in casual flings with married men. She dated Sammy who told the press, 'Her name is pronounced "My" and I say, "My, my", every time I see her.'

Sammy and May planned to get married with Frank as best man. Such a marriage would have been against the law in 31 states. Sammy didn't think that it was a problem or if it was, his stardom would rise about it. Joe Kennedy told Sinatra to stop it as this could lose the party votes and even cost Jack the presidency. Sinatra told Sammy and May to delay the wedding and it was deferred until after the election.

One of Sinatra's biographers, Richard Havers, says, 'Frank Sinatra was becoming a millstone around the Kennedys' necks. The Rat Pack and politics made sense while Kennedy was the candidate but it should have been clear to Sinatra that it wasn't going to mix if Kennedy became President.'

As much as Frank wanted to be involved in the presidential campaign, he had to work and he was committed to flying to Maui, Hawaii in October 1960 to make *The Devil at 4 O'Clock*. It was an early example of a disaster movie, costing $5m, the same as *The Guns of Navarone*, though the characters are more rounded than the ones usually in disaster movies.

The Devil at 4 O'Clock was based on a novel by Max Catto but it's one thing to write about a disaster and quite another to film it. A whole village had to be built and then destroyed. The film was produced and directed by Mervyn LeRoy, who as a child had lived through the San Francisco earthquake in 1906.

Frank knew Spencer Tracy from his time with Humphrey Bogart and was keen to work with him. He was happy to give him top billing although Frank was the bigger draw. The fee of $600,000 (12% of the budget!) might have had something to do with it.

Father Doonan (Spencer Tracy) is a missionary who had wanted to build a hospital for children with leprosy but the residents thought that this would affect tourism and so he could only build it in the mountains and, as it happens, rather too close to a volcano. Over the years, Father Doonan had setbacks and at the start of the film, he's seen as a drunken, disillusioned priest who has lost his faith.

Frank Sinatra played a prisoner who had brought in to help him. We don't know why he was doing time but we did see him steal from a poor box and take advantage of a blind girl. He married the girl and then he gradually emerged as a decent person. Indeed, both Tracy and Sinatra found redemption by sacrificing themselves to save others. Sinatra said to him, 'Just you and me, pops, New Jersey and New York.'

Sinatra was able to undertake some campaigning while making the film. In the morning he would go round the islands with Peter Lawford in his private plane and then return for the shoot. Tracy was amazed by his lack of sleep and indeed it was Tracy who caused the real problems as he had a lung condition. Tracy took time off to attend Clark Gable's funeral.

At first Sinatra was fine. He liked Tracy and he liked working with children and when LeRoy turned 60, he threw a party for him and had Sammy Cahn write special lyrics. As everyone called Sinatra 'Mr S', Tracy insisted on being 'Mr T'. Unfortunately he and Tracy fell out, probably some drunken row, and then Tracy referred to him only as 'the other fella'. Most of all Mr T realised that Mr S was not very professional. At one point Tracy had to do his death scene without Mr S around. He did it by talking to a stick with a cap on. Tracy said, 'That's it. We can't get it any better with that son of a bitch.'

The Maui shoot wrapped up on 1 November, and Sinatra went straight to a Dean Martin TV special arriving late, but he and Dean worked happily together without rehearsal. There was some further studio work on *The Devil at 4 O'Clock* but Tracy never wanted to see the rushes as he didn't want to look at his ageing features on a large screen. He and Sinatra made it up, possibly because Frank was hoping he could get him a cameo in *Judgment at Nuremberg*, which Tracy was making in 1961.

The special effects in *The Devil at 4 O'Clock* were very good but the film was too long and the trek from the mountains went on forever. Nevertheless, the film was Tracy's biggest success since *Father of the Bride* (1950) but it only did moderately well. It became a TV favourite with the years.

Two days before the election, Jack Kennedy came to Palm Springs and stayed with Sinatra. Sinatra later put up a plaque that he had slept there but wanted to add 'and numerous whores'.

The media built up the Kennedys as though they were America's Royal Family. They had wealth and glamour and the public loved them. Kennedy had a structured mind and came across as youthful and efficient. He had a monotonous voice but somehow he got away with it.

With his full head of hair and square-cut face, there was a Hollywood film star image about Jack Kennedy. This was borne out in a TV debate where his Republican opponent, Richard Nixon had a five o'clock shadow and looked sinister, although Kennedy in reality was just as slippery. Privately, Dean Martin was unimpressed: 'Any country that has to choose between Nixon and Kennedy is in bad shape.' It was a victory for Kennedy but Joe, ever the schemer, did say to Nixon, 'If my boy can't make it, I'm for you.'

His boy did make it, though election night was a close call. When it looked as though Kennedy was going to win, Sinatra called Richard Nixon's office and asked to be put through. He wanted him to concede defeat. He told the switchboard, 'Don't you know who this is? This is Frank Sinatra and I want to talk to Richard Nixon.' He wasn't connected. No matter as Nixon soon gave way and Kennedy had won by a slender margin. At the age of 43, the 35th President of the United States was the youngest to date. Jack and Jacqui's second child, John, was born a few days later as if to emphasise how young the President was. In his inaugural address, Kennedy referred to the torch being passed to a new generation. His brother, Bobby, who had never been in a court room, was appointed Attorney General.

Frank Sinatra had heard Vic Damone with some swinging arrangements at the Sands and he asked him about the arranger. He was 35-year-old Johnny Mandel, a jazz based musician who had been strongly influenced by Billy May and he had written and arranged the score for the prison drama, *I Want To Live!* (1958). Mandel went to see him when he was filming *The Devil at Four O'Clock* to discuss the songs for his first Reprise album, which, in keeping with his Rat Pack persona, would be called *Ring-A-Ding-Ding!* The soft-spoken Sonny Burke was to produce most of his Reprise sessions. The album was recorded over three days in LA, just before Christmas, but as Mandel had not completed his arrangements in time, two of the songs were arranged by Skip Martin and Dick Reynolds.

Frank had no intention of ringing the changes on his first Reprise album and indeed *Ring-A Ding Ding!* is surprisingly similar to *Sinatra's Swingin' Session!!!* Perhaps he just wanted to show that he could do it better at Reprise, but the casual listener certainly would not be able to differentiate which track belonged to which album. Frank had a dog called Ring-A Ding Ding, who was constantly soiling his neighbour's garden in Mulholland Drive, Santa Monica, the neighbour being Peggy Lee.

As with so many of his Capitol albums, Frank asked Sammy Cahn and Jimmy Van Heusen for a title song. Frank often used the expression, particularly on *The Red Skelton Show* where 'Ring-a-ding ding' had been substituted for the punchline of a risqué joke. It was another wedding song, although it was meant to be celebrating the bachelor life style. The lyric is okay, but the melody could have been stronger. Emil Richards' wide selection of chimes and bells was impressive but when he used his chimes to replicate Big Ben on 'A Foggy

Day (In London Town)', it's corny.

One of the great moments on the album is when Sinatra sings the little-known introductory verse to 'Let's Fall in Love' and then pauses. The song itself comes in as a delightful surprise. Johnny Mandel commented, 'One good example of his musicality was to have the two bar break after the verse on 'Let's Fall in Love'. The verse of that song never usually gets done. He suggested the break, right off the cuff, and he was totally right.'

There are superb versions of 'Let's Face the Music and Dance' and 'In the Still of the Night'. You get Sinatra's hip phrasing on 'I've Got My Love to Keep Me Warm' where he sings staccato lyrics which assume that the listeners know what the words are. There are some odd pronunciations in 'A Fine Romance' but this is a fun song. The most underrated song on the album is a re-run of Bob Hilliard and Dick Myles' witty 'The Coffee Song', kitted out with a pulsating rhumba beat.

When Jimmy Stewart sang 'You'd Be So Easy to Love' in the film, *Born to Dance* (1936), Cole Porter noted, 'He sings far from well, although he has nice notes in his voice.' Stewart couldn't reach the high notes but had an aw, shucks personality that enabled him to get away with it. Sinatra gave the song a gently swinging arrangement. Both Frank and Dean loved to mimic Jimmy Stewart and the way he often repeated syllables, rather like Elvis.

Frank recorded but discarded 'Have You Met Miss Jones', a song written to introduce two characters in Rodgers and Hart's *I'd Rather Be Right* (1937). It is given a lovely slow arrangement by Mandel but Sinatra says on the session tapes, 'This sounds like a different album. This doesn't belong on an album called *Ring-A-Ding-Ding!*' The song was later used to describe a fictional Miss Jones in *Bridget Jones' Diary* (2001). At the other end of the scale, Sinatra decided that 'Zing! Went The Strings of My Heart' was too fast for the album.

In 2013 *Ring-A-Ding-Ding!* was reissued in a 2CD package with the second disc consisting of outtakes. There is an alternative performance for every song thereby dispelling the notion that Frank invariably recorded only one take. However, for this album, he didn't need to go further than Take 4. The conversation is revealing as he is in good humour, displaying a strong and keen knowledge of what he wants and he is very much in charge. The good humour could stem from the fact that Kennedy had won the election.

As well as the album, Frank recorded two new Cahn and Van Heusen songs, one being the underrated 'The Last Dance' with a neat twist on a familiar theme ('Save me the first dance in your dreams tonight'). The other was the classic, 'The Second Time Around', one of the first songs for the over-40s, with its epigrammatic line, 'Love like youth is wasted on the young.'

Sammy Cahn said, "'The Second Time Around' is one of the most important songs I've written, because when people say to me, "You've written my song", they invariably mean 'The Second Time Around". It is a hymn of hope for failed romance or whatever. That song was written for the film, *High Time*, in which Bing Crosby plays a widower who has achieved everything in life. He goes back to college and he meets a French teacher who's a widow. I said to Van Heusen, "What are we going to write for a widower and a widow? 'I'm glad that you're dead, You rascal you.' 'You'll be the death of me'." We kicked around some funny titles and I said to him, "Are we going to be the only team that couldn't come up with a ballad for Bing Crosby? What do you think of the title, 'The Second Time Around'? "Love is wonderful the second time around, Just as beautiful with both feet on the ground." He said, "No, 'Love is lovelier the second time around, Just as wonderful with both feet on the ground'." The song was then written very quickly. We sang it to Bing Crosby and he just nodded. The great, great artists know that you are doing your part, so it is very simple to write for them.'

The song resonated with Van Heusen too who was hoping to impress and marry Shirley MacLaine, but it didn't happen. Shirley also had her Sam Giancana stories. She once pulled out a toy water pistol and Giancana had reached for his gun. Giancana once insisted that she had pasta. Sammy Davis said, 'Go easy on her. She's on a diet' and Giancana hit him in the stomach.

Sam Giancana had thought he was being offered a 'get out of jail free card'. He had done as Joe Kennedy requested and he thought he would not be pursued for Mafia activities. Who knows if this *quid pro quo* was really given, but it didn't mean anything as Bobby Kennedy as Attorney General, was to come down heavily on the Mob. From then on, Giancana referred to Bobby as the 'little punk' and Sinatra as the 'piece of shit'. He told Sinatra, 'I don't know how you are still living.'

CHAPTER 12

War games

'In the stormy east-wind straining,
The pale-yellow woods were waning,
The broad stream in his banks complaining,
Heavily the low sky raining.'

Alfred Lord Tennyson, The Lady Of Shalott, 1842

I. The Sound of Middle-Aged America

1960 had been one of Frank Sinatra's busiest years: indeed, he was never happier than when he had several projects on the go. The film, *Can-Can*, was a major success and he had made his first Rat Pack film, *Ocean's 11*. He had returned to the charts with 'Ol' MacDonald' and had made the biggest album of his career with *Nice 'n' Easy*. Throughout the year, he had played a significant, not to say crucial, role in the election of President Kennedy. Yes, it was a very good year.

Against all this was a backcloth of Frank Sinatra establishing his own record company, Reprise. It was an open secret with rumours and rumblings in the music press for most of the year and it was officially announced in December 1960. Sinatra had started the company because he was so annoyed with his royalty rates at Capitol and he hadn't been able to renegotiate his contract to what he wanted. So his plan was to get out as quickly as he could and establish his own independent label.

Oddly enough, it was the very success of Capitol Records that gave him the encouragement to start Reprise. Capitol had been started by the film producer Buddy DeSylva, the songwriter Johnny Mercer and the record store owner Glenn Wallichs. They hadn't planned it this way but 1942 had been the worst time to start a record company. America had joined the war and the availability of shellac had been much reduced. Would there still be customers for records and could they even be made as the American Federation of Musicians had called a strike? Capitol made some bad business decisions but they made a major right one: unlike the other record companies, the label realised that constant radioplay would not deter potential purchasers but actually encourage them.

The three executives knew that these bad times wouldn't last unless the Allies somehow lost the war. They decided that if they made quality records the public would come to them, and so they signed Nat 'King' Cole, George Shearing, Dean Martin and Peggy Lee. Frank Sinatra joined them in 1953 when LPs were the growing trend. They decided to release many concept albums with well-chosen covers to match. Their sales dipped during the rock'n'roll era but they still fared well in the new teenage market with Gene Vincent, Tommy Sands and the Kingston Trio.

By the mid-50s Capitol was no longer an independent label. It had grown to be one of the biggest labels in the country with its own huge head office (the Capitol Tower), its own recording studios and its own pressing plant. In 1955, the British company EMI paid $8m for a 95% controlling interest in Capitol. Glenn Wallichs stayed on as the president of the company and although he had his arguments with Sinatra, Frank was still immensely impressed with all Wallichs had achieved.

Sinatra had the money to start Reprise and the disc jockey William B Williams called him 'The Chairman of the Board', which stuck. Although he spent excessively, he had been in the Top Ten of highest earning movie stars for five years.

Initially Frank Sinatra had set up Reprise for himself investing $200,000 of his own money. He would be able to determine what he would sing and with whom he would record and so he would have complete artistic control over his product. He had extreme confidence in himself and his ability to make records that the public would want to buy. Provided he could get the distribution and the sales right, he would make considerably more money from his hit records than at Capitol. Because of distribution deals, he also knew that he needed a regular stream of releases to make the label work and when he told Dean Martin and Sammy Davis Jr, they both wanted to join him. Frank promised them, as he did to all his artists, higher royalty rates and the rights to own those recordings after a certain period of time. This was extremely generous and really came down to his altruistic decision not to profit from his friends.

Sinatra said that he did not want to stifle creativity which meant that artists who felt hemmed in at their current labels were anxious to join. He intended the packaging to be different and, years ahead of his time, he was even talking about different coloured vinyl, although this didn't happen at Reprise.

During 1960 he had been signing up his first artists and the first sessions were with the jazz saxophonist Ben Webster, whom he had enticed away from Norman Granz's Verve. In December 1960, he recorded his first album for the label, *Ring-a-Ding-Ding!*, and his first single, neatly titled, 'The Second Time Around', and coupled with a song for his young daughter, 'Tina'.

Outside of Frank Sinatra's own releases, the Reprise catalogue for the first year in business was impressive, although there were no big sellers. The most popular were Sammy Davis's *The Wham of Sam!* (great title) and *Sammy Davis Jr Belts the Best of Broadway*. His version of 'Thou Swell', arranged and conducted by Marty Paich, was up there with the best of Sinatra.

There were blues albums from Al Hibbler, Mance Lipscomb and Jimmy Witherspoon. Mavis Rivers, released a couple of albums that were as close as you get to Ella Fitzgerald and there were jazz LPs from trumpeter Jack Sheldon and pianist Calvin Jackson. There were albums of gospel music and Israeli hits. There were novelty performances from Lou Monte and Soupy Sales, a solo album from Tony Williams of the Platters, a twist collection from Aki Aleong and his Licorice Twisters and stand-up from Joe E Lewis and Mort Sahl. In 1962, Reprise issued an LP about space exploration with the astronaut John H Glenn. Most of them were within Frank's own sphere of interest, although Soupy Sales was included because Tina was such a fan. Back in the UK, the jazz musician Monty Babson told the *NME* that he was joining Reprise. Although it didn't happen, it shows that Sinatra was casting his net wide.

Reprise released 40 singles in 1961 and they were a very diverse collection, though many of them were used to promote albums. The first single was an instrumental 'Big Mr C', a tribute to Ray Charles from the Link Eddy Combo, which made the R&B charts. Although it meant nothing in sales terms, Sammy Davis released a sensational and even better tribute to Ray Charles, 'One More Time'. In June 1961, Frank attended a recording session for Ray Charles and Betty Carter, which might suggest that he was hoping to capture Ray for

Reprise. It's surprising too that he didn't pick up on Betty Carter whose career was otherwise in limbo at the time.

Mo Ostin had originally said 'No rock'n'roll', which was in line with Frank's thoughts and would give the label an identity, albeit an old-fashioned one. However, Nancy wanted to make records and they realised she might be successful in the Annette vein, hence her first single, 'Cuff-Links and a Tie Clip'. It wasn't really nepotism as she clearly had the ability to make hit singles and she was unlucky to miss out with 'Like I Do' in 1962. Reprise signed the rock'n'roll singer Dorsey Burnette, the Chiffons and Danny Kaye with a tongue-twisting song for the LA baseball team, Dodgers.

Dean Martin was out of his Capitol contract at the end of 1961. His agent Herman Citron had suggested that he formed his own Claude Productions and then lease the tapes to Reprise for release. His first recording for Reprise was an Italian song, 'Senza Fine'.

Buddy Greco recalls, 'When I left Columbia, Frank asked me if I would join his label. At the time he had signed Keely Smith and Sammy and Dean. I was overwhelmed and I said, "Oh my god, of course I will, what a thrill." I joined his label for about two years. Most of the people he signed were his friends so it was something special. You had more freedom on Reprise. In a sense, I became the A&R man and the arranger, which is what I really wanted to do. A song I remember from that period was 'Girl Talk'. I still do that every night as I get so many requests for it. Neal Hefti and Bobby Troup were wonderful musicians. Bobby Troup wrote a lot of wonderful songs and Neal is a great arranger that both Sinatra and Basie used. I was totally surprised when they gave me that song. When I first sang it, I knew it was wonderful material and it's about my favourite subject – I love women!'

But by the end of 1962 Reprise was a sinking ship. The label had an impressive roster but many of the releases were too specialist to become best sellers. All this would have been okay if Sinatra himself was having big sellers, but he wasn't. Alan Livingston at Capitol had decided that he could, at long last, teach him a lesson. Capitol had forced Sinatra to record new tracks in 1961 and they had a back catalogue of several hundred tracks. They could release one single after another which would act as spoilers for his new Reprise singles.

In 1961 Frank made five albums – three for Reprise and two for Capitol – but that wasn't all. Budget-priced albums were in their infancy and didn't usually feature big names. Livingston flooded the market with cheap Sinatra product with decent packaging so that listeners would be totally confused as to which were the new releases, although the price of $2.98 was a giveaway in more ways than one. Some of Capitol's albums were very attractive, including compilations by songwriter, and they did impact on Sinatra's new releases. In the UK, for example, Capitol released a series of 10 four-track EPs, devoted to songwriters, such as *Frank Sinatra Sings Jimmy McHugh*.

Alan Livingston remarked that the lawyers had a field day and that 'Frank Sinatra was the worst enemy you could possibly have. People said I was going to get my knees broken.' In 1962 Livingston met Sinatra in a dressing-room when he was making a TV special with Judy Garland, then a Capitol artist. Frank turned his back to him.

As it turned out, the budget albums were good for Sinatra in the long run as many record-buyers picked up on his work through cheap LPs and became fans for life, myself included.

Instead of aggro, Sinatra should have decided to record only new material or songs that he had never done before but he didn't – he often cut old favourites and so it's little wonder that the public were confused. What's more, if he had found some great new songs (not too difficult – he was after all Frank Sinatra), he could have had hit singles and then named the albums after the hits.

There had been hundreds of independent record labels prior to Reprise but Reprise was one of the earliest of the artist-owned companies. His move encouraged others including Herb Alpert (with Jerry Moss) with A&M, the Beatles with Apple, the Moody Blues with Threshold and Led Zeppelin with Swan Song.

II. Day In–Day Out, 1961–1963

Frank Sinatra was always a juggler. He rarely concentrated on one aspect of his life and for most of the time, he was recording, broadcasting, performing and making films, often involved in production. He could be dating several women at the same time and at the start of 1961, he wanted to be best friends with the President of America. Although numerous factors were at play, he certainly believed that his actions had swung the election and he had got Kennedy into the White House. He was a bit suspicious of Kennedy as he was, when all was said and done, a 'Mick', but this also worked in reverse. Dean Martin saw what Frank was too blind to see: Italians were not welcome in Camelot. Kennedy knew that Sinatra operated in the dangerous but highly enticing world of playboys and playgirls, not to mention the Mafia.

Although Frank was officially an item with Juliet Prowse, his latest flame was the unpredictable and highly strung film actress, Marilyn Monroe. Frank loved her beauty but was unsure about her vulnerability, telling her at one party, 'Toughen up, baby, or get the hell out. I ain't no babysitter.' She did, however, disappear one day and Frank went to find her, thinking she might have had another breakdown. It was nothing dramatic as she had only gone shopping. As a result, Frank missed lunch with the President.

The meeting was over the planning for the Inaugural Ball in Washington on 19 January 1961. Frank was executive producer, calling in favours and inviting star names wherever they happened to be working. Ella Fitzgerald came from Australia, Sidney Poitier from France, and Gene Kelly from Switzerland. Frank even reached an arrangement with the Broadway production of *Gypsy* to enable Ethel Merman to come to Washington for the day. The *New York Times* called it 'the most stunning assembly of theatrical talent ever brought together for a single show.'

It would have been even better if the weather hadn't been so dreadful – heavy snow and blizzards, and traffic at a standstill. Several performers and many guests didn't make the ball; Sammy Davis hadn't been invited. Despite the bad weather, the Inaugural Ball was an immense success, raising $1.5m for the Democrat's funds when they had a deficit of $4m.

Peter Lawford was overseeing what Sinatra was doing and when he had criticised the running order Frank had walked out, saying, 'Let the fucking Englishman sing 'The House I Live In'.' Sinatra did perform 'The House I Live In' as well as a new song, 'Walking Down To Washington', arranged by Nelson Riddle and conducted by Leonard Bernstein.

The next day was Inauguration Day itself. Kennedy, inspired by Churchill's 'We shall fight them on the beaches' speech, said, 'We shall pay any price, bear any burden, meet any hardship, support any friend, oppose any foe , in order to assure the survival and the success of liberty.' At one point Kennedy excused himself to visit Sinatra's private party at the Hilton, no doubt to assure the survival and the success of liberty.

Sammy Davis was back with Frank and Dean for an appearance at the Southern Christian Leadership Conference at Carnegie Hall. This was to mark Martin Luther King's release from prison in Georgia for a non-violent demonstration without a permit, which had been organised by Harry Belafonte. King was moved to tears when he heard Sinatra sing 'Ol' Man River', which he was now singing better than ever.

Then the battle between Capitol and Reprise began in earnest. Capitol issued 'The

Moon Was Yellow' at the same time as the first Reprise single, 'The Second Time Around'. 'The Second Time Around' made No.50 but in view of its standing today, it should have done much better. Capitol issued two albums, *Sinatra's Swingin' Session!!!* and *All The Way* while Reprise offered *Ring-a-Ding-Ding!* All were Top 10 albums with the Reprise album doing best at No.3.

Despite this conflict, Sinatra was still required to complete his contract for Capitol. He made a new album with Billy May, *Come Swing with Me!* It was formed in the main from big band remakes of old favourites but without saxophones and strings – 'Yes Indeed', 'American Beauty Rose', 'Almost Like Being in Love' and 'Day by Day' – so no wonder one track was called 'I've Heard That Song Before'. Actually, Frank hadn't recorded 'I've Heard That Song Before' before.

There is an exhilarating four-minute version of 'That Old Black Magic' which Frank had been singing as 'That Old Jack Magic'. Notice how Frank deliberately goes 'You (pause) are the lover.' The song had been a US hit for Glenn Miller and his Orchestra (1943), Sammy Davis (1955) and Louis Prima and Keely Smith (1958), but it would be Bobby Rydell, copying Bobby Darin, who would return it to the charts in 1961.

Although 'Paper Doll' was a huge success for the Mills Brothers in 1943, the sheet music placed Frank Sinatra on the cover along with the caption, 'Featured by Frank Sinatra, the voice that is thrilling millions'. This, 18 years later, was his first studio recording of 'Paper Doll' and the introduction suggests that this should not to be dismissed as a lightweight composition. In a way it is the first hit song about a lads' mag.

At the same time and even on the same day, Frank was recording a new album for Reprise, *I Remember Tommy*, a tribute to Tommy Dorsey with arrangements from Sy Oliver. The album started magnificently with Dorsey's signature tune, 'I'm Getting Sentimental over You' taken slowly and beautifully, and this was followed a very strong performance of 'Imagination'. The main difference from the Dorsey originals was Frank was now centre stage and not confined to a one minute vocal. There was a poignant 'Without a Song' with the bass trombone playing behind Sinatra throughout. It's good to hear the lesser-known 'Take Me', although it sounded like a 1920s operetta and it was odd that Frank didn't reprise 'I'll Never Smile Again'.

Since Tommy Dorsey's days, 'I'll Be Seeing You' had become popular as Liberace's mawkish signature tune, but Frank told Sy Oliver, 'Tommy said "Swing it, Buster", so we swung it." Frank emphasises the point by singing "I will dig you in the early bright."

In an interview to promote the album, Frank was asked what he had learnt from Tommy Dorsey and said, 'To treat every record as if it's the last song I'll ever sing.' For all I criticise Sinatra for reworking his old songs, this album clearly hit a nerve as it had advance orders of 200,000 and reached No.3 on the album charts.

The release of *I Remember Tommy* was held up until November 1961 and not just for the reason of picking up seasonal sales. Frank knew that Capitol was to release *Come Swing With Me!* on 14 August 1961 and as Billy May was out of his Capitol commitments by May 1961, he asked him to conduct and arrange a new set for Reprise which he would call *Swing Along With Me*. Childish, or what? Capitol objected as this sounded too close to their title and Reprise was forced to change it to *Sinatra Swings*. Both were Top 10 albums with *Sinatra Swings* doing slightly better, but these were expensive days for Sinatra devotees.

For the first time, Sinatra recorded the Gershwin's 'Love Walked In'. It was a glorious recording but no doubt Ira was irritated by Sinatra's padding of 'Love walked right in'. The very lively 'Please Don't Talk About Me When I'm Gone' found Frank adding, 'Dig this. Not a word about me when I'm gone' There was a very bright 'You're Nobody Till Somebody

Loves You', although Frank simply sang the refrain three times. The Notorious B.I.G. must have known this song to come up with 'You're Nobody (Til Somebody Kills You)' and, in 2013, James Arthur had the audacity to release a new song called, 'You're Nobody 'Til Somebody Loves You',

Frank was enjoying the sessions adding 'It's a ring-a-ding world loving wonderful you' to 'It's a Wonderful World' and "My little Hindu!" to "Moonlight on the Ganges'. Maybe it's just as well that 'Moonlight on the Ganges' is largely a showcase for Billy May. At the end of 'Granada', the band shouts 'cha-cha-cha'. 'The Curse of an Aching Heart' harked back to his days with the Hoboken Four, while 'I Never Knew' was a success for Gene Austin from 1926. 'Don't Cry Joe' was another excellent track, sounding like the advice the barman might have given Frank if he'd a speaking role in 'One for My Baby'.

There appears to be no particular reason for it but Sinatra didn't make another complete album with Billy May until 1979. May did however make an album with Ethel Merman for Reprise and worked for the Reprise Repertory Company in 1963.

On 7 June 1961 Frank was at the Sands and hosting a party for Dean's 44th birthday. The manager of the Sands, Jack Entratter, send two memos to his staff. Firstly, 'Miss Monroe will be registered in Mr Sinatra's suite. Under no circumstances is she or Mr Sinatra to be disturbed by telephone calls or visitors before 2pm.'

Fair enough, but how about this one? 'Under no circumstances is any backstage photographer permitted to photograph Mr Sinatra and Miss Marilyn Monroe together at the cocktail reception to follow the performance on 7 June. This is not only a Sands requirement: it is a requirement of Mr Sinatra himself.'

The party was a lavish affair with a guest list including Elizabeth Taylor and Eddie Fisher. Marilyn was so entranced by the guests that she found a photographer and asked him to take some shots. The photographer was attacked as soon as Frank saw him.

In the summer of 1961 Joe and Rose Kennedy hosted a cruise on the Riviera with Frank, Peter and Pat Lawford and Jimmy Van Heusen among the guests. The highlight would be a charity performance for Princess Grace by Frank at the International Red Cross Ball in Monaco. Along the way, they met Dean who had a singing engagement in Frankfurt on 7 August.

Although married, Dean had picked up a new date along the way, but when they all attended a cocktail party, Peter Lawford ignored Pat and left early with the girl. Both Frank and Dean thought this was inexcusable behaviour: you didn't take a fella's girl like that. On a whim, Frank decided to leave the cruise and go to Frankfurt and meet up with Dean and be an unbilled attraction on his show. The charity, through no fault of its own, was left floundering, but fortunately Sammy was arriving for the show and rose to the challenge.

During the cruise, Peter and Pat Lawford learnt that their daughter Robin, who had been born in July, was choking and had been rushed to hospital. They decided not to cut the trip short. Three days later, the baby was admitted to hospital with abdominal pains and then they returned home. The press got wind of this but they didn't respond to the negative publicity. In August, Peter Lawford was back in France to film his role as an aristocrat in *The Longest Day*.

After Frankfurt, Frank and Dean flew to London for a cameo appearance as spacemen in *The Road to Hong Kong*, starring Bing Crosby and Bob Hope. Despite Frank and Dean's spacesuits (while Bing and Bob were playing Chinamen!), this was a dated comedy which suggested that all four should have stayed at home. Although there were only on the set for a day, Joan Collins was hoping for a quick fling with Sinatra but her stand-in beat her to it.

Various projects to star Sinatra and Monroe had fallen apart. One was a remake of a the

1950 film, *Born Yesterday,* as a musical; another, was *The Great Train Robbery*, a concept owned by Peter Lawford for both the Rat Pack and Monroe; and yet another, a musical of the 1945 film, *A Tree Grows in Brooklyn*, but none of them ever happened.

Frank had enjoyed making *Ocean's 11* and it had been especially lucrative. He decided to make further Rat Pack films though his company, Essex, in conjunction with United Artists, perhaps as many as five in five years. Sinatra was fond of Rudyard Kipling and his epic poem about an English soldier in India, *Gunga Din* had been filmed in 1939 and then recast as a western for *Soldiers Three* in 1951. Somehow Frank had thought that all this was out of copyright – and this from a man who had already clashed with the Kipling estate. Once the film had been made, his company received a bill for the rights.

Initially, Frank was going to call his film, *Soldiers 3,* but there had been that MGM film called *Soldiers Three*. In exchange for MGM waiving their objection, Frank would make a guest appearance in *How the West Was Won* free of charge. In the end, Sinatra didn't take the role and his film emerged as *Sergeants 3*.

The film was shot in Bryce Canyon National Park in Utah, with the cast and crew stationed at Kanab, a one-horse town by Rat Pack standards and – what's worse for their hedonistic tastes – in Mormon country. Joey Bishop commented, 'The Dairy Queen was open until 11pm. You'd better have two scoops because after that there wasn't a damn thing to do.' Frank insisted on connecting doors being constructed in the hotel to link the rooms for the leading players. As the film featured mayhem and destruction almost on a *Raiders of the Lost Ark* level, the hotel reconstruction didn't add much to the total cost.

The potential for the film was strong as it had a decent storyline and the director John Sturges had just made *The Magnificent Seven*. However, that did not allow for Rat Pack indulgence. Although he is not in the film, Tony Curtis was doing a photo-assignment for *Ebony* magazine about life on the set – but the Rat Pack was silly rather than cooperative. The film seems very politically incorrect now with its treatment of American Indians, not to mention Sammy Davis. Nevertheless, Davis rated this as the best of the Clan films. He is said to have worn the same hat as John Wayne in *Stagecoach* but that is ridiculous as Wayne was twice his size. There is inherent racism as Sinatra, Martin and Lawford are sergeants and he is a bugler. Oddly, there was also a fourth sergeant in Joey Bishop – but who's counting?

The film does not know what it wants to be: action movie, slapstick comedy or a repository for in-jokes. If it is a comedy, then why does it begin with the massacre of a whole town, and what happened to the corpses? The bloodbath is shot well but it belongs in another film. Frank and Dean did their own stunts and Frank had to be dragged under a runaway wagon with Dean stomping on his fingers as he fought above him. It's not as dangerous as it looks but most stars would have used stand-ins. Indeed, Dean confused fireworks with dynamite when he was filming one scene and most of the time he was suffering from an arthritic back.

Peter Lawford alleviated the boredom by overeating, so much so that he gained two stone during the filming. Sinatra would look at the rushes and say, 'Here comes Fat Boy.' Lawford got back to normal by taking Dexedrine. During the film, he says to Sinatra, 'I don't know how to say this after all we've been through together but you're a louse', which is something he probably said off-screen too.

Sinatra gave bit parts to three of Bing Crosby's sons – Phillip, Dennis and Lindsay – as soldiers who guard Dean Martin in the stockade. The score was written by Billy May who is in full blast for the final skirmish though it's hard to tell what is happening.

The film was released six months later, in January 1962, with a charity screening for handicapped children. The reviews were poor with *Time* calling it the $4m home movie, which was about right. It did reasonably well at the box office, generating $4.3m so at least it broke even. A couple of years later, James Stewart went to Kanab to make a western and found that the quiet town was still recovering from their revelry.

At the time, Juliet Prowse was also dating Elvis Presley and Eddie Fisher. In September, Frank and Marilyn Monroe invited some friends onto his yacht and sailed to Santa Catalina Island off the California coast on a four day cruise.

It was good for a performer's prestige to have the Rat Pack in the audience but they could ruin the act. Frank and Dean spoilt Eddie Fisher's opening at the Coconut Grove in Los Angeles. Eddie opened by singing 'That Face' to Elizabeth Taylor and Dean yelled, 'If I were you, I wouldn't be working here. I'd be at home fucking her!' Uninvited, Frank, Dean and Sammy joined Eddie for an evening of impressions, limericks, racial jokes and drunken songs. They asked the audience to sing 'God Bless America' and show their allegiance to Kennedy.

The Rat Pack all loved the comedian Don Rickles, who was a lovable teddy bear, but he had found making jokes about the Rat Pack, both individually and collectively, was good for his act. He even joked about Frank's ladies. Frank decided to teach him a lesson. They all went to his show in Vegas one night and when he came on stage, they all held up newspapers and started reading.

Frank Sinatra's style was the inspiration for a new show in London's West End by Anthony Newley and Leslie Bricusse. Newley said, 'Lord Delfont asked me I wanted to do a stage show and Leslie Bricusse and I came up with *Stop the World – I Want to Get Off*. It would never have happened had I not got an audience from my rock'n'roll records. I went to Bricusse and I said, "I want to do a show with a dozen girls and me in a dinner-jacket and it'll be very sexy and I'll be like Frank Sinatra." Once we got to work of course, it became an entirely different show.'

Stop the World – I Want to Get Off was a cynical show about how a teaboy (Littlechap) became a millionaire. Newley who directed the show had elements of Charles Aznavour, Charlie Chaplin and Marcel Marceau in his performance. The score included 'Gonna Build a Mountain' (now associated with Matt Monro) and 'What Kind of Fool Am I'. The show transferred to Broadway with equal success. To my surprise, Tony Newley recalled, 'The first person in America to record 'What Kind of Fool Am I' was not Sammy Davis but Jerry Lewis. To hear stars like Sammy and Big Tone (Tony Bennett) sing our songs was such a turn-on for us and they sang them everywhere they went.'

In Liverpool, the Beatles were starting to make an impact at a basement club, the Cavern. Bob Wooler, the club's DJ, said, 'One day in 1961 the Beatles did the Cavern lunchtime session and afterwards we went to drink at the Mandolin which was an old cinema in Windsor Street, just outside the city centre, run by Harry the Pole. John sat on a settee with a girl in the club, and Paul went over to the upright piano on stage and played a song. When he came across to where I was sitting, he said it was called 'Suicide', and I told him that was a strange and uncommercial title for a song.' In *Many Years From Now*, Paul McCartney recalls how Frank Sinatra asked him for a song and he sent him 'Suicide'. 'He thought it was an almighty piss-take,' Paul recalls, 'I think he sent the demo back.'

Sinatra's arranger, Axel Stordahl, had cancer but he wanted to make one final album with Frank. The Capitol studio was booked for two days in September and the album was called *Point of No Return*. Several arrangements were written by Heinie Beau as Stordahl was not well enough to complete them.

It's a shame that there wasn't a title song, as this would have been an ideal subject for Cahn and Van Heusen. It was lonely songs of lost love, but the liner notes sought to make it something different: 'On other occasions Frank has sung for *Only the Lonely* and he's sung about the times when *No One Cares*. This album has the same universal appeal as those earlier best sellers, but now there's an extra ingredient that intensifies the lonely mood. For these songs all express the special longing that come with the memory of a September not spent alone or an April when someone did care. Every one of them is a revelation of a human being with a heart that beats experiencing a sort of moment of truth – the *Point of No Return*.'

Frank was showing extreme kindness to his old friend, but otherwise, he was his usual non-comprising self. The producer, Dave Cavanaugh, would ask him for another take and he would say, 'I'm sorry. Next number!' When Frank had hit a bad note at the end of 'These Foolish Things', he refused to redo it. Fortunately there had been an earlier take and Dave Cavanaugh was able to splice them together. Only a few months earlier, he had been quoting Tommy Dorsey's advice 'to treat every record as if it's the last song I'll ever sing', but he was taking little notice.

Still, *Point of No Return* was a fine album, offering dramatic versions of Noël Coward's 'I'll See You Again' and Kurt Weill's 'September Song'. Earlier in the year he had recorded a swing version of 'I'll Be Seeing You' for *I Remember Tommy* and this time he gave it a ballad treatment. There is a lovely Stordahl arrangement for 'There Will Never Be Another You'. Surprisingly, 'I'll Remember April' came from the Abbott and Costello film, *Ride 'Em Cowboy* (1942).

The clearest example of an opportunity lost in Sinatra's career came with the French chanson, '(Ah, the Apple Trees) When the World Was Young'. It is a strong acting performance from Sinatra and it begs the question as to why he didn't do more of this. He knew Charles Aznavour well and yet he never sang his songs. I'm sure he could have been easily persuaded to cut an album of chansons. After all, what is 'It Was a Very Good Year' but American chanson?

Bill Miller suggested to Frank that he might like to work with the conductor and arranger Don Costa at Reprise. He had been born Dominick Costa into an Italian-American family in Boston in 1925 and as a guitarist, had been a member of the CBS radio orchestra. He began arranging in the 1950s and made a name for himself as A&R manager for ABC-Paramount Records. He arranged and conducted hit records for Paul Anka (including 'Diana' and 'Lonely Boy'), Lloyd Price, Steve Lawrence and Eydie Gorme. Frank told him that he wanted to record standards for an album to be called *Sinatra and Strings*. It was the only time that Costa worked with him on such a project as his later work with Sinatra was more contemporary.

The most famed track on the album is Hoagy Carmichael's 'Stardust' and it's famous for what was left out. Everybody else sings the body of song (that is, 'Sometimes I wonder...') and a few attach the introduction ('And now the purple dusk of twilight time'). Sinatra had performed the song before, but here Costa and Sinatra only performed the introduction, causing Hoagy Carmichael to remark, 'But I wrote a whole song!' Frank was making the point that the introduction was complete in itself and is an exquisite tone poem.

'I Hadn't Anyone Till You' was a throwback to Sinatra's days as a bobbysox idol, and girls would have similarly swooned over Russ Columbo's 'Prisoner of Love', soon to be revamped by James Brown. There is an old-fashioned feel to Jerome Kern's 'Yesterdays' as who in the 1960s would rhyme 'yesterdays' with 'sequesterdays'? The key changes in 'It Might as Well Be Spring' are deliberate so as to give the effect of someone who is jumpy and can't believe what is happening. Don Costa claimed that 'Come Rain or Come Shine' was 'the best chart I ever wrote'. Frank sent the record to the songwriter Harold Arlen with a note, 'Play it loud!'

Errol Garner's piano instrumental 'Misty' had been recorded in 1954 but Johnny Burke had added a lyric, his last major work, and it brought Johnny Mathis a gold disc in 1959. Sinatra wanted to show he could match Mathis whom he referred to as 'the African queen'. 'Misty' was a hit with a country music arrangement for Ray Stevens in 1975.

Bobby Darin was still on his mind. Darin had swung 'That's All' for the title track of an album in 1959. Here Sinatra presented it as a ballad. Who knows what was going through Sinatra's mind but he did offer Bobby Darin a contract with Reprise when his time with Atco was finished. Darin went with Capitol because he wanted to record in the Tower with Nelson Riddle and Billy May. Nelson at the time was enjoying his own chart success with the theme from the TV series, *Route 66*, but he was about to be on the move himself.

It's possible that Livingston signed Darin to annoy Sinatra but it does seem odd that he replaced one temperamental prima donna with another one. Whereas Sinatra always sounded like Sinatra, Darin had a range of voices and could write and sing in almost any genre. One of his first hits at Capitol was with an excellent country song '18 Yellow Roses', while his finger-snapping 'A Nightingale Sang in Berkeley Square' with Billy May was join-the-dots Sinatra.

Nelson Riddle joined Frank for the title song for the film, *A Pocketful of Miracles*, which was directed by Frank Capra and starred Bette Davis and Glenn Ford. It was a Top 40 single but Sammy Cahn and Jimmy Van Heusen were hoping to repeat the success of 'High Hopes'. Two of Nelson's children, Chris and Rosemary, sang in the children's chorus. The film was a remake of *Lady for a Day* (1933) and Frank had agreed to play Dave the Dude until he saw the script.

Frank Sinatra recorded his sixth album of the year with a live concert from the Sands with the hotel's regular director of music, Antonio Morelli. Morelli conducted many albums from the Sands, but this not one was not released at the time. Sinatra was happy with the performance but the market was being flooded with his product and he had to hold back. It's a good well-chosen 18 song set including 'In the Still of the Night', 'The Second Time Round' and 'Here's That Rainy Day' but not 'I've Got You Under My Skin', 'All the Way' or 'One for My Baby'.

In 1960 Bobby Kennedy had published *The Enemy Within*, a book which exposed how deep corruption was in American business and how powerful the Mafia was. Maybe Frank Sinatra had offered Sam Giancana a safe passage, but on whose authority? In December 1961, the FBI caught Sam Giancana discussing Sinatra's ability to intercede on the Mob's behalf. Whether he knew it or not before, Bobby now knew that his father had made a deal with the Mafia to help his brother get elected President. Both brothers then agreed that Joe had to be cut off from giving them advice.

On 9 January 1962 Sinatra got engaged to Juliet Prowse, a dancer from South Africa who was 20 years his junior. The director George Cukor was having trouble filming Marilyn Monroe on *Something's Gotta Give* with Dean Martin and Cyd Charisse. He recalled that when Frank and Juliet became engaged, Marilyn went mad, knocking her head against a wall. The film was never completed although Marilyn's nude poolside sequence became world famous. Dean Martin said it was impossible to work with her and he informed the press, no doubt jokingly, that he was 'the highest paid golfer in history'.

The engagement only lasted a few weeks, although they were to remain friends, and Johnny Carson cracked, 'Frank has had longer engagements in Las Vegas.' One of the problems was that Frank didn't want to meet her parents.

The romance had also cooled after she was entertaining another man in her apartment and she had refused to let Frank enter. Frank, in his normal happy way, threatened to kill her but he soon cooled and neither party seemed particularly upset. Frank sent her a mink coat with a note, 'This is your swan song.' But it was never going to work. While he was with Ava, he hated been thought of as Mr Gardner, so he wasn't keen on having a permanent partner who would continue her career.

The February 1962 issue of *Playboy* featured a long and candid interview with Frank about his life and loves. How much of it was actually said by Frank? Probably very little – but the views expressed did match his thoughts. He said, 'I'm for anything that gets you through the night, be it prayer, tranquillisers or Jack Daniel's.' Cue for a song, Mr Kristofferson.

On 15 January 1962 Frank was a pallbearer at the funeral for the comic and TV actor, Ernie Kovacs, who had died in a car accident. In the evening, he began a new Reprise album with Gordon Jenkins. The original idea had been to call the album, *Come Waltz with Me*, but the troubles with Capitol had put paid to that. Cahn and Van Heusen wrote a title song and, although it was recorded, the song was passed to Steve Lawrence.

As an album title, *Come Waltz with Me* implied something rather cheerful and upbeat. Next Gordon Jenkins was contracted to arrange a collection of lost love songs in waltz time and the LP was named after one of them, *All Alone*, with the emphasis being on compositions by Irving Berlin. Berlin had written 'All Alone' in the early 1920s and it had done well for John McCormack and Al Jolson. He wrote 'When I Lost You' in 1912 when his wife had died five months after their wedding, and 'What'll I Do' is a similar picture of helplessness.

The Hungarian waltz, 'Charmaine', had been made famous by Mantovani in 1951 and it was good to hear Frank's vocal version of a song that would provide a 1963 hit for the Bachelors. In 1961 Connie Francis had had a hit with the oldie 'Together', here performed as a stately waltz. Unlike Elvis Presley, he chose to drop the narration on 'Are You Lonesome Tonight' although he could have done it extremely well. The most recent song was 'Indiscreet', a Cahn and Van Heusen title song for the 1958 film starring Cary Grant and Ingrid Bergman.

There had been speculation about Sinatra starring in *The Actor*, based on a Clifford Odets story but it never happened. Instead, Frank made *The Manchurian Candidate*, which was based on a novel by Richard Condon and directed by John Frankenheimer. Because it was about brainwashing, political manipulation, communist infiltration and how somebody could be trained to assassinate the President, Sinatra thought that it might alienate him from the Kennedys. It could have been embarrassing if it was released while Kennedy was trying to improve relations with Russia, particular as the countries had been on the brink of a nuclear war a few months earlier. Sinatra asked Kennedy if they should make it. Kennedy knew the book and said, 'Who's going to play the mother?'

Having Kennedy's approval reassured United Artists' executives who were wary about the project, feeling that the film might be blacklisted, and it might not have been made at all without Sinatra battling for it. Sinatra wanted the film to be made immediately. George Axelrod had written 20 pages of script and Sinatra asked, 'Can't you write the rest over the weekend?'

The black comedy was set in 1954 when a brainwashed war hero (a zombie-like Laurence Harvey) was involved in a plot to place a very right wing senator into the White House. His mother (Angela Lansbury) was behind the plot and appeared as manipulative as Joe Kennedy, hence JFK's interest in who was going to play her. She was perfectly cast although in the reality, she was 36 and Harvey 33.

The filming began on 22 January 1962 and was made in a very commendable 39 days. The dream sequence in which the New Jersey flower arrangers changed into Communist agents took six of those days. That was filmed in every conceivable combination to give

Frankenheimer a wide choice for the final cut. Sinatra was restless but it was something to have held onto him for that long. The resulting opening sequence was unlike any other film and was as unnerving as Salvador Dali's dream sequence for Alfred Hitchcock's *Spellbound* (1945). There were striking images throughout the film: a senator dying with, seemingly, milk pouring out of his veins. Dali proved to be another of Ava conquests but she couldn't take him seriously.

Laurence Harvey had little regard for his own safely and his walk into the frozen lake at Central Park was filmed in one take without a wet suit. During the karate fight with Sinatra and Henry Silva, Sinatra broke the little finger on his right hand, which remained permanently broken. He said that Silva had difficulty in deciding which was left and which was right and so made the wrong move. Sinatra was most impressed with Harvey's performance saying, 'I wouldn't have known how to play Larry's role.'

When Sinatra confronted Harvey with a pack of cards (actually all Queens), he was out of focus. Frankenheimer said that it would have to be done again but Sinatra stated that they could make do with what they had. When the film was released, critics praised the scene as it looked as though Frank was being viewed from Laurence Harvey's perspective. There are, as usual, little sequences that showed Sinatra's influence, notably a few minutes in Jilly Rizzo's bar. All this helped to keep Sinatra sweet and he gave the best performance of his career.

The Manchurian Candidate was previewed when Sinatra was in London in June 1962. The film was highly acclaimed and Angela Lansbury was nominated for an Oscar but the public wasn't interested. Frank always wondered whether Lee Harvey Oswald had seen it. Pauline Kael was surprised that such a thought-provoking film could have stemmed from Hollywood, saying 'Although it's a thriller it may be the most sophisticated political satire ever made in Hollywood.' Tina was taunted at school and informed that her father must be a Communist with the result that Frank had to visit the school and talk to the pupils.

After Kennedy's assassination in November 1963 the film went out of circulation. For some reason Sinatra did not realise that he owned the rights. When it was reissued on video in 1988 the copyright was 'Frank Sinatra Trust No.10'. For the DVD version, Frankenheimer, Axelrod and Sinatra met up again for an extra feature. They were very easy with each other and there were no indications of any trouble with the picture.

In February1962 Dean Martin left Capitol and joined Reprise, immediately releasing the Italian 'Senza Fine'. Frank had considered singing a couple of songs in Italian but he wasn't happy with his pronunciation.

On 25 February both Frank and Dean were guests on *The Judy Garland Show*, directed by Norman Jewison, and they worked exceptionally well together. Frank and Dean wanted to record with her on Reprise but received a definite no from Alan Livingston, who had her under contract to Capitol.

The Broadway actress Elaine Stritch attended a dinner party at Frank's home in Palm Springs. When a recent performance of Frank performing 'The Lady Is a Tramp' came on TV, Stritch remarked, 'My, that man can still sing!' Sinatra responded with 'I hear that you're on Broadway, Miss Stritch. You just ain't going anywhere.' 'And tell me, Mr Sinatra,' said Stritch, 'Just where are you going these days?' Sinatra shouted, 'Get that broad out of my house!' and she had to leave.

In February 1962 some FBI agents informed J Edgar Hoover that Judy Campbell was having an affair with the President. He knew that Campbell was Sam Giancana's girlfriend and it didn't take him long to realise that Frank Sinatra was involved. A few days later, Sinatra cancelled an appearance at the White House for Kennedy, claiming a bad throat, but he might have been ordered not to go. A couple of months later, the Mafia boss, Lucky Luciano, died in Naples. In his pocket, the police found a gold cigarette case with the inscription, 'To Charlie, from your pal, Frank Sinatra''.

Anthony Newley's UK hit, 'Bee Bom' was covered by Sammy Davis Jr and one of Reprise's first successes. Newley said, 'I was told that 'Bee Bom' was President Kenney's favourite tune and that he used to make love to it. I don't know whether to believe that or not but it's a nice thought. I like to believe he did. I never did as I don't know how you can keep up that kind of pace.'

In March 1962 Capitol, just to be awkward, insisted that Frank Sinatra owed them one more track. Although he might have been retaliated in kind, he loved the swinging arrangement that Skip Martin had written for the 1932 song, 'I Gotta Right to Sing the Blues' and he left the label in fine style.

It was planned that President Kennedy would spend a weekend in Palm Springs at Frank Sinatra's house. Jackie Kennedy would be in India, so we can guess what kind of a boys' weekend was planned. However, the FBI advised Kennedy that this would not be wise; Judy Campbell had been seeing Kennedy and Giancana at the same time, all engineered by Sinatra. In anticipation of the President's visit, Frank had been making alterations to his house and grounds including creating a heliport.

When Kennedy told Peter Lawford to break the news to Frank that he would not be coming, Frank went berserk, at first smashing up his heliport with a sledgehammer. However, he soon had his repairs made good and found the heliport very useful for himself – until he was stopped by noise abatement laws. Although it was hardly Lawford's fault, Frank told him that he would never speak to him again. Puccini's, the Hollywood restaurant that they co-owned, was sold.

What particularly annoyed Sinatra was when learning that the President would be staying nearby in Bing Crosby's house – and Bing was a Republican! The overflow would be staying at Jimmy Van Heusen's house as Jimmy lived next door to Bing. Frank had just recorded a new Van Heusen song, 'Cathy', with an arrangement from Billy May. He told Van Heusen, 'Tell you what, Chester. Why don't you get Jack Kennedy to record the fucking song and then see how many it sells?' The track has never been released, but Van Heusen passed the song to Vic Damone.

In April 1962 the most perplexing single of Frank Sinatra's career was released. Many cite it as the worst record ever made. It was 'Everybody's Twistin'' in which Frank followed Chubby Checker, Joey Dee and Sam Cooke by making a record for the current dance craze, the Twist. It was submitted by two old-time songwriters, Ted Koehler and Rube Bloom and Koehler was one of Frank's neighbours. Frank mentioned Checker in the lyric and Chubby was so pleased that he uses Sinatra's record as a stage introduction to this day. The song was a simple rewrite of their 1935 recording 'Truckin'' for Fats Waller. It was good fun and was a small hit in both the US and the UK.

As a new staff producer at Reprise, Neal Hefti had arranged and conducted 'Everybody's Twistin'' and he was given a more serious assignment. It was another album of standards, this time with the title, *Sinatra and Swingin' Brass*. Why did Sinatra persist with these *Swingin'* titles given that the law of diminishing returns was settling in? Still, it was better than an alternative suggestion, *Hefti Meets the Thin One*. Frank re-recorded 'I Get a Kick Out Of You', but that was because he then had a Reprise version to sell.

It was a very good album but with a feeling of déjà vu. There was a marvellous 'I'm Beginning to See the Light' in which Sinatra sang in harmony with the trumpets. It does sound odd the first time round but play it again and the ploy works. Sinatra was in fine voice and he held the final note on 'They Can't Take That Away from Me' for ten seconds. At the end of 'Don'cha Go 'Way Mad', which was originally the instrumental 'Black Velvet' for Illinois Jacquet, Frank repeated 'baby' twelve times.

The actor Monty Woolley, one of Cole Porter's best friends, bet him that he couldn't do anything with the title, 'I Love You'. In 1944 Cole was writing a musical, *Mexican Hayride*, and one of the characters is given the task of writing his first love song, hence the banal title. It was a clever trick as, by its very nature, it has to be banal with one cliché following another. Cole Porter did what he set out to do but I'm not sure that this song worked without knowing the background.

Sinatra bounced around on 'Goody Goody' and was at his most amusing on 'Love Is Just Around the Corner', a song like Chuck Berry's 'Too Much Money Business' namechecking the Venus de Milo. The first time round Sinatra sings, 'You're cuter than Venus, What's more you've got arms.' The second time he is in Louis Prima mode for 'You gotta de arms' and has the musicians join him for a response. He ended similar interplay on 'Pick Yourself Up' with 'That's enough now'. I was going to add that Frank then put on his hat and went home, but there was no need. He wore his hat for all the sessions.

Even before Sinatra fell out with the Kennedys he knew that his public image needed a makeover. A lot of people enjoyed his Rat Pack antics but he knew that the public perception of endless hedonism turned off many more. It didn't bother Dean, who played along with it, but Dean was Frank-lite, and Frank, unlike Dean, saw himself as a serious artist. Frank didn't want to break with the Rat Pack (excepting Peter) but it would be good to be away from them for a while.

The newspapers kept dragging up Sinatra's Mob connections. They hadn't hard evidence and they didn't know of the potential scandal around Judy Campbell. Around the same time, the Profumo scandal which had many parallels brought down the UK government.

Frank Sinatra thought it called for drastic action and, completely out of character, he announced a ten-week world tour with 30 concert dates. The shows would be for children's charities and he would be visiting orphanages and hospitals wherever he went. It could be argued that Sinatra was being completely altruistic, which is possible, but he knew that by being benevolent he could improve his own image. For this to work meant that Frank would have to be on good behaviour for over two months, and he never enjoyed travelling. As you might have guessed, there were some hairy moments. He was prone to tantrums and bad manners and he never mastered the art of counting to ten before he said anything untoward.

Because Frank was meeting the costs from his own pocket, although some concerts were sponsored, he did not want to tour with a full orchestra. He asked Bill Miller to form a sextet, rather like George Shearing's group but with a saxophonist, and they would accompany him. Frank could play around with some old favourites and freshen them up from night to night. The musicians selected were Al Viola, Ralph Peña, Irv Cottler, Emil Richards and Harry Klee. The guitarist Al Viola was to work with Frank until 1980, even though he did blot his copybook by working on the soundtrack for *The Godfather.*

Although this was a world tour involving dates in Africa, Asia, Australia, Europe and South America, Sinatra did not include America itself. If he had done this, he thought that the US newspapers would be describing his tour as some sort of tax loss. The tour started in Mexico City on 15 April, which went fine. The show wasn't too lively but then Sinatra had to get used to the musicians.

Next stop, Japan. Frank was given the keys to Tokyo and the citation said that many Japanese had learnt to speak English through listening to Frank Sinatra's records. Admittedly, his diction was perfect but what did they make of 'the kookoo wind in her hair'? The open air concert amidst the cherry blossoms in Hibiya Park has been released by the budget label

Acrobat and it is an excellent set with little concession to an audience who might not have understood him. He laughed in 'Imagination' with 'Ha ha, you want me too'; he did 'a zillion things' in 'I Could Have Danced All Night'; and said he knew 'a cat who danced with his wife' in 'Chicago', which might have perplexed anyone who was taking him literally. He was moved when he was shown hundreds of orphaned children living in boxcars.

Frank performed for American servicemen in Korea and then moved to Hong Kong. He played seven concerts in nine days in Israel; a documentary film, *Sinatra in Israel*, was released later in the year. He showed his compassion but he also said, 'These children are tapped out in the seeing department, no sight, just high hopes' – an out-of-character plug for one of his singles.

Then it was Greece, with a concert in Athens. In Italy Frank played an amphitheatre in Verona. It was raining throughout so Frank added 'Pennies from Heaven' to the set list. He made sure that the musicians were under cover even if the audience wasn't. There were further dates in Rome and Cinisello Balsamo, Milan. The Milan concert was sponsored by Perugina Confectionary and he only performed 12 songs instead of the customary 18.

While Sinatra was in Madrid, he looked up Ava Gardner for a few days' holiday and naturally they fell out. In subsequent performances of 'I Get a Kick Out of You', he would go 'Some like the perfume from Spain – ugh!' or something similar.

The *NME* wrote about Frank coming to the UK but he was the victim of a practical joke. Frank was travelling on his plane, 'Christina', but the *NME* printed the name as 'El Dago'.

On 1 June 1962 Frank gave a midnight concert at the Royal Festival Hall in the presence of Princess Margaret and Lord Snowdon. It was filmed by ITV and half of the set was broadcast the following night. Frank had required three rows of seats at the front for his friends. On being told that they had all been sold, he ordered them to put in another three rows at the front. One friend happened to be Nelson Riddle, who was in the UK to record and tour with Shirley Bassey.

The following day Frank gave a concert for the British Heart Foundation at the Odeon, Leicester Square and was introduced by Peter Sellers. Frank was given a Silver Heart for his charitable work.

When Frank visited a home for disabled children, a blind girl asked him, 'What colour is the wind?' and he responded beautifully with 'No one knows because it blows so fast.' This exchange inspired Charlie Landsborough's country song, 'What Colour Is the Wind' (1994), which has been sung by both Jack Jones and Pat Boone. Had he written it earlier, it would have been perfect for Frank.

On 3 June Frank gave two concerts at the Gaumont, Hammersmith, presented by Harold Davison. Featuring John Dankworth and Cleo Laine and the King Brothers in support, this would be Sinatra's last UK concert for eight years.

The *New Musical Express* was desperate for an interview but Harold Davison knew that he would be unlikely to agree to a one-to-one. He told the news editor, Derek Johnson, to join the party for lunch on Sunday but he would have to pretend that he was a doctor. Of course the inevitable happened. Sinatra said, "Oh, doctor, I've been having these headaches and no one in America can cure them." Thinking on his feet, "Dr" Johnson said, "I always find the simplest solutions are the best. Just take some Aspirin and you should be okay." Sinatra said, "Harold, have you got any Aspirin?" An hour later, Sinatra said to him, "You know, I have being paying specialists a lot of money to get rid of these headaches and you've just solved the problem. Thank you very much."

On 5 June 1962 Frank Sinatra made his French début at the Lido, Paris, singing love songs in the world's most romantic city and introduced by Charles Aznavour. Aznavour told him, 'Paris belongs to you' and it did. The concert was professionally recorded and would have made a great double-album – 25 songs in 74 minutes – but again, Frank decided that there was too much product around. In 1994 it was issued on CD as *Sinatra in Paris* and ranks amongst the finest of Sinatra's live recordings.

Frank opened with a brisk 'Goody Goody' and he relished the lyric of 'Imagination' although the line about a bee imagining honey was forced. Being in France, he offered a cool jazz version of 'April in Paris'. There was a double joke when he announced he was going to sing 'about my favourite city' as he paused and said 'Helsinki' and then went into 'A Foggy Day (In London Town)'. Nobody applauded when he started this so maybe they had been expecting 'I Love Paris', which did come later.

When Bill Miller played the intro to 'My Funny Valentine', he commented, 'That kind of note can give you a headache, daddy.' 'The Second Time Around' with Bill Miller playing like Erroll Garner was marvellous, but the highlight was 'Night And Day', spotlighting the dexterity of Al Viola. At the end Sinatra remarked, 'If you weren't looking at him, you'd swear he was an octopus.'

I am glad that Reprise issued the full performance as it is part of the package to hear him trying jokes which don't work. This was Paris, not Vegas, and the locals spoke a different language for a start, so why did he do it? His impersonations – Jimmy Cagney, twice – were not that hot either. When he came to the line, 'fighting vainly the old ennui', he added, 'That's French.' He said of 'One for My Baby': 'It's obvious what his trouble is, girls, *cherchez la femme*, which means in French, "Why don't you share the broad with me?"'

The ethnic jokes sound appalling today but you could argue that he was poking fun at bigotry. After performing a sublime 'Ol' Man River' to rapturous applause, he said, 'That was a song about Sammy Davis's people and this is a song about my people,' before going into 'The Lady Is a Tramp'. When the concert was eventually issued in 1994, *Rolling Stone* commented, 'Given a microphone to speak into, Sinatra can always be counted on to embarrass himself.'

As always, the stage was his platform for bellyaching and he told his audience, 'The onion soup was great but don't eat it before you have to sing here.' He commented on the weather – 'I'm crazy about Paris in the winter' and provided too much information amid 'I Love Paris': 'Holy Christ, do I love Paris because my love is here. She's in Room 542 at the hotel.' When he coughed, he repeated the old vaudeville joke, 'Gotta stop sleeping in the park.'

Anyway, no harm was done as the state presentation of a gold medal to Sinatra was made at the Olympia in Paris two days later. There were few recipients outside of France and they included Albert Schweitzer and John F Kennedy.

Despite the problems a year earlier year when he snubbed a charity gala in Monaco, Princess Grace welcomed him for a new benefit performance in Monte Carlo on 9 June.

Frank returned to London to record the album, *Great Songs from Great Britain* with Robert Farnon conducting, the only studio album that Sinatra made outside America. Farnon wrote ambitious and lush charts which stretched Sinatra's voice. All proceeds were to a children's fund chaired by the Duke of Edinburgh. Sinatra wanted Churchill to paint the cover but he declined. It was promoted with a BBC Light programme special, *Frank Sinatra Personally Presents Great Songs from Great Britain*, an early example of a musician hosting a radio show around his own album.

Sinatra dined with the journalist Kenneth Allsop who had written a book on bootlegging in the Capone era. He told Allsop that boxers should be made to give one-third of their fees to the government so that they could be provided with pensions in later life.

Frank was very keen to make the album as he was so fond of the UK and because he often recorded British songs, he knew that there would no drop in quality. He didn't want to follow *Mel Tormé Meets the British* in which Mel was singing 'I've Got a Lovely Bunch of Coconuts' and 'My One and Only Highland Fling' and thus turning his project into a novelty.

Because of the long tour, Sinatra's voice was showing some wear and the slow tempos didn't help, but he was reluctant to cancel the 40-piece orchestra which had been booked and he was keen to make the album. It was produced by Pye's A&R manager, Alan A Freeman, with 22-year-old Tony Hatch in the control booth, but he had flown in his regular engineer, Bill Putnam, to advise them. Naturally, the final decisions were made by Sinatra himself. Freeman and Farnon had given Sinatra a choice of 70 songs and he chose well, but added 'Now Is the Hour' and 'Garden in the Rain', which stretched the concept as they came from New Zealand and America respectively

As in America, Frank was happy to invite well-wishers to the sessions and 50 people were sitting around the sides of the studio. Nelson Riddle was one spectator and he remarked that Frank seemed happy even though the arrangements put demands on his voice. Noël Coward wanted to attend as Frank was recording his song, 'I'll Follow My Secret Heart', but he was in France. A short while later he happened to be at Abbey Road and thought he heard Frank's voice coming from a studio but it was Matt Monro's.

Perhaps because it did not get a US release at the time, this has become an underrated album. Another reason could be because there is nothing contemporary about the arrangements, but this is why it works so well: Sinatra is simply giving beautiful performances of beautiful songs. *Melody Maker* stated that 'Sinatra has not exactly pulled out the punches' but that is the point. Bobby Darin had just recorded a swinging up-tempo 'Roses of Picardy' with Billy May at Capitol, but this was 100% Sinatra and Sinatra wanted to sing it as the songwriters intended. When Farnon ran down the arrangement, Sinatra remarked, 'I can't even talk in that key.' Encouraged by Farnon, he looked up at the ceiling and said, 'Don't just sit there. Come down and help me.' Frank gave a superlative performance but it was omitted from the original album.

The warm and romantic 'If I Had You' was a 1929 hit by Rudy Vallée, enhanced by a celesta used by Bill Miller because the piano was out of tune. There was a lovely version of 'The Very Thought of You', which betters Bing's hit from 1934, one of the few recordings in which Bing went for a high note.

Alan A Freeman and Robert Farnon, backed up by Nelson Riddle, questioned Frank's phrasing on 'The Gypsy' but he wouldn't budge. As a result, it was Farnon's least favourite track, but that's being picky – it sounds fine to most listeners.

It's great to hear Frank singing 'A Nightingale Sang in Berkeley Square' with an excellent trombone solo from Harry Roche, who was associated with Ted Heath and his Orchestra. Frank fluffed a line at the end and he said, remarkably for him, 'We'll pick up on the recording as the trombone solo was excellent.' Harry regarded Sinatra's praise as the highspot of his life. The song had been written by the BBC executive, Eric Maschwitz, in 1940 and had been a wartime hit for Glenn Miller and Ray Noble and their orchestras. London was being bombed and this offered an affectionate portrait of the city. The song has often been criticised because there are no nightingales in Berkeley Square but surely that's the point. The singer swears he hears the bird because he's in love. This wartime optimism is also evident in 'We'll Meet Again' and 'We'll Gather Lilacs'.

Over the years Frank made 44 recordings of 36 different British songs. Earlier he had cut a beautiful version of 'London by Night' and Capitol had reissued this to promote his time in the city. A Liverpool comic, Norman Vaughan, made the UK charts in 1962 with a Sinatra pastiche, 'Swingin' In The Rain', helped by the Corona Kids.

The world tour had been immensely successful on all fronts, raising over $1m for charity and showing that Frank was a kind and sympathetic individual. He had distanced himself from the Mafia and from the Rat Pack's idiocy. He was shown reading serious books – a biography of Michelangelo and Sinclair Lewis's *It Can't Happen Here*. Maybe he was thinking of Sinclair Lewis's novel about a dictator taking over America as a possible follow-up to *The Manchurian Candidate*.

But absolutely everything was about to go wrong.

In a new spirit of contriteness, Frank rang Pat Lawford to say that he was sorry that he had shunned Peter and that he realised he was only the messenger when he told Frank that Kennedy couldn't stay at his compound. Frank wanted to make it up to them and asked if they would visit the new look Cal-Neva for the weekend. Some improvements had been made and it was now on a par with the best Vegas casinos. He was playing there and Buddy Greco was in the lounge. He would provide a plane to take them to Nevada.

There was a catch – there was always a catch with Sinatra – Marilyn Monroe would be on that plane. She hadn't been in the best of health and Frank wanted Pat to maintain a watchful eye. They flew up on Friday 27 June, but Monroe was in a worse state than Frank could have imagined. She was depressed and, as well as drinking heavily, she was injecting drugs. When Frank saw her, he said, 'Get her out of here!' Frank certainly didn't want her to die at Cal-Neva, especially when he owned a substantial slice of it.

Monroe returned from Cal-Neva on 29 July. She consoled herself by playing Sinatra's melancholy records over and over, identifying with the lyrics and with his voice as she tried to sleep. She died on 5 August. Joe DiMaggio felt that she had been let down by her friends, notably Sinatra and the Kennedys. Norman Mailer was to write a biography in which he considered the Kennedys were involved in her death, but that is speculation. As the song in *Cabaret* says, 'That's what comes of too much pills and liquor.'

Frank recorded a new single on 27 August. The A-side was a ridiculous novelty, 'The Look of Love', not worthy of him, the arranger Nelson Riddle nor its writers, Sammy Cahn and Jimmy Van Heusen. According to the song, the look of love is 'more surprising than an elephant's sneeze'. Where had that come from? The B-side, or at least the first B–side, was far more stimulating.

'I Left My Heart in San Francisco' had been written in 1953 by two amateur writers, Douglas Cross and George Cory who had come from San Francisco but lived in New York. They gave it to the light opera singer, Claramae Turner, who sang it on stage but never recorded the song. Additionally, Tennessee 'Ernie' Ford turned it down. Then Tony Bennett was booked to play some club dates at the San Francisco's Fairmont Hotel in December 1961. He wanted a song about San Francisco to make his act complete and his pianist Ralph Sharon, who knew Cross and Cory, gave him the song. It so happened that the Mayor of San Francisco was there and thought it was great. Tony Bennett recorded the song in January 1962 and it was released the following month as the B-side to 'Once Upon a Time', a perfectly decent ballad, which Frank sang in 1965 and is sometimes used in funeral services now.

Frank Sinatra recorded 'San Francisco' while it was still unknown and released it on the B-side of 'The Look of Love'. At the time he hadn't heard Tony Bennett's version, but the radio disc-jockeys had latched onto the fact that 'Once Upon a Time' had an even better B-side and it looked as though the song would be a hit. You might have thought Sinatra, owning Reprise, would have told his people to push his own version, but not a bit of it.

When he heard Tony Bennett's version, he thought it was much better than his own and reissued 'The Look of Love' with 'Indiscreet' on the B-side. It's hard to say whether Sinatra would have stolen Bennett's thunder, but Bennett was relieved. The Mayor of San Francisco presented Tony with his gold disc, and he later said, 'That song helped make me a world citizen. It allowed me to live, work and sing in any city on the globe.'

Quite possibly Frank Sinatra could have had Reprise's first Top 20 hit with 'I Left My Heart in San Francisco' but instead the honour went to Sammy Davis who took 'What Kind of Fool Am I' into the charts in October 1962.

In 1962 Frank told Nelson Riddle to write him a concerto for Spanish guitar that he could conduct. Nothing came of that but Frank did pick up the baton for the awkward-sounding *Frank Sinatra Conducts Music from Pictures and Plays*. It is a good middle-of-the-road album but you will wish Sinatra had been singing 'Exodus', 'Maria', 'If Ever I Would Leave You' or even 'Tammy' instead.

In October 1962 Frank Sinatra made an album with Count Basie and his Orchestra. The songs were expertly chosen to bring out the best in Sinatra and the musicians and the arrangements were written by Neal Hefti. The album was called *Sinatra-Basie* but it could have been named after one of the songs, 'Looking at the World through Rose Coloured Glasses', as this is one of the most joyous affirmations of life that has ever been recorded. The album had the subtitle, 'An historic musical first' and Reprise was right.

Frank regarded it as a perfect mix. Basie maintained a brilliant band and he never veered much from his 1930s sound. Even his album, *Basie's Beatles Bag* (1966), didn't sound particularly contemporary. Frank however was not on best form for the first day of the sessions as he had been shouting himself hoarse for the Dodgers.

When he was in London, Ira Gershwin had seen a cartoon in *Punch* that featured the exchange, "Nice work if you can get it" and "Won't you show me how?" This became 'Nice Work If You Can Get It', which is one of the most exhilarating openings to any album at any time.

Basie had assembled a great, swinging jazz orchestra but he himself was something of a minimalist. Very often he just played the piano with one or two fingers, which gave the album a distinctive feel. This was particularly effective in their leisurely stroll through 'I Won't Dance'. Sinatra adapted the same approach to his singing in 'I'm Gonna Sit Right Down and Write Myself a Letter' in which he often didn't sing complete lines but just a word here and there. The wonderful orchestra is strongly featured in 'Learnin' the Blues' and note Sinatra's delight, going 'ooooo' as he glides back into the vocal in 'I Only Have Eyes for You'.

The *tour de force*, if not the *tour de farce*, is 'My Kind of Girl'. Matt Monro's original had been very like Sinatra and Riddle but now it was recorded with great fun. The drums sound like a plodding elephant as Frank sings, "She walks like an angel walks".

Leslie Bricusse says, 'I didn't write 'My Kind Of Girl' for Matt. I entered it in a song competition on ITV and they cast him to sing it. My wife Evie was Yvonne Romain and she was doing a Hammer film with Oliver Reed at Bray Studios called *The Curse of the Werewolf* and I drove her out there and dropped her off at 7am. I was thinking about her and I wrote that song sitting by the River Thames in Bray. It was the first of what became known as the 'Evie songs'. There is a song in every score I write that is an 'Evie song'. I married her for my copyrights! 'My Kind of Girl' was the only song of mine that all the Rat Pack sang – Frank, Dean and Sammy, and Nat 'King' Cole did a lovely version of it as well.'

The album was called *Sinatra-Basie* and Hefti felt that it should be *Sinatra-Basie-Hefti* with his picture on the cover. When he saw that this wouldn't happen, he asked for more money, and Frank told him that he wouldn't work for him again. The album made No.5 on the US charts and remained on the listings for 42 weeks.

Frank and Sammy decided to make a single of 'Me and My Shadow' with an arrangement by Billy May. It had been written for the revue, *Harry Delmar's Rebels* (1927) and been a success for 'Whispering' Jack Smith and Al Jolson as well as providing the closing theme for bandleader, Ted Lewis. It had never been recorded like this. The way their voices wove in and out of the song is magical and the new lyrics are topical and funny: 'We're closer than smog when it clings to LA, We're closer than Bobby is to JFK'. It is performed with great affection but it could be seen as politically incorrect now as the black man is the white man's shadow. 'Me and My Shadow' became a hit record but it should have been an international smash. The B-side, 'Sam's Song', with Sammy and Dean was equally entertaining

'Me And My Shadow' coupled with 'Sam's Song' is a 45rpm which summed up the Rat Pack. It contained their jargon ('Ring-a-ding-ding, happy new year') and in-joke references to Jilly's and Toots Shor's restaurants, both in Manhattan. Well ahead of the game, Toots Shor had made an asset out of a liability during the war by promoting its great vegetarian menu.

The 'Jilly' was Ermenigildo Rizzo, who had grown up among street gangs in the 1930s and he was a 'deez, dem and doze' guy. He had opened his restaurant in the 1950s and he had befriended Frank when he was in Miami. He and his wife, Honey, were always arguing and Dolly called him 'Fuckface' – and to his fuckface, apparently. He was friendly but there was always something sinister and menacing about him. He possessed a dangerous punch and usually had a police blackjack up his sleeve.

There was a special chair and table kept for Sinatra in the back room at Jilly's. When he was there, friends and acquaintances would come and pay their respects to him. Remind you of anyone?

Hank Sanicola and Frank fell out over Sam Giancana as Hank had told Frank to keep his distance from him. To keep in with the Kennedys, Frank had to sell his stake in Cal-Neva which he thought was ridiculous. Ever the diplomat, he called Bobby Kennedy and complained, 'Look, you little rat bastard, after I went through hell with your brother's campaign getting him elected, you're doing this to me.' Bobby Kennedy replied, 'I have to follow the regulations.' 'Well,' said Frank, 'I am no longer a Democrat.'

Frank and Hank Sanicola parted company, although Hank was given Frank's share of the Barton publishing company. With Hank out of the picture, Jilly Rizzo became his manager and fixer. Jilly's brother took over the day-to-day running of the restaurant but kept the name.

The UK manager, Tony Cartwright, who often saw him in Las Vegas, says, 'Jilly Rizzo doesn't get the credit he deserves. When he managed Sinatra, he tripled his earnings. He was also his confidant, his bouncer and his friend, and he owned a restaurant in New York, which Frank loved. Sinatra hated photographers and if he saw one, he was likely to shove him and so Jilly had a lot of hassle with Sinatra.'

Although Sinatra kept insisting there was no such thing as the Clan or the Rat Pack, there certainly was – and it was part of the group's marketing strategy. The gambling, the endless parties, the drinks in hand, the girls, the narcissism of it all made them attractive, drawing headlines if not always transferring to record sales.

But all this could have been fiddling while Rome burns. In October 1962 the world was in a precarious state. When Kennedy came to power, first the Soviet leader Nikita Khrushchev had not seen him as a threat. He said, lightheartedly, that he had children older than the US president – he had too.

The botched 'Bay of Pigs' invasion of Cuba in April 1961 by some Cuban exiles trained by the CIA and with the object of deposing Fidel Castro reflected badly on Kennedy. It prompted Khrushchev to establish nuclear missile sites in Cuba, all pointing at America, and Russian ships were to deliver the weapons. The philosopher Bertrand Russell remarked, 'Macmillan, Kennedy and Khrushchev are the wickedest people in the history of man.'

Kennedy ordered a blockade of the Russian ships and during some very tense days, it could not be predicted who would back off. The Americans already had nuclear bases in Turkey and so could launch an attack on Russia at any time. In the end, Khrushchev backed down, saying quite correctly that only somebody who was stupid would start a nuclear war. Khrushchev took great criticism from within the Kremlin for his remarks and was replaced in 1962, but the crisis was over. It has been estimated that the chance of a nuclear war had been about 1 in 6, the same as playing Russian roulette.

Kennedy was able to return back to his marital infidelities including Judy Campbell. In 1983, Peter Lawford admitted, 'I was Frank's pimp and Frank was Jack's. It sounds terrible now but then it was really a lot of fun.'

Sam Giancana owned a restaurant in Northbrook, Illinois, which was northwest of Chicago. It was frequented by the Mob but Giancana converted it to an up-market nightclub, the Villa Venice Supper Club. It was set in eight acres and the grounds had been renovated with canals and gondolas. Giancana was owed favours for getting Kennedy elected and so Frank persuaded Sammy and Dean to join him for expenses only for Thanksgiving week from 26 November 1962. Later, Sinatra told the FBI that he was working for the club manager, Lee Olsen, and didn't know Giancana was involved. What a tangled web we weave.

Sinatra arranged for all 16 sets to be recorded and then edited for a live album. 'What are we going to call it,' joked Dean Martin, '*The Mafia's Greatest Hits?*'

The standard format was that they would each perform for 15 minutes and finish with a 15 minute free-for-all, though the free-for-all did sometimes start much earlier. They were so confident that they never had a serious rehearsal and it showed. The album was not issued at the time as it would have been too ramshackle. However, the tapes are a valuable social document today, even if all three performers were better on their own. The tapes convey the camaraderie between the three entertainers. They seem so hip and so cool and you wonder how many female companions were waiting for them when they came off stage.

Dean Martin was introduced as 'directly from the bar', but the comic lyrics sung to 'The Lady Is a Tramp' could only have been performed sober. One of the few songs that Dean sang straight was 'I Left My Heart in San Francisco', which he never recorded in a studio. When Dean crooned 'Where or When' and got to the line, 'The clothes you are wearing are the clothes you wore,' Frank added, 'Better get dressed and out of here because the cops are coming up the stairs.' What is this? A joke about underage sex?

As Sammy sang 'Hey There', Frank and Dean chimed 'better forget her' behind him. He had to take the usual humiliation when he sang 'What Kind of Fool Am I'. When he and Dean duetted on 'Sam's Song', Dean asked for the lyric sheet, another indication that so much of this was under-rehearsed.

There were plenty of one-liners, often directed at gays. When Frank asked Dean if he had a fairy godmother, he replied, 'No, but I've an uncle we watch closely.'

Dean asked Frank if he knew how to make a fruit cordial. When Frank said no, Dean responded, 'Be nice to him.' Big laugh.

After that joke, Frank asked him backstage, 'How come you always get the laughs and I don't?' to which Dean replied, 'You're not funny', not an assessment that others would have said to Sinatra's face. Frank said they would reverse the lines at the next show and see what happened. This time Frank said, 'Be nice to him' and there was a small titter, followed by

Dean giving an 'oh dear' look to the audience which got the biggest laugh of the evening.

The Villa Venice was more than a supper club as Giancana was running an illegal casino in a hut on the grounds. The week was a great success and Giancana took $3m from his customers. However, a few weeks later, the casino was raided by police and the club was closed.

Ultimately, the threat to Sinatra's supremacy was not from the Mafia but from the Beatles. As the Rat Pack clowned around in Chicago, four Liverpool lads were entering the UK charts with their first Parlophone single, 'Love Me Do', and popular music would never be the same again.

On 28 November 1962 Frank took a quick flight to Chicago to host a press reception for Duke Ellington. Duke was going to join Reprise and he started work the next day on *Will the Big Bands Ever Come Back*. The bandleader had *carte blanche* to do what he wanted but this sounded like a Sinatra idea: 'Duke, I'd like to hear you playing 'Sentimental Journey'.' Then came *Duke Ellington's Greatest Hits* and *Duke Ellington Plays Mary Poppins* – hardly Ellington's finest hour – but we might not have had the album with Sinatra if he hadn't been at Reprise. At the outset, Duke Ellington said, 'I thought it would be a very good idea to be contracted to some company which is controlled by an artist rather than a businessman. It gives the soul a better opportunity.'

Frank's first recording of 1963 was on January 21. 'Call Me Irresponsible' was written by Sammy Cahn and Jimmy Van Heusen and arranged and conducted by Nelson Riddle. The old team was back in action. Frank was keen to get this right and didn't mind several takes, at one point singing, 'Call me wrong note irresponsible'. He told the string section, 'Have more than strings to your bow as the strings might break.'

'Call Me Irresponsible' has an ingenious lyric, involving five syllable words. Sammy Cahn explained how the song came about: 'It was written for Fred Astaire to sing in the film, *Papa's Delicate Condition*, but he never made the film. He never recorded the song and that is one of the disappointments of my life. The greatest thrill of my entire life was standing in front of Fred Astaire and doing the song. I came to the lines,

'Do my foolish alibis bore you,
Well, I'm not too clever,
I just adore you'

and Astaire said, "Stop!" Van Heusen almost fell off his piano bench as this had never happened before. Astaire said, "That is one of the best songs I've ever heard." I said, "That is one of the best half-songs you've ever heard. May I finish it?" He said, "That's a great, great song. Would you like to know how you got this job? Johnny Mercer wasn't available." I said, "I consider that a high compliment." He said, "No, I'll give you the high compliment now. The next time Mercer leaves town, I won't worry."' Although the song has become a standard, and deservedly so, it failed to make the Top 40 in the US and didn't figure on the UK charts.

The other song at the session was the title song from *Come Blow Your Horn*, a song of male dominance, again written by Cahn and Van Heusen, but this time far more routine. Note the references to Brando, 'Make like a Mr Mumbles and you're a zero.' Frank hit the last note, put his coat on and was out of the door before Nelson had finished conducting.

The playwright Neil Simon had had a Broadway success with his comedy, *Come Blow Your Horn*, writing about Jewish family life as usual and with the central character being based around the playboy lifestyle of his brother, Danny. This Lothario role was offered to Frank Sinatra and his mother was going to be played by Maureen Stapleton who was 10 years younger than Frank. She had just played Dick Van Dyke's mother in *Bye Bye Birdie* and they were the same age. She decided that playing mothers of middle-aged men was not going to be good for her career, so the role went to Molly Picon, one of the few Jewish actors in the cast. The play had to be rewritten for gentiles.

Tommy Sands declined the role of Frank's brother on the grounds of miscasting and it would have been curious if he was playing the brother of his real life father-in-law. The producers went with Tony Bill, who was 22 playing 31, whereas Frank was 47 playing 39 and acting younger. Although he is acting well, Frank is not youthful enough for the role and anyway he was only a few years away from 'My Way'.

Frank was unsure about Lee J Cobb playing his father as he had been disappointed by his evidence to the Un-American Activities Committee. Cobb had been a Communist and he told Sinatra that the pressure had brought about a nervous breakdown in his wife and that he'd become a friendly witness to avoid her suffering further distress. Sinatra accepted his explanation and they became friends. The dialogue between them often sparkled. Frank: 'You don't even treat me with the same respect as the night watchman.' Lee J Cobb: 'At least I know where the night watchman was last night.'

Frank was pushing all the time to make the film quickly. This speed was evident in the film itself. When Tony Bill stumbled on the word 'television', note how Sinatra picked up on it and ran it into the scene. Sinatra threw in impersonations of Kennedy and Bogart and there were in-jokes about Paramount in the script, which was written by Norman Lear, best known for the TV sitcom, *All in the Family*.

There are many Sinatra touches in the film. One setting in a lavish bar took place in Toots Shor's restaurant in New York City and in Frank's bachelor pad; in each location there was a turntable featuring a Reprise LP. This was appropriate as the Reprise repertoire was music for playboys. When Dean Martin visited Frank on the set, they dressed him as a tramp and, in an improvised scene, Frank gave him the steak he was using for his black eye. Phyllis McGuire appears in two scenes, cast as a favour to Sam Giancana, and she is fine, as is Jill St John who was one of Frank's girlfriends in real life as well as on the screen. Sinatra's song, 'Come Blow Your Horn' fits in with his brother Buddy getting his new look.

Frank pushed for everything to be done quickly. The director Bud Yorkin didn't mind as he was used to making TV variety shows. However, Sinatra became so exasperated with the set up for one New York street scene that he lost patience. He said, 'I'm doing the take now.' He marched down the street as requested and then hailed a cab and drove away. As a result of Sinatra's pushing, the film was brought in a week under schedule and under budget. Barbara Marx was planning a charity preview of a forthcoming film in Palm Springs but when it wasn't ready, she asked Frank if he could help. He gave them *Come Blow Your Horn*, some four months before its official release in June. It did reasonably well at the box office.

Frank's first album with Nelson Riddle for Reprise was a sombre affair, an album that said, 'I am a very serious and committed artist.' It was an album of heavily orchestrated show tunes called, *The Concert Sinatra*, but it was not a live recording despite its title. As six of the eight songs had music by Richard Rodgers, it could, with two changes, have been called *Frank Sinatra Sings the Richard Rodgers Songbook*, though neither of them would have liked that. Rodgers referred to Sinatra as his 'foul weather friend', though he was impressed with the results. The album was made at the Goldwyn Studios in Hollywood as the studio had to take a 70-piece orchestra.

This was as close to a classical album as Sinatra would get and the tracks could have been more adventurous as Sinatra was often singing songs he had performed before, albeit never so grandly. 'Ol' Man River' was a truly magnificent performance. Note how Sinatra held his note for 15 seconds on 'lands in jail' and then added 'I get weary' without pausing for breath. Again, 'Lost in the Stars' was much more impressive and dramatic than his earlier recording from 1946.

Of the Richard Rodgers' songs, the desperate 'This Nearly Was Mine' called for big notes and a big finish, and got them, but 'You'll Never Walk Alone' was not as dramatic as it could have been. He is acting out the lyrics so much on 'I Have Dreamed' from *The King and I* that he should have tried a stage musical in Broadway or the West End. It is a strikingly unusual song, highlighted by writing the rhyming pattern – ABCADEFFEE.

'Bewitched, Bothered And Bewildered' from *Pal Joey* didn't fare so well in this context as Lorenz Hart's lyric called for a lighter touch, and another Rodgers and Hart song, 'My Heart Stood Still', sounded better with one of Sinatra's swinging arrangements.

The highlight was the eight minute 'Soliloquy' from *Carousel*, but it even omitted a portion of the lyric. The song was both aggressive and tender and Sinatra and Riddle captured the changes very well. It had a positive message as the gadfly roustabout intended to be responsible and settle down. Interestingly, Sinatra followed this song with 'Nancy' on a later compilation, *A Man and His Music*. It was a great album and even Richard Rodgers was impressed.

Waste not, want not. While recording with the big orchestra, Sinatra and Riddle cut three more songs. Cahn and Van Heusen were rarely away from any of his projects and this time they had written 'California' with the hope of it becoming the state song. A huge choir came in halfway through to bog it down, but the lyric was doing that perfectly well anyway. Sinatra could do little with lines like 'A land that paradise could well be jealous of' – give me 'California Here I Come' and 'California Dreamin''. 'America the Beautiful' is Frank Sinatra being patriotic with a huge choir – fine if you like that sort of thing. The third recording was a sparkling arrangement of a Maurice Chevalier success, 'You Brought a New Kind Of Love to Me'.

In May 1963 Frank Sinatra met the singer and guitarist who would become Reprise's first big commercial discovery, a Mexican cabaret entertainer, Trini Lopez, who was performing in Beverly Hills. 'I had seen Sinatra about a year before when I was at Ye Little's and he gave me a dirty look. Then he saw me at PJ's and told my manager that he wanted to meet me. When he was in a good mood, everything was great, but when he wasn't, oh boy, you had to look out. Thank God that my first three or four albums, all recorded live, were all big hits.' Indeed. Trini's first single, the highly infectious 'If I Had a Hammer' from *Trini Lopez at PJ's* was an international hit, selling millions of copies, the very thing Sinatra wanted when he was negotiating a price for his label.

For his next Reprise album, Frank wanted to record new versions of his biggest successes for an album called *Sinatra's Sinatra*. The songs were all arranged by Nelson Riddle and often set in different keys and tempos from the originals. Sinatra's voice was getting lower and the booze and cigarettes didn't help. They were still very good performances and the only weak point was when he added, 'Oh, you're a fine witch' in a silly voice at the end of 'Witchcraft' – why did he keep doing things like that?

'In the Wee Small Hours of the Morning' was lighter than the original version, almost given a *Nice 'n' Easy* treatment. Now with the enhancement of stereo, Frank performed a magnificent version of 'I've Got You Under My Skin', but there didn't seem much point in revisiting 'The Second Time Around' as it was already in the Reprise catalogue, but the second time around Nelson was able to conduct.

The most interesting track is 'Nancy'. I would have expected Frank to have updated the line 'She has no sister' but he leaves it alone. He does however add;

'Keep Audrey Hepburn and keep Liz Taylor,

Nancy's the feature, they're just the trailer.'

Frank's new 'All the Way' had a new lease of life in 1999 when Celine Dion added a vocal track and similarly, 'Young at Heart' was released in 2007 with added Aznavour.

Another aborted project involved Frank and Kim Novak making a film about international movie making, *Le Mépris (aka Contempt)*, directed by Jean Luc Godard. The roles finally went to Brigitte Bardot and Jack Palance.

Next Frank made a guest appearance in John Huston's spoof thriller, *The List of Adrian Messenger*. It was a spot-the-guest-stars movie including Burt Lancaster (as a female fox hunt protester), Tony Curtis, Robert Mitchum and Frank Sinatra. Sinatra played an Irish gypsy stableboy but because he was in disguise, he realised that he could use a lookalike character actor, Dave Willock, for much of his role. It is possible, and I certainly like to believe it, that Sinatra only appeared to rip his mask off at the end. If so, whoever guessed it was him, was wrong. Sinatra was paid $75,000 which included a secrecy clause in that he wasn't to reveal he was involved in the film – but for $75,000, I wouldn't tell anyone either. Indeed, I wouldn't want to.

Robert Mitchum gave a rare laugh when he took off his mask and no wonder, it was money for old rope. What's more, he was obviously Robert Mitchum even when he had the make-up on. The film was rubbish: the acting ham off the bone and the ridiculous plot gave no indication as why the killings took place or why the victims have been executed in such a convoluted way. On IMDB, it says, 'The plot synopsis is empty'. Indeed.

The film was shot on the cheap, perhaps because the cameos were so expensive. It is obvious that they filmed a fox hunt and then stuck their actors in front of it. I'll tell you for nothing that Kirk Douglas was the assassin, but do I have to give the $75,000 back now?

Frank recorded 'Have Yourself a Merry Little Christmas' with Gus Levene and his Orchestra for the soundtrack of the film, *The Victors,* a World War II film starring Vince Edwards, Albert Finney, Peter Fonda and George Hamilton. Only a brief snatch was heard in the film but Sinatra was able to use the track as a Christmas single.

The noted film director Robert Aldrich once reflected, 'I'm just one of those who thought they could direct Sinatra. It's like being one of the girls who thought they'd get Howard Hughes to marry them.' He couldn't claim inexperience as at the time he wrote and directed *4 for Texas*, he had completed the grotesque but compelling *What Ever Happened To Baby Jane* with two monstrous egos, Bette Davis and Joan Crawford. Still, *4 for Texas* didn't work and Aldrich called it a total failure, saying he had no rapport with Sinatra. It's not that bad but it does resemble a below par TV movie.

A spoof western *4 for Texas* isn't a Rat Pack film as both Sammy Davis and Joey Bishop were making a gangster flick, *Johnny Cool,* for Peter Lawford's company at the time. Made in June 1963, the film starred Frank and Dean with Anita Ekberg (who had been in two Martin and Lewis films) and Ursula Andress as the four for Texas, along with Charles Bronson, Victor Buono (oddly cast as a corrupt banker but he was taking Lawford's role) and the always sinister Jack Elam.

There was a good opening sequence in which Frank and Dean out in the desert are attempting to get the better of each other. It set the tone as both Frank and Dean were depicted smiling as they shot their victims. The whole film had a casual disregard for the loss of life. Okay, it's only a film so who cares, but would a banker arrange for a ship to sink for insurance purposes, knowing that lives would be lost?

There was no dramatic tension whatsoever and Dean only happened to have more lines than Frank because he showed up when Frank didn't. Dean's best line, surely a reflection of himself, was 'I'm anybody's man, mostly my own.' Dean forgot to duck when Frank hit him in a fight; he fell to the floor and gnawed at Frank's ankle.

The film would have stood a better chance at the box office if the busty co-stars had taken their clothes off, but the Three Stooges did deliver a nude portrait of Ursula Andress to the riverboat casino. With Dean, they went through a comic routine about pointing to the right. We never learnt how these two European girls happen to be in Galveston.

Ursula Andress's career was certainly taking some strange twists. The Swiss beauty had appeared in some Italian films in her teens and had been brought to Hollywood by Marlon Brando. Her first international success was in *Dr No* in 1962 and then she supported Elvis Presley in *Fun in Acapulco*, though rather unfun in Acapulco. Quite possibly, Frank wanted Ursula Andress in the film because he wanted to andress, sorry, undress her. It's likely that Frank and Dean were not too successful with their costars as they flew in some hookers from Vegas. These girls ended up in the saloon scene in the Antler bar and also offered their services after hours. Stag nights a speciality, I presume.

When the bad guys come along at the end of the film, it is not only hard to determine what's going on but even harder to care. Hundreds of extras were involved in the final scene. The film had been completed in 37 days.

The score was written by Nelson Riddle and released on LP, one piece being called 'Girls of the Antler Bar'. The editing was poor. Dean and Ursula talked about the trouble with some crockery and yet that scene had been deleted. The film was released for Christmas 1963 and only had poor reviews. Still, it passed a pleasant, inconsequential evening if you were a young lad with a date, and you could at least say that one of the Three Stooges had a Beatle haircut.

The Three Stooges did however seem almost normal when compared to Jerry Lewis, who like Dean was now a solo star. While Dean appeared to be uninterested in what his former partner was doing, Jerry was intrigued by Dean's development. Although they weren't speaking, he did sneak into a Rat Pack show at the Sands. He commented that Dean had replaced him with four other guys.

Jerry Lewis was starring, writing and directing his own movies, having two roles in *The Nutty Professor* (1963), a comic take on *Dr Jekyll and Mr Hyde*. In the film, Professor Kelp's alter ego was a smooth-talking, handsome night club singer called Buddy Love, who was unpleasant and cruel but the girls all loved him. Although Lewis said it was unintentional, the criticism of Dean seemed obvious and revealed how Lewis was thinking. Possibly it was even accurate from Lewis's perspective but most people found Dean generous and good-natured.

Indeed, Johnny Prophet (real name, John Profeta) was a big band singer in the 1940s who had hit bad times and Dean Martin wanted to do something for him. He arranged with Frank that he could make an album with Reprise, one that enabled Prophet to relaunch his night-club career.

Probably promoted by *The Concert Sinatra*, Frank conceived and produced four albums by the Reprise Repertory Theatre. He would take great, post-war musical scores from Broadway and have the songs performed by top singers and arranged by Nelson Riddle, Billy May and the like, all being conducted by Morris Stoloff. Frank had wonderful scores and casts to work with and derived much pleasure in finding the right songs for the right singers. He insisted that the full score be recorded with the introductory verses, and each album started with an overture.

Frank sang 'Some Enchanted Evening' on *South Pacific* and was joined by Rosemary Clooney for the reprise. Sammy Davis was dazzling on 'There Is Nothing Like a Dame' and, in a brilliant move, Frank had him sing 'Carefully Taught', a song of racial equality where Oscar Hammerstein was saying the opposite of what he thought. Frank and Keely

Smith handle 'Twin Soliloquies' where the man and the woman separately thought that they would not meet their partner's expectations. Keely has some strange pronunciation on 'A Wonderful Guy' and Frank should have told Debbie Reynolds that she didn't have to play the character performing 'Happy Talk', but just sing the song well. In an album of highlights, Dinah Shore outshone them all with 'I'm Gonna Wash That Man Right Outa My Hair'.

Guy and Dolls was ideal for Frank, Dean and Sammy and it's amusing to hear Bing with Dean and Frank on 'The Oldest Established (Permanent Floating Crap Game in New York)', which was arranged by Billy May. At last Frank sang the warm, romantic ballad, 'I've Never Been in Love Before' which was dropped from the film and when he swaggered through Billy May's brilliant arrangement for 'Luck Be a Lady', he said, at the end of the recording, 'That'll show Mumbles!' Brando had not been invited to join the project. There was a spectacular 'Sit Down, You're Rockin' the Boat' from Sammy Davis and the only drawback on this project was Debbie Reynolds again adopting an annoying accent for 'Adelaide's Lament', but she did perform 'Sue Me' with Allan Sherman.

Frank Loesser wrote his musical about downtrodden hustlers in New York and Sinatra was giving *Guys and Dolls* all the glitz and glamour of Las Vegas. When Frank, Dean and Sammy performed together at the Sands in September, they included songs from *Guys and Dolls* in the act as well as 'Call Me Irresponsible'.

Frank, Dean and Sammy delivered 'We Open in Venice' from *Kiss Me Kate* and when Frank and Dean started joking about Italy, Sammy added, 'Here we go, back to the home country again.' 'So In Love' was sung twice on the album, first by Johnny Prophet and then as a duet between Frank and Keely. Pride of place must go to Phyllis McGuire who sang the hilarious 'I Hate Men' – wonder why Frank had given her that song.

Finian's Rainbow was the weakest score but it had many highlights. Frank sang a fine 'Old Devil Moon' with Nelson Riddle arranging and the curious 'When I'm Not Near the Girl I Love'. How would you rhyme 'bosom'? How about 'refuses 'em', 'pursues 'em' and 'woos 'em'. Rosemary Clooney asked 'How Are Things in Glocca Morra' and the McGuire Sisters are very entertaining on 'The Begat'.

Sinatra decided to cut his losses as Reprise's sales had been disappointing and the label was making losses. He had done it his way and it wasn't fully working. He had been Reprise's biggest artist and he had been continually undermined by Capitol's vengeful marketing.

After several months of negotiation, he made a deal with Jack Warner. He sold two-thirds of the label to Warner Brothers along with his own acting services and his casino holdings, which we shall come to, for $3.5m and in return he would pay $2m for one-third ownership of the Warner/Reprise labels. So Warners took over the label, dropping many of his loss-making acts, mostly jazz performers, but the hitless Nancy Sinatra could stay. Sonny Burke remained Sinatra's producer at Reprise until his death in 1980 and Mo Ostin was label manager until 1994.

Reprise became one of the most progressive labels in the world. It's easy to imagine Sinatra approving of Gordon Lightfoot, Ry Cooder and Joni Mitchell and even, at a push, Kenny Rogers and Arlo Guthrie but how about Neil Young, the Electric Prunes, Captain Beefheart, Frank Zappa and Tiny Tim? Reprise signed Randy Newman, who satirised Sinatra in 'Lonely at the Top', and the cutting edge comedian Richard Pryor. They secured the licensing rights for the Kinks and Jimi Hendrix in the US, but just what did Frank make of Wild Man Fischer?

At one point, the conglomerate WEA (Warner-Elektra-Atlantic) under the Kinney Corporation decided that the label would only continue for Frank Sinatra but Neil Young refused to budge to W, E or A, meaning that Frank Sinatra and Neil Young were the only current artists on the label. When Neil Young left for Geffen in 1982, the label stopped making new recordings. It was revived in 1986 with Dwight Yoakam and then Enya and Dream Academy, eventually building a new roster of country, gospel and rock acts with Neil Young and Kenny Rogers returning to the fold.

On 9 September 1963, 19-year-old Frank Sinatra Jr made his professional debut with the Tommy Dorsey Band, such as it was, at the Americana Hotel in Manhattan. Frank said encouragingly, 'The kid sings better than I did at that age. He's way ahead of me because he's a studied musician which I am not.' Maybe, but no matter how good he was, it was an ill-advised move to start your professional career by singing your dad's songs and telling your dad's jokes with your dad's old band and, indeed, using the name Frank Sinatra Jr.

In October 1963 Frank played Carnegie Hall for the first time, supported by Lena Horne, for two nights for a children's charity. Meanwhile, Frank's old rival, Dick Haymes, relocated to the UK, a broken man. He was drinking heavily; his personal relationships were bad; his bookings were poor; and he hoped that this would be a new start. Haymes found work on the chicken-in-a-basket venues in the north of England and he dated Wendy Smith, an actress who had played nude volleyball in Michael Winner's sexploitation movie, *Some Like It Cool*. The Cavern's DJ, Bob Wooler saw him at the Empress Club in Widnes. 'It was so terrible to see him doing 'It's a Grand Night for Singing' to a noisy audience. It was pathetic that they treated him that way.' In January 1964, he repeated the title line of 'What Kind of Fool Am I?' over and over again in one drink-sodden performance. Dick Haymes told one reporter, 'I've never been a good businessman. Things would have been a lot different for me if I'd been as bright as Frank Sinatra.'

But at that time it wasn't much better being Frank Sinatra.

The Nevada authorities had told Sam Giancana that he was blacklisted and not allowed to visit casinos in the State. He was being watched constantly by the FBI but he won a strange court injunction in which he claimed the surveillance was treating him like a prisoner. The court determined that no more than a carload of FBI agents could tail him and if he were playing golf, there had to be a disinterested foursome between Giancana's party and the G-men. This was tough on the unfortunate party who had gone golfing and found themselves piggy in the middle.

Sam Giancana was *persona not grata* at the Cal-Neva but he was there while Sinatra was there, and Sinatra was one of the owners. What's more, he was involved in a very public row with the manager of the McGuire Sisters. As a result, Frank Sinatra was seen as an unsuitable owner for the Cal-Neva. His lawyer, Mickey Rudin, could prove that he had not invited Giancana personally but it was to no avail.

Frank owned 50% of the Cal-Neva and 9% of the Sands, and Jack Warner told him that he would have to drop his interest if he was to join Warners. He decided not to contest the charges as he felt he would lose anyway. Better to sell his holdings and move on. His manager, Hank Sanicola, who owned 33% of the Cal-Neva, thought he should have challenged it. They fell out and Jilly Rizzo replaced him as Frank's manager. The press had a field day, deriding Sinatra at every opportunity, which damaged his reputation.

In November Frank was filming another Rat Pack movie, this time a 1920s gangster flick for Warners called *Robin and the 7 Hoods or Who Maid Marian?* It starred Frank, Dean and Sammy with Bing Crosby stepping into Peter Lawford's role. How curious that Frank should have given the role to Bing, the source of his resentment with Lawford. The script was changed to accommodate Bing by giving him a couple of songs, and this film, with a score by Sammy Cahn and Jimmy Van Heusen, was the most musical of the Rat Pack films. It was directed by Gordon Douglas, who seemed especially fond of filming female backsides, so he undoubtedly fitted in well with the rest of the gang. As gangster films go, this is extremely mild with only one killing being shown on screen.

Frank had been hoping that Gene Kelly would play the rival gangster, but Kelly had seen enough of Sinatra's working methods to realise it wouldn't be to his liking if Frank was in control. Instead, he hired Peter Falk to play a gangster who wanted all the clubs in Chicago with Frank owning the club that he particularly prized.

Sinatra hardly knew Falk but had sent him a script. Falk wanted to get away from playing gangsters and was hoping to be cast as a doctor in another film. Frank said, 'Do what you think is best, but the part in the picture is yours until we start shooting.' The medical role fell through so he took Sinatra's offer. He was mortified when Sammy Cahn gave him a song. He had never thought of himself as a singer and here he was making his singing début in a film with Frank, Dean, Sammy and Bing. When Peter Falk complained about some of the dialogue, Frank tore out the page and said, 'Say what you want.'

Although Edward G Robinson only made a cameo appearance as Big Jim, his scene was hugely enjoyable as was the remarkable moment when a casino transforms into a temperance hall, an incredible set being constructed for a wildly improbable, one-line joke.

Sammy Davis was desperate to make the film because he had been spending lavishly. He was performing at the Sands but he commuted to Los Angeles whenever he was required. As a result, he had little to do in the film but he did perform a sensational song and dance routine for 'Bang Bang'.

In a similar routine to the title song in *Come Blow Your Horn*, Frank and Dean gave Bing Crosby a makeover in 'Style' but it was the old-fashioned Bing who got the girl, Barbara Rush. Bing was enjoying himself in 'Mr Booze', gently mocking his ba-ba-ba-booing image. His children's song, 'Don't Be a Do-Badder' is fine if you like that sort of thing (I don't).

Dean Martin crooned 'Any Man Who Loves His Mother' while playing pool, but his winning pool shots were made by Milton Berle, doubling for him and good enough to have been a professional. While shooting the picture, Gordon Douglas made a short with Dean about funding the US team at the 1964 Olympics, which was widely shown in cinemas before the feature.

The hit song of the movie was 'My Kind of Town', a second song about Chicago and just as well known. When it was released as a single, the promotions executive at Warners, Joe Smith had *Playboy* bunnies in Chicago deliver the single to influential disc-jockeys, which might explain some of the airplay. It was not a singles hit nationally but the soundtrack album made the Top 40.

'My Kind of Town' had a famed Nelson Riddle arrangement which started quietly and built up. Sinatra mentions the Ripley Building and Union Stockyard, and this is parodied by Randy Newman at the end of 'Rednecks'. 'My Kind of Town' is a great record but albeit a shallow song. It received an Oscar nomination but lost out to an even shallower one, 'Chim Chim Cheree' from *Mary Poppins*, so maybe they should have nominated 'Don't Be a Do-Badder' instead. It is easy to understand Sammy Cahn's annoyance when Frank's song, 'I Like to Lead When I Dance' was dropped from the film, as it is amongst their best compositions and well in line with Sinatra's personality. There was a very good reason for the song being dropped. Frank mimed poorly and didn't go for another take. In a behind the scenes documentary, the cast is pictured performing another song, 'Charlotte Couldn't Charleston'.

On November 21, Sinatra rang his daughter Tina and found that she was going to see Johnny Mathis with her mother, Nancy. He informed them that they should have better taste. While Frank was shooting in a cemetery in Burbank, he noticed a tombstone for a John F Kennedy, who had died in 1940.

The following day the cast had just started work on location in a cemetery in Burbank when Frank received the news that Kennedy had been shot in Dallas and he told the production team. The next report confirmed that he had been assassinated and so Frank told Gordon Douglas that they would finish the scene so that they would not have to return the next day. Whatever Kennedy's shortcomings, he had been a very popular president and the country was in mourning.

After Kennedy's death, Frank shut himself in his bedroom in Palm Springs for three days. He felt snubbed at not been invited to the funeral. Peter Lawford later said, "He was too much of an embarrassment to the family." A benefit concert for Martin Luther King in Santa Monica with Frank and Count Basie and his Orchestra on 26 November was cancelled.

A keen Democrat, Judy Garland had been friendly with Kennedy but not in a sexual way. She called him Mr President and he called her Madame Ambassador. Sometimes if the day was getting too much for him, he would call her and say, 'Sing 'Over The Rainbow' to me' – and wouldn't it be fabulous to do that if you'd had a lousy day? In 1963 she making a TV series, *The Judy Garland Show*, and she wanted to record a whole episode of patriotic songs in his memory. 'No, no,' said CBS, 'it's too much. We will never beat *Bonanza*!' Allowed one patriotic number to close the show; with a single spot, she sang, almost shouted, 'The Battle Hymn of the Republic'. It was a crowning moment in her career and the audience gave her a standing ovation.

Frank returned to filming and on 3 December, he entered a studio to record the main theme for the film, *The Cardinal*, 'Stay with Me'. The film, directed by Otto Preminger, was about the dilemmas facing a priest from Boston who became a cardinal. It was a long slow film that would test anyone's faith to watch it through. Decent song though.

On 8 December 1963, Frank Sinatra Jr was singing with the Dorsey band as an out-of-season lounge act at Harrah's club in Lake Tahoe. He was in a hotel room with the trumpeter John Foss at 9pm when there was a knock on the door. Two gunmen were there and kidnapped them both, though they soon let Foss go. They proved incompetent kidnappers as the getaway car soon ran out of petrol. Having no money, the abductors had to take it from Frank Jr, whom they held captive in San Fernando Valley.

Frank Jr was reported missing and his father finally received a call the next day at 5pm. He was told that the kidnappers would ring with their demands the following day at 9am. They wanted $240,000 in used notes in a suitcase and, if their demands were met, Sinatra could collect his son four hours after the money was delivered. The press had got hold of the story and it had become the biggest kidnapping in modern times.

The money was paid and Frank Jr was eventually found wandering on the San Diego Highway. He celebrated his father's birthday and the joy of his release with a meal at the Sands with his dad's current squeeze, Jill St John.

The main kidnapper, Barry Keenan was an estate agent, needing quick money for drugs and the effect of a costly divorce. He had talked his friend, John Amsler into helping him. The duo approached a painter and decorator, John Irwin, who had a commanding voice for ransom demands. He was given $40,000 for his efforts, but then he foolishly told his brother about the plot. His brother went to the police and all three were arrested on 14 December. At the trail, the kidnappers claimed it had been a publicity stunt for Frank Jr's career. This was easily discounted but the story has stuck. It's hard to have been a kidnapping victim and then have everyone believe it was a set up.

In December 1965 Sinatra won libel damages against the ITV company, Associated-Rediffusion, which had broadcast that the kidnapping had been a publicity stunt.

CHAPTER 13

Making it with the moderns

'Frank Sinatra is the Mercedes-Benz of men.'
(Marlene Dietrich, and she should know)

I. Beatleland

The Beatles had lightning success in the UK in early 1963 and then around Europe. Few British acts had had success in America and their manager, Brian Epstein had learnt from previous failures, notably with Cliff Richard, and other performers as well. Although the Beatles were unknown to Americans in December 1963, the next two months were extraordinary as they took the country by storm.

Dennis Locorriere from Dr Hook was born in 1949 and he recalls when he first saw the Beatles. 'Before *The Ed Sullivan Show*, there was a little clip on *The Jack Paar Show* which he regarded as an oddity, you know, "Wow, look at this freaky thing from across the ocean." It was like he had discovered aliens. It was a pretty dark clip from some club. I first really noticed them when I heard 'I Want to Hold Your Hand' on the radio. It jumped off the radio; the cymbals were so bright and vibrant. It made me want to play something, bang on a box with spoons I suppose, but it got me going.'

Early in 1964, with Beatlemania rampant in the UK, the Beatles topped the US charts with 'I Want to Hold Your Hand' and became a sensation on *The Ed Sullivan Show*. As George Harrison said, 'There had been cover stories on European Beatlemania in *Life* and *Newsweek* so it wasn't too difficult a job for Capitol to follow through. And the song itself was very catchy anyway.'

There were many reasons as to why the Beatles made such a huge impact in America. Timing was certainly a factor and the scenario would surely have been very different if the Beatles' first visit had been scheduled for the end of November 1963.

Beatles' author Bruce Spizer discounts the Kennedy effect. 'It is there but it has been exaggerated. It is hogwash to say the youth of America was despondent and needed the Beatles. This is over a month later and life goes on. One of the main things about the Beatles is that it was a fun story, and even if a reporter hated the band, he would have fun writing about it. The press gave the Beatles terrific coverage and that helped fuel Beatlemania. Sure, the music cheered us up, but it was great music.' In other words, the main factor was their talent.

In April 1964, in an unprecedented coup, the Beatles held the top five positions on the *Billboard* Hot 100. In 1964 alone, the Beatles had 19 Top 40 hits in America including six No.1s. This was staggeringly impressive and there has been nothing like it before or since. The reasoning is simple: no record company wants to promote more than four or five singles by the same act in a year. What took place was saturation marketing gone berserk and any promotion man would fear that the public would be turned off by the over-exposure. That it didn't happen is testimony to the originality and enduring appeal of the Beatles' records.

It was never intended that the Beatles should be competing with themselves on the charts and it only happened through a mixture of one man's incompetence and the aversion of the Capitol label for its British owners.

EMI with its subsidiary labels was the biggest record company in the UK. It relied upon licensing agreements with American labels to release their product in the UK but having established the popularity for certain artists, it was always possible that the American labels might move elsewhere. Having established Elvis Presley in the UK, RCA Victor then switched from EMI to the Decca group, setting up their own label in the process.

In order to maintain stability, EMI bought Capitol Records in 1955. One of Capitol's founders, Glenn Wallichs, joined the EMI board and in 1956, both EMI and Capitol had bumper years, a good portion of being due to Frank Sinatra's recordings. In 1957, EMI consolidated its American operations by merging EMI (US) Ltd with Capitol.

So far so good but there were problems. Some of the key personnel at Capitol resented their British owners and ignoring the quality of what was on offer, did not want to release EMI's product in the US. Capitol had a US No.1 with Laurie London's 'He's Got the World in His Hands' in 1958, but issued Cliff Richard's 'Move It' with no promotion. Some major British hits were licensed to other US labels after Capitol had turned them down. How could Capitol have missed the potential of 'Living Doll' (Cliff Richard), 'Portrait of My Love' and 'My Kind of Girl" (both Matt Monro) and "I Remember You" (ironically, written by Capitol's founder, Johnny Mercer, and here revived by Frank Ifield), especially when they were getting those rights for free?

The Capitol executive Dave Dexter listened to EMI's UK releases and decided what was suitable for America. He had been with the company since the 1940s and preferred jazz and blues. He thought there would be little interest for British acts in America. Dexter turned down 'Love Me Do', 'Please Please Me', 'From Me to You' and 'She Loves You'. Bizarrely, Dexter's recommendation, Freddie and the Dreamers' 'I'm Telling You Now', was released by Capitol in October 1963. The Beatles' product was licensed to smaller labels, Vee-Jay and Swan, which issued them without much fanfare.

Brian Epstein was dismayed when Capitol rejected their strongest single to date, 'I Want to Hold Your Hand' and he telephoned Alan Livingston, now the president of the company. Livingston admitted that he had never even heard the Beatles and relied upon Dexter's recommendations. Appreciating that Epstein had EMI's support, Livingston overruled Dexter and persuaded Swan Records to drop their option for 'I Want to Hold Your Hand'.

Brian Epstein played a blinder by insisting that Capitol spend around $40,000 promoting the single. For some crazy reason, Livingston agreed to this; perhaps he thought it would get the English off his back if it failed to sell. The promotion emphasised the length of the Beatles' hair as much as the group's talent, even so, the single exploded onto the charts. At nearly every stage of the Beatles' career, they were supported by top class people who were sympathetic to what they were doing. The only instance where it went horribly wrong is with Dave Dexter, but even then it worked to their advantage.

Capitol's publicity had been sensational and 'I Want to Hold Your Hand' had sold over 1.5m copies before the Beatles had arrived in New York in February 1964. They were greeted at the newly renamed John F Kennedy Airport on a cold and blustery day but over 3,000 screaming fans were at the airport. Ringo, asked what he thought of Beethoven, said 'Great, especially his poems' Everybody loved their humour, which was something new for press conferences. If only the Rat Pack had given press conferences in such an off-beat way.

Admittedly some publicity was tacky as Capitol executives were wearing Beatle wigs;

why had no one thought of marketing Sinatra wigs? One factory was said to be manufacturing 35,000 wigs a day. There were Beatle T-shirts, Beatle buttons, Beatle hats, Beatle wallpaper and Beatle pillows. Paul McCartney said at the time, 'We didn't want to appear like a gang of idiots', but much of the publicity was perilously close to that. Every radio station was playing the Beatles' records – endlessly. The radio DJ, Murray the K (Murray Kaufman), who had once played Sinatra over and over, now became so close to the group that he started calling himself the Fifth Beatle.

Up until this point Dave Dexter had hardly released any British product, but he didn't admit his mistake or change his views. Cilla Black and Peter and Gordon were released on Capitol, but he passed on the Hollies and Billy J Kramer (both Imperial), the Animals and Herman's Hermits (both MGM), Gerry and the Pacemakers (Lauric), Manfred Mann (Ascot) and the Dave Clark Five (Epic).

Acknowledging the new order, Elvis had sent the Beatles a good luck telegram but Ed Sullivan was cantankerous, disliking the hordes of screaming girls. However, he didn't criticise his guests publicly, no matter what he thought. Contrast this with Dean Martin who made his disdain for the Rolling Stones apparent when he introduced them on *The Hollywood Palace Show* in June 1964. He introduced a daredevil circus act as 'the father of the Rolling Stones. He's been trying to kill himself ever since.' It was the long hair that got to him – he hated it. Although Dean didn't know it, one of his daughters had a brief fling with Brian Jones. 'Dean Martin was just a drunk,' says Bill Wyman, 'and he took us on face value. He didn't think that we took baths and he didn't know how to treat people who were different from himself.'

Ed Sullivan was to say that paying for the Beatles was the greatest single investment in the history of American television. His first programme with them had 73m viewers which was 40% of the population. 60% of all US televisions were tuned to the Beatles that night. Even the evangelist Billy Graham, who campaigned against television on Sundays, switched on. Graham said that the Beatles' performance displayed 'all the symptoms of the uncertainty of the times and the confusion about us.' President Johnson said they needed haircuts.

The blues rocker, George Thorogood remarked, 'Kennedy had been assassinated a few months before and so the Beatles couldn't have hit at a better time. They didn't sound or look like anything we had heard or seen before. On Monday in school I was in the cafeteria eating lunch and the guy next to me was screaming in my ear about them. Everybody – the cooks, the janitors, the teachers, the police, every kid in school – was talking about the Beatles and talking at the top of their lungs.'

The music critic of the *New York Times*, Theodore Strongin wrote, 'The Beatles have a tendency to build phrases around unresolved leading tones. This precipitates the ear into a false modal frame that temporarily turns the fifth of the scale into the tonic, momentarily suggesting the Mixolydian mode. But everything always ends a plain diatonic all the same.' Ringo commented, 'Why couldn't he say whether he liked us or not?'

One encouraging moment for the old guard was when Louis Armstrong found himself high in the singles charts alongside the Beatles and even deposed them with 'Hello Dolly!' The single was on Kapp; Frank must have wondered why he couldn't do the same at Reprise. However, MGM had cold feet over a lavish musical about Irving Berlin, *Say It with Music,* for which Berlin, had written ten new songs. It was to star Frank Sinatra and Judy Garland with cameos from Fred Astaire, Bing Crosby, Ethel Merman, Johnny Mathis, Connie Francis, Robert Goulet, Julie Andrews and Pat Boone. Then, for the opening number, the cast of *The Beverly Hillbillies* would perform a Berlin song. The advent of the Beatles meant that the project's success was no longer assured and it was dropped.

The jazz guitarist Barney Kessel said, 'I wouldn't rate the Beatles at all. I wouldn't go across the street to see them. It's not my music and it's not for me. It doesn't stack up to Duke Ellington or Cole Porter. There's no malice in what I say. It's like saying "I don't care for peppermint or tobacco or a certain kind of candy bar"; it doesn't mean I hate it.'

Social commentator and jazz vocalist, George Melly, had a different take on that. 'They haven't got the glittering, chromium sophistication of Cole Porter, but their songs will last as long. There's room for more than one kind of song-writing in the world and into the Beatles' songs do things that were certainly not in Cole Porter's. There's the influence of George Formby on 'When I'm 64' and the portrayal of provincial Liverpool. There's room for that as well as Cole Porter's Manhattan or Paris.'

Nearly everybody wanted a slice of the action. Dan Rickles put Beatle jokes into his act and Cassius Clay (later Muhammad Ali) broke from his training for a humorous photo-shoot. Clay told them that his favourite singers were Lloyd Price and Little Richard.

On 20 August 1964 the Beatles were in Sinatra territory, but with a difference. They played the Convention Centre at the Sahara Hotel in Las Vegas. The convention centre heralded the new look Vegas which would cater to sales conventions and other corporate events. The Beatles appeared in two shows to a total audience of 16,000, many of them young fans. It was the first time that parents had brought their children to Vegas and there was a huge shout of 'Ringo for President!' as the Beatles came on stage.

The king of Las Vegas, Liberace, saw the Beatles between shows and George Harrison noted that Pat Boone had brought his daughters. He said, 'I think the first four rows were filled up by Pat Boone and his daughters. He seemed to have hundreds of them.' (He had four.)

In January 1965 Brian Epstein returned to America to resolve the dates for the next tour. Playing to 17,000 fans at once as they had done at Hollywood Bowl intrigued him and large stadiums became the norm. He took out insurance with Lloyd's, fearing that the group might be torn apart. Their tours were staggeringly successful and they created the template for top musical acts, including Sinatra in the 1970s, playing multi-purpose arenas. Maybe that was why Frank Sinatra invited them to a late night dinner party after their concert at Shea Stadium. The security arrangements made that impossible. Instead Frank was invited to meet them in their hotel suite but he declined: there had to be some protocol here. A pity. They could have had summit meetings with Elvis and Frank within days of each other.

Unlike the rock'n'roll revolution of the mid-1950s, this music was not confined to the young. It would have been unusual to have found a 40-year-old loving Elvis Presley and Little Richard, but everyone flocked to the Beatles, admittedly liking them for different reasons. Many MOR singers and instrumentalists recorded the Beatles' originals with 'Yesterday' becoming their most recorded songs of all-time.

Frank recorded 'Yesterday' and 'Something'; Ella Fitzgerald gave a display of vocal gymnastics on 'Can't Buy Me Love'; Buddy Rich played 'Norwegian Wood'; Maurice Chevalier recorded 'Yellow Submarine' in French; and Perry Como, Al Martino and Ray Charles all sang 'Yesterday'. When it comes to albums, there's *Basie's Beatle Bag, Keely Smith Sings the John Lennon – Paul McCartney Songbook* and Bing Crosby's *Hey Jude/ Hey Bing!* Barney Kessel says, 'Who knows what their motives were? It might be that they liked the songs; it might be that their producers insisted that they did them to sell records; it might be that they felt intimidated and said, "I want to reach younger people so I'm going to do something they will identify with." The record company may say, "Look, we are paying you what you want. Now, give us the chance to sell some records. This is what we want you to do." If they did those songs for any other reason than that they loved them, then they were not true to themselves.'

The orchestra leader Stanley Black commented, 'I am strictly a middle-of-the-road man. My ideal artists are Frank Sinatra and Ella Fitzgerald, so when the Beatles burst upon the scene, I wasn't entirely grabbed by their music. It took somebody else's recording, an American singer called Keely Smith, to make me realise, for the first time, that they wrote wonderful songs. The Beatles never grabbed me as performers but they did as songwriters.'

Curtis Stigers adds, 'Tony Bennett threw up before he went in the studio because of the things that he had to sing for Mitch Miller at Columbia. Sinatra did 'Something' and you gather that it may not have been his best choice when he says 'Jack' in the middle of it. There are some questionable decisions when these pop and jazz singers were trying to stay in vogue. They couldn't compete with the Beatles and the Stones and perhaps they should have taken the decade off and gone to the beach.'

In March 1966 a profile of John Lennon by Maureen Cleave was published in the London newspaper, *Evening Standard*. It had the clumsy title, *How Does a Beatle Live? John Lennon Lives Like This*, but it was well-written and revelatory. Although Cleave knew John well, it was not a flattering feature, showing him to be listless and bored. There was no mention of any drug habits although that could easily be read into the text.

Lennon was dipping into several books, one of them being *The Passover Plot* by an academic Hugh J Schonfield, who commented that Jesus was convinced that he was the Messiah and lived and died to that end. His followers were simple, uneducated men. Taking his lead from this book, John said, 'Christianity will go. It will vanish and shrink. I needn't argue about that; I'm right and I will be proved right. We're more popular than Jesus now; I don't know which will go first – rock'n'roll or Christianity. Jesus was all right but his disciples were thick and ordinary. It's them twisting it that ruins it for me.' Brian Epstein had said in 1962 that his group was going to be bigger than Elvis, but he hadn't expected John Lennon to say the Beatles were bigger than Jesus.

Paul laughed it off: 'In order to burn our records, you've got to buy them, so it's no sweat off us, mate. It's not compulsory to play them.'

Rt Rev Kenneth Maguire, the Bishop of Montreal, agreed with John. 'I wouldn't be surprised if the Beatles actually were more popular than Jesus. In the only popularity poll during Jesus' lifetime, he came out second to Barabbas.'

The commentator, Jonathan Miller, thought the Beatles were the new Jesus: 'They have become a religion. All over the place there are icons, devotional photos and illuminated missals which keep the tiny earthbound fans in touch with the provocatively absconded deities.'

II. Day In Day Out, 1964–1966

Strange days indeed. It was January 1964 and, motivated by Judy Garland's touching performance of 'The Battle Hymn of the Republic', Frank decided to record an album of patriotic songs, *America, I Hear You Singing*, performed by Bing Crosby and himself with Fred Waring and the Pennsylvanians. He recalled the first thanksgiving with 'Early American' and stressed the importance of living in a democracy in 'You're a Lucky Fellow, Mr Smith'. 'The House I Live In' was ideal for this project and he sang it with a huge choir. He and Bing stressed the value of Holy Communion in 'Let Us Break Bread Together' and there was a new Sammy Cahn and Jimmy Van Heusen composition, 'You Never Had It So Good'. It's odd to hear them singing a slogan associated with the British Prime Minister, Harold Macmillan, but Frank had taken it from the 1952 Democratic campaign.

With the Oscar season imminent and Frank hosting the ceremony, he made an album of Oscar-winning songs, ridiculously called *Frank Sinatra Sings Days of Wine and Roses, Moon River and Other Academy Awards Winners*. How could anyone go into a shop to ask for that?

The contents were not difficult to admire, as, unlike today, the standard of new songs for films was high and all the major writers wrote for the cinema. Frank chose 11 songs: 'The Continental' (Fred Astaire and Ginger Rogers, 1934), 'The Way You Look Tonight' (Fred Astaire, 1936), 'Swinging on a Star (Bing Crosby, 1944), 'It Might As Well Be Spring' (Jeanne Crain but associated with Dick Haymes, 1945), 'In The Cool, Cool, Cool of the Evening' (Bing Crosby and Jane Wyman, 1951), 'Secret Love' (Doris Day, 1953), 'Three Coins in the Fountain' (Frank Sinatra, 1954), 'Love Is a Many-Splendored Thing' (Four Aces, 1955), 'All The Way' (Frank Sinatra, 1957), 'Moon River' (Audrey Hepburn but associated with Andy Williams, 1961) and 'Days of Wine and Roses' (Henry Mancini Orchestra and Chorus but associated with Andy Williams, 1962). Several of the songs he had sung before and three he had introduced, so he could have been more ambitious – there could have been a swinging 'Zip-A-Dee-Doo-Dah' or a dramatic 'High Noon' and it's surprising that he didn't go for 'Mona Lisa' as Nelson Riddle had arranged the song for Nat 'King' Cole.

The recordings were excellent and included swinging versions of 'The Continental' and 'The Way You Look Tonight'. Frank had fun with the lighthearted 'In the Cool, Cool , Cool of the Evening', but if you haven't seen it, do catch Bing Crosby and Jane Wyman's original from Frank Capra's *Here Comes the Groom* on YouTube. The way they cavorted through several interiors as they sang live, clearly in one take, was brilliant. They sing 'ah, ee, oh, ah, ah', something which was purloined by Sheb Wooley for 'Purple People Eater'.

When the producer Marty Rakin saw a rough cut of *Breakfast at Tiffany's,* he said, 'I tell you one thing, that song can go.' That song was 'Moon River'. Nelson Riddle knew Henry Mancini well; they were both very talented but Henry (or Hank as he was known) could write simple, very commercial tunes and Nelson couldn't. He was always envious of this talent as it was a gateway to riches.

There were no Sammy Cahn songs on the album as he had been nominated for an Oscar 13 times and never won. That changed when 'Call Me Irresponsible' was a winner, and Reprise, issuing the album after the Oscar ceremony, should have added the song and retitled the product. Nevertheless, it was a Top 10 album.

Oscar-nominated or not, there were no major roles coming Frank's way in 1964. He sang 'The Girl Who Stole the Eiffel Tower' on the soundtrack of a romantic comedy *Paris When it Sizzles* and took part in a party scene with Marlene Dietrich and Fred Astaire. The film starred Audrey Hepburn and William Holden, but Holden was a drunk playing a drunk, even running into a brick wall.

Another light-hearted comedy, *What a Way to Go!,* with Shirley MacLaine, Paul Newman and Dean Martin was made, but not with Frank Sinatra who demanded $200,000 for two weeks' work, the asking price indicating that he didn't want to do it. Robert Mitchum took his place. Another Frank Capra project, *Marooned,* about astronauts lost in space didn't get off the ground: Capra was 50 years ahead of his time here.

Frank Sinatra did produce *For Those Who Think Young,* the only Sinatra production not to feature Frank himself although it did star his daughter Nancy. As the title implies, this was a teen movie (and a surfing one, to boot) also featuring James Darren, Dean's daughter Claudia, Ellen Burstyn and the vintage actor with Mafia connections, George Raft.

Nelson Riddle was also thinking young when he recorded the orchestral album, *The Greatest Hits Of 1964,* for Reprise. Such titles as 'Hello, Dolly!' (Dolly Sinatra's favourite song), 'Charade' and 'I Wish You Love' were obvious candidates, but he must have been winding Frank up to include 'I Want To Hold Your Hand' and Elvis Presley's nondescript 'Kissin' Cousins'. The oddest choice was a song Frank had rejected, 'My Heart Cries for You', which had been revived on a single by Ray Charles.

The album of patriotic songs with Frank Sinatra and Bing Crosby with Fred Waring and his Pennsylvanians had only limited sales (No.116 on the album charts) but Frank felt it was the right thing to do. In June the same team came together to make *12 Songs of Christmas*. Bing was more comfortable than Frank in this homely setting and it was a companion to the first album in that 'I Heard the Bells on Christmas Day' was a plea for world peace. Frank played the little drummer boy and, best of all, they did 'Go Tell It on the Mountain' as finger-snapping acappella (if that is not a contradiction in terms).

Sinatra's pianist, Bill Miller lived in a house on a hill in Burbank and, in 1964, his house was washed away in a mudslide in which his wife, Aimee, was killed. His daughter was rescued and so was Bill himself who was found clinging to a car. Because of Miller's injuries, Frank identified Aimee's body at the morgue. He told Miller, 'If it's any consolation, there wasn't a mark on her.' 'It wasn't any consolation,' said Miller.

Lou Levy replaced Bill Miller until he was fit: Lou had accompanied Nat 'King' Cole and Peggy Lee. He said, 'Nat Cole was fantastic as everything he did was effortless, but I really learned the value of a lyric when I worked for Peggy Lee because she is so dramatic. She becomes an actress when she sings. I liked playing with Frank, especially when it was just him and me. The first half of 'Angel Eyes' before the orchestra comes in was just us and he would be rephrasing it from night to night.'

Frank's next film was a Japanese/American production involving both Warners and his own company, Artanis, *None but the Brave*. It is the only film where Sinatra was officially the director – though there are plenty where he assumed the role. While making the film, he told the press, 'Directing is my favourite medium. It keeps me busy and I like that. I also like the sense of responsibility.' He remarked, 'I have found out how difficult actors can be and wondered: am I that difficult when I am working for another director?' He knew the answer was yes.

None but the Brave was filmed in Kauai, Hawaii in April and May 1964. The plot evolved around some American servicemen who'd crashed on a Pacific island and a Japanese platoon that was already there. They all knew that the war would soon be over and an uneasy truce developed between the two sides. However, both camps had a hothead as second in command.

Making good use of subtitles, *None but the Brave* worked well and Sinatra was at his best when he as a medic had to visit the Japanese camp to amputate a soldier's leg when he had never been trained in this. It was an anti-war film at the time of Vietnam and instead of 'The End', the final caption is 'Nobody ever wins'. A comparison can be made with Clint Eastwood's *Letters from Iwo Jima* (2006).

The cast included Clint Walker, Tommy Sands, Brad Dexter, who is the one you won't remember from *The Magnificent Seven,* plus Dick Sinatra, the son of the bandleader Ray Sinatra. Tatsuya Mihashi (Lt Kuroki) had a crucial role, speaking both languages, although his English sometimes faltered. These were servicemen in tense situations but the film worked without swearing, the closest to an expletive being Tommy Sands' 'Son of a buck'.

Tommy Sands had one of the leading roles, although his marriage to Frank's daughter was failing. He said of his father-in-law, 'The relationship was a little strained but nothing bad really happened. Making the film was all so easy and effortless as he was a marvellous director and a nice, easy man to work with.'

Ah yes, Tommy Sands. Sands had enrolled at Lee Strasberg's school of acting in 1960 and, in my view, was entitled to a full refund. It could be argued that he was acting as a shrill, obnoxious loudmouth deliberately. After all, why would Sinatra want to ruin his own film? It might have been what Frank wanted; he loved Shirley MacLaine's acting style.

While making the film, Frank went swimming with the producer's wife, Ruth Koch, in Wailua Bay. When Ruth floundered, he swam out to save her. She made it back but Sinatra was then in danger and Brad Dexter was said to have rescued him. It turned out to be a passing man on a surfboard but Frank gave Brad Dexter the credit for saving his life. Joey Bishop sent Frank a cable, 'You must have forgotten who you were. You can walk on water.'

None but the Brave received bad reviews with the LA Times suggesting that Sinatra should have avoided nepotism by not casting Sands, saying he had a 'cartoonish officious role'. Tommy Sands admits, 'I got so mad that I drove to the reviewer's office and beat him up. I'm not proud of that but it did happen.'

Constantly busy, Frank was planning his next album with Count Basie and his Orchestra, *It Might as Well Be Swing,* this time incorporating a string section. The arranger, Quincy Jones, visited him on the film set and wrote some arrangements while he was there.

Cy Coleman and Carolyn Leigh had written 'The Best Is Yet to Come' for Frank Sinatra in 1959 but after he had sat on it for a year, they gave it to Tony Bennett. Frank got round to it at last with a superlative recording. He was again in Tony Bennett territory for 'I Wanna Be Around', a song that Johnny Mercer had written after a doctor's wife, Sadie Vimmerstedt, had sent him a potential title line, 'I wanna be around to pick up the pieces when somebody breaks your heart'.

There is a third song associated with Tony Bennett, 'The Good Life', although it was written by another performer, Sacha Distel. In the early 1960s, Distel was having highly publicised romances with Brigitte Bardot, Juliette Gréco and the skiing champion, Francine Bréaud, so no wonder he wrote a song called *La Belle Vie*. His American publisher, Duke Niles, suggested that it should have English words and Tony Bennett recorded *The Good Life* for the US market. The song is so associated with Tony Bennett that it is the title of his autobiography, but the Basie/Sinatra version is equally strong.

When Sinatra sang another French song, Charles Trenet's 'I Wish You Love', he changed the tempo towards the end, and exclaimed, 'Hot damn! I wish you love, all kinds of love!'

The pianist, Bart Howard, accompanied well-known acts at New York's Blue Angel night-club, and in 1954 he wrote a waltz, *In Other Words*, which was recorded by Kaye Ballard and then Nancy Wilson. Peggy Lee liked the song but changed the title to *Fly Me to the Moon*. Frank Sinatra upped the tempo for a Las Vegas showroom performance, also more in keeping with the space race of the 60s. In 1969, the astronauts took a portable tape recorder with them so that Frank's record would be the first music played on the moon. Prior to landing, Buzz Aldrin played Tony Bennett's 'The Best Is Yet To Come'. Rather more grounded in reality, the 1987 film, *Wall Street*, started with commuters coming into the city and Frank is heard singing 'Fly Me to the Moon'.

'I Believe in You' was a curious song from Frank Loesser's *How to Succeed in Business without Really Trying* as it is about a man singing to himself in the bathroom mirror and doesn't work out of context. On the other hand, it's good to hear Frank acknowledging the rising potential of Burt Bacharach and Hal David with 'Wives and Lovers', but Burt Bacharach commented, 'When I heard Sinatra doing 'Wives And Lovers' with Count Basie, I called Q and said, "Q, how come it's in four/four? It's a waltz." He said, "The Basie band doesn't know how to play in three/four." (Laughter)'

Frank loved playing around with words, adding lines to Don Gibson's country song, 'I Can't Stop Loving You', now associated with Ray Charles. He recorded other country songs, such as 'I Can't Believe I'm Losing You', with Don Costa and 'Anytime at All' with Ernie Freeman, but unlike Dean, who had considerable success in that genre, these were not for him. (Several books assume that Sinatra recorded the Beatles' 'Anytime At All' but this was a different song.)

It was inevitable that he and Basie would get round to 'Hello, Dolly!' and it was a wonderful version full of asides from Frank. He tells Satch to 'Blow your horn, Louis. Sing up a great big storm, Louis,' incidentally calling him Lou-ee and not the more common Lewis of today. As Sinatra's mother was called Dolly, it's surprising that she didn't get a shout-out.

Reprise wasn't making money and Sinatra had to make concessions. He knew nothing about rock and didn't want to but he was recommended to a man who did. Jimmy Bowen had seen chart success as a performer with Buddy Knox and his Rhythm Orchids in 1957 and he was producing Frankie Avalon and Johnny Rivers for Chancellor Records.

Bowen felt more comfortable behind the controls and he made Jack Nitzsche's album, *Lonely Surfer*, for Reprise in 1963. Bowen came to Reprise with Ernie Freeman, a jazz musician from the 1940s who had had success with Gene McDaniels and Bobby Vee at Liberty. They brought in younger musicians to work on Reprise recordings like Glen Campbell, Leon Russell and Hal Blaine, and Jimmy Bowen would sneak in backbeats and triplets whenever he could. Leon Russell says, 'I used to work for Jimmy Bowen and he did a lot of those guys - Frankie Laine, Dean Martin, Keely Smith - and I played on their records. When I did the Sinatra sessions, there were armed guards on the door which I thought was extraordinary. He was not my cup of tea really.'

Frank wasn't sure that he wanted a makeover himself but Dean didn't mind. Well, Dean would never mind as long as it didn't take much effort or time. However, he had his mind set on another retro project. Dean preferred the golf course or drinking with his buddies, but sometimes in the wee small hours, after playing the main room at the Sands, Dean would drift into the lounge and sing moody songs with his pianist, Ken Lane. He wanted to make an album of such material called *Dream with Me*.

Dean and Jimmy picked the songs and Ernie wrote the arrangements. Fortunately, Ken Lane thought an old song of his, 'Everybody Loves Somebody', might be right for the album. It had been recorded by Dinah Washington and Peggy Lee, but the first person placing it on record had been Frank himself in 1947 and what's more, Frank owned the publishing.

Jimmy Bowen recorded 'Everybody Loves Somebody' with Dean. It sounded okay but it wasn't a hit single. However, Jimmy realised that it could be. Ray Charles had created a new genre by taking country songs like 'I Can't Stop Loving You' and 'Take These Chains from My Heart' and recording them with singalong choirs. He told Ernie Freeman to give 'Everybody Loves Somebody' the same treatment.

The radio stations picked up on this infectious single and soon the whole of America was singing 'Everybody Loves Somebody' and mimicking Dean's easy delivery. The single soared up the US charts and to Frank and Dean's surprise, it knocked the Beatles' 'A Hard Day's Night' from No.1 in August 1964. The *Everybody Loves Somebody* album was only kept from the top by the soundtrack for *A Hard Day's Night*. It's not overstating things to say that Dean Martin had saved his buddy's label.

'Everybody Loves Somebody' became Dean's theme song for his new TV series and set the path for a long trail of easy listening country albums. One was even called *Dean 'Tex' Martin Rides Again*. Dean the Italian cowboy: they should have put him in spaghetti westerns. Dean and Jimmy would choose the songs in late night sessions with their friend, Jack Daniels. Dean could have made the albums in his sleep and probably did.

Dean's son Dino was 14-years-old and was singing with his friends, Desi Arnaz Jr, the son of Lucille Ball and Desi Arnaz, and Billy Hinsche, whose father owned a casino. 'No problem,' said Dean, 'I'll get you on Reprise.' Recording teenage acts had been Jimmy's speciality so he took Dino, Desi and Billy into the Top 20 with 'I'm a Fool' in July 1965. Then Dean had another Top 10 hit with more of the same, 'The Door Is Still Open to My

Heart'. Frank was delighted as the hits gave Reprise commercial viability, but he hadn't had a Top 20 hit himself since 'Witchcraft' in 1958.

Dean Martin starred with Kim Novak in *Kiss Me, Stupid!*, an adult comedy directed by Billy Wilder about a horny Las Vegas crooner. Wonder what made Billy Wilder think of Dean? It's an entertaining film but what made it particularly interesting is that Dean sang some new Ira Gershwin lyrics for melodies that brother George had left behind.

Sinatra told Bowen to find a song that would restore him to the charts. The song he chose was Matt Monro's UK hit from 1962, 'Softly As I Leave You', an Italian song with an English lyric by the publisher, Hal Shaper. Arranged by Ernie Freeman, it was a very good recording but not, to my ears, as good as Monro's which had a better vocal and a more poignant string arrangement. Hal Shaper recalled, "Softly' started slowly in America although it was a Top 40 record for Matt Monro. Then Doris Day recorded it and after that Andy Williams and Brenda Lee. In those days, if you had a hit with a ballad, a number of wonderful singers would include it on their next album, which doesn't happen anymore. Then in 1964 Frank Sinatra recorded it and it was that version which kicked the song off into glory, although I have never heard anyone sing it better than Matt. I've always loved his version.'

It led to an album, *Softly As I Leave You*, which was a mishmash with various arrangers and producers. There were songs from recent films including his own *Come Blow Your Horn*. Nelson Riddle arranged another Henry Mancini song, this time 'Dear Heart', an Andy Williams song from the film starring Geraldine Page and Glenn Ford. Johnny Mercer's song 'Emily' came from *The Americanisation of Emily* with James Garner, while 'Pass Me By' stemmed from *Father Goose* starring Cary Grant and Leslie Caron. Arranged by Billy May, this sounded like a music hall song for Stanley Holloway and it was hard to imagine Frank's trousers 'tied up with a laundry line'. The song fared much better as a march in Peggy Lee's version.

On 20 June 1964 Tina Sinatra had her 16th birthday. The previous year she had had a motorcycle accident, which wasn't serious but could have been. Frank did not like the idea of his daughter riding a motorcycle and always said that you were safer in a car. So Tina was given a Pontiac Firebird convertible for her birthday.

Meanwhile, Nancy Sinatra and Tommy Sands divorced after three and a half years of marriage. Nancy later said, 'I made the colossal blunder of leaving college to have sex with a man I married because you didn't have sex unless you were married. I was stupid and la-di-da like Annie Hall.'

In August and September, Frank Sinatra played some dates in Sweden, Tel Aviv and Paris, ending up on the French Riviera. He raised money for a youth centre in Tel Aviv, which was named after him and intended to encourage friendship between Jewish and Arabian adolescents.

Whilst in Tel-Aviv he filmed a brief cameo for *Cast a Giant Shadow*, a film being produced by John Wayne and starring Kirk Douglas and Angie Dickinson. Frank was a fighter pilot whose plane was attacked but in order to save money, the plane that attacked him came from footage taken for the film, *633 Squadron*.

At a preview for *Robin and the 7 Hoods*, the screenwriter Harry Kurnitz told Frank that he had to stop making home movies. 'Okay,' said Frank, 'What book should I buy?' Harry sent him *Von Ryan's Express*.

Many war films were made in the 1960s and as *Von Ryan's Express* was being made at the same as *Morituri* (with Marlon Brando and Yul Brynner) and *The Sound of Music*, there was a run on German uniforms. *Von Ryan's Express* was a train variant of *The Great*

Escape (1963). Produced and directed by Mark Robson, it was one of the last CinemaScope productions, being filmed for Twentieth Century Fox. Shot in Italy in August and September 1964, it was then completed in a Hollywood studio in October.

Von Ryan's Express was no *Saving Private Ryan*. This was straightforward family entertainment, a good old-fashioned action pic with strong performances from the leading actors, Frank Sinatra and Trevor Howard. Frank had wanted Richard Burton but found that the film company was in litigation with him over *Cleopatra*. Trevor Howard had endured a frustrating and harrowing time with Marlon Brando making *Mutiny on the Bounty* and he found Sinatra affable by comparison. Howard was tipsy most of the time, but he would drink heavily, throw up and then act immaculately. After Brando, he was pleased to work with someone who wanted to move on when he was satisfied with a take.

British pop star, John Leyton, who had also been in *The Great Escape*, recalls, 'Sinatra is someone whom I had admired over the years and working with him was one of the bonuses of my life. I remember arriving on the set of *Von Ryan's Express* and meeting with the director. My first scene was with Frank Sinatra and Trevor Howard and within one minute of meeting Sinatra, I was working with him as an actor which was a bit overpowering. He was very professional and very nice to me and my admiration for him grew as we were making the film.'

Sinatra was soon fed up with working in Italy and he wanted his scenes to be shot quickly and consecutively which was impossible as they involved several different locations. Sometimes he walked off the production but this only slowed down the filming. Sinatra was on a share of gross profits while Robson was on a percentage of the net, so the director saw his rewards decreasing with Sinatra's awkwardness. The film had a high body count and it might have been higher as Sinatra and Robson were so often at loggerheads. Robson was an experienced director, having made *Peyton Place* (1957) with Lana Turner and *The Inn of Sixth Happiness* (1958) with Ingrid Bergman, and he didn't want any nonsense from Sinatra.

Von Ryan's Express was set in 1943 just after the allies' invasion of Sicily. Sinatra played an American pilot who was shot down and put in a prison camp with British POWs under Trevor Howard whose mission was to escape. Sinatra, being a colonel, pulled rank and placed himself in charge. He said that there was no need to escape as the war was almost over. He made mistakes, in particular saving a German officer from death, which led to the demise of some POWs. Howard said Sinatra's character would win the Iron Cross and he was dubbed Von Ryan.

The film was spectacular especially when the prisoners hijacked a train, the Von Ryan's Express of the title. The plan depended upon the British chaplain's ability to speak German, but surely his accent would have aroused suspicion. Ryan had to shoot an Italian girl who would have given them away. The producers had been thinking of a sequel but Sinatra insisted that his character must die for shooting a woman. It was the fifth time he had been killed in a film. He refused to do an alternative ending for comparison as he said that the producers would pick the wrong one.

Sinatra refused to stay in Rome itself as he had been booed off stage there in the 1950s. Instead he stayed in a villa outside the city which had its own helipad. The director John Huston was in Rome making *The Bible – In The Beginning...*, really the story of Genesis, and the cast included Ava Gardner and Peter O'Toole. To the delight of the paparazzi, Sinatra saw her from time to time. Another time Peter O'Toole was in a fight with the paparazzi. When the police came to question him, his stunt double (for God!) pretended he was O'Toole while O'Toole escaped wearing a beard. Because both O'Toole and Richard Harris were in the production, Sinatra called the film, *The Gospel According to Mick*.

Fuelled by booze, Peter O'Toole assembled a group of actors who vowed not to work in Rome again until the problem with the paparazzi had been resolved. A ridiculous idea but as 'A' as any A-list can be: Peter O'Toole, Frank Sinatra, Albert Finney, Richard Burton, Elizabeth Taylor and Ava Gardner.

For all that, the newspapers were missing the main story. George C Scott, who played Abraham, had been pursuing Ava. She went into his apartment and cut off all his shirts, sweaters and suits at the shoulder. When she went to London for a weekend, he followed her and broke down a door at the Savoy. Ava sought solace with Frank, whose behaviour was normal by comparison.

While Frank was in Italy making *Von Ryan's Express*, he had a brief fling with Burt Bacharach's former girlfriend, Slim Brandy, also known as Shirley Parker. Burt called her while she was dining with Frank and when she returned he said, 'Who were you on the phone too for all that time?' She said, 'My ex, Burt Bacharach.' 'He's a lousy writer,' said Frank, and Slim retorted, 'You couldn't even hum his music let alone sing it, it's so complicated.' During the evening a photographer snatched a picture of Frank and Slim. Frank grabbed the camera and broke the photographer's arm.

On last day of shooting in Torremolinos, Frank Sinatra and Brad Dexter were detained by police as a young woman accused them of assault. They had to be bailed out by the producer, Saul David, but the matter was settled with little fuss and they could leave the country.

When Sinatra arrived home he went to visit Nat 'King' Cole who was in hospital. He was not allowed visitors but naturally Frank Sinatra waltzed in as he pleased. Cole died in February 1965.

While the cast was completing the film in Hollywood in October, Mia Farrow who was making the TV series, *Peyton Place*, strolled across to see John Leyton as they had been in *Guns at Batasi* earlier in the year. John introduced her to Sinatra, who was immediately struck with her elfin looks. He gave her a silver cigarette case and she kept her joints in it.

At the wrap party, which was thrown by Sinatra, Trevor Howard was plastered and found his car was hemmed in. He went forward and rammed the one in front and then did the same in reverse. He went berserk and had to be forcibly stopped. It was the most expensive day of his life as he had to pay for the damage.

In November Frank recorded a song written by Russell Faith, who had written for Frankie Avalon and Fabian, though this fact might have been kept from him. It was the singalong 'Somewhere in Your Heart', completely predictable, the easiest of easy listening, but the arrangement by Ernie Freeman aped Bert Kaempfert, who had topped the US charts with 'Wonderland by Night' in 1961. Kaempfert himself would soon be involved in Sinatra's revival and this record, which made the Top 40, showed that Sinatra had latched onto his sound.

Lyndon Johnson won the Presidency in his own right and his inauguration was on 20 January 1965. Frank Sinatra never expected to be invited as they were not keen on each other. Apparently, Sinatra snubbed Sam Rayburn, the Speaker of the House, at the 1956 Democratic Convention and Johnson thought this showed how ill-mannered Sinatra was. Sinatra did have a meeting with Johnson about the awkwardness of the press but Johnson could only see Sinatra during his massage. Sinatra joked that he wasn't allowed to have his picture taken with the President.

Rock'n'roll had suffered two major blows. One of its most talented practitioners, Sam Cooke, had the potential to be a major star. Blessed with exceptional good looks, Cooke was a gospel singer who turned to rock'n'roll and his two live albums, one from a club in

Harlem and one at the Copa, showed just how wide his talent and his repertoire were, his voice proving quite different on those sets. He idolised Nat 'King' Cole and, like Bobby Darin, his career could have gone in any number of directions. His self-penned 'A Change Is Gonna Come' became a civil rights anthem. Although he was shown as a family man, he had a bad boy side to him and a liaison with a prostitute resulted in his death in a motel in November 1964.

On the same day as the inauguration, the DJ Alan Freed, the man who had named rock'n'roll, died from alcoholic poisoning at age of 38. He had been caught up in the payola scandals – that is, disc-jockeys playing rock'n'roll records for cash – and also found guilty of tax evasion. Freed had been impressed with Sinatra's bobbysoxer following at the Paramount and had sought to emulate it with his rock'n'roll concerts, at one stage being arrested for inciting a riot. After the payola scandal in 1961, the radio station WINS played three days of continuous MOR records by the likes of Frank Sinatra as his records had not been tainted with payola, which is strange considering his dubious friends. When George Raft was found guilty of tax evasion in April 1965, Frank sent him a blank cheque 'to use if you need it'.

Payola had been removed from the industry or at least there were more subtle ways of making a record a hit. There is no doubt that the charts accurately reflected the sales figures for the Beatles as the demand for their records was so high. Sinatra still didn't care for their music but he agreed to an unlikely request when Ringo Starr married a Liverpool hairdresser, Maureen Cox, whose favourite artist was Frank Sinatra. One year Adam Faith recorded a tribute song for her birthday; next year it was Frank Sinatra, merging 'The Lady Is a Tramp' with 'But Beautiful'.

Sammy Cahn told the story, 'Frank called me one time and said, "Ringo Starr's getting married and his bride is my No.1 fan and she is also having her birthday, and I want you to write something that I could sing to her." So I wrote special lyrics for Ringo's bride, Maureen. They were thrilled." The special lyrics are:

'There's no one like her,
But no one at all,
And as for charm,
Hers is like wall to wall.
She married Ringo
And she could have had Paul,
That's why the lady is a champ.
'Creates excitement
Whenever it's dull,
She just appears
And there goes the lull.
She merely smiles
And you're out of your skull,
That's why the lady is a champ.
'The folks who do and who don't meditate
Agree she's great,
They mean
Maureen,
I've got more lyrics right after this vamp,
Because the lady is a champ.
'Though we've not met
I'm convinced she's a gem,

I'm just F S
But to me she's Big M,
Mainly because she prefers to me to them,
That's why the lady is a champ.
'I've lots of fans, well, at least one or two,
But Peter Brown called me to tell me it's true,
She sleeps with Ringo but she thinks of you,
That's why the lady is a champ.
'But I can boast, boast as much,
As much as I please,
The fact is that she's
His wife,
But that's life,
But it's her day so I whistle and stamp,
Because the lady, the charming lady, Mr Ringo's lady, is a champ.
'May I toast you all the way
Lift my glass and softly say
I have thoughts for you this day
But beautiful.
Thoughts for you and for your Ringo
That I must express
With the warm and deep affection of F S.
Would you kindly ask the guys
If they'd grab a glass and rise
'Cause I think we'd harmonise
But beautiful.
May your birthdays and birthday candles
Softly gleam and glow
For that would be
But beautiful I know.'

Sinatra was working at the Sands in February 1965 and after making *Von Ryan's Express*, he had invited John Leyton to come there as his guest. He was introduced to a small, middle-aged man who asked him about his career. John Leyton said, 'And what do you do for a living?' and the man replied, 'I own Chicago.' It was Sam Giancana.

Frank's romance with Mia was blossoming. He held a 20th birthday party for her at Chasen's in Los Angeles on 9 February 1965. There was a 30-year age gap between them; she was five years younger than his daughter Nancy. Dean Martin said on stage, "I've got Scotch older than Mia Farrow."

In June and July 1965 Frank played dates with Count Basie and his Orchestra with Quincy Jones conducting, including the Newport Jazz Festival and a prison concert, part of which was televised as a news item. A clip of 'Fly Me to the Moon' is on YouTube. After seeing a prisoner with a scarred face, Sinatra is shown with his neck scar very visible as if to say, 'I could be one of the inmates.' They scored a triumph at the Newport Jazz Festival on 4 July. Sinatra flew in by helicopter and left straight after performing. Despite it being a jazz festival, he opened with the show tune, 'Get Me to the Church on Time'.

The most significant date, however, was on 20 June when Sinatra and Basie were joined by Dean Martin, Sammy Davis and Johnny Carson for a charity event at the Kiel Opera House, St Louis. It was filmed for closed circuit screening as a Frank Sinatra spectacular.

Sammy was taking a short break from his Broadway success, *Golden Boy*. Johnny Carson said he was standing in for Joey Bishop 'who had slipped his disc backing out of Frank's presence.'

The show started with Dean with his winning smile and drunk act. He changed the words in 'Everybody Loves Somebody' to 'If I had you in my shower' and, sensing he had a new career, sang the country songs, 'Send Me the Pillow that You Dream On' and 'King of the Road'. He ended with 'Volare' and 'On an Evening in Roma' and concluded, 'I'd like to do some more for you but you're lucky I remembered these.'

Sammy pulled out all the stops for 'My Shining Hour' and 'Who Can I Turn To' and then with Michael Silver (drums) and Johnny Mendoza (congas), he turned 'I've Got You Under My Skin' into a long medley which incorporated 'You Came a Long Way from St Louis', 'What'd I Say', 'You Are My Sunshine' and a great 'Bee-Bom.' He demonstrated contemporary dances such as the Mashed Potato and the Swim. His 'One for My Baby' included accurate impressions of Nat 'King' Cole, Billy Eckstine, Vaughn Monroe, Frankie Laine, Louis Armstrong, Dean Martin and Jerry Lewis. Really breathtaking.

Frank blasted away with 'Get Me to the Church on Time' and offered a sublime 'Fly Me to the Moon'. 'Luck Be a Lady' was sung superbly but his continual blowing and throwing of imaginary dice was irritating. When he sang 'Please Be Kind', both Dean and Sammy added backstage comments, while 'My Kind of Town' is here dedicated to St Louis. In their final minutes together, Frank said, 'Sam is going to do a medley of race riots', to which Sam replied, 'If we ever get in the lead, you two cats are first.' After this absurd banter, they go into 'Birth of the Blues'.

On 23 June 1965 *Von Ryan's Express* received its première at Loew's State Theatre, New York. At the same time, his hands and footprints were preserved in cement in the Hollywood Walk of Fame outside Grauman's Chinese Theatre. Everyone was confident about its success and Sinatra gave custom-made toy trains to the main members of the cast and crew as mementos. Judging by the number of times it appears in the TV schedules, Frank Sinatra had made his most popular film and he trousered $2m from his percentage deal.

Columbia wanted Frank to star in another POW drama, *King Rat*, but the director, Bryan Forbes, insisted that he was too old and went with George Segal, some 20 years younger. Otto Preminger wanted Sinatra as the investigating policeman in the film of Truman Capote's true crime book, *In Cold Blood*, but the rights had gone to another director, Richard Brooks. Otto Preminger was so annoyed that he had an argument in a restaurant with Capote's agent, Irving Lazar, who was also Sinatra's agent.

Brad Dexter tried to persuade Frank to film *Harper*, a *film noir* which had a script by William Goldman, but Frank was dating Mia and felt he had enough projects on the go. The role went to Paul Newman and possibly it was another encounter with Shelley Winters that put him off.

Most intriguingly, Brad Dexter tried to interest Frank Sinatra in *A Clockwork Orange*, but Frank thumbed through Anthony Burgess's novel and said he couldn't understand a word of it. He didn't seek Mia's advice – he wasn't interested.

Frank and Mia had a holiday in a yacht off New England but this ended in tragedy, through no fault of their own. A crew member fell into the water and drowned while he was sailing to Frank's yacht.

While dating Mia Farrow, Frank told the press that he was thinking of casting her as his daughter in his next film, *Community Property*, later called *Marriage on the Rocks*. The role went to Nancy Sinatra, playing his daughter but said to be 18.

Because Frank's company partly produced *Marriage on the Rocks*, he could as usual fill

it with his friends. His co-star was Dean Martin and the Reprise artist, Trini Lopez, sang 'There Once Was a Sinner Man' in a club sequence. Nelson Riddle contributed a rather too swinging score.

Marriage on the Rocks was the only film in which Frank played a conventional family man, here with a wife and two kids. He ran an advertising agency which had few original ideas and his deputy, Dean Martin, only wanted to put a scantily-clad model in every ad.

With cracks in his marriage, Frank planned to take his wife (Deborah Kerr) to Mexico for a second honeymoon. In a series of mishaps, she found herself married to Dean Martin. This was a workable idea with comic potential but Kerr was a terrible comedienne, emphasising her lines for (non-)comedic effect. The tall actress had to wear a green chiffon dress for several scenes and Frank and Dean referred to her on set, but sadly not in the film, as the Jolly Green Giant. But there's worse: Hermione Baddeley was truly awful as her over-the-top bagpipes-playing mother. Dean coasted through the film but even he couldn't save it. Frank did have to play a character who was bored, so you could argue that he was acting well.

Frank was go-go dancing with a teenage girl in one scene, but the best moment was when he was framed in the doorway of a lawyer's office. The notice above the door says, 'Divorce your loved one with dignity.'

The film was directed by Jack Donohue, who had been Frank's dance teacher and had worked on TV with Frank and Dean so he should have had the measure of them. Frank called him 'The Fat Director'. However, he hadn't directed since *Babes in Toyland* with Annette and Tommy Sands in 1961 with Sands, very much a former teen idol playing Tom, Tom, the Piper's son. Considering the star power of the cast, there were few close-ups and it is like watching a stage play with sets made on a shoestring. The Sinatra books invariably tell you that *The Kissing Bandit* is his worst film, but it isn't.

When *Marriage on the Rocks* was released in September 1965, the Mexican government declared it to be racist because of Cesar Romero's comic attorney and Sinatra's remark 'The secret is not to come to this place at all.' What did the authorities make of the western *Django* with Franco Nero?

In a similarly lightweight mode, Frank had two small hits on the US charts with 'Tell H (You Love Her Each Day)', a cheerful commercial radio friendly song, and 'Forget Doma an Italian song with an English lyric from Norman Newell and written for the film, *Yellow Rolls-Royce*. It was a novelty to hear Frank with Neapolitan mandolins and repea an Italian word, but even more unlikely was its nod to disco.

In September 1965 Frank started filming *Assault on a Queen*, again directed by Donohue. The title was misleading as this film was about robbing the Queen Mary. Bogart-styled role, Frank played a war veteran who longed for excitement. Some tre seekers were looking for a Spanish galleon in the Bahamas but found a 20-year-old Ge submarine with only a corpse aboard. Their immediate thought was to hijack the C Mary and steal £1m from its vaults. They repair the German U-boat in record time, som ignoring all the corrosion.

This film was a disaster in many ways. The producer Bill Goetz was an odd cha he and his wife Edie, the daughter of Louis B Mayer, would pledge money at fund dinners and then dishonour them. Edie was obsessed with Sinatra and had an affair w during the making of the film, but that didn't keep him happy.

Sinatra got bored and the double in his diving sequences looked nothing like h only thing he did like was snogging Virna Lisi. When Donahue yelled 'Cut!', they co kissing and Donahue said, 'If you ever get through, let me know. I'm running out

There was no tension to the heist and the only merit is Duke Ellington's score, although he had little to work from. Sinatra's non-cooperation added to the films budget and when it was screened in July 1966 it sank like the U-boat. Bill Goetz never made another film.

In December 1965 Frank Sinatra was going to be 50 years old and he thought he would celebrate it in two ways. He issued a double album for his birthday, *A Man and His Music*. In the liner notes, Sinatra thanked 'DJs brave enough to give me equal time in Beatleland', but there weren't many of them. The album featured previously released Reprise recordings of his successes. Frank narrated the album, telling some good anecdotes, but the script had been written for him. It was, in equal measures, funny and tiresome. Capitol could still cause mischief as they compiled a competing triple-LP set, *The Great Years*.

Although Sinatra acted and behaved as though he were younger and had a young girlfriend, he wanted to make an album which reflected his age, hence, *September of my Years*. His core audience was getting older and they would appreciate songs which put their age into context. Nobody had made such a concept album before. Gordon Jenkins was the ideal arranger and Frank asked Sammy Cahn and Jimmy Van Heusen to write a title song. However, the album, although superb, is a bit like *Songs from the Rest Home*, when Frank had yet to reach 50.

As the jazz critic Gene Lees wrote, 'He made a retrospective of his career and a retrospective of his life. The latter comprised material about growing old. You could sense a qualitative change in the man: a real and heavy despair. It is the darkest album he's ever made, and his eyes during that period, the loneliest eyes I have ever seen, seemed to verify that he meant every word of it.'

Indeed. Cahn and Van Heusen thought they had written a song that was too dark for him and submitted it as 'September of His Years' but Frank changed it back to 'September of My Years'. He reflects, 'How quickly seasons go' and acknowledged that he has always had 'wandering ways'. Not only did the song open his album, it closed his retrospective package, *A Man and His Music*. It hadn't been his intention. Cahn and Van Heusen had written a song called 'A Man and His Music' but Sinatra didn't care for it.

Although the songs are written by others, this was close to being an autobiographical album. Other performers would have seen different aspects in ageing, such as watching their children grow. There is only one song on the album, another Cahn and Van Heusen composition, 'It Gets Lonely Early', which acknowledges the benefits of a family.

Gordon Jenkins wrote two songs for the album; 'How Old Am I' and 'This Is All I Ask', which Billy May called a beautiful song. 'How Old Am I' was a song for an ageing Lothario and was directed at Mia Farrow: 'If I make you happy, I'm the perfect age', while 'This Is All I Ask' acknowledged the power of music. As might be expected, Alec Wilder's 'I See It Now' was a beautiful song looking back on adolescent memories, while Bart Howard's 'The Man in the Looking Glass' was about being confronted by thoughts while shaving, containing the strange line, 'How's your sacroiliac today?'

Kurt Weill and Maxwell Anderson's 'September Song' was an old favourite but now he had grown into the lyric. He sang both the verse and the refrain and although comparing your life to the seasons was a cliché, it worked beautifully. Nobody could touch Sinatra when he sounded like this. There was no purpose served by including 'When the Wind was Green' as this too contrasted the seasons with the age of man.

The *tour de force* was Ervin Drake's song, 'It Was a Very Good Year', which compared former relationships to vintage wine. It had been recorded in a folksy version by the Kingston Trio in 1961 and had been turned into a slow ballad by Lonnie Donegan two years later. Lonnie said, 'The Kingston Trio had recorded it before I did but you'd hardly know that we were singing the same song. After I'd done it, I was having lunch with my agent in New York

and a bloke came up to our table and asked me if I was Lonnie Donegan. He had written 'It Was a Very Good Year' and he said, "I cried when I heard what you'd done with that song. It was beautiful. You put things in there that I had never written." A short time later Frank Sinatra recorded the song and as his arrangement was so similar to mine, I can only conclude that he had heard my version. Incidentally, I secured the publishing rights for the UK and so quite literally, I had Frank Sinatra working for me.'

Gordon Jenkins' string arrangement was outstandingly good and this is one of Sinatra's greatest recordings. Scott Walker has said, 'To me, the greatest soul singer in the world is Frank Sinatra. I'd like to be able to put the same styling into a song that Sinatra does in 'It Was a Very Good Year'.'

When Frank Sinatra performed this song on *A Man and his Music*, it was split into sections, each section introducing a different song. It seemed an indignity but worse was to come. In 2001, part of Sinatra's vocal was removed to make way for Robbie Williams for a duet track on *Swing When You're Winning*. Admittedly, it was a No.1 album and so commercially was the right thing to do, but it was hard to justify artistically as a magnificent Frank Sinatra record, a beautiful work of art, was being vandalised. On the plus side, Sinatra's version was still available and there may have been thousands of Robbie Williams fans who sought it out.

The September of My Years album made No.5 on the US charts, his most successful Reprise album for two years, and stayed on the listings for over a year. He had a Top 30 single with 'It Was a Very Good Year', but in retrospect it is hard to see why this single didn't restore him to the Top 10. Frank won well-deserved Grammys for Best Album (*September of My Years*) and Best Solo Vocal Performance ('It Was a Very Good Year'). He had beaten *Help!* and 'Yesterday', respectively.

Frank was capable of flooding the market even without his old Capitol recordings as he released a third album to tie in with his 50th birthday, *My Kind of Broadway*, but it was mostly material he had previously recorded. There were two songs from *Skyscraper*, Sammy Cahn and Jimmy Van Heusen's only Broadway musical: the beautiful 'I'll Only Miss Her When I Think of Her' with Laurindo Almeida on guitar, and 'Everybody Has the Right To Be Wrong (At Least Once)', which was hardly his own philosophy. Perhaps that's why his invited friends applauded so loudly at the end of the take. In his autobiography, Cahn calls the musical 'a devastating experience' and the mistake was probably to cast a non-singer, Julie Harris, in the main role. The musical ran for a few months but largely due to the introduction of 'twofers', two tickets for the price of one.

Frank's albums, *A Man and his Music* and *September of My Years*, were promoted in a birthday show for NBC, naturally called *A Man and His Music*. It won Emmys for lighting and production. As well as his TV special, another network, CBS presented an unofficial tribute, *Sinatra: An American Original*, hosted by Walter Cronkite. Frank's publicist asked him if he wanted to write personally to the producer, Don Hewitt, and he responded, 'Can you send a fist through the mail?'

On 12 December 1965 his former wife Nancy threw a black tie party for him at the Beverly Wilshire Hotel in Beverly Hills. It was staged by Jack Haley, and Sammy Davis emerged from a cake singing 'My kind of man, Sinatra is'. Tony Bennett was the main attraction and Nancy sang a parody from Sammy Cahn:

'Who in the 40s was knocking them dead,
My daddy, my daddy, my daddy,
The rug he once cut he now wears on his head,
My daddy, my daddy, my daddy.'

Mia was not at the birthday party, but her present to him was her new hairstyle: a boyish crop. 'Aha,' said Ava Gardner, 'I always knew he would end up sleeping with a boy.'

Sinatra couldn't afford to have tantrums: he had a 30% holding in Warner/Reprise; he had his own airline; he owned property in Palm Springs and New York and around 75 people depended on him for their livelihood.

At the end of November, Sinatra had spent two days recording *Moonlight Sinatra* (great title!) with Nelson Riddle. It was a collection of songs with moon in their titles, most of them associated with Bing Crosby and Glenn Miller. It represented good thinking as it was so topical: the space race was on and the ambition was to land a man on the moon. It would have been even better had a new song touched on that.

André Kostelanetz had become one of the cornerstones of Easy Listening music. His version of 'With a Song in My Heart' was the signature tune of the BBC radio programme, *Two-Way Family Favourites*. His composition, 'Moon Love', was adapted from the second movement of Tchaikovksy's Fifth Symphony, so maybe it wasn't his composition after all. It had been successful for both Glenn Miller and Mildred Bailey. Nancy Sinatra considers among her father's finest recordings.

Glenn Miller had written 'Moonlight Serenade' as 'Now I Lay Me Down to Sleep' but Robbins Music changed the title, making it a companion to Miller's 'Sunrise Serenade'. Mitchell Parish added a moon-and-June lyric, but a good one. 'Gee, that is a nice tune,' said Frank as Nelson ran through the arrangement. A better crafted lyric comes from the poet Dorothy Parker who had written 'I Wished on The Moon' for Bing in 1936, while the best song was 'Moonlight Becomes You', again associated with Bing, this time in 1942, but here given a dramatic arrangement that started with the middle section. Released in April 1966, *Moonlight Sinatra* was only a moderate success but remained very pleasant listening.

Frank Sinatra loved his live shows with Count Basie and his Orchestra and he decided to record the ten shows at the Sands between 26 January and 1 February 1966. On the flight to Vegas on 24 January, Sinatra said to Quincy Jones, 'Q, wouldn't it be kooky if we added Johnny Mandel's new song 'The Shadow Of Your Smile' to the show?'

'Okay,' said Q, liking a challenge, 'but can you learn the lyric by tomorrow?'

Sinatra got out a pad and wrote the lyric over and over, something he often did to get the words into his brain.

That night before the first show, he was drinking heavily with Basie and he said to him, 'If I miss a note along the way, follow me through so that it will sound all right.' Basie replied, 'We play the notes as written. The rest is up to you.'

There was an audience of around a thousand for each show and Sinatra opened with the line, cribbed from Dean, 'How did all these people get into my room?' The double-album, *Sinatra at the Sands*, was largely a magical experience as Sinatra and Basie had become used to working with each other and the arrangements by Quincy Jones brought out the best in everyone. 'Don't Worry 'Bout Me', written for a Cotton Club show in 1939, was especially good. 'I've Got a Crush On You' was a playful duet with the tenor saxophonist, Lockjaw Davis, and had Frank adding, 'You wanna meet Monday and we'll pick out the furniture.'

What is especially welcome is that only 'Fly Me to the Moon' was repeated from the two studio albums. There were no studio performances of Sinatra singing 'The Shadow of Your Smile' but this live version was lovely. The song won an Oscar in 1965 and came from *The Sandpiper*, which starred Hollywood's new golden couple, Elizabeth Taylor and Richard Burton.

As you might expect, Sinatra was full of his hip jargon ('You're such a kookoo individual', 'I'll beat your bird') and there's a ding-dong at the end of 'Get Me to the Church on Time'.

Frank described 'It Was a Very Good Year' as 'an awfully pretty folk song' and concluded, 'It was a mess of good years' at which the audience chuckled. Sinatra missed out words on 'Where or When' and concluded, 'I'm through, this is boozing time. One more. One more what? I'm going to the bar.'

Sinatra had taken to performing his songs with short introductions and then rapping towards the end, usually with a cup of tea. There is a 12-minute monologue on *Sinatra at the Sands*. Jilly's had recently opened a branch in Palm Springs and now Frank said, 'Welcome to Jilly's West.' Soon there would be a Jilly's South in Miami. Dorothy Kilgallen, a journalist who had often criticised him, had died in November 1965: Frank had often commented on her from the stage and he said, 'Well, I guess I gotta change my act.'

The monologues were never very good as Frank didn't have Dean's timing and so many of his jokes were dubious. Here he said, 'Dean Martin has been stoned more often that the United States Embassies'" and that he was bringing in Sammy Davis from *Golden Boy* 'just to clean'. The most remarkable comment was about the extensions to the Sands. He says, 'We got $3m from the local bank and $8m from the cocktail waitresses.'

But if these were ill-advised jokes, consider the brash and insensitive outtakes from other performances. He talked about George Raft's pants being part of his tie and that Raft wore a corset. He said, "I'm a wopaho from Sicily, that's an Indian tribe that they have over there, next door to the Navajews,'and commented that 'Xavier Cugat switches Indians like Louis Prima does.' He announced that he had brought in Bill Miller to the Basie orchestra to 'break up the colour scheme'. Dean's film *10,000 Bedrooms* was declared 'nearly as bad as Sammy's first television show'. After spotting the Righteous Brothers in the lounge, he joked, 'They are better known as Frick and Frack', comparing them to a pair of comedy ice skaters from the 1940s. He often referred to Basie as Splank, 'as that's what he does with his right hand – splank, splank, splank.' You do wonder what planet he is on. Oh yes, Planet Sinatra.

The Righteous Brothers was the first rock act to do well in Vegas and Bill Medley says, 'Frank Sinatra brought us to the Sands in 1965. Bobby and I were 25 and in the middle of Sinatra and all his people. Sinatra would come into the lounge after his show and as he attracted the full Hollywood set, he was allowed to approve the lounge acts. He called us "the kids". He said, "I don't understand rock'n'roll but you kids are doing a good version of it. He gave us a lot of great tips about saving our voices. It's very dry in the desert and it can wreck your voice, and we were doing three shows a night. He said, "Come to the health club with me" and he showed us the importance of using steam for your vocal cords. It was no big deal to see Sinatra around. When Elvis came to Vegas later on, you never saw him as he was like Howard Hughes.'

Frank had turned 50 and he was making good records but they were only appealing to a limited market. His singles in particular had a look of desperation about them.

Something had to be done about the poor sales of the Sinatra record releases.

That's Frank and Nancy.

What record label perseveres with a singer who has had 10 flop singles? Well, Reprise for one. Nancy Sinatra's singles were nondescript and inconsequential and Nancy was no Sinatra – only she was, genetically. The very name went against her because the public and the DJs alike thought that she only had a record contract because Daddy owned the company.

Maybe with all his connections, Frank could have bought her into the charts. With a snap of his fingers, he could have offered a weekend in Vegas with a few broads to influential DJs but the payola scandal at the start of the 1960s meant that the authorities were watching. If his daughter suddenly had a hit record, they might ask questions and it could rebound on his own career. The public might even think that his records had been bought into the charts.

So that was out.

Jimmy Bowen was friendly with a maverick songwriter and producer called Lee Hazlewood. He had made his name writing and producing hit records for the guitarist Duane Eddy, using an echo chamber of his own invention. Everything he wrote was quirky and he had sung his own album, *Trouble Is a Lonesome Town*, in a deep, cavernous voice. Jimmy asked him to join Reprise and told him, 'I'll do the mamas and papas and you do thc kids.'

Lee Hazlewood was assigned to establishing Nancy Sinatra, now 25 and getting a bit old for the charts. She had been recording drippy teen songs like 'Cuff Links and a Tie Clip'. There were no real direction to her career and she needed some killer songs. Hazlewood supplied both. 'It wasn't a big problem,' said Hazlewood, 'she'd got the genes, and she was smart too, but that's the genes again.'

Lee Hazlewood wanted her to sing something with more bite. He said to her, 'You're not a virgin: you're a grown woman and we have to reflect that.'

Cue for a song.

Lee Hazlewood wrote an incredibly catchy song to capture Nancy's mood, 'These Boots Are Made for Walkin'. As idiosyncratic as ever, it had a sadistic element, especially when Nancy sang it in long boots on TV. She was walking over Sands all right, but she came to regret the tough, trampling 'Boots'. 'The image created by 'Boots' isn't the real me,' says Nancy Sinatra, 'Lee taught me how to sing lower and how to sing tough. 'Boots' was hard and I'm as soft as they come.'

Tommy Sands remarked, 'Lee Hazlewood told me that I was the sole reason that those boots were made for walking. (Laughs) So I take that as the truth and I don't mind it one bit. I like being the inspiration for that song.'

In February 1966 'These Boots Are Made for Walkin'' became Reprise's second No.1 record and was also No.1 in the UK and, indeed, around the world. It sold six million copies and even her father hadn't had a record as big as that. The image of Nancy with her full head of blonde hair and kinky boots was ideal for what was now being called, with no reference to Frank, the Swinging 60s. 'I should have gone into the boots business,' said Nancy.

As Lee Hazlewood recalled, the accountants were raining on Nancy's parade. 'This was before the days of computers and nobody had noticed that Nancy's contract with Reprise had expired. When 'Boots' was No.1 in half the countries in the world, Nancy came over to my house and she was crying. She said, "They didn't pick up on my option at Reprise and they said that I owed them $12,000." I said, "You're kidding, we've got the biggest record in the world." I rang my lawyer in New York and I rang Nancy the next day and said, "How would you like $1m? I've got three labels that are offering that for you right now, and I can get something pretty good for myself as well." She talked to Daddy who said she could write her own contract with Reprise – after all, she was selling more records than him at the time. I said, "Okay, what'll we'll say is – you never pay any musicians; you never pay for studio time; and after three years, you own your masters." She said, "That sounds good." I said, "Just don't tell them it was me as I've got to work with the other artists here."'

Nancy and Lee followed 'Boots' with 'How Does That Grab You, Darlin''. It was not so much a new song as a rewrite of 'Boots', but it did the job and made the Top 10. Later in the year they would have another international smash with 'Sugar Town', a song that referred to the amount of drugs available in LA. It had crept under the radar at Reprise as Frank was so against youth culture and regarded rock as the road to hard drugs. Frank would never record a Bob Dylan song, but when Dylan released *Blonde on Blonde* in 1966, his organist Al Kooper remarked, 'Nobody has captured the sound of 3am better than that album. Nobody, not even Sinatra, gets it that good.'

In 1967 Frank heard the Doors' 'Light My Fire' which he maintained was the worst record that had ever been made. I wonder if Sinatra ever heard Jimi Hendrix inserting some notes from 'Strangers in The Night' into 'Wild Thing' at the Monterey festival.

Frank knew he was an albums artist but somehow he wanted to appeal to the kids. If Dean could have hits, so could he. If Nancy could do it, so could he. He was a better singer than both of them combined, though that was part of the problem. Vocal perfection was not the order of the day, and Jimmy Bowen had to come up with something.

The bandleader, Bert Kaempfert, was a German Lawrence Welk, a purveyor of cheesy listening, and he had topped the US charts with the instrumental, 'Wonderland by Night'. He was also known for the insidious 'A Swingin' Safari'.

Kaempfert could write catchy tunes but he never seemed to put himself out. He would craft a commercial main theme and that would be it. His songs were full of repetition and he didn't write bridges or middle eights. What's the point? They could be used instead for another composition. Sometimes Kaempfert didn't even write the tune: he found an old German folk song which became 'Wooden Heart' for Elvis Presley.

To a degree, his international songwriting success had been unexpected. He had served as a bandsman in the German navy during the war. After his service, he played clarinet and piano in orchestras and then discovered and established Schlager acts for Polydor in Hamburg. In 1961 he had spotted the Beatles playing in St Pauli and had recorded 'My Bonnie', which made the German charts – their first hit anywhere in the world.

Kaempfert was enjoying a lucrative sideline through American writers putting English lyrics to his songs. Wayne Newton had his breakthrough hit with 'Danke Schoen' in 1963 and Nat 'King' Cole recorded his brain dead 'L-O-V-E' the following year. You may wonder why a sublime performer like Cole should record 'L-O-V-E' and the answer was M-O-N-E-Y. Kaempfert's 'Moon Over Naples' was given a lyric by Charles Singleton and Eddie Snyder and was now 'Spanish Eyes'.

'Blue Spanish eyes
Prettiest eyes in all Mexico.'

So a German musician wrote a Neapolitan tune, which was turned into a song about a Mexican girl that became a hit for an Italian-American crooner, Al Martino.

Kaempfert had written the score for his first Hollywood movie, a spy caper, *A Man Could Get Killed*, starring James Garner, Melina Mercouri and Sandra Dee. When the music publisher, Hal Fine, was trying to interest Bowen in some material, he played him the main theme, then called 'Beddy-Bye'. Bowen said, 'Get me some lyrics for this and I'll give it to Sinatra, but don't call it 'Beddy-Bye'.'

Fine agreed but Bowen didn't like the first lyric he submitted. Nor the second. Fine commissioned a third lyric, this time from Charles Singleton and Eddie Synder, who had written 'Danke Schoen' and 'Spanish Eyes' and should have been given the job in the first place.

They took their cue from the film where James Garner and Melina Mercouri were exchanging glances in a bar and by the end of the film were in love forever. 'That was all we needed,' said Snyder, but he told Kaempfert, who happened to be in Hollywood, that there must be a bridge and they worked something out.

Hal Fine passed the song, now called 'Strangers in The Night', to Jimmy Bowen. He loved it and Frank could see its potential. Thinking that Bowen might be stringing him along, Fine played it to Bobby Darin, who was about to divorce Sandra Dee, and to Jack Jones.

Bobby Darin responded immediately. 'Strangers in The Night' was a hit song and he recorded it on March 23, 1966. Then Jack Jones recorded it on April 8.

Oh dear.

Jimmy Bowen knew Frank would be furious if he found that the song had been given to rival acts and the last thing Frank wanted was to be in a chart race and lose. Frank might hire stranglers in the night to teach him a lesson.

Bowen had to act fast. He had an album session scheduled with Dean Martin and an orchestra for Monday evening, 7pm–10pm, April 11. Dean, as if to rub it in Frank's face, was making an album which would be called *The Hit Sound of Dean Martin*. So an orchestra was available on that date although it wasn't Frank's crowd as they weren't the old big band guys.

Dean recorded quickly and Jimmy Bowen knew he could ask him to come in an hour late. In that spare hour, he would record 'Strangers in The Night' with Sinatra. Bowen asked Ernie Freeman to write an arrangement over the weekend and the lead guitarist from his own records, Donny Lanier, would conduct.

As was often the case with Dean and Frank, there were onlookers in the recording studio. Indeed, it gave the sessions a live feel but they had to be quiet and not applaud until the end. Mitchell Torok was a friend of Jimmy Bowen and he and his wife had been invited to the session as Dean was recording one of his songs. 'There was a list of names on the inside of the door at the big Sunset Recording Studios on Sunset Boulevard. They liked to invite their friends to sit around the edge of the studio while they were recording, and sometimes they could be a hundred people sitting in chairs, right round the walls. Nobody coughed; nobody dropped anything; nobody sneezed.'

Mitchell Torok recalled that particular session: 'That night Frank was going to cut a record first and he'd picked 'Strangers in the Night'. Electricity went through the room when he walked in with his entourage. There was a 35 piece orchestra and they jumped up and saluted. It was like God walking in. He shook hands with the conductor, took off his hat and his coat, and loosened his tie.'

Amongst the musicians was a hot, young guitarist, Glen Campbell, but he couldn't read music. The UK impresario Jeff Kruger recalls, 'Glen Campbell didn't know the song and had been brought in at the last minute. Glen hadn't heard the demo and he was busking on the first take but listening to the melody. When it was through, Sinatra yelled out, "Is that guy with us or is he sleeping?" Well, Glen was learning the song and he came up with that famous guitar phrase which helped to made it a hit.'

'I could appreciate a great session whether it was country, rock or whatever.' said Glen Campbell, 'Like 'Strangers in the Night'. It was the first session that I did with Sinatra and I loved it straight off. I loved the song and I loved the way it was being done. It was commercial pop as far as I was concerned with that typical big band sound of Sinatra.' 'It was an easy session for me,' says the drummer Hal Blaine, 'I was just playing what I had done on the Ronettes' 'Be My Baby'.'

Sinatra heard the orchestration and was ready to record. The red light went on. Mitchell Torok continues, 'The orchestra started a take but someone blew it when Sinatra was going pretty good. Sinatra said, "Okay, boys, we're going to do it again. I'm going to sing it one more time and if you don't get it right, I'm gone." Talk about pressure, but that is the take that the world heard. He added that 'Dooby, dooby, doo' on the end and it gives me goosepimples just talking about it, to think that I was there. Sinatra adjusted his tie, put his hat on and said, "I'm going to eat."' He had first used 'Dooby, dooby, do' during a performance of 'Please Be Kind' on a TV show with Count Basie in 1965. It's not too far from Yogi Bear's catchphrase, which suggests that Frank had been watching *Huckleberry Hound*.

The jazz writer Gene Lees wrote, 'Even if he doesn't like the material, he reveals himself in his approach to it. 'Strangers in the Night 'is dreck. Frank Sinatra recorded it. He stated his contempt with the 'dooby, dooby, doo' he attached to the end of it. He thereby told us that he's a snob about material. But then he told us something that he didn't intend to: that there was a streak of hypocrisy in him. If he didn't respect the song, he shouldn't have recorded it – even for money, which he hardly needed at that point.'

About 20 minutes later, Dean Martin parked his red sports car outside the studio and ambled in. Unlike Sinatra, he started cracking jokes and everybody loved him. He was recording Mitchell Torok's '(Open Up The Door) Let The Good Times In'. Mitchell says, 'It was a novelty song, a fun song, but Dean misread the lyric saying the word 'cat' instead of 'rat'. I said, "Jimmy, Jimmy, he's singing the wrong words." Jimmy looked at me and said, "You wanna go down there and tell him?"(Laughs) The wrong lyric appeared on the album.'

Once Jimmy Bowen had 'Strangers in the Night' on tape, he prepared advance copies and sent them to the main radio stations. This gave Frank a head start on Jack Jones, whilst Bobby Darin's performance has never been released. Jack Jones's version was slower and more reflective than Sinatra's and he repeats 'Strangers in the night' at the end., adding not a single 'dooby, dooby, do'.

The song's message of casual sex was in line with the Swinging 60s, or was it? Dean Martin teased Frank when he heard that the single was being rush-released, he said, 'Frank, what are you singing that song for? It's about two faggots and I turned it down.' But Dean was always winding Frank up. In Dean's first Matt Helm film, *The Silencers*, Stella Stevens put on the radio and Frank's voice came out of the speakers. 'Oh turn him off,' said Dean, 'he's terrible.'

In June 1966 Dean and Frank celebrated Dean's birthday at Chasen's in Beverly Hills with Richard Conte and Jilly Rizzo. Two businessmen at a nearby table found them noisy and vulgar. When one of them, Fred Weisman, complained, Frank said, 'You're out of line, buddy' and added something about 'this fucking Jew bastard'. Fred Weisman objected and Frank threw a telephone at him, hitting him on the head. Dean pulled Frank off him but when Weisman called them 'dirty wops', he hit him himself. Weisman was taken to intensive care and cranial surgery was needed to save his life. No charges were ever pressed.

Frank and Brad Dexter had bought the film rights to the cold war thriller, *The Naked Runner* by Francis Clifford, and they recruited the director Sidney Furie, who had had success with *The Ipcress File*. The script was written by Stanley Mann (*The Collector*) and it was the third film Frank would make about political assassination, but he did enjoy making films that might get America talking. Not that this was one of them.

Frank plays a widowed American industrialist about to attend trade show in East Germany and living in London with his young son Patrick (Michael Newport). He is a former agent from World War II. His mission was to assassinate a freed political prisoner before he revealed state secrets to the Kremlin, and his son would be killed if he refused to cooperate, an extraordinary method of coercion by the secret service.

On 5 July, his first day of shooting, Frank spent the evening at the *Playboy* club and somehow that made him want to marry Mia Farrow.

Another bride, another, er, July.

The production was shut down so that Charlie Brown could marry Babyface (their nicknames for each other) at the Sands on 19 July. They were married in Jack Entratter's suite. Although ill, Spencer Tracy attended the wedding reception, and Audrey Hepburn accompanied George Cukor, the bride's godfather.

Dean was asked to tell Frank's daughter, Tina, about the marriage and she said, 'Well, he's got a great mother-in-law', a reference to the actress Maureen O'Sullivan. Mia's father, the film director John Farrow, was a drinker and a womaniser like Frank. Ava had made a terrible western *Ride, Vaquero!* in Utah with him in 1952. Farrow had been so bored that he had flown hookers in from Los Angeles and Ava disliked his cruelty to horses. Frank was soon to fall out with his mother-in-law in a strange argument at a restaurant in Beverly Hills which ended with him turning the table over his agent, Swifty Lazar.

They returned to London on 25 July and in between honeymooning in France, some filming was slotted in. The *Daily Mirror* journalist, Donald Zec, got wind of what had happened and wrote about it. He received a curt note from Sinatra: 'You've blown it.'

The film was made with a local cast including Peter Vaughan, Edward Fox and Derren Nesbitt in London. But the weather was bleak, hardly providing a suitable setting for Swinging London. When a helicopter was lost in the fog on the Thames, Frank said that he would do the rest of his acting from Palm Springs, Furie refused to continue but Dexter told Sinatra of the losses they would incur if either of them left. Sinatra agreed to three more days in London and then some further shooting in Copenhagen. After that, he was going to Los Angeles to support the Democratic candidate Edmund Brown who was standing against Ronald Reagan in California. Sinatra said he wasn't coming back. Furie had to do the best he could, sometimes using stand-ins for the back of Sinatra's head. Maybe he left his toupée behind. Dexter and Furie reworked the script and used a double, subsequently editing in close-ups of Sinatra. When Dexter handed the film to Jack Warner on completion, Warner fired him.

If Sinatra had stayed longer and been in a better mood, he would have made a second UK album, but this time more contemporary and under the control of Tony Hatch. The sessions were arranged but he cancelled them. A session singer, Mike Redway, recalls, 'Tony Hatch rang me to say that an orchestra had been booked for Sinatra and he wasn't coming. Could I sing the songs in his place? The studio was packed with musicians, bigger than anything I had ever worked with. Unfortunately the arrangements were a bit low for me but I did five tracks, and they were never released. I did get a TV series out of that as I had some acetates and I played them to John Ammonds who wanted a singer for *Don't Ask Us, We're New Here*. So something good came out of it.'

Frank's single of 'Strangers in the Night' had been rush-released by Reprise and Frank had the satisfaction of having a No.1 hit on his own record label. It was his first No.1 since 'Learnin' the Blues' in 1955. It removed 'Paperback Writer' from the No.1 slot in the US and the Rolling Stones' 'Paint It Black' in the UK.

Although Frank loved being at No.1, he still hated the song and he told Nelson Riddle that they were going to make a contemporary album where every track would outshine 'Strangers in the Night'. Probably not knowing what Sinatra wanted (and nor did he), the sessions were utterly bizarre and overrun by a Hammond organ. There were leaden attempts at 'My Baby just Cares for Me' and 'Yes Sir That's My Baby' and possibly the worst 'Downtown' that has even been recorded as he sings 'Yuk, downtown', possibly playing to the gallery. Its composer Tony Hatch says, 'You can tell from the record that Frank wasn't comfortable with 'Downtown'. The arrangement is weird as well. It's as if he said to Nelson Riddle, "Let's do 'Downtown Hong Kong'."' All is not lost as there is a decent version of another Tony Hatch song, 'Call Me'.

Frank brought an ultra-hip Sammy Davis styled performance to Rodgers and Hart's 'The Most Beautiful Girl in the World', usually a waltz and now full of organ licks and frenzied bongos. All this and yet Frank makes mention of his slippers.

Frank and Nelson are floundering as they are so far out of their comfort zone and making the album without much care. Note how Sinatra stumbles over a word on 'You're

Driving Me Crazy' and it was never corrected.

Scott Walker commented, 'Sinatra degrades himself by doing this rubbish. Listening to him doing numbers like 'Downtown' is like trying to watch an old man jive.'

In later years, Frank would work with Bob Gaudio of the Four Seasons. Perhaps he should have done that in 1966. Frankie Valli recalls, 'We played a date in Florida and then we went to see Sinatra who was amazing. Bob Gaudio rang me at three in the morning and he said, "This can't wait. We've gotta do 'I've Got You Under My Skin'." I said, "How can we make it better?", and he said, "Trust me." We did with a great symphonic arrangement and it was a big hit.'

The best track, even better than 'Strangers in the Night' in my opinion, is 'Summer Wind' which did okay but not great as the follow-up single: US 25, UK 36. It is a German song with an English lyric by Johnny Mercer, previously recorded by Wayne Newton and Roger Williams. The song was given a gentle swing arrangement and in this instance, the electric organ definitely worked.

The album was released with the asinine title, *Strangers in the Night – The Popular Sinatra Sings for Moderns*, but what do I know? This was his first No.1 album in the US for six years and it stayed on the charts for a year. On the other hand, Nelson Riddle never made another album with Sinatra.

Naturally, Sinatra had to add 'Strangers in the Night' to his set list but he never grew to love it. It's entertaining to go through his live concerts to hear how he introduces 'Strangers in the Night':

'Here's a song I can't stand, but what the hell!'

'If you like this song, you must be crazy about pineapple yogurt.'

'This song helped keep me in pizza for a long time.'

And, most of all, 'This is one of the worst songs I ever sang in my life.'

Sometimes Sinatra would amend the lyrics, replacing 'Love was just a glance away, a warm embracing dance away' with 'Love was just a glance away, a lonesome pair of pants away.'

Still, as a result of 'Strangers in the Night', Bert Kaempfert became an answer in *Trivial Pursuit* as the only man who has worked with Elvis Presley, the Beatles and Frank Sinatra. It turned out so right for Eddie Snyder, who said, 'It made a bum out of me because I didn't have to work anymore.'

Possibly Sinatra thought that singing for moderns was the right thing to do as he had married Mia Farrow, a flower power girl and actress less than half his age. In a good example of car crash television, Mia Farrow was the mystery guest when Frank was a panelist on the quiz show, *What's My Line?* Asked 'Have you ever performed with Frank Sinatra?', Mia answered, 'No.' Frank asked her if she has tasted the food at Toots Shor's restaurant (product placement again) and then said, 'You got the same name as me?' He didn't look happy when he found the answer was yes. He normally did the practical jokes. Frank told one Vegas audience, 'I finally found a broad I can cheat on.' Mia was in tears but Frank said he was kidding.

Although Frank had had antipathy towards one of the regular panelists, Dorothy Kilgallen, he was very friendly with the publisher and founder of Random House, Bennett Cerf and his wife, Phyllis. Once they told him that they needed a big picture for the living-room wall. While they were away, their maid let him in and he put up a painting for them of his own New York, New York. However, Frank always turned down Bennett Cerf's suggestion that he should write his autobiography.

Frank could joke about his relationship with Mia but that was off limits to anybody else except Dean. When the comedian Jackie Mason came to Vegas, he talked about Frank's hair transplants and elevator shoes and described the couple's going-to-bed ritual. He was told to lay off by Sinatra's people and when he didn't, three shots were fired into his hotel room from the balcony. The story made the press and Jackie Mason said on TV, 'I have no idea who it was who tried to shoot me. After the shots were fired, all I heard was someone singing "Dooby, dooby, do".' A few months later some thug with a fistful of metal broke Jackie Mason's nose.

During 1966 the singer and songwriter, Kelly Gordon, took 'That's Life' to Warners and the executive Russ Regan said, 'How badly do you want to record this song yourself? I want to give it to Frank Sinatra.' As it happens, it had already been recorded by Marion Montgomery and O C Smith. Inspired by Ray Charles' current hit, 'Let's Go Get Stoned', Ernie Freeman wrote an arrangement that incorporated a gospel choir. When Jimmy Bowen produced Sinatra, he was happy with what he had, but he ran out after him and requested one more take. As he hoped, Sinatra was angry and that anger came over in the recording. In a sense, it's Frank's most rebellious performance and it went to No.4 in the US. The arrangement suited Frank fine as he had previously informed *Life* magazine that Ray Charles was 'the only genius in our business'.

The *That's Life* album followed the same path as *Strangers in the Night* but, aside from a ghastly 'Winchester Cathedral', the arrangements by Ernie Freeman were more suited to Sinatra and to the mid-60s. 'Somewhere My Love' doesn't work as a swinger but the Ray Conniff-slanted 'What Now My Love' was fine. There was a French feel to the album with Michel Legrand's 'I Will Wait for You' and Gilbert Bécaud's 'Sand and Sea'. Mia Farrow suggested 'The Impossible Dream' and although Sinatra was none too keen, he did it well. Possibly Sinatra viewed it as a Sammy song as he loved songs with a positive message like 'A Lot of Livin' To Do' and 'Gonna Build a Mountain'.

A sleazy tale of Hollywood life, *The Oscar,* was filmed in 1966 with Stephen Boyd in the main role. The unscrupulous character, Frankie Fane, expected to win an Oscar but he is beaten in the film by another Frankie, Frank Sinatra, who is congratulated by his daughter, Nancy. Frank has one line: 'Thank you very much.' The film is unintentionally funny and the best moment has to be Jill St John's striptease. The worst, Tony Bennett's acting.

In December 1966 CBS screened about a follow-up TV special, *A Man and His Music II,* where he doesn't even sing 'Strangers in the Night'. He called 'The Most Beautiful Girl in the World' the fastest arrangement he'd ever sung. His current single, 'That's Life' was 'a good tune and something to think about' and he told us that he preferred baths to showers. He and Nancy performed a medley of 'Yes Sir That's My Baby' and 'Downtown' and he was still going 'Yuk, downtown', but singing it as though he were Anthony Newley. The show won a Grammy for sound, more for how it was reproduced than what the results were.

CHAPTER 14

The first goodbye

'If you ring this bell, you better have a damn good reason.'
Brass plate on Frank Sinatra's gate

I. The Record Shows I Took the Blows

Once I happened to be at an audition for the ITV talent show, *Opportunity Knocks*, when the producer was addressing the young (and not so young) hopefuls. 'Give your music to the pianist,' he said, 'but please, no more 'My Ways'.'

'My Way' is any impassioned singer's calling-card, which renders the song meaningless as any performer is, *ipso facto*, doing it someone else's way. 'My Way' is a karaoke favourite and became the most mauled song of the 20th century. The lyric is half-sung, half-spoken, and, to be performed convincingly, it needs an intensity that matches Robert De Niro's acting. To quote an editorial in *The Times* commenting on Radio 2's *Songs of the Century*, ''My Way' may have been intended as a hymn to individuality, but paradoxically it is a favourite of the common herd.'

Most people think that 'My Way' is a song that Paul Anka wrote for Frank Sinatra but the story is far richer and much more complex than that. Indeed, rarely have so many people been involved in one song.

The story begins in 1965 when the songwriting team of Gilles Thibault (words) and Jacques Revaux (music) wrote a pop song, a French *chanson* called 'Comme d'habitude'. A direct English translation would be 'As Usual' but the theme is different from Brenda Lee's 1964 hit of the same title. The French song is about a one-way love affair ('I touch your hair while you're asleep as usual'), while in Brenda Lee's 'As Usual', the affair is definitely over.

Thibault and Revaux had written for several French artists but none of their songs were known internationally. As they were not established as performers, they passed their new composition to one of France's biggest stars, Claude François. (If you want to see Revaux, he is in the 1967 film *The Young Girls of Rochefort (Les Demoiselles de Rochefort)*.)

Claude François was born in Ismailia, Egypt, in 1939. His father was an engineer who worked for the Suez Canal Company and who found himself without a job when the Egyptians assumed control in 1956. The promise of employment in France came to nothing and the family found themselves with little money in Monte Carlo, surely the worst place in the world to be without money. His father died, totally disillusioned, a few years later and, in interviews, François was very critical of the French government.

François could play drums and sing and was determined to become a performer. He watched Frank Sinatra in rehearsal, although he had no idea that their paths would cross a few years later. François' first wife left him for the singer, Gilbert Bécaud, and then in 1962 he had his first hit with a cover of Steve Lawrence's lightweight 'Girls, Girls, Girls', now called 'Belles, Belles, Belles'. He sang twist songs and had further hits with 'Si J'Avais

Un Marteau (If I Had A Hammer)', performed Trini Lopez-style, and, surprisingly, Noël Coward's 'Poor Little Rich Girl'. He was a heart-throb and the girls called him Clo-Clo.

Claude's girlfriend was France Gall, who won the Eurovision Song Contest for Luxembourg in 1965 with a Serge Gainsbourg song, 'Poupée de Cire, Poupée de Son'. He was sad when they broke up, so he could identify with the latest song in his in-tray, 'Comme d'habitude'. He made a few adjustments to the melody and claimed a songwriting credit. 'Comme d'habitude' stormed up the French charts.

Several songwriters including Gilbert Bécaud, Charles Aznavour and Georges Moustaki had done well in the English-speaking world, but usually their songs had been translated. A UK publisher was asked to supply an English lyric for 'Comme d'habitude' and find a suitable performer. The song was passed to an up-and-coming singer planning a cabaret act, David Bowie. He took the melody and wrote a new lyric, rather than a translation, 'Even a Fool Learns To Love'. A demo recording was made, but the lyric was not accepted.

Paul Anka, a pop singer with a surname ideal for limericks, was born in Ottawa in 1941. He found international fame when only 15 with a song about having the hots for a babysitter, 'Diana'. Over the next few years, he became Canada's greatest musical export, writing and recording such hits as 'Lonely Boy', 'Puppy Love' and 'Put Your Head on My Shoulder'. He wrote Buddy Holly's posthumous UK No.1, 'It Doesn't Matter Anymore', the theme for the film, *The Longest Day* and the music for Johnny Carson's long-running *Tonight Show*. In the documentary, *Lonely Boy*, released in 1962, Paul Anka's manager says, 'God gave Paul something I don't think has been given to anyone in the last 500 years.' I wonder what it was and whether Paul would share it with the rest of us.

Paul Anka was, and still is, a competent but not great songwriter; unlike Burt Bacharach, he didn't have a readily identifiable style. He was a jobbing songwriter who could turn his hand to commissions for other artists, film songs and TV themes. One underrated song is 'Love Me Warm and Tender', which was covered, excellently, by Arthur Alexander. In 1963 Anka recorded an album, *Songs I Wish I'd Written* and no doubt the songwriters were planning to strike back with *Songs We're Glad He Didn't*.

Like Neil Sedaka and Carole King, Paul Anka's ability to write hit songs faded in the mid-1960s. He kept going with TV shows and appearances in Las Vegas, but his smugness prevented him from becoming a major star. His official website says that he has achieved 'unprecedented success in every venue: stage, screen, television and recording', so you can see what I mean. Still, if your manager says you're the best thing for 500 years, you're bound to have some delusions of grandeur. He enjoyed working in Vegas but the slogan said it all, 'It's Sinatra's world, we just live in it.' He wanted to write for Frank, saying 'He's the only one who can put you in a mood within five seconds no matter what he's singing.'

In 1968 a publisher was talking to Paul Anka at a music festival in Cannes and asked him to write an English lyric for 'Comme d'habitude', although he'd had no experience of reworking European hits. He liked the melody and he had an idea one rainy night while winding down after a performance in New York. By five in the morning, he had the lyric he wanted – 'My Way'. Like many adaptations of continental songs, it bore no relation to the original lyric, but the new words said everything about Frank Sinatra's turbulent life.

Paul Anka wrote it as a journalist, writing from the standpoint of someone 25 years his senior, 'I sat at the typewriter and started typing the words, 'And now the end is near...' That really got it going. The moment I got the first two lines out, I was focused entirely on Sinatra, trying to portray everything indigenous to his life and what he was about.'

Everyone knew about Frank Sinatra's life – the saloon singer with the portable saloon, the rat in the Rat Pack, the Chairman of the Flawed. Counting the women in Kitty Kelley's salacious biography, *His Way*, I found 60 named lovers as well as hundreds of showgirls and prostitutes. He was a man's man, who treated women appallingly (and Sammy Davis like a lackey). He beat them up, if Kelley is to be believed, and yet they loved him. Or some of them did – he had lost favourites along the way. Like his Scotch, his current marriage to the hippie actress Mia Farrow was on the rocks, largely because he objected to her pursuing her own career with the film, *Rosemary's Baby*. Sinatra's career had the ups and downs of a roller-coaster and currently he was on top, part-owning his record label, Reprise, and even appealing to teenage record-buyers with 'Strangers in the Night' and 'Somethin' Stupid' (a duet with daughter Nancy). He'd faced it all and he'd stood tall – you see how it is easy to associate the lyric with Frank's life.

Anka said, 'I would never normally write something so chauvinistic, narcissistic, in your face and grandiose.' He loved Frank Sinatra's personality. The character in the song is a driven man, often misunderstood but always true to himself, a man who can transform failure into triumph. Frank had sung about 'High Hopes' but that was a kids' song. Here was a lyric that got under his skin, one that he could identify with in every respect. Because of his contretemps with the press, Frank Sinatra gave few interviews, and none at all which would trespass on his psyche. Instead, via 'My Way', Frank could make a defiant statement to the world, give everyone the finger if you like,

'The record shows I took the blows,
And did it My Way!'

His way, according to the song, was wholly admirable and he was to be congratulated for his independence. It was a brilliant lyric as in a few short stanzas, Paul Anka had captured the very essence of being Frank Sinatra. 'I can't believe songs like 'No Regrets' or 'My Way',' says the country songwriter Gretchen Peters. 'Everybody has some regrets. They are really songs of bluster and bravado.'

Another songwriter, Tony Hazzard, who wrote 'Fox on the Run', says, 'To me 'My Way' is bad lyric writing. The sentiment seems wrong. Sinatra is saying that he did it his way, but was it a good way? Not necessarily, but we aren't told. 'I saw it through without exemption' is terrible. I'm a songwriter and I know that's the sort of word you squeeze in when you can't think of anything else. The lyric doesn't flow well at all and the whole thing is too artificial for me.'

'My Way' was a psychological Full Monty, but it was also an appalling lyric and little better than the couplets in his first hit, 'Diana'. It's unthinkable that Sammy Cahn would have ever rhymed 'mention' with 'exemption'. What does 'I saw it through without exemption' mean? Possibly, I didn't neglect my duties and I got through difficult times. 'I saw it through without exception' would be better, or how about this, 'I saw it through until my pension'. Well, at least it rhymes.

Try this:

'Regrets, I've had a few,
But then again too few for naming,
I did what I had to do
And saw it through without complaining.'

Also, Anka is tied to finding rhymes for 'my way' itself, which leads, in desperation, to

'To think I did all that,
And may I say, not in a shy way,
Oh no, oh no, not me,
I did it my way.'

Again, how about this?

'To think I did all that,
And rising high up in the skyway.
I saw the light, I did it right,
I did it my way.'

Unlike, say, Herbert Kretzmer's elegant lyric for Charles Aznavour's 'She', 'My Way' is not well-crafted, but if Paul Anka had tinkered with it as Paul Simon would, it might have lost its potency. For all its clumsiness, 'My Way' does work, and it certainly works with Sinatra singing it. Considering that Paul Anka's track record was not that great, he excelled himself with 'My Way'.

Keen fans have transcribed the lyrics of well-known songs for the internet. One of the Nina Simone websites, not the official one, contains the worst transcription of 'My Way' imaginable. It makes you wonder what listeners actually hear. This is a sample:

'Oh, I've laughed and cried, had my fill my share of losing,
And now, as tears subside, counted all music
To think like the old lad
And may I say not in a sky away
Oh no no no, you're not me, I did it my way.'

Don Costa had been the musical director on Paul Anka's hit records and now he was working for Frank Sinatra. RCA wanted Anka to keep the song for himself, but Paul passed the song to Don Costa, who noted that it had much in common with Sinatra's reflective songs for his 50th birthday: 'September Song', 'The September of My Years' and 'It Was a Very Good Year'. It was with some trepidation that he recommend 'My Way' to Frank Sinatra. You never knew which way Frank would jump and he might have thought that they were mocking him.

Fortunately, Paul Anka had met Frank Sinatra before, most recently while he was filming *Tony Rome* in Florida and Anka was at the Fontainebleau. Frank was thinking of retiring and making a final album with Don Costa. He played him 'My Way'. Sinatra recognised its potential, although he wasn't sure whether he wanted to expose himself in this way. He did do things his way, he knew that, but he wasn't sure that he wanted to say so. In concert, Paul Anka says that he was forced to give the song to Sinatra rather than keep it for himself, but this is simply so he can follow it with a good one-liner, 'I didn't want to find a horse's head in my bed.'

Considering how heavily Frank Sinatra smoked and drank, it is remarkable that he retained his voice. He didn't undertake vocal exercises, but somehow it stayed in shape, deeper than it had been, but then Sinatra was 53.

The 'My Way' session was scheduled for the afternoon of 30 December 1968, Sinatra's first session for six weeks and the only song he recorded on that day. Don Costa rehearsed the orchestra and Sinatra came in when Costa was ready. He did two takes and within half an hour, he was gone.

A month later, Paul Anka got a call from Frank, who said, 'Hey, kid, listen to this', and he put the phone close to the audio speaker so that he could hear 'My Way'. 'I cried,' said Anka, 'I hadn't had a hit record or written a good song for five years. It was a traumatic period for me. I can't describe the thrill of hearing Sinatra sing that song. It was one of the milestones of my career.'

'My Way', as released, was a combination of the two takes. You can hear the splice just before 'I've loved, I've laughed and I've cried.' Sinatra goes from a bravura voice to an intimate one and I'm told that it would be impossible to do that naturally. Even for Sinatra.

Strangely, 'My Way' was not a huge US hit for Frank Sinatra, peaking at No.27. In 1970

Brook Benton took the song into the US charts but fared no better. Meanwhile, Paul Anka, regenerated, was writing songs as though they were going out of fashion. In 1971 Tom Jones went to No.2 in the US with Anka's song, 'She's A Lady', and its B-side was 'My Way'.

'My Way' fared much better in the UK. Frank Sinatra's record reached No.5. It remained on the charts for a remarkable two years, thus proving more enduring than Sinatra's follow-ups. The first was Rod McKuen's folky 'Love's Been Good to Me' (No.8) and then Paul Ryan, noted for teenage songs with his twin brother Barry, had a fair stab at writing a song for the older Sinatra with 'I Will Drink the Wine' (No.16).

Dorothy Squires was an argumentative, litigious British singer whose career had been as stormy as Sinatra's. Her show-business marriage to Roger Moore had been a disaster and she was dogged by controversy. By being written in non-specific terms, 'My Way' suited her life as much as Sinatra's. Her version of 'My Way' made the UK Top 30 and prompted her to book the London Palladium for a major concert return. Defying expectations, the concert sold out, and 'My Way', naturally, was her show-stopper.

'My Way' achieved an additional resonance in 1971 when Frank Sinatra announced his retirement. He gave his final concert in Los Angeles. He finished dramatically with 'My Way', but returned for an encore. He sat on a stool and sang the intimate 'Angel Eyes' in a solitary spotlight. It was great theatre. The final words were ''Scuse me while I disappear' and then he was gone, leaving behind his cigarette smoke. Possibly he was retiring because he couldn't grasp the changes in popular music; this man hated rock'n'roll, so what did he make of Jimi Hendrix? ''Scuse me while I kiss the sky' had become more relevant than ''Scuse me while I disappear'.

By now, everyone wanted to sing 'My Way' as their personal statement, and possibly one reason for its great popularity was that audiences identified with the lyric: everyone wants to do things their way but most of us haven't got the nerve. Hank Snow and Don Gibson treated it as a country song, while Nina Simone and Eartha Kitt were feisty females who could identify with the lyric. Middle-of-the-road treatments came from Acker Bilk and Mantovani. It was recorded by the Treorchy Male Voice Choir and by St Paul's Cathedral Choir, all of whom presumably believed that they were doing it their way.

David Bowie, intrigued by the impact of 'My Way' and possibly thinking that his own lyric had been better, wrote 'Life on Mars'. His 1973 hit, 'Life on Mars', though you'd never know it, was a parody of 'My Way', and Bowie said in 1993, 'There was a sense of revenge because I was angry that Paul Anka had done 'My Way'. I thought I'd write my own version. There are snatches of melody in 'Life on Mars' that are definite parodies.' Bowie's fascination with Sinatra continued when he was scheduled to play him in a bio-pic, although it never happened. Judging by the closing notes on 'Life on Mars', Bowie would have struggled vocally with 'My Way'.

Sinatra started performing again in 1973. His new album was *Ol' Blue Eyes Is Back* and the single, appropriately titled 'Let Me Try Again', was tailored by Sammy Cahn and Paul Anka from a French song, 'Laisse Moi Le Temps'. It sounded like Anka too was moving into parody. Back on stage, Sinatra introduced 'My Way' with the words, 'We're about to sing the national anthem, but you needn't rise.' Sinatra gave Anka namechecks but he was less inclined to mention the other writers. He would identify Anka's collaborator as General de Gaulle.

A reviewer for the magazine, *Woman's Wear Daily*, said: 'The Voice is now the void and it is a performance of self-destructive vulgarity. It is the ego-infested arrogance of a man who has made the sentiment of 'My Way' stand as his musical epitaph and he has totally surrendered any musical relevance by catering to the coarse and useless windbag within.'

In 1974 Paul Anka recorded '(You're) Having My Baby', an international hit to be sure, but one that angered women's groups everywhere. With a few adjustments, this need not have been a controversial song at all. Perhaps Anka wanted it that way or perhaps Anka, as with 'My Way', never spent enough time completing his lyrics. Don Costa gave Anka some additional royalties by arranging a new version of 'Puppy Love' for Donny Osmond, a UK No.1.

Meanwhile, Claude François, plagued by depression and insomnia, kept performing and maintained his business interests which included an agency with 40 models on its books. When his marriage to Isabelle ended, he wrote two notable songs about their relationship. In 1971 Richard Harris recorded one as 'My Boy' and he had his own UK hit with the other, 'Tears on the Telephone', in 1976. This prompted him to appear with his dance troupe, the Claudettes, at the Royal Albert Hall and although this was very successful, it did him little good. He died in 1978 in bizarre circumstances. He was electrocuted while changing a lightbulb in his bathroom whilst soaking wet. Presumably he had missed out on physics at school.

Gripped by the success of 'My Way', many international cabaret stars wanted a song about their long and winding roads. I had assumed that Sammy Davis, typically, had followed his master's voice with 'I've Gotta Be Me', but I was wrong because Davis recorded 'I've Gotta Be Me' before Sinatra sang "My Way", and his record was a US Top 20 hit in January 1969. The song came from the stage musical, *Golden Rainbow*, which in turn was based on the 1959 Frank Sinatra film, *A Hole in the Head*. The 1968 musical was a showcase for those singing sweethearts, Steve Lawrence and Eydie Gormé, but Davis was quick to pick up on its key song, 'I've Gotta Be Me', which had the same pomposity as 'My Way' – it tied in with what came to be known as Me Generation:

Whether I'm right or whether I'm wrong,
Whether I find a place in this world or never belong,
I've gotta be me, I've gotta be me
What else can I be, but what I am?'

Feuds between top singers are not confined to Liam Gallagher and Robbie Williams. Johnnie Ray had recorded for Sinatra's label, Reprise, in 1966 but Ray blamed Sinatra when the recordings were shelved. He dated it back to 1952 when Sinatra was jealous of Ray's friendship with his wife, Ava Gardner. So, in 1966, Johnnie did it his way: in a fit of rage, he burnt all his Sinatra albums. He didn't record again for several years, and then he made an album in London, *Yesterday, Today and Tomorrow*, produced by Tony Hiller. One of Hiller's songs was styled on 'My Way' and used Ray's key word, 'cry' – 'I Cry in My Sleep':

'And what about me and what of my life,
Well, I've had success, I've tasted the wine,
I try to forget but your cut was deep,
And God only knows, I cry in my sleep.'

The relationship between Frank Sinatra and Bing Crosby had never been perfect, but it reached rock bottom when John F Kennedy chose to stay with Crosby rather than Sinatra in 1962. Sinatra wouldn't even speak Crosby's name and referred to him as 'The other singer'. Crosby wanted a 'My Way' and he helped shape the lyric of 'That's What Life Is All About', a radio favourite in 1975. Bing's approach to life was very different to Sinatra's and Sinatra would never have sung the line, 'I was never too courageous'. The two songs, played back to back, tell us much about Der Bingle and the Hoboken Heart-throb:

'I've known some success, some mild acclaim,
And thinking of it gives me pleasure,

I've had some stress, the scars remain,
When Lady Luck gave me short measure.'

Hal Shaper and Cyril Orandel wrote 'At My Time of Life', which was sung by Sir John Mills in the 1975 West End musical of Charles Dickens' *Great Expectations*. Hal Shaper recalls, 'I had gone to America because we handle the publishing of over 100 Sinatra standards, but Frank felt that the song was too old for him. When I got back to London, Bing Crosby was in town and I passed the song to his producer, Ken Barnes. They liked it enough to ask if there was anything else in the show they could do, and they cut two songs, 'At My Time of Life' and 'Children', and they are lovely recordings.''

'At My Time of Life' is more Bing than Frank, who was 12 years older than Frank:

'Puffing my pipe and watching the smoke rings fly,
Doing my best
And as for the rest
Just letting the world go by.'

One of the best 'career songs' was 'If I Never Sing Another Song', by the manager/lyricist, Don Black, for his artist, Matt Monro. Don Black told me, 'It has nothing to do with 'My Way', nothing at all, although they are both songs for mature singers. 'My Way' is about somebody who says, "No matter what has come along, I've been all the way through it." 'If I Never Sing Another Song' is a story, a heartbreaking story of a singer, who has had an unbelievable share of success, looking back over a long career and trying to shrug off the fact that he is not so popular now. "So what if I never sing another song, I'll get by," he says, but he adds, "I don't know how." It's a very sensitive song and it's a million miles away from 'My Way', which is showbiz nonsense. 'My Way' is the sort of cabaret song that Americans love to sing but it doesn't bear close examination. "I ate it up and spit it out, And did it my way", what does it all mean?'

Don Black's chorus is:

'If I never sing another song, it shouldn't bother me,
I've had my share of fame, you know my name.
If I never another song or take another bow,
I would get by, but I'm not sure how.'

The song was also recorded by Frankie Laine, who told me at the time, 'It's the same sort of song as 'My Way', although it isn't the real me speaking in those lyrics. Don Black has the singer saying, "If I never sing another song, it wouldn't bother me." Well, of course it would. It matters a lot and I hope that nobody thinks that I'm giving up because I've recorded that song.'

Don Black continues, 'I know it was Matt Monro's favourite song of all the ones that he recorded. It will become a major, major song one day. Singers keep singing it, particularly in Las Vegas. It's an anthem for someone who has been in the business a long time, and it could turn out to be a major, major copyright. As it is, Shirley Bassey and Connie Francis sing it. It suits everyone who's had a dodgy career with its highs and lows.'

There are many show songs which can be reworked as 'career songs'. Stephen Sondheim's superb musical, *Follies*, includes 'I'm Still Here', which has been associated at different times with Yvonne De Carlo, Dolores Gray and especially Eartha Kitt. It is down to Eartha as she sings:

'I've been through Reno,
I've been through Beverly Hills,
And I'm here.
Reefers and vino,

Rest cures, religion and pills,
But I'm here.'

Shirley Bassey and Helen Shapiro sang 'Nobody Does It Like Me' from the 1974 musical by Dorothy Fields, *Seesaw,* which also contained 'It's Not Where You Start (It's Where You Finish)', which Shirley MacLaine performed. 'I Am What I Am' from *La Cage Aux Folles* (Gloria Gaynor and Bassey again) was the 'My Way' for the 1980s and is now a gay anthem. Ms Bassey belted out the Les Reed and Johnny Worth song, 'Does Anybody Miss Me', and Norman Newell's translation of 'La Vita', 'This Is My Life', and so could build a whole act from career songs. You could argue, with perverse logic, that John Lennon's 'Working Class Hero' was a career song of sorts and his response to 'My Way'.

In 1975 Jerry Leiber and Mike Stoller wrote and produced a remarkable album for Peggy Lee, *Mirrors.* It's a brave singer who would tackle 'Ready to Begin Again':

'But I put in my teeth and I put on my hair
And a very strange thing occurs when I do,
For my teeth start to feel like my very own teeth
And my hair like my very own too.'

Peggy Lee recorded their most original song, 'Is That All There Is', a US Top 20 hit from 1969, which is, to my ears at any rate, superior to 'My Way'. Its jaded lyric tells how disillusioned she is with life and how nothing excites her anymore. Even when her house burns down, she says, 'Is that all there is to a fire?' Curiously, the song was covered by Dorothy Squires, whose own, underinsured house had burnt down. 'Is That All There Is' has travelled in the other direction as it has been recorded in French by Sacha Distel. Dorothy Squires recorded the masochistic 'I the Chosen One' which is so full of disasters that you wonder how the singer could still be around to sing it.

As singers now want to show their youthfulness and appear younger than their years, there are few career songs today. When Paul McCartney sings 'The Long and Winding Road', it can sound like a career song, such was the cleverness of his writing, but I doubt that he will write a genuine one. Mick Jagger certainly won't, and I can't imagine Cliff Richard recording one either. Possibly Tim Rice will write something for Elton John, whose career has been as public and as colourful as Sinatra's, but Elt has already used the perfect title, 'I'm Still Standing'. For all that, the versions of 'My Way' proliferate, and even Jimmy Nail has sung it with philharmonic orchestras.

Elvis Presley was smitten with two career songs: 'The Impossible Dream' from the 1965 musical, *Man of La Mancha* and 'My Way'. Elvis sang 'My Way' on his 1973 TV special, *Aloha from Hawaii,* and some thought it was a tribute to Sinatra. In view of the tensions between them (chiefly over Juliet Prowse), I doubt that very much. Possibly Elvis wanted to demonstrate that he could sing the song better than Sinatra, and he identified with the lyric, although he spent most of his time doing it Colonel Parker's way. In later years he liked songs which mirrored his relationship with Priscilla, hence, his hit recording of that other François song, 'My Boy'.

Doc Pomus would have been the perfect lyricist for an Elvis's 'My Way' song, but it never happened. Instead, Elvis empathised with the sentiments of the folk songs comprising 'American Trilogy' while Doc, with another Doc (Dr John), wrote the staggeringly good 'There Must Be a Better World Somewhere' for B B King.

'Flying high, some joker cuts my wings,
Just because he gets a kick out of doing those kind of things,
I keep on falling in space or just hanging in mid-air
But I know there's just gotta be a better world somewhere.'

According to Paul Anka, Presley's 'My Way' changed the nature of the song: 'That song had resonance for him but not in the way I intended. Given his pathetic state at the end, it was the opposite sense of what the words meant for Sinatra. There was nothing defiant or heroic about Elvis at that point.'

Elvis was performing until his death but his concerts had become erratic and shambolic. He struggled through songs he had sung with ease. You'll have seen him out of breath, looking as though he will never finish 'My Way'. Sinatra at 53 had been too young to sing, 'And now the end is near, And so I face the final curtain', but Elvis at 42 was perfect.

Elvis Presley's 'My Way' was the first single to be released after his death and it went to No.9 in the UK and by reaching No.22 became the highest-placed version of the song on the US chart. Curiously, another casualty, Sid Vicious of the Sex Pistols chose to spit out the words on a solo single, made with jazz musicians in France, and his version was a UK Top 10 hit in 1978, helped by a video in which he gunned down all in sight before collapsing himself. This version was used with surprising effect at the end of Martin Scorsese's *Goodfellas*. Another wrecked celebrity, Shane McGowan of the Pogues, returned the song to the Top 30 in 1996.

Sinatra continued to perform and as he regarded his concerts as *The Main Event*, it was appropriate that he should have been presented by the boxing promoter, Frank Warren, in London's Docklands in 1990. 'My Way' was perfect for all his retirements and comebacks and despite an enormous repertoire, he commented that it had 'done more for my career than any other song.' When Mia Farrow told him about her troubles with Woody Allen, she repeated the conversation to a journalist: 'Frank never lets you down. He even offered to break Woody's legs.'

By then, Sinatra had become the Chairman of the Bored. He did 'My Way' at every concert but because the setting for each stanza is identical, he would get lost. It was as though he was making it up as he went along. Like Elvis singing 'My Way' in 1977, it became irresistible theatre. Even Luciano Pavarotti got in on the act. A fast-ageing Sinatra was in the audience when the Three Tenors belted it out and he recorded it as a duet with Pavarotti for his eightieth birthday. In 1998 Frank's original recording of 'My Way' was doctored so that it could be a duet with Paul Anka.

Unlike Sinatra, Paul Anka had a happy family life. He was married to Anne (Marie Anne De Zogheb) for many years and their children were named Amelia, Anthea, Alicia, Amanda and Alexandra. Fats Domino also gave his children names beginning with A and it must have created havoc when the mail arrived. However, Anka possessed a temper, and a tape has been circulated of him remonstrating with his musicians for playing badly. Anka said that when he is on stage, he calls the shots. 'Even if Jesus comes onto the stage,' he said, 'you watch me.' Really? He tells the musicians that they have to tighten up their act. 'It's either 'My Way' or the highway," he said, "Take your pick."

In 2012 the BBC Radio 4 programme *Desert Island Discs* published statistics from its castaways. The Beatles had been chosen 252 times; Frank Sinatra 240; and Bing Crosby 166, being the top three. As the programme had started in 1942, some 20 years before they recorded, the Beatles' achievement is remarkable, especially as Bob Dylan could only muster 91 selections and Elvis Presley 73. However, the BBC has admitted that Frank has been held back. A spokesman said, "My Way' is not banned but in the past guests have been greatly encouraged to think of something else to prevent the song becoming a cliché.' Among those who have chosen 'My Way' are Michael Caine, Geoff Boycott and David Frost.

II. Day In–Day Out, 1967–13 June 1971

In the mid-1960s Frank Sinatra is celebrated for such tracks as 'It Was a Very Good Year', 'Strangers in the Night', That's Life' and 'My Way', but artistically the high spot was much more low key, both in terms of commerciality and the sound itself. When Frank Sinatra collaborated with the Brazilian musician, Antonio Carlos Jobim, he joked, 'I haven't sung so soft since I had laryngitis.'

Antonio Carlos Brasileiro de Almeida Jobim (known as Tom) was born in Rio de Janeiro on 25 January 1927 and he planned to be an architect but his musical talents took control. Making his recording début in 1954, he sang in a quiet, restrained manner and he played both piano and guitar. In 1956 he wrote the score for a play, *Orfeo da Conceição*, which was set in, and performed at, a carnival in Rio de Janeiro. This, in turn, became the film, *Black Orpheus* (1959). Jobim said that his inspiration came from the birds of the Brazilian forests.

In the spring of 1961 the jazz guitarist Charlie Byrd was sent on a cultural visit to South America by the US government. The intention was that he would generate an interest in American jazz. That may have happened, but what was far more important was what he brought back home. He met the saxophonist Stan Getz in Washington and played him records by Jobim and the Brazilian guitarist, João Gilberto. Getz and Byrd made an album, *Jazz Samba*, which to everyone's surprise, topped the album charts. The opening cut, 'Desafinado', was a singles hit and Jobim performed at Carnegie Hall with Getz, Byrd and Dizzy Gillespie.

'Bossa nova' itself meant 'new appeal' and soon everybody in the Brill Building was writing Brazilian songs. Eydie Gorme had a hit with 'Blame It on the Bossa Nova' and Elvis Presley with 'Bossa Nova Baby'. Pat Boone sang Norman Gimbel's lyric for Jobim's 'Meditation (Meditacáo)' and Ella Fitzgerald recorded 'Stardust Bossa Nova', about the coolest of cool jazz performances, but it wasn't until 1981, that she recorded a songbook album, *Ella Abraca Jobim*.

Nat 'King' Cole had made the album, *Cole Español*, in 1958, but his health prevented him for exploring the possibilities of the bossa nova, a shame as he would have been an ideal vocalist. Doris Day recorded *Latin for Lovers* in 1964.

Stan Getz had another successful album with *Big Band Bossa Nova* and then he teamed up with Jobim for *Jazz Samba Encore*, which, in 1964, was only kept from the top of the US album charts by the Beatles' soundtrack, *A Hard Day's Night*. Bossa nova was seen as 'making out' music so it is surprising that Frank didn't start recording it until 1967.

The American jazz pianist George Shearing said, 'I love the bossa nova and Latin American music and it has rhythmically a lot more going for it than jazz. I knew Antonio Carlos Jobim as he lived very close to me. He was more Brazilian in his approach than Latin-American, which is Cuban really. So the bossa nova and the samba are very different musical approaches. You have to play the bossa nova very lightly and the Americans generally do not play it lightly enough. The basic approach should be boom boom boom and not BOOM BOOM BOOM. It is still bossa nova but that is wrong. When you know Jobim and the way he sings and the way he plays, it is the utmost in emotional delicacy. It is not pie-in-the-face rhythm that is being thrown at you.'

Jobim did not consider himself a jazz musician but a samba player and the bossa nova can be seen as a muted version of that carnival dance. In 1964 Getz had another million seller record with 'The Girl from Ipanema', which featured not only João Gilberto, but also a breathy vocal from his wife, Astrud, who sang the lyric because she was only female around who could speak English fluently. João murmured the Portuguese lyric first and then Astrud took over with words from Norman Gimbel. The chart book entries for Astrud Gilberto say

'See Getz, Stan' and indeed, a relationship between the two of them ended her marriage.

Just as the Beach Boys' songs capture images of Californian life on the beach, so too does Jobim with his songs about Brazil's natural beauty – and beauties. Jobim had written 'The Girl from Ipanema' about a girl Heloísa Pinheiro, who walked past a bar where Jobim was a regular. With another musician, Brough Moraes, they looked at the girl and wrote 'Menina Que Passa (The Girl Who Passes By)', which became 'The Girl from Ipanema'. Heloisa has since appeared in TV documentaries and magazine articles, a starting point for any 'person behind the song' features.

Sinatra was looking forward to making an album with Jobim but, as always in Frank's life, many things were happening and first he had to give evidence to a federal grand jury about his knowledge of the Mafia. In highly unusual circumstances, it was agreed that he could give his testimony behind closed doors in Las Vegas. This took place on 26 January 1967.

So, from 30 January 1967 for three days, Frank and Tom made the amusingly titled *Francis Albert Sinatra and Antonio Carlos Jobim*, which was as good as anything either of them recorded, though Jobim is not on all the tracks. And when he is, you can hardly hear him. The credits say. 'Vocal support by Antonio Carlos Jobim' but so what does he do? He sings softly in Portuguese or hums behind Sinatra. It was all understated and very charming: instead of a bombastic brass section, there is a single trombone from Dick Noel. Indeed, at one stage, he put a felt hat over his horn and he said, 'If I blow any quieter, it will be coming out of my neck.'

The arrangements were written by Claus Ogerman, who had come to America from Poland and had his first success by arranging 'It's My Party' for Lesley Gore in 1963. He had met Jobim in 1962 and had arranged several of his albums. While working on this project, Ogerman asked the lyricist Gene Lees to be Sinatra's stand-in. Lees wrote the English words for 'Dindi', which would have worked as one of Sinatra's saloon songs. Ignoring false modesty, Gene Lees wrote that it was 'one of the most exquisite things ever to come out of American popular music. It is filled with longing. It aches. Somewhere within him Frank Sinatra aches. Fine. That's the way it's always been. The listener's pleasure derives from the artist's pain.' Both Keely Smith and Nancy Sinatra attended the sessions and were very impressed.

Gene Lees also wrote the English lyric for 'Quiet Night of Quiet Stars (Corcovado)' which was another wonderful, understated performance from Sinatra. The song had been recorded before and Lees said, 'No singer had ever sung it absolutely accurately, but he got it right.' He certainly did and it's miles away from Vegas.

'The Girl from Ipanema' was another highlight as Sinatra sang in English and then Jobim in Portuguese, before trading phrases and then singing together. The vocal performance did not work so well on 'How Insensitive (Insensatez)' as it sounded like Frank was telling the story and then Jobim came in, rather distractingly. It's an intriguing song though, based on Chopin's *Prelude in E Minor* and it was also recorded by the Monkees, Iggy Pop, Liberace and William Shatner – there's an eclectic bunch for you.

As well as Jobim's songs, Claus Ogerman was asked to orchestrate three American standards with Brazilian rhythms. Based on a Russian melody, the insidious 'Baubles, Bangles and Beads' from *Kismet* opened with Jobim's wordless vocals and then went into Sinatra. The jangling of the bangles at the end was a cliché but it was a tremendous performance.

Cole Porter's 'I Concentrate on You' was transformed into a Jobim song and there was a glorious performance of Irving Berlin's 'Change Partners' with Al Viola on guitar. The song came from the film, *Carefree* (1938), in which a radio singer, Ginger Rogers, went to see a hypnotist Fred Astaire in the hope that he can make her fall in love with Ralph Bellamy, and you can guess the outcome. Change partners, of course. It's unethical, to say the least and Fred would struck off today.

One exceptional performance, Johnny Mercer's saloon song, 'Drinking Again', was kept over until the next album, *The World We Knew*. Although the album only made No.19 on the US album charts, it was on the listings for seven months, an impressive performance particularly as he hadn't gone for the more full-bodied commercial songs like 'Blame It on the Bossa Nova'.

The session on 1 February 1967 was a split session as Frank was to record a duet with Nancy Sinatra, arranged by Billy Strange. Nancy's producer, Lee Hazlewood, had found her a little-known beat-ballad, 'Somethin' Stupid', which had been recorded by its writer, C Carson Parks, and he wanted her to record it. Nancy thought it would work better as a duet and showed it to her dad.

They recorded 'Somethin' Stupid', but there were doubts within Warners/Reprise as to whether a father and daughter act should be singing a love song. Would they be mocked for it? Frank Sinatra told them not to worry and bet Mo Ostin a couple of dollars that it would make the Top 10. 'Somethin' Stupid' topped the charts in both the UK and the US. In France, a cover version from Sacha Distel and Joanna Shimkus was the hit, now called 'Ces Mots Stupides'. Sinatra framed his two dollars with a note from Mo saying, 'You were right'.

It's corny but it worked and, funnily enough, it did have a bossa nova beat. Sinatra called it 'The Dumb Dumb Song' but the public jokingly renamed it 'The Incest Song', although nobody thinks 'Leavin' on a Jet Plane' by Peter, Paul and Mary was about a threesome. Both Frank and Nancy were amused by this analysis.

The Sinatra expert Will Friedwald has written that 'It may be the most un-Frankish performance Sinatra ever recorded, with the two Sinatras chanting away in bland folkish harmony.' The co-producer Jimmy Bowen said, 'I do know that Frank was pleased with the results of 'Somethin' Stupid'.' Of course he was. It was going to win him teenage fans but he did think that the song lived up to its title. For his first take, he sang the song as Daffy Duck but unfortunately that has never been released.

Mo said to him, 'We should do a sequel,' to which Sinatra replied, 'You mean, something even more stupid?' Frank and Nancy never made an album together, although the famous picture of them touching noses would have made a brilliant cover shot. Their only other duets are on light-hearted novelties and Christmas songs.

In 1995 Ali Campbell revived 'Somethin' Stupid', with his daughter, Kibibi, but despite considerable airplay, the Christmas single only reached No.30. Following her success in the film musical *Moulin Rouge*, Nicole Kidman sang 'Somethin' Stupid' with Robbie Williams and the song returned to the top of the UK charts.

In April 1967 Frank started filming *Tony Rome* in Miami and to keep himself occupied, he accepted three-week booking at the Fontainebleau as well. He gave his warm-up act, Shecky Greene, a few lines in the film. Several of Frank's friends are on screen including the restaurant owners, Jilly Rizzo and Mike Romanoff.

This was a crime thriller set in Florida, directed, once again, by Gordon Douglas. Tony Rome was a private investigator, an ex-cop, gambler and skirtchaser. The film played ideally into Frank's preoccupations and his desire to be like Humphrey Bogart. Cast in the title role, Frank was a wise-cracking, cynical but romantic, tough guy. The music was by Billy May but the theme song was sung by Nancy and written by Lee Hazlewood. Frank (sorry, Tony) ogled a bikini-clad bottom as the last line of the song played.

Frank's co-star was Jill St John who had been Dean's girl and then Frank's and was known as the Paramount on Parade. She described Miami as 'twenty miles of sand looking for a city'. However, she was last week's news as far as Frank was concerned. He may have been married to Mia Farrow but his latest flame was a B-movie actress and *Playboy* model, Tiffany Bolling, also in *Tony Rome*. He gave her a diamond watch at the wrap-up party. The film had been scheduled for 45 days but with Frank's speed, it was made in 28. In one scene, he delivered a line too early and he then paused to led Simon Oakland speak.

Frank already had ideas for his next album. At long last he was going to record *The Italian Songbook* and Don Costa wrote arrangements for 'Anema E Core', 'Malafemmena' and 'Al De La'. Among the other songs he had chosen were 'La Strada', 'Arrivederci Roma', 'Dicitencello Vuie (Just Say I Love Her)' and 'Non Dimenticar'. The album never went ahead and nor did an album with Ella Fitzgerald which would have included 'A Taste of Honey' and 'Necessity' from *Finian's Rainbow*.

Frank Sinatra's close friend, Spencer Tracy, died in June 1967, shortly after making one of his greatest films, *Guess Who's Coming to Dinner*. Frank was a pallbearer at his funeral.

Then, quite unexpectedly, Las Vegas was shaken up in a way that no one would believe – and it had nothing, and yet everything, to do with the atomic testing in Nevada. The industrialist Howard Hughes had been born in Houston on Christmas Eve, 1905 – it would have been fitting if it was Christmas Day, but we can't change history – and when he was 18, he inherited his father's business, the Hughes Tool Company, which manufactured oil-drilling equipment. In 1926 he started ploughing his profits into Hollywood films and he made his name by discovering the platinum-blonde Jean Harlow and shooting the spectacular aerial scenes in *Hell's Angels* (1930). His other successes included *The Front Page* (1931) and *Scarface* (1932).

Hughes learnt how to design, build and fly advanced forms of aircraft. In 1935 he broke the world's speed record and in 1938 he flew round the world in four days. He returned to films and made Jane Russell a star in *The Outlaw*, even designing a bra to display her cleavage to best advantage. He loved beautiful woman and had affairs with several including Gingers Rogers, Katherine Hepburn and Ava Gardner, who seems to crop up everywhere. Because of their shared love for Ava Gardner, he and Sinatra detested each other.

During the war Hughes designed a huge wooden seaplane, the Hercules (popularly known as the Spruce Goose), but it was only flown once. Although a costly mistake, it helped the development of the aviation industry. In 1946 Hughes nearly died when he had a flying accident and it turned him from being a playboy to a recluse, only conducting his business (and there was much of it) through trusted employees. His last public appearance was to the Senate committee investigating what went wrong with the Hercules. That was in 1947; he lived until 1976.

Hughes owned the RKO film studios but it floundered without his day-to-day control, although he was able to sell it as a profit. He made a fortune when he sold his shares in the airline, TWA. By the 1960s he was one of the world's richest men.

As a film producer, Hughes had made many westerns. They had usually been shot in Nevada and he had found the resident American Indians very cooperative. They lived on reservations, fished for salmon in the Colorado River and had a healthy lifestyle. In the 1960s he heard of serious illnesses within their community and he wondered about the cause. He discovered that the American government was undertaking nuclear testing in the area, known as Area 51, and he assumed that there was a connection. He wanted to expose what was happening.

On Thanksgiving Day, 24 November 1966, Hughes came to Vegas by train and moved into the penthouse suite in the Desert Inn. He wasn't in Las Vegas because he loved it but to use it as a base to find out about the atomic testing. When he was asked to leave a few weeks later, he avoided conflict by buying the Desert Inn outright and that penthouse suite became both his home and the hub of his empire.

Hughes' main aim was still to end the testing in Nevada and he was horrified when the Desert Inn trembled with shock waves after one test. He offered $1m to both President Johnson and President Nixon to stop the testing, but even Hughes was unable to stop this on his own.

Hughes hadn't intended to transform Las Vegas but that seemed a good idea. He wanted to rid the city of its Mob image and its crooked gaming tables. He spent over $300m in acquiring local TV stations and newspapers and he bought further properties including the Sands for $14.6m in August 1967. Johnny Carson joked that he was playing *Monopoly* for real.

The casinos were to be as tightly run as banks, and cameras were installed to prevent the skimming of profits. The girls were forbidden to have sex with the high rollers. An air force major general, Ed Nigro, was made general manager but Hughes retained Jack Entratter as the director of operations.

Sinatra had an existing contract with the Sands for September 1967. He agreed to honour it but wanted more money. Hughes was not prepared to do that: a contract was a contract. Sinatra was rebuffed when he tried to see him in his penthouse. He cancelled his first show in protest but started playing the others. He was bad-tempered and screaming unnecessarily at the hotel staff; he hated working for Howard Hughes.

At one point the right leg of Bill Miller's piano began to give away and he had to prop it up while still playing. 'Look at that,' said Sinatra, 'A $20m hotel and $1.98 piano.'

Sinatra had made the Sands rich from his appearances and previously nobody had thought twice about giving him credit. One evening he was entertaining some Apollo astronauts who had come for his show. He went to the tables and was informed in front of his guests that his credit had been cut off by order of Howard Hughes.

Sinatra went to the switchboard room and demanded to be put through to Hughes. He spoke to his second-in-command, Carl Cohen. He was in bed and he told Sinatra no, he had no credit. Berserk and drunk, Sinatra jumped in a golf buggy and crashed it through a plate glass window in the hotel's shopping arcade.

When Carl Cohen arrived in the casino, Sinatra said, 'I'll break your legs, you motherfucker' and threw hot coffee over him. Cohen, a pleasant man but 18 stone, hit Sinatra so hard that the punch knocked out his front teeth. Hughes' men threw him out onto the Strip. Jilly Rizzo held himself and his men back as he knew it would be unwise to retaliate. They could all end up in the desert. Frank flew to LA the next day for dental work and Frankie Avalon stood in for the rest of his dates. He had a tough job as the patrons were expecting to see Sinatra.

Howard Hughes decreed that Sinatra would never appear at the Sands again, so Sinatra signed a $3m contract to appear exclusively at Caesars Palace. It guaranteed him $100,000 a week, at that time the highest salary paid to a Vegas performer. When Frank told his friend Kirk Douglas about the fight, he said, 'Kirk, I've learned one thing. Never fight a Jew in the desert.' In November, when there were local elections in Vegas, a series of mocking posters appeared around town: Frank had his teeth blacked out and the slogan was 'Carl Cohen for Mayor'.

But Frank didn't learn from his experience. He never did. In 1970 he won $2m playing baccarat at Caesars Palace, but he soon lost it. He was playing $8,000 a hand and he owed $400,000, such is the nonsense of this world. He was refused further credit and he went berserk. His former friend and casino executive, Sanford Waterman, pulled a gun on him. Jilly Rizzo knocked it out of his hand. Waterman ran into the cashier's room. Sinatra followed and his arm was trapped when the door closed on him. There was blood everywhere and he needed surgery. Frank said that he never play Nevada again and he didn't return until 1974.

For therapeutic relief, the songwriter Alec Wilder would write letters to his friends, which he never mailed. More's the pity that his cleaner didn't one day think, 'Oh, I'll just post these letters for Mr Wilder.' Some of the correspondence was published posthumously in *Letters I Never Mailed* and there is one to Frank: 'I continue to believe that despite your political capitulation, your strange bedfellows, your often unfortunate choice of songs, and saddest of all, your silence, that you would be, given a sane society and time for a deep breath, once again my active friend and once again we could sit in a room locked against the intrusion of the leeches, the court jesters, the presidents of vice, the dreary little girls, and we could talk about beliefs and longings and wonderments. To boot, and praise be, we might even laugh.' He said that he wanted to find out 'if the man I knew is still there hiding behind the garish, the violent, the reactionary and the lost.'

Frank made his third special in the NBC series, *A Man and His Music*, this time largely featuring himself with Ella and Antonio Carlos Jobim. Ella was strongly featured and they duet on 'The Song Is You', 'They Can't Take That Away from Me',' Stompin' at the Savoy' and 'The Lady Is a Tramp'. Frank had to be at the top of his game to match Ella and this was jazz at its finest. There is a light moment where Frank and Ella sing the theme from *Tony Rome* and the film was due for release on 13 November 1967, two days after the broadcast. The TV special was directed by Michael Pfleghar who dated Tina Sinatra and they set up home in Munich. Frank visited them in June 1968 and had good things to say about Germany at the airport.

Nancy Sinatra followed 'Somethin' Stupid' with a playful country duet with Lee Hazlewood, 'Jackson'. Possibly Frank had been considered as a duet partner but he couldn't have matched Hazlewood's deep Johnny Cash-styled vocal. Indeed, the rival version of this Billy Edd Wheeler song came from Johnny Cash and June Carter. Sinatra's follow-up single was a Bert Kaempfert song that was as awkward as its title, 'The World We Knew (Over And Over)'. It's unnerving to hear Frank with a fuzz guitar and it shows that some of his 1960s recordings are more dated that ones he made 20 years earlier.

The World We Knew was equally directionless, one of his worst albums, although, to be fair, it was more ambitious than most middle of the road albums of the time. The title implied that Frank was looking back but he was trying to be contemporary. On the face of it, 24 July 1967 was his most productive day in the studio with six masters being recorded. In reality, it was the most unproductive day as the six masters are nearly all terrible. He and his arrangers were lost. Maybe Nancy Sinatra should have been singing the songs. Around the same time, Desmond Dekker was making the UK charts with '007' which made reference to *Ocean's 11*.

There was a weak cover of Matt Monro's 'Born Free' as Sinatra hadn't worked out which notes he should stretch. This is followed by the second Gordon Jenkins arrangement, 'This Is My Love', a nondescript song with a nondescript performance.

While making *The Countess from Hong Kong*, Charlie Chaplin had written 'This Is My Song' for Al Jolson, little realising that he was dead. Petula Clark made a good record from weak material but Sinatra and Clark's original arranger, Ernie Freeman, wasn't interested in doing much with it. Still, it's serviceable, certainly compared to Freeman's arrangement of another Clark hit, 'Don't Sleep in the Subway', which was an even bigger disaster than 'Downtown'. Frank lost the melody and only sang one verse, which happened to be the first two lines of the second verse and the last two of the first and would you believe it, they didn't rhyme. He didn't correct 'N, nothing' and he added, 'Take your boots off, my sweet.' His girl was living on the street and he concluded, rather improbably, 'I got candy, I got flowers, I got kisses, I got pumpkin.' Totally meaningless.

Ernie Freeman, Billy Strange and Lee Hazlewood were all involved in the score for the teen movie, *The Cool Ones*, and they thought it was a good idea for Frank to record Lee's song, This Town'. The lyric said, 'This town is a quiet town' and yet Frank was going for an all-out assault. Even worse was H B Barnum's overbearing jazz arrangement of 'Some Enchanted Evening' and Frank's vocal was shoddier than the arrangement. Frank didn't get on with Richard Rodgers so surely he was mocking him.

The album was filled out with a decent ballad, 'You Are There' from *The Naked Runner*, typical of Scott Walker. The song left over from the Jobim session, 'Drinking Again', was easily the best cut on the album.

When Frank was questioned about recording new material, he said, 'Hell, I've run out of the Cole Porter and Rodgers and Hart and Gershwin repertoire – the standards that have always meant the most to me. And I can't go rock. But I'm going to do an album of country and western that Lee Hazlewood is putting together for me, so I guess the old dog will be learning a few new tricks.' Totally untrue – there were plenty of great songs he hadn't sung and the country and western album was never made.

The guitarist James Burton remembered, 'Jimmy Bowen booked me for three days with Sinatra. Frank came in and said that he didn't think his voice was good enough. He was going to Palm Springs for some golf and Jimmy could reschedule the sessions for when he returned. When he left, Jimmy said, "Don't worry: the sessions are cancelled but you'll all be paid." You have never seen such a scramble for the phones as everyone wanted to get back the work that they'd lost for this. Another time Sinatra cancelled a session because Telly Savalas came to see him and they went off together.' No wonder Reprise had cash-flow problems.

Duke Ellington had written the score for Frank's film, *Assault on a Queen*, and now he was signed to Reprise, it was inevitable that he would make an album with Frank. The album, *Francis A and Edward K* was recorded at the start of December 1967 and released with very little publicity in February. Still, it was a strong collection of performances that were arranged and conducted by Billy May. Unlike the albums with Basie, Sinatra was not interjecting his own comments into the lyrics.

The album featured eight lengthy tracks, only one of which was written by Ellington. 'I Like the Sunrise' comes from *The Liberian Suite* which was presented in front of the President of Liberia at Carnegie Hall on Boxing Day 1947. The President was more entranced by the weather as he had never seen anything as pretty as snow before. Al Hibbler sang it that night and Frank rang him after the session and said, 'You're still the only guy in the world who can sing that goddamned thing.'

In 1916 the songwriters, John Golden and Raymond Hubbell, wanted to cash in on the popularity of Puccini's opera, *Madam Butterfly*. Although 'Poor Butterfly' was intended as a catchpenny composition, its beautiful melody has endured and become a jazz standard, being recorded by Nat 'King 'Cole and Barney Kessel. This was a fine interpretation but without the Oriental overtones.

'Indian Summer', which was written by Victor Herbert in 1919, was perfect for Ellington and Sinatra, with Nelson Riddle citing it as a classic arrangement. When Johnny Hodges played his alto solo, Frank said, 'My god, that's unbelievable, John.' Hodges asked Frank if he had sung it before and he said, 'Yes, with Tommy Dorsey, and Dorsey refused to transfer the arrangement from Jack Leonard's key. My eyeballs would fall out every time on the top note.'

There are two Alan Jay Lerner songs: the melancholy 'Follow Me' from *Camelot* might have had Sinatra reflecting on Kennedy whilst 'Come Back to Me' from *On a Clear Day You Can See Forever* is a frenzied song about wanting your girl back. The full lyric includes a reference to *Waiting for Godot* but is omitted here.

'All I Need Is the Girl', a Stephen Sondheim and Jule Styne song from *Gypsy,* was given a smart jazzy arrangement. Sondheim's rhyming was superb and as he wrote an alternative lyrics 'All I Need Is the Boy' for Carol Burnett, it's a pity that no one thought of merging the two for a duet for, say, Frank and Ella.

The album was completed by the mellow ballad, 'Yellow Days', which referred to sunshine and has been recorded by Johnny Mathis and Tony Bennett, plus a laidback jazzy reading of a contemporary hit, Bobby Hebb's 'Sunny'. Duke sent roses and champagne to Sinatra, which he generously shared with the band. 'I didn't buy the Dom Perignon for the band,' laughed Duke.

While there were no bad tracks on this album, it was not as exhilarating as it could have been, perhaps because Ellington's own contribution was not substantial. There are too many slow songs and Billy May was to comment, 'That was a hard album and there is some disastrous shit in there, but some of it is awfully good.'

Sinatra had thought of *Tony Rome* as his final film, but the director Gordon Douglas persuaded him to make another in the same genre, *The Detective*, based on a best-selling book by a former policeman, Roderick Thorp. It was about a middle-aged man who was driven to murder through being gay, though clearly that wasn't Frank's role. He was the detective. The poster said the film offered 'an adult look at a police detective' and the script was full of police brutality and corruption with considerable sexual frankness. The NYPD cooperated with the making of the film, allowing several scenes to be shot in their police stations, so presumably they did not object to the corruption in the script. Frank handles his role well and it is easy to how he would have suited *Dirty Harry*.

Frank had wanted Mia Farrow to play the widow of someone who had committed suicide but she was making *Rosemary's Baby*, which was overrunning. Frank told her to walk away from the film and she refused. This being Sinatra's world, she received her divorce papers the next day. *Rosemary's Baby* had been the last straw: he hated the concept of the film and he had had many arguments with Mia. She had been distraught when he set off a cherry bomb next to her cat and the cat left home for good. (That would have wrecked most marriages too.) Mia said, 'Looking back, I think our ages finally mattered. I was too ill at ease with his remoteness and unable to fathom his complexities.'

Sinatra also hated Bob Evans, the studio executive in charge of *Rosemary's Baby*. He had been cast as a matador in the film of Ernest Hemingway's *The Sun Also Rises* in 1957. They had wanted to drop him but the producer Darryl Zanuck had uttered the famed, final decision, 'The kid stays in the picture.'

Mia's role went to Jacqueline Bisset and as Sinatra was having an affair with his co-star Lee Remick, he was not too cut up about his break-up with Mia. The cast included Robert Duvall with guest appearances from Sugar Ray Robinson and Jilly Rizzo as a bartender. The music was by Jerry Goldsmith who had worked on *Von Ryan's Express* in 1965.

Nancy Sinatra made her first TV special, *Movin' with Nancy*, with Frank, Dean and Sammy, which suggested that she was as unsure about her image as Frank. Frank sang 'Younger than Springtime', a curious choice for a teenage show. The best moments were her duets with Lee Hazlewood, who definitely knew what he was doing. Nancy married for the second time on his birthday, this time to Hugh Lambert. She commented, 'Daddy likes to give things away on his birthday.'

The jokes about Frank and Mia were rife throughout the media. Johnny Carson joked, 'Hear about the trouble at Frank Sinatra's house? Mia Farrow dropped her Silly Putty in Frank's Poli-Grip?' It was never going to work and in November, Frank and Mia agreed to a trial separation. In January 1968 she and her sister, Prudence, joined the Beatles in India where they received instruction from Maharishi. The Beatles recorded 'Dear Prudence' and revealed how the Maharishi had shown himself to be all too human when it came to Prudence in 'Sexy Sadie'.

Caesars Palace opened in 1966, which even by Vegas standards was a monument to kitsch. There was a preposterous invitation designed like a Roman medallion for Frank's first appearance in 1968. Frank had assumed that Dean and Sammy would shortly be joining him at Caesars Palace but Dean entered into negotiations at the Riviera and Sammy stayed at the Sands, which Frank took as a personal affront.

When Frank caught pneumonia, he stayed in Miami and Dean did not call him. The press sensed a rift but Dean couldn't care less. Frank told reporters, 'I feel like I'm cheating people when the voice is bad. They don't pay out that kind of dough to listen to a bullfrog.' He appeared at the Fontainebleau, Miami and would party at Jilly's South as he never slept before 4am. The restaurant had five go-go girls on platforms: 'I don't go for topless,' said Sinatra.

Tony Rome had done well and *The Detective* which opened in June 1968 was another success. However, the major success of the year was Roman Polanski's *Rosemary's Baby*, which was a box office hit as well as a critical success. Sinatra may have hated the film because his wife had been following her own career and not taking his advice, but he didn't get horror films, never making one himself.

Quite possibly, he could have been in the biggest film of 1969 as he was offered a co-starring role with Barbra Streisand, who was recreating her Broadway success in *Funny Girl*. It was a clash of egos. Despite the title, he would only accept top billing and he demanded extra songs, which did not go down well with Streisand. Also, he still felt aggrieved at the way its composer Jule Styne had betrayed him and surely he would have demanded the song, 'People'. Furthermore, Frank turned down the role of the psychiatrist in Streisand's 1970 film, *On a Clear Day You Can See Forever*.

In his personal diaries, Richard Burton wrote about the death of Elizabeth Taylor's father in November 1968. He described the hundreds of letters of commiserations but added, 'A notable exception was Frank Sinatra. What a petulant little sod he is.' Apparently, Elizabeth had once interceded on Mia's behalf.

The Indian-born balladeer Engelbert Humperdinck, after many unsuccessful years as Gerry Dorsey, had topped UK charts with 'Release Me', which had kept the Beatles' 'Penny Lane'/'Strawberry Fields Forever' from the UK No.1 spot during 1967. His manager Gordon Mills knew that he was right for Vegas and asked his road manager, Tony Cartwright, to accompany him for his first shows at the Riviera. He says, 'There weren't many at the first show but Juliet Prowse told me that Dean, Frank and Sammy would be at the second. The protocol was that the star introduced other performers and personalities in the audience and Engelbert did the second show and came off stage ready for the encore. I gave him the list of the celebrities in the house and I had put them in order. You always put the most important celebrity last. I had written, Juliet Prowse, Sammy Davis Jr, Frank Sinatra and Dean Martin. Engelbert said, "You've have done that wrong. It should be Dean Martin before Frank Sinatra." I said, "No, who's paying our wages?" Engelbert went out and sang 'Release Me' and read out the names in the order I gave him. Fifteen minutes later, we were relaxing with champagne after the show and Dean and Frank came in. Dean patted him on the back and said, "That's my boy, you got it right, Humpy." He snapped his fingers and said, "Frank, this is my place." The headline in the Vegas paper the next day was *Dean Gets the Hump with Humpy* and that created a lot of attention. It was all very tongue-in-cheek and the Americans loved it. After that night, the show was sold out for every performance.'

It wasn't long before Engelbert was enjoying the Vegas ways. Tony Cartwright recalls, 'I could see Engelbert looking at Juliet Prowse as though he wanted to bed her and she said that she would make him a curry. Engelbert loves curry and they wound up sleeping together. He was cutting it fine as she was still seeing Sinatra from time to time and Sinatra was playing Vegas. He came looking for her and she had to concoct some excuse as Engelbert had been with her for a couple of hours. I said to Engelbert, "You must be mental. You know what Sinatra can do when he's had a few drinks."'

In July 1968 Frank started recording two albums simultaneously; *Cycles* and *The Sinatra Family Wish You a Happy Christmas*. The title song, 'Cycles', was written by Gayle Caldwell of the New Christy Minstrels, but the title was badly placed and many listeners must wondered what the song was called. Don Costa was about to give this song a strong rock treatment but Nancy persuaded him and her father that it needed a country approach. The final line is 'I'll keep on trying to sing but please don't ask me how.' Even odder is Bert Kaempfert's 'My Way of Life' which sounded like an anthem for a stalker and was described by Gene Lees as 'flamboyant and pretentious, weird, ghastly lyric, psychotic in its possessiveness.'

Frank's version of 'By the Time I Get to Phoenix' is the best of his country performances, though he was not as convincing as Dean when performing such material as 'Gentle on My Mind' and 'Little Green Apples', which has a dreary arrangement from Don Costa. His comment at the end of Pat Boone's 'Moody River', 'I ain't going swimming in that', revealed what he was thinking. If only he had spent more time on Joni Mitchell's 'Both Sides Now'. However, as Frank's contemporary albums went, *Cycles* was decent enough and it did make the US Top 20.

On the day that Frank's divorce came through, 16 August 1968, Frank was due to record his TV special, *Francis Albert Sinatra Does his Thing* with Diahann Carroll and Fifth Dimension. He was too upset to perform that day and the dress rehearsal, filmed the previous day, was screened instead. The Fifth Dimension performed Laura Nyro's 'Stoned Soul Picnic' and were then joined by Frank as a sixth Dimension, wearing a Nehru jacket and beads, for another Nyro song, 'Sweet Blindness'. Frank prefaced 'Cycles' with the words, 'The records they're buying these days have simple tunes and simple words, but sometimes they manage to express some very profound thoughts.' Did he know Leonard Nimoy was also going to record this song?

Meanwhile, Mia was refusing press interviews in London as she was making the psychodrama *Secret Ceremony* with Elizabeth Taylor and Robert Mitchum. She did not want to talk about their marriage and she did not want any cash settlement so she and Frank remained friends.

By its very nature, *The Sinatra Family Wish You a Happy Christmas* had to be a predictable album, but there was a beautiful new song from Jimmy Webb, 'Whatever Happened to Christmas'. The Sinatra family comprised Frank and his three children. We can all guess what Frank or their 'loving dad' would want for Christmas but in this reworking of 'The Twelve Days of Christmas', it is such items as 'nine games of Scrabble'. 'I Wouldn't Trade Christmas' has some neat harmonies in Swingle Singers mode, while Nancy sang 'It's Such a

Lonely Time of Year', dedicated to soldiers serving in Vietnam.

Starting in February 1968 Frank made his third crime thriller with the director Gordon Douglas, *Lady in Cement*, this time reprising Tony Rome and again set in Miami. When diving for treasure, Tony Rome found a nude lady in cement, which led to threatening scenes with implausible dialogue. When someone had a gun pointed at him, the victim said, 'Don't do that, mister. I only have six payments left on my Ford.' The violence could be graphic hence an X certificate.

Sinatra didn't have his mind on the job as he was appearing at the Fontainebleau throughout March. The owner of the club, Ben Novack, wore a hearing aid and Sinatra called him 'Deafy', at one point setting off a cherry bomb to test his hearing. Another time he put cherry bombs around the piano in his apartment. The club, over-decorated and tasteless, was losing custom in any event. A rival club, Eden Roc, built next door was stealing the business.

Most of the time Sinatra was feeling sorry for himself because of his third failed marriage. When he caught pneumonia, the cast had to shoot around him. However, he did have some hookers to cheer him up and he did enjoy eating ham and eggs off their flat, little stomachs – Juliet Prowse has confirmed that this was one of Frank's 'eccentricities'.

His leading lady, Raquel Welch, was depressed as she wanted to be accepted as an actress in roles where she could keep her clothes on. However, she was wooden throughout, the worst moment being when a policeman says, 'We don't want to alarm you but there's a killer on the loose' and she responds, 'Oh, well, if I see a killer, I'll call.'

The cast included Richard Conte and Lainie Kazan with small roles for Sinatra's chums. Jilly's Saloon was one of the locations and Jilly Rizzo himself played a man in the toilet. Joe E Lewis made an appearance as a customer in a massage parlour but when Pat Henry, who was opening for Frank, messed up three takes in a row, Frank hit him. The score was by Hugo Montenegro was a plus, but this was little more than a TV movie. Sinatra never cared for *Lady in Cement* and later, when he wanted guests to leave, he would threaten them with the film.

Frank was becoming a laughing stock and *Mad* magazine featured him over and over. They showed Frank and Mia holding up Oscars for Best Performances in a Romantic Farce. Frank was shown reading a book, *Who's Who at the Bottom of the East River*. When Sammy Davis talked of advances being made by black artists, Frank called him and he answered, 'Yes, master.'

Litigation was always a difficult matter: some magazines couldn't pay you if you won and very often you created more controversy and more attention when you sued, and it looked like you couldn't take a joke. This was brought into relief when Garry Trudeau in his syndicated *Doonesbury* strip told a deliberately skewed version of Frank's life. Frank decided to let it go but it was a close call.

In February 1969, Frank returned to recording studios for further tracks with Antonio Carlos Jobim. The arrangements this time were written by Eumir Deodata and the intention was to make something a little more high powered than the previous collaboration. It didn't always work as there was too much orchestration on 'Someone to Light up My Life'. Not enough tracks were recorded and the album, *Sinatra And Company*, released in 1971, included songs from other sessions.

The best performance was 'Wave' where Sinatra's deep notes at the end matched the instruments. Several songs have been written about songwriting and Jobim's was 'One Note Samba (Samba De Uma Nota So)', another good performance and Jobim was less inhibited than usual in the bridge. Together they sang 'Desafinado' which had a new English lyric from

Jon Hendricks, and their blend of voices worked well on 'Drinking Water (Aqua De Beber)', which is partly sung in Portuguese by Sinatra. 'Don't Ever Go Away (Por Causa De Voce)' was a reflective song about marriage breaking up.

The main event in February 1969 was to make a contemporary album with Don Costa, which would be named after the single, My Way. There was one connection to Jobim though as Sinatra performed an early bossa nova song, 'A Day in the Life of a Fool', which had been written for Orfeu Negro (Black Orpheus), though not by Jobim. Tori Amos recorded this song in 2000 for Mission: Impossible 2. There was only one song from Sinatra's past, a remake of 'All My Tomorrows' which was an improvement on the original.

Of the contemporary composers, Sinatra held Jimmy Webb in highest regard and he recorded a very sensitive 'Didn't We', which had originally been sung by Richard Harris. Sinatra held back on additions to the lyric and while 'Didn't we, girl' would have seen right for him, he just sings 'Didn't we'. He recorded his first Beatle song, 'Yesterday', with a slow, regretful string arrangement. In 1980, he said on stage that 'Yesterday' was the best song of the last 30 years.

Who knows what Sinatra was thinking when he sang 'Mrs Robinson' from The Graduate? He drops the reference to Joe DiMaggio, and instead of Jesus, he sings, 'Jilly loves you more than you will know', a fine example of product placement for his favourite restaurant owner. He added Rat Pack chat like 'How's your bird, Mrs Robinson' and inexplicably added, 'The PTA, Mrs Robinson, won't okay the way you do your thing, ding ding ding.' It has to be heard to be disbelieved.

Did Frank know that Ava had turned down the role of Mrs Robinson?

Ron Miller, who wrote special material for nightclub entertainers, composed For Once in My Life in 1965. It impressed the singer, Carmen McRae, who recommended the song to Tony Bennett. Bennett recorded it and although the song is now associated with him, his version hardly dented the US Top 100. In 1968 Stevie Wonder upped the tempo with a punchy Motown arrangement and turned the song an international hit. Frank also is on fire via a swinging big band version decked out with an excellent vocal.

Michel Legrand's 'Watch What Happens' from Les Parapluies de Cherbourg has the easy swinging brass feel of 'Nice 'n' Easy'. 'If You Go Away' was a Jacques Brel song with a lyric from Rod McKuen and was another immaculate performance, leading onto his next project.

Rod McKuen had been around the music industry since the mid-50s and he was a Grade A trier. He had had a US Top 20 hit as Bob McFadden and D'or (Rod backwards) with 'The Mummy' and had gone on the road promoting his dance single, 'The Oliver Twist'. He strained his voice and ended up with a permanent raspy whisper. He became a best-selling poet with books like Lonesome Cities and Listen to the Warm, writing romantic free verse about one-night stands and his love of cats and sheepdogs. He wrote occasional hit songs ('Ally Ally Oxen Free' for the Kingston Trio) and he was known for providing English lyrics for French successes ('The Importance of the Rose', 'Seasons in the Sun', 'If You Go Away'). In 1968 he wrote the score for The Prime of Miss Jean Brodie and several MOR artists had recorded the saccharine 'Jean'. He was a popular stage and TV performer, ambling on in sweatshirt, jeans and sneakers, once observing quite correctly, 'I have a style that is uniquely mine. There is only one Rod McKuen.'

For some years, McKuen had been trying to contact Sinatra and when they did meet socially, he didn't waste the opportunity. He said, 'Let me put together a whole album of poems and songs for you.' 'Okay,' said Frank, 'let's see what you got.'

McKuen said, 'I'd written 20 new songs for Frank's album but he wanted to sing 'Love's Been Good to Me' which I had written in 1963. I was very pleased because I had written that song for him and had never been able to get it to him. Frank worked very hard on that album. 'Empty Is' was a very difficult piece and he did it beautifully. I don't know whether here's any significance but Frank announced his retirement shortly after the album came out.'

A Man Alone featured six songs and four poems plus 'Empty Is' which was both. Frank recorded them on three consecutive days in March 1969. 'A Man Alone' had been the title of a Ray Milland western in 1955 and the reflective song has a strong melody which suited Frank very well. The folky and tender 'Love's Been Good to Me' was ideal for Frank's image and falls in line with both 'It Was a Very Good Year' and 'My Way'. Some of the words would have sounded embarrassing from another performer but Frank made it work;

'All the beautiful strangers
All in the afternoon
Who praised my flat little stomach
And came back to my room.'

Very true, no wonder Frank approved.

A Man Alone was released in July 1969 and it was a Top 30 success in both Britain and America. 'Love's Been Good to Me' was a UK Top 10 single, though at the time the biggest-selling Reprise single was Fleetwood Mac's 'Oh Well'. How times had changed.

Although Frank had made some dismissive remarks about Burt Bacharach, he genuinely admired him and wanted Burt and his lyricist Hal David to write a concept album for him, which Bacharach could arrange and produce. Burt said, Yes, they would like to do it but it would have to wait until they had finished their Broadway show, *Promises, Promises*. As usual, Frank wanted it now so he said, "Forget it" and put the phone down.

Mia Farrow had encouraged Frank to sing contemporary material and he had liked 'Goin' Out of My Head', written by Teddy Randazzo and recorded by Little Anthony and the Imperials in 1964. He had sung it in cabaret and performed it with Ella very effectively on TV. He finally recorded it for a single in August 1969 but it only made the bottom rungs in the US Hot 100. He'd missed the boat as the Lettermen had taken into the Top 10 in 1968.

Little Anthony says, 'That song was recorded by artists throughout the world. It was a publisher's dream. Sinatra had done me a favour, he had got me out of a jam with another company that didn't want to give me a release. He said, "Tell the kid he sings good." I didn't meet him but Don Costa was his conductor and arranger and he heard 'Goin' Out of My Head' and he decided to do it on a TV special with Ella Fitzgerald. That was great and then he recorded it as a single. He really liked it.'

In June 1968 the session guitarist James Burton had not been able to work on Elvis Presley's comeback special for NBC because he was working for Sinatra. In 1969, when Elvis was forming a road band, he trusted Burton enough to say, 'What you want is what we get.' Elvis loved the band but he was real nervous that first night at the International in Las Vegas. According to Burton, 'he was wearing out the carpet but I told him, "Elvis, don't worry, it's too late to cancel."' Starting 31 July 1969, Elvis played a month of shows at the International. Frank and Dean had reigned supreme for 10 years but Elvis was so successful that Vegas was about to undergo a transformation towards the rock acts.

When Frank had Richard Burton and Elizabeth Taylor to stay at his home in Palm Springs, they played tennis with Frank's neighbour, Barbara Marx. Burton admired Barbara's legs and Liz said, 'What about mine, Burton?' Burton replied, 'They are stubby as your fingers.' At which point, Liz replied, 'In that case, I want the biggest diamond in the world for this stubby finger.' Burton spent $1m on the diamond from Cartier and Frank blamed Barbara for Burton's extravagance.

Such extravagance had fuelled Charles Manson's thoughts that the rich must die.

In August 1969 Charles Manson and his so-called Family committed murder and other atrocities on the Hollywood elite. One of his victims was Sharon Tate, a beautiful young actress married to the director Roman Polanski. When Manson was arrested, the police found a list of potential victims which included Frank Sinatra. The intention was for Sinatra to have sex with one of Manson's teenage disciples (which wouldn't have been difficult to arrange) and he would be castrated while having sex.

Many of the tracks on *A Man Alone* had been written earlier as Rod McKuen had written them for himself, but the next album was a wholly original work, *Watertown*, created by Bob Gaudio from the Four Seasons and the singer/songwriter Jake Holmes. It had been set up by Frankie Valli who had told Frank that they would be perfect for him. Gaudio and Holmes had previously written a concept album for the Four Seasons, *Genuine Imitation Life*, which hadn't sold but had been well received critically.

In terms of feelings and its interplay of narration and song, it is a companion to *A Man Alone*. Bob Gaudio explains, 'I wrote *Watertown* with Jake Holmes, who became the king of New York commercials. We had some meetings with Sinatra and then we locked ourselves away for four weeks at my house in Mount Clair, wrote the songs and made the demos. Sarge Weiss who handled Frank's publishing said, 'Guess what? Frank wants to record all of them', but I was so cocky then that I just thought, 'Well, of course he does.' It was a concept album about a man in a small town in New York State and it was what he went through with his wife leaving him. It is dark and lamenting, maybe suicidal – no, it is suicidal – but fortunately Frank felt very comfortable doing it. It was supposed to be a TV show, a one man special, but he didn't feel up to doing TV and the album came out on its own. We had no temperament problems with Sinatra at all, which was just as well as I was only in my early twenties.'

Watertown was austere, dark and introspective, the story of a haunted man. The orchestral tracks were recorded in New York in July 1969 and Frank added his vocals in Los Angeles a few weeks later. Such a recording schedule is commonplace today but this was a new technique for Frank. Al Viola overdubbed some classical guitar on 'Goodbye (She Quietly Says)'.

Most unusually for a Sinatra album, his face was not shown on the cover of his new album: instead, there was a gatefold drawing of Watertown with the lyrics on the inside. *Watertown* was not highly esteemed at the time, perhaps seen as too progressive and only selling 35,000 copies, but today it is among Frank's great albums. It was a poignant collection of songs about a man who, even if he knew the outcome, would not have changed his behaviour – Frank all over. He showed his surprise at his wife leaving him in the key song, 'I Would Be in Love (Anyway)'. Although the song was not about her, Frank sent a demo of 'Elizabeth' to Elizabeth Taylor for her birthday. Similarly, Bob Gaudio and Jake Holmes had not intended 'Lady Day' to be about Billie Holiday but as Sinatra took it that way, why not?

Frank had bought his parents a large house in Fort Lee, New Jersey for their 50th wedding anniversary in 1963, but they didn't enjoy it for long. Marty had suffered from asthma all his life and this had developed into emphysema. He had circulatory problems in his left arm which might have been a boxing legacy. He had heart and lung problems and Frank paid for expert medical attention. He was at his father's side when he died on 24 January 1969 at the age of 74. There were 75 limousines at the funeral service and a short while later, Dolly moved to the west coast so that Frank could look after her. She was still the same old Dolly, swearing in polite company and swinging her handbag at anyone who used the word 'wop'.

In November 1969 CBS broadcast another Sinatra special. They had decided that putting Sinatra with the Fifth Dimension was a step too far and this new special was simply called *Sinatra*. For once, the comedy worked as Frank took a light-hearted trawl through his film appearances. The arrangements were by Don Costa and it was a mixture of the old and the recent including 'My Way', 'A Man Alone', 'Goin' Out of My Head' and 'Little Green Apples' and, naturally, as it was now the most topical of topical songs, 'Fly Me To The Moon'.

After *Lady in Cement*, a few roles fell through. He was to make a film about losers in Las Vegas, *The Only Game in Town*, with Elizabeth Taylor. He would be a piano player for whom 'dice was his vice'. The film was postponed when Taylor had a hysterectomy. Sinatra went into Caesars Palace instead. The film eventually surfaced in 1970 with Elizabeth Taylor and Warren Beatty in the leading roles.

Sinatra had not wanted to do anything too heavy after the death of his father and he thought a comedy would be therapeutic. However, Sinatra should have stuck with *The Only Game in Town* because *Dirty Dingus Magee*, made in February 1970 for the producer and director, Burt Kennedy, was a disaster. It was based on a novel by David Markson and the hero is only 19 in the book. The script by Joseph Heller, who wrote *Catch-22*, is terrible and full of innuendo: 'dingus' is Yiddish slang for 'penis, but who got that? It is as though Sinatra, in a frightful wig and an orange nightshirt, had been cast in a *Carry On* film. Sinatra even laughed like Sidney James.

Dirty Dingus Magee was the country's most unwanted outlaw with only a $10 price tag on his head, but his squaw calls him 'the hottest pistol in the west'. When someone is ordered to circle the wagons, the response is 'We haven't enough men.' 'Then make a half moon.' It's a bad film but it's no fault of the cast which includes George Kennedy, Harry Carey Jr and Jack Elam as John Wesley Hardin. Frank had a brief relationship with Lois Nettleton who plays a schoolteacher. Perhaps she was wooed by all the double entendres in the script. Sinatra played a character with complete disdain for the consequences of his actions, so typecast again. Shortly after this dreadful film was released, Frank announced his retirement.

It would have been better if Frank had been cast as Dirty Harry rather than Dirty Dingus Magee. John Wayne had been unhappy with the role, not liking his habits, and Robert Mitchum and Paul Newman also said no. Sinatra liked *Dirty Harry* but he was having difficulty with his right hand. It was giving him pain as he held his microphone and the consultant said that he needed surgery for Dupuytren's contracture, otherwise his hand would become a claw. Instead of putting *Dirty Harry* on hold, Clint Eastwood stepped into the role.

Sinatra's hands were an important ingredient of his act. One programme note advised, 'Watch out for the left hand, the one that isn't holding the mike, as it traces poetic patterns in the air to accentuate a certain part of a lyric.'

One of the key characters in Mario Puzo's novel, *The Godfather*, was a singer called Johnny Fontane. In the book, Johnny Fontane was a Catholic and a skinny band singer who married his childhood sweetheart and had a couple of children. His best friend, Nino Valenti, was another Italian singer whom we worked with on occasion. His wife tolerated his affairs as he became a solo star. Then he divorced her and married a Hollywood star, who bedded everyone. He went to propose to her in Spain where she was making a film. Fontane was balding and obsessed about his lack of hair. He lost his singing voice and he wanted a role in a new war film from a major studio but the producer hated him and didn't want to give him the role. Remind you of anyone?

Sinatra loathed the book but had decided that legal action could be embarrassing for himself as he didn't know the extent of Puzo's knowledge. Otto Preminger planned to direct the film version and he wanted Frank to play the Mafia head. Sinatra was tempted but didn't want to be in a film where one character was playing a younger version of himself. Preminger asked him if he would do it if he dropped the Fontane character, but before they had worked out a deal, Preminger had abandoned he project, passing it over to Francis Ford Coppola.

Gianni Russo, who played Carlo in *The Godfather*, says, 'I know that Mario had Sinatra in mind in that book as I spent so many days with him. Mario was a degenerate gambler and he died broke unfortunately. He definitely wrote it about Frank and that is why Frank was so mad, but the Mob didn't get Frank the part in *From Here to Eternity*. He hated *The Godfather* book and so he didn't want to be in the film. Vic Damone was offered Johnny Fontane first. Sinatra called him and told him not to do it. Frank was calling everybody that was being cast and saying, "Don't do it." He called me, I am 27 years old, and he said, "You're a friend of mine, right?" I said, "Yeah, Frank, I love you, man." I had met him when I was 18 so this is nine years later. He said, "Vic was cast for the part and he turned it down, all my friends are turning it down. I want you to turn it down." I had to think for a minute. I wanted to do this movie and I said I'd get back to him. About three days past and I called Dorothy in his office and I said, "Dorothy, is the old man around?" She got Frank on the phone and I said, "Frank you're a friend of mine, right?" He said, "Of course." I said, "Can I ask you a question? If I had asked you not to do *From Here to Eternity*, would you have still done it?" He hung up on me. (Laughs) He realised I would do it and for three years he didn't talk to me.'

But the role of Johnny Fontane was greatly reduced for the film. 'It wasn't cut down because of Sinatra,' says Gianni Russo. 'It was because Al Martino was the worst actor for the role. I was in the room when he was doing that scene with Marlon Brando. He was so intimidated by Brando. Al kept flubbing his lines, he did about 10 takes. Then Brando took over and he went 'Act like a man, don't cry like a baby', that was ad libbed and then he was done with it. Al Martino could sing lyrics but he couldn't act.'

Frank and Barbra Streisand hosted a charity event in Hollywood called *The Movies*, which was packed with classic clips from famous films. The montages were put together by George Cukor who had to be talked out of using long clips from his own films.

Princess Grace was in attendance and while she was in Hollywood, Gregory Peck asked her to present a lifetime achievement award to Cary Grant. This was a controversial award as he had been critical of the Academy and just before the ceremony, details of an affair were leaked to the press. Princess Grace felt that she could not be involved in anything controversial and so Frank Sinatra stepped in to present the award. Two years later, Frank received a humanitarian award at the Oscars.

Richard Burton had hopes of winning an Oscar for *Anne of the Thousand Days* and Frank lent them his Gulfstream Jet so he and Liz could fly from Puerto Vallarta in Mexico to Hollywood for the ceremony. The sentiment though was high for John Wayne who won the award for *True Grit*. Elizabeth Taylor called Richard Burton 'the Frank Sinatra of Shakespeare'. Burton wanted a jet like Frank's but they cost $3.5m. If he had won an Oscar, his earnings would have risen and he could have bought one.

Richard Harris said that 'Frank could be your best friend or your worst enemy.' When his marriage was breaking up and he was playing King Arthur in *Camelot* in 1967, Frank offered him his jet to fly back to his wife. He told Harris, 'You can't make love long distance.'

Richard Burton's diaries reveal how unhappy Sinatra was. He was plagued by questions regarding his associations with gangsters. Burton describes his house as being like a super motel with every possible gadget in your room. His rumpus room contained a pool table and 'a magnificent toy train set given to Frank by the manufacturers.' Burton comments that he is 'a very nice man in short doses but I imagine a bore to live with. I've seen lots of copies of *Encounter* around and I'm bloody sure Francis doesn't read that.' Burton describes Brando as 'a smugly pompous little bastard' and few escape in his diaries, but he, Liz, Brando and Sinatra carry something sanguicolous, that is parasites in the blood stream, and that parasite is press-envy. Other actors like Paul Newman and John Voight don't have it at all and so the press doesn't come after them.

In May 1970 Frank Sinatra came to London with Count Basie and his Orchestra for a series of concerts. There had been talk of the Queen attending a charity concert at the Royal Albert Hall but the Metropolitan Police Commissioner wondered if this was wise. He wrote to J Edgar Hoover, who responded that Sinatra's associations with hoodlums were well known. The Queen did not attend.

Because of the expense, Count Basie hadn't brought his whole orchestra over and he supplemented the personnel with local musicians. The trombonist Don Lusher was there: 'I found out that Sinatra hated a band with just one dynamic. The loud sessions had to be loud, and then it had to be just a whisper when we were quiet.' The concerts went very well with Sinatra excelling himself on 'Ol' Man River' and 'Yesterday' and, in Churchillian tones, he was to call the concerts his finest hour. A sign that he enjoyed himself is that he was on stage for 90 minutes, not his usual hour. On one show he improvised 'This Love of Mine', one of the few lyrics he had written, but then he forgot the words.

By contrast, in July, Dick Haymes played a week's cabaret in Manchester with rarely more than 20 in the audience. He had added 'My Way' to his repertoire and a regional newspaper called him 'plodding and predictable'.

The British singer Malcolm Roberts had some dates in Vegas. 'I was opening for Nancy Sinatra at the Sahara and I had my pale blue suede suit on and I was signing autographs with women all around me. Across the room, I could see these eyes and it was him. He was just sitting there and when the last one went, he came over. He said, "I hear you're a singer. Are you any good?" I said, "I'm great", and he said, "You are. I've seen you and you are fantastic." He invited me to his house and he was very kind and generous, although I knew he could go the other way if I said something wrong. He used to read the papers every day and if he read about somebody who needed an operation, he would pay for it. He was a wonderful host and I found out that he gave presents to everyone.'

In one extraordinary week, Frank, Nancy and Frank Jr were all playing different venues in Vegas. Frank Jr said on stage, 'I'm going to devote exactly five minutes to my father because, as he once confided in a moment of weakness, that's exactly how much time he devoted to me.'

In October 1970 Frank recorded what he intended would be his final sessions with Don Costa. It included an arrogant comment on flower power, 'I Will Drink the Wine', written for him by Paul Ryan, whose stepfather was Harold Davison. It's a curious lyric ('I will give you back your flowers and I will take the land.') but it had enough resonance to become a UK Top 20 singles in March 1971.

Frank showed little interest in recording children's songs so 'Bein' Green', written by Joe Raposo, was a strange choice. The song only made sense when it was sung by Kermit the frog in *The Muppet Show*, but as it was also recorded by Diana Ross and Ray Charles, they might have considered it a comment on race relations. Frank liked Raposo's work so much that he did think of coming out of retirement with an album of his songs.

There were John Denver songs, the charming 'My Sweet Lady', an overblown 'Leaving on a Jet Plane' and the little-known 'The Game Is Over', which was the last song he recorded before his retirement. Sinatra should have spent more time on Burt Bacharach and Hal David as they could have tailored an album for him. When he recorded 'Close to You', the second song of that title he had recorded, it should have had a more intimate arrangement.

There were two duets with Nancy Sinatra, 'Feelin' Kinda Sunday' and 'Life's a Trippy Thing', written by Nino Tempo and Howard Greenfield respectively. Austin Powers would have loved them. 'I mean just what I sing, Life is such a trippy thing.' Really? Frank ended the second song with the words, 'That's silly.'

He also recorded a couple of arrangements from Lena Horne's husband, Lennie Hayton. One was the Brel/McKuen song, 'I'm Not Afraid', which seemed to have two tunes and two tempos, and the other, George Harrison's 'Something', which goes from a jazzy arrangement into a ballad.

The Cavern DJ Bob Wooler said astutely, 'Most people think that George Harrison's 'Something' is a wonderful song, but "Something in the way she moves, Something in the way she woos me" is hardly commendable rhyming. Okay, Frank Sinatra recorded the song, but he was jumping on the bandwagon. I adore Sinatra but he was totally wrong to record that and also 'Downtown' and 'Winchester Cathedral'. It was not his scene and it would be like the Beatles' recording 'I Left My Heart in San Francisco'. When singers bandwagon, they are out of their depth – they are not liked by the people who revere them and they are disliked even more by the people who don't revere them. Everyone thinks, 'What are they doing that for?' To be fair to Sinatra, maybe the quality songwriters had dried up and were no longer producing the type of songs he preferred to record.'

Sinatra was back in the UK in November 1970 for two charity concerts at the Royal Festival Hall with Bob Hope as the opening act. Princess Grace of Monaco introduced the second show, which was televised by the BBC.

The Scottish songwriter Bill Martin was in the audience. 'I was out to impress Jan, my future wife, and the tickets were £100, an extortionate amount, but it was for charity. We were in the fourth row and we had two seats in the aisle. Then along came a television camera and I had two huge backsides in front of me and the cameramen were talking. When Bob Hope came out, they were nattering all the time. In the interval, I went to the organiser, Jeffrey Archer, who was there with his wife and I said, "I have paid all this money for tickets and yet I am sitting behind the camera and I am not going to see Frank Sinatra. You've got to give us better tickets or I'll kick those cameras out of the way." He said, "Take my tickets." They were in the fourth row too but they had better seats. So we sat right in the middle of the fourth row and Jan said, "This is great, fantastic."'

So far so good. 'Frank Sinatra came out, bouncing across the stage, with a long microphone lead. He was singing 'The Lady Is a Tramp' and there was a guy in front of me with a huge Afro, the biggest Afro I have ever seen, and he was swinging along in time, I will give him that. Jan said, "Don't you dare speak to him, we have had enough trouble. Don't poke him in the back." Frank finished the song and said, "And that's for my friend in the third row, the best set of pipes in the music business, Mr Tony Bennett." It was Tony Bennett in a ridiculous wig. I looked across to Jeffrey Archer and as they had moved the camera, they had perfect seats, while I was watching Sinatra through a black fuzz.'

In March 1971 Frank Sinatra did two unusual things. He announced that he would be retiring in June after a charity concert in Los Angeles. Secondly, he had wanted ringside seats for the championship fight between Muhammad Ali and Joe Frazier and when he had not been able to get them, he told *Life* magazine that he would take some photographs for them. They accepted this so Frank got what he wanted and *Life* magazine had a photospread from Frank with text by Norman Mailer.

Tony Cartwright recalls an incident in April 1971: 'I was flying in a private plane, an eight seater, for the 450 mile journey from Las Vegas to Lake Tahoe. It was Frank's plane and my travelling companions included Frank, Dean and Sammy. They were all going to perform at Cal-Neva. We landed on Bill Harrah's landing strip and he had another hotel and casino where Engelbert Humperdinck was to perform. When we got off, we went one way and the others went to Cal-Neva. I went across to Cal-Neva that night as Joe Frazier was going to be there. The previous month he had had beaten Muhammad Ali at Madison Square Garden and he had become the heavyweight champion of the world. He was a decent singer and guitarist and he was performing with his band. You could still see some injuries and although the music was good, the audience was really paying homage to him. Frank, Dean and Sammy were falling over him. I guess they were as impressed by celebrity as the rest of us.' And childish fun. One day when Dean was drunk, Frank got an actor in a bear suit to chase him round Lake Tahoe.

What was intended as Sinatra's final album, *Sinatra and Company*, was released in April 1971. One side was devoted to Sinatra/Jobim and the other to miscellaneous songs he had recorded six months earlier. 'Lady Day' which had been left off the *Watertown* album was included. Despite the publicity over Frank's imminent retirement, it was not a big seller in the US although it went Top 10 in the UK.

Frank was also keen to give charity concerts so it was fitting that his farewell performance should be for the Motion Picture and Television Relief Fund and it was staged by his friend Gregory Peck. It was a lavish affair with tickets costing $250, and he was accompanied by the Los Angeles Philharmonic Orchestra conducted by Zubin Mehta. Because of the rigidity of the arrangements, he couldn't take his usual liberties.

So on 13 June 1971 Barbra Streisand sang 'Oh Happy Day' in his honour, rather an ambiguous choice it would seem, and after being introduced by the actress Rosalind Russell, Frank Sinatra performed his farewell set at the Ahmanson Theatre in the Los Angeles Music Centre. It was a show that encompassed his career – 'All or Nothing at All' and 'I'll Never Smile Again' from the big band days; 'Ol' Man River' and 'Try a Little Tenderness' from Columbia; 'I've Got You Under My Skin' and 'The Lady Is a Tramp' from Capitol; and 'Fly Me to the Moon', 'That's Life' and 'My Way' from Reprise. He came back for an encore and he lit a cigarette and ended with the saloon song, 'Angel Eyes' with its final line "'Scuse me while I disappear."

And with that he was gone, leaving just the smoke behind.

CHAPTER 15

Intermission

'Frank Sinatra was the Mozart of popular singers. I particularly love his masterpieces, 'Strangers in the Night' and 'My Way'.'

Luciano Pavarotti

Day In–Day Out, 14 June 1971–1973

A few days after Frank Sinatra had announced his retirement, Jack Benny did the same thing and Frank sent him a one-word telegram, 'Copycat'. Benny responded by saying, 'I would like to retire, only I can't afford to.' It was good knockabout stuff, but it emphasised an intriguing issue. Just who had retired before, especially when they were still in good health?

There were special cases such as Greta Garbo who wanted to be alone but, by and large, there was no need for any performer to retire. It wasn't as though a performer was clocking in every day and then stopped. A performer could take time out whenever he or she liked and there was no compulsion to return.

It might have been better if some performers had retired, the sad case of Dick Haymes being evidence for that. But on the whole, performers didn't retire because they were drawn to the applause. No one would be clapping if they were just putting out the refuse or walking the dog, and it meant that many artists were performing long after their sell-by date. Indeed, Jimmy Stewart had said to him, 'Why did you do it, Frank? I never want to quit. I'll do commercials. I'll do anything. I just need to work.'

At the time, the only comparable case to Sinatra's was Gracie Fields. She said 'Wish me luck as you wave me goodbye' time and again. She didn't want to leave her home on the Isle of Capri, but she kept being offered farewell tours. I interviewed the country singer, Slim Whitman, when he was doing his farewell tour of the UK. He told me that he didn't know until he arrived that this was his farewell tour as he had every intention of returning. The term had been used to generate ticket sales. I interviewed Tom Paxton on what he had agreed would be his farewell tour, only to find that he was back on the road a few years later. After a long layoff which looked suspiciously like retirement, David Bowie returned in 2013. His new single, 'Where Are We Now', was promoted on news bulletins – how's that for brilliant PR?

There was no financial incentive for Frank Sinatra to retire: he could simply have taken a year or two off and then returned so why did he do it?

He wasn't nursing any serious doubts about his abilities. His recent films had done okay, notably *Tony Rome,* and he had recorded two landmark songs, no matter what he thought of them: 'Strangers In The Night' and 'My Way'. Artistically, he had had musical adventures with Antonio Carlos Jobim and been well up to the challenge. Maybe he was fed up and he certainly wanted more time to paint and play golf as well as manage his investments. He had executive duties at Warner/Reprise and Jack Daniel's had made him a Tennessee Squire and given him land in Lynchburg.

Golf was not the perfect game for Sinatra whose temperament was more suited to the hundred yards dash. Dean Martin was an exceptionally good golfer and played from scratch. He hated playing with Frank who would suggest skipping holes. In Palm Springs, the freeway for one of the holes at the Tamarisk Country Club backed onto his house, so if Frank was bored, he could stroll home.

One thing was certain. He told several reporters, 'I won't do a book.'

But his past kept coming back.

The Mafia links wouldn't go away. In a testimony to the New Jersey State Commission in February 1970 he said that he knew Sam Giancana but it was 'never brought to my attention that he had connections to the Mafia or Cosa Nostra'.

Now he had been subpoenaed to appear before Senate Select Committee on Crime. This was wearing him down and if he were no longer a public figure, he would have more time to prepare for his appearance and it was possible that the authorities would no longer come after him. He gave his evidence on 18 July 1972 when he was asked a series of questions about his private life.

Sinatra was asked about a $50,000 investment in the Berkshire Downs racetrack in Massachusetts and had he known that the property was partly owned by two Mobsters, Raymond Patriarca and Tommy Lucchese. He responded, 'That's their problem, not mine. Let's dispense with that kind of question.' Considering the size of some of Sinatra's investments and the money needed to maintain a racetrack, this was a relatively trivial amount. However, the gangsters were using Sinatra's name to encourage other investors.

Thoroughly rattled, Sinatra put his name to a letter for the *New York Times,* which was published six days later. He maintained that the Committee had become a forum for 'gutter hearsay' and, anyway, all such questions should have been asked privately. He said that many stars were subject to gossip and speculation but 'it is complicated in my case because my name ends in a vowel'. He claimed that even many liberals believe such accusations if they are connected to an Italian-American name.

Sinatra hinted at a more sinister motive. He had been called to Washington in an election year. He felt that he had been victimised by the Committee and 'if this sort of thing could happen to me, it could happen to anyone.' He had written the letter calling for 'this sort of nonsense to end once and for all.'

The letter is so considered and so well-written that it clearly was drafted by a lawyer for Sinatra but he surely meant every word. It was nonsense though. Dean was Italian-American and the Committees had never come after him, and would anyone have bothered if Sinatra hadn't dabbled in politics?

His time with the Kennedys was highly contentious. After John F Kennedy's assassination, he became disenchanted with the Democrats as both Lyndon Johnson and Bobby Kennedy had little to do with him. For the moment he remained a Democrat. In 1966 he campaigned against the Hollywood star Ronald Reagan who wanted to become Governor of California. He even signed a newspaper ad which declared, 'We believe very strongly that the skills an actor brings to his profession are not the skills of governing.' Ouch!

It didn't work. Reagan was elected Governor, a post he held for eight years, and then, in 1980, he campaigned for President. According to Peter Lawford, Sinatra disliked Reagan 'almost as much as Richard Nixon'.

Much, much more than the politics, Frank Sinatra loved winners, but by switching to Republican, he was also following what a lot of older voters did in middle age. The only issue where he strongly opposed Reagan was over abortion, as Reagan was staunchly pro-life.

As a Catholic, Sinatra might have been expected to support him but he had seen too many problems amongst his showgirl and Hollywood friends.

So in 1966 he campaigned against Reagan and in 1970 he was campaigning for him. Maybe he liked the shock value in changing his mind as in private he made many comments about Reagan: 'He's such a bore. Every time you get near the bastard he makes a speech and he never knows what he's talking about.'

With Reagan, he supported US forces in Vietnam and he loathed student demonstrations. In this view, if students were privileged enough to attend university, then they shouldn't be criticising government policy. Reagan stood up to the students at the University of Berkeley and had told the authorities, 'Throw them out, They don't deserve the education they're getting.' Sinatra agreed 100%.

There were 300 protesters outside one fundraising event. It was recommended that Reagan and his principal guests including Sinatra should leave by a side door, but John Wayne refused to be intimidated and strolled out of the front door.

Sinatra, who had kept Bill Miller on a retainer, appeared for Reagan on fundraisers in Los Angeles, San Francisco and San Diego. At every fundraiser he would dedicate 'Nancy' to his wife, and this was one reason for Sinatra's change of heart. He had known Nancy Reagan, formerly a Hollywood actress, since the 1940s and they were very fond of each other. Sometimes when he sang 'The Lady Is a Tramp', he added, 'She hates California, It's Reagan and damp' – but was this anything more than a humorous remark?

Richard Burton commented in his diary entry for 15 July 1970, 'I read yesterday that Frank Sinatra has "come out for Reagan". I shouldn't think that either of them has had a thought of their own in their lives except about themselves. Even Frankie, despite his monomania, should be able to see that Reagan is patched cardboard and dangerously stupid.'

In memory of his father, Frank established the Martin Anthony Sinatra Medical Education Centre in Palm Springs. Both Reagan and his fellow Republican, Spiro Agnew were at the opening. Frank had donated $800,000 and he received an honorary medical degree. Dr Sinatra will see you now.

The Sinatra files on the FBI website reveal he, Jilly Rizzo and a mobster, Carlo Gambino made a bad investment in Computer Files Expressway. The shares fell from $12 to just seven cents and the New York stockbroker Ronald Alpert who had recommended this investment felt his life was under threat.

If Frank suffered loss of memory, he would have no trouble remembering his address as Wonder Palms Road had been renamed Frank Sinatra Drive. His address was 70588 Frank Sinatra Drive, Rancho Mirage, California – this for a man who loved privacy. His compound has a plaque on the gates, 'Never mind the dog, Beware of the owner.'

Many ladies knew the address. He dated Eva Gabor, sister of Zsa Zsa, for some months. Her last husband had been her plastic surgeon and she saw a psychiatrist about her wish to marry Sinatra. The psychiatrist told her that he had three other patients who wanted to marry Sinatra. Frank proposed to the English socialite, Pamela Churchill Heyward, who had been married to Winston Churchill's son, Randolph, but they knew it wouldn't work. She became the US Ambassador to France. He approached a pretty, flower child actress, Peggy Lipton, with a line in keeping with his age, 'Would you let an old man buy you a cup of coffee?' Later, Peggy had affairs with Sammy Davis and Elvis Presley and she married (and divorced) Quincy Jones.

When the Temptations played the Talk of the Town in London in 1971, they were invited to Ava Gardner's apartment in Mayfair. They went with their British minder, Malcolm Cook, and she asked him who he was. He told her and she said, 'Ah, another fucking hanger-on.'

On a small table, he noted several Dunhill lighters all engraved from Frank Sinatra, so she still carried a torch for the man who had been supplanted by a bullfighter.

In 1971 Dick Haymes had been declared bankrupt in London. The Official Receiver said he had been living in the past and had his head in the clouds. His fortunes improved when he returned to the States and was reunited with his family. He appeared on a TV special, *The Fabulous Forties*, hosted by Tennessee 'Ernie' Ford. He sang 'The More I See You' to Betty Grable as he had done originally. He did well in cabaret at the Coconut Grove in Los Angeles and received an encouraging telegram from Sammy Davis, 'With Frank retiring, it's a good feeling to know that there are still some of us left and cookin'.' In an interview with Gene Lees, Haymes said that he only blamed himself for his troubled past.

With Sinatra's retirement, Bobby Darin might have stepped forward to claim his crown, but Darin was no longer interested. He had campaigned for civil rights issues and in 1966 he had switched to the emerging folk-rock sounds, having one of his biggest successes with 'If I Were a Carpenter'. He supported Bobby Kennedy in his bid for the presidency and had attended his funeral. Then he grew a moustache and developed a new repertoire of protest material as 'Bob Darin'. When he played the Sahara in Las Vegas in 1969 he ignored requests for 'Mack the Knife' and 'Beyond the Sea' and was booed. He took out newspaper ads denouncing the American invasion of Cambodia and was considering political office when he received a bombshell. He found out that his sister was his mother and his mother was really his grandmother; he was only given this information because its detection could have ruined his political campaign. In 1971 Darin had heart surgery, but he returned to performing. He made an album for Motown in 1972 and one of his compositions, 'Something in Her Love', would have been perfect for Sinatra. He starred in a summer replacement series for Dean Martin but the billing *Dean Martin Presents the Bobby Darin Amusement Company* bruised his ego. Dean was taking top billing and wasn't even in the series! Bobby Darin divorced Sandra Dee and married Andrea Yaegar in June 1973. In December 1973, he died on the operating table. He was 37 years old.

In 1972 Peter Lawford, desperate for work, filmed *Return to the Land of Oz* and *They Only Kill Their Masters*, the final film to be made on MGM's backlot before it was sold to developers. He had a new wife but he couldn't get decent work.

In June 1972 Frank came to Europe on holiday but he also had business meetings. Alan Jay Lerner and Fritz Loewe were working on the score for a children's film, *The Little Prince* and they thought that Sinatra, although retired, might agree to play the Pilot. The role had been offered to Richard Burton who declined. Although Sinatra was keen, the director Stanley Donen did not want to work with him and all his attendant problems again. The role went to Richard Kiley who had starred in *Man of La Mancha* on Broadway and also featured Gene Wilder and Bob Fosse. Lerner complained that their score was unrecognisable which was particularly sad as it was Loewe's last score.

Frank Sinatra had an eventful evening in Monte Carlo in July 1972. He put a firecracker under the seat of the perfume millionairess, Hélène Rochas, and was punched by her husband. Then he threw another firecracker at a student he mistook for a press photographer. He ripped the clothes off the student's back and threw his camera into the sea. He paid compensation and he was lucky not to be arrested.

In 1972 Richard Nixon and his running mate, Spiro Agnew, defeated George McGovern and Sargent Shriver in the presidential election. Nixon represented California and he made it a Hollywood election by eliciting support from Frank Sinatra, John Wayne, Bob Hope, Charlton Heston and Clint Eastwood. Tina Sinatra was campaigning for the Democrats and she told her father, 'I'm out there registering voters and impressing nobody and you come out for a candidate and sway a million votes.' 'That's the way it is, sweetheart,' said Sinatra, 'You go and be a celebrity.'

In October 1972, despite being retired, he sang at a *Young Voters For Nixon* rally, not that Nixon would be likely to have many. Sammy Cahn was instructed to change sides too and wrote new lyrics for 'The Lady Is a Tramp':

They're both unique,
Quaker and Greek,
They make this Italian want to whistle and stamp,
Because each gentleman is a champ.'

Frank became particularly friendly with Spiro Agnew, who would stay at his house in Palm Springs. He fell out with his friend Dinah Shore when she came to the house and asked Agnew awkward questions. His neighbour Barbara Marx, now separated from Zeppo, was one of their tennis partners. Frank had hopes that Nixon would reward him by making the US Ambassador to Italy, but it never happened.

On New Year's Eve 1972 Sinatra went to a New Year's Eve party with Barbara Marx. She had a bright and warm personality and they got on well. She started divorce proceedings in January. Zeppo remarked, 'She left me with a deck of cards and some old Sinatra albums.' She was awarded $1,500 a month alimony but she wasn't going to need it.

Frank found Barbara calm and reassuring and for the moment, she was happy to do whatever he wanted. Dolly who was now living in Palm Springs didn't think that she was right for her son. She wanted Frank to marry a good Catholic girl, not a Protestant, and told Frank in her usual blunt way, 'Aren't there enough whores around? Why do you have to go with your friend's wife?'

Not that everything in their romance was plain sailing. When they played charades, Barbara would stick to the rules and said, 'Your three minutes are up. You didn't get it.' Frank was furious and smashed the clock. 'What was it?' he snarled. Pat Henry said, "As Time Goes By" and everybody laughed.

Barbara Marx would become Frank's fourth wife. When she complained about being in the press, Swifty Lazar told her, 'If you don't want to be written about, you should have stayed married to Zeppo.'

Sinatra agreed to compère one of Nixon's inauguration events. Although he wanted to add Pat Henry at the last minute, the security staff wouldn't allow him through. Then he was accosted by a journalist, Maxine Cheshire, from the *Washington Post*. She asked him if President Nixon would find his support as embarrassing as it was for President Kennedy. The fuse was lit. Sinatra yelled, 'You're nothing but a $2 whore!' He stormed out of the theatre and didn't return.

On another occasion, Sinatra was dining at Chasen's in New York and Mario Puzo, the author of *The Godfather*, was sitting with a millionaire at another table. He said that he would introduce him to Frank. Puzo did not want to do this but the millionaire insisted. 'I'd like you to meet my good friend, Mario Puzo,' said the millionaire.

'I don't want to meet him,' said Frank.

'Listen, it wasn't my idea,' said Puzo.

Frank thought he was apologising for the character Johnny Fontane in *The Godfather*. 'Who told you to put that in the book,' he said, 'Your publisher?'

Puzo said, 'I didn't mean that. I meant being introduced to you.'

Sintatra shouted abuse, decrying Puzo as worst than a pimp. Puzo started coughing and walked out of the restaurant. 'There you go,' yelled Sinatra, 'Go ahead and choke.'

On 17 April 1973 President Nixon, hoping for better behaviour, invited Frank to sing for the Italian Prime Minister, Giulio Andreotti, at the White House. He was back with Bill Miller on piano and Nelson Riddle conducting. He received a standing ovation, his first for many months, and he realised that he couldn't give it up.

At the end of 1972 Dean and Jeannie Martin were divorced. Their assets were valued at over $6m. On 25 April 1973 Dean married 24-year-old Kathy Hawn; Frank Sinatra was best man. Dean gave him a golden cigarette lighter with an obscene inscription. The newly-weds carved their names in an ice sculpture. The marriage was not built to last. Dean walked out after three years and his new squeeze was Bing Crosby's daughter-in-law, Peggy Crosby.

By now Frank was determined to return to performing and he wanted to start with a new album. He would choose songs that he had not recorded before along with several new compositions. He would have liked Joe Raposo to write him a whole album but *A Man Alone* and *Watertown* had shown him that limiting the songs to one composer or songwriting team might not generate big sales. He asked Don Costa and Gordon Jenkins to provide the arrangements.

On 29 April Frank was back in a recording studio in Hollywood putting down three songs, but he wasn't happy at how he sounded and he cancelled the sessions for the following day. He ordered the tapes to be destroyed, an instruction he had borrowed from President Nixon. April 29 was an infamous day in American history as Nixon was on TV agreeing that the Watergate tapes could be released, but there were some notorious gaps. Sinatra knew the game was up so possibly his mind was on this. Even when Nixon resigned, Frank didn't desert him. He would say, 'Everybody makes mistakes.'

In July 1973 the popularity of Frank's repertoire was given an unexpected boost with the release of Nilsson's *A Little Touch of Schmilsson in the Night*. As a performer, Harry Nilsson had been hard to categorise. He was an excellent songwriter but his biggest successes were with songs he had not written: Fred Neil's 'Everybody's Talkin'' and Badfinger's 'Without You'. He was quirky and outrageous but he held his natural instincts back for an album of standards, arranged and conducted by Gordon Jenkins. Jenkins planned this as an intimate album and the mood was only broken when Nilsson added some lyrics to 'It Had To Be You' by saying his girl was seven foot two.

Gordon Jenkins must have found it similar to working with Sinatra as Nilsson was constantly smoking and imbibing whiskey, but the album cover was completely unSinatra with Nilsson, holding a spliff, looking dishevelled in his dressing-gown. During the BBC documentary on the album, you can see the harpist passing a joint to a cellist.

Tony Hazzard, composer of 'Fox on the Run', says, 'Frank Sinatra is very cool and slick and I can admire the musicianship and the arrangements, but they don't do much for me. I like him best when the song is a really good idea. "I get no kick from champagne but I get a kick out of you" is tremendous, and comparing your life to vintage wine in 'It Was a Very Good Year' is brilliant. I don't like 'All the Way' as you can imagine someone sitting down in an office and writing that to order. On the whole his records leave me cold. I would much prefer to hear Harry Nilsson singing 'Without You'. The strings go up the octave as he sings the title line and it hits me in the guts everytime.'

Gordon Jenkins was also back with Frank, but the first song was out of Jenkins' comfort zone. Sonny Bono wrote 'Bang Bang (My Baby Shot Me Down)' for his wife Cher. It was about two children playing cowboys 'on horses made of sticks' and the boy, the bad guy, always won. In the middle section they get married and in the final verse, he leaves her and once again 'My baby shot me down.' The song was a Top 10 hit in the UK and US, whilst there was a superb, more melancholy album version from Nancy Sinatra highlighted by a haunting guitar-based arrangement from Billy Strange. Frank liked this so much that he insisted Nancy perform it on one of his TV specials, *A Man and His Music II*. He came to the song himself in 1973 and it had a string-based arrangement from Gordon Jenkins. It's odd to hear a man nearing 60 remembering playing western games but it was a fine performance. It should have been featured on his comeback album, but was held back. Frank did like the arrangement and he recorded it with Gordon Jenkins again in 1981. By that time, Frank had come to know Sonny Bono who became Mayor of Palm Springs between 1988 and 1992 and was then elected to Congress. Nancy's version of 'Bang Bang' was used behind the credits in the Quentin Tarantino film, *Kill Bill, Vol.1*.

You can sense the reasoning: let's find a French song, give it an English lyric and create another 'My Way'. To be fair, they got close. With an English lyric from Sammy Cahn and Paul Anka combined, 'Let Me Try Again' was a perfect song for someone making a comeback album but it seemed too calculated and too obvious. The reflective verses came off better than the bombastic choruses.

Sinatra was championing the *Sesame Street* songwriter, Joe Raposo, but his four songs fell a long way short of Cole Porter and Irving Berlin. Sinatra called 'You Will Be My Music' 'my protest song' and it was the opening cut on his comeback album. The song complains about the music of the day: 'When all the songs are out of tune, And all the rhymes ring so untrue.' He described his contemporaries: 'When I hear lonely singers who are just as lost as me, Making noise, not melody.' When Frank recorded this, he said to Barbara, 'This is our story, baby.'

'You Will Be My Music' was tolerable, but Raposo's 'Noah (Walk with the Lions)' was possibly the worst song that Sinatra ever recorded, certainly the most bizarre. The world is an ark afloat in space and we're all Noah trying to keep the darkness out. It's a way of saying we should live in love and harmony. The song was published by Instructional Children's Music so there you have it. Another Raposo song, 'Winners', praised heroes: 'Here's to winners and most of all me.' More Instructional Children's Music. 'There Used To Be a Ballpark' is better, a nostalgic song decrying the loss of a sports field and a fairground.

If Sinatra had wanted to make an album of one writer's compositions, he should have chosen Stephen Sondheim. Sinatra had wanted to record was 'Send in the Clowns' by Stephen Sondheim from his show, *A Little Night Music*. Frank said, 'I love 'Send in the Clowns' because it is an unusual song. It's been years since Cole Porter or one of those guys put together that kind of sophistication in the lyric.' The song was ideal for a Gordon Jenkins arrangement who commented, 'Frank sings the word 'farce' and your whole life comes up in front of you.' You actually have to be very careful when you sing 'farce' in that song: if you don't have a little pause, the lyric, 'Don't you love farce?' becomes 'Don't you love arse?'

Sondheim has said, 'Why so many fine (and not so fine) singers have recorded 'Send in the Clowns' in a mystery to me. Not that I don't think the song is eminently worth singing, but why this ballad of all the ones I've written? Judy Collins recorded it in England, where it incomprehensibly became a hit, after which Frank Sinatra's recording made it an even bigger one, and soon virtually everyone in the pop field climbed on the bandwagon.' Frankie Laine admitted that he had no idea what 'Send in the Clowns' was about when he recorded it; it is a difficult song if you haven't seen *A Little Night Music*.

Sinatra might also have considered an album of Kris Kristofferson's songs, especially as he had unknowingly inspired 'Help Me Make It Through the Night'. Ray Price in 1970 and Perry Como in 1973 had huge success with 'For the Good Times' and here Frank chose the wrong song. 'Nobody Wins' was okay, but it lacked the bite of his other world-weary compositions.

The other tracks on his comeback album were inconsequential. Teddy Randazzo's

'You're So Right (For What's Wrong in my Life)' was a dreary ballad, but a clumsy title invariably means a clumsy song. Don Costa thought 'Dream Away' was the best track on the album. It was a pleasant lullaby and maybe if it sent the listener to sleep, it achieved its purpose.

The initial thought had been to call the new album, *Let Me Try Again*, but Lee Solters from the Warners press team came up with the term, Ol' Blue Eyes and hence the album was brilliantly called *Ol' Blue Eyes Is Back*. It was released with full publicity in October 1973 and made the Top 20 on the album charts in both Britain and America. It sold enough to be awarded a gold album although it isn't among his best work.

Frank starred in a one hour TV special, *Ol' Blue Eyes Is Back*, which was broadcast on 18 November 1973. The guest star was Gene Kelly and instead of Sammy Cahn, the special material came from Liza Minnelli's writers, Fred Ebb and John Kander. Nancy Sinatra's husband, Hugh Lambert, arranged the choreography although he didn't have to teach Gene Kelly much. Sinatra opened with his new battle-cry, 'You Will Be My Music' and performed 'Let Me Try Again' and 'Send in the Clowns' from the new album. Frank and Gene had a song and dance routine, 'We Can't Do That Anymore' and Gene danced while Frank sang 'Nice 'n' Easy'.

Frank wore a yellow sweatshirt proclaiming 'Ol' Blue Eyes is back'. He was older but as we shall find out, not much wiser. The most controversial episode in his career was still to come and was only a few months away. In July 1974 he might well have considered retiring again.

CHAPTER 16

Let me try again

'There are no second acts in American life.'
F Scott Fitzgerald

Day In–Day Out, 1974–1979

At the end of January 1974 Frank Sinatra started performing in earnest once more, beginning with a short season at Caesars Palace. Outside the venue, a banner said, 'Hail Sinatra, the Noblest Roman has returned.' When Bob Hope remarked, 'Frank found Caesars paid better than social security', Frank retorted, 'I just figured I'd do some work. It's no fun trying to hit a golf ball at eight at night.'

Frank added that he had come back because the telephone operators had forgotten how to spell his name. He had wandered into a bar in Palm Springs later one night and heard a woman ask, 'Do you have a jukebox?' 'No,' said the barman. Frank chipped in, 'If you want, I'll sing for you.' The woman said, 'No, thank you' and walked out. The barman said, 'She didn't recognise you, Mr Sinatra.' 'Maybe she did,' said Frank, and if that isn't a cue for a song, I don't know what is.

Frank opened with 'Come Fly with Me' and dedicated 'My Funny Valentine' to Barbara whom he introduced as 'my roommate'. The dubious jokes were back and he commented, 'The Polacks are deboning the coloured people and using them for wet suits.' His opening actor Pat Henry said, 'I wish they'd make Frank Pope because then I'd only have to kiss his ring.'

On 27 January 1974 Frank's daughter Tina married the songwriter and record producer, Wes Farrell. His successes as a songwriter included: 'Boys' (Shirelles, Beatles), 'Baby, Let Me Take You Home' (Animals), 'Hang on Sloopy' (McCoys) and 'Come a Little Bit Closer' (Jay and the Americans). He had written many of the songs for the Partridge Family. Meanwhile, Frank's former wife, Mia Farrow, was the first guest ever on *The Muppet Show*.

On 3 March 1974 Frank had to introduce Doris Day at the American Film Institute and he chose his words with care. He called her 'the lady all of us love all of the time' which was so blatantly untrue that Doris would know he didn't mean a word of it. Later in the year, Doris Day went to Vegas to see Ella Fitzgerald and Frank Sinatra with the Count Basie Band. She met Ella before the show but Frank ignored her. Doris received a standing ovation when entering the auditorium. On the other hand, when the comic actor, Bud Abbott, died penniless in April, Frank Sinatra paid the funeral expenses.

On 8 April Frank started a US tour at Carnegie Hall and introduced his saloon songs with this preamble, 'I've prided myself through the years in being identified as a saloon singer. I've worked in a lot of saloons, and consequently, you usually do a saloon song, so to speak. You know, in the old days, they had 'Ace in the Hole' and 'Jack of Diamonds' and whatever those things were. Then we came up to date with songs like 'One for My Baby' and beautiful things like that. So I would like to do a trilogy of saloon songs for you. These all tell of unrequited love, obviously: where the chick has flown the coop, and she not only took the bread, but she took the grass and everything that was laying round in the kitchen. So we are now about to view a cat who's been living it up by himself for sometime. He's consumed a substantial amount of John Barleycorn or whatever, and one morning he wakes and decides that he's going to go out among us and see if he can get back into the mainstream again, and he falls into a small saloon and proceeds to tell his story to the bartender.'

Frank had no intention of resting on his laurels and his next album was to be *Some Nice Things I've Missed* featuring his own interpretations of current favourites. If he believed that these were the best songs he'd missed, then he'd lost the plot. The album was arranged by Don Costa and the best known track is 'Bad, Bad Leroy Brown', a semi-spoken story about a dubious character in Chicago. It had been a US No.1 for its writer, Jim Croce, in 1973. Croce's lyric writing (rhyming 'junkyard dog' with 'King Kong') sounded like a first draft and as Frank ended his big band treatment with a quiet 'ruff, ruff', he was harking back to 'Mama Will Bark'.

Sinatra was perfectly at home with 'You Are the Sunshine of My Life', revelling in Don Costa's big band arrangement. There's a nod to the Doors' hated 'Light My Fire' at the end. Although Bread had the potential to be cutting edge, they got caught in whimsy, one example being the mawkish sentimentality of David Gates' 'If', taking its title from Rudyard Kipling's poem. Sinatra enjoyed a song when he could give a performance but here he took it too slowly. What would have happened if he had narrated the whole lyric? In 1975 Telly Savalas had a UK No.1 by doing just that.

Sinatra liked the overblown writing of Neil Diamond and he went for that deep Diamond sound on 'Sweet Caroline'. He slurred the lyric and judging by his phrasing, he may not have read the lyric before he started. The jazz bassist Dave Finck says, 'Frank can sing right on the beat without ever sounding stiff, even when he does 'Sweet Caroline'. It's a terrible song, but he gives it a really strong quarter-note, on the beat feeling.'

Tony Orlando and Dawn had an international hit with 'Tie a Yellow Ribbon Round the Ole Oak Tree' or as Sinatra sang, 'Tie a yella ribbon'. This was a big, brassy arrangement and for once, Don Costa made good use of Sinatra's studio audience by encouraging them to yell on 'the whole damn bus is cheering' and applaud at the end.

One of the principal songwriting teams of his comeback was Michel Legrand with the husband and wife lyricists, Alan and Marilyn Bergman. Here Sinatra sang two of their film songs, 'The Summer Knows' from the 1971 film, *Summer of '42* and 'What Are You Doing the Rest of Your Life' from 1969's *The Happy Ending*, starring Jean Simmons. The latter performance was particularly good, especially as Sinatra sang the little-known verse.

'Empty Tables' was a new and superbly crafted saloon song from Johnny Mercer and Jimmy Van Heusen. Sinatra could easily have slotted this into his set, but other songs would have had to make way.

There were two songs from the Disney writer, Floyd Huddleston. The opening line of 'I'm Gonna Make It All the Way' suggested suicide but the singer then poured out a torrent of lyrics rather in the vein of 'Gentle on My Mind', only not as strong. 'Satisfy Me One More Time' would be a song for an S&M couple: 'Let's smother each other in a good stranglehold', Frank's laugh suggesting that he knew the song was ridiculous. Although Kim Carnes wrote 'You Turned My World Around', it is no more than a typical reflective ballad from the period.

There was one track which didn't come to fruition: 'If You Could Read My Mind', written by the Canadian singer/songwriter, Gordon Lightfoot, who recorded for Reprise, 'I was signed by Mo Ostin who was Sinatra's right hand man in that department,' says Gordon, 'Sinatra almost did some of my tunes but it didn't work out. I was at the session when he did Stevie Wonder's 'You Are the Sunshine of My Life', which he did great but he wasn't satisfied with his performance. He then threw 'If You Could Read My Mind' on the floor and said, "I can't sing this."' What diplomacy.

On 22 May Nancy gave birth to her first child, Frank's first granddaughter, Angela Jennifer. Frank told his daughter, 'I hope you'll consider having another baby. It was very lonely for me as a child.' He added that he would never let the child see *The Kissing Bandit*. He told the press, 'I wish her 100 times the fun I've had and 100 times as many guys as I've had broads,' which presumably was a compliment.

Frank had had minor hits with 'Let Me Try Again' and 'Bad, Bad Leroy Brown' and the signs were encouraging as his new album, *Some Nice Things I've Missed*, entered the US album charts. The audiences loved him and fans had started bringing stuffed toys to the concerts for his granddaughter.

In July Sinatra went to Australia for concert appearances in Sydney and Melbourne and he arrived a few days early in Sydney so that he and Barbara could do some sightseeing. The concerts were sell-outs, so no additional publicity was needed, and much to his annoyance, Frank found that a press conference had been scheduled. The Australian press was notorious for goading its subjects and he called them all 'a bunch of goddamn liars'. The male reporters were 'a bunch of fags' and one hapless female reporter was no better than 'a two dollar whore'.

The union leader Bob Hawke (later the Australian Prime Minister) instructed his members to boycott Sinatra and his team and requested solidarity with the other unions. As a result, Sinatra was front page news, imprisoned in his hotel room without food and drink. He could not leave the country because no one would service his private plane. Bob Hawke said that he must apologise before the concerts went ahead. After he had stopped laughing, Buddy Rich commented, 'Apologise! Oh yeah, that'll be the day when Frank apologises to those assholes.' After much negotiation, Bob Hawke came to a deal with Sinatra and the shows were reinstated together with an additional concert for charity.

In 2006 an Australian production company made the film, *The Night We Called It a Day*, directed by Paul Goldman. As Sinatra was played by that most sinister of actors, Dennis Hopper, you can sense Paul Goldman's stance. Hopper does well, miming to an impersonator, but nobody ever employed Dennis Hopper as a nice guy. This is Cranky Franky but it is an enjoyable film with much to commend it, although Melanie Griffith is stuck in a thankless role as Barbara Sinatra.

The Australian music writer Glenn A Baker says, 'We have a history of giving foreign performers the full honours or telling them to get out. The unions got together and locked him in his hotel. They wouldn't refuel his plane and no cab driver would take him to the airport because he said that Australian female journalists were like two dollar hookers. But that didn't begin there. The Who and the Small Faces came to Australia in early 1968. Keith Moon wore a blue singlet and ordered a beer on an early morning flight. A hostess freaked out and they rang the Commonwealth Police and they circled the plane in Melbourne and wanted to deport them. Pete Townshend said he was never coming back. When the Beatles came, they were told that they were not getting a police escort in New Zealand, "We are in no position to do this for pop stars." The whole city exploded and they had to do it. It seems to me that we were pleased to be connected with the top half of the world but we almost resented it. We were supposed to behave in a certain way and we didn't want to.'

The controversy became big news in America, and Bob Hope cracked, 'They let Frank

Sinatra out of Australia after the union boss found a kangaroo head on his pillow.' Instead of ignoring the incident, Frank revelled in it, even joking about it in a huge Thanksgiving concert at Madison Square Garden. When he appeared at Harrah's in Lake Tahoe with Nancy and Frank Jr, he apologised to any hookers out there for comparing them to journalists.

Still, everybody now knew that ol' blue eyes was back and was just as much a bad boy as before. A folk singer from Australia, Gary Shearston, revived 'I Get A Kick Out of You' in a soft, low-key way with a rock beat and had a best seller.

Frank Sinatra was receiving movie offers but he, James Cagney and Sir Laurence Olivier all turned down *Harry and Tonto*, a road film about a pensioner and his cat. Sinatra did not like the idea of playing someone ten years old than himself. Never mind, the role went to Art Carney and he won an Oscar, beating Al Pacino in *The Godfather, Part 2* and Jack Nicholson in *Chinatown*. At the same ceremony, Nelson Riddle won an Oscar for scoring *The Great Gatsby* starring Robert Redford and Mia Farrow.

Frank provided an off-screen narration in MGM's tribute to its musical heritage, the highly successful *That's Entertainment*, which included footage from several Sinatra films. It was followed by *That's Entertainment Part II* in 1976 in which Gene Kelly narrated a section devoted to Sinatra. Much later, there were Sinatra clips in *That's Entertainment Part III* (1994).

Frank was discovering that the music world was changing. Arena tours were in vogue with the innovation of video screens, and big, big bucks could be made. As he was not making best-selling records, Frank realised he could spend his time more profitably by giving concerts. The promoter Jerry Weintraub persuaded Sinatra that he should move away from his usual haunts – Chicago, New York, Atlantic City, Lake Tahoe and Vegas. Very conveniently, Sinatra determined that he wouldn't have to make many changes: he would still talk to the audiences on a one to one and even with a huge audience, he could still sing a saloon song with a solo pianist.

In 1972 Elvis Presley released an album from Madison Square Garden and followed it the next year with a close circuit TV and album package, *Aloha from Hawaii*, which was seen around the world via satellite. Frank wanted some of this.

Frank had a love of boxing so the idea grew for an arena tour in October 1974. He was accompanied by Woody Herman and the Young Thundering Herd, conducted by Bill Miller, and the concerts were recorded, leading up to a television special, *The Main Event – Live*, before 20,000 people at Madison Square Garden on 13 October. Frank was introduced by the fight commentator Howard Cosell. The live album, although giving the impression that all the songs were taken from the Garden, featured tracks from Philadelphia, Buffalo and Boston too. Frank commented from the stage, '*Sinatra – The Main Event*. That's class. In the old days, they would say, "Let's go see Bones at the Paramount".' All the songs had been previously recorded and he retained his joke about 'My Way' being the national anthem.

Frank played around with 'I've Got You Under My Skin' – 'Now the Woody Herman band is gonna wail at you. Light 'em up, light 'em up!' and 'Where does it hurt you, baby? Under my skin!' At the end of 'My Kind of Town', the Herd started chanting the title line of 'Chicago'.

Frank talked affectionately about being a grandfather and of his recent material, he sang 'Let Me Try Again', which he called 'a wonderful song, great song' and 'Bad, Bad Leroy Brown', which worked better live. Before 'Angel Eyes', he says that the only other saloon singers are 'Tony Bennett and Drunkie Dean'. The best performance is a sublime 'Autumn in New York' and what an achievement to perform such an intense, quiet song to an audience of 20,000. Dick Haymes watched the concert on TV and noted in his diary, 'Saw the Sinatra special. Not impressed but the fans loved him; mostly old fans and Hollywood devotees. I'll do my own thing.'

Frank was asked if he would like to join the Knights of Malta – an organization which went back to the Crusades. He would become Sir Francis and be given a scroll with a papal blessing and a diplomatic passport. He could fly their flag from his home. There would a ceremony with red silk robes, rather akin to *The Godfather Part 3*, and Frank thought it would delight Dolly as well as appealing to his own sense of self-importance. He had to make a charity commitment which, in his case, would be four performances over two days.

This was before the internet, so it was easier to be duped. There was a prestigious Knights of Malta, but this offer was a high class scam. It was run by Ivan Markovics, a Hungarian who settled in Australia during the war. He claimed to be the Ambassador for Special Missions with the United Nations.

At the Oscar ceremony in 1975, the rebellious film producer Bert Schneider, who had made *Easy Rider*, accepted an award for a documentary about Vietnam, *Hearts and Minds*. He read out a telegram from the head of the North Vietnamese delegation to the peace talks. It thanked the anti-war movement 'for all they have done on behalf of peace.'

Bob Hope was furious that the Oscars were being hijacked for political ends and he insisted that a statement be read out to the effect that the Academy was non-political. Hope drafted the statement and gave it to Sinatra, who delivered it amidst boos and cheers. When he came off stage, Shirley MacLaine screamed at him (and boy, can she scream), 'Why did you do that? You said you were speaking on behalf of the Academy, but I'm a member of the Academy and you didn't ask me.' Later in the evening, Warren Beatty came on stage and called Sinatra 'an old Republican'.

Again Dick Haymes was watching at home and he recorded in his diary: 'I saw Sinatra on the Awards show tonight and had to admire his guts but I'm taking over; he's had his run and since I'm better, it's my turn. I'm being guided.' To give Haymes some credit, he did well as an opening act at the MGM Grand in Las Vegas and at the Copacabana in New York and he appeared on a radio special singing the songs of Harry Warren. Inspired by *A Star Is Born*, Dick Haymes wrote a film script about an ageing singer and an aspiring young singer: he called it *Reprise*.

In April 1975 Frank Sinatra reached No.75 on the US charts with a new Paul Anka song, 'Anytime (I'll Be There)', which had an enticing Latin rhythm. Anka felt that the song could be more successful and his version became a Top 40 hit in 1976. Another single, the pleasant rock ballad, 'I Believe I'm Gonna Love You', reached No.2 on the new US AOR charts for Frank. The phrase 'adult oriented rock' had replaced 'middle of the road' but AOR or MOR was much the same thing.

In Germany, *Der Spiegel* published a critical article about his performance on *The Main Event* and further articles noted that his singing voice was damaged, how badly he handled the press in Australia, how he still chased woman and how he loved his Mob connections. Sinatra was coming to Germany and this was so negative that it discouraged many fans from buying tickets. Additionally, Sinatra had been offered 100,000 DM for a 10 minute spot but the TV company promptly withdrew its offer.

On 23 May Sinatra appeared at the Olympiapark, Munich – a venue built for the 1972 Olympic Games – and then moved onto Frankfurt. His conductor, Don Costa, took ill and was replaced by Bill Miller. The Berlin and Hamburg concerts were cancelled because Bill Miller could not be ready in time. That's the official line (and clearly nonsense) but it was mooted that Sinatra cancelled the concert either because of poor sales (no one wanted him) or because of a kidnapping threat (someone wanted him). It's hard to say, because Sinatra often acted illogically, but surely he had a duty to those who had bought tickets and 3,000 patrons at an 11,000 venue was still a lot of customers.

He referred to 'those Germans', called them gangsters and said he had kept quiet because 'I could have mentioned Dachau.' The remarks were reported in Germany as though he detested the whole country and its people. For the next 10 years, there was mostly hostile press in Germany, although in 1980, both the editor of *Der Spiegel* and a feature writer apologised on air for their treatment of Sinatra.

Frank played two nights at the Royal Albert Hall, renaming the venue the 'Francis Albert Hall' and singing a generous 20 songs in his 90 minute sets. One reviewer, Clive James, commented that he had said 'more goodbyes than Sarah Bernhardt'.

'My Way' had been such a big record in the UK that it was a total showstopper. It was a break from singing love songs, although the song is about self-love. It was in line with Sinatra's view of himself. Nevertheless, it seemed as though Sinatra had to be forced to sing it and he said one night, 'You sing this song for eight years and you'd hate it too.' Among his other remarks from the stage were, 'I got a letter from a chick who had my face tattooed on her rear end. Her cheeks are filled out as fat as mine.'

When everything was running right, Sinatra was fine. One of his stipulations was that a show must not start late. The orchestra would be cued at 7.59pm and the show would begin at 8pm. There was a practical reason for this: once he had put his stage suit, he remained standing. There would not be creases in his clothes when he walked out on stage.

Considering the requirements of today's superstars, his contractual requests were basic – Campbell's soup, tea and honey, LifeSavers and Tootsie Rolls. Frank had rules for the orchestra – no long hair, no pierced ears and no beards. The UK concerts were a great success as were the ones in Monte Carlo, France, Austria and Holland.

Things were not going so well for Sam Giancana. Fed up with the constant wiretapping and scrutiny, Sam Giancana left the US in 1967 but he was deported back from Mexico in 1974 and returned to live outside Chicago. He was told to appear before a Senate Committee investigating John F Kennedy's death. He would have liked Kennedy out of the way but whether he hatched a plot to kill him is not known. The police had his house under surveillance but they were recalled on 19 June 1975. It remains a mystery as to who went to see Giancana that night but they shot him in the back as he was cooking and then turned the body over and shot him several times in the face.

In August 1975 Frank Sinatra was back at Harrah's in Lake Tahoe but this time as a double-top with John Denver. The package sold out and they performed some songs together. Meanwhile Sammy Davis was becoming an unpredictable as Frank. In the summer of 1975 he went to Monte Carlo to star at a charity ball. Something went wrong and he wasn't met at the airport and so he simply left the country. Fortunately, Burt Bacharach and Bill Cosby were going to the fundraiser as part of the audience and they had two days in which to get a show together.

A new road film with Hope and Crosby called *The Road to the Fountains of Youth* mercifully fell by he wayside, but Mel Brooks parodied Sinatra and his Nelson Riddle arrangements alongside Alfred Hitchcock in the film, *High Anxiety* (1977).

In September 1975, Frank was working with Ella Fitzgerald and the Count Basie band at the Uris Theatre in New York. Frank said that he could be billed third as he would be 'beneath two real legends'. While in New York, he met with Jackie Onassis, formerly Kennedy and working as an executive for Viking books, to discuss his memoirs. He did considered a ghosted autobiography with Pete Hamill but nothing came of it because Frank didn't want to tell his story, no matter how tempting the offer.

In November, Frank returned to the London Palladium, this time with Sarah Vaughan and the Count Basie band. The promoter, Malcolm Feld, recalls, 'I was with MAM and Harold Davison sent round a note to say that Frank Sinatra was coming to play a week at the London Palladium and he would be staying at the Savoy but only Liz Petty who was Harold's secretary could go backstage or anywhere where he was. We had tickets for the opening night and he was sensational and my car was parked by the stage door and as we were coming out I bumped into Liz, and I was with my sister and some friends. They said, "Malcolm knows Frank." I said, "I haven't seen him for 20 years: he won't remember me". Liz invited me backstage and my bosses were sitting there – Colin Berlin, Barry Clayman and Harold Davison. They gave me looks which suggested I was going to lose my job. Liz said, "Here's someone who would like to meet you" and Frank goes, "Hi, it's, er, Malcolm isn't it?" After all that time, he had remembered.'

By all accounts, this was a very happy week for Sinatra. He was pleasant backstage, talked to fans and met Prime Minister Harold Wilson in Downing Street. He and Sarah Vaughan ended the show together with 'The Song Is You', 'They Can't Take That Away from Me' and 'The Lady Is a Tramp'. He gave her a compliment, Sinatra-style. He told her that he wanted to cut his wrists and bleed to death while she sang to him. Not that he enjoyed her company too much; she was obsessed about not sweating and always had her hotel suites icily cold.

When Frank was given the telephone number of Radio 1 DJ, Tony Blackburn, he rang and asked him for a request. Tony thought it was a joke and put the phone down, now saying that he is the only person to have put the phone down on Sinatra and lived.

Frank recorded a Christmas single of a nauseous John Denver song, 'A Baby just like You', the theme being that Jesus was a baby just like you. He concluded the single by saying, 'Merry Christmas little Angela, Merry Christmas everyone.' On 17 March 1976 Frank became a grandfather again as Nancy and Hugh had their second child, Amanda Katherine.

Frank brought in the New Year with a spectacular stadium concert in Chicago. There followed a short season at Caesars and then on 25 January he celebrated the bicentennial by performing on the steps of the Jefferson Memorial with the Marine Corps band. Peter Lawford, still looking for work, was a host on a cruise, Sail with the Stars. One of Frank's most unlikely bookings was a concert in the Grand Ole Opry House in Nashville on 10 May 1976 as part of a US tour, but he performed his standard show.

Why did he do it? Just when everything was going so well, Frank had his photograph taken with some mobsters at the Westchester Premier Theatre in Tarrytown, just north of New York City.

When the theatre was being built in the early 1970s, the trust received a major donation from Carlo Gambino, a known mobster, and he brought in two other characters with doubtful pedigrees, Gregory DePalma and Richard Fusco. The theatre had been opened by Diana Ross in 1975 and both Frank and Dean played there. The management was operating a skimming operation similar to that of Vegas in the 1960s where money was being taken from the top. Either knowingly or not, Frank Sinatra and his management received $50,000.

In November 1977 the theatre filed for bankruptcy after its president Eliot Weisman resigned amid charges of racketeering. This led to Weisman being arrested for fraud and for failing to disclose that the theatre was run on Mafia money. Apparently, Weisman was offered a deal – testify against Frank Sinatra or go to jail. Weisman went to jail, receiving six years, and after he had done time, the Sinatra organisation gave him a job and he promoted the Together Again tour.

Sinatra's recording sessions in 1976/7 were haphazard as though he wasn't sure what to do. He recorded a couple of singles and the first session featured Sam Butera on tenor saxophone. During the Dixieland arrangement of Neil Diamond's 'Stargazer', Sinatra goes, 'Jump on it, Sam, get all over that thing.' Another Neil Diamond composition, 'Dry Your Eyes', was about the youthful ideals of the 1960s, hardly a Sinatra subject. Considering the size of John Denver's repertoire he could have done better than the repetitive 'Like a Sad Song'. Paul Anka's 'Everybody Ought To Be in Love' was so derivative of 'Everybody Loves Somebody' that it should have gone to Dean.

Bruce Johnston of the Beach Boys had written a terrific song about songwriting, 'I Write the Songs'. When Barry Manilow recorded the song, it went to the top of the US charts. Frank saw it as a potential 'My Way', even opening some of his concerts with it. He did however change the title to 'I Sing the Songs' and his version was released as a single.

Bruce Johnson says, 'If he had listened closely closely to the lyrics, he would have realised that Barry Manilow or whoever wasn't saying that they wrote the songs. Their role was on a much higher plane, a spiritual one if you like, a force that is within men and women for them to be creative and write songs. The song is about where creativity comes from. If you take it further, it is the creative mom helping the children with their homework or the father doing something to help them. It is not about Barry Manilow going, 'Hey, look at me, I write the songs'. If it was, I don't think it would have sold 14 million copies and won a Grammy.'

Nevertheless, Bruce gave Frank permission to change the lyric: 'He rang and asked me. My wife Harriet and I flew to Caesars Palace and we went there to hear it. He made me stand up and take a bow. I looked at this grey-haired genius with this great body of work and thought, he has been alive forever and he did sing the very first song. He and Bing Crosby invented pop music. I did explain to him why I had written 'I Write the Songs' but he told me why he wanted to say 'I Sing the Songs'. I thought that it worked. It was a great point of view as people will look at him as someone who really was the first pop star.'

Frank recorded the title song from a forthcoming Broadway show, *I Love My Wife*, which was written by Cy Coleman and Michael Stewart. The lyric was ideal for Sinatra and was touching when you think of his life.

My mind at times may dwell on sex
If someone's rating dreams, mine, I guess, are double X,
So dimpled knees delight me,
Well, that's life,
But in just case you haven't heard,
I love my wife.'

David Niven saw a show-biz feature in a newspaper about awkward Brando and Sinatra had been and how unlike he and Roger Moore they were, both of whom had always been charming with their fans. At that point David Niven and Roger Moore were having difficulty in getting good film roles and Niven sent the clipping to Moore with the comment, 'It pays to be a cunt.'

On 11 July 1976 Frank married for the fourth time, this time 45-year-old Barbara Marx, at his Rancho Mirage compound. Dolly attended the ceremony although she did not approve of Barbara and said so openly. Frank Jr did not attend but sent his father a sex manual. When Frank heard the words, 'for richer or poorer', he said, 'For richer! For richer!' His net worth was $15m. Jimmy Van Heusen played 'True Love' but still Barbara had to sign a pre-nup. On his death, she would receive an allowance and a share in future earnings. She commented, 'I've found a new kind of tranquility.' I'd have thought 'tranquility' was the last thing you would find with Frank Sinatra. Tina, who didn't approve, said, 'He has finally married his mother.'

It seems that for one reason or another, no one was very happy that day: Frank, Barbara, Dolly, Nancy or his children. For some time, Frank had been anti-Catholic calling it 'a tough religion to live by, a great one to die by'. He went to the occasional midnight mass but now he wanted his first marriage annulled and Barbara to become a Catholic so that he could marry her in church. There was no good reason why Frank wanted this other than he had been told he couldn't have it. The only grounds for annulment were non-consummation of marriage, insanity, and non-disclosure of important information by one party before the marriage, none of them applying here. Rather like Henry VIII, if Frank wanted something, he wanted it and to be told no raised the challenge. He knew holy men in high places, very high places; he had met Popes and cardinals.

And he got it.

This is a strange business. A marriage annulled in the eyes of church is effectively saying that it didn't take place. But how could this be when there was a family of three children? Would this have been allowed if this was somebody other than Frank Sinatra? Did Frank make the Vatican an offer it couldn't refuse? Nothing needed to be done about his second or third marriages as they were not in church. So Frank remarried Barbara in a church ceremony in 1978. His children were furious and his first wife Nancy stopped going to church.

Every year Jerry Lewis hosted a fundraising TV special for muscular dystrophy, which was broadcast live with all manner of guest stars. In September 1976 the show was from the Sahara while Frank was at Caesars Palace. Frank agreed to make a guest appearance and he brought along a special friend, Dean Martin. Jerry had no idea that he was going to meet Dean that night. With a brilliant adlib, Jerry Lewis got over the shock by asking him, 'Are you working?' This gave Dean the opportunity to plug his appearances at the MGM Grand.

As usual Frank was scheduled to play Caesars Palace in January. Frank and Barbara were already there and on 6 January Dolly was flying from Palm Springs to join them. She hadn't come with the main party as her friend had been delayed at the hairdresser's. The plane hit Mount San Gorgonio and Dolly and the pilot were killed. Frank cancelled his engagement and Phyllis McGuire and Johnny Carson filled in for him. At her funeral on 12 January the pallbearers included Jimmy Van Heusen, Dean Martin and Jilly Rizzo. In November Frank held a dinner in Dolly's memory at the Stardust Hotel in Las Vegas at $500 a plate.

And then there's Saturday Night Sinatra. Who on earth thought that Frank Sinatra should enter the Bee Gees' territory? Well, the arranger Joe Beck for one. Maybe even Sinatra himself who told one reporter he had recorded a hustle. The song he chose to hustle was 'Night and Day' and he also recorded 'All or Nothing at All' with a disco beat. You should be dancing? I don't think so. Sinatra did perform this arrangement of 'Night and Day' from time to time, but then at Caesars Palace in 1979, he stopped the band and said, 'Throw it on the floor.' From then on, it was back to Nelson Riddle.

Luckily, the single didn't sell and so Sinatra jumped off the bandwagon before he made an album in the same vein. It wasn't original but he thought he would make an album, *Here's to the Ladies,* where each title would feature a girl's name. The album would be produced by Frank Sinatra Jr who, although certainly capable, had a fraught (and fought) relationship with his father.

In her final years, Dolly Sinatra had tried to impove the relationship between Frank and his son. It can be difficult to be the son of a major star and even worse when your name is the same. Gianni Russo says, 'To me Frank Jr is an idiot and I would tell him that to his face. He got so fat and he looked stupid. He hated his father and I was once in the audience with his father at the Tavern on the Green in New York and a couple of mobsters. Frank's mother Dolly told him, "Your son is in town, you gotta go see him." We were sitting there and Frank Jr kept referring to his father as "Frank did this" and "Frank did that", and Louis Domes stood up and said, "Frank is your father, you asshole. He is sitting here. Show him respect." Twenty guys then got up and walked out. Frank Jr always sided with his mother: that was the problem.'

When Nelson Riddle was to be honored by his fellow musicians, he wanted Sinatra to make the keynote speech. Frank agreed and the date was arranged to accommodate him. Then Sinatra did not turn up. Riddle should have expected this but he took umbrage and didn't speak to Frank for some years. However, in March 1977, he came back to Frank to orchestrate some songs and they began with a new arrangement of 'Nancy', which now owed something to 'Maria' from *West Side Story*.

Just as 'Nancy' had been written for his baby daughter, 'Linda' had been written for Linda Eastman, the daughter of a show business lawyer, in 1947. The song had been a success for both Ray Noble's orchestra with Buddy Clark and Paul Weston's with Matt Dennis. Frank gave a fun-loving performance in an arrangement featuring electric organ.

In the ghost story, *The Uninvited* (1944), directed by Lewis Allen, Ray Milland played the piano. When he is asked the title, he says it was a serenade called 'To Stella by Starlight'. The lyricist Ned Washington had to write a lyric to fit. The song had a suitably moody presence and was ideal for Sinatra.

Sinatra sang 'Emily', a Johnny Mercer song written for the Julie Andrews film, *The Americanisation Of Emily* (1964), but only heard on the soundtrack album. The one new song on the session was 'Barbara', written by Jimmy Van Heusen with Hal David's brother, Mack. It was surprising that Frank hadn't had a hand in the lyric himself. He sang the song first in Las Vegas so that Barbara would get a surprise. The line 'Wherever she is, I'll be there' might have been more accurately written as 'Wherever I am, she'll be there.' And she was. Five good performances had been recorded for *Here's to the Ladies* but then Sinatra lost interest and the album wasn't completed.

And talking of losing interest, 52-year-old Peter Lawford, stoned on Quaaludes, married 25-year-old Deborah Gould in Virginia. The next morning he couldn't remember getting married, but they kept it together for a couple of months.

In March 1977 Frank was back in London, the first performer to play a week of concerts at the Royal Albert Hall. He was supported by a large orchestra, the comedian Pat Henry and Fifth Dimension. Both Princess Margaret and Ava Gardner came to see him. Unusually, he was trying new songs on stage: Barry Manilow's 'Why Don't You See the Show Again', 'I Love My Wife' and Elton John's 'Sorry Seems to Be the Hardest Word', certainly a title that would appeal to him. Sinatra had plans to record 'Why Don't You See the Show Again' but Streisand told him that the lyric wasn't right for him and he dropped it.

Frank recorded a TV special, *Sinatra and Friends*, which was broadcast in April. The celebrity-packed guest list was Tony Bennett, Natalie Cole, John Denver, Loretta Lynn, Dean Martin, Robert Merrill and Leslie Uggams, and the whole cast sang 'Where or When' and Paul Anka's 'Everybody Ought To Be in Love'. John Denver, some 28 years younger than Frank, was a mismatched partner for 'September Song' and Loretta Lynn stepped away from country for a disco duet of 'All or Nothing at All'. He, Dean and Robert Merrill sang a big-voiced 'The Oldest Established' from *Guys and Dolls*.

The British songwriter Bill Martin recalled, 'Jan and I met Frank Sinatra personally in 1977. Sammy Cahn had given me a letter to see Sinatra in Las Vegas. It was in Caesars Palace and I was with Larry Page, the Teenage Rage, and our wives as his wife Lee was my wife's best friend. We got a call from Jilly Rizzo and we were told that we could see Mr Sinatra but we were not to shake hands. Sinatra never shook hands as he said that was how you caught germs. Also, we weren't to take photographs and there must be no kissing. We went up to see him and as soon as he saw Jan, who was very attractive, he said, "Oh, hi" and kissed her. He said, "I am really sorry, kids. I am not singing tonight because I have got the desert throat, but I have got a great replacement and you will love him." It was Paul Anka. I didn't like to say, "Oh, shit", but I was so disappointed. Paul Anka was good but he was no Frank Sinatra.'

In 1977 Elvis's former bodyguards wrote a warts-and-all book about their life with the King: well, just warts, really. Frank was horrified by this lack of trust and rang Elvis and told him that he could use his influence to have the book pulped and his bodyguards punished. Elvis, deciding things were bad enough already, wisely decided that this might make it worse. Whether Frank could have delivered on his promise is another matter.

Elvis Presley died in August 1977, aged 42 and a victim of his own excesses; Bing Crosby died on a Spanish golf course, aged 74 in October. Bing had died happy, his final words being, 'That was a great game of golf, fellas.' Frank had been used to his friends dying of unnatural causes but now they had reached the age where they were dying of natural causes.

In October 1977, Frank was eating in Patsy's restaurant in New York and he found that the Yankees were celebrating their World Series victory over Frank's team, the LA Dodgers. He told their shortstop, Bucky Dent, 'Kid, you cost me a lot of money but you played a great game.' Frank then picked up the tab for their meal.

Frank had been a forerunner in a campaign to discourage the identification of gangsters in ethnic terms. The release of *The Godfather* put paid to all that. As Frank had loathed *The Godfather* and hated TV movies, it seemed odd that he agreed to star in a TV movie about the Mafia, *Contract on Cherry Street*. However, it was based on a novel that Dolly Sinatra had recommended to him. The film, in which he co-starred with Martin Balsam, was made on location in New York. Sinatra played a tough cop but he was called Inspector Clouseau after a botched bust, which only strengthened his resolve. After his partner was killed, he wanted to bring the killers to justice. He broke the rules and somehow kept his job and stayed out of jail. Jay Black of Jay and the Americans was one of the gangsters and took part in the final shoot out with Sinatra. The reviews were mixed but Sinatra was praised. Sinatra commented, 'I'm dying to do a good comedy right now, but try and find one.'

In 1978 Frank was back in the UK, this time at the Royal Festival Hall with Guys 'n' Dolls, Lennie Bennett and Jerry Stevens. Bill Miller was conducting but the pianist Vinnie Falcone, was being groomed to take over. This time he included 'Remember' from Elton John and Bernie Taupin, 'The Groom Couldn't Get In', a comedy number from Joe E Lewis's set, 'That's What God Looks Like', and as a tribute to English bandleader and songwriter, Ray Noble, who had died in April 1978, 'I Hadn't Anyone Til You'. The *New Musical Express* commented that he was 'more multi-dimensional than Tony Bennett'.

On a charity show in Israel, Frank sang Eric Carmen's US hit, 'All by Myself' but it wasn't too much of a stretch for him as it was based on Rachmaninov's 2nd piano concerto.

In May 1978 Plastic Bertrand (Roger Jouret) from Belgium has an international hit with 'Ça Plane pour Moi' and said his ambition was to be the next Frank Sinatra. We're still waiting. Nobody wanted to be the next Dick Haymes. In 1978 his marriage broke up and he was arrested for drunk driving. He was playing to senior citizens in small clubs. He wrote in his diary, 'I feel I am sucking on the blood of bloodless old people for money.'

Sammy Davis starred in a Broadway revival of *Stop the World – I Want To Get Off*, which opened to mixed reviews. Sammy said, 'Sinatra and I have the closest of relationships. When I did *Stop the World*, there were six notices: three were great, one was mediocre and two were terrible. Sinatra was so upset. He sent me a cable telling me not to make excuses or to put myself down.'

An early example of car crash television was the TV roasting of well-known personalities. Dean Martin had started a *Roast of the Week* on *The Dean Martin Show*, the first one being Ronald Reagan, the event being hosted by the celebrities' charity, the Friars Club. By 1975 there was a full-blown programme, *Dean Martin's Celebrity Roast* in which Dean would host a meal with famous friends who told scurrilous stories about the man or woman of the hour. The first ones in 1975 were with Lucille Ball and Jackie Gleason; NBC regarded them as expensive, special events which would be much talked about. They ran two a year. It was a nasty programme, dishing up the dirt but expecting the subject to a good sport and laugh about it. Thankfully, Dean knew how to keep the whole thing good-natured. In November 1976 Frank had appeared on the roasting of John Wayne.

In 1978 it was his turn. The programme came from the Ziegfeld Room at the MGM Grand. Dean started the ball rolling with, 'Nobody knew Frank Sinatra had lent money to New York until they found the Statue of Liberty with her arms broken.' On the same theme, Gene Kelly said, 'If you said you liked his tie, he would send you one. If you liked his suit, he would send you one. If you said you liked his girl, he would send round two guys.' Dean Martin joked, 'His hobby as a child was amateur gynaecology,' and he added, 'When he dies, they're going to hang his zipper in the Hall of Fame.' Milton Berle said, 'Frank, I'm really glad you came out of retirement – too bad your voice didn't join you.' These were exactly the kind of insults that would have them ostracised if they'd been said at a party, and judging by Frank's face, the whole show was a bit touch-and-go. Perhaps the most telling remark came from Jilly Rizzo. He said that his most regular line to Frank was 'I'll be waiting in the car.'

Sonny Burke had worked out a concept for a triple album by Frank Sinatra called *Trilogy*. It would be in three sections: Past, Present and Future. The Past would find Sinatra recording standards that he had not performed before; the Present would be songs of today; and the Future would be looking forward where Gordon Jenkins would put some of Sinatra's reflections to music. *The Future* was mirroring the concept albums, *A Man Alone* and *Watertown* and his single, *The House I Live In*. Sinatra hadn't done any serious recording for five years but Burke knew he would fall for this. He did. Sinatra said, 'We will not do another thing until we do this.'

Sinatra chose to make *The Past* with Billy May and of the three albums, it is the most successful. Unfortunately, as so often happened, Frank retreated to his comfort zone by reviving familiar items. Still, he has never sung 'Let's Face the Music and Dance' with such gusto before. Both Frank and the arrangement are full of humour and there is an exhilarating instrumental section. When Frank was looking over the score, he said to Billy May, 'What's that at the end?' 'Wait and see,' said Billy May, 'You'll like it.' Frank gave the song all he'd got and then there is a coda, not of fiddlers, but a brass riff which is a nod to mariachi bands. As it might be associated with bullfights, this might even be a sly reference to Ava, who knows? Nevertheless, Frank liked it.

Sinatra had not recorded the Gershwin's 'But Not for Me' before. It came from *Crazy Girl* (1930) where it was sung by Ginger Rogers, but it is more associated with *Girl Crazy* (1943) and Judy Garland. Frank sang the introductory verse and the reference to Beatrice Fairfax is to a prototype agony aunt. Similarly, 'When a feller needs a friend' was a reference to a cartoon series by Clare Briggs. The trombonist Dick Nash was asked to revive his 'Tommy Dorsey shit' and the vocal group aped the Pied Pipers. Plus there's a little pun at the end 'No knot for me'. This recording was used in both Woody Allen's *Manhattan* and the British rom-com *Four Weddings and a Funeral*.

Sinatra had recorded 'Street of Dreams' twice before and he wanted to record it again. Billy May said he couldn't get excited about it because the song was too short. Indeed, the

Ink Spots had sung the same section three times. Sinatra pointed out that there was a verse, which had been performed by Bing Crosby (1932) and Tony Bennett (1959), but which anchored the lyric to drug addiction.

'Come on and trade in your old dreams for new
Your new dreams for old
I know where they're bought
I know where they're sold
Midnight, you've got to get there at midnight
And you'll be met there by others like you
Brothers as blue
Smiling on the street of dreams.'

'Fuck it,' said Sinatra, 'We'll just make a short record.' Billy May wrote a long outro, which continued for 40 seconds after Sinatra stopped singing. Sinatra thought the ending could be employed as a concert closer, a good way to scram at the end of a show, but after 'New York, New York' became such a hit, it could only be that.

Frank must have thought of recording 'It Had To Be You' many times but he didn't get round to it until now. It had been introduced by Eddie Cantor in 1924 and Sinatra was on top form. The song was revived with great success by Harry Connick Jr on the soundtrack of *When Harry Met Sally...* in 1989, a film which performed a valuable public service by introducing pre-war standards to a young audience.

The Gershwins' 'They All Laughed' was introduced by Fred Astaire and Ginger Rogers when they danced on a rooftop restaurant in Manhattan in *Shall We Dance* (1937). Billy May's humorous arrangement included guffaws from the band (Frank's idea) and it takes time to realise that this is a love song. It's very enjoyable but sadly, the only recording by Frank of this classic song verged on novelty.

Another new song for Sinatra was 'I Had the Craziest Dream', a success for Harry James with Helen Forrest in 1943. The singer blended beautifully with the chorus, but, by Sinatra standards, this was a deadpan vocal. The trumpeter, Charlie Turner, who played with Sinatra on the road, captured Harry James' style.

Also new to Sinatra was Johnny Mercer and Harold Arlen's 'My Shining Hour', which came from *The Sky's The Limit* (1943), the same source as 'One for My Baby. Frank told the orchestra, 'I can't believe I never got to this one.' It's a lovely performance and sung like an anthem. On hearing the take, Frank said, 'That's nice.'

'More than You Know' came from the Broadway show, *Great Day* (1929), which was unlucky enough to open the day before the stock market crashed. A film version was halted after Joan Crawford rebelled against speaking 'baby talk'. Still, it was a nice ballad which Streisand sang in *Funny Lady*. Sinatra gave it a blues feel and Chuck Finley's improvised a flugelhorn solo. Frank liked saying to people, 'Do you know 'More Than You Know'? That's an oxymoron.'

At the last minute, Sinatra dropped 'The Surrey with the Fringe on Top' declaring the Rodgers and Hammerstein song 'a bunch of shit'. He replaced it with 'All of You' from the Broadway musical, *Silk Stockings* (1955). The backstage shenanigans for the musical would make a play in itself as one key person after another was replaced. The constant factor was Cole Porter's score, which included a love song that was sung by Don Ameche, 'All of You'. The stage musical became a film in 1957 starring Fred Astaire and Cyd Charisse. The song sounds tame today but the idea of wanting all of you was controversial. Sinatra sang an unobjectionable lyric, opting for 'The sweet of you and the pure of you' over "I'd love to make a tour of you'.

There were another 10 songs on *The Present*, eight of which were new to Sinatra. He had previously sung 'Love Me Tender' on his 1960 TV special with Elvis Presley. As it went back to the 19th century, it hardly qualified for *The Present* but the track itself was pleasant enough.

Sinatra sang George Harrison's 'Something' again, this time with a Nelson Riddle arrangement and conducted by Vinnie Falcone. The critic Will Friedwald wrote that Sinatra 'makes Something out of nothing', an amusing critique but unfair. It was an excellent song and the arrangement made very good use of violins. Sinatra emerged from the bridge with a small, trembling voice which was very effective. However, his comment, 'You hang around, Jack' misfired. Like Paul Simon with 'Mrs Robinson', George Harrison didn't care for these embellishments but, unlike Simon, he took it in good spirits. When he appeared on tour in Japan with Eric Clapton, he was adding comments about Jack to his own performances, revealing once again his sense of humour.

Curtis Stigers comments, 'There are some questionable moments like that 'Jack' in 'Something' when those pop/jazz singers like Frank Sinatra and Tony Bennett were trying to keep in vogue. They couldn't compete with the Beatles and the Stones and perhaps they should have taken the decade off and gone to the beach. I wouldn't do a swing version of 'Stairway to Heaven' but I have become more daring. I have been looking at some Kinks songs as Ray Davies writes these really cool tunes – strange but cool. It is worth turning these songs into standards but 'Something' was a good choice for Sinatra as it was already a little jazzy.'

Chris Riddle, Nelson's son, confides, 'My father was troubled by the onslaught of rock'n'roll. He felt that it was replacing him and his type of music. He viewed it as a threat but as with all threats, you have got to make peace with it as it was here to stay. He wrote arrangements for some Beatle tunes, not least of which is 'Something', which does have some old-fashioned romanticism about it. I think that when Frank put the 'Jack' in, he was saying, 'This is mine now.' It's like a dog or cat marking out its territory.'

But there is evidence that Frank liked George Harrison's songwriting. George's sister, Louise says, 'George was not over impressed when Sinatra recorded 'Something' and on one occasion at the Plaza, he spent the whole evening hiding in a closet as Frank's people were looking for him. Frank wanted George to write a whole album for him and they were not the kind of people he wanted to be involved with. There is a photo of the two of them together on the back of an album so they got together later on.'

Barney Kessel said, 'When you are performing standards, you are not living in the past because we find these songs – the songs of Kern, Gershwin, Porter and Berlin – so superior to most of the songs today. If you're going to do a play, you might as well do Shakespeare as there is so much more content to it. I just want to play beautiful songs that have been well conceived by someone with good musical taste and 90% of what I hear today is rubbish. It is only made for the money. It is made to sell sexual innuendoes and to appeal to a drug-oriented society and these songs have no appeal to me. I'm living in the present, but I do like old songs. Good music is timeless, just like Shakespeare, just like Keats and Byron, just like the Rolls-Royce automobile and Sir Laurence Olivier. Time does not deteriorate their worth.'

The most uncomfortable arrangement was for Kris Kristofferson's 'For the Good Times' as Sinatra shares the song with the operatic soprano Eileen Farrell. It's a curious mix and the wrong song for the purpose. Sinatra did this better on his own in concert.

Michael Feinstein comments, 'Many extraordinarily talented opera singers cannot sing popular songs very well. There are a few notable examples, but most of them have not done it successfully. Dorothy Kirsten did some beautiful recordings of Gershwin and Kern in the 1950s. I'm not crazy about the way Eileen Farrell sang popular songs. Her voice as an opera singer was exquisite, and her voice as a pop singer I thought was very average.'

When Frank had been at the Royal Albert Hall, the Australian singer/songwriter Peter Allen had given him a new song, 'We Wanted It All'. Don Costa came up with a strong arrangement and he changed the title to 'You and Me'. Vinnie Falcone was asked to conduct this as his audition piece, and then he replaced Bill Miller as Frank's concert conductor. When Alice Cooper was on the BBC programme, *Desert Island Discs*, this was one of his eight selections.

Frank Sinatra singing 'MacArthur Park' sounded intriguing. It could easily be a triumph or a disaster, but, as it happens, it was neither. This is like 'Stardust' where Sinatra sang only the least-known section; here there was nothing about a cake being out in the rain. It became a reflection of lost love, rather like 'Lush Life'.

Originally Frank had intended to sing 'Just the Way You Are' as a ballad in the Billy Joel tradition. Vinnie Falcone suggested that he could swing it and so Don Costa gave it the Basie treatment. It's a very full sound with 55 musicians and Sinatra loved the dynamics of the arrangement. Another track from the sessions, Stevie Wonder's 'Isn't She Lovely', wasn't released at the time but it's another arrangement which would have suited the Basie band.

The vocal chorus of Neil Diamond's 'Song Sung Blue' was corny but maybe that's the point. The song was about how music can make you happy and was only one up from a nursery rhyme. It's unusual for a Sinatra record to fade out and even though it didn't stretch him, the musicians applauded after the take. It's banal and it was chosen in preference to a new Elton John and Bernie Taupin song, 'Remember', which had been written for him. Frank recorded the track but it was not issued at the time.

Barbara was taking a keen interest in her new husband's activities and she recommended 'New York, New York', the theme from a 1977 film which had starred Robert DeNiro as a saxophonist and Liza Minnelli as an aspiring singer. Minnelli had made the song her own and Barbara thought that it would suit Frank. He said, 'No, that's Liza's song. I couldn't possibly do it.' Barbara wouldn't take no for an answer; she had ways of making him change his mind. Frank hated the silent treatment and Barbara was good at that.

'New York, New York' had a brash, swaggering arrangement from Don Costa which epitomised New York. It is a brilliant performance of a song denoting worldly success, although the composers had intended some irony. It became a showstopper and Sinatra used the opening vamp to tease audiences. Soon it was being sung at the end of the New York Yankees' games.

The Bergmans and Michel Legrand are represented by 'Summer Me, Winter Me', which harked back to the sound of *Sinatra and Strings* and had originally been recorded by Johnny Mathis. The weakest track was a new song, 'That's What God Looks Like', in which Lois Irwin and Lan O'Kun had converted his musings on about religion from the 1962 *Playboy* interview into a song. It set the scene for *The Future*, which is a fantasy built around Sinatra's thoughts and dreams.

The Future is the most difficult part of the package. It was totally written, arranged and conducted by Gordon Jenkins and it was recorded in December 1979 at the Shrine Auditorium because a smaller studio couldn't accommodate 150 musicians and singers. Unfortunately, nobody let a decent melody into the room and most of the time Sinatra is rabbiting away about peace and space travel.

While the orchestra tuned up, Sinatra introduced himself. He talked about the future and sang about visiting other planets. He will know Heaven if he is greeted with a cheese and tomato pizza and red wine. (Honest, I'm not making this up.) There was a hymn to end fighting, 'World War None!', and Sinatra sang that 'A bombsite can't replace a stained glass window.'

'The Future' itself opened with a 12-bar blues sung by Jenkins' wife, Beverly Mahr. There followed a bombastic instrumental section as Sinatra reflected on conducting. Then Sinatra sang a song that he hoped everybody would understand 'I've Been There!', leaving the opera singers, Loulie Jean Norman and Beverly Jenkins, to ask what he would do now.

The finale, 'Before the Music Ends', was a rambling Vegas monologue set to music. Where was he going? Voices urged him, 'Francis, don't go home again.' When Frank mentioned Lefty, he was referring to Gordon Jenkins. His reference to 'baby having 57 pairs of shoes' may be about Barbara. Who knows and who cares? Frank delivered all this nonsense with conviction, clearly flattered by the whole nonsensical project.

It is hard to decry *The Future* when it has been made with so much effort but you lose the will to live as you listen. Where's Rod McKuen now that we need him? The reviews of *The Future* were almost universally terrible – Sinatra's equivalent to Bob Dylan's *Self Portrait* or Lou Reed's *Metal Machine Music*. Sinatra shrugged it off. He said that critics who put down *The Future* didn't understand it. But nor did the fans. What's more, the years have not been kind to *The Future*. Unlike *Watertown*, it has not been reappraised. It does have some supporters but they're wrong.

Frank himself lived with this curious mixture of past, present and future. In September 1979 he was back playing with Harry James in Caesars Palace, and in December 1979 NBC hosted a 40th anniversary special in Caesars Palace titled *The First 40 Years*. Two huge oil paintings of Sinatra were erected outside Caesars Palace, and over 1,000 friends and associates were there to greet him. The event, which was televised by NBC in January 1980, was hosted by Cary Grant and included performances from Paul Anka (singing 'My Way' to Frank), Tony Bennett, Sammy Davis and Harry James as well as Frank himself. Dean Martin, Orson Welles, Glenn Ford and Gene Kelly were amongst those who paid tribute. The high point was when Robert Merrill put all Frank's film titles into one song.

Tommy Roe, who is known for 'Sheila' and 'Dizzy' recalls, 'I have been married 33 years to Josette Banzet, who is a very talented actress. She was in *The Other Side Of Midnight* and *Rich Man, Poor Man*. She won a Golden Globe for *Rich Man, Poor Man*. She had a home in Palm Springs two doors down from Frank Sinatra and she knew him very well. We went to a restaurant one evening and Frank and his crew were sitting in the corner. Josette sees him and says, "Hey Frank. look at my bodyguard" as Josette liked to call him my road manager her bodyguard as he was 6 foot 7 and weighed 280, a huge guy. Frank came over and gave her a big hug and said, "Hey, baby, how ya doing?" She says, "Frank, I want you to meet my boyfriend, Tommy Roe, and this is my bodyguard Ken." Frank laughed, "You don't need a bodyguard when I'm around, baby. I'm your bodyguard." He was a great guy with incredible charisma, both on and off stage.'

Apart from his world tour in 1962, Frank had not travelled much during his career, but now with Barbara beside him, he would go wherever the money was right and there was potential for much greater rewards outside Vegas. In September 1979, he gave a concert in front of the Pyramids with the audience seated on Persian rugs. He wanted to appear in China and Russia and although he asked the State officials to help, nothing came of it.

The awards were coming in thick and fast. He received an honorary diploma from Hoboken High and a Frank Sinatra Chair was established at Santa Clara University in California. There was the opening of the Frank Sinatra International Student Centre in Jerusalem.

Frank rejected the role of a patriarch modelled on Joe Kennedy in *Winter Kills*, based on Richard Condon's novel. The role was played by John Huston and the cast included Jeff Brides, Tony Perkins, Eli Wallach and Elizabeth Taylor. Anyone versed in Sinatra's way would have known he wouldn't do it. Frank never played any character older than himself.

CHAPTER 17

They can't take that away from me

'You only live once, and the way I've lived, once is enough.'
Frank Sinatra

'When you've loved and lost the way Frank has, then you know what life is all about.'
Chauffeur, *This Is Spinal Tap*, 1984

Day In–Day Out, 1980–1998

In January 1980 Frank was back for his customary New Year's season at Caesars Palace at $35 a ticket, but for that you were getting an overhaul. He gave a one hour show and included four songs from *Trilogy* – 'I've Been There', 'It Had to Be You', 'Summer Me, Winter Me' and naturally 'New York, New York'. He opened with 'I Hear Music' and he sang 'The Best Is Yet to Come', and in a way it was.

The pinnacle of Sinatra's career came on 26 January 1980 when he performed for the largest paying audience ever assembled for a solo performer. 175,000 fans saw him at a huge sporting arena, the Maracana Stadium in Rio de Janeiro. It was hot, humid and had been raining heavily but he gave the performance of his career, opening, amusingly, with 'The Coffee Song'. The Brazilian press said that Sinatra, by using an American orchestra, was siphoning money from their economy and taking it to the States, but Sinatra, who was never short of an answer, said in his usual diplomatic way that Pelé had been taking money from America and bringing it to Brazil.

On 15 February 1980, Barbara organised a charity gala in Palm Springs, *Frank, his Friends and Food*. She tried a few new recipes and indeed a Frank Sinatra cook book was on the way.

Dick Haymes died of lung cancer on 28 March 1980. During his final weeks, he kept asking if Frank Sinatra had called, but he heard nothing. The publicity had never gone his way – he had been seen as a draft dodger and an abusive husband and had never had a second chance like Frank. He had become a grumpy alcoholic. Most of all, he regretted never becoming friendly with Frank. Frank said from time to time that he had admired his phrasing but that was it. The following year the vocalist Bob Eberly died, also from cancer. Frank had taken care of both the hospital and the funeral bills as Eberly had little money.

The First Deadly Sin was a best-selling crime novel by Lawrence Sanders and the intention was to film it with Marlon Brando as the rule-bending New York detective with Roman Polanski as the screenwriter and director. The project was dropped in 1977, when Polanski fled the country on a rape charge, but was picked up by Brian Hutton who had directed *Where Eagles Dare* and *Kelly's Heroes*.

Frank Sinatra, who had read and enjoyed the book, agreed to play for the first time in his life someone who was about to retire, although he wanted to nail a serial killer first.

Faye Dunaway played Sinatra's sick wife, a role that called for little speech and much less movement, yet somehow her agent secured $750,000 for this performance. Martin Gabel stumbled over a line but that could be because Frank was not doing retakes. David Dukes was concurrently playing a prisoner in a concentration camp in *Bent* on Broadway and so he wore a hairpiece for his role as the killer. It's more fun trying to spot Bruce Willis in an uncredited role than working out the plot.

New York was depicted as dark and desolate and *The First Deadly Sin* was relentlessly depressing with a downbeat ending. Sinatra commented, 'They've given us an R rating, we can't understand why.' The intention to make a sequel fell to pieces when it had a commercial and critical drubbing.

Sinatra never made another feature film, although there were possibilities. The writer and director Peter Bogdanovich pitched a movie about a team of gamblers who didn't speak to each other until the end of the film. He thought it might be a Rat Pack project. Sinatra said okay but Dean's response was 'Who gives a fuck?', thereby putting an end to it.

There was talk of a Frank Sinatra bio-pic. When he learnt that he was going to be played by David Bowie, he went into overdrive saying that he was not going to be 'played by a faggot'. Frank didn't make the more obvious criticism, that David Bowie could hardly match Sinatra's singing voice.

While in New York, Frank associated with Luciano Pavarotti. He wanted to keep his voice in shape and he was gathering tips from the best. He said to Pavarotti, 'How do you end a long crescendo?' 'That's easy,' said Pavarotti, 'You just shut your mouth.'

Sinatra stopped smoking, although he still had a cigarette as a prop for his saloon songs. He no longer drank Jack Daniel's before a show and turned more towards tea and honey. Not that you would have thought that judging by the cover of his next album, *She Shot Me Down* (1981): he was covered in smoke, drinking Jack Daniel's and to add to the coolness, was wearing a black leather jacket.

But when he wasn't working Frank was still drinking heavily. He could drink a bottle of Jack Daniel's in a day. Barbara commented that he was an entertaining drunk on whiskey but gin made him mean. Once he was so drunk that he threatened to tear up the bar at the Waldorf-Astoria. Barbara received a 4am call to come and deal with him, and she managed to sort it out.

The three-LP set, *Trilogy*, had been priced at $21 and despite a higher price than its competitors, it made the US Top 20 albums and sold 500,000 copies. Customers had to purchase *The Past*, *The Present* and *The Future* together, but *The Past* was the most popular album and in most cases *The Future* would only have been played once – or perhaps twice if somebody couldn't believe what they were hearing. By default, Gordon Jenkins' monstrosity was a best seller.

The score for *The First Deadly Sin* was composed and conducted by Jenkins and although *Trilogy* gave the appearance of being Frank's last word, he talked him into making another album while he was filming in New York. *She Shot Me Down* (1981) is a good album if somewhat underrated and is far, far better than anything on *The Future*. Indeed, Gordon Jenkins' own song about how opposites attract, 'I Loved Her', is delightful. Sinatra sang, 'She was Boston, I was Vegas' and 'She was Mozart, I was Basie' and I wished that they had been a little more of the same.

There were two excellent love songs from Alec Wilder. Sinatra dismissed the cool look on his girl's face and said he was heading 'South – To A Warmer Place'. 'A Long Night' was a dramatic saloon song, as bleak as *film noir*. 'No daylight,' sang Sinatra, 'just a long night for me.'

The theme of lost love ran through the album. 'Monday Morning Quarterback' was about the ease of seeing things with hindsight whether it be a football game or a relationship and 'Thanks For The Memory' had been given new lyrics about his time in London and Malibu, although it's hard to believe that Frank went jogging in London. There was 'Hey Look, No Crying' from *Pieces from Eight*, a little-known musical by Jule Styne and Susan Birkenhead.

After eight years, Frank and Gordon returned to 'Bang Bang', and this time the track was released, effectively the title song. Cher almost dismissed the line 'Just for me the church bells rang' but Gordon Jenkins turned into an orchestral spectacular.

The album included two tracks with Don Costa. Sammy Cahn's 'Say Hello' had an old razzle dazzle workout while 'Good Thing Going', a Sondheim song from *Merrily We Roll Along*, became a Bacharach ballad. Vinnie Falcone had the concept of merging two Nelson Riddle arrangements for the medley, 'The Gal that Got Away'/'It Never Entered My Mind'. Meanwhile, Nelson Riddle was busying himself by writing the arrangements for *Top Hat*, an instrumental tribute to Fred Astaire from Yehudi Menuhin and Stéphane Grappelli.

Sinatra came to London in September 1980 for a week of concerts at the Royal Festival Hall, which Sinatra declared had 'the finest acoustics in the world, better than Carnegie Hall.' This was followed by a week at the Royal Albert Hall and in both series of concerts he was supported by Sergio Mendes Brasil '88, although not working with them. Sinatra told the press, 'I could have ended with a bombastic ballad but I put 'Chicago', 'A Foggy Day (In London Town)' and 'New York, New York' together. I got the idea on the plane coming over. The audiences really jumped and down with that 'New York' thing. I had a marvellous time.' On a couple of occasions, tears were streaming down Frank's face as he came off stage.

Sammy Cahn talked about the big surprise of the concerts, 'When he came to London in 1980, he asked me to write him new lyrics to Cole Porter's 'Let's Do It'. He called me and said, "Sam, you did some lyrics for Vegas. Could you change them for London?" I said, "When do you want them?" He said, "Now." I said, "Why didn't you call me from the stage?" I called Jackie Collins, who lives in Beverly Hills, and I said, "Jackie, I need some information about England." She gave that to me and some names like Mrs Whitehouse went into the lyric. It was incredibly well received.' The lyric included:

'Birds do it, bees do it,
History proves a few MPs do it,
Let's do it, let's fall in love.
And likewise,
Lords do it, earls do it,
Boys with boys and girls with girls do it,
Let's do it, let's fall in love.
'And Margaret Thatcher I hear does it
And the Prime's in her prime,
With cool veneer does it
When does she find the time?'

'The thing about Frank Sinatra, Nat 'King' Cole and Dean Martin is that they had the greatest songwriters of the twentieth century waiting to get calls from them,' says Curtis Stigers, 'They might call Sammy Cahn and have him write another verse to something: "I'm doing a show in Baltimore and I need a verse about Baltimore." It was an amazing period. I was either born too late or too early I'm not sure which.'

Mark Ellen was on the editorial staff at the *New Musical Express*, now fervently promoting the new punk sounds. 'It is exciting to think that I even saw Sinatra. I was working with Anton Corbijn, now a great photographer and film director, and we were living in a terrible old squat and we used to love Sinatra. We had very broad tastes and the *NME* was a very narrow church, very parochial. Ant and I went to see Frank Sinatra and we didn't dare tell anybody in the office that we were doing it. It was a sackable offence. He was a weird, orange skinned man and these heavily made up matrons would go up and leave very expensive gifts on the stage. There seemed something decadent about it all as if he didn't care, but he did produce his music in a fond way. He sang really well but I remember laughing with Anton and thinking, 'Rock'n'roll will never come to this. It will never be turned into a monstrous cabaret, but of course it has.'

In July 1981, Sinatra created controversy by appearing at Sun City, Bophuthatswana, but it was a complex issue. Bophuthatswana had been declared an independent state by the South African government, although it was still South Africa to the rest of the world. There was a 6,000 seat auditorium and as they could provide gambling and nude shows, it became a holiday resort for residents in Johannesburg. The UN had imposed a cultural and sporting boycott on South Africa so long as it practised apartheid, but some entertainers convinced themselves that it was okay to play Sun City. Among those who went to Sun City were Frank Sinatra, Paul Anka, Rod Stewart and Elton John, Sinatra being the first major stars to play there. Frank maintained that playing Sun City was part of his campaign against apartheid, but he was being used by the apartheid government.

In October 1981 Frank appeared in concert with Fifth Dimension and Bob Newhart for St John's Health Centre, a Roman Catholic hospital in Santa Monica. They raised $1m, a spectacular amount for a night's work.

Frank made another TV special which was broadcast in November 1981. For most of the show, he was working with Don Costa and his Orchestra, but he also performed 'Pennies from Heaven' and 'The Best Is Yet to Come' with Count Basie and his Orchestra along with a short Latin section accompanied by the guitarist Tony Mottola.

Nancy Reagan wanted to initiate the Foster Grandparents Programme and she asked Frank about a theme song. Hal David and Joe Raposo wrote 'To Love a Child', which was recorded by Frank and Don Costa's nine-year-old daughter, Nikka. Her album, *Nikka Costa*, was already a best seller in Italy. As well as recording the song, they performed it on the White House launch for the charity.

In 1982 Sinatra was again the nearly man when it came to some big movies. A number of leading actors – Robert Redford, William Holden, Dustin Hoffman, Roy Schneider and Cary Grant – turned down the lead role in *The Verdict*, a courtroom drama written by David Mamet. The producers thought that Sinatra could play the alcoholic and ageing lawyer as indeed he could. The director, Sidney Lumet, felt he would be too much trouble and went with Paul Newman.

In that same year, Martin Scorsese needed a comic host like Johnny Carson to play alongside Robert DeNiro in *King of Comedy*. He tried Carson himself but Carson didn't think he would transfer well to the big screen. Then he considered Frank Sinatra and Dean Martin before settling on Jerry Lewis, whom, it must be said, was a revelation. He acted like Ed Sullivan or Milton Berle, who were both expressionless with jerky movements, and the film was very successful.

There was also talk of making a new version of *Born Yesterday*, a 1950 film starring Judy Holliday, Broderick Crawford and William Holden. The new version would star Al Pacino and Frank Sinatra but nothing came of it; the film was remade in 1993 with neither of them.

On 24 January 1982 Frank recorded a concert at Radio City Music Hall where he was backed by George Shearing. He also sang 'Santa Lucia' and 'O Sole Mio' with Pavarotti. He commented, 'It would be fun to be a tenor. They make such an exciting sound.'

Frank took part in the inaugural gala for President Reagan. He was very well received but he was upstaged by the comic Rich Little giving a masterclass in how to perform like Sinatra. It involved lots of pointing. Frank was reunited with Nelson Riddle for this event and they considered completing *Here's to the Ladies* although Nelson thought they should work on standards that Frank had never recorded. However, his only vocal session in 1982 was for two songs by Sammy Cahn and Jule Styne, 'Love Makes Us Whatever We Want to Be' and 'Searching'. Neither was released at the time.

Barbara wanted to promote a new range of Italian food under Sinatra's name, but unfortunately, Paul Newman was launching his Italian products at the same time. The public found Newman's food more appetising and after 18 months, the Sinatra brand had disappeared from the shelves. While promoting *The Verdict*, Paul Newman commented, 'I ran Sinatra out of the spaghetti sauce business.' He was probably taken off Sinatra's Christmas card list.

Around 40 years earlier, Billie Holiday had introduced Frank to the New York song stylist, Sylvia Syms. She was short and round and called herself 'a dumpy little Jewish broad from Brooklyn.' She had a lived-in voice but used to it to her advantage on well-chosen material. She said, 'This voice isn't clear or beautiful but it's me and it's real.' Frank used to call her 'Buddha' and he had wanted to make an album with her for some time. Both of them are shown on the cover of *Syms by Sinatra*, but Sinatra doesn't sing a note although she wanted him on 'Honeysuckle Rose'. She sang well despite poor health as she had had a lung removed due to cancer and suffered from emphysema. She could hardly climb the stairs. In 1992 she collapsed and died while singing 'My Heart Is so Full of You' from *The Most Happy Fella* at the Algonquin Hotel in New York.

After the newspaperman Frank Garrick let Frank down in 1932, Dolly cut him off and never spoke to him again. It is unlikely that Frank would have repaired the friendship during Dolly's lifetime. In 1982 he met up with the 85-year-old Garrick and his wife who lived in sheltered accommodation in Hoboken. He came with Jilly Rizzo and his secretary, Dorothy Uhlemann and he gave them a fruit basket and $500.

In July 1983, Frank made a guest appearance in *Cannonball Run II*, which starred Burt Reynolds, Dean Martin, Sammy Davis and Shirley MacLaine. MacLaine said that no one had bothered to read the script before shooting. During his four hours on set, Sinatra engaged in some light-hearted banter with Burt Reynolds and that's about it. He came and left by helicopter with Jilly Rizzo permanently at his side. The film included some outtakes at the end where Frank was amused when Dom DeLuise fumbled his lines. The film opened in Japan six months before the US, which said it all really.

Frank and Buddy Rich had repaired their on-off relationship and they did some concerts together. In August, their performance in the Dominican Republic was filmed and shown as a TV special, *Concert for the Americas*, in November. As well as Frank doing his standards, Tony Mottola accompanied him for 'Send in the Clowns' and Buddy Rich played his electrifying suite from *West Side Story*.

On 13 September 1982, while out driving in Monaco, Princess Grace had a stroke and crashed down a mountainside. She was 52 years old and she died in hospital the following day. Her daughter, Princess Stéphanie suffered a serious cervical fracture. Prince Rainier never remarried and in 2005 he was buried alongside her. James Stewart said in his eulogy, 'You know, I just love Grace Kelly. Not because she was a princess, not because she was an actress, not because she was my friend, but because she was just about the nicest lady I ever met.' Frank took part in a charity event for the Red Cross that was staged in Monte Carlo in her honour in August 1983.

Frank still looked for opportunities. In 1984 Frank and Willie Nelson played a double-top at the Golden Nugget but Sinatra had to drop out after the first night because of a problem with his throat. He did think of making an album with Willie, which would have been interesting as they both had very esoteric phrasing. However, he didn't like Willie's dress: it was not the slightest bit classy. Frank asked Jimmy Webb to write a cycle of songs about the seasons for him: Webb wrote some of it but the project never came to fruition. Another aborted project was to make an exhilarating Latin album with the Puerto Rican bandleader, Tito Puente.

Most mouth-wateringly, Sinatra planned a three album set of 36 songs with Lena Horne and an all-star jazz band, arranged by Quincy Jones and conducted by Don Costa. They went as far as choosing the songs and Quincy wrote the arrangements. The songs included Scott Joplin's 'The Entertainer' with lyrics, 'Whatever' with guest artist Michael Jackson, and a new Barry Mann and Cynthia Weil song, 'We're Dangerous'. It's not known why this project hit the rocks but the poor health of Don Costa had something to do with it. He was a heavy smoker and drinker and he had to have open heart surgery.

Frank was having to deal with a succession of deaths – his second cousin Ray Sinatra, Jack Benny's partner, and Harry James who said he was going to do one-nighters with Gabriel. Gordon Jenkins suffered injuries in a car crash and also was suffering was a wasting disease; he died in 1984. Peter Lawford married his fourth wife in July 1984, but he died on Christmas Eve of kidney and liver failure.

Woody Herman had bought Bogart's old house, but his finances were grim, largely because of his bad bookkeeping. He owed back taxes and Frank and some of his wealthier friends bailed him out so that he didn't lose his home. He performed until 1985 and died two years later.

The avant-garde choreographer Twyla Tharp staged a modern dance work around Sinatra's songs, *Songs by Sinatra*, using them to show a developing relationship between a man and a woman. It was performed by Mikhail Baryshnikov and Eliain Kudo of the American Ballet Theatre.

In October 1983 Capitol issued a huge box set of Sinatra albums. This was an assertion that Sinatra was the most important artist of the twentieth century. A reviewer for *Atlantic Monthly* wrote, 'The albums explore knowledge, reflection, friendship, travel, swinging and finally, accomplishment and power, every avenue except religion.' The huge package was priced at $350 but maybe it wasn't such a good investment as CDs were just around the corner.

Between 1979 and 1982, Frank had been performing 40 shows a year for the Resorts group at $40,000 a show. The appropriately named Steve Wynn, whose father had run a bingo hall, was the chairman of the group which owned casinos in Las Vegas and Atlantic City. He made Sinatra an improved offer for 1983, particularly because he wanted to establish the Golden Nugget, which opened in Atlantic City in November 1982 as a major major attraction. Frank would receive $10m over three years. Wynn said, 'Great as he is, he's not the main attraction. The Golden Nugget is. If every time you wanted to get customers, you needed to have Frank Sinatra, you'd go broke. It might be Sinatra who brings people into the Golden Nugget, but it's the staff who keep them here.' Frank made TV commercials with Wynn, and met the high rollers. One TV ad even said, 'Be sure to look me up', so was this a new hospitable Sinatra? He had become, not the Italian ambassador for the US, but the goodwill ambassador for the Golden Nugget, and it paid much better.

Frank and Dean starred in a High Rollers weekend at the Golden Nugget. The invitation referred to meeting Nathan Detroit, although surely that's the last person a high roller would want to meet. While Frank and Dean did their work, the Nugget's customers gambled $22m. The total gross for the year for the seven casinos in Atlantic City was $804m. In 2013 Steve Wynn was declared the richest man in the world, although the real richest man in the world probably didn't tell anyone about it.

Frank's guitarist Ron Anthony recalls, 'When we worked in Atlantic City, they had a private club in the casino where we could go and they didn't charge for drinks. They normally would close at 2am or 3am but Frank would come in with his friends, and people would just stare at him as this was pretty much his home town. There were some security guys around but he was always very nice and he would sit there and drink and then Barbara would say, 'Frank, I'm going to bed, I'll see you later', and the bar would never close until Frank left. When we went into a casino to work, the money that they took was probably trebled and so everyone was happy. He was being treated like a god.'

Over the years, Sinatra had raised millions for Variety Clubs International, often done anonymously and aware from public glare. They acknowledged his contribution by constructing a hospital wing in Hoboken, the Sinatra Family's Children's Unit for the Chronically Ill. There was a televised birthday concert to honour him and Steve Lawrence and Vic Damone performed an engaging, eight minute A to Z of Sinatra, arranged by Nelson Riddle and running through song titles from 'All or Nothing at All' to 'Zing! Went the Strings of My Heart'. Richard Burton saluted his humanitarian work as 'Mr Anonymous' and said, 'I have never sung a song with Frank Sinatra, never acted with him, shared his stage, nor been a member of an orchestra under his baton. We are however old friends of some 30 years.'

In December, Ronald Reagan gave Sinatra a presidential honour at the Kennedy Centre, and he said, 'Art is the shadow of humanity. You have spent your life casting a magnificent and powerful shadow.' Gene Kelly added, 'There is not the remotest possibility that you will have a successor.'

Even then after all this acclaim, there was a feeling that things could go wrong in an instant. The CBS Evening News showed a tape of Frank in Las Vegas where he was ordering a Chinese blackjack dealer to disobey the rules regarding multiple decks. He snarled, 'If you don't want to play with just one deck, you can go back to China.'

Stepping on stage, Frank dismissed the CBS news anchor Dan Rather as a 'yuk' and said that Barbara Walters was 'a real bow-wow, a pain in the ass'. Another journalist Liz Smith wrote, 'Why doesn't this great big bully just shut up and sing?' Frank responded that she was 'a dumpy, fat, ugly broad'.

Sinatra spent July and August 1984 holidaying on the French Riviera. He appeared with Elton John in Monte Carlo. On stage at the Royal Albert Hall in September, he said, 'There are no other saloon singers left except for ol' red eye,' a reference to Dean Martin. He said that he was going to do a song by General de Gaulle and sang 'My Way'. He did 'Luck Be a Lady' from *Guys and Dolls* and said that it had been sung in the film by 'America's greatest baritone, Marlon Brando': even 30 years on, this still rankled.

The album project with Lena Horne had been dropped but Quincy Jones produced a solo album by Sinatra, *L.A. Is My Lady*. The title song was written and scored by Quincy with a lyric from the Bergmans and had been used at a celebration in Los Angeles. It's an excellent performance with George Benson on guitar, but the song was forced as though it was putting elements of 'New, York, New York' into a song about L.A. The theme of the city being a woman was hackneyed and how many cities could Frank praise without sounding ridiculous?

Sinatra had wanted to sing 'How Do You Keep the Music Playing', written by the Bergmans with Michel Legrand. It's a very good song that had been recorded by Tony

Bennett. A legacy from the Lena Horne project was her success, 'Stormy Weather', which Sinatra sang very well with Lee Ritenour on guitar. There was a frantic rush through Cole Porter's 'It's All Right with Me', and at the end of take, Frank gasped, 'We all finished together anyway.'

Q couldn't persuade Frank to revive 'Body and Soul'. 'I did it for Columbia,' said Frank, 'and I can't bring anything new to it.' 'But we have much better microphones now,' said Q. Still no. On the other hand, 'Teach Me Tonight' was a rarity: a famous Sammy Cahn song which Sinatra had not recorded before. Sammy had tailored the lyric for him:

'I've played love scenes in a flick or two
And I've also met a chick or two,
But I still can learn a trick or two,
Teach me tonight.'

Sammy Cahn had also updated one of his first songs, 'Until the Real Thing Comes Along', recorded by Fats Waller in 1936 but a hit for Andy Kirk and his Twelve Clouds of Joy. Sinatra added a Vegas veneer with lines like 'I would drive the Chrysler, Leave the Rolls for you' (what's the hardship in that?) and 'I'd even punch out Mr T for you.'. Another example of Frank's high living was Kander and Ebb's 'The Best of Everything'. He wished his girl the best of everything including 'a Rembrandt hanging on the wall'.

'After You've Gone' was nearly as old as jazz itself as it was introduced by Al Jolson and Sophie Tucker in 1918. It became a downhearted blues for Bessie Smith and hundreds of performers have recorded it, a fact that has been beneficial for the Great Ormond Street Hospital. The songwriter Turner Layton was in England in 1918 and after his child was treated successfully at the hospital, he gave them the royalties on his next song, which, fortunately for them, happened to be 'After You've Gone'. Sinatra gave it a superb jazz treatment and although George Benson's headphones slipped off, he kept playing his Django-style guitar perfectly. The song had a punchy ending and as the track concluded, Frank took a towel and fanned the trumpet section.

'Mack the Knife' had been written in 1928 by Kurt Weill and Bertolt Brecht for *Die Dreigroschenoper (The Threepenny Opera)*. It was originally called 'Moritat', which means 'murderous deed' and it had been a hit for Louis Armstrong in 1956. Three years later Bobby Darin gave it a sparkling, Frank Sinatra-styled treatment and, here 25 years later, was Frank himself. Everyone was trying too hard to match Darin, but this was an honorable failure.

Frank Foster recalls, "Quincy Jones and Ol' Blue Eyes chose the songs together for that and they were all great songs. Frank was relaxed and easy going and enjoying himself. He called everybody 'baby' including me. Most of them only took a couple of takes. I wrote a couple of arrangements, one for 'Mack the Knife' and another for 'After You've Gone'. Frank used the arrangement of 'Mack the Knife' on the road, so I guess he liked it. Your vocal range descends as you get older and so I wrote in the lower range for the most part.'

The album packaging for *L.A. Is My Lady* is pretentious and the credits seem endless; did anyone ever read them? The lyric sheet covered not only the words but also Sinatra's asides. There was a photograph of Michael Jackson, who was produced by Quincy, visiting the sessions but he did not appear on the record. Although Quincy Jones produced the 'We Are the World' single, Frank was not there so we can only presume that he didn't want to do it.

President Reagan was re-elected and as in 1981, Frank produced the inaugural gala. While this was happening, the *Washington Post* dredged up Mafia stories. When questioned by Barbara Hower for *Entertainment Tonight*, he pointed his finger at her and said, 'You're dead.' More controversy, but he later said that it was nothing personal and the gesture meant that the press didn't exist for him anymore.

Nelson Riddle's son, Chris, remembers, 'Frank Sinatra called my father in December 1984. They had had a rift and it was all Frank's fault, but Frank wanted to make it up and work with him again. He asked my father to be the music director on Ronald Reagan's second inaugural, which was to take place on January 20, 1985 in Washington DC. The last time my father and Frank had worked on a similar project was John F Kennedy's inauguration on January 20, 1961, so my father graciously said, "Yes, Frank". My father lived in Los Angeles and Frank was calling from Washington. At one point Frank realised it was 6.15 in the morning where my father was, and 9.15 where he was. Frank became a little uncomfortable about calling him so early. He said, "Nelson, I am really sorry." My father had a dry wit and he said, "That's alright, Frank, I had to get up to answer the telephone anyway." If my father was at an airport and saw someone with a sign saying 'Nelson Riddle', he would walk to him and say, "Funny that's my name too."'

The inaugural concert passed without incident. Frank led Ray Charles to the piano for 'America the Beautiful' and the performers gathered around including Dean Martin and James Stewart. When Kevin Spacey met James Stewart, he said to him, 'You're one of the greatest actors ever, but you're probably sick of hearing that.' 'Not at all,' said Jimmy, 'Say it again.'

In April 1985 Sinatra played the Budokan Hall in Tokyo. When he sang, 'My Kind of Town' he started 'My kind of town, Yokohama is' and for 'New York, New York' he sang 'Kyoto, Kyoto'. Frank sang "Ruck be a rady" and did a Japanese 'dooby dooby do'. He referred to 'Come Rain Or Come Shine' as his favourite song".

On 23 May1985 he received two awards in one day, one in New York, the other in Washington. First he was made an Honorary Doctor of Engineering degree from the Stevens Institute of Technology, Hoboken – not bad for a couple of weeks study, but then honorary alumni are often chosen, quite calculatedly, for their wealth. And what was he planning to do with this degree? Then President Reagan awarded Frank a Medal of Freedom, the highest civilian honour in the US. Reagan spoke of Sinatra's 'love of country, his generosity for those less fortunate, his distinctive art, and his winning and compassionate persona.' Sinatra said afterwards that it was the proudest day of his life.

At the meal, Frank was sat by Henry Kissinger and he told him, 'I'm not associated with the Mafia.' 'I'm very disappointed, Frank,' said Kissinger, 'Who is going to take care of my enemies?'

Nancy Sinatra's husband, Hugh Lambert, died from throat cancer in August and although Frank could be uncaring in some family matters, he was perfect for dealing with his grandchildren and the questions they would ask. 'He always told the truth,' said Nancy, 'He taught me that communicating with children is just like communicating with adults.'

The fact that Nelson hadn't been working with Frank hadn't bothered him too much as he had made some of the biggest albums of his career with Linda Ronstadt. Very influenced by *In the Wee Small Hours*, she recorded three albums of torch songs: *What's New* (1983), *Lush Life* (1984) and *For Sentimental Reasons* (1986). Although a bit samey, they were beautifully performed and recorded and a huge commercial success, selling over 7 million copies in the US alone.

Nelson had given Frank a list of over 250 songs that he didn't think Frank had recorded, the idea being that he would choose from them and then add some choices of his own. Frank and Nelson wanted to bring something new to the songs. Indeed, when Jeri Southern recorded 'Dancing on the Ceiling', Frank sent her a note, 'No one should record 'Dancing on the Ceiling' after what you have done with it.' Getting wind of this project, *Rolling Stone* suggested more contemporary songs that Frank should consider: Sam Cooke's 'Mean Old World', Van Morrison's 'Moondance' Randy Newman's 'Sail Away' and Elvis Costello's 'Shipbuilding'.

It's worth speculating on the album that Frank Sinatra never made. There were so many songs that he could have done. He never sang 'Ev'ry Time We Say Goodbye', possibly because Ella Fitzgerald was his favourite singer and this was her legendary performance. He never sang 'St Louis Blues', 'I Got Rhythm', 'Beyond the Sea', 'Mountain Greenery', 'Don't Blame Me, 'Smoke Gets in Your Eyes' (perfect!), 'Long Ago and Far Away', 'Satin Doll' and 'They Didn't Believe Me'. He could have fun with ''S Wonderful'. He could have recorded a definitive version of Tim Hardin's 'Misty Roses' and brought something unique to David Bowie's 'Life on Mars'. Ron Anthony and Sammy Cahn's saloon, 'It's Almost 4am' has Frank written all over it. He never sang any Charles Aznavour, Hank Williams or Neil Sedaka songs and very few by Anthony Newley and Leslie Bricusse, certainly by Sammy Davis's standards. I'd like have heard him whistling 'Big Noise from Winnetka'.

In September 1985, while Sinatra was doing two weeks at Carnegie Hall with George Shearing, Nelson Riddle was conducting for Ella Fitzgerald at the Hollywood Bowl but he was feeling ill. He had hepatitis and while he was in hospital, Frank sent him a note, 'Get your strength back. The next album is with you.' It wasn't as Nelson Riddle died on 6 October.

The jazz pianist Lou Levy sometimes played at Sinatra's house on Christmas Eve. When he arrived with a stick because of a back injury, Sinatra arranged for his treatment and paid his hospital bills.

Frank had personal problems in 1986. He and Barbara were arguing in public and they did talk of getting divorced. Part of Frank's irritability came from an attack of diverticulitis which involved him having a colostomy bag for a couple of months.

His wife was the driving force behind some charity work at the Eisenhower Medical Centre in Palm Springs which led to the juvenile ward being renamed the Barbara Sinatra Children's centre.

In 1986 Kitty Kelley published her gossip-driven biography, *His Way*, which had something distasteful on nearly all of its 500 pages. Like Albert Goldman with Elvis Presley and John Lennon, she sought to make the worst out of every situation. Frank was mortified by her attack on his mother and by the suggestion that he had had an affair with the current First Lady, Nancy Reagan. He commented, 'I hope the next time Kitty Kelley is crossing the street, four blind guys come around the corner driving fast cars.'

Around this time, I met Lonnie Donegan who was reading *His Way*. I asked him what he thought of it. 'Well, I believe all that stuff about the Mafia. I saw it myself. I could have worked for Sinatra in Las Vegas, but it would have been working for the Mafia, so I came home.'

On 14 March 1986 Frank gave a concert, performing in the round at the Meadowlands Sports Complex, New Jersey, only five miles from Hoboken. As he told the audience, 'It's a hell of a lot better than playing Atlantic City.' The concert was released on CD in 2009 and it is an excellent performance from his later years. The overture, conducted by Bill Miller, contained snatches of nine songs, but as Frank only sang one of them, Bill had presumably picked up the wrong sheets. When he sings, 'It Was a Very Good Year', he comments, 'It's not exactly about my life but anybody's life who is getting on in years.' He adds to the phrase, 'When I was 17' – 'Holy Jesus, 17!' You can tell that Sinatra was really enjoying himself.

There was talk of Frank and Dudley Moore starring in the American film version of the gay comedy, *La Cage aux Folles*. It was bizarre casting and it was Dudley who backed out not wanting to play a female impersonator. The film was made in 1995 as *The Birdcage* with Robin Williams, Nathan Lane and Gene Hackman.

Frank had a harrowing role as a retired policeman in an episode of the TV crime series show, *Magnum PI*, in which he joined Tom Selleck to track down his granddaughter's killer. The viewing figures were extremely high but Selleck's moustache and hairy chest had a lot to do with that.

In November 1986 Frank was admitted to hospital in Palm Springs for diverticulitis and underwent an emergency operation to remove yards of infected intestine. Now, there's a souvenir hunter's dream! At the same time, Ava Gardner was in hospital in Santa Monica, suffering from the aftermath of a stroke. Both of them were released later in the month; Frank was soon performing again in Vegas.

On 20 March 1987 Dean Martin's son, Dean Paul, who was a pilot for the air force, crashed into the same mountain which had killed Dolly Sinatra. At the funeral, his fellow pilots flew in an incomplete V out of respect for their missing colleague. Dean stopped drinking; he would never be the same again.

In January 1988 Frank Sinatra was back in Australia and by now Bob Hawke was Prime Minister. There was no controversy and Sinatra gave a concert for 40,000 fans with Peter Allen in support and Clive James hosting. He gave James a short interview in which he talked about his recording plans. He was still thinking of recording ballads that he had not sung before with 'nice and easy arrangements from Billy May'. He said, 'Rock is out of the question' and added, 'Why did Jimmy Webb stop writing?' Jimmy Webb hadn't stopped writing but presumably had decided that the Seasons project was never going to happen. There had been talk of Frank making an album of Tom Waits' songs but Frank ignored the suggestion, no doubt put off my Waits' wardrobe. Waits did write a song for him, 'Empty Pockets', but it was never recorded by Frank or even released by Tom.

Dean was mourning the loss of his son and Frank thought that it would be a good idea to put the Rat Pack together for a tour, billed as *The Ultimate Event*, and taking place in arenas. It was a great idea as Frank, Dean and Sammy had never toured together and unless you had gone to the Sands or some other casino you would never have seen them. Sammy had been out of favour with Sinatra for some years as Frank disapproved of his cocaine habit. He had to be clean to tour with Frank.

Sammy had had some rocky years. His talent was unquestionable but he had alienated black audiences, albeit unintentionally. The photograph of him hugging President Nixon on stage and Nixon looking so uncomfortable had gone around the world. At a time of black empowerment, this was totally the wrong image and it implied that he was selling out. The fact that he hadn't stood up to Frank and Dean's jibes went against him. While black artists like James Brown, Marvin Gaye, Stevie Wonder and the Temptations had been promoting the black cause, he had been singing 'The Candy Man' with the Mike Curb Congregation. It had stemmed from a children's film, *Willy Wonka and the Chocolate Factory* and it had made him look corny and trite. Davis was aware of this himself and at a restaurant he once wrote 'Where does brown begin?' on a napkin to Jimmy Webb and asked him to use it for a song title. The song was perfect for him but he decided against it and Jimmy Webb gave it to the Supremes.

But there was worse. His appearances on *Rowan and Martin's Laugh In* were spectacularly ill-judged. He seemed to be making fun of being black. Then he kissed the racist Archie Bunker on the TV sit-com, *All in the Family*. These cameos can be taken two ways, but the public turned against him. He could have been a role model but he was making black people a laughing stock. For a man to whom timing was everything, he was spectacularly out of touch and had become an Uncle Tom.

Sammy had rather liked his own candy man. He and his wife were heavily into drugs and he embraced Satanism and pornography in the most open of open marriages. He had huge debts particularly to the IRS and if he didn't pay up soon, he'd be in jail. Quincy Jones wanted to write a Broadway musical around his autobiography, *Yes I Can*, but there were too many problems in Sammy's personal life and he put the idea on hold.

Sammy still worked the casinos. He had recently been working very successfully as a double-top with, of all people, Jerry Lewis. However, the billing of Frank, Sammy, Dean and Jerry would have been several steps too far. There is a poignant shot of the three of them announcing the tour, all dressed in black leather jackets as though it made them look younger and cooler.

It was a familiar format. Dean would come on first, then Sammy, and after an intermission, Frank. They would get together at the end for 20 minutes of nonsense and a few songs. Dean would have to shake off his gloom for an hour a night but otherwise it was easy money as he trotted through his hits. However, for once, he wasn't confident. Unlike Frank, he wasn't used to stadiums and he wasn't sure that his intimate act would transfer. Also, he had some problems with his false teeth and his bad back and he felt that the medication was affecting his memory. Frank himself wasn't feeling too good: he was sleeping badly, possibly the consequence of all his nightcaps, and he was having urinary problems.

Paul Anka had met Dean shortly before the tour and asked him how he was doing. He replied, 'Just waiting to die, pally.' He didn't want to tour. Dean called Frank a couple of days beforehand and said, 'Is it too late to call the whole thing off?' The answer was yes and the tour started with considerable tension between Frank and Dean. The first three nights went well but Dean was not putting any effort into it.

During the third show, Dean had flicked a burning cigarette into the crowd and Frank was furious. After the show, Dean had ordered spaghetti and was watching a western on TV. Frank came to see him, grabbed hold of his plate and poured the spaghetti over his head. The next morning Dean checked out of the hotel, caught a plane and said he wasn't coming back. Sammy thought that they should continue with Jerry Lewis but Frank chose Liza Minnelli. She called him Uncle Frank. She did astonishingly well at such short notice and geed up Sammy and Frank. After Frank sang 'All or Nothing at All', Sammy said to Liza, 'This was before our time', and Frank responded, 'This was before everybody's time.'

To avoid being sued, Dean's manager told him to check into a hospital. The press reported that he had a kidney condition. A month later, Dean did some solo gigs and he cracked, 'Frank sent me a kidney, but I don't know whose it was.'

A huge all-star event was planned for 11 May 1988 to celebrate Irving Berlin's 100th birthday. Berlin with his customary wit said, 'I might screw up all your plans. I might die before my hundredth birthday.' The writer and broadcaster, Garrison Keillor, recited the words of 'All Alone' which he described as 'a poem of 81 words without one unnecessary word.' Frank Sinatra sang 'Always'.

In June 1988 Frank Sinatra was going to record Billy May's arrangement of 'My Foolish Heart', a film song from 1949 made famous by Billy Eckstine. Sinatra arrived at 7.50pm and did several takes. He left at 8.45pm and didn't bother with any other songs. He thought his voice was not up to par and the proposed album was abandoned.

With the 25th anniversary of the Kennedy assassination, there was renewed interest in the 1962 film, *The Manchurian Candidate*. It had not been seen for many years and it was thought that it could be given a cinema showing in the States, followed by a DVD release and TV sales. Sinatra put forward a $2m guarantee and easily got his money back. Sinatra sang

'Witchcraft' as an animated singing sword in the cartoon feature, *Who Framed Roger Rabbit*.

If that wasn't bizarre enough, Frank Sinatra Jr, looking like a younger but fuller faced version of his dad, joined Was (Not Was) for 'Wedding Vows In Vegas'. Most of time, Frank Jr was working with his dad: he was starting to conduct the orchestra with Bill Miller playing piano. Frank Jr enjoyed the work but there was no doubt who was boss and Frank thought nothing of demeaning him in front of the orchestra.

For Barbara's birthday on 16 October, Frank had decided to cancel the pre-nup as her birthday present. This would give Barbara joint tenancy for their properties and also the rights to his personal effects. The children were understandably unhappy and thought that he had been set up for this.

Much to Barbara's annoyance, Tina had already been given the Sheffield company which had the rights to market his image and his name. Frank didn't want to be seen on coffee mugs but he did like the silk ties which were based on his paintings. Frank did not seem keen on writing an autobiography and when a proposed ghost writer died, he took that as an omen not to do it. He did authorise a TV mini-series and Tina was spending her time resolving these issues.

In December 1988, Frank, Sammy and Liza were on the road with Frank Jr conducting and this time they had integrated their acts into a continuous whole. The orchestra opened with 'Strangers in the Night' but they were anything but as they came on together and sang 'Style'. Frank sang 'Witchcraft' and let Liza sing 'Say Liza' and Sammy 'Talk to the Animals'. They kept this up all evening and the songs included Stephen Sondheim's 'Old Friends' and concluded with them all singing 'New York, New York' with Sammy adding, 'You ganging up on me.' Frank's 'Soliloquy' had a new dimension as it sounded like a grandfather reminiscing. He half-spoke 'Where or When' which built into a big finish and introducing 'One for My Baby', he remarked, 'He's been hurt very badly, ask Eddie Fisher. He cried a long time. I lent him twelve handkerchiefs.' The whole show had been directed by George Schlatter but as Liza said, 'When it comes to choreography, we work around Frank.'

The Ultimate Event came to Europe in April 1989 with five concerts scheduled for the Royal Albert Hall. From time to time, Frank was doing a new Jerry Leiber and Mike Stoller song on stage, 'The Girls I Never Kissed' and although he recorded it with Billy May, it was not released at the time. Leiber and Stoller had written the heartrending 'Is That All There Is' for Peggy Lee and this song tapped into the same vein. Reprise should have had more confidence in this track.

As a consequence of too much smoking, Sammy Davis had contracted throat cancer and a tribute for him had been arranged at the Shrine Auditorium. He was able to attend but was too ill to perform.

Sinatra's influence had penetrated Russia. When Mikhail Gorbachev allowed neighbouring Warsaw Pact countries to determine their own internal affairs, it was known as the 'My Way' or 'The Sinatra Doctrine'.

On 25 January 1990 Ava Gardner, who had been living in London, died from pneumonia. She had had a stroke and been ill for years so her death was not unexpected. She never lost her love for Sinatra and would play his records when she felt depressed. When she died, Frank was due to appear for 17,000 admirers at the new Knickerbocker Arena in Albany. He didn't feel like appearing and Liza Minnelli was asked to stand by. He sat by himself at home all day but he pulled himself together and gave a great show. Artie Shaw told the press, 'There's nothing to talk about. She ruined my life.' Frank at times felt the same way.

On 16 May 1990 Sammy Davis died. Frank was with him at the end and he was very disturbed when he saw how much his health had deteriorated. At least *The Ultimate Event* had meant that he had returned to something close to his peak. His finances were in an even worse state that anyone imagined. Knowing that the IRS was going to lay claim to his assets, his friends and employees had been purloining his assets when they visited him.

Sinatra was still regularly performing in Las Vegas and Atlantic City and he and Barbara now planned the *Golden Jubilee World Tour*. In July 1990 Frank appeared at the London Arena in the Docklands, performing in the round for five nights to 11,000 fans each night. This was a new venue but actually was making good use of a former aircraft hanger on the Isle of Dogs. The audience paid between £35 and £100 to sit on plastic chairs on a stone floor with brick walls all around – but that's normal today. The venue was going to be used for boxing championship fights and the promoter Frank Warren paid $4.5m to secure Sinatra's services. Frank also played his first concert in Scotland since 1953 at the Ibrox Stadium in Glasgow.

The bandleader Syd Lawrence, commented, 'The tickets for Frank Sinatra at £92 would be cheap at twice the price. The man is a legend and not many people have had to chance to see him live in the UK. He is still magic. He can't sing as he did 20 years ago but he still has a voice and a good voice and he is, after all, Frank Sinatra.'

One evening the blind BBC journalist Mark Turnbull met Frank Sinatra in the Savoy Hotel's American Bar, a favourite watering hole where Frank could have a gin and tonic and relax. The meeting ended up in a late-night jam session with Turnbull playing the piano for Frank.

A new award had been instituted at the Society of Singers. It was called an Ella and the first recipient in 1989 was Ella Fitzgerald herself. In December 1990, she presented the second Ella to Frank Sinatra. Even though she had been ill they did a great 'Lady Is a Tramp' together. This performance was included in the two-hour TV special, *Sinatra 75: The Best Is Yet to Come*, which was broadcast to celebrate his birthday.

Despite making *The Godfather*, Francis Ford Coppola was on friendly terms with Frank. He offered him the role of a senior Mafia figure, Don Artobello, in *The Godfather, Part 3*. Oddly enough, Frank liked the idea but he decided against it as he didn't like location work. In a neat reversal, the role went to Eli Wallach. In 1991 Maurice Jarre and Sammy Cahn asked Frank if he would sing the title song for a Japanese film, *The Setting Sun*. It was a good ballad, typical of Sinatra, but he didn't think strong enough and the song was performed by Ella Fitzgerald instead.

Frank's only recording session in 1991 was a private recording of 'Silent Night' with Frank Jr on piano, copies of which were sent out as Christmas gift. However, all was not well in the family as Frank had signed a new will allocating even more of his assets to Barbara. There was a family meeting where the following exchange took place:

Tina: 'Did you understand what you were signing?'

Frank: 'I'm not sure.'

Tina: 'Were you represented by an attorney?'

Frank: 'No I wasn't.'

Now 75, Frank came to the UK for more appearances at the Royal Albert Hall. Tony Bennett was in the audience and Frank introduced him and said, 'If Tony Bennett is singing as well as he's singing right now when he's my age, he's gonna beat me.' Frank looked bewildered at the end of one concert and had to be shown his way off stage. There were indications that Frank was forgetting his lyrics and he had teleprompters. Don Rickles joked, 'Frank has Sicilian Alzheimer's – he only remembers the grudges.'

But that embarrassment was nothing compared to Dean's final shows in December 1991. He started talking about Dean Paul and asking, 'Hey, God, why didn't you take me instead?' The uncomfortable audiences had no idea what he was going to say next.

After Frank Sinatra, Mia Farrow married the composer and conductor, André Previn, their partnership lasting throughout the 1970s. Then she had a 12-year-relationship with the writer and director, Woody Allen. They had separate homes and adopted two children, Dylan (later Eliza) and Moses. They had one child together, Ronan, or did they? Mia claimed in 2013 that his father was Frank Sinatra as they had never really ceased their sexual relationship. Looking at Ronan, it was easier to see a link to Frank Sinatra than to Woody Allen.

Allen had a relationship with the adopted daughter of Mia and André Previn, Soon-Yi, which led to their break-up. He is with Soon-Yi to this day, but during a battle for custody, Farrow claimed that he had molested her daughter, Eliza. The judge said that the charges were inconclusive, but nevertheless, Farrow won custody of the children. Mia discussed the case with Frank, who took Mia's side. He offered to hire someone to break Allen's legs, but Mia thought that was a step (or a broken leg) too far.

Sinatra came to the UK for six shows over consecutive nights at Royal Albert Hall with the John Dankworth Orchestra, conducted by Frank Sinatra Jr. His final appearance on 31 May 1992 was his last UK concert appearance. John Dankworth himself was impressed: 'He was severely limited technically but able to use his lifetime of experience.' Frank didn't stay in the UK for a tribute to Sammy Davis, also at the Royal Albert Hall, but he sent a taped message.

When Frank appeared in Dublin, he said from the stage, 'I'd like to introduce someone everybody's been talking about: Bono. I'm told that you're very important and you make a lot of money so will you please stand up and take a bow.' Bono stood up and bowed, and Frank added, 'Since you're so important and make so much money, why don't you invest some in your wardrobe?'

As well as acting as Frank's personal manager and running his own restaurants, Jilly Rizzo was involved in a fraud to obtain money from a New York bank. He confessed that he and his associates obtained a huge bank loan by giving shares to the wife of the bank's president. The resort was never built and Rizzo, because of his age, avoided jail and was given community service. On 6 July 1992 Rizzo was about to celebrate his 75th birthday with some friends in Palm Springs but unfortunately had a car crash and burned to death. Frank greatly missed his old friend and but, encouraged by Barbara, he continued to perform.

Frank performed 84 dates in 1992, sometimes with Shirley MacLaine. Strangely, MacLaine was the most apprehensive as she not done stadium dates before. His health was not good and his Alzheimer's was becoming more marked. Because he had cataracts, he couldn't read the teleprompters, so much bigger print was introduced. When he forgot the words to 'You Make Me Feel so Young', Shirley MacLaine stepped on stage to get him back on track. He became increasingly aware that he was letting down the public and he would often end his concerts by saying, 'Thank you for letting me sing to you.'

His guitar Ron Anthony recalls, 'Sometimes he could see the words but the continuity wasn't there. Something was wrong. He was taking some medication and he used to drink with it and that got in the way of his concentration. A lot of times though he was okay and didn't need the teleprompter. He might be fine for two-thirds of the show and then he would start losing a little bit and would get confused. Sometimes Frank Jr who was conducting would feed him the lyrics but the audience didn't care, they loved him and he could do no wrong. Many times we would go through this but he could still give the ballads a wonderful dramatic reading. Sometimes he would have a night that was just like the old days and I would think, 'Why can't he do that all the time?' He always had a drink on stage but then they decided that if he didn't take his medication then he would do a better show. It was great to hear those wonderful arrangements night in and night out. He was happy as he would much rather sing than do anything else. He had a 35 piece band, sometimes 50, and he had the best musicians in the world and an audience that loved him. What more could a singer ask? It was very satisfying.'

When Frank introduced 'One for My Baby' at Radio City Music Hall, he poured himself some bourbon and said, 'You killed my old man but I'll get even with you.' Possibly he had said that because if his father had still been alive, he would have been 100 years old. A few blocks away at P J Clarke's, Johnny Mercer had written the lyric in 1943 as he talked to the barman, Tommy Joyce.

Frank was on the ball when George Michael was complaining about the price of fame to the *LA Times*. Frank wrote, 'Come on, George. Loosen up. Swing, man. Dust off those gossamer wings and fly yourself to the moon of your choice and no more talk about the tragedy of fame. The tragedy of fame is when no one shows up and you're singing to the cleaning lady in some empty joint that hasn't seen a paying customer since St Swithin's Day.'

Tony Bennett recorded an affectionate tribute album, *Perfectly Frank* with the Ralph Sharon Trio. Having a small rhythm group was a smart move on Bennett's part as he didn't have to compete with Sinatra's arrangements.

In 1989 Hank Williams Jr had had a country hit by singing with his late father on 'There's a Tear in my Beer'. At the time it was a novelty but then, in 1991, Natalie Cole turned her father's hit single 'Unforgettable' into a duet and toured with footage of her father over which she added a live vocal. The record industry was realising that there might be endless possibilities here. In 1992 there was a new Christmas duet – Cyndi Lauper and Frank Sinatra with 'Santa Claus Is Comin' to Town'. A casual listener might have assumed that Frank was in good voice, but then he had recorded his contribution 45 years earlier. Luckily no one thought of putting their versions of 'Time After Time' together because they were different songs.

Sinatra, the authorised TV series produced by Tina, was ready to be screened. It had an 18m budget with the Broadway actor, Philip Casnoff, as Frank. Her original choice, Ray Liotta, had turned the part down although he appeared as Sinatra in *The Rat Pack* (1998). Casnoff didn't have to sing as he was lip-syncing to performances from Tom Burlison and Frank Jr. Olympia Dukakis played Dolly who, quite outspokenly for a TV movie of the time, kept calling Frank 'a little son of a bitch'. At the start of his career, someone in a bar says to Sinatra, 'Here's a penny. Sing with feeling', and Frank responds, 'Feeling costs a nickel.'

As far as the Sinatra family was concerned, the film was to counteract the stories which had appeared in the Kitty Kelley biography. Here it was clever Hollywood lawyers not the Mafia who extricated him from his contract with Tommy Dorsey. Tina said, 'I didn't try to evaluate him in the movie. How could I? He doesn't understand himself.' Tina had stopped the film at 1974; she wasn't going to include the very thing she couldn't understand: his marriage to Barbara Marx.

Frank had surgery on his cataracts in 1993 but it was not wholly successful. As a result, he had to stop painting and reading. He continued to work saying, 'If I stop working, I know I'll be next.' But nearly every show was fraught with difficulty. In Richmond, Virginia, in March 1993 he blacked out while performing 'My Way'. In Westbury, New York, he apologised for 'a throat that sounds like I ate a piece of broken glass.'

The poor sod should really have retired for a second time but he went on another European tour at the end of May 1993. He played open air concerts in Germany and made his final appearance in Europe in Cologne on 6 June. This time the tickets were selling out fast in Germany. The critic, Werner Burkhardt compared him to the Lieder singer, Dietrich Fischer-Dieskau.

The American government had long acknowledged that the American Indians had been treated abominably and by way of compensation, they came up with the curious notion that they could run casinos. They would be getting their birthright back – one punter at a time. You couldn't make this up. The Foxwoods Resort Casino in Connecticut was a complex of six casinos. The American Indians turned out to be exceptionally good at running casinos: they were very well organised and more to the point, there was no dirty money. The Mob was not involved at all.

Unfortunately for the Rat Pack, all this potential for extra work came too late. By now Dean and Sammy had died, but Frank did open the resort on 17 November 1993. It was a sad performance as he got lost in 'My Way' – an easy song to get lost in as the structure of each verse is so similar – and at the end of the show he confessed, 'I'm not in tip-top shape.'

For a few years, Sinatra and his associates had been considering a final album, but what should it be? In the end, it was determined that he would return to Capitol and record some old favourites with the original arrangements and then the songs would be turned into duets by performers from around the world, but mostly America. This would make things easy for Sinatra as he would not need to socialise with the performers or prepare the duets in any way, but there was a danger as electronic duets were usually no more effective than electronic cigarettes.

The producers would be Hank Cattaneo, who staged his concert appearances, and Phil Ramone who had recorded duet albums with Ray Charles and Tony Bennett, admittedly with their guests live in the studio. They devised a wish list but Phil Collins turned the opportunity down because he wouldn't meet Sinatra. Ella Fitzgerald said no: she had retired and meant it. Although he'd often worked with Phil Ramone, Paul Simon felt insecure about singing standards with Sinatra. It's not known if Bob Dylan was offered a track but such a pairing would have shown that Frank's voice hadn't fared too badly with the years. Another omission was Rod Stewart who would make a series of best-selling albums called *The Great American Songbook*. The final choice was Sinatra's. He would say, 'Yes, I want to sing with that person.'

Mark Hudson, who wrote 'Livin' on the Edge' for Aerosmith, was working for Phil Ramone. 'Phil Ramone was my mentor and I trained under him for three years. I got so comfortable that I didn't want to leave and I was there the entire time of the *Duets* album with Sinatra. Everybody wanted to sing with him and so the phone would ring and it might be Madonna or Bono or Natalie Cole. Phil is a beautiful man and an incredible producer and everybody was flocking to him because his work ethic was so good.'

To avoid complex negotiations over fees, it was determined that all vocals would be recorded for free but the artists would be allowed to put the tracks on their own solo albums or release them as singles after a year. In 2014 Barbra Streisand included her duet on her best-selling *Partners*.

Thus, *Duets* was recorded using the old arrangements with a sympathetic conductor, Pat Williams, and Bill Miller on piano. Frank heard a few arrangements on the first day but said that his voice wasn't up to it but on 1 July 1993 he recorded eight songs, another seven on 6 July and four more on 9 July. Later in the year, they recorded another batch of titles so that there would be enough for a second volume. Frank would sing the complete song and then Phil Ramone would remove sections of his vocals to make way for his partners. There were 13 duets on the first volume and 14 on the second.

Frank was treating the sessions as live performances and was still apt to say, 'Next song' when he did a good take. After one take, he said, 'If you don't like that, you don't like ice cream' and Frank Sinatra always loved ice cream.

'Frank didn't want to sing with other singers live as he thought he might be embarrassed, that he wouldn't be as good as he used to be,' says guitarist Ron Anthony, 'He did everything live with a 50-piece orchestra in the Capitol Studios, and although they had built a special booth for him, he wanted to sing with the orchestra. The first couple of days he had laryngitis and he couldn't sing and he got bad-tempered. He didn't have much patience and they said, 'Frank, we brought you down so that you could get used to the room and hear the musicians and just get a feel for everything.' The third night he came in we did eight songs in a six hour session. He was really turned on by it. The band stood up and applauded. Some of the guys had been with him in the early days. He was a pro, he could be tough on conductors, but he was even tougher on himself. He wanted things to be just right.'

Mark Hudson recalls, 'Sinatra's people came into the room and I was being funny and they liked me and I got too excited and I said that Sinatra might forget his lyrics and the whole room went silent. Phil Ramone had me against the wall and he said, "If you say that again, I will kill you." Cut to Frank in the Capitol studio, sitting on a chair in his red cardigan and smoking a cigarette. He had been told about my rude comment. Phil went, "Frank wants to meet you" so these two huge Italian guys took me into the studio. Frank moved his hand as if to say, "Come closer to me." Then he said, "What makes you such a smart ass?" I answered immediately, "Because I'm Italian", because I am. His eyes smiled and he laughed and then he slapped me. I am talking boom!, a hard slap. "Now get out of here." It was such a huge moment for me to be slapped by a legend.'

The first duet was with the soul singer Luther Vandross, who had said, 'Why, Phil? He's never heard of me.' 'The Lady Is a Tramp' was a strange song to give Vandross but he added some excellent falsetto and when Sinatra heard it, he said, 'That's wonderful.' On the other hand, Aretha Franklin was terrible on 'What Now My Love' all grace notes or rather screeching and it was a relief when Sinatra sang on his own. Gloria Estefan added little to 'Come Rain or Come Shine' and you may wonder why Anita Baker is on 'Witchcraft'; surely there were 100 better-known and more accomplished contenders.

Dean was too ill to appear on the album and indeed, there are few artists from Frank's generation. Charles Aznavour and Frank Sinatra fit together so well on 'You Make Me Feel so Young' that it was hard to believe that they weren't together in the studio. Julio Iglesias turned 'Summer Wind' into a buddy song and Frank and Tony Bennett da-da-da'd amusingly on 'New York, New York'. Liza Minnelli, who recorded her vocal in Rio de Janeiro, added little to 'I've Got the World on a String', but it's a good track. Natalie Cole contributed some scat singing to 'They Can't Take That Away from Me' but fancy having to say 'the way you sing off-key' to Frank Sinatra.

There's worse. Imagine calling Sinatra 'you old fool' which Bono did on 'I've Got Under My Skin', the hit single from the album. It sounded like a father and son duet with Bono sniping, 'Don't you know, Blue Eyes, you never can win.' The critic Will Friedwald commented that it was 'an attack on all that Sinatra stands for... Like a stoned punk with a karaoke machine...'

Still, Frank appeared to like it and he welcomed Bono to Palm Springs for the making of a video. Bono wrote 'Two Shots of Happy, One Shot of Sad' for him, and although he didn't record it, Bono sang the song with U2 at Sinatra's 80th birthday tribute and Nancy Sinatra included it on an album.

Carly Simon had refused to sing 'One for My Baby' on the grounds that it advocated dangerous driving. They settled for a medley of 'Guess I'll Hang My Tears Out to Dry' and

'In the Wee Small Hours of the Morning', which was a thoroughly bad idea. It's a bit like playing two CD players at once and hearing one song on top of the other.

The saxophonist Kenny G played 'All the Way', which was added to Frank's 'One for My Baby', so this is misrepresented as a duet. 'Man, it's long,' said Frank, when he heard it and the critic Will Friedwald called it 'unspeakably awful'. It's not as a bad as that and 'One for My Baby' does benefit from knowing Sinatra's age and his back story.

Streisand, being Streisand, had to do it differently. She took Frank's vocal from 'I've Got a Crush on You' and added her own orchestral accompaniment. Then she sent it back to Frank for some asides. It could have been a recipe for disaster but it works well and it does sound like they are together and enjoying one another's company.

Capitol had promised a big promotional campaign for *Duets* and the results exceeded their expectations. There was a chance that the album would be dismissed as a gimmick but that didn't happen. The album sold over 2m copies in the US, second only to Mariah Carey, and internationally it was his biggest album ever. It created interest in his back catalogue and there were many reissues. There was a one hour TV special on the making of *Duets*, so Capitol wasn't concealing the way in which the album had been made.

Duets was so successful that Ramone and Cattaneo continued with *Duets II*, released in 1994. The big guns had been on the first volume but this was still an impressive collection of names. The duet of 'For Once in My Life' with Gladys Knight had the added bonus of Stevie Wonder's harmonica and is a fine opener. Another soul diva, Patti Labelle, like Aretha Franklin, goes for overkill on 'Bewitched'.

It was good to hear Frank with Lena Horne on 'Embraceable You': they sounded like two old friends, though the best track on both *Duets* albums had to be 'Where or When' with Steve and Eydie. With skilful electronic trickery, the trio ended up sounding like Lambert, Hendricks and Ross.

Linda Ronstadt was a shoo-in but 'Moonlight in Vermont' is not very exciting. Frank was reunited with Antonio Carlos Jobim for 'Fly Me to the Moon', which starts with scat singing from Jobim. Jobim was not suited to swinging but waste not, want not as this track was also used for George Strait and included on one of his country albums. Strait handled the arrangement better than Jobim but the end result was not as satisfying. The original thought had been to put Willie Nelson with 'South of the Border', as they had worked well together on 'A Foggy Day', although it would have been better to have had Frank going country with Willie.

What on earth was another country singer, Jimmy Buffett, doing with 'Mack The Knife', which incidentally listed the songwriter as 'Bert Brecht'? The ad-libs (or rather ad-fibs as they were planned) worked fine but Buffett sounded like Liberace and isn't much more than a backing vocalist. I'd rather have heard Frank singing 'Margaritaville' with him. Yet another country star, Lorrie Morgan, joined Frank for a medley of 'How Do You Keep the Music Playing' and 'My Funny Valentine', which was much better than the Carly Simon mishmash on the first album.

Two Latin American stars, Luis Miguel and Jon Secada, joined Frank for 'Come Fly with Me' and 'The Best Is Yet To Come' respectively. 'My Kind of Town' was with Frank Jr and sounds like Frank duetting with a younger version of himself; now that would have been a good idea.

Chrissie Hynde's slurred vocal didn't lend itself to 'Luck Be a Lady' but nothing prepared you for the final track – the final track on the last studio album Sinatra ever recorded. In essence, it was his goodbye and it is, beyond belief, ghastly, kitsch to the nth degree. I can see the logic of asking Neil Diamond to sing 'The House I Live In' as he excelled in powerful, overblown ballads, but this vocal was so bad that it detracted from the beauty and the memory of Sinatra's original recording.

A recording of 'My Way' had also been put down but this was the song in search of a duet partner. The producers tried it at different times with Willie Nelson and Jon Seceda but in neither case were satisfied. In 2013 Willie and Frank's version of 'My Way' was released on an expanded version of *Duets*, along with Frank and the country singer Tanya Tucker on 'Embraceable You'.

Sinatra's first public outing in 1994 was attending the memorial service for Swifty Lazar and then on 17 January 1994, he was at home when a considerable earthquake struck in the San Fernando Valley, He was not directly affected but there were 60 deaths and many injuries and the thought was that it could happen again. Was it worth living in such a beautiful area? His former wife Nancy thought so as she moved closer to Frank and Barbara on Frank Sinatra Drive. But Barbara and Frank themselves were thinking of moving. In 1995, they sold the compound to a Canadian entrepreneur, Jim Pattison, and moved to Los Angeles. They had a beach house in Malibu.

On 1 March 1994 Frank attended the Grammys at Radio City Music Hall and was given the Legend award. Bono presented the award and, to be fair, his citation was very good. At first Frank responded well by saying, 'This is more applause than Dean had in his whole life.' Then he started rambling and was confused, so the producer cut him short by cueing the orchestra. The producer later apologised to the Sinatra family.

Five days later Sinatra collapsed while singing 'My Way' at the Mosque Auditorium in Richmond, Virginia to an audience of 4,000. He said to one of the staff, 'Can you get me a chair?' and was rushed to hospital. He was discharged after three hours and then returned home.

In December 1994 Frank, supported by Natalie Cole, gave his last ever concerts at the Fukuoka Dome in Japan. He didn't want to go and he drank his way across the ocean, but he performed two good shows. He felt tired and he decided that there would be no more shows, but he didn't want an announcement as things might change.

Nancy Sinatra still had the figure from her youth and quite unexpectedly, she received an offer to reveal all in *Playboy*. She told her father about it who asked, 'How much are you getting?' When she told him, he said, 'Double it and do it.' She did too. At the time Nancy was putting the finishing touches to an illustrated book, *Frank Sinatra – An American Legend*, which was published for his 80th birthday. It was a very good book too, taking in account that the family were in denial about his negative side. As Frank had collaborated, it is the closest that he came to writing an autobiography, but the book does read like the case for the defence. The book ignored Barbara wherever possible as the three Sinatra children considered her a golddigger, and she in turn thought that his children were ungrateful. There is little doubt, however, that Frank genuinely loved her.

On 25 February 1995 Frank hosted the Frank Sinatra Desert Classic golf tournament in Palm Springs. He performed a short set with Bill Miller on piano and ending with 'The Best Is Yet to Come'. It was the last time that Sinatra would sing in public.

In November 1995 Frank had both Bruce Springsteen and Bob Dylan round for dinner. The pianist Lou Levy was also invited and they performed Frank's songs together. After they'd gone, Frank said to Barbara, 'Great guys, let's have them over once a month' to which Barbara replied, 'Over my dead body.'

Having released the *Duets* albums in 1993/4, Barbara hit on a 2CD compilation for his 80th birthday, *Sinatra 80th All the Best*, and the final track merged Frank's and Nat 'King' Cole's recordings of 'The Christmas Song', recorded 1957 and 1946 respectively. There was also a compilation of performances from shows over the past 10 years – Barbara had recorded everything. This album was misleadingly called *Sinatra 80th Live in Concert*. Frank added a dedication, 'The beautiful music on this album is dedicated to my wife, Barbara, the love of my life.'

His introductions were often worth hearing. He considered 'My Heart Stood Still' 'one of the best stories that anyone could speak or sing', while 'What's New' was 'a sad but beautiful song'. When he sang the verse of 'In the Still of the Night', he said, 'It'll be Ash Wednesday before I get to the chorus.' Considering his advanced age, his 'Soliloquy' was a considerable achievement. He credited songwriters but when he got to 'Strangers in the Night', he said, 'I don't even know who the hell these guys are. Oh, you know this one, huh?' and he did a mock dooby, dooby, do at the end. He had added 'Maybe This Time' from *Cabaret* to his repertoire and made a decent job of it.

Guitarist Ron Anthony says, 'Most of the things I recorded with him I wasn't crazy about with the exception of *Sinatra 80th*, I like that record. There is a little piece I played behind him when he hit the last note on 'What's New', and that was nice. Unfortunately I never did anything with just the two of us because he didn't think he could handle the exposure of just his voice and guitar anymore; with the piano it was different. He knew his voice wasn't what it had been.'

During 1993, Frank and Barbara had been to see the Three Tenors at Dodger Stadium in Los Angeles. The tenors had sung 'My Way' directly to him and blown him kisses. Now Luciano Pavarotti agreed to record a duet of 'My Way'. Third time lucky (though Pavarotti might not have known this), Phil Ramone and Hank Cattaneo added his voice to Frank's. The track was used in 1995 for the album, *Sinatra 80th Live In Concert*. This is kitsch in overdrive but why did Capitol stick it on the end of a live album, especially when a compilation of studio recordings was also being issued?

There was a two-hour TV special, *Sinatra: 80 Years My Way*, produced by George Schlatter and taped at the Shrine Auditorium in Los Angeles. It featured many of the usual suspects but also Little Richard, Bob Dylan, Bruce Springsteen (performing 'Angel Eyes', one Jersey boy to another) and Hootie and the Blowfish (performing 'The Lady Is a Tramp'). Paul Anka was amused, 'Frank couldn't stand the sound of rock music and never wanted to sing it. He hated the sound of Dylan's voice, and yet there was Dylan at Sinatra's 80th birthday celebration singing 'Restless Farewell'. Go figure.' Maybe, but 'Restless Farewell' does share the same sentiments as 'My Way', and Dylan ended his performance with the quirky, 'Happy birthday, Mr Frank'. Don Rickles said to Dylan, 'You know your problem? You gotta stop mumbling when you sing.' At the end of the show, everybody sang 'New York, New York' and Frank himself let rip on the last line.

When Sinatra was 80, the Empire State Building glowed blue for his birthday and on Christmas Day, the lights were dimmed around Las Vegas to remember Dean Martin. Dean died on Christmas Day 1995 and among his final words was 'I have no regrets'. He asked for donations to be given to Barbara's children's centre. His former partner Jerry Lewis was enjoying great success in a revival of *Damn Yankees* on Broadway and it was now a national tour.

In July 1996 Frank and Barbara renewed their vows for their twentieth wedding anniversary. .He had been with Barbara far longer than any of his other wives: it depends on how you measure it but he was living with her longer than all three combined, In October Frank made his final public appearance at the Carousel of Hope ball in Los Angeles.

Frank's former fiancée, Juliet Prowse, died from cancer in September 1996. She had always maintained her friendship with Frank and her life story had been a rollercoaster ride, both with him and without. She had been married to Eddie Fisher for a couple of years and she had lost an ear when she was mauled by a leopard when filming; it was sewn back on. Frank's friend and neighbour, Peggy Lee, had suffered respiratory problems for years and when she toured she would refer to seeing 'Charlie', which meant her oxygen cylinder in the wings. She was hooked on anti-depressants and the voice, which had been cool and sexy, sounded spooky. She would, however, outlast Frank, dying in October 1998. Frank heard a little of *Keely Smith Sings Sinatra* before he died and remarked how good 'Angel Eyes' was.

In November 1996 Frank went to hospital to recover from pneumonia but he wasn't in for long. In December, Nancy's daughter made Frank banana shortcake for his birthday. She said, 'What do you wish for?' and he replied, 'Another birthday.' In January 1997 Frank was hospitalised with a heart attack. Joey Bishop sent him a get well card: 'Frank, you've got to get well because I haven't worked since you got sick.'

In April 1997 Congress awarded Frank Sinatra the Congressional Gold Medal. The previous recipient had been the Rev Billy Graham and before that, Mother Teresa.

By 1998 the children had fallen out with Barbara because she wasn't keeping them up to date with his progress. One problem was coming after another – he had cardiac and respiratory problems, Alzheimer's disease, high blood pressure, pneumonia and bladder cancer. He was still smoking but he thought, 'What the hell?' He would spend his whole day in his pyjamas and dressing-gown, and Michael Jackson offered him his personal oxygen tent. Frank told Roger Moore, 'You gotta love livin', kid, 'cause dying is a pain in the ass.'

Frank Sinatra died on 5 April 1998. Although Tina and Nancy lived close to the hospital, they were not informed until he had actually gone. In a *Citizen Kane* moment, his final words were 'Oh dear Lord, oh mother'. Tina Sinatra remarked, 'My father did not die. He escaped.'

Frank had said, 'I want fireworks lighting up the sky, all the former Presidents in attendance and Pavorotti singing 'Ave Maria'.' He didn't get that but he came close. President Clinton said that the coffin should be covered with an American flag. He said, 'I think every American would have to smile and say he really did do it his way.' Possibly – one cartoon showed a wreath from the Mafia with the note, 'He did it our way'.

The music critic Andrew Doble says, 'By and large, I am in the 'Sinatra leaves me cold' camp but that does not imply a lack of respect for his artistry. I was in Paris when he died and was struck by the warm tributes in the French press, as if he were one of their own. 'It Was a Very Good Year' is a contender for Frank's finest performance. In a stylistic departure from the standard American Songbook, Ervin Drake portrayed the cycle of ageing very tenderly and eloquently unlike the bombast of 'My Way', which nevertheless works because of its bold, arrogant stance, its melodic sweep and a bravura performance.'

The burial service was at the Good Shepherd Catholic Church in Beverly Hills and the mass was celebrated by the Cardinal of Los Angeles. Dozens of security staff were recruited and helicopters hovered over the church. A skywriter wrote Frank's initials and drew a heart. Frank had notched up four weddings and a funeral.

The pallbearers were Tony Bennett, Ernest Borgnine, Steve Lawrence, Wayne Newton and Don Rickles. They were carrying Frank, dressed in his finest suit, a flask of Jack Daniel's and a Zippo lighter, as well as a Tootsie roll (from Nancy) and a ring with "love" on it (from Mia Farrow). On top of the coffin it said, 'The best is yet to come.'

Kirk Douglas, Gregory Peck and Frank Sinatra Jr spoke at the funeral. A 65 strong choir sang the 23rd Psalm; Bill Miller and two musicians played his music and 'Put Your Dreams Away' was heard over the speakers. Over on the east coast, a freak storm had broken out in Hoboken.

The guests included Mia Farrow, Ronald Reagan, Robert Wagner, Gregory Peck, Liza

Minnelli, Sophia Loren, Jack Lemmon, Sidney Poitier, Bruce Springsteen, Tony Bennett. Tony Curtis and Paul Anka. Jo Stafford commented, 'It's starting to look like it's more fun on the other side – so many of the good ones are over there.' That could be true. Frank Sinatra was buried in the Desert Memorial Park in Cathedral City, California, next to his father and mother. Jilly Rizzo, who was buried there, may still be looking after him while Jimmy Van Heusen could be lining up the girls and pushing his songs.

Ron Anthony says, 'Considering how he lived, Frank was lucky to get to 82. Without a doubt, he lived a full life. If only we could all live a full life like that.'

CHAPTER 18

The ghost of swingers past

'My work in every field has been criticised, good and bad, for years and none of it ever meant crap to me because the people who criticise me do not have the calibre of my musicianship and performing know-how.'

Frank Sinatra, 1980

Frank Sinatra had left the building... or had he?

Since their deaths, huge cults have developed around Elvis Presley and John Lennon that could be branded as new religions. This hasn't happened for Frank Sinatra, but his legacy has been just as lucrative as he was in life.

Whether he would like it or not, it is the Rat Pack image that has endured.

A couple of years before he died, Sinatra was approached about a film based on the Rat Pack. The film company did not want his advice so much as his guarantee not to sue. He was paid $250,000 for agreeing to this, and the film received its première on HBO some four months after his death.

The Rat Pack was impressively cast with Ray Liotta (Frank Sinatra), Joe Montagna (Dean Martin) and Don Cheadle (Sammy Davis), although Liotta looked too young. The characters were prone to say, 'Hi, my name is John Kennedy' but it was confusing as nicknames were used such as 'Cyril' for Peter Lawford and 'Momo' for Sam Giancana. In the film, Sinatra secured Kennedy's nomination for West Virginia which was said to be 95% Protestant. The film trod familiar ground and recreated news cuttings rather than delving into original research. In a first-rate scene, the new Rat Pack performed 'High Hopes' at the 1960 Democratic Convention. Frank was depicted behaving like a spoilt child throughout, especially when being informed that Kennedy wouldn't be staying at his Compound, but that incident is borne out by fact.

There were many effective lines in the script. Ava said to Frank, 'You're an angel when you sing. Why don't you just stick with that?' The most poignant moment went to Sammy Davis, who said, 'Sometimes Frank and the guys cross the line and yes, it hurts, and I get a little dirt on my uniform but so what? The point is that I'm circling the bases and the fellas that come up after me are gonna have it easier.' *The Rat Pack* was written with hindsight; in 1961, would Sinatra have made a joke about Reagan going into politics?

Many aspects of American culture in the mid-50s/early 60s resonate today – Marilyn Monroe, James Dean and Elvis Presley, for starters. The Rat Pack with their fashionable clothes and quick quips are seen as cool and chic, even though their attitudes (older man, younger woman; picking up showgirls; racist quips; continual smoking and drinking) are out of step. Compare their popularity with Bing Crosby. Nobody would think of being a Bing Crosby imitator today – and is he known for any other record but 'White Christmas'? Would the BBC spend two hours on an *Arena* documentary as was done with Sinatra in 2005 and which has been repeated endlessly ever since?

The Rat Pack's most successful film, *Ocean's Eleven*, was remade in 2001 with the Brat Pack and directed by Steven Soderbergh. The film had the brilliant but rather wasted cast of George Clooney (as Danny Ocean), Matt Damon, Andy Garcia, Brad Pitt and Julia Roberts. Although the plot still involved a heist in Las Vegas, very little of the original was kept and its main purpose was to recapture that Rat Pack coolness. Angie Dickinson who played Sinatra's wife in the original had a bit part. Technically, it was streets ahead of the original, but it was not as memorable and should have been better. Still, its box office success led to the instantly forgettable *Ocean's Twelve* and *Ocean's Thirteen*.

Ocean's Thirteen is a ridiculous film with six plots going on at the same time, so it is very easy to lose interest. As Al Pacino and Eddie Izzard had been brought into the franchise, the cast was stunning but it was all to waste. *Ocean's Thirteen* is the only film in the series to make direct reference to Sinatra – there is solidarity with those who have shaken hands with Sinatra who include George Clooney and Al Pacino's characters. There is also 'This Town' on the soundtrack, played in full. The films are directed by the highly-rated Steven Soderbergh, but he's not rated highly by me.

For some years, Martin Scorsese had been planning to make a film about the Rat Pack or just Frank. Frank himself had intimated that he wanted to be played by Scorsese's key actor, Robert DeNiro. It was once reported that Scorsese would make a film about Dean Martin or about the Rat Pack, the latter to have starred Tom Hanks and John Travolta. In 2013, Scorsese announced he was making a drama about Sinatra for his centenary, but this has been deferred. Instead, we have two official two-hour documentaries, *All Or Nothing at All*, produced by HBO, but screened in four one-hour instalments in the UK.

Since 2000, a stage show, *The Rat Pack Live from Las Vegas* has been in and out of the West End and touring the UK The initial cast was Louis Hoover (Frank Sinatra), Clive Carter (Dean) and Peter Straker (Sammy Davis). The show is predictable and provides a good night's entertainment so long as you are not looking for insights.

Prior to a TV special in the 1960s, Sinatra had gone through his songs with just Bill Miller on piano so that the crew could work out camera angles. For 'All of Me', he was moving around on a crane dolly. This film had been preserved and both Tina and Nancy thought it could be integrated into a stage show. With a budget of £5m, *Sinatra at the London Palladium* came to the West End in a highly skilled production which merged the film and its soundtrack with a swinging live band and dancers. The show told his life story, highly selectively, and incorporated news footage including John F Kennedy being shot in Dallas. The audiences loved it and the aficionados were treated to previously unheard vocals from Sinatra. This was revived with continued success in 2015.

In 2013 *From Here to Eternity* was staged as a West End musical with lyrics by Tim Rice and music by Stuart Brayson. It was a very good production with a brilliant staging of the Pearl Harbour invasion, but the production only lasted six months. There were several reasons for this but the obvious ones were no stars in the major roles and no hit songs, although 'Fight the Fight' and 'Love Me Forever Today' had potential. I was pleased that the author Bill Oakes had gone back to James Jones' novel and so the production was much more graphic than the film with sex scenes, brothels and swearing, but this could have been its downfall as it ruled out the family audiences. A shame that it didn't last as it could have been part of Sinatra's centenary celebrations.

Since his death, there have been squabbles and in-fighting over Frank's inheritance, which has been estimated at $200m. It was impossible for Frank to write a will which would satisfy all parties, the split between Barbara and his children proving the most problematic.

At least Frank hadn't done a Sting, who says that his family will not benefit from his fortune. Frank left a generous donation to the Barbara Sinatra Children's Centre and in the years since his death, Barbara has kept their charities alive and promoted his name positively. Quincy Jones has been so impressed with Barbara's efforts that he sends her heart-shaped cookies every Valentine's Day.

With one exception, Barbara has kept the jewellery that Frank bought her. She sold the so-called 'holy shit' necklace, made of emeralds and diamonds and originally made for Madame Cartier.

Nancy has continued to promote her father but she has her own career, cutting new records and making her first concert appearance in the UK at the Royal Festival Hall in 2004. She was part of the Meltdown festival curated by Morrissey. She sang 'It's For My Dad' for her father as well as Bono's song about him, 'Two Shots of Happy, One Shot of Sad'. I was disappointed that she sang 'Boots' while walking around the audience, but then she returned to the stage for a full concert version. She said that she couldn't do the duets without Lee Hazlewood. Nancy performed for 90 minutes and received a standing ovation after which it was time to start walkin', Boots.

If imitation is the sincerest form of flattery, then Frank Sinatra, Elvis Presley and the Beatles are the most flattered artists of the twentieth century. There are tribute acts to Frank Sinatra in every city. Although he wouldn't think of himself as such, the most acclaimed tribute act has to be Frank Sinatra Jr, who is now 70. He sings like him, he talks like him, dresses like him, and copies his mannerisms. Plus he has his name, though it must be disconcerting for someone of that age to be known as Jr. But, and this is a big but, he lacks his father's warmth on stage; you watch him perform and you wonder what is actually going through his mind. He does it well but what's the point? The American commentator Jon Stewart, in joking about religion, remarked, 'Why worship the Son of God? Who buys Frank Sinatra Jr records?'

There are poor facsimiles of Frank Sinatra everywhere. They toss the microphone around and throw leads over their shoulder but they don't have his style or class. The whole point of 'My Way' is that the lyrics say, 'I am better than anybody', so should anyone sing 'My Way' as a tribute perfomer? These are the people who are definitely not doing it their way. In the Philippines, there was a murder in a karaoke bar over 'My Way'. I wondered if 'My Way' was used for the final curtain when the victim was cremated. 'My Way' is still a favourite on TV talent shows and the judges highly commended the Jack Pack on their version on ITV's *Britain's Got Talent* in 2014. It's a shame that Plato isn't around to judge them. He wrote that poor copies detracted from the originals, which might contain essential truths.

The problems of being a Sinatra tribute act were very well highlighted by the actor Ian Hart in *Strictly Sinatra* (2001), which was written and directed by Peter Capaldi. In the Bruce Willis film, *A Good Day to Die Hard* (2013), a Russian cabbie lets customers off their fares if they can recognise his Sinatra impersonation.

Tribute acts by their very nature lack originality but Frank Sinatra Jr offers nothing new. The best of the New Sinatras is the Canadian Michael Bublé and his tracks are often alongside Sinatra's and Tony Bennett's on CD compilations. He has recorded a classy 'Fever' which Frank never sang, and transformed Paul Anka's 1959 hit, 'Put Your Head on My Shoulder'. Sinatra should have thought of that one for himself. Maybe though the New Sinatra is female, namely, Diana Krall, who works with one of Sinatra's arrangers, Claus Ogerman. Her phrasing on albums like *The Look of Love* (2001) is as unique and idiosyncratic as Frank's.

Then there are the occasional wannabe Sinatras, the stars who want to do a few dooby, dooby, doos. The prime example is Robbie Williams, a bad boy of rock who loves the Rat Pack cool. He made *Swing When You're Winning* (2001) in the Capitol studios with Sinatra's arrangements. He performed a good 'Mack the Knife' and 'Beyond the Sea', but he still sounded like Robbie Williams. His mistake was to perform 'It Was a Very Good Year' as a duet with Frank Sinatra; true, an electronic duet endorsed the product but this was the wrong song and just made you realise how perfect Sinatra's version was. In 2013 he returned to the era with *Robbie Williams Swings Both Ways*, a collection of standards and new songs with some guest artists.

Many other artists have recorded albums of standards including Bryan Ferry, Boz Scaggs, k.d.lang and Barry Manilow. *Manilow Sings Sinatra* (2006) included a tribute song, 'Here's to the Man'. The seemingly interminable volumes of Rod Stewart's *The Great American Songbook* are as puzzling as they are successful. The arrangements are lifeless with the drummer thumping his way through the songs and Rod Stewart, so animated with rock material, is soporific. Still, it had been a long-standing ambition and the albums have sold millions. After all, in 1964 when Decca released 'Good Morning Little Schoolgirl' (a song no singer would dare release today for fear of misunderstanding), his stated ambition on the press release as 'to sing with Count Basie'.

But whom does Frank pass his hat to? At first Harry Connick Jr and Peter Cincotti took on much of Sinatra's persona but since then they have branched out into their own songs and style. Connick's role in *Hope Floats* (1998) is pure Sinatra, a tough guy with a lonely heart.

Even when the unkempt grunge look was at its height, there were still sharp dressers around. In 1996 Vince Vaughn starred in a new comedy about the joys of having a life style like Sinatra's called *Swingers*. The easy listening music of the Vegas era was now called lounge and if you like, many youngsters were trying their grandparents' look. Leonard Cohen, a grandfather himself, returned to the stage looking immaculate in fedora and grey suit. He was even playing Vegas, which would never have happened in the 1960s. There was also the anti-Sinatra. You wore the clothes but looked rebellious in them – Tom Waits and Nick Cave are like the antithesis of the saloon bar crooner, the Trash Can Sinatras if you like.

No matter who you are: the name or the image of Sinatra can be used to add commercially viability. Frank was outspoken in his disdain for rock and yet he had a rock persona incorporating sex, swagger, attitude and danger. Certainly not in music, certainly not in dress, but there is a clear link between Frank Sinatra and the rappers. Like the Rat Pack, the rappers are often in gangs; they are fearless and involved in fights and fracas. They speak frankly and crudely using terms like 'bitch' and 'ho' for their women. In 1998 the R&B star Usher called his album *My Way* and it sold three million copies. One single was called 'Nice and Slow'. The Hoboken group Skanatra performed Sinatra songs in Bob Marley's style, and a previously unissued 1970s track 'Hoboken (Be a Friend)' was released by Sly Stone in 2013.

Sinatra sells products too. Nearly every year there is some big campaign involving Sinatra. 'Come Fly with Me' is a given for airlines. In 2002 'I've Got Under My Skin' was used with positive results in basketball commercials. In 2008 the US Postal Service issued a 42 cent Frank Sinatra commemorative stamp.

In 2001 the Las Vegas authorities declared that 12 December should be Frank Sinatra Day. The old Las Vegas has gone. The Mafia no longer own the casinos and nearly all of them have been rebuilt. The new high-tech Las Vegas is theme park city – still featuring casinos and adult entertainment but providing thrills and spectacles for the whole family as well as facilities for corporate functions. It has become one of the rock capitals of the world and the shows are invariably contemporary. The dress code has gone: you can gamble in T-shirt and shorts.

The Mafia's huge influence has now been dissipated or at least been driven underground, although it surfaces in the news from time to time. In 2014 there were moves to deport Domenico Rancadore, allegedly a Mafia boss, from the UK. He was said to have sent a lamb's head and some bullets to a prison chaplain in Palermo who had spoken out about the Mafia with the note, 'One is for your head and one for your heart. One is for the coup de grâce. This is your final warning.'

With impressive modesty, Tony Bennett founded the Frank Sinatra School of the Arts in Queens, New York. He often paints pictures of Sinatra, but a major difference between them is that Bennett has led a relatively normal life and walks his dog around Manhattan without an entourage.

There are few Sinatra recordings of unreleased songs which have not been issued, and they were usually held back for good reason. In 2013 there was a CD release of alternative takes from *Ring-A-Ding Ding*, and more are bound to follow. Another recent release has been the 4CD set, *New York*, offering Sinatra performances in his home city from 1955 to 1990.

Barbara Sinatra recorded all Frank's concerts from 1976 and although there has only been a trickle of live albums since his death, the pace is hotting up as more and more concerts are issued. *Caveat emptor* applies as it can be hard to determine which concerts have been professionally recorded and which are from an audience member with a hand-held recorder; always check the Amazon reviews.

The Elvis Presley market has been saturated with alternative takes and live performances and he has had far more releases since his death than in his lifetime. This has resulted in overkill as no one wants 30 different live versions of 'Can't Help Falling in Love', but the specialist Follow That Dream releases show what can be done with multiple takes. Sinatra's legacy should be treated this way. In 2013 came the release of the conversations between Louis Armstrong and Oscar Peterson in which they discussed their collaboration and if such things exist for Sinatra it would be good to hear them.

With a few exceptions, Frank Sinatra's films are dated, but the best of his music endures and the tracks sound as good as when they were made. Forget the Mafia connections, the Rat Pack silliness, the excessive hedonism, the bad behaviour, the wrongdoing – the final word belongs to Frank Sinatra, the musician, and that legacy will be there for generations to come. Still, those in the new generations are often drawn to his music because of that bad behaviour: 'He was a cocky bastard, that was part of his charm,' said Ava Gardner.

Amy Winehouse told *Word* that the title of her 2003 album, *Frank*, was because her former boyfriend had bought her *In the Wee Small Hours*, which is "one of the classic heartbreak albums". She said, "Sinatra had an emotional connection with his music. That was his thing. He had the tone in his voice. But singer? I know a hundred singers that piss on Frank. And just as a person: he was an arsehole. But he had an emotional connection to songs that touched everyone."

Arsehole or not, everybody is celebrating Frank in 2015 and it's partly because they are fascinated by him. His son, Frank Sinatra Jr, has been in the UK presenting *As I Remember It*, a multimedia event with family film as well as concert performances of his father's best songs. It is said that Frank Sinatra still earns around $5m a year for his estate: it will be several times that in 2015.

In contrast, Frank's 'Witchcraft' is presented rather differently in the film, *50 Shades of Grey*, and amazingly, Bob Dylan topped the UK album charts in February 2015 with his tribute to Sinatra, *Shadows in the Night*. Dylan said that he was lifting the songs "out of the grave and bringing them into the light of day", and despite his tumbledown voice, it works. Maybe we shouldn't have been too surprised as Dylan sang Dean Martin's 'Return to Me' in both English and Italian on the soundtrack for *The Sopranos* in 2001.

In August the BBC Proms had a special evening devoted to *Late Night Sinatra* and the conductor and orchestrator John Wilson has said that his golden period was the late 50s. "He made seven indisputably masterpiece LPs with that theme, beginning with the genius that is *In the Wee Small Hours*, for me the absolute high watermark when it comes to concept albums. A phenomenal piece of work." Indeed, there is going to be so much Sinatra on the box that I will end up Ol' Square Eyes.

The overwhelming theme of this book has been the significance of Sinatra's Italian-American background. It is said that there are now 20 million citizens in America who could call themselves Italian-American – but do they? With each succeeding generation, the Italian legacy becomes ever more distant and most of these people will regard themselves as American. Hence, the story as to how they got to America becomes historical, which is where we came in.

Bibliography

Almost every book that has been written about Frank Sinatra and hundreds of articles have been read during the research for this book as I didn't want to miss anything. Here are the more important sources:

Sammy Davis with Jane and Burt Boyar, *Yes I Can* (Farrar, Strauss & Giroux 1965)

Alan Frank, *Sinatra* (Hamlyn 1978)

Richard Peters, *The Frank Sinatra Scrapbook* (Souvenir 1982)

Kitty Kelley, *His Way* (Bantam 1986)

Nick Tosches, *Dino: Living High in the Dirty Business of Dreams* (Martin Secker & Warburg 1992)

Nancy Sinatra, *Frank Sinatra: An American Legend* (Virgin 1995)

Steven Petkov & Leonard Mustazza (Editors), *The Frank Sinatra Reader* (Oxford University Press 1995)

Will Friedwald, *Sinatra! The Song Is You* (Da Capo 1997)

Shawn Levy, *Rat Pack Confidential* (Fourth Estate 1998)

Gary Giddins, *Bing Crosby: A Pocketful of Dreams* (Little, Brown 2001)

George Jacobs & William Stadiem, *Mr S: The Last Word on Frank Sinatra* (Sidgwick & Jackson 2003)

Richard Havers, *Sinatra* (Dorling Kindersley 2004)

Charles Pignone, *The Sinatra Treasures* (Bulfinch 2004)

Lee Server, *Ava Gardner: Love Is Nothing* (Bloomsbury 2006)

Linda Chase, *Picturing Las Vegas* (Gibbs Smith 2009)

James Kaplan, *Frank: The Making of a Legend* (Doubleday 2010)

Lois Banner, *Marilyn: The Passion and the Paradox* (Bloombury 2012)

Chris Williams (ed.), *The Richard Burton Diaries* (Yale University Press 2012)

21 January '88

Dear Stan Britt:

You write a hell of a letter. Extremely persuasive — and courteous.
But I am a sick, dull old man after 6 strokes in 6 days three
years ago. My vision is poor and getting worse and I have so
little energy.

I feel, moreover, that FS is one of the vilest, unadmirable men on
Planet Earth and has been since I first met him in October '39
when he was with Harry James in Chicago at a time when I was
editing Down Beat.

So Stan, I have minimum interest in commenting additionally on
the man, though I'd like to be of help to you. The Kelly book
handled the case well.

Voyle Gilmore produced FS records for Capitol several years but
FS fired him for no reason. And Axel Stordahl worked loyally
when I signed FS to Capitol and was dumped after a
couple of months. Both Voyle and Ax are long deceased.
Your project is important, yet I feel I can't contribute much
that you can use inasmuch as FS refused to work with me when I
lifted him off the floor and strived to bring him back from
oblivion.

I have difficulty writing. Perhaps I could do better talking — briefly.
My number is 1-800-808-990-8911 if you care to call from
noon to 11 p.m. Pacific Coast time. But I'm not sure I can
help you substantially, Stan. My old brain no longer functions
normally.
        I wish you extreme success with your book and I regret I am
of so little help to you.   Sincerely,
                                        Dave.

UK journalist Stan Britt asked Dave Dexter to help him with a Sinatra biography.
Dave doesn't pull his punches, 1988.